Fodor's 8th Edition

Maine, Vermont, New Hampshire

The Guide
for All Budgets

Completely
Updated

Where to Stay, Eat,
and Explore

On and Off
the Beaten Path

When to Go,
What to Pack

Maps, Travel Tips,
and Web Sites

D1044292

Excerpted from *Fodor's New England*

Fodor's Travel Publications • New York, Toronto, London, Sydney, Auckland
www.fodors.com

Fodor's Maine, Vermont, New Hampshire

EDITORS: Shannon Kelly, William Travis

Editorial Contributors: Andrew Collins, Satu Hummasti, Laura Kidder, Hilary M. Nangle, Bill Scheller, Kay Scheller

Editorial Production: Ira-Neil Dittersdorf

Maps: David Lindroth, *cartographer*; Rebecca Baer and Bob Blake, *map editors*

Design: Fabrizio La Rocca, *creative director*; Guido Caroti, *art director*; Jolie Novak, *senior picture editor*; Melanie Marin, *photo editor*

Cover Design: Pentagram

Production/Manufacturing: Colleen Ziemba

Cover Photo (Marshall's Point Lighthouse near Owl's Head on Maine Coast): Peter Guttman

Copyright

Eighth Edition

ISBN 1–4000–1073–X

ISSN 1073–6581

Important Tip

Although all prices, opening times, and other details in this book are based on information supplied to us at press time, changes occur all the time in the travel world, and Fodor's cannot accept responsibility for facts that become outdated or for inadvertent errors or omissions. So **always confirm information when it matters,** especially if you're making a detour to visit a specific place.

Special Sales

Fodor's Travel Publications are available at special discounts for bulk purchases for sales promotions or premiums. Special editions, including personalized covers, excerpts of existing guides, and corporate imprints, can be created in large quantities for special needs. For more information, contact your local bookseller or write to Special Markets, Fodor's Travel Publications, 1745 Broadway, New York, NY 10019. Inquiries from Canada should be directed to your local Canadian bookseller or sent to Random House of Canada, Ltd., Marketing Department, 2775 Matheson Boulevard East, Mississauga, Ontario L4W 4P7. Inquiries from the United Kingdom should be sent to Fodor's Travel Publications, 20 Vauxhall Bridge Road, London SW1V 2SA, England.

PRINTED IN THE UNITED STATES OF AMERICA

10 9 8 7 6 5 4 3 2 1

CONTENTS

ON THE ROAD WITH FODOR'S

A trip takes you out of yourself. Concerns of life at home completely disappear, driven away by more immediate thoughts—about, say, what marvels will beguile the next day, or where you'll have dinner. That's where Fodor's comes in. We make sure that you know all your options, so that you don't miss something that's around the next bend just because you didn't know it was there. Mindful that the best memories of your trip might have nothing to do with what you came to Maine, Vermont, and New Hampshire to see, we guide you to sights large and small all over the region. You might set out to discover the Maine's southeastern coast, but back at home you find yourself unable to forget driving in fall under canopies of trees, ablaze in shades of oranges and reds, in Vermont. With Fodor's at your side, serendipitous discoveries are never far away.

About Our Writers

Our success in showing you every corner of Maine, Vermont, and New Hampshire is a credit to our extraordinary writers. Although there's no substitute for travel advice from a good friend who knows your style, our contributors are the next best thing—the kind of people you would poll for travel advice if you knew them.

Hilary M. Nangle, formerly travel editor for a daily newspaper in Maine, is now a freelancer based in the state's scenic midcoast. Her Fodor's beat is Maine, and she writes regularly about travel, food, and skiing for publications in the United States and Canada.

Former Fodor's editor and New England native **Andrew Collins,** who updated and expanded the New Hampshire chapter as well as the Martha's Vineyard, Berkshires, and Pioneer Valley sections of Massachusetts, is the author of several books on travel in New England, including handbooks on Connecticut and Rhode Island.

Kay and Bill Scheller, who updated the Vermont chapter have a total of more than 30 years' experience as contributors to Fodor's guides. They are the authors of several books on travel in New England

and the Northeast. The Schellers live in northern Vermont.

You can rest assured that you're in good hands—and that no property mentioned in the book has paid to be included. Each has been selected strictly on its merits, as the best of its type in its price range.

How to Use This Book

Up front is Smart Travel Tips A to Z, arranged alphabetically by topic and loaded with tips, Web sites, and contact information. Destination: Maine, Vermont, New Hampshire helps get you in the mood for your trip. Subsequent chapters in *Fodor's Maine, Vermont, New Hampshire* are arranged regionally. All chapters are divided geographically; within each area, towns are covered in logical geographical order, and attractive stretches of road between them are indicated by the designation En Route. To help you decide what you'll have time to visit, all chapters begin with our writers' favorite itineraries. (Mix itineraries from several chapters, and you can put together a really exceptional trip.) The A to Z section that ends every chapter lists additional resources.

Icons and Symbols

★ Our special recommendations
✕ Restaurant
🏠 Lodging establishment
✕🏠 Lodging establishment whose restaurant warrants a special trip
⚠ Campgrounds
☝ Good for kids (rubber duck)
☞ Sends you to another section of the guide for more information
✉ Address
☎ Telephone number
☉ Opening and closing times
💰 Admission prices (those we give apply to adults; substantially reduced fees are almost always available for children, students, and senior citizens)

Numbers in white and black circles ③ ❸ that appear on the maps, in the margins, and within the tours correspond to one another.

For hotels, you can assume that all rooms have private baths, phones, TVs, and air-conditioning unless otherwise noted and that all hotels operate on the European Plan (with no meals) if we don't specify another meal plan. We always list a property's facilities but not whether you'll be charged extra to use them, so when pricing accommodations, do ask what's included. For restaurants, it's always a good idea to book ahead; we mention reservations only when they're essential or are not accepted. All restaurants we list are open daily for lunch and dinner unless stated otherwise; dress is mentioned only when men are required to wear a jacket or a jacket and tie. Look for an overview of local dining-out habits in Smart Travel Tips A to Z and in the Pleasures and Pastimes section that follows each chapter introduction.

Don't Forget to Write

Your experiences—positive and negative—matter to us. If we have missed or misstated something, we want to hear about it. We follow up on all suggestions. Contact the Maine, Vermont, New Hampshire editors at editors@fodors.com or c/o Fodor's at 1745 Broadway, New York, NY 10019. And have a fabulous trip!

Karen Cure

Karen Cure
Editorial Director

Maine, Vermont and New Hampshire

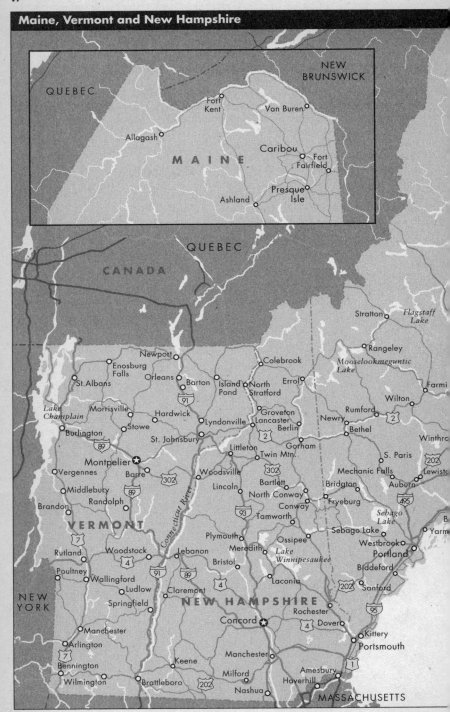

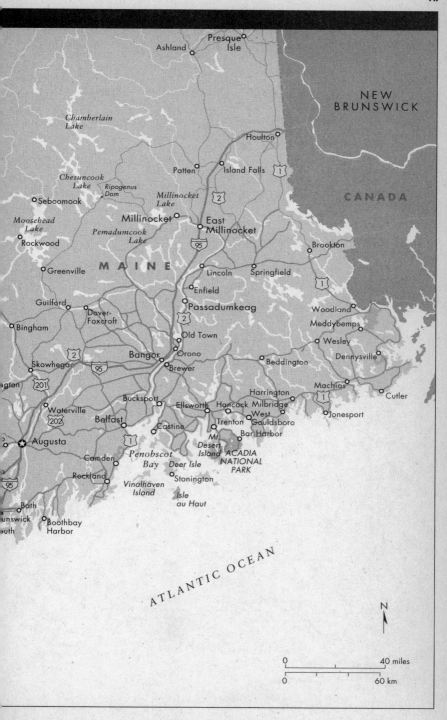

New England

CANADA — **QUÉBEC**

Stratton

Newport
Rangeley
Colebrook
Mooselookmeguntic
Lake

Enosburg
Falls
St. Albans
Orleans — Barton
Island
Pond
North
Stratford
Errol
Wilton

Lake
Champlain
Morrisville
Hardwick
Lyndonville
Groveton
Rumford
Newry

Burlington
Stowe
St. Johnsbury
Lancaster
Berlin
Bethel

Montpelier
Barre
Littleton
Gorham
S. Paris
Mechanic Falls

Vergennes
Woodsville
Lincoln
Twin Mtn.
Bridgton
Auburn

Middlebury
Randolph
Bartlett
North Conway
Conway
Fryeburg
Sebago
Lake

Brandon
VERMONT
Tamworth
Sebago Lake
Westbrook
Portland

Rutland
Woodstock
Lebanon
Meredith
Ossipee
Lake
Winnipesaukee
Biddeford

Wallingford
Bristol
Laconia
Stratford

Poultney
Ludlow
Claremont
Rochester

Springfield
NEW HAMPSHIRE
Dover

Manchester
Concord
Portsmouth

Arlington
Manchester
Amesbury
Newburyport

Bennington
Keene
Milford
Haverhill
Gloucester

Wilmington
Brattleboro
Nashua
Lawrence
Danvers
Beverly

Williamstown
Athol
Fitchburg
Lowell
Salem

Greenfield
Gardner
Concord
Lexington
Cambridge

Pittsfield
Leominster
Marlborough
Boston

Northampton
MASSACHUSETTS
Worcester
Braintree
Brockton

Stockbridge
Chicopee
Springfield
Bridgewater
Plymouth

Sandisfield
Putnam
Providence
Taunton
Sandwich

Winsted
Windsor
Locks
Manchester
Willimantic
Warwick
Fall River
Cape

Torrington
New Britain
Hartford
Bristol
New Bedford
Hyannis

Bristol
CONNECTICUT
**RHODE
ISLAND**
Newport
Falmouth

Waterbury
Meriden
Middletown
Norwich
Oak Bluffs
Martha's
Vineyard

Danbury
Wallingford
Wakefield

New
London
Westerly
Block
Island Sound

New Haven
Long Island Sound
Block
Island

Bridgeport
Long Island (N.Y.)

Norwalk

**NEW
YORK**

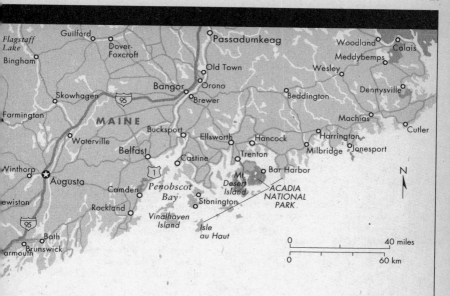

Flagstaff Lake
Guilford
Dover-Foxcroft
Passadumkeag
Woodland
Calais
Bingham
Meddybemps
Old Town
Wesley
Skowhegan
Bangor
Orono
Beddington
Dennysville
Brewer
MAINE
Farmington
Bucksport
Machias
Waterville
Ellsworth
Hancock
Harrington
Cutler
Belfast
Trenton
Milbridge
Jonesport
Castine
Winthrop
Augusta
Bar Harbor
Mt. Desert Island
ewiston
Camden
Penobscot Bay
ACADIA NATIONAL PARK
Rockland
Stonington
Vinalhaven Island
Bath
Isle au Haut
armouth
Brunswick

N

0   40 miles
0   60 km

ATLANTIC OCEAN

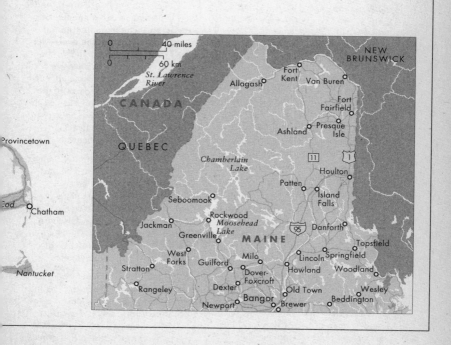

NEW BRUNSWICK
0   40 miles
0   60 km
St. Lawrence River
Allagash
Fort Kent
Van Buren
CANADA
Fort Fairfield
Ashland
Presque Isle
QUEBEC
Chamberlain Lake
Houlton
Patten
Seboomook
Island Falls
Provincetown
Rockwood
Moosehead Lake
Jackman
Danforth
Greenville
MAINE
Topsfield
Cod
Chatham
West Forks
Milo
Lincoln
Springfield
Stratton
Guilford
Howland
Woodland
Nantucket
Dover-Foxcroft
Rangeley
Dexter
Old Town
Wesley
Newport
Bangor
Brewer
Beddington

ESSENTIAL INFORMATION

AIR TRAVEL

Most travelers visiting Maine, Vermont, and New Hampshire head for a major gateway and then rent a car to enjoy the sights. The states form a fairly compact region, with few important destinations more than six hours apart by car. Intraregional air transportation facilities are mainly patronized by business travelers. Should you wish to fly, be advised that intraregional fares can be high and flights limited.

CARRIERS

➤ MAJOR AIRLINES: **American** (☎ 800/433–7300). **Continental** (☎ 800/525–0280). **Delta** (☎ 800/221–1212). **Northwest** (☎ 800/225–2525). **Southwest** (☎ 800/435–9792). **Sun Country** (☎ 800/359–5786). **TWA** (☎ 800/221–2000). **United** (☎ 800/241–6522). **US Airways** (☎ 800/428–4322).

➤ REGIONAL AIRLINES: **Midway** (☎ 800/446–4392).

➤ FROM THE U.K.: **American** (☎ 0345/789–789). **British Airways** (☎ 0345/222–111). **Virgin Atlantic** (☎ 01293/747–747).

➤ FROM AUSTRALIA AND NEW ZEALAND: **Qantas** (from Australia, ☎ 13–1313, 0800/808–767, or 09/357–8900; from New Zealand, outside Auckland, ☎ 0800/808–767; from Auckland area, ☎ 09/357–8900).

CHECK-IN AND BOARDING

Always **ask your carrier about its check-in policy.** Plan to arrive at the airport about 2 hours before your scheduled departure time for domestic flights and 2½ to 3 hours before international flights. Assuming that not everyone with a ticket will show up, airlines routinely overbook planes. When everyone does, airlines ask for volunteers to give up their seats. In return, these volunteers usually get a certificate for a free flight and are rebooked on the next flight out. If there are not enough volunteers, the airline must choose who will be denied boarding. The first to get bumped are passengers who checked in late and those flying on discounted tickets, so **get to the gate and check in as early as possible,** especially during peak periods.

Always **bring a government-issued photo ID to the airport;** even when it's not required, a passport is best.

CUTTING COSTS

The least expensive airfares to Maine, Vermont, and New Hampshire are priced for round-trip travel and must usually be purchased in advance. Airlines generally allow you to change your return date for a fee; most low-fare tickets, however, are nonrefundable. It's smart to **call a number of airlines,** and when you are quoted a good price, **book it on the spot**—the same fare may not be available the next day. Always **check different routings** and look into using alternate airports. Also, price off-peak flights, which may be significantly less expensive than others. Travel agents, especially low-fare specialists (☞ Discounts and Deals), are helpful.

Airlines often post discounted "cyberfares" on their Web sites. The best bargains are on unsold seats on upcoming flights. If your plans are flexible, you can often save 60% to 70% by booking on-line. Discount travel Web sites such as Travelocity and Priceline.com also offer reduced fares (☞ Discounts and Deals).

Consolidators are another good source. They buy tickets for scheduled international flights at reduced rates from the airlines, then sell them at prices that beat the best fare available directly from the airlines. Sometimes you can even get your money back if you need to return the ticket. Carefully read the fine print detailing penalties for changes and cancellations, purchase the ticket with a credit card, and **confirm your consolidator reservation with the airline.**

➤ CONSOLIDATORS: **Cheap Tickets** (☎ 800/377–1000 or 888/922–8849, WEB www.cheaptickets.com). **Discount Airline Ticket Service** (☎ 800/576–1600). **World Travel Network** (☎ 800/409–6753).

FLYING TIMES

Flying time to Boston is 1 hour from New York, 2 hours and 15 minutes from Chicago, 6 hours from Los Angeles, 4 hours from Dallas, and 8 hours from London. Flying time from Sydney, Australia, to Boston (via Los Angeles) is 20 hours; flying time from Auckland, New Zealand, to Boston (via Los Angeles) is 17 hours.

RECONFIRMING

Check the status of your flight before you leave for the airport. You can do this on your carrier's Web site, by linking to a flight-status checker (many Web booking services offer these), or by calling your carrier or travel agent.

AIRPORTS

The main gateway to Maine, Vermont, and New Hampshire is Boston's Logan International Airport, the region's largest. Additional airports served by major carriers include Manchester Airport in New Hampshire (a rapidly growing, lower-cost alternative to Boston); Portland International Jetport (PWM) in Maine; and Burlington International Airport (BTV) in Vermont. Other airports are in Bangor, Maine; Albany, New York; Rutland, Vermont; near Hartford, Connecticut; and near Montréal, Québec.

➤ AIRPORT INFORMATION: **Albany International Airport** (ALB; ✉ 737 Albany-Shaker Rd., Albany, NY, ☎ 518/242–2200, WEB www.albanyairport.com). **Bangor International Airport** (BGR; ✉ 287 Godfrey Blvd., Bangor, ME, ☎ 207/947–0384, WEB www.flybangor.com). **Bradley International Airport** (BDL; ✉ Schoephoester Rd., Windsor Locks,

CT, ☎ 860/292–2000, WEB www.bradleyairport.com). **Burlington International Airport** (BTV; ✉ 1200 Airport Rd., South Burlington, VT, ☎ 802/863–1889, WEB www.burlingtonintlairport.com). **Logan International Airport** (BOS; ✉ 600 Tower Rd., East Boston, MA, ☎ 800/235–6426, WEB www.massport.com/logan). **Manchester Airport** (MHT; ✉ One Airport Rd., Manchester, NH, ☎ 603/624–6539, WEB www.flymanchester.com). **Montréal-Dorval International Airport** (YUL; ✉ 975 Roméo-Vachon Blvd. N, Dorval, QC, ☎ 514/394–7200, WEB www.admtl.com). **Portland International Jetport** (PWM; ✉ 1001 Westbrook St., Portland, ME, ☎ 207/774–7301, WEB www.portlandjetport.org). **Rutland State Airport** (RUT; ✉ 1002 Airport Rd., N. Clarendon, VT, ☎ 802/786–2579).

BIKE TRAVEL

Cyclists favor Maine, Vermont, and New Hampshire because overnight destinations are seldom far apart. Inns and B&Bs are plentiful, and some operators provide guided inn-to-inn tours. Except for far northern Maine, northern New England has the some of the best cycling opportunities in the country, with plenty of lightly traveled secondary roads and pleasant small towns to explore en route. Make sure you're in shape if you plan to tackle the hills of Vermont and New Hampshire, and **consider a mountain bike** if you're going to be on dirt roads. Both mountain and touring bikes are available for rent in resort areas and in most larger towns and cities for as little as $20 a day.

BIKES IN FLIGHT

Most airlines accommodate bikes as luggage, provided they are dismantled and boxed; check with individual airlines about packing requirements. Airlines sell bike boxes, which are often free at bike shops, for about $15 (bike bags start at $100). International travelers often can substitute a bike for a piece of checked luggage at no charge; otherwise, the cost is about $100. Domestic and Canadian airlines charge $40–$80 each way.

BOAT AND FERRY TRAVEL

Many ferry routes provide access to islands off the Maine coast. In addition, ferries cross Lake Champlain between Vermont and upstate New York. International service between Portland and Bar Harbor, Maine, and Yarmouth, Nova Scotia, is also available. With the exception of the Lake Champlain ferries, which are first-come, first-served, car reservations are always advisable.

FARES AND SCHEDULES

For reservations made by phone, MasterCard and Visa are universally accepted; many ferry services also accept American Express and Discover. When picking up tickets at the station, travelers' checks, credit cards, and cash are approved forms of payment.

BUS TRAVEL

Maine, Vermont, and New Hampshire have bus service; fares are generally moderate and buses normally run on schedule, although service can be infrequent and travel time can be long due to traffic and frequent stops. Be sure to arrive at the terminal at least one hour before the bus is scheduled to depart. Smoking is not permitted on buses.

CUTTING COSTS

Greyhound offers Ameripass, which allows riders to travel throughout New England at discounted fares for varying lengths of time from 7 to 60 days. Tickets purchased at least 7 days in advance are discounted. A Companion Fare, purchased at least 3 days in advance, allows a companion to ride for free (not available in some destinations and at certain times of the year).

PAYING

Tickets can be purchased at the terminal or by phone; Greyhound offers on-line ticket sales. All major credit cards are accepted.

RESERVATIONS

Greyhound does not accept advance reservations. The only way to reserve a seat on the bus is to purchase a ticket in advance.

➤ BUS INFORMATION: **Concord Trailways** (☎ 800/639–3317). **Greyhound** (☎ 800/231–2222; 888/454–7277 Ameripass; WEB www.greyhound. com). **Peter Pan Bus Lines** (☎ 800/343–9999). **Vermont Transit** (☎ 800/642–3133 in Vermont; 800/552–8737 elsewhere).

BUSINESS HOURS

Banks are generally open weekdays 9 AM–3 PM, with longer hours on Thursday and Friday. Post offices are open weekdays 8 AM–5 PM; many branches operate Saturday morning hours. Business hours tend to be weekdays 9–5. Banks and post offices close on all national holidays; retail businesses generally close only on Thanksgiving, Christmas, New Year's Day, and Easter. Convenience stores, especially in urban areas, are often open year-round.

GAS STATIONS

Except along major highways, gas stations frequently close at around 10 or 11 PM and reopen at 5 or 6 AM.

MUSEUMS AND SIGHTS

While some major museums and attractions are open daily—at least during peak tourist season, Memorial Day to Columbus Day—Monday closings are common. In resort areas, museums and attractions are frequently closed or on significantly reduced schedules from mid-October to late May. Hours of sights and attractions are denoted throughout this book by the clock icon, ☉ .

PHARMACIES

In larger cities, pharmacies near hospitals and/or medical centers generally stay open 24 hours.

SHOPS

Many stores may not open until 10 or 11 AM, but they remain open until 6 or 7 PM; most carry on brisk business on Saturday and Sunday as well. Suburban shopping malls are generally open seven days a week, with evening hours every day except Sunday. Convenience stores sell food and sundries until about 11 PM. Along the highways and in major cities you can usually find all-night diners, supermarkets, pharmacies, and convenience stores.

CAR RENTAL

Rates begin at around $25 a day and $160 a week for an economy car with air-conditioning, an automatic transmission, and unlimited mileage. This rate does not include taxes and surcharges, which can add as much as 25% if you rent a car at the airport.

➤ MAJOR AGENCIES: **Alamo** (☎ 800/327–9633; WEB www.alamo.com). **Avis** (☎ 800/331–1212; 800/879–2847 in Canada; 02/9353–9000 in Australia; 09/526–2847 in New Zealand; 0870/606–0100 in the U.K.; WEB www.avis.com). **Budget** (☎ 800/527–0700; 0870/156–5656 in the U.K.; WEB www.budget.com). **Dollar** (☎ 800/800–4000; 0124/622–0111 in the U.K.; where it's affiliated with Sixt; 02/9223–1444 in Australia; WEB www.dollar.com). **Hertz** (☎ 800/654–3131; 800/263–0600 in Canada; 020/8897–2072 in the U.K.; 02/9669–2444 in Australia; 09/256–8690 in New Zealand; WEB www.hertz.com). **National Car Rental** (☎ 800/227–7368; 020/8680–4800 in the U.K.; WEB www.nationalcar.com).

CAR TRAVEL

Because public transportation is spotty or completely lacking in the outer reaches of Maine, Vermont, and New Hampshire, a car is the most convenient means of transportation. The region is well served by the interstate highway system, on which you can expect to average 65 mph, except near major metropolitan areas (in rush hour around Hartford and Boston, you will cut that average in half). On other federal and state highways, your average will more likely be 40–50 mph. East–west travel is notoriously slow, due to several mountain ranges and no limited-access highways.

GASOLINE

Self-service gas stations are the norm in Maine, Vermont, and New Hampshire, though in some of the less-populated regions you'll find stations with one or two pumps and a friendly attendant who provides full service (pumping your gas, checking your tires and oil, washing your windows). Stations are plentiful. Most stay open late (24 hours along large highways and in big cities), except in rural areas, where Sunday hours are limited and where you may drive long stretches without a refueling opportunity. At this writing, rates for unleaded regular gas at self-service stations in Maine, Vermont, and New Hampshire are about $1.40 per gallon; rates at full-service stations are often slightly more.

ROAD CONDITIONS

Federal and state highways throughout the area are maintained in excellent condition and are promptly plowed and salted in winter. Secondary roads maintained by local municipalities are sometimes in poor repair, especially in spring, when frost heaves—bumps and dips in the pavement—are caused by melting ground frost. There are many miles of unpaved roads, but these are usually well graded and pleasant to travel, except in mud season during late March and early April. Far northern Maine is crisscrossed by privately owned logging roads, for which a pass is frequently required (pay at gates at entrances to logging company lands).

City traffic can be particularly trying in New England, as many streets were laid out centuries ago. Boston's traffic snarls are legendary, which can add serious time to your journey if you plan to fly into Logan Airport. Rush hours in the city run roughly from 6 to 9 AM and from 4 to 7 PM.

ROAD MAPS

Each state makes available a free map that has directories, mileage, and other useful information—contact the state offices of tourism (☞ Visitor Information). Delorme publishes topographical atlases of Maine, New Hampshire, and Vermont that include most back roads and many outdoor recreation sites. The maps are widely available in these states.

RULES OF THE ROAD

The speed limit in much of Maine, Vermont, and New Hampshire is 65 mph on interstate and some limited-access highways (55 mph in densely populated areas) and 50 mph on most other roads (25–30 mph in towns and cities). Speed limits are stringently enforced throughout the region, particularly in populated areas. Fines can easily exceed $100 for driving 15–20 mi above the speed limit. Drivers can turn right at a red light (unless signs indicate otherwise) providing they come to a full stop and check to see that the intersection is clear first.

There is zero tolerance for drunk driving. The blood alcohol content that defines legal intoxication for adults varies between .08 and .10 percent, depending on the state, and penalties are severe.

Always **strap children under age 4 or under 40 lbs., regardless of age, into approved child-safety seats.** Children must wear seat belts regardless of where they're seated.

CHILDREN IN MAINE, VERMONT, AND NEW HAMPSHIRE

In New England, there's no shortage of things to do with children. Major museums have children's sections, and you'll find children's museums in cities large and small. Many tourist areas have roadside attractions, and miniature golf courses are easy to come by. Attractions such as beaches and boat rides, parks and planetariums, lighthouses and llama treks can be fun for youngsters, as can special events such as crafts fairs and food festivals.

Be sure to plan ahead and **involve your youngsters** as you outline your trip. When packing, include things to keep them busy en route. On sightseeing days try to schedule activities of special interest to your children. If you are renting a car, don't forget to **arrange for a car seat** when you reserve. For general advice about traveling with children, consult *Fodor's FYI: Travel with Your Baby* (available in bookstores everywhere).

FLYING

If your children are two or older, **ask about children's airfares.** As a general rule, infants under two not occupying a seat fly at greatly reduced fares or even for free.

Experts agree that it's a good idea to use safety seats aloft for children weighing less than 40 pounds. Airlines set their own policies: U.S. carriers usually require that the child be ticketed, even if he or she is young enough to ride free, since the seats must be strapped into regular seats. Do **check your airline's policy about using safety seats during takeoff and landing.** Safety seats are not allowed everywhere in the plane, so get your seat assignments as early as possible.

When reserving, **request children's meals or a freestanding bassinet** (not available at all airlines) if you need them. But note that bulkhead seats, where you must sit to use the bassinet, may lack an overhead bin or storage space on the floor.

LODGING

Chain hotels and motels welcome children, and Maine, Vermont, and New Hampshire have many family-oriented resorts with lively children's programs. You'll also find farms that accept guests and can be lots of fun for children. Rental houses and apartments abound, particularly around ski areas; off-season, these can be economical as well as comfortable touring bases. Some country inns, especially those with a quiet, romantic atmosphere and those furnished with antiques, are less enthusiastic about little ones, so **be up front about your traveling companions** when you reserve. Many larger resorts and hotels will provide a baby-sitter at an additional cost. Others will provide a list of sitters in the area.

Most hotels in New England allow children under a certain age to stay in their parents' room at no extra charge, but others charge them as extra adults; be sure to **find out the cutoff age for children's discounts.**

Most lodgings that welcome infants and small children will provide a crib or cot, but **be sure to give advance notice** so that one will be available for you. Most resort and hotels with extended amenities will also arrange to have a baby-sitter come to your room. Many family resorts make special accommodations for small children during meals. Be sure to ask in advance.

SIGHTS AND ATTRACTIONS

Places that are especially appealing to children are indicated by a rubber-duckie icon (🦆) in the margin.

TRANSPORTATION

Each New England state has specific requirements regarding age and weight requirements for children in car seats. If you're renting a car, **be sure to ask about the state(s) you're planning to drive in.** If you will need a car seat, make sure the agency you select provides them and **reserve well in advance.**

CONSUMER PROTECTION

Whether you're shopping for gifts or purchasing travel services, **pay with a major credit card** whenever possible, so you can cancel payment or get reimbursed if there's a problem (and you can provide documentation). If you're doing business with a particular company for the first time, **contact your local Better Business Bureau and the attorney general's offices** in your state and (for U.S. businesses) the company's home state as well. Have any complaints been filed? Finally, if you're buying a package or tour, always **consider travel insurance** that includes default coverage (☞ Insurance).

➤ BBBs: **Council of Better Business Bureaus** (✉ 4200 Wilson Blvd., Suite 800, Arlington, VA 22203, ☎ 703/276–0100, FAX 703/525–8277, WEB www.bbb.org).

CRUISE TRAVEL

Several cruise companies have ships that set sail from Boston to cruise north to Canada, stopping in Montréal or Halifax. To learn how to plan, choose, and book a cruise-ship voyage, consult *Fodor's FYI: Plan & Enjoy Your Cruise* (available in bookstores everywhere).

➤ CRUISE LINES: **American Canadian Caribbean Line** (☎ 800/556–7450). **Clipper Cruise Line** (☎ 800/325–0010). **Royal Caribbean International** (☎ 800/327–6700).

CUSTOMS AND DUTIES

IN AUSTRALIA

Australian residents who are 18 or older may bring home A$400 worth of souvenirs and gifts (including jewelry), 250 cigarettes or 250 grams of tobacco, and 1,125 ml of alcohol (including wine, beer, and spirits). Residents under 18 may bring back A$200 worth of goods. Prohibited items include meat products. Seeds, plants, and fruits need to be declared upon arrival.

➤ INFORMATION: **Australian Customs Service** (Regional Director, ✉ Box 8, Sydney, NSW 2001; ☎ 02/9213–2000 or 1300/363263; 1800/020504 quarantine-inquiry line; FAX 02/9213–4043; WEB www.customs.gov.au).

IN CANADA

Canadian residents who have been out of Canada for at least seven days may bring in C$750 worth of goods duty-free. If you've been away fewer than seven days but more than 48 hours, the duty-free allowance drops to C$200; if your trip lasts 24 to 48 hours, the allowance is C$50. You may not pool allowances with family members. Goods claimed under the C$750 exemption may follow you by mail; those claimed under the lesser exemptions must accompany you. Alcohol and tobacco products may be included in the seven-day and 48-hour exemptions but not in the 24-hour exemption. If you meet the age requirements of the province or territory through which you reenter Canada, you may bring in, duty-free, 1.5 liters of wine *or* 1.14 liters (40 imperial ounces) of liquor *or* 24 12-ounce cans or bottles of beer or ale. If you are 19 or older you may bring in, duty-free, 200 cigarettes and 50 cigars. Check ahead of time with the Canada Customs and Revenue Agency or the Department of Agriculture for policies regarding meat products, seeds, plants, and fruits.

You may send an unlimited number of gifts (only one gift per recipient, however) worth up to C$60 each duty-free to Canada. Label the package UNSOLICITED GIFT—VALUE UNDER $60. Alcohol and tobacco are excluded.

➤ INFORMATION: **Canada Customs and Revenue Agency** (✉ 2265 St. Laurent Blvd. S, Ottawa, Ontario K1G 4K3, ☎ 204/983–3500, 506/

636–5064, 800/461–9999, WEB www. ccra-adrc.gc.ca/).

IN NEW ZEALAND

All homeward-bound residents may bring back NZ$700 worth of souvenirs and gifts; passengers may not pool their allowances, and children can claim only the concession on goods intended for their own use. For those 17 or older, the duty-free allowance also includes 4.5 liters of wine or beer; one 1,125-ml bottle of spirits; and either 200 cigarettes, 250 grams of tobacco, 50 cigars, *or* a combination of the three up to 250 grams. Meat products, seeds, plants, and fruits must be declared upon arrival to the Agricultural Services Department.

➤ INFORMATION: **New Zealand Customs** (Head office: ✉ The Customhouse, 17–21 Whitmore St., Box 2218, Wellington, ☎ 09/300–5399 or 0800/428–786, WEB www.customs. govt.nz).

IN THE U.K.

From countries outside the European Union, including the United States, you may bring home, duty-free, 200 cigarettes or 50 cigars; 1 liter of spirits or 2 liters of fortified or sparkling wine or liqueurs; 2 liters of still table wine; 60 ml of perfume; 250 ml of toilet water; plus £145 worth of other goods, including gifts and souvenirs. Prohibited items include meat products, seeds, plants, and fruits.

➤ INFORMATION: **HM Customs and Excise** (✉ Portcullis House, 21 Cowbridge Rd. E, Cardiff CF11 9SS, ☎ 029/2038–6423 or 0845/010–9000, WEB www.hmce.gov.uk).

DINING

Thoughts of dining in New England center on seafood, and the coast and many inland locations have restaurants specializing in lobster, clams, scallops, and fresh fish. City restaurants have an impressive variety of menus and price ranges. The best dining in rural areas is often to be found in country inns, the larger of which are often quite proud of their chefs and their commitment to using local meats and produce.

Restaurant prices in Maine, Vermont, and New Hampshire are generally on a par with those elsewhere in the country, but travelers may experience sticker shock at even more modest seafood restaurants. Catch limits on many favorite ocean species, as well as the premium charged for lobster and other shellfish, have sent prices soaring. Lobsters are sold by the pound ("market price" is the phrase that appears on many menus), and a $20 lobster dinner or a $10 lobster roll is not uncommon.

The restaurants we list are the cream of the crop in each price category. Properties indicated by an ✕🍴 are lodging establishments whose restaurant warrants a special trip. Following is the price chart used in this book; note that prices do not include tax, which is 5% in Maine (7% on alcohol), 8% in New Hampshire, and 9% in Vermont (10% on alcohol).

CATEGORY	COST*
$$$$	over $25
$$$	$17–$25
$$	$9–$16
$	under $9

per person, for a main-course dinner

MEALTIMES

In general, the widest variety of mealtime options in Maine, Vermont, and New Hampshire is in larger cities and at resort areas.

For an early breakfast, pick places that cater to a working clientele. City, town, and roadside establishments specializing in breakfast for the busy often open their doors at 5 or 6 AM. At country inns and B&Bs, breakfast is seldom served before 8; if you need to get an earlier start, ask ahead of time if your host or hostess can accommodate you.

Unless otherwise noted, the restaurants listed in this guide are open daily for lunch and dinner. Lunch generally runs from around 11 to 2:30; dinner is usually served from 6 to 9 (many restaurants have early-bird specials beginning at 5). Only in the larger cities will you find full dinners being offered much later than 9, although you can usually find a bar or bistro serving a limited menu late into the evening in all but the smallest towns.

Many restaurants are closed on Mondays, although this is never true in resort areas in high season. However, resort-town eateries often shut down completely in the off-season.

Credit cards are accepted for meals throughout Maine, Vermont, and New Hampshire in all but the most modest establishments.

RESERVATIONS AND DRESS

Reservations are always a good idea; we mention them only when they're essential or not accepted. Book as far ahead as you can, and reconfirm as soon as you arrive. (Large parties should always call ahead to check the reservations policy.) We mention dress only when men are required to wear a jacket or a jacket and tie.

WINE, BEER, AND SPIRITS

New England is no stranger to microbrews. Following the lead of Boston's independent beer maker Samuel Adams, in offering hearty English-style ales and special seasonal brews, are breweries such as Vermont's Long Trail, Maine's Shipyard, and New Hampshire's Old Man Ale.

Vermont is getting into the wine-producing business with its new Snow Farm Vineyard in the Lake Champlain Islands and Boyden Valley Winery in Cambridge.

Although a patchwork of state and local regulations affect the hours and locations of places that sell alcoholic beverages, licensing laws are fairly liberal. State-owned or -franchised stores sell hard liquor in New Hampshire, Maine, and Vermont; many travelers have found that New Hampshire offers the region's lowest prices. Look for state-run liquor "supermarkets" on interstate highways in the southern part of the state; these also have good wine selections.

DISABILITIES
AND ACCESSIBILITY

➤ LOCAL RESOURCES: The **New Hampshire Office of Travel and Tourism Development's** (☞ Visitor Information) *New Hampshire Guide Book* includes accessibility ratings for lodgings and restaurants. **Vermont Chamber of Commerce** (☞ Visitor

Information) includes accessibility codes for attractions in the *Vermont Traveler's Guidebook*. **VSA** (✉ 2 Boylston St., Room 211, Boston 02116, ☎ 617/350–7713, WEB www. accessexpressed.net) sells "Access Expressed! New England."

LODGING

Despite the Americans with Disabilities Act, the definition of accessibility seems to differ from hotel to hotel. Some properties may be accessible by ADA standards for people with mobility problems but not for people with hearing or vision impairments, for example.

If you have mobility problems, ask for the lowest floor on which accessible services are offered. If you have a hearing impairment, check whether the hotel has devices to alert you visually to the ring of the telephone, knock at the door, and a fire/emergency alarm. Some hotels provide these devices without charge. Discuss your needs with hotel personnel if this equipment isn't available, so that a staff member can personally alert you in the event of an emergency.

If you're bringing a guide dog, get authorization ahead of time and write down the name of the person you spoke with.

RESERVATIONS

When discussing accessibility with an operator or reservations agent, **ask hard questions.** Are there any stairs, inside *or* out? Are there grab bars next to the toilet *and* in the shower/tub? How wide is the doorway to the room? To the bathroom? For the most extensive facilities meeting the latest legal specifications, **opt for newer accommodations.** If you reserve through a toll-free number, consider also calling the hotel's local number to confirm the information from the central reservations office. Get confirmation in writing when you can.

SIGHTS AND ATTRACTIONS

In Kennebunkport, as in many of Maine's coastal towns south of Portland, travelers with mobility impairments will have to cope with crowds as well as with narrow, uneven steps and sporadic curb cuts. L. L. Bean's outlet in Freeport is fully accessible, and Acadia National Park has some 50 accessible miles of carriage roads that are closed to motor vehicles. In New Hampshire, many of Franconia Notch's natural attractions are accessible.

TRANSPORTATION

Many major rental agencies provide special cars for people with disabilities on request. Most ask that you provide your own handicapped sticker or plate, which will be honored throughout the region. Be sure to reserve well in advance.

➤ COMPLAINTS: **Aviation Consumer Protection Division** (☞ Air Travel) for airline-related problems. **Departmental Office of Civil Rights** (for general inquiries, ✉ U.S. Department of Transportation, S-30, 400 7th St. SW, Room 10215, Washington, DC 20590, ☎ 202/366–4648, FAX 202/366–3571, WEB www.dot.gov/ost/docr/index.htm). **Disability Rights Section** (✉ NYAV, U.S. Department of Justice, Civil Rights Division, 950 Pennsylvania Ave. NW, Washington, DC 20530; ☎ ADA information line 202/514–0301, 800/514–0301, 202/514–0383 TTY, 800/514–0383 TTY, WEB www.usdoj.gov/crt/ada/adahom1.htm).

TRAVEL AGENCIES

In the United States, the Americans with Disabilities Act requires that travel firms serve the needs of all travelers. Some agencies specialize in working with people with disabilities.

➤ TRAVELERS WITH MOBILITY PROBLEMS: **Access Adventures** (✉ 206 Chestnut Ridge Rd., Scottsville, NY 14624, ☎ 716/889–9096), run by a former physical-rehabilitation counselor. **Accessible Vans of America** (✉ 9 Spielman Rd., Fairfield, NJ 07004, ☎ 877/282–8267; 888/282–8267 reservations; FAX 973/808–9713; WEB www.accessiblevans.com). **CareVacations** (✉ No. 5, 5110–50 Ave., Leduc, Alberta T9E 6V4, Canada, ☎ 780/986–6404 or 877/478–7827, FAX 780/986–8332, WEB www.carevacations.com), for group tours and cruise vacations. **Flying Wheels Travel** (✉ 143 W. Bridge St. [Box 382, Owatonna, MN 55060], ☎ 507/451–

5005, FAX 507/451–1685, WEB www.flyingwheelstravel.com).

➤ TRAVELERS WITH DEVELOPMENTAL DISABILITIES: **Sprout** (✉ 893 Amsterdam Ave., New York, NY 10025, ☎ 212/222–9575 or 888/222–9575, FAX 212/222–9768, WEB www.gosprout.org).

DISCOUNTS AND DEALS

Be a smart shopper and **compare all your options** before making decisions. A plane ticket bought with a promotional coupon from travel clubs, coupon books, and direct-mail offers or purchased on the Internet may not be cheaper than the least expensive fare from a discount ticket agency. And always keep in mind that what you get is just as important as what you save.

DISCOUNT RESERVATIONS

To save money, **look into discount reservations services** with Web sites and toll-free numbers, which use their buying power to get a better price on hotels, airline tickets, even car rentals. When booking a room, always **call the hotel's local toll-free number** (if one is available) rather than the central reservations number—you'll often get a better price. Always ask about special packages or corporate rates.

➤ AIRLINE TICKETS: ☎ **800/AIR–4LESS. Travelocity** (www.travelocity.com). **Priceline.com** (www.priceline.com).

➤ HOTEL ROOMS: **Accommodations Express** (☎ 800/444–7666, WEB www.accommodationsexpress.com). **Central Reservation Service** (CRS; ☎ 800/548–3311, WEB www.roomconnection.net). **Hotel Reservations Network** (☎ 800/964–6835, WEB www.hoteldiscount.com). **Quikbook** (☎ 800/789–9887, WEB www.quikbook.com). **RMC Travel** (☎ 800/245–5738, WEB www.rmcwebtravel.com). **Steigenberger Reservation Service** (☎ 800/223–5652, WEB www.srs-worldhotels.com). **Turbotrip.com** (☎ 800/473–7829, WEB www.turbotrip.com).

PACKAGE DEALS

Don't confuse packages and guided tours. When you buy a package, you travel on your own, just as though you had planned the trip yourself. Fly-drive packages, which combine airfare and car rental, are often a good deal.

ECOTOURISM

Many state parks in Maine, Vermont, and New Hampshire request that you dispose of your trash after you leave the grounds. Maine and Vermont recycle cans and bottles and charge 5¢–15¢ per unit at time of purchase, refundable when the can or bottle is returned to a store or recycling center.

Throughout the region, particularly on beaches and in areas with high cliffs, markers forbid trespassing. These are generally nesting areas for endangered species, such as peregrine falcons in Smugglers' Notch, Vermont.

GAY AND LESBIAN TRAVEL

As one of the country's most socially and politically progressive regions, New England is almost invariably accepting of gay and lesbian travelers. Some exceptions might be found in areas less frequented by visitors, but in general, people in the tourism business here are hospitable to travelers regardless of sexual orientation. Most sizable college and university towns have gay communities. Alternative publications in all of these areas carry listings of gay bars, nightclubs, and special events.

➤ GAY- AND LESBIAN-FRIENDLY TRAVEL AGENCIES: **Different Roads Travel** (✉ 8383 Wilshire Blvd., Suite 902, Beverly Hills, CA 90211, ☎ 323/651–5557 or 800/429–8747, FAX 323/651–3678). **Kennedy Travel** (✉ 314 Jericho Turnpike, Floral Park, NY 11001, ☎ 516/352–4888 or 800/237–7433, FAX 516/354–8849, WEB www.kennedytravel.com). **Now, Voyager** (✉ 4406 18th St., San Francisco, CA 94114, ☎ 415/626–1169 or 800/255–6951, FAX 415/626–8626, WEB www.nowvoyager.com). **Skylink Travel and Tour** (✉ 1006 Mendocino Ave., Santa Rosa, CA 95401, ☎ 707/546–9888 or 800/225–5759, FAX 707/546–9891, WEB www.skylinktravel.com), serving lesbian travelers.

GUIDEBOOKS

Plan well and you won't be sorry. Guidebooks are excellent tools—and you can take them with you. You may want to check out color-photo-illustrated guides such as the Maine and Vermont guides in the Compass American series—thorough on culture and history. *Fodor's Road Guide USA: Maine, Vermont, and New Hampshire* is packed with hotel, restaurant, and attractions listings. All are available at on-line retailers and bookstores everywhere.

HEALTH

LYME DISEASE

Lyme disease, so named for its having been first reported in the town of Lyme, Connecticut, is a potentially debilitating disease carried by deer ticks, which thrive in dry, brush-covered areas, particularly on the coast. Always **use insect repellent;** outbreaks of Lyme disease all over the East Coast make it imperative that you protect yourself from ticks from early spring through summer. To prevent bites, **wear light-colored clothing and tuck pant legs into socks.** Look for black ticks about the size of a pinhead around hairlines and the warmest parts of the body. If you have been bitten, **consult a physician, especially if you see the telltale bull's-eye bite pattern.** Influenza-like symptoms often accompany a Lyme infection. Early treatment is imperative.

PESTS AND OTHER HAZARDS

New England's two greatest insect pests are black flies and mosquitoes. The former are a phenomenon of late spring and early summer and are generally a problem only in the densely wooded areas of the far north. Mosquitoes, however, can be a nuisance just about everywhere in summer—they're at their worst following snowy winters and wet springs. The best protection against both pests is repellent containing DEET; if you're camping in the woods during black fly season, you'll also want to **use fine mesh screening in eating and sleeping areas, and even wear mesh headgear.** A particular pest of coastal areas, especially salt marshes, is the greenhead fly. Their bite is nasty, and they are best repelled by a liberal application of Avon Skin So Soft.

SHELLFISHING

Coastal waters attract seafood lovers who enjoy harvesting their own clams, mussels, and even lobsters; permits are required, and casual harvesting of lobsters is strictly forbidden. Amateur clammers should be aware that New England shellfish beds are periodically visited by red tides, during which microorganisms can render shellfish poisonous. To keep abreast of the situation, inquire when you apply for a license (usually at town halls or police stations) and pay attention to red tide postings as you travel.

HOLIDAYS

Expect banks and post offices to be closed on all national holidays. Exceptions are restaurants and hotels, which, depending on location, may be even busier at holiday times. Christmas in ski country, for instance, will require early advance dining and lodging reservations. Public transportation schedules will also be affected on major holidays; in general, schedules will be similar for those of normal Sundays.

Major national holidays include New Year's Day (Jan. 1); Martin Luther King Jr. Day (3rd Mon. in Jan.); Presidents' Day (3rd Mon. in Feb.); Memorial Day (last Mon. in May); Independence Day (July 4); Labor Day (1st Mon. in Sept.); Thanksgiving Day (4th Thurs. in Nov.); Christmas Day (Dec. 25); and New Year's Eve (Dec. 31).

INSURANCE

The most useful travel-insurance plan is a comprehensive policy that includes coverage for trip cancellation and interruption, default, trip delay, and medical expenses (with a waiver for preexisting conditions).

Without insurance you will lose all or most of your money if you cancel your trip, regardless of the reason. Default insurance covers you if your tour operator, airline, or cruise line goes out of business. Trip-delay covers expenses that arise because of bad weather or mechanical delays. Study the fine print when comparing policies.

Always **buy travel policies directly from the insurance company**; if you buy them from a cruise line, airline, or tour operator that goes out of business you probably will not be covered for the agency or operator's default, a major risk. Before making any purchase, **review your existing health and homeowner's policies** to find what they cover away from home.

➤ TRAVEL INSURERS: In the United States: **Access America** (✉ 6600 W. Broad St., Richmond, VA 23230, ☎ 800/284–8300, FAX 804/673–1491 or 800/346–9265, WEB www. accessamerica.com). **Travel Guard International** (✉ 1145 Clark St., Stevens Point, WI 54481, ☎ 715/345–0505 or 800/826–1300, FAX 800/955–8785, WEB www.travelguard.com).

FOR INTERNATIONAL TRAVELERS

For information on customs restrictions, *see* Customs and Duties.

CAR TRAVEL

Interstate highways—limited-access, multilane highways whose numbers are prefixed by "I–"—are the fastest routes. Interstates with three-digit numbers encircle urban areas, which may have other limited-access expressways, freeways, and parkways as well. Tolls may be levied on limited-access highways. So-called U.S. highways and state highways are not necessarily limited-access but may have several lanes.

Along larger highways, roadside stops with rest rooms, fast-food restaurants, and sundries stores are well spaced. State police and tow trucks patrol major highways and lend assistance. If your car breaks down on an interstate, pull onto the shoulder and wait for help, or have your passengers wait while you walk to an emergency phone. If you carry a cell phone, dial *55, noting your location on the small green roadside mileage markers.

Driving in the United States is on the right. Do **obey speed limits** posted along roads and highways. Watch for lower limits in small towns and on back roads. On weekdays between 6 and 9 AM and again between 4 and 7 PM **expect heavy traffic.** To encourage carpooling, some freeways have special lanes for so-called high-occupancy vehicles (HOV)—cars carrying more than one passenger.

Bookstores, gas stations, convenience stores, and rest stops sell maps (about $3) and multiregion road atlases (about $10).

For more information, *see* Car Travel.

CONSULATES AND EMBASSIES

➤ AUSTRALIA: **Consulate** (⊠ 150 E. 42nd St., 34th floor, New York, NY 10017, ☎ 212/351–6500).

➤ CANADA: **Consulate** (⊠ 3 Copley Pl., Suite 400, Boston, MA 02216, ☎ 617/262–3760).

➤ NEW ZEALAND: **Consulate** (⊠ 780 3rd Ave. NW, Suite 1904, New York, NY 10017-2024, ☎ 212/832–7420)

➤ UNITED KINGDOM: **Consulate** (⊠ 600 Atlantic Ave., Boston, MA 02210, ☎ 617/248–9555).

CURRENCY

The dollar is the basic unit of U.S. currency. It has 100 cents. Coins include the copper penny (1¢); the silvery nickel (5¢), dime (10¢), quarter (25¢), and half-dollar (50¢); and the golden $1 coin, replacing a now-rare silver dollar. Bills are denominated $1, $5, $10, $20, $50, and $100, all green and identical in size; designs vary. At this writing, the exchange rate is US$1.53 per British pound, $.98 per European Union euro, $.66 per Canadian dollar, $.51 per Australian dollar, and $.49 per New Zealand dollar.

ELECTRICITY

The U.S. standard is AC, 110 volts/60 cycles. Plugs have two flat pins set parallel to each other.

EMERGENCIES

For police, fire, or ambulance, **dial 911.**

INSURANCE

Britons and Australians need extra medical coverage when traveling overseas.

➤ INSURANCE INFORMATION: In Australia: **Insurance Council of Australia** (⊠ Level 3, 56 Pitt St., Sydney, NSW 2000, ☎ 02/9253–5100, FAX 02/9253–5111, WEB www.ica.com.au). In Canada: **RBC Insurance** (⊠ 6880 Financial Dr., Mississauga, Ontario L5N 7Y5, ☎ 905/816–2400 or 800/668–4342, FAX 905/813–4704, WEB www.rbcinsurance.com). In New Zealand: **Insurance Council of New Zealand** (⊠ Level 7, 111–115 Customhouse Quay, Box 474, Wellington, ☎ 04/472–5230, FAX 04/473–3011, WEB www.icnz.org.nz). In the United Kingdom: **Association of British Insurers** (⊠ 51 Gresham St., London EC2V 7HQ, ☎ 020/7600–3333, FAX 020/7696–8999, WEB www.abi.org.uk).

MAIL AND SHIPPING

You can buy stamps and aerograms and send letters and parcels in post offices. Stamp-dispensing machines can occasionally be found in airports, bus and train stations, office buildings, drugstores, and the like. You can also deposit mail in the stout, dark blue steel bins at strategic locations everywhere and in the mail chutes of large buildings; pickup schedules are posted.

For mail sent within the United States, you need a 37¢ stamp for first-class letters weighing up to 1 ounce (23¢ for each additional ounce) and 23¢ for postcards. You pay 80¢ for 1-ounce airmail letters and 70¢ for airmail postcards to most other countries; to Canada and Mexico, you need a 60¢ stamp for a 1-ounce letter and 50¢ for a postcard. An aerogram—a single sheet of lightweight blue paper that folds into its own envelope, stamped for overseas airmail—costs 70¢.

To receive mail on the road, have it sent c/o General Delivery at your destination's main post office (use the correct five-digit ZIP code). You must pick up mail in person within 30 days and show a driver's license or passport.

PASSPORTS AND VISAS

When traveling internationally, **carry your passport** even if you don't need one (it's always the best form of ID) and **make two photocopies of the data page** (one for someone at home and another for you, carried separately from your passport). If you lose your passport, promptly call the nearest embassy or consulate and the local police.

Visitor visas are not necessary for Canadian citizens, or for citizens of Australia and the United Kingdom who are staying fewer than 90 days.

➤ AUSTRALIAN CITIZENS: **Australian State Passport Office** (☎ 131–232, WEB www.passports.gov.au). **United States Consulate General** (✉ MLC Centre, 19–29 Martin Pl., 59th floor, Sydney, NSW 2000, ☎ 02/9373–9200, 1902/941–641 fee-based visa-inquiry line, WEB www.usis-australia. gov/index.html).

➤ CANADIAN CITIZENS: **Passport Office** (to mail in applications: ✉ Department of Foreign Affairs and International Trade, Ottawa, Ontario K1A 0G3, ☎ 819/994–3500 or 800/ 567–6868, WEB www.dfait-maeci.gc. ca/passport).

➤ NEW ZEALAND CITIZENS: **New Zealand Passport Office** (☎ 04/474– 8100 or 0800/22–5050, WEB www. passports.govt.nz). **Embassy of the United States** (✉ 29 Fitzherbert Terr., Thorndon, Wellington, ☎ 04/462– 6000 WEB usembassy.org.nz). **U.S. Consulate General** (✉ Citibank Bldg., 3rd floor, 23 Customs St. E, Auckland, ☎ 09/303–2724, WEB usembassy. org.nz).

➤ U.K. CITIZENS: **London Passport Office** (☎ 0870/521–0410, WEB www. passport.gov.uk). **U.S. Consulate General** (✉ Queen's House, 14 Queen St., Belfast, Northern Ireland BT1 6EQ, ☎ 028/9032–8239, WEB www.usembassy.org.uk). **U.S. Embassy** (enclose a SASE to ✉ Consular Information Unit, 24 Grosvenor Sq., London W1 1AE, for general information; ✉ Visa Branch, 5 Upper Grosvenor St., London W1A 2JB, to submit an application via mail; ☎ 09068/200–290 recorded visa information or 09055/444–546 operator service, both with per-minute charges; WEB www.usembassy.org.uk).

TELEPHONES

All U.S. telephone numbers consist of a three-digit area code and a seven-digit local number. Within most local calling areas, you dial only the seven-digit number. Within the same area code, dial "1" first. To call between area-code regions, dial "1" then all 10 digits; the same goes for calls to numbers prefixed by "800," "888," and "877"—all toll-free. For calls to numbers preceded by "900" you must pay—usually dearly.

For international calls, dial "011" followed by the country code and the local number. For help, dial "0" and ask for an overseas operator. The country code is 61 for Australia, 64 for New Zealand, 44 for the United Kingdom. Calling Canada is the same as calling within the United States. Most local phone books list country codes and U.S. area codes. The country code for the United States is 1.

For operator assistance, dial "0." To obtain someone's phone number, call directory assistance, 555–1212 or occasionally 411. To have the person you're calling foot the bill, phone collect; dial "0" instead of "1" before the 10-digit number.

At pay phones, instructions are usually posted. Usually you insert coins in a slot (10¢–50¢ for local calls) and wait for a steady tone before dialing. When you call long-distance, the operator tells you how much to insert; prepaid phone cards, widely available in various denominations, are easier. Call the number on the back, punch in the card's personal identification number when prompted, then dial your number.

LODGING

Hotel and motel chains provide standard rooms and amenities in major cities and at or near traditional vacation destinations. At small inns, where each room is different and amenities vary in number and quality, price isn't always a reliable indicator; fortunately, when you call to make reservations, most hosts will be happy to give all manner of details about their properties, down to the color scheme of the handmade quilts—so **ask all your questions before you book.** Also **ask if the property has a**

Web site; sites may have helpful information and pictures, although it's always wise to confirm how up-to-date the information is. The rooms in the lodgings reviewed here have private baths unless otherwise indicated.

The lodgings we list are the cream of the crop in each price category. We always list the facilities that are available—but we don't specify whether they cost extra. When pricing accommodations, always ask what's included and what costs extra. Lodgings are indicated in the text by a little house icon, 🏠 ; lodging establishments whose restaurants warrant a special trip, by ✕🏠 . Following is the price chart used in this book; note that prices do not include tax, which is 5% in Maine, 8% in New Hampshire, and 9% in Vermont.

CATEGORY	COST*
$$$$	over $180
$$$	$130–$180
$$	$80–$130
$	under $80

*All prices are for a standard double room during peak season and not including tax or gratuities. Some inns add a 15% service charge.

Assume that hotels operate on the **European Plan** (EP, with no meals) unless we specify that they use the **Continental Plan** (CP, with a Continental breakfast), **Breakfast Plan** (BP, with a full breakfast), **Modified American Plan** (MAP, with breakfast and dinner), or the **Full American Plan** (FAP, with all meals).

APARTMENT RENTALS

If you want a home base that's roomy enough for a family and comes with cooking facilities, **consider a furnished rental**. These can save you money, especially if you're traveling with a group. Home-exchange directories sometimes list rentals as well as exchanges. In New England, you are most likely to find a house, apartment, or condo rental in areas in which ownership of second homes is common, such as beach resorts and ski country. A good strategy is to **inquire about rentals in what would be the off-season** for those resort areas—for instance, it's fairly easy to

rent ski chalets during the summer. Home-exchange directories sometimes list rentals as well as exchanges. Another good bet is to **contact real estate agents in the area in which you are interested.**

➤ INTERNATIONAL AGENTS: **Hideaways International** (✉ 767 Islington St., Portsmouth, NH 03801, ☎ 603/430–4433 or 800/843–4433, FAX 603/430–4444, WEB www.hideaways.com; membership $129).

➤ LOCAL AGENTS: **Cyberrentals.com** (✉ 110 Main St., Ludlow, VT 05149, ☎ 802/228–7158, FAX 815/461–5569, WEB www.CyberRentals.com). **Go New England** (✉ Box 322, Harwich Port, MA 02646-0322, WEB www.gonewengland.com).

BED-AND-BREAKFASTS

The bed-and-breakfasts and small inns of Maine, Vermont, and New Hampshire offer some of the region's most distinctive lodging experiences. Some are homey and casual, others provide a stay in a historic property in a city or out in the country, and still others are modern and luxurious. At even the poshest country inns, rooms frequently lack telephones or televisions; many proprietors feel that their guests are actively escaping from the modern world. These properties are also not likely to have air-conditioning, which is often superfluous in New England's mountains or seashore. Most inns offer breakfast—hence the name bed-and-breakfast—yet this formula varies; at one B&B you may be served muffins and coffee, at another a multicourse feast with fresh flowers on the table. In keeping with the preferences of their guests, most inns and B&Bs prohibit smoking, and some of the inns with antiques or other expensive furnishings do not allow children. Almost all say no to pets. Always be sure to **ask about any restrictions** when you're making a reservation. It's also necessary to **inquire about minimum stays**; many inns require a two-night stay on weekends, for example.

CAMPING

The state offices of tourism (☞ Visitor Information) supply information about privately operated campgrounds and ones in parks run by state agencies and the federal government.

HOME EXCHANGES

If you would like to exchange your home for someone else's, **join a home-exchange organization,** which will send you its updated listings of available exchanges for a year and will include your own listing in at least one of them. It's up to you to make specific arrangements.

➤ EXCHANGE CLUBS: **HomeLink International** (✉ Box 47747, Tampa, FL 33647, ☎ 813/975–9825 or 800/638–3841, FAX 813/910–8144, WEB www.homelink.org; $106 per year). **Intervac Home Exchange** (✉ 30 Corte San Fernando, Tiburon, CA 94920, ☎ 800/756–4663, FAX 415/435–7440, WEB www.intervacus.com; $93 yearly fee includes one catalog and on-line access).

HOSTELS

No matter what your age, you can **save on lodging costs by staying at hostels.** In some 4,500 locations in more than 70 countries around the world, Hostelling International (HI), the umbrella group for a number of national youth-hostel associations, offers single-sex, dorm-style beds and, at many hostels, rooms for couples and family accommodations. Membership in any HI national hostel association, open to travelers of all ages, allows you to stay in HI-affiliated hostels at member rates; one-year membership is about $25 for adults (C$35 for a two-year minimum membership in Canada, £13 in the U.K., A$52 in Australia, and NZ$40 in New Zealand); hostels run about $10–$30 per night. Members have priority if the hostel is full; they're also eligible for discounts around the world, even on rail and bus travel in some countries.

➤ ORGANIZATIONS: **Hostelling International—American Youth Hostels** (✉ 733 15th St. NW, Suite 840, Washington, DC 20005, ☎ 202/783–6161, FAX 202/783–6171, WEB www.hiayh.org). **Hostelling International—Canada** (✉ 400–205 Catherine St., Ottawa, Ontario K2P 1C3, ☎ 613/237–7884 or 800/663–5777, FAX 613/237–7868, WEB www.hihostels.ca).

Youth Hostel Association of England and Wales (✉ Trevelyan House, Dimple Rd., Matlock, Derbyshire DE4 3YH, U.K., ☎ 0870/870–8808, FAX 0169/592–702, WEB www.yha.org.uk). **Youth Hostel Association Australia** (✉ 10 Mallett St., Camperdown, NSW 2050, ☎ 02/9565–1699, FAX 02/9565–1325, WEB www.yha.com.au). **Youth Hostels Association of New Zealand** (✉ Level 3, 193 Cashel St., Box 436, Christchurch, ☎ 03/379–9970, FAX 03/365–4476, WEB www.yha.org.nz).

HOTELS

Hotel and motel chains are amply represented in Maine, Vermont, and New Hampshire. Some of the large chains, such as Holiday Inn, Hilton, Hyatt, Marriott, and Ramada, operate all-suites, budget, business-oriented, or luxury resorts, often variations on the parent corporation's name (Courtyard by Marriott, for example). Though some chain hotels and motels may have a standardized look to them, this "cookie-cutter" approach also means that you can rely on the same level of comfort and efficiency at all properties in a well-managed chain, and at a chain's premier properties—its so-called flagship hotels—the decor and services may be outstanding.

Maine, Vermont, and New Hampshire are liberally supplied with small, independent motels, which run the gamut from the tired to the tidy. Don't overlook these mom-and-pop operations; they frequently offer cheerful, convenient accommodations at lower rates than the chains.

While reservations are always a good idea, they are particularly recommended in summer and winter resort areas; in college towns during September and at graduation time in the spring; and at areas renowned for autumn foliage.

Most hotels and motels will hold your reservation until 6 PM; **call ahead if you plan to arrive late.** All will hold a late reservation for you if you guarantee your reservation with a credit-card number.

When you call to make a reservation, **ask all the necessary questions up**

front. If you are arriving with a car, ask if there is a parking lot or covered garage and whether there is an extra fee for parking. If you like to eat your meals in, ask if the hotel has a restaurant or whether it has room service (most do, but not necessarily 24 hours a day—and be forewarned that it can be expensive). Most hotels and motels have in-room TVs, often with cable movies, but verify this if you like to watch TV. If you want an in-room crib for your child, there will probably be an additional charge.

➤ TOLL-FREE NUMBERS: **Best Western** (☎ 800/528–1234, WEB www. bestwestern.com). **Choice** (☎ 800/ 221–2222, WEB www.choicehotels. com). **Clarion** (☎ 800/424–6423, WEB www.choicehotels.com). **Colony Resorts** (☎ 800/777–1700). **Comfort Inn** (☎ 800/424–6423, WEB www. choicehotels.com). **Days Inn** (☎ 800/ 325–2525, WEB www.daysinn.com). **Doubletree and Red Lion Hotels** (☎ 800/222–8733, WEB www.hilton. com). **Embassy Suites** (☎ 800/362– 2779, WEB www.embassysuites.com). **Fairfield Inn** (☎ 800/228–2800, WEB www.marriott.com).**Four Seasons** (☎ 800/332–3442, WEB www. fourseasons.com). **Hilton** (☎ 800/ 445–8667, WEB www.hilton.com). **Holiday Inn** (☎ 800/465–4329, WEB www.sixcontinentshotels.com). **Howard Johnson** (☎ 800/654–4656, WEB www.hojo.com). **Hyatt Hotels & Resorts** (☎ 800/233–1234, WEB www. hyatt.com). **La Quinta** (☎ 800/531– 5900, WEB www.laquinta.com). **Marriott** (☎ 800/228–9290, WEB www. marriott.com). **Quality Inn** (☎ 800/ 228–5151, WEB www.choicehotels. com). **Radisson** (☎ 800/333–3333, WEB www.radisson.com). **Ramada** (☎ 800/228–2828; 800/854–7854 international reservations; WEB www.ramada.com or www. ramadahotels.com). **Sheraton** (☎ 800/325–3535, WEB www. sheraton.com). **Sleep Inn** (☎ 800/ 424–6423, WEB www.choicehotels. com). **Westin Hotels & Resorts** (☎ 800/228–3000, WEB www. starwood.com/westin).

MAIL AND SHIPPING

➤ OVERNIGHT SERVICES: FedEx (☎ 800/463–3339). UPS (☎ 800/742– 5877).

MEDIA

NEWSPAPERS AND MAGAZINES

The *New York Times* and the national *USA Today* are available in all but the most remote regions of Maine, Vermont, and New Hampshire; of the two, the *Times* is by far the more thorough and is considered the U.S. States newspaper of record. The *Boston Globe,* a respected morning daily, is also available throughout the region. Most cities with 10,000 or more inhabitants generally have their own daily newspapers, many of which carry comprehensive listings of local events at least once a week. Larger cities and college towns often have at least one alternative publication that provides extensive coverage on the local cultural and social scene. Among regional magazines, the most noteworthy are *Yankee, Vermont Life,* and *Down East* (Maine).

RADIO AND TELEVISION

As in the rest of the United States, talk shows are usually found on AM radio stations, while FM stations are devoted primarily to music. National Public Radio (NPR), which has FM affiliates in Maine, Vermont, and New Hampshire, provides a combination of both, including *Morning Edition* and *All Things Considered,* the most comprehensive radio news programs in the United States.

Although major metropolitan areas each have their own local television stations and public television affiliates, cable and satellite TV bring dozens of channels to most hotels and motels. Cable News Network (CNN) offers the most comprehensive national and international news coverage. Boston's public television affiliate, WGBH, is a flagship station of the U.S. Public Television Network.

MONEY MATTERS

It costs about the same to travel in Maine, Vermont, and New Hampshire as it does throughout the rest of the northeastern United States. As a rule, this is slightly more expensive than touring just about anywhere else in the country, with the exception of metropolitan California and major resort areas. Out in the countryside, or in lesser metropolitan centers, you'll find consistent good value, with the exception of fall foliage season along well-traveled routes.

British, Australian, and New Zealand travelers will find hotel and restaurant tariffs comparable to those they're familiar with at home; Canadians, however, may be in for a bit of sticker shock due to the prevailing exchange rate between the two currencies. However, a number of hotel and resort operators, and places frequented by Canadian travelers, often offer exchange rates at or close to par as a promotional come-on.

Unless you're out slumming or deliberately going posh, figure on paying about $1 for a cup of coffee in Maine, Vermont, or New Hampshire, $2–$3 for a draft beer, and $4 for a ham sandwich with a few pickles and chips.

Prices throughout this guide are given for adults. Substantially reduced fees are almost always available for children, students, and senior citizens. For information on taxes, see Taxes.

ATMS

Automatic teller machines (ATMs) are a useful way to obtain cash. A debit card, also known as a check card, deducts funds directly from your checking account and helps you stay within your budget. When you want to rent a car, though, you may still need an old-fashioned credit card. Although you can always *pay* for your car with a debit card, some agencies will not allow you to *reserve* a car with a debit card.

ATMs are located just about everywhere in Maine, Vermont, and New Hampshire, from big-city banks to Vermont general stores.

CREDIT CARDS

Using a credit card on the road allows you to delay payment and gives you certain rights as a consumer (☞ Consumer Protection).

Throughout this guide, the following abbreviations are used: AE, American Express; D, Discover; DC, Diners Club; MC, MasterCard; and V, Visa.

➤ REPORTING LOST CARDS: **American Express** (☎ 800/441–0519). **Discover** (☎ 800/347–2683). **Diners Club** (☎ 800/234–6377). **MasterCard** (☎ 800/622–7747). **Visa** (☎ 800/ 847–2911).

NATIONAL PARKS

Look into discount passes to save money on park entrance fees. For $50, the National Parks Pass admits you (and any passengers in your private vehicle) to all national parks, monuments, and recreation areas, as well as other sites run by the National Park Service, for a year. (In parks that charge per person, the pass admits you, your spouse and children, and your parents, when you arrive together.) Camping and parking are extra. The $15 Golden Eagle Pass, a hologram you affix to your National Parks Pass, functions as an upgrade, granting entry to all sites run by the NPS, the U.S. Fish and Wildlife Service, the U.S. Forest Service, and the Bureau of Land Management (BLM). The upgrade, which expires with the parks pass, is sold by most national-park, Fish-and-Wildlife, and BLM fee stations. A percentage of the proceeds from pass sales funds National Parks projects.

Both the Golden Age Passport ($10), for U.S. citizens or permanent residents who are 62 and older, and the Golden Access Passport (free), for those with disabilities, entitle holders (and any passengers in their private vehicles) to lifetime free entry to all national parks, plus 50% off fees for the use of many park facilities and services. (The discount doesn't always apply to companions.) To obtain them, you must show proof of age and of U.S. citizenship or permanent residency—such as a U.S. passport, driver's license, or birth certificate—and, if requesting Golden Access, proof of disability. The Golden Age and Golden Access passes, as well as the National Parks Pass, are available at any NPS-run site that charges an entrance fee. The National Parks Pass is also available by mail and via the Internet.

➤ PASSES BY MAIL AND ON-LINE: **National Park Foundation** (WEB www.nationalparks.org). **National Parks Pass** (✉ 27540 Ave. Mentry, Valen-

cia, CA 91355, ☎ 888/GO–PARKS
or 888/467–2757, WEB www.national-
parks.org); include a check or money
order payable to the National Park
Service for the pass, plus $3.95 for
shipping and handling.

OUTDOORS AND SPORTS

See Destination: Maine, Vermont, and
New Hampshire (Chapter 1) for a
summary of sporting opportunities.
For further information, call state
information offices (☞ Visitor Information).

BIKING

➤ BIKING: **Vermont Bicycle Touring**
(✉ Box 711, Bristol, VT 05443,
☎ 802/453–4811 or 800/245–3868)
operates tours throughout the region
and overseas.

HIKING

➤ HIKING: **Appalachian Mountain
Club** (✉ Box 298, Gorham, NH
03581, ☎ 603/466–2725). **Audubon
Society of New Hampshire** (✉ 3 Silk
Farm Rd., Concord, NH 03301,
☎ 603/224–9909). **Green Mountain
Club** (✉ Rte. 100 [Box 650, Waterbury, VT 05677], ☎ 802/244–7037).
White Mountain National Forest
(✉ 719 N. Main St., Laconia, NH
03246, ☎ 603/528–8721).

SKIING

See Destination: Maine, Vermont, and
New Hampshire for a skiing information and destination map.

PACKING

The principal rule on weather in
Maine, Vermont, and New Hampshire
is that there are no rules. A cold, foggy
morning in spring can and often does
become a bright, 60° afternoon. A
summer breeze can suddenly turn
chilly, and rain often appears with
little warning. Thus, the best advice on
how to dress is to **layer your clothing**
so that you can peel off or add gar-
ments as needed for comfort. Showers
are frequent, so **pack a raincoat and
umbrella.** Even in summer you should
bring long pants, a sweater or two,
and a waterproof windbreaker, for
evenings are often chilly and sea spray
can make things cool.

Casual sportswear—walking shoes
and jeans or khakis—will take you

almost everywhere, but swimsuits and
bare feet will not: shirts and shoes are
required attire at even the most casual
venues. Dress in restaurants is generally casual, except at a handful of
distinguished restaurants. Upscale
resorts will, at the very least, require
men to wear collared shirts at dinner,
and jeans are often frowned upon.

In summer, **bring a hat and sun-
screen.** Remember also to **pack insect
repellent**; to prevent Lyme disease
you'll need to guard against ticks
from early spring through the summer (☞ Health).

In your carry-on luggage, **pack an
extra pair of eyeglasses or contact
lenses and enough of any medication**
you take to last a few days longer
than the entire trip. You may also ask
your doctor to write a spare prescription using the drug's generic name,
since brand names may vary from
country to country. In luggage to be
checked, **never pack prescription
drugs or valuables.** And don't forget
to carry with you the addresses of
offices that handle refunds of lost
traveler's checks. Check *Fodor's How
to Pack* (available in bookstores
everywhere) for more tips.

To avoid customs and security delays,
carry medications in their original
packaging. Don't pack any sharp
objects in your carry-on luggage,
including knives of any size or material, scissors, manicure tools, and
corkscrews, or anything else that
might arouse suspicion.

CHECKING LUGGAGE

You are allowed one carry-on bag
and one personal article, such as a
purse or a laptop computer. Make
sure that everything you carry aboard
will fit under your seat or in the
overhead bin. Get to the gate early, so
you can board as soon as possible,
before the overhead bins fill up.

If you are flying internationally, note
that baggage allowances may be
determined not by piece but by
weight—generally 88 pounds (40
kilograms) in first class, 66 pounds
(30 kilograms) in business class,
and 44 pounds (20 kilograms) in
economy.

Airline liability for baggage is limited to $2,500 per person on flights within the United States. On international flights it amounts to $9.07 per pound or $20 per kilogram for checked baggage (roughly $640 per 70-pound bag) and $400 per passenger for unchecked baggage. You can buy additional coverage at check-in for about $10 per $1,000 of coverage, but it excludes a rather extensive list of items, shown on your airline ticket.

Before departure, **itemize your bags' contents** and their worth, and label the bags with your name, address, and phone number. (If you use your home address, cover it so potential thieves can't see it readily.) Inside each bag, **pack a copy of your itinerary.** At check-in, **make sure that each bag is correctly tagged** with the destination airport's three-letter code. If your bags arrive damaged or fail to arrive at all, file a written report with the airline before leaving the airport.

PASSPORTS AND VISAS

For information on passports for non-U.S. citizens, *see* For International Travelers.

➤ U.S. CITIZENS: **National Passport Information Center** (☎ 900/225–5674 or 888/362–8668, WEB www.travel.state.gov/passport services; calls to the 900 number are 35¢ per minute for automated service, $1.05 per minute for operator service); calls to the 888 number, for Visa, Master-Card, or American Express card holders, are billed at a flat rate of $4.95.

SAFETY

Rural New England is one of the country's safest regions, so much so that residents often leave their doors unlocked. In the cities, observe the usual precautions; it's worth noting, however, that crime rates have been dropping in metropolitan areas. You should avoid out-of-the-way or poorly lit areas at night; clutch handbags close to your body and don't let them out of your sight; and be on your guard in subways, not only during the deserted wee hours but in crowded rush hours, when pickpockets are at work. Keep your valuables in hotel safes. Try to use ATMs in busy, well-lighted places such as bank lobbies.

If your vehicle breaks down in a rural area, **pull as far off the road as possible,** tie a handkerchief to your radio antenna (or use flares at night—check if your rental agency can provide them), and stay in your car with the doors locked until help arrives. Don't pick up hitchhikers. If you're planning to leave a car overnight to make use of off-road trails or camping facilities, **make arrangements for a supervised parking area** if at all possible. Cars left at trailhead parking lots are subject to theft and vandalism.

The universal telephone number for crime and other emergencies throughout Maine, Vermont, and New Hampshire is 911.

SENIOR-CITIZEN TRAVEL

To qualify for age-related discounts, **mention your senior-citizen status up front** when booking hotel reservations (not when checking out) and before you're seated in restaurants (not when paying the bill). Be sure to have identification on hand. When renting a car, ask about promotional car-rental discounts, which can be cheaper than senior-citizen rates.

Members of AARP, an organization for people 50 years of age and older, are often eligible for discounts at attractions, lodgings, and restaurants.

➤ EDUCATIONAL PROGRAMS: **AARP** (✉ 3200 E. Carson St., Lakewood CA 90712, ☎ 800/424–3410). **Elderhostel** (✉ 11 Ave. de Lafayette, Boston, MA 02111-1746, ☎ 877/426–8056, FAX 877/426–2166, WEB www.elderhostel.org). **Interhostel** (✉ University of New Hampshire, 6 Garrison Ave., Durham, NH 03824, ☎ 603/862–1147 or 800/733–9753, FAX 603/862–1113, WEB www.learn.unh.edu).

SHOPPING

SMART SOUVENIRS

Distinctive northern New England souvenirs include Blue Hill pottery—sturdy, brightly colored tableware made in Blue Hill, Maine, and available at several shops in the area; Bennington Pottery, attractive, utilitarian items made in the Vermont town (Bennington Potters North in Burlington sells inexpensive seconds); moccasins of moose and deer hide made by Maine Native Americans and sold throughout the state; and whimsical animal prints by Woody Jackson (cows) and Stephen Huneck (dogs), available at several Vermont galleries.

WATCH OUT

When you're looking for pure maple syrup, a sugarhouse can be the most or the least expensive place to shop, depending on how tourist-oriented it is. Small grocery stores are often a good source of less-expensive syrup. **Look for the word "pure" and the state designation;** much artificially flavored sugarcane syrup is sold as "maple."

With any crafts item, always **be aware that some vendors substitute mass-produced imports** for the real thing; if the price seems too good to be true, it probably is.

As the United States is signatory to treaties involving trade and products made from endangered animal species, you won't need to worry about purchasing souvenirs that you won't be able to bring into your home country. Visitors to New Hampshire should be aware that one item for sale in this state—fireworks, found at many roadside stands—is strictly forbidden as airline baggage and cannot be imported into most countries.

STUDENTS IN MAINE, VERMONT, AND NEW HAMPSHIRE

Most major attractions throughout the region offer discount admissions to students.

➤ IDS AND SERVICES: **Council Travel** (✉ 205 E. 42nd St., 15th floor, New York, NY 10017, ☎ 212/822–2700 or 888/226–8624, FAX 212/822–2719, WEB www.counciltravel.com). **Travel Cuts** (✉ 187 College St., Toronto, Ontario M5T 1P7, Canada, ☎ 416/979–2406 or 888/838–2887, FAX 416/979–8167, WEB www.travelcuts.com).

TAXES

See Dining *and* Lodging for information about taxes on restaurant meals and accommodations.

SALES TAX

Sales taxes in this region are as follows: Maine 5%; Vermont 5% (with an exemption on purchase of individual clothing items costing under $110). No sales tax is charged in New Hampshire. Some states and municipalities levy an additional tax (from 1% to 10%) on lodging or restaurant meals. Alcoholic beverages are sometimes taxed at a higher rate than that applied to meals.

TIME

Maine, Vermont, and New Hampshire are in the eastern time zone.

TIPPING

At restaurants, a 15% tip is standard for waiters; up to 20% is expected at more expensive establishments. The same goes for taxi drivers, bartenders, and hairdressers. Coat-check operators usually expect $1; bellhops and porters should get $1 per bag; hotel maids should get about $1.50 per day of your stay. Hotel concierges should be tipped if you utilize their services; the amount varies widely depending on the nature of service. On package tours, conductors and drivers usually get $10 per day from the group as a whole; check whether this has already been figured into your cost. For local sightseeing tours, you may individually tip the driver-guide $1–$5, depending on the length of the tour and the number of people in your party, if he or she has been helpful or informative.

TOURS AND PACKAGES

Because everything is prearranged on a prepackaged tour or independent vacation, you spend less time planning—and often get it all at a good price.

BOOKING WITH AN AGENT

Travel agents are excellent resources. But it's a good idea to collect brochures from several agencies, as some agents' suggestions may be influenced by relationships with tour and package firms that reward them for volume sales. If you have a special interest, **find an agent with expertise in that area**; the American Society of Travel Agents (ASTA; ☞ Travel Agencies) has a database of specialists worldwide.

Make sure your travel agent knows the accommodations and other services of the place being recommended. Ask about the hotel's location, room size, beds, and whether it has a pool, room service, or programs for children, if you care about these. Has your agent been there in person or sent others whom you can contact?

Do some homework on your own, too: local tourism boards can provide information about lesser-known and small-niche operators, some of which may sell only direct.

BUYER BEWARE

Each year consumers are stranded or lose their money when tour operators—even large ones with excellent reputations—go out of business. So **check out the operator.** Ask several travel agents about its reputation, and try to **book with a company that has a consumer-protection program.** (Look for information in the company's brochure.) In the United States, members of the National Tour Association and the United States Tour Operators Association are required to set aside funds to cover your payments and travel arrangements in the event that the company defaults. It's also a good idea to choose a company that participates in the American Society of Travel Agents' Tour Operator Program (TOP); ASTA will act as mediator in any disputes between you and your tour operator.

Remember that the more your package or tour includes the better you can predict the ultimate cost of your vacation. Make sure you know exactly what is covered, and **beware of hidden costs.** Are taxes, tips, and transfers included? Entertainment and excursions? These can add up.

➤ TOUR-OPERATOR RECOMMENDATIONS: **American Society of Travel Agents** (☞ Travel Agencies). **National Tour Association** (NTA; ✉ 546 E. Main St., Lexington, KY 40508, ☎ 859/226–4444 or 800/682–8886, WEB www.ntaonline.com). **United States Tour Operators Association** (USTOA; ✉ 275 Madison Ave., Suite 2014, New York, NY 10016, ☎ 212/599–6599 or 800/468–7862, FAX 212/599–6744, WEB www.ustoa.com).

TRAIN TRAVEL

The *Down Easter* connects Boston with Portland, Maine. Amtrak services include the *Vermonter* between Washington, D.C., and St. Albans, Vermont, and the *Ethan Allen* between New York and Rutland, Vermont. These trains run on a daily basis. Amtrak sells passes good for travel within specific regions for a set period of time and also has a schedule of reduced children's fares. Reservations are required for certain trains and for all overnight accommodations. As a general policy, Amtrack does not permit smoking on its trains. To avoid last-minute confusion, allow 15 to 30 minutes to make train connections.

Private rail lines have scenic train trips throughout New England, particularly during fall foliage season. Several use vintage steam equipment; the most notable is the Cog Railway to Mt. Washington in New Hampshire.

➤ TRAIN INFORMATION: **Amtrak** (☎ 800/872–7245, WEB www.amtrak. com).

TRANSPORTATION AROUND MAINE, VERMONT, AND NEW HAMPSHIRE

If you plan to travel around a sizable portion of the region, a car or car rental is a *must*. Rail connections are infrequent and regional travel by air is expensive. Buses connect major cities and towns, but schedules are often inconvenient and routes are generally not the most scenic. Since one of New England's primary attractions is its picturesque countryside and innumerable small villages, only the automobile traveler (or bicyclist) can really appreciate all the region has to offer.

TRAVEL AGENCIES

A good travel agent puts your needs first. Look for an agency that has been in business at least five years, emphasizes customer service, and has someone on staff who specializes in your destination. In addition, **make sure the agency belongs to a professional trade organization.** The American Society of Travel Agents (ASTA)—the largest and most influential in the field, with more than 24,000 members in some 140 countries—maintains and enforces a strict code of ethics and will step in to help mediate any agent-client disputes involving ASTA members if necessary. ASTA (whose motto is "Without a travel agent, you're on your own") also maintains a Web site that includes a directory of agents. (If a travel agency is also acting as your tour operator, *see* Buyer Beware *in* Tours and Packages.)

➤ LOCAL AGENT REFERRALS: American Society of Travel Agents (ASTA; ⊠ 1101 King St., Suite 200, Alexandria, VA 22314, ☎ 800/965-2782 24-hr hot line, FAX 703/739-3268, WEB www.astanet.com). Association of British Travel Agents (⊠ 68-71 Newman St., London W1T 3AH, ☎ 020/7637-2444, FAX 020/7637-0713, WEB www.abtanet.com). Association of Canadian Travel Agents (⊠ 130 Albert St., Suite 1705, Ottawa, Ontario K1P 5G4, ☎ 613/237-3657, FAX 613/237-7052, WEB www.acta.net). Australian Federation of Travel Agents (⊠ Level 3, 309 Pitt St., Sydney, NSW 2000, ☎ 02/9264-3299, FAX 02/9264-1085, WEB www.afta.com.au). Travel Agents' Association of New Zealand (⊠ Level 5, Tourism and Travel House, 79 Boulcott St., Box 1888, Wellington 10033, ☎ 04/499-0104, FAX 04/499-0827, WEB www.taanz.org.nz).

VISITOR INFORMATION

Each state provides a helpful free information kit, including a guidebook, map, and listings of attractions and events. All include listings and/or advertisements for lodging and dining establishments. Each state also has an official Web site with material on sights and lodgings; most of these sites have a calendar of events and other special features.

➤ TOURIST INFORMATION: **Maine Tourism Association** (⊠ 325-B Water St. [Box 2300, Hallowell, ME 04347], ☎ 207/623-0363 or 888/624-6345, WEB www.visitmaine.com). **New Hampshire Office of Travel and Tourism Development** (⊠ Box 1856, Concord, NH 03302, ☎ 603/271-2343; 800/258-3608 seasonal events; 800/386-4664 brochures; WEB www.visitnh.gov). **Vermont Chamber of Commerce,** Department of Travel and Tourism (⊠ Box 37, Montpelier, VT 05601, ☎ 802/223-3443, WEB www.VTchamber.com). **Vermont Department of Tourism and Marketing** (⊠ 134 State St., Montpelier, VT 05602, ☎ 802/828-3237; 800/837-6668 brochures; WEB www.1800VT.com).

➤ IN THE U.K.: **Discover New England** (⊠ Admail 4 International, Greatness La., Sevenoaks, England TN14 5BQ, ☎ 01732/742777, WEB www.discovernewengland.org).

WEB SITES

Do check out the World Wide Web when planning your trip. You'll find everything from weather forecasts to virtual tours of famous cities. Be sure to **visit Fodors.com** (www.fodors.com), a complete travel-planning site. You can research prices and book plane tickets, hotel rooms, rental cars, vacation packages, and more. In addition, you can post your pressing questions in the Travel Talk section. Other planning tools include a currency converter and weather reports, and there are loads of links to travel resources.

MAINE

MaineToday.com provides travel information at WEB travel.mainetoday.com. Maine's **Nordic Ski Council** provides cross-country info at WEB www.mnsc.com. The site of **Ski Maine** (WEB www.skimaine.com) has information about alpine snow sports.

NEW HAMPSHIRE

For information on downhill and cross-country skiing, WEB www.skinh.com is the site of **Ski New Hampshire.**

VERMONT

The **Vermont Ski Areas Association** covers the downhill scene at WEB www.skivermont.com. Up-to-date foliage reports are given at WEB www.1800vermont.com.

GENERAL INTEREST

The Great Outdoor Recreation Page (WEB www.gorp.com) is arranged into three easily navigated categories: attractions, activities, and locations; within most of the "locations" are links to the New England state parks office. The **National Park Service** site (WEB www.nps.gov) lists all national parks and has extensive historical, cultural, and environmental information. **Visit New England** (WEB www. visitnewengland.com) covers the entire region.

WHEN TO GO

Maine, Vermont, and New Hampshire are year-round destinations. But you might want to **stay away from rural areas during mud season in April and black-fly season from mid-May to mid-June.** Many smaller museums and attractions are open only from Memorial Day to mid-October, at other times by appointment only.

Memorial Day is the start of the migration to the beaches and the mountains, and summer begins in earnest on July 4. Those who are driving along the Maine coast in July or August should know that Friday and Sunday are the days weekenders clog the coastal roads and feeder routes I–95 and U.S. 1; a better time to visit may be after Labor Day.

Fall is the most colorful season in Maine, Vermont, and New Hampshire, a time when many inns and hotels are booked months in advance by foliage-viewing visitors. The region's dense hardwood forests explode in color as the diminishing hours of autumn daylight signal trees to stop producing chlorophyll. As green is stripped away from the leaves of maples, oaks, birches, beeches, and other deciduous species, a rainbow of reds, oranges, yellows, purples, and other vivid hues is revealed. The first scarlet and gold colors emerge in mid-September in northern areas; "peak" color occurs at different times from year to year. Generally, it's best to **visit the northern reaches in late September and early October** and move southward as October progresses.

All leaves are off the trees by Halloween, and hotel rates fall as the leaves do, dropping significantly until ski season begins. November and early December are hunting season in much of the region; those who venture into the woods should wear bright orange clothing.

Winter is the time for downhill and cross-country skiing. Major ski resorts in Maine, Vermont, and New Hampshire are well equipped with snowmaking equipment if nature falls short. Along the coast, bed-and-breakfasts that remain open will often rent rooms at far lower prices than in summer.

In spring, despite mud season, maple sugaring goes on in Maine, New Hampshire, and Vermont, and the fragrant scent of lilacs is never far away.

CLIMATE

In winter, coastal areas are cold and damp; inland temperatures may be lower, but generally drier conditions make them easier to bear. Snowfall is heaviest in the interior mountains and

BURLINGTON, VT

Jan.	29F	– 2C	May	67F	19C	Sept.	74F	23C
	11	–12		45	7		50	10
Feb.	31F	– 1C	June	77F	25C	Oct.	59F	15C
	11	–12		56	13		40	4
Mar.	40F	4C	July	83F	28C	Nov.	45F	7C
	22	6		59	15		31	– 1
Apr.	54F	12C	Aug.	79F	26C	Dec.	31F	– 1C
	34	1		58	14		16	– 9

PORTLAND, ME

Jan.	31F	– 1C	May	61F	16C	Sept.	68F	20C
	16	– 9		47	8		52	11
Feb.	32F	0C	June	72F	22C	Oct.	58F	14C
	16	– 9		54	15		43	6
Mar.	40F	4C	July	76F	24C	Nov.	45F	7C
	27	– 3		61	16		32	0
Apr.	50F	10C	Aug.	74F	23C	Dec.	34F	1C
	36	2		59	15		22	– 6

can range up to several hundred inches per year in northern Maine, New Hampshire, and Vermont. Spring is often windy and rainy; in many years it appears as if winter segues almost immediately into summer. Coastal areas can be quite humid in summer, making even moderate temperatures uncomfortable. One of the delights of inland northern New England, particularly at higher elevations, is the prevalence of cool summer nights. Autumn temperatures can be quite mild in more southerly areas well into October, although northern portions of the region can be quite cold by Columbus Day. In some years, a period of unseasonably mild weather occurs in late October and early November.

➤ FORECASTS: **Weather Channel Connection** (☎ 900/932–8437), 95¢ per minute from a Touch-Tone phone.

FESTIVALS AND SEASONAL EVENTS

➤ JANUARY: The Bethel (ME) **Winter Festival** has snowshoe and cross-country races, sleigh rides, and a snowman contest. Stowe's (VT) festive **Winter Carnival** heats up late in the month. Brookfield (VT) holds its **Ice Harvest Festival,** one of New England's largest. The weeklong **Winter Carnival** in Jackson (NH) includes ski races and ice sculptures.

➤ FEBRUARY: The Camden Snow Bowl in Camden (ME) is the site of the **U.S. National Toboggan Championships.** On tap at the **Brattleboro Winter Carnival** (VT), held during the last week of the month, are jazz concerts and an ice fishing derby. The **Mad River Valley Winter Carnival** (VT) is a week of winter festivities, including dogsled races and ski races and fireworks; Burlington's **Vermont** **Mozart Festival** showcases the Winter Chamber Music Series.

➤ MARCH: This is the season for **maple-sugaring festivals and events:** throughout the month and into April, New England sugarhouses demonstrate procedures from maple-tree tapping to sap boiling. During **Maine Maple Sunday** Maine sugarhouses open for tours and tastings. Maine's Moosehead Lake has a renowned **Ice-Fishing Derby.** Rangeley's (ME) **New England Sled Dog Races** attract more than 100 teams. Stratton Mountain (VT) hosts the U.S. **Open Snowboarding Championships.**

➤ APRIL: During **Reggae Weekend** at Sugarloaf/USA (ME), Caribbean reggae bands play outdoors and inside. At Sunday River's (ME) annual **Bust 'n' Burn Mogul Competition,** professional and amateur bump skiers test their mettle. You can gorge on sea grub at Boothbay Harbor's (ME) **Fishermen's Festival,** held on the third weekend in April. At the **Maple Festival,** held early each April in St. Albans (VT), you can try Sugar on Snow, a taffylike treat.

➤ MAY: The Shelburne Museum in Shelburne (VT) is awash in purple glory in mid-May, when the **Lilac Festival** blossoms. If you want to see a moose, visit Greenville (ME) during **Moosemania,** which runs from mid-May to mid-June. Events include moose safaris and mountain bike and canoe races.

➤ JUNE: In Vermont, you can listen to jazz at Burlington's **Discover Jazz Festival.** Lake Champlain International Fishing Derby (VT) entices anglers to try their fishing skills. The **Boothbay Harbor Windjammer Days** starts the high season for Maine's boating set. **A Taste of Hartford** lets you eat your way through Connecticut's capital city while enjoying outdoor music, dance, comedy, and magic. Burlington, Vermont's **Green Mountain Chew Chew** offers a variety of entertainment including outdoor music and comedy. During the **Strawberry Festival** in Wiscasset (ME), you can get your fill of strawberry goodies.

➤ JULY: During Bath's (ME) **Heritage Days,** Independence day is celebrated with concerts, family entertainment, an art show, a parade, and fireworks. Exeter (NH) holds a **Revolutionary War Festival** at the American Independence Museum with battle re-enactments and period crafts and antiques.The **Marlboro Music Festival** presents classical music at Marlboro College (VT). The **Bar Harbor Festival** (ME) hosts classical, jazz, and popular music concerts into August. Glorious outdoor concert sites and sumptuous picnics are sidelines to fine music at the **Vermont Mozart Festival,** held throughout central and northern Vermont in July and August. The two-day **Stoweflake Hot Air Balloon Festival** in Stowe (VT) is one of the state's most popular events. Admire the furnishings of homes during **Open House Tours** in Camden (ME). The **Yarmouth Clam Festival** (ME) is more than a seafood celebration—expect continuous entertainment and a crafts show throughout the three-day event.

➤ AUGUST: Stowe (VT) hosts a popular **Antique and Classic Car Rally.** The **Southern Vermont Crafts Fair** in Manchester (VT) features popular arts, crafts, and antiques. Sellers and collectors throng to the **Maine Antiques Festival** in Union. Waterfront activities, arts and crafts, entertainment, and succulent Maine lobster feature prominently at Rockland's (ME) **Lobster Festival.** Everything's coming up blueberries at the **Wild Maine Blueberry Festival** in Machias (ME). In Rangeley Lake (ME), the blueberry is king at the annual **Blueberry Festival.** Brunswick's **Maine Festival** is a four-day celebration of Maine arts. Maine's **Annual Maine Highland Games** features traditional Scottish athletic events and music entertainment.

➤ SEPTEMBER: New England's Labor Day fairs include the **Vermont State Fair** in Rutland, with agricultural exhibits and entertainment. The **International Seaplane Fly-In Weekend** sets Moosehead Lake (ME) buzzing. The **Champlain Valley Fair,** in Burlington (VT), has all the features of a large county fair. Many of the country's finest fiddlers compete at the **National Traditional Old-Time Fiddler's Contest** in Barre (VT). Folk music is the highlight at the **Rockport Folk Festival** in Rockport (ME). In Stratton (VT), artists and performers gather for the **Stratton Arts Festival.** The **Common Ground Country Fair** in Unity (ME) is an organic farmer's delight. The **Deerfield Fair** (NH) is one of New England's oldest agricultural fairs. The six small Vermont towns of Walden, Cabot, Plainfield, Peacham, Barnet, and Groton host the weeklong **Northeast Kingdom Fall Foliage Festival.** The **Eastport Salmon Festival** (ME), the first Sunday after Labor Day, hosts entertainers and crafts artists. At the **Annual Seafood Festival** in Hampton Beach (NH), you can sample seafood specialties, dance to live bands, and watch fireworks.

➤ OCTOBER: The **Fryeburg Fair** (ME) presents agricultural exhibits, harness racing, and a pig scramble. **Hildene Farm, Food and Crafts Fair** in Manchester (VT) has farm activities, entertainment, and lots of events for kids.

➤ NOVEMBER: The **International Film Festival** presents films dealing with environmental, human rights, and political issues for a week in Burlington (VT). The **Bradford Wild Game Supper** (VT) draws thousands to taste large and small game animals and birds.

➤ DECEMBER: Historic **Strawbery Banke** (NH) has a Christmas Stroll, with carolers, through nine historic homes. **Christmas Prelude** in Kennebunkport (ME) celebrates winter with concerts, caroling, and special events. The final day of the year is observed with festivals, entertainment, and food in many locations during **First Night Celebrations.** Some of the major cities hosting First Nights are Portland (ME); and Burlington, Montpelier, and St. Johnsbury (all in VT).

1 DESTINATION: MAINE, VERMONT, NEW HAMPSHIRE

Deep Roots in Stony Soil

What's Where

Pleasures and Pastimes

Fodor's Choice

Great Itineraries

DEEP ROOTS IN STONY SOIL

BACK IN THE 1940S photographer Paul Strand took two pictures that capture the essence of northern New England. One photograph, "Susan Thompson, Cape Split Maine," shows a late-middle-aged woman standing perfectly still at the entrance to her barn. She stands, as if pausing in her work, with her worn hands resting at her sides and her wistful, rather tired eyes just averted from the camera. Susan Thompson has the composure of a person who has lived long and hard in a single place.

The second picture, "Side Porch, New England," is a stark, almost abstract composition. Broad, rough-sawn, white painted boards frame the porch. A ladder-back chair with a cane seat (unoccupied) stands on the cracked, weathered boards of the porch floor. A broom and a wire rug-beater hang from nails on the wall. The scene is one of poverty, but not of neglect. The broom has obviously swept the porch clean that very morning, and, though the house has not been painted in years, one imagines that the rugs inside receive regular and thorough beatings.

Susan Thompson is gone, and so, most likely, is the old farmhouse with the clean-swept side porch. But even today, you don't have to travel far off the interstates that knife through Maine, Vermont, and New Hampshire before you run across people and houses and landscapes that are hauntingly similar to those Paul Strand photographed 50 years ago. The serenity, the austere beauty, the reverence for humble objects, the unassuming pride in place, the deep connection between man and landscape—all of these remain very much alive in northern New England.

In northern New England, the people and the land (and in Maine, the sea) seem bound by a marriage that has withstood many hardships. The relationship derives its character in part from the harsh climate. Spring withholds its flowers until mid-May, winter blows through in November, and a summer sunny spell is interrupted by rainstorms before it's had time to settle in properly. (There's a saying that there are two seasons in the north country—winter and July.)

There is a heritage here of self-reliance: the hardship of scratching out a living in small farms; the loneliness of sailing onto the cold northern waters to fish. In some places, isolation and hardship breed suspicion and meanness of spirit; in northern New England, they have engendered patience, endurance, a shrewd sardonic humor, and bottomless loyalty.

People sink deep roots in the thin, stony soil. They forgive the climate its cruelty. The north has a way of taking hold of the body and the spirit, as if weaving a kind of spell. It's not just the residents who are susceptible; summer visitors who have endured years of humid, overcast Julys and fog-shrouded Augusts keep coming back.

Distinct as they are in landscape, geology, and feeling, Maine, Vermont, and New Hampshire are linked by their northerness. There is something pure and fine and mystical about the North, just as there is something lush and soft and voluptuous about the South. You can feel the spirit of the North in the very light. The sun seems to burn more sharply and cleanly in the north country: It scours the rocks on the Maine coast, fills Vermont valleys with powdered gold in September, and turns the new snow of January into sapphires and diamonds.

Even more evocative than the light are the sounds of the North: the mournful, five-note whistle of the white-throated sparrow piercing the stillness of a June morning; the slap of lake water against a sandy shore; or the more insistent murmur of the sea reaching into a cove.

The explosions of warfare have not sounded in northern New England since the War of 1812, but throughout the 19th century the explosions of the industrial revolution ripped through the rural quiet in parts of these three states, particularly in southern New Hampshire. But eventually the noise of this revolution subsided. For the first half of the 20th century, the history of northern New England was primarily a history of decline. Mills and quarries were closed. Farms were abandoned. Fishing villages dwindled to a handful of old folks. Fields were overgrown by maple and spruce.

It was only when Americans began to have the time, money, and inclination to travel that the region had a resurgence. Motor courts popped up along Maine's coastal Route 1 during the 1950s. Ski chalets peeked above the pines in Vermont and New Hampshire. Artists, teachers, and urban professionals snatched up the old farmhouses, and hippies set up communes in southern Vermont.

In the 1970s and '80s gentrification began to alter the towns and villages of the North. Second homes and condominiums went up in record numbers on the shores of Lake Winnepesaukee, alongside Maine's Casco and Linekin bays, and throughout the green countryside of southern Vermont.

Gentrification looks lovely compared with some of the other changes that have overtaken northern New England in the past couple of decades. Strip development has swallowed long stretches of Vermont's Route 4, especially around Rutland; and a good deal of southern New Hampshire has a distinctly suburban cast. Factory-outlet fever has reached epidemic proportions in Maine and New Hampshire. It used to be that tourists came to northern New England to buy a jug of maple syrup or a little pillow stuffed with balsam needles—now it's a pair of Bass shoes or Calvin Klein jeans.

Equally distressing are the crowds that have brought urban headaches into the heart of the northern wilderness. An endless caravan of leaf peepers crawls along the Kancamagus Highway in late September. The lift lines at Mt. Snow or Killington can be long enough to make you want to trade skiing for shopping at Manchester's boutiques and outlets. I have found few vacation experiences more depressing than slogging up the long, increasingly steep trail of Vermont's Camel's Hump mountain only to find the summit mobbed with fellow hikers. "Do we seat ourselves, or should we wait for the maitre d'?" one hiker remarked as he surveyed the scores of picnickers who had beat him to the top.

But even in the midst of the changes and crowding of the present, the eternal images, tastes, and experiences of the North

endure. The steam of boiling maple sap still rises from sugarhouses all over the Green and White mountains every March. In May, lilacs bloom in fragrant, extravagant mounds beside seemingly every old farmhouse in the North. Loons flapping through the dawn mist rising off a lake, a scarlet-maple branch blazing beside a white church, sows grazing on a lush, green hillside—these images have become cliches, but they are nonetheless stirring and satisfying.

Whenever I feel the first chill of autumn in the air, whenever I see a flock of geese winging north, whenever I come upon a stand of spruce and white pine rising at the end of a freshly mown hay field, I feel the tug of northern New England. The drive north from my home outside New York City is long and dull, and, on the way up, there always comes a moment of doubt: Will it be worth the time and money? Will it have changed? Will it rain or fog the entire time?

Then I see the first ramshackle house with a side porch, the first rough pasture strewn with stones and humps of grass, the first kind wistful face, and I know it will be all right.

— David Laskin

David Laskin has written for the *New York Times* and *Travel and Leisure*.

WHAT'S WHERE

Maine

Maine is by far the largest state in New England. At its extremes it measures 300 mi by 200 mi; all other New England states could fit within its perimeters. Due to overdevelopment, Maine's southernmost coastal towns won't give you the rugged, "Down East" experience, but the Kennebunks will: classic townscapes, rocky shorelines punctuated by sandy beaches, quaint downtown districts. Purists hold that the Maine coast begins at Penobscot Bay, where the vistas over the water are wider and bluer, the shore a jumble of granite boulders. Acadia National Park is Maine's principal tourist attraction; Bar Harbor is one of the park's gateway towns. Bangor is north of Penobscot Bay on the

Penobscot River. The vast North Woods region is a destination for outdoors enthusiasts.

Vermont

Southern Vermont has farms, freshly starched New England towns, quiet back roads, bustling ski resorts, and strip-mall sprawl. Central Vermont's trademarks include famed marble quarries, just north of Rutland, and large dairy herds and pastures that create the quilted patchwork of the Champlain Valley. The heart of the area is the Green Mountains, and the surrounding wilderness of the Green Mountain National Forest. Both the state's largest city (Burlington) and the nation's smallest state capital (Montpelier) are in northern Vermont, as are some of the most rural and remote areas of New England. Much of the state's logging, dairy farming, and skiing takes place here. With Montréal only an hour from the border, the Canadian influence is strong, and Canadian accents and currency common.

New Hampshire

Portsmouth, the star of New Hampshire's 18-mi coastline, has great shopping, restaurants, music, and theater as well as one of the best historic districts in the nation. Exeter is New Hampshire's enclave of Revolutionary War history. The Lakes Region, rich with historic landmarks, also has good restaurants, several golf courses, hiking trails, and antiquing. People come to the White Mountains to hike and climb, to photograph the dramatic vistas and the vibrant sea of foliage, and to ski. Western and central New Hampshire have managed to keep the water slides and the outlet malls at bay. The lures here include Lake Sunapee and Mt. Monadnock, the second-most-climbed mountain in the world.

PLEASURES AND PASTIMES

Beaches

Long, wide beaches edge the coast in southern Maine; the York County coast is the most popular beach area. Many beaches are maintained by state and local governments and have lifeguards on duty; they may have picnic facilities, rest rooms,

changing facilities, and concession stands. Depending on the locale, you may need a parking sticker to use the lot. The waters are at their warmest in August, though they're cold even at the height of summer along much of the Maine coast. Inland, small lake beaches abound, most notably in New Hampshire and Vermont.

Bicycling

Favorite areas for bicycling are the New Hampshire Lakes Region, and Vermont's Green Mountains and Champlain Valley. Biking in Maine is especially scenic in and around Kennebunkport, Camden, Deer Isle, and the Schoodic Peninsula. The carriage paths in Acadia National Park are ideal. Many ski resorts allow mountain bikes during the summer months.

Boating

Along many larger lakes, sailboats, rowboats, canoes, and outboards can be rented at local marinas. Sailboats are available for rent at a number of seacoast locations; you may, however, be required to demonstrate competence. Lessons are also frequently available. Maine's Penobscot Bay draws boaters, including windjammers. Lakes in New Hampshire and Vermont are splendid for all kinds of boating. Maine's Allagash Wilderness Waterway is one of the region's premier places to canoe.

Dining

Seafood is king throughout New England. Clam favorites include chowder, made with big, meaty quahogs (with milk or cream, unlike the tomato-based Manhattan version); fried clams; and steamers. Some lobster classics include plain boiled lobster—a staple at "in the rough" picnic-bench-and-paper-plate spots along the Maine coast—and lobster rolls, a lobster meat and mayo (or just melted butter) preparation served in a hot dog bun. The leading fin fish is scrod—young cod or haddock—best sampled baked or broiled.

Inland specialties run to the plain and familiar dishes of old-fashioned Sunday-dinner America—pot roast, roast turkey, baked ham, hefty stacks of pancakes (with local maple syrup, of course), and apple pie. One regional favorite is Indian pudding, a long-boiled cornmeal and molasses concoction that's delicious with vanilla ice cream. As for ethnic menus, Maine, Vermont, and New Hampshire have welcomed Chinese, Thai, Middle Eastern, and all the other international cuisines popular in America. The pork pie (*tortière*) and pea soup of northern New England's French-Canadians is one of the region's deeper ethnic traditions.

Fishing

Anglers will find sport aplenty throughout the region—surf-casting along the shore; deep-sea fishing in the Atlantic on party and charter boats; fishing for trout in streams; and angling for bass, landlocked salmon, and other fish in freshwater lakes. Maine's Moosehead and Rangeley lakes regions are draws for serious anglers, as are Vermont's Lakes Champlain and Memphremagog and the Connecticut Lakes of far northern New Hampshire. Sporting-goods stores and bait-and-tackle shops are reliable sources for licenses—necessary in fresh waters—and for leads to the nearest hot spots.

Golf

Golf caught on early in New England. Maine, Vermont, and New Hampshire have an ample supply of public and semiprivate courses, many of which are attached to distinctive resorts or even ski areas. One dilemma facing golfers is keeping their eyes on the ball instead of the scenery: in Manchester, Vermont, the Gleneagles Course at the Equinox Hotel is ringed by mountain splendor, as are the links at the Balsams Grand Resort in Dixville Notch, New Hampshire, and the nearby course at the splendid old Mount Washington Hotel in Bretton Woods. During prime season, make sure you reserve ahead for tee times, particularly near urban areas and at resorts.

Hiking

Probably the most famous trails are the 255-mi Long Trail, which runs north–south through the center of Vermont, and the Maine-to-Georgia Appalachian Trail, which runs through New England on both private and public land. The Appalachian Mountain Club (AMC) maintains a system of staffed huts in New Hampshire's Presidential Range, with bunk space and meals available by reservation. Good hiking can also be found in state parks.

National and State Parks and Forests

National parks and forests provide myriad facilities, including campgrounds, picnic grounds, hiking trails, nature walks, boating, and ranger programs. Contact the state tourism offices or specific national park or forest headquarters for more information on any of these.

Maine. Acadia National Park, which preserves fine stretches of shoreline and high mountains, covers much of Mount Desert Island and more than half of Isle au Haut and Schoodic Point on the mainland. The 6,700-acre Moosehorn National Wildlife Refuge, in the eastern quarter of Maine near the New Brunswick border, is bounded by Cobscook Bay and the mouth of the Dennys and Whiting rivers. Baxter State Park comprises more than 200,000 acres of wilderness surrounding Katahdin, Maine's highest mountain. Hiking and moose-watching are major activities. The Allagash Wilderness Waterway is a 92-mi corridor of lakes and rivers surrounded by vast commercial forest property. A number of state parks line Maine's fabled rock-bound coast; at Camden Hills State Park, an auto road winds to the top of Mt. Battie for spectacular views of Penobscot Bay.

Vermont. Vermont has one of the Northeast's best developed systems of state parks, many of which are along the shores of lakes ideal for swimming, fishing, and boating. Most have campsites and boat rentals. Several of the most attractive are among the islands of northern Lake Champlain. At the Green River Reservoir in north-central Vermont, you'll find primitive camping along the shores of the motorboat-free reservoir. The 350,000-acre Green Mountain National Forest consists of separate northern and southern portions in the center of the state. Hikers treasure the more than 500 mi of trails; canoeists work its white waters; and campers and anglers find plenty to keep them happy. Among the most popular spots are the Falls of Lana and Silver Lake near Middlebury; Hapgood Pond between Manchester and Peru; and Chittenden Brook near Rochester. The Marsh-Billings-Rockefeller National Historical Park, in Woodstock, is dedicated to the legacy of conservation and land stewardship associated with the trio of local luminaries for which it is named. On the shores of Lake Champlain in the state's northwestern corner, the Missisquoi National Wildlife Refuge provides superb wildfowl habitat; in the Connecticut River Watershed of the state's Northeast Kingdom, the Sylvio Conte National Wildlife Refuge protects thousands of acres of undeveloped lands.

New Hampshire. New Hampshire state parklands vary widely, even within a region. Major recreation parks are at Franconia Notch, Crawford Notch, and Mt. Sunapee. Rhododendron State Park near Fitzwilliam in the Monadnock region has a singular collection of wild rhododendrons; Mt. Washington Park (White Mountains) is on top of the highest mountain in the Northeast. Along New Hampshire's short coastline, Hampton Beach and Odiorne Point state parks provide fine ocean swimming. The White Mountain National Forest covers 770,000 acres of northern New Hampshire, including 6,288-ft Mt. Washington, highest point in the Northeast, and the other peaks of the Presidential Range. Several federally designated Wilderness areas lie within its boundaries. Near the city of Portsmouth, Great Bay National Wildlife Refuge has fine birding and canoeing opportunities on a shallow backwater of the Piscataqua River.

Outdoor Activities
Whether you want to cast a line, ski down a snowy mountainside, or just relax on a beach, options abound throughout northern New England. Biking is a wonderful way to explore such areas as the lakes of New Hampshire or Vermont's Champlain Valley, and hikers can be challenged by the Appalachian Trail or hundreds of other trails in numerous parks. Fishing choices vary from a secluded lake in Maine to the lure of the open Atlantic. Kayakers and canoeists will find challenging white water as well as more tranquil lakes and rivers, and Maine is known for windjamming cruises and fine sailing. Outdoor fun does not stop in the winter, either. Skiers have been drawn to the softly rounded peaks of New England for a full century; the New England Ski Museum in Franconia, New Hampshire, tells the story. Today resorts from small to large cater to both beginners and experts.

Shopping
Antiques, crafts, maple syrup and sugar, and fresh produce lure shoppers to New England's flea markets, bazaars, yard sales, country stores, and farmers' markets.

Antiques. Particularly in the Monadnock region of New Hampshire, dealers abound in barns and home stores strung along back roads—along Route 119, from Fitzwilliam to Hinsdale; Route 101, from Marlborough to Wilton; and in the towns of Hopkinton, Hollis, and Amherst. In southern New Hampshire, shops flourish along the stretch of U.S. 4 between Durham and Concord. In Vermont, antiques shops and barns are scattered just about everywhere but are especially concentrated along the southern portions of U.S. 7 and along Route 30, particularly in and around Newfane. In Maine, antiques shops are clustered in Wiscasset and Searsport and along U.S. 1 between Kittery and Scarborough.

Crafts. In Vermont, galleries in Burlington, Middlebury, and Windsor sell work by some of the best of the state's craftspeople, although artisans have set up shop throughout the state. The League of New Hampshire Craftsmen operates seven fine shops, including locations in Concord, Exeter, and North Conway. On Maine's Deer Isle, Haystack Mountain School of Crafts attracts internationally renowned craftspeople to its summer institute. The Schoodic Peninsula is home to many skilled artisans. Passamaquoddy baskets can be found in Eastport.

Produce. Opportunities abound for obtaining fresh farm produce from the source; some farms allow you to pick your own strawberries, raspberries, blueberries, and apples. October in Maine is prime time for pumpkins and potatoes. Maple-syrup producers demonstrate the process to visitors, most notably in Vermont. Maple syrup is available in different grades; while Grade AA, "fancy," is the lightest in color and the most refined, many Vermonters prefer grade B, which has a deeper flavor and is often used in cooking. Grade A, medium amber in color, has a light caramel flavor and is often used with pancakes and hot cereals.

FODOR'S CHOICE

Dining
White Barn Inn, Kennebunkport, ME. One of Maine's best restaurants, it combines fine dining with unblemished service in a rustic setting. *$$$$*

Fore Street, Portland, ME. From the open kitchen, two of Maine's best chefs create culinary magic at this restaurant near the city's Old Port. $$–$$$

Lobstermen's Co-op, Round Pond, ME. For lobster-in-the-rough, you can't beat this dockside takeout. $–$$

The Balsams Wilderness, Dixville Notch, NH. The summer buffet lunch is heaped upon a 100-ft-long table; dinners might include salmon with caviar. $$$$

Porto Bello Ristorante Italiano, Portsmouth, NH. Pure Italian food is served at this downtown family-run establishment that overlooks Portsmouth Harbor. $$

Hemingway's, Killington, VT. The chic seasonal menu celebrates native game and fresh seafood in such dishes as Vermont venison with pumpkin pudding. $$$$

Prince & the Pauper, Woodstock, VT. A Colonial dining room is the setting for creative French and American dishes prepared with Vermont accents. $$$–$$$$

Lodging

Blair Hill Inn, Greenville, ME. Beautiful gardens and a hilltop location with marvelous views over Moosehead lake distinguish this 1891 estate. $$$$

Ullikana, Bar Harbor, ME. Within this Tudor mansion is a riot of color and art. Water views and delicious breakfasts make it a real treat. $$$–$$$$

Manor on Golden Pond, Holderness, NH. The rooms in this English-style manor are filled with luxurious touches. $$$$

Snowvillage Inn, Snowville, NH. Rooms in this book-filled inn near North Conway are named after authors; the nicest, with 12 windows, is a tribute to Robert Frost. $$$–$$$$

West Mountain Inn, Arlington, VT. A former 1840s farmhouse anchors a llama ranch with 150 acres of glorious views. $$$$

Inn at Shelburne Farms, Shelburne, VT. This Tudor-style inn sits on the edge of Lake Champlain. $$–$$$$

Memorable Sights

Sunrise from Cadillac Mountain, Mount Desert Island, ME. From the summit you have a 360-degree view of the ocean, islands, woods, and lakes.

Yacht-filled Camden Harbor, from the summit of Mt. Battie, ME. Mt. Battie may not be very tall, but it has a memorable vista over Camden Harbor, which shelters a large fleet of windjammers.

Early October views, Kancamagus Highway, NH. The White Mountain vistas on this 34-mi drive burst into color each fall.

Journey up Mt. Washington, NH. Whether you hike, drive the toll road, or take the Mt. Washington Cog Railway, the trek up the Northeast's tallest mountain yields spectacular panorama.

The Appalachian Gap, Route 17, VT. Views from this mountain pass near Bristol are a just reward for the challenging drive.

Village green, Woodstock, VT. The spirit of New England's past is preserved in the lovely Federal homes that surround the green in this handsome town.

Ski Resorts

Big Squaw Mountain, ME. A down-home laid-back atmosphere prevails at this resort overlooking Moosehead Lake. This is no frills, big mountain skiing at bargain basement prices.

Sugarloaf/USA, ME. At 2,820 ft, Sugarloaf/USA's vertical drop is greater than that of any other New England ski peak except Killington.

Sunday River, ME. Good snowmaking and reliable grooming ensure great snow from November to May.

Attitash Bear Peak, NH. Something innovative is always happening here—from demo days to race camps.

Jay Peak, VT. Jay gets the most natural snow of any Vermont ski area.

Mad River Glen, VT. The apt motto at this area owned by a skiers cooperative is "Ski It If You Can."

Smugglers' Notch, VT. Morse Mountain at Smugglers' is tops for beginners.

Sugarbush, VT. Sugarbush is an overall great place to ski; nearly everyone will feel comfortable.

GREAT ITINERARIES

Highlights of Maine, Vermont, and New Hampshire

4 to 5 days. In a nation where distances can often be daunting, Maine, Vermont, and New Hampshire pack their highlights into a remarkably compact area. Understanding Yankeedom might take a lifetime—but it's possible to get a good appreciation for the six-state region in a 2- to 2½-week drive.

Manchester and Concord *(1 day)*. Manchester, New Hampshire's largest city, holds the Amoskeag Textile Mills, a reminder of New England's industrial past. Smaller Concord is the state capital. Near the State House is the fine Museum of New Hampshire History, housing one of the locally built stagecoaches that carried Concord's name throughout the West. ☞ *Western and Central New Hampshire in Chapter 4.*

Green Mountains and Montpelier *(1 or 2 days)*. Route 100 travels through the heart of the Green Mountains, whose rounded peaks assert a modest grandeur. Vermont's vest-pocket capital, Montpelier, has the gold-dome Vermont State House and the quirky Vermont Museum. ☞ *Central Vermont and Northern Vermont in Chapter 3.*

White Mountains *(1 day)*. U.S. 302 threads through New Hampshire's White Mountains, passing beneath brooding Mt. Washington and through Crawford Notch. In Bretton Woods the Mt. Washington Cog Railway still chugs to the summit, and the Mount Washington Hotel recalls the glory days of White Mountain resorts. ☞ *The White Mountains in Chapter 4.*

Portland *(1 day)*. Maine's maritime capital shows off its restored waterfront at the Old Port. Nearby, two lighthouses on Cape Elizabeth, Two Lights and Portland Head, stand vigil. ☞ *Portland to Waldoboro in Chapter 2.*

Kancamagus Trail

3 to 7 days. This circuit takes in some of the most spectacular parts of the White

and Green mountains, along with the upper Connecticut River valley. In this area the antiques hunting is exemplary and the traffic is often almost nonexistent. The scenery evokes the spirit of Currier & Ives.

Lakes Region and White Mountains *(1 to 3 days)*. From the New Hampshire coast, head northwest to Wolfeboro, perhaps detouring to explore around Lake Winnipesaukee. Take Route 16 north to Conway, then follow Route 112 west along the scenic Kancamagus Pass through the White Mountains to the Vermont border.

Connecticut River Valley *(1 to 2 days)*. Head south on Route 10 along the Connecticut River, past scenic Hanover, New Hampshire, home of Dartmouth College. At White River Junction, cross into Vermont. You may want to follow Route 4 through the lovely town of Woodstock to Killington, then travel along Route 100 and I-89 to complete the loop back to White River Junction. Otherwise, simply proceed south along I-91, with stops at such pleasant Vermont towns as Putney and Brattleboro.

Scenic Route 119 *(1 to 2 days)*. Take Route 119 east to Rhododendron State Park in Fitzwilliam, New Hampshire. Nearby is Mt. Monadnock, the most-climbed mountain in the United States; in Jaffrey take the trail to the top. Dawdle along back roads to visit the preserved villages of Harrisville, Dublin, and Hancock, then continue east along Route 101 to return to the coast.

Fall Foliage Tour

4 to 7 days. In fall, New England's dense forests explode into reds, oranges, yellows, and purples. Nature's schedule varies from year to year; as a rule, this trip is best begun around the third week of September. Book accommodations well in advance.

Northwestern Vermont *(1 or 2 days)*. In Burlington the elms will be turning color on the University of Vermont campus. A ferry ride across Lake Champlain affords great views of Vermont's Green Mountains and New York's Adirondacks. After visiting the resort town of Stowe, continue beneath the cliffs of Smugglers' Notch. The north country's palette unfolds in Newport, where the blue waters of Lake Memphremagog reflect the foliage. ☞ *Northern Vermont in Chapter 3.*

Northeast Kingdom *(1 day).* After a side trip along Lake Willoughby, explore St. Johnsbury, where the St. Johnsbury Athenaeum and Fairbanks Museum reveal Victorian tastes in art and natural-history collecting. In Peacham, stock up for a picnic at the Peacham Store. ☞ *Northern Vermont in Chapter 4.*

White Mountains and Lakes Region *(1 or 2 days).* In New Hampshire, I–93 narrows as it winds through craggy Franconia Notch. Watch for the Old Man of the Mountain, a natural rock profile. The sinuous Kancamagus Highway passes through the mountains to Conway. In Center Harbor in the Lakes Region, you can ride the M/S *Mount Washington* for views of the Lake Winnipesaukee shoreline, or ascend to Moultonborough's Castle in the Clouds for a falcon's-eye look at the colors. ☞ *The White Mountains and Lakes Region in Chapter 4.*

Mt. Monadnock Region *(1 or 2 days).* In Concord stop at the Museum of New Hampshire History and the State House. Several trails climb Mt. Monadnock, near Jaffrey Center, and colorful vistas extend as far as Boston. ☞ *Western and Central New Hampshire in Chapter 4.*

The Seacoast

3 to 5 days. For history buffs, the Maine and New Hampshire coast provides vivid links to the days when the sea was the region's lifeblood; for water-sports enthusiasts, it's a guarantee of fun on the sandy shores. A journey along the coast also brings the promise of fresh seafood, incomparable sunrises, and a quality of light that has entranced artists from Winslow Homer to Edward Hopper.

New Hampshire and Southern Maine *(1 or 2 days).* New Hampshire fronts the Atlantic for a scant 18 mi, but its coastal landmarks range from honky-tonk Hampton Beach to quiet Odiorne Point State Park in Rye and pretty Portsmouth, whose Georgian- and Federal-style mansions once sheltered the cream of pre-Revolutionary society. Visit a few at Strawbery Banke Museum and elsewhere. Between here and Portland, Maine's largest city and the site of a waterfront revival, you will find ocean-side resorts such as Kennebunkport. Near Portland is Cape Elizabeth, with its Portland Head and Two Lights lighthouses. ☞ *The Coast in Chapter 4, and York County Coast and Portland to Waldoboro in Chapter 2.*

Down East *(2 or 3 days).* Beyond Portland ranges the ragged, island-strewn coast that Mainers call Down East. On your first day, travel to Camden or Castine. Some highlights are the retail outlets of Freeport, home of L.L. Bean; Brunswick, with the museums of Bowdoin College; and Bath, with the Maine Maritime Museum and Shipyard. Perhaps you'll think about cruising on one of the schooners that sail out of Rockland. In Camden and Castine, exquisite inns occupy homes built from inland Maine's gold, timber. On your second day, visit the spectacular rocky coast of Acadia National Park, near the resort town of Bar Harbor. If you have another day, drive the desolately beautiful stretch of Maine's granite coast to the New Brunswick border, where President Franklin Roosevelt's "beloved island," Campobello, and Roosevelt Campobello International Park lie across an international bridge. ☞ *Portland to Waldoboro, Penobscot Bay, Mount Desert Island, and Way Down East in Chapter 2.*

2 MAINE

At its extremes Maine measures 300 mi by 200 mi; all the other states in New England could fit within its ample perimeters. The Kennebunks hold classic townscapes, rocky shorelines, sandy beaches, and quaint downtown districts. Portland has the state's best selection of restaurants, shops, and cultural offerings, and Freeport draws outlet shoppers. North of Portland, sandy beaches give way to rocky coast and treasures such as Acadia National Park. Outdoors enthusiasts head to inland Maine's lakes, mountains, and the vast North Woods.

By Hilary M. Nangle

O N THE MAINE–NEW HAMPSHIRE BORDER is a sign that plainly announces the philosophy of the region: WELCOME TO MAINE: THE WAY LIFE SHOULD BE. Local folk say too many cars are on the road when you can't make it through the traffic signal on the first try. Romantics luxuriate in the feeling of a down comforter on an old, yellowed pine bed or in the sensation of the wind and salt spray on their faces while cruising in a historic windjammer. Families love the unspoiled beaches and safe inlets dotting the shoreline and the clear inland lakes. Hikers and campers are revived by the exalting and exhausting climb to the top of Katahdin. Adventure seekers raft the Kennebec and Penobscot rivers or sea-kayak along the coast, and skiers head for the snow-covered slopes of western and northern Maine.

There is an expansiveness to Maine, a sense of distance between places that hardly exists elsewhere in New England and, along with the sheer size and spread of the place, a variety of terrain. People speak of "coastal" Maine and "inland" Maine as though the state could be summed up under the twin emblems of lobsters and pine trees. Yet the topography and character in this state are a good deal more complicated.

Even the coast is several places in one. Portland may be Maine's largest city, but its attitude is decidedly more big town than small city. South of this rapidly gentrifying city, Ogunquit, Kennebunkport, Old Orchard Beach, and other resort towns predominate along a reasonably smooth shoreline. North of Portland and Casco Bay, secondary roads turn south off U.S. 1 onto so many oddly chiseled peninsulas that it's possible to drive for days without retracing your route. Slow down to explore the museums, galleries, and shops in the larger towns and the antiques and curio shops and harborside lobster shacks in the smaller fishing villages on the peninsulas. Freeport is an entity unto itself, a place where numerous name-brand outlets and specialty stores have sprung up around the retail outpost of famous outfitter L.L. Bean. And no description of the coast would be complete without mention of popular Acadia National Park, with its majestic mountains, and the rugged scenery of the less-visited towns that lie way Down East.

Inland Maine likewise defies easy characterization. For one thing, a lot of it is virtually uninhabited. This is the land Henry David Thoreau wrote about in his evocative mid-19th century portrait, *The Maine Woods*; aside from having been logged over several times, much of it hasn't changed since Thoreau and his Native American guides passed through. Ownership of vast portions of northern Maine by forest-products corporations has kept out subdivision and development, but this, too, is changing; many of the roads here are private, open to travel only by permit.

Wealthy summer visitors, or "sports," came to Maine beginning in the late 1800s to hunt, fish, and play in the clean air and clean water. The state's more than 6,000 lakes and more than 3,000 mi of rivers and streams still attract such people, and more and more families, for the same reasons. Sporting camps still thrive around Greenville, Rangeley, and in the Great North Woods.

Logging in the north created the culture of the mill towns, the Rumfords, Skowhegans, Millinockets, and Bangors that lie at the end of the old river drives. The logs arrive by truck today, but Maine's harvested wilderness still feeds the mills and the nation's hunger for paper.

The hunger for potatoes has given rise to an entirely different Maine culture, in one of the most isolated agricultural regions of the country.

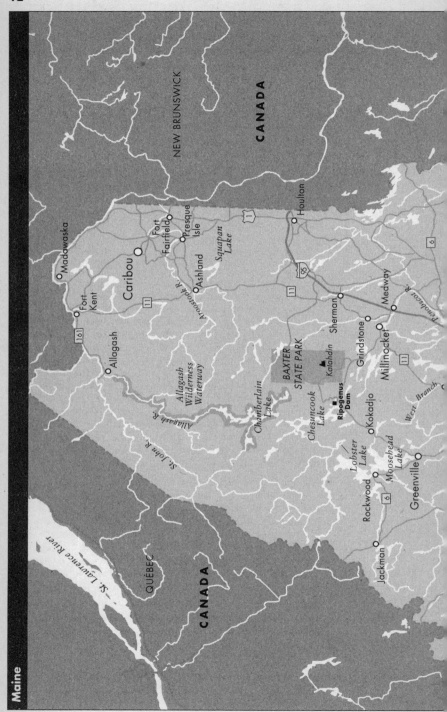

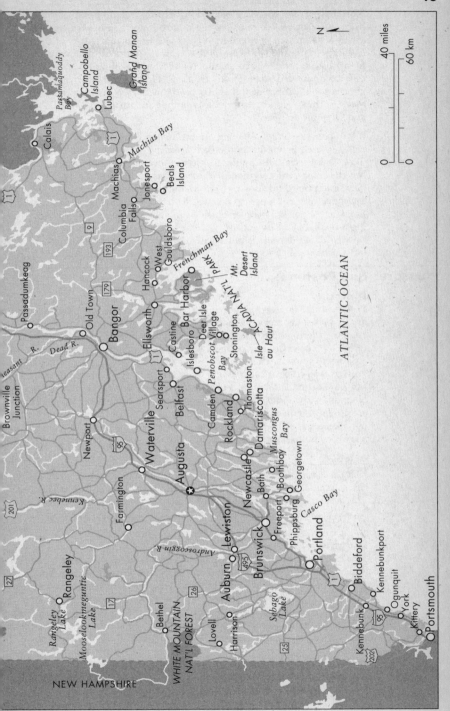

Northeastern Aroostook County is where the Maine potatoes come from. In what was once called the Potato Empire, however, farmers are now as pressed between high costs and low prices as any of their counterparts in the Midwest, and a growing national preference for Idaho baking potatoes to small, round Maine boiling potatoes has only compounded Aroostook's troubles. However, the arrival of an international-caliber winter sports center in 1999 is giving a renewed focus to this region by hosting events that are attracting World Cup and Olympic competitors.

If you come to Maine seeking an untouched fishing village with lo-cals gathered around a potbellied stove in the general store, you'll likely come away disappointed; that innocent age has passed in all but the most remote villages. Tourism has supplanted fishing, log-ging, and potato farming as Maine's number one industry, and most areas are well equipped to receive the annual onslaught of visitors. But whether you are stepping outside a motel room for a walk or watch-ing a boat rock at its anchor, you can sense the infinity of the natu-ral world. Wilderness is always nearby, growing to the edges of the most urbanized spots.

Pleasures and Pastimes

Dining

Lobster and Maine are synonymous. As a general rule, the closer you are to a working harbor, the fresher your lobster will be. Aficionados eschew ordering lobster in restaurants, preferring to eat them "in the rough" at classic lobster pounds, where you select your dinner out of a pool and enjoy it at a waterside picnic table. Shrimp, scallops, clams, mussels, and crabs are also caught in the cold waters off Maine. Restau-rants in Portland and in resort towns prepare shellfish in creative com-binations with lobster, haddock, salmon, and swordfish. Wild blueberries are grown commercially in Maine, and local cooks use them generously in pancakes, muffins, jams, pies, and cobblers. In 1999, Maine passed a law prohibiting smoking in restaurants.

CATEGORY	COST*
$$$$	over $25
$$$	$17–$25
$$	$9–$16
$	under $9

*per person, for a main-course dinner

Lodging

The beach communities in the south beckon with their weathered look. Stately digs can be found in the classic inns along the York County Coast. Bed-and-breakfasts and Victorian inns furnished with lace, chintz, and mahogany have joined the family-oriented motels of Ogunquit, Boothbay Harbor, Bar Harbor, and the Camden–Rockport region. Although accommodations tend to be less luxurious away from the coast, Bethel, Carrabassett Valley, and Rangeley have so-phisticated hotels and inns. Greenville has the largest selection of restaurants and accommodations in the North Woods region. Lake-side sporting camps, which range from the primitive to the upscale, are popular around Rangeley and the North Woods. Many have cozy cabins heated with woodstoves and serve three hearty meals a day. At some of Maine's larger hotels and inns with restaurants, rates may in-clude breakfast and dinner during the peak seasons.

CATEGORY	COST
$$$$	over $180
$$$	$130–$180
$$	$80–$130
$	under $80

All prices are for a standard double room during peak season and not including tax or gratuities. Some inns add a 15% service charge.

Outdoor Activities and Sports

BOATING

Maine's long coastline is justifiably famous: be sure to get on the water, whether on an excursion headed for Monhegan Island for the day or on a windjammer for a relaxing vacation. Windjammer trips last from just a few hours to a full week. Longer trips include hearty, home-style meals and a traditional lobster bake often held on a remote island. Windjammers may sail past long, craggy fingers of land that jut into a sea dotted with more than 2,000 islands. Sail among these islands and you'll see hidden coves, lighthouses, boat-filled harbors, and quiet fishing villages. Some windjammers, traditional two- or three-masted tall ships, are historic vessels that have been modified to carry human cargo while others have more modern amenities. Most windjammers depart from Rockland, Rockport, or Camden, all ports on Penobscot Bay. Boating trips, including whale-watching, run in season, from mid- to late May through September or mid-October.

HIKING

From seaside rambles to backwoods hikes, Maine has a walk for everyone. This state's beaches are mostly hard-packed and good for walking. Many coastal communities, such as York, Ogunquit, and Bar Harbor, have shoreside paths for people who want to keep sand out of their shoes yet enjoy the sound of the crashing surf and the cliff-top views of inlets and coves. Those who like to walk in the woods will not be disappointed: 90% of the state is forested land. Acadia National Park has more than 150 mi of hiking trails, and within Baxter State Park are the northern end of the Appalachian Trail and Katahdin. At nearly 1 mi high, Katahdin is the tallest mountain in the state.

SKIING

Weather patterns that create snow cover for Maine ski areas may come from the Atlantic or from Canada, and Maine may have snow when other New England states do not—and vice versa. Sunday River and Sugarloaf, both operated by the American Skiing Co., are the state's largest ski areas. Both are full-service destination resorts with a choice of lodging, dining, and shopping as well as more than enough terrain to keep skiers and riders content for days. It's worth the effort to get to Sugarloaf, which provides the only above-tree-line skiing in New England and also has a lively base village.

Saddleback, in Rangeley, has big-mountain skiing at little-mountain prices. Its lift system is sorely out of date, but many would have it no other way, preferring its down-home wilderness ambience. Squaw Mountain in Greenville is similar in character. Its remote location ensures few crowds, and its low prices make it an attractive alternative to other big mountains.

WHITE-WATER RAFTING

From early May through September, Maine has consistent white-water rafting on three dam-controlled, Class III–V rivers: the Kennebec, the Penobscot, and the Dead. About a dozen outfitters are based in and around the Forks, Maine's white-water capital, where the Kennebec and the Dead rivers meet. Both are good day trips, with the Kennebec being the most popular—like a white-water roller coaster; big thrills but few chills. The Penobscot, which flows near Baxter State Park in the shadow of Mt. Katahdin, provides a remote trip with challenging white water and beautiful views of the mountain. It's not uncommon to see moose or deer while on the river. Most outfitters have facilities in this area, and most offer both day and overnight trips.

Exploring Maine

Maine is a large state that offers many different experiences. The York County Coast, in the southern portion of the state, is easily accessible and has long sand beaches, historic homes, and good restaurants. The coastal geography changes in Portland, the economic and cultural center of southern Maine. North of the city, long fingers of land jut into the sea, sheltering fishing villages. Penobscot Bay is famed for its rock-bound coast, sailing, and numerous islands. Mount Desert Island lures crowds of people to Acadia National Park, which is filled with stunning natural beauty. Way Down East, beyond Acadia, the tempo changes; fast-food joints and trinket shops all but disappear, replaced by family-style restaurants and artisans' shops. Inland, the western lakes and mountains provide an entirely different experience. Summer camps, ski areas, and small villages populate this region. People head to Maine's North Woods to escape the crowds and to enjoy the great outdoors by hiking, rafting, camping, or canoeing.

Numbers in the text and in the margin correspond to numbers on the maps: Southern Maine Coast, Portland, Penobscot Bay, Mount Desert Island, Way Down East, Western Maine, and the North Woods.

Great Itineraries

You can spend days exploring just the coast of Maine, as these itineraries indicate, so plan ahead and decide whether you want to ski and dogsled in the western mountains, raft or canoe in the North Woods, or simply meander up the coast, stopping at museums and historic sites, shopping for local arts and crafts, and exploring coastal villages and lobster shacks. Trying to see everything in one visit is complicated by the lack of east–west roads in the state and heavy traffic on popular routes, such as U.S. 1 and U.S. 302. Build extra time into your schedule and relax. You'll get there eventually, and in the meantime, enjoy the view.

IF YOU HAVE 2 DAYS

A two-day exploration of the southern coast provides a good introduction to different aspects of the Maine coast. Begin in **Ogunquit** ③ with a morning walk along the Marginal Way. Then head north to **Kennebunks** ⑤, allowing at least two hours to wander through the shops and historic homes around Dock Square. Relax on the beach for an hour or so before heading to ⊡ **Portland** ⑦–⑫. If you thrive on arts and entertainment, spend the night here. Otherwise, continue north to ⊡ **Freeport** ⑮, where you can shop all night at L.L. Bean. On day two, head north, stopping in **Bath** ⑰ to tour the Maine Maritime Museum, and finish up with a lobster dinner on **Pemaquid Peninsula** ⑳.

IF YOU HAVE 4 DAYS

A four-day tour of midcoast Maine up to Acadia National Park is one of New England's classic trips. From New Harbor on **Pemaquid Peninsula** ⑳, take the boat to ⊡ **Monhegan Island** ㉔ for a day of walking the trails and exploring the artists' studios and galleries. The next day, continue northeast to **Rockland** ㉕ and ⊡ **Camden** ㉖. On day four, visit the Farnsworth Museum in Rockland, hike or drive to the top of Mt. Battie in Camden, and meander around Camden's boat-filled harbor. Or bypass midcoast Maine in favor of ⊡ **Mount Desert Island** ㊱–㊹ and Acadia National Park. To avoid sluggish traffic on U.S. 1, from Freeport, stay on I–95 to Augusta and the Maine Turnpike; then take Route 3 to Belfast and pick up U.S. 1 north there.

IF YOU HAVE 8 DAYS

An eight-day trip allows time to see a good portion of the coast. Spend two days wandering through gentrified towns and weather-beaten fishing villages from ⛔ **Kittery** ① to ⛔ **Portland** ⑦–⑫. On your third day explore Portland and environs, including a boat ride to **Eagle Island** ⑭ or one of the other Casco Bay islands and a visit to Portland Head Light and Two Lights in Cape Elizabeth. Continue working your way up the coast, letting your interests dictate your stops: outlet stores in **Freeport** ⑮, Maine Maritime Museum in ⛔ **Bath** ⑰, antiques shops in **Wiscasset** ⑱, fishing villages and a much-photographed lighthouse on **Pemaquid Peninsula** ⑳. Allow at least one day in the **Rockland** ㉕ and ⛔ **Camden** ㉖ region before taking the leisurely route to **Bar Harbor** ㊱ via the **Blue Hill** ㉚ peninsula and ⛔ **Deer Isle Village** ㉛. Finish up with two days on ⛔ **Mount Desert Island** ㊱–㊹.

When to Tour Maine

From July to September is the choice time for a vacation in Maine. The weather is warmest in July and August, though September is less crowded. In warm weather, the arteries along the coast and lakeside communities inland are clogged with out-of-state license plates, campgrounds are filled to capacity, and hotel rates are high. Midweek is less busy, and lodging rates are often lower then than on weekends.

Fall foliage can be brilliant in Maine and is made even more so by its reflection in inland lakes or streams or off the ocean. Late September is peak season in the north country, while in southern Maine the prime viewing dates are usually around October 5 to 10. In September and October the days are sunny and the nights crisp.

In winter, the coastal towns almost completely close down. If the sidewalks could be rolled up, they probably would be. Maine's largest ski areas usually open in mid-November and, thanks to excellent snowmaking facilities, provide good skiing often into April.

Springtime is mud season here, as in most other rural areas of New England. Mud season is followed by spring flowers and the start of wildflowers in meadows along the roadsides. Mid-May to mid-June is the main season for black flies, especially inland. It's best to schedule a trip after mid-June if possible, though this is prime canoeing time.

YORK COUNTY COAST

Maine's southernmost coastal towns, most of them in York County, won't give you the rugged, wind-bitten "Down East" experience, but they are easily reached from the south, and most have the sand beaches that all but vanish beyond Portland. These towns are highly popular in summer, an all-too-brief period. Crowds converge and gobble up rooms and dinner reservations at prime restaurants. You'll have to work a little harder to find solitude and vestiges of the "real" Maine here. Still, even day-trippers who come for a few fleeting hours will appreciate the magical warmth of the sand along this coast.

North of Kittery, the Maine coast has long stretches of hard-packed white-sand beach, closely crowded by nearly unbroken ranks of beach cottages, motels, and oceanfront restaurants. The summer colonies of York Beach and Wells Beach have the crowds and ticky-tacky shorefront overdevelopment, but quiet wildlife refuges and land reserves promise an easy escape. York's historic district is on the National Register of Historic Places. Ogunquit is more upscale and offers much to do, from shopping to taking a cliff-side walk.

More than any other region south of Portland, the Kennebunks—and especially Kennebunkport—provide the complete Maine-coast experience: classic townscapes where white clapboard houses rise from manicured lawns and gardens; rocky shorelines punctuated by sandy beaches; quaint downtown districts packed with gift shops, ice cream stands, and visitors; harbors where lobster boats bob alongside yachts; lobster pounds and well-appointed dining rooms. As you continue north, the scents of french fries, pizza, and cotton candy hover in the air above Coney Island–like Old Orchard Beach, known for its amusement pier and 7-mi-long shoreline. These towns are best explored on a leisurely holiday of two days—more if you require a fix of solid beach time. U.S. 1 travels along the coast. Inland, the Maine Turnpike (I–95) is the fastest route if you want to skip some towns.

Kittery

❶ *55 mi north of Boston; 5 mi north of Portsmouth, New Hampshire.*

Kittery, which lacks a large sand beach of its own, hosts a complex of factory outlets that make it a popular destination. As an alternative to shopping, drive north past the outlets and go east on Route 103 for a peek at the hidden Kittery most people miss: hiking and biking trails and, best of all, great views of the water. Also along this winding stretch are two forts, both open in summer.

Built in 1872, **Ft. Foster** (✉ Pocahontas Rd., Kittery Point, ☎ 207/439–3800) was an active military installation until 1949. **Ft. McClary** (✉ Rte. 103, Kittery Point, ☎ 207/384–5160), which dates from 1715, was staffed during five wars.

Dining and Lodging

$–$$ ✕ **Warren's Lobster House.** A local institution, this waterfront restaurant specializes in seafood and has a huge salad bar. The pine-sided dining room leaves the impression that little has changed since the restaurant opened in 1940. In season, you can dine outdoors overlooking the water. ✉ *U.S. 1 and Water St.,* ☎ *207/439–1630. AE, MC, V.*

$$$ ▥ **The Inn at Portsmouth Harbor.** This brick Victorian built in 1889 on the old Kittery town green overlooks the Piscataqua River and Portsmouth Harbor. An easy walk over the bridge takes you to nearby Portsmouth, New Hampshire. English antiques and Victorian watercolors decorate the inn. ✉ *6 Water St., 03904,* ☎ *207/439–4040,* FAX *207/438–9286,* WEB *www.innatportsmouth.com. 5 rooms. In-room data ports, cable TV; no kids under 16, no smoking. AE, MC, V. BP.*

$ ▥ **Academy Street Inn.** Antiques, family photos, and a collection of sleds and snowshoes adorn this grand 1903 home within walking distance of two historic houses, Hamilton House and Sarah Orne Jewett's home. Its location on the New Hampshire border is convenient for exploring both southern Maine and New Hampshire. Rates include big breakfasts served in the formal dining room. ✉ *15 Academy St., South Berwick, 20 mi northwest of Kittery, 03908,* ☎ *207/384–5633. 5 rooms. No air-conditioning, no room phones, no room TVs, no kids under 10, no smoking. AE, D, MC, V. BP.*

Nightlife and the Arts

Hamilton House (✉ 40 Vaughan's La., South Berwick, 20 mi northwest of Kittery, ☎ 603/436–3205; ▱ $5), the Georgian home featured in Sarah Orne Jewett's historical novel *The Tory Lover,* presents "Sundays in the Garden" in July, a series of concerts ranging from classical to folk music. Concerts ($6) begin at 4. You can also visit **Jewett's**

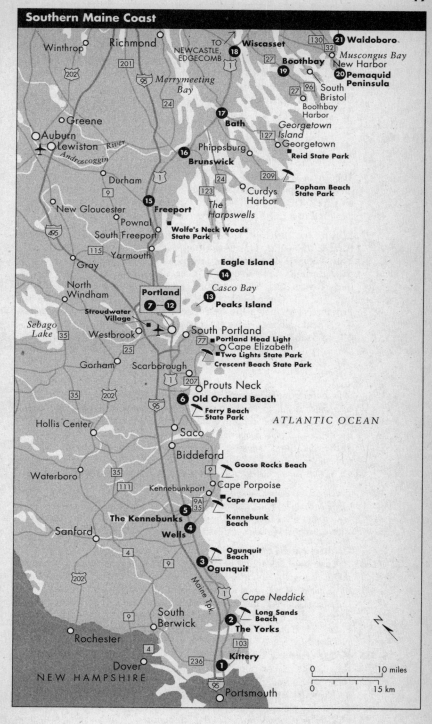

Southern Maine Coast

Winthrop
Richmond
Greene
Auburn
Lewiston
Durham
New Gloucester
Pownal
South Freeport
Yarmouth
Gray
North Windham
Westbrook
Gorham
Scarborough
Hollis Center
Waterboro
Sanford
South Berwick
Rochester
Dover

NEW HAMPSHIRE

Portsmouth

Merrymeeting Bay
Androscoggin River
Sebago Lake

18 Wiscasset
TO NEWCASTLE, EDGECOMB
21 Waldoboro
130
32
27 Boothbay
Muscongus Bay
New Harbor
19
20 Pemaquid Peninsula
27 **96** South Bristol
Boothbay Harbor
17 Bath
Georgetown Island
127
Georgetown
Reid State Park
16 Phippsburg
Brunswick
209
Popham Beach State Park
24
123
Curdys Harbor
15 Freeport
The Harpswells
Wolfe's Neck Woods State Park

Portland
7 **12**
14 Eagle Island
Casco Bay
13 Peaks Island
Stroudwater Village
South Portland
Portland Head Light
Cape Elizabeth
77
Two Lights State Park
Crescent Beach State Park
207 Prouts Neck
6 Old Orchard Beach
Ferry Beach State Park

ATLANTIC OCEAN

Saco
Biddeford
9 Goose Rocks Beach
Kennebunkport
Cape Porpoise
9A **35** Cape Arundel
5 The Kennebunks
Kennebunk Beach
4 Wells
Ogunquit Beach
3 Ogunquit
Maine Tpk.
Cape Neddick
2 Long Sands Beach
The Yorks
103
Kittery
236
1

0 ___ 10 miles
0 ___ 15 km

home (✉ 5 Portland St., South Berwick, ☎ 207/436–3205, ✍ $5, ⊙ Wed.–Sun. 11—5, with tours on the hour until 4) during summer.

Shopping

Kittery has more than 120 outlet stores. Along a several-mile stretch of U.S. 1 you can find just about anything, from hardware to underwear. Among the stores are Crate & Barrel, Eddie Bauer, Jones New York, Esprit, Waterford/Wedgwood, Lenox, Ralph Lauren, Tommy Hilfiger, DKNY, and J. Crew.

The Yorks

2 *4 mi north of Kittery.*

The Yorks—York Village, York Harbor, York Beach, and Cape Neddick—are typical of small-town coastal communities in New England and are smaller than most. Many of their nooks and crannies can be explored in a few hours. The beaches are the big attraction here.

Most of the 18th- and 19th-century buildings within the **York Village Historic District** are clustered along York Street and Lindsay Road in York Village; seven are owned by the Old York Historical Society and charge admission. You can buy tickets for all the buildings at the **Jefferds Tavern** (✉ U.S. 1A at Lindsay Rd.), a restored late-18th-century inn. The **Old York Gaol** (1720) was once the King's Prison for the Province of Maine; inside are dungeons, cells, and the jailer's quarters. Theatrical jailbreak tours are staged Friday and Saturday nights. The 1731 **Elizabeth Perkins House** reflects the Victorian style of its last occupants, the prominent Perkins family. ☎ 207/363–4974, WEB *www.oldyork.org.* ✍ *All buildings $7.* ⊙ *Mid-June–mid-Oct., Mon.–Sat. 10–5.*

The waterfront **Sayward-Wheeler House** (1718) mirrors the fortunes of a coastal village in the transition from trade to tourism. Jonathan Sayward prospered in the West Indies trade in the 18th century; by 1860 his descendants had opened the house to the public to share the story of their Colonial ancestors. The house, accessible only by guided tour, reflects both eras. ✉ *79 Barrell La., York Harbor,* ☎ *603/436–3205.* ✍ *$5.* ⊙ *June–mid-Oct., weekends 11–5; tours on the hr 11–4.*

If you drive down Nubble Road from U.S. 1A and go to the end of Cape Neddick, you can park and gaze out at the **Nubble Light** (1879), which sits on a tiny island just offshore. The keeper's house is a tidy Victorian cottage with gingerbread woodwork and a red roof.

Dining and Lodging

$$–$$$$ ✕ **Cape Neddick Inn.** Chef Jonathan Pratt's French-based American menu changes frequently at this restaurant and art gallery. Past entrées have included poached lobster in vermouth cream and sautéed sweetbreads in caper parsley butter. Tables are well spaced in the bi-level dining room, which is accented by local artwork. ✉ *1233 U.S. 1, Cape Neddick,* ☎ *207/363–2899. AE, MC, V. Closed Mon., Mar., and Nov. No lunch.*

$–$$$ ✕ **Cape Neddick Lobster Pound.** At this casual harborside restaurant, the nautical decor reflects the menu. All kinds of seafood, including lobster, is served. A children's menu and outdoor dining are available. ✉ *Shore Rd., Cape Neddick,* ☎ *207/363–5471. MC, V. Closed Jan.–Mar.*

$$ ✕⌂ **York Harbor Inn.** A mid-17th-century fishing cabin with dark
★ timbers and a fieldstone fireplace forms the heart of this inn, to which wings and outbuildings have been added over the years. The rooms are furnished with antiques and country pieces; many have decks over-

looking the water, and some have whirlpool tubs or fireplaces. The nicest rooms are in two adjacent buildings, Harbor Cliffs and Harbor Hill. The dining room ($$$–$$$$; no lunch off-season) has great ocean views. For dinner, start with Maine crab cakes and then try the lobster-stuffed chicken breast or the scallops Dijon. ⊠ *U.S. 1A (Box 573, York Harbor 03911),* ☎ *207/363–5119 or 800/343–3869,* FAX *207/363–7151,* WEB *www.yorkharborinn.com. 47 rooms, 2 suites. Restaurant, pub, cable TV, meeting rooms; no smoking. AE, DC, MC, V. CP.*

$$–$$$$ 🏠 **Edward's Harborside.** This turn-of-the-20th-century B&B sits on the harbor's edge and is just a two-minute walk from the beach. Rooms share baths, are spacious, and have big windows to take in the water views. One room has a whirlpool tub. ⊠ *Stage Neck Rd. (Box 866, York Harbor 03911),* ☎ *207/363–3037,* FAX *207/363–1544,* WEB *www. edwardsharborsideinn.com. 4 rooms without bath, 3 suites. Cable TV, dock; no kids under 8, no smoking. MC, V. CP.*

$$ 🏠 **The Riverbed.** An oasis of calm, this clapboard home dating from before the American Revolution provides a nice counterpoint to busy York Beach, a short walk away. Each room is carefully furnished with antiques and family pieces and has a private deck; a private sitting room has TV and phone. The shared back deck, with hot tub, slopes gently down to the Cape Neddick River. ⊠ *154 Cape Neddick Rd. (Rte. 1A), 03910,* ☎ *207/363–3630. 3 rooms. Outdoor hot tub, boating; no air-conditioning, no room phones, no room TVs, no smoking. MC, V. Closed Columbus Day–Memorial Day weekend. BP.*

Nightlife and the Arts

Inn on the Blues (⊠ 7 Ocean Ave., York Beach, ☎ 207/351–3221) is a hopping blues club that attracts national bands.

Outdoor Activities and Sports

U.S. 1A runs right behind **Long Sands Beach,** a 1½-mi stretch of sand in York Beach that has roadside parking and a bathhouse. **Short Sands Beach** in York Beach has a bathhouse and is convenient to restaurants and shops. **Capt. Tom Farnon** (⊠ Rte. 103, Town Dock No. 2, York Harbor, ☎ 207/363–3234) takes passengers on lobstering trips, weekdays 10–2.

Ogunquit

❸ *10 mi north of the Yorks, 39 mi southwest of Portland.*

Probably more than any other south-coast community, Ogunquit blends coastal ambience with style and good eating. The village became a resort in the 1880s and gained fame as an artists' colony. A mini Provincetown, Ogunquit has a gay population that swells in summer; many inns and small clubs cater to a primarily gay and lesbian clientele. Families love the protected beach area and friendly environment. Shore Road, which takes you into downtown, passes the 100-ft Bald Head Cliff, with views up and down the coast. On a stormy day the surf can be quite wild here.

Perkins Cove, a neck of land connected to the mainland by Oarweed Road and a pedestrian drawbridge, has a jumble of sea-beaten fish houses. These have largely been transformed by the tide of tourism to shops and restaurants. When you've had your fill of browsing and jostling the crowds, stroll out along the **Marginal Way,** a mile-long footpath that hugs the shore of a rocky promontory known as Israel's Head. Benches along the route give walkers an opportunity to stop and appreciate the open sea vistas, flowering bushes, and million-dollar homes.

The small but worthwhile **Ogunquit Museum of American Art,** dedicated to 20th-century American art, overlooks the ocean and is set amid a 3-acre sculpture garden. Inside are works by Henry Strater, Marsden Hartley, Winslow Homer, Edward Hopper, Gaston Lachaise, Marguerite Zorach, and Louise Nevelson. The huge windows of the sculpture court command a superb view of cliffs and ocean. ⊠ *543 Shore Rd.,* ☎ *207/646–4909.* 🎫 *$4.* ☉ *July–mid-Oct., Mon.–Sat. 10:30–5, Sun. 2–5.*

Dining and Lodging

$$$$ ✕ **Arrows.** Elegant simplicity is the hallmark of this restaurant in an 18th-century farmhouse, 2 mi up a back road. Grilled salmon and radicchio with marinated fennel and baked polenta, and Chinese-style duck glazed with molasses are typical entrées on the daily-changing menu. The Maine crabmeat mousse and lobster risotto appetizers and desserts such as strawberry shortcake with Chantilly cream are also beautifully executed. ⊠ *Berwick Rd.,* ☎ *207/361–1100. Reservations essential. MC, V. Closed Mon. and mid-Dec.–mid-Apr. No lunch.*

$$$–$$$$ ✕ **98 Provence.** Country French ambience provides a fitting backdrop
★ for chef Pierre Gignac's French fare. Begin with the duck foie gras or country-style rabbit pâté, and follow it up with a cassoulet or medallion of veal tenderloin with a wild mushroom cream sauce. ⊠ *104 Shore Rd.,* ☎ *207/646–9898. Reservations essential. MC, V.*

$$–$$$ ✕ **Gypsy Sweethearts.** The multiethnic fare at this popular bistro ranges from shrimp margarita to chili-crusted rack of lamb to Jamaican jerk-rubbed chicken. In the dining area, cobalt-blue glassware accents the white-draped tables. ⊠ *10 Shore Rd.,* ☎ *207/646–7021. MC, V. Closed Mon. and Jan.–Apr. No lunch.*

$$–$$$ ✕ **Hurricane.** Don't let the weather-beaten exterior or the frenzied atmosphere inside deter you—this small seafood bar and grill with spectacular views of the crashing surf turns out first-rate dishes. Start with lobster chowder or a chilled fresh-shrimp spring roll. Entrées may include lobster cioppino, rack of lamb, and fire-roasted red snapper. A second Hurricane is on Dock Square, in Kennebunkport. ⊠ *Oarweed La., Perkins Cove,* ☎ *207/646–6348 or 800/649–6348. AE, D, DC, MC, V. Closed early Jan.*

$$$$ 🏨 **Cliff House.** Elsie Jane Weare opened the Cliff House in 1872, and her granddaughter Kathryn now presides over this sprawling oceanfront resort atop Bald Head Cliff. All rooms have ocean views. Those who favor country decor, intimate areas, and artsy touches may find the rooms lack warmth, but the resort's facilities are the best in the region. A new resort center with full health spa, new pools, and 32 oversize rooms with gas fireplaces opened in 2002. This place has a loyal following, so reserve well in advance. ⊠ *2 E. Shore Rd. (Box 2274, 03907),* ☎ *207/ 361–1000,* 📠 *207/361–2122,* 🌐 *www.cliffhousemaine.com. 194 rooms, 2 suites. Restaurant, in-room data ports, cable TV, 2 pools (1 indoor), hot tub, sauna, spa, 2 tennis courts, health club; no smoking AE, D, MC, V. Closed mid-Dec.–late Mar.*

$$–$$$$ 🏨 **The Rockmere.** Midway along Ogunquit's Marginal Way, this shingle-style Victorian cottage is an ideal retreat from the hustle and bustle of Perkins Cove. All the rooms have corner locations and are large and airy, and all but one have ocean views. You'll find it easy to laze the day away on the wraparound porch or in the gardens. ⊠ *150 Stearns Rd. (Box 278, 03907),* ☎ *207/646–2985,* 📠 *207/646–6947,* 🌐 *www.rockmere.com. 8 rooms. Cable TV; no air-conditioning, no phones, no kids under 16. AE, D, V. CP.*

Nightlife and the Arts

Much of the nightlife in Ogunquit revolves around the precincts of Ogunquit Square and Perkins Cove, where people stroll, often enjoying an after-dinner ice cream cone or espresso. Ogunquit is popular with gay and lesbian visitors, and its club scene reflects this.

Jonathan's Restaurant (⊠ 2 Bourne La., ☎ 207/646–4777) hosts live entertainment, usually blues, during peak season, from June to mid-October. The **Ogunquit Playhouse** (⊠ U.S. 1, ☎ 207/646–5511), one of America's oldest summer theaters, mounts plays and musicals with name entertainment from late June to Labor Day.

Outdoor Activities and Sports

Ogunquit Beach, a 3-mi-wide stretch of sand at the mouth of the Ogunquit River, has snack bars, a boardwalk, rest rooms, and, at the Beach Street entrance, changing areas. Families gravitate to the ends; gay visitors camp at the beach's middle. The less-crowded section to the north is accessible by footbridge and has portable rest rooms, all-day paid parking, and trolley service. **Finestkind** (⊠ Perkins Cove, ☎ 207/646–5227) operates cocktail cruises, lobstering trips, and cruises to Nubble Light.

Wells

4 *5 mi north of Ogunquit, 34 mi southwest of Portland.*

This family-oriented beach community has 7 mi of densely populated shoreline, along with nature preserves where you can explore salt marshes and tidal pools and see birds and waterfowl.

Extensive trails in the **Wells Reserve** lace the 1,600 acres of meadows, orchards, fields, and salt marshes, as well as two estuaries and 9 mi of seashore. Laudholm Farm, an 18th-century saltwater farm, houses the visitor center, where an introductory slide show is screened. Five rooms have exhibits. In winter, cross-country skiing is permitted. ⊠ *342 Laudholm Farm Rd.,* ☎ *207/646–1555.* ⊡ *$2 July–Aug. and weekends Sept.–mid-Oct.* ☉ *Grounds daily 8–5. Visitor center May–Dec., Mon.–Sat. 10–4, Sun. noon–4; Jan.–Apr., Sat. 10–4, Sun. noon–4.*

Rachel Carson National Wildlife Refuge (⊠ Rte. 9, ☎ 207/646–9226) has a mile-long-loop nature trail through a salt marsh. The trail borders the Little River and a white-pine forest where migrating birds and waterfowl of many varieties are regularly spotted.

☾ A must for motor fanatics and youngsters, the **Wells Auto Museum** has 70 vintage cars, antique coin games, and a restored Model T you can ride in. ⊠ *U.S. 1,* ☎ *207/646–9064.* ⊡ *$5.* ☉ *Memorial Day–Columbus Day, daily 10–5.*

Dining and Lodging

$$–$$$$ ✕ **Billy's Chowder House.** Locals head to this simple restaurant in a salt marsh for the generous lobster rolls, haddock sandwiches, and chowders. Big windows in the bright dining rooms overlook the marsh. ⊠ *216 Mile Rd.,* ☎ *207/646–7558. AE, D, MC, V. Closed mid-Dec.–mid-Jan.*

$$–$$$ ✕▥ **Grey Gull Inn.** This Victorian inn, built in 1893, has views of the open sea and rocks on which seals like to sun themselves. Most of the unpretentious rooms have ocean views. The restaurant ($$–$$$$) serves excellent seafood dishes such as soft-shell crabs almandine and regional fare like Yankee pot roast and chicken breast rolled in walnuts. ⊠ *475 Webhannet Dr., at Moody Point,* ☎ *207/646–7501,* FAX *207/646–0938,* WEB *www.thegreygullinn.com. 5 rooms, 4 with bath. Restaurant, cable TV; no smoking. AE, D, MC, V. CP.*

$$–$$$$ ▥ **Haven by the Sea.** Spacious rooms, some with marsh views, provide comfort at this renovated 1920s church. One block from the beach, it has four common areas, including one with a fireplace. ⊠ *59 Church St., 04090,* ☎ *207/646–4194,* FAX *207/646–6883,* WEB *www.havenbythesea.com. 6 rooms, 2 suites, 1 apartment. Cable TV,*

*Internet, meeting rooms; no kids under 12, no smoking. AE, MC,
V. BP.*

Outdoor Activities and Sports

Kayaking is popular along the coast, and **World Within Sea Kayaking**
(☎ 207/646–0455) conducts guided tours with lessons.

Shopping

Douglas Harding Rare Books (✉ 2152 Post Rd. [U.S. 1], ☎ 207/646–
8785) has more than 100,000 old books, maps, and prints. The **Lighthouse Depot** (✉ U.S. 1, ☎ 207/646–0608) calls itself the world's
largest lighthouse gift store, with lighthouse-themed gifts and memorabilia. **R. Jorgensen** (✉ 502 Post Rd. [U.S. 1], ☎ 207/646–9444) stocks
18th- and 19th-century formal and country antiques from the British
Isles, Europe, and the United States.

The Kennebunks

❺ *5 mi north of Wells, 29 mi southwest of Portland.*

The Kennebunks encompass Kennebunk, Kennebunk Beach, Goose
Rocks Beach, Kennebunkport, Cape Porpoise, and Arundel. This cluster of seaside and inland villages provides a little bit of everything, from
salt marshes to sand beaches, jumbled fishing shacks to architectural
gems.

Handsome white clapboard homes with shutters give Kennebunk, a
shipbuilding center in the first half of the 19th century, a quintessential New England look. If you enjoy shopping, plan to spend the better part of a day exploring the boutiques and galleries in Dock Square.
People flock to Kennebunkport mostly in summer; some come in early
December when the **Christmas Prelude** is celebrated on two weekends.
Santa arrives by fishing boat, and the Christmas trees are lighted as
carolers stroll the sidewalks.

Route 35 south leads to Kennebunk's Lower Village. Continue south
on Beach Avenue for Kennebunk Beach. To reach Kennebunkport, head
east on Route 9/Western Avenue and cross the drawbridge into Dock
Square. Continue east on Route 9, or take scenic Ocean Avenue and
Wildes District Road to quiet Cape Porpoise. To access Goose Rocks
Beach continue east on Route 9, which is now called the Mills Road.
Arundel is nestled between Kennebunk and Kennebunkport.

The cornerstone of the **Brick Store Museum,** a block-long preservation
of early 19th-century commercial buildings, is **William Lord's Brick
Store.** Built as a dry-goods store in 1825 in the Federal style, the building has an open-work balustrade across the roof line, granite lintels
over the windows, and paired chimneys. Exhibits chronicle Kennebunk's relationship with the sea. The museum leads architectural walking tours of Kennebunk's historic Summer Street. ✉ *117 Main St.,
Kennebunk,* ☎ *207/985–4802,* WEB *www.brickstoremuseum.org.* 🖭 *$5.*
⊙ *Apr.–Dec., Tues.–Sat. 10–4:30.*

The drive from Kennebunk to Kennebunkport will take you by the **Wedding Cake House** (✉ 104 Summer St./Rte. 35, Kennebunk). The leg-
end behind this confection in fancy wood fretwork is that its builder,
a sea captain, was forced to set sail in the middle of his wedding; the
house was his bride's consolation for the lack of a wedding cake. The
home, built in 1826, is not open to the public.

Route 35 merges with Route 9 in Kennebunk and takes you right into
Kennebunkport's **Dock Square,** the busy town center. Boutiques, T-shirt
shops, art galleries, crafts stores, and restaurants encircle the square

and spread out alongside streets and alleys. Although many businesses close in winter, the best bargains often are had in December. Walk onto the drawbridge to admire the tidal Kennebunk River.

The **Nott House,** also known as White Columns, is an imposing Greek Revival mansion with Doric columns that rise the height of the house. The 1853 house is furnished with the belongings of four generations of the Perkins-Nott family. It is a gathering place for village walking tours; call for the schedule. ⊠ *8 Maine St., Kennebunkport,* ☎ *207/ 967–2751,* WEB *www.kporthistory.org.* ⊡ *$5.* ☉ *Mid-June–mid-Oct., Tues.–Fri. 1–4, Sat. 10–1.*

Ocean Avenue follows the Kennebunk River from Dock Square to the sea and winds around the peninsula of **Cape Arundel.** Parson's Way, a small and tranquil stretch of rocky shoreline, is open to all. As you round Cape Arundel, look to the right for the entrance to former president George Bush's summer home at Walker's Point.

★ ℃ The **Seashore Trolley Museum** displays streetcars built from 1872 to 1972 and includes trolleys from major metropolitan areas and world capitals—Boston to Budapest, New York to Nagasaki, and San Francisco to Sydney—all beautifully restored. Best of all, you can take a trolley ride for nearly 4 mi over the tracks of the former Atlantic Shoreline trolley line, with a stop along the way at the museum restoration shop, where trolleys are transformed from junk into gems. Both guided and self-guided tours are available. ⊠ *195 Log Cabin Rd., Kennebunkport,* ☎ *207/967–2800,* WEB *www.trolleymuseum.org.* ⊡ *$7.50.* ☉ *Early May–mid-Oct., daily 10–4:30; reduced hrs in spring and fall.*

Dining and Lodging

$$$$ ✕ **White Barn Inn.** Formally attired waiters and meticulous servers and
★ exquisite food have earned this restaurant accolades as one of the best in New England. Regional New England fare is served in a rustic but elegant dining room. The three-course, prix-fixe menu, which changes weekly, might list steamed Maine lobster nestled on fresh fettuccine with carrots, ginger, and snow peas. ⊠ *37 Beach Ave., Kennebunkport,* ☎ *207/967–2321. Reservations essential. Jacket required. AE, MC, V.*

$$$–$$$$ ✕ **Seascapes.** The emphasis is on seafood at this pretty harbor-front restaurant where the view takes center stage. You can begin with Seascapes smoked chowder, then move on to grilled diver-harvested scallops or try the ginger-garlic rack of lamb. Accompany it all with a selection from the excellent wine list. ⊠ *77 Pier Rd., Cape Porpoise,* ☎ *207/967–8500. AE, D, DC, MC, V. Closed late Oct.–Apr.*

$$$–$$$$ ✕ **Windows on the Water.** Big windows frame Dock Square and the working harbor of Kennebunkport, and almost every window in the airy dining room shares the view. Lobster ravioli and classic Spanish paella are two noteworthy entrées. ⊠ *12 Chase Hill Rd., Kennebunkport,* ☎ *207/967–3313. Reservations essential. AE, D, DC, MC, V.*

$$ ✕ **Grissini.** This popular trattoria draws high praise for its northern Italian cuisine. Dine by the stone hearth on inclement days or on the patio when the weather's fine. Mix and match appetizers, pizzas, salads, pastas, and entrées from the menu to suit your hunger and budget. ⊠ *27 Western Ave., Kennebunk,* ☎ *207/967–2211. AE, MC, V.*

$–$$ ✕ **Cape Pier Chowder House.** You can watch the surf crash over distant ledges near the Goat Island lighthouse and see lobster boats returning with their day's catch at this oceanfront lobster shack. Seating is on the deck or inside. The fare includes lobster, clams, and fried foods. ⊠ *15 Pier Rd., Cape Porpoise,* ☎ *207/967–4268 or 800/967–4268. MC, V. Closed early Nov.–mid-Apr.*

$$$–$$$$ ✕⊡ **Cape Arundel Inn.** This shingle-style inn commands a magnificent ocean view that takes in the Bush estate at Walker's Point. The spacious rooms are furnished with country-style furniture and antiques, and most have sitting areas with ocean views. You can relax on the front porch or in front of the living-room fireplace. In the candlelit dining room ($$$–$$$$), open to the public for dinner, every table has a view of the surf. The menu changes seasonally. ✉ *208 Ocean Ave., Kennebunkport 04046,* ☎ *207/967–2125,* ℻ *207/967–1199,* ⱲⱭⒷ *www.capearundelinn.com. 13 rooms, 1 suite. Restaurant; no air-conditioning, no room phones, no TV in some rooms, no smoking. AE, D, MC, V. Closed Jan.–Feb. CP.*

$$$$ ⊡ **The Beach House.** Gooch's Beach is out the front door of this elegant late-19th-century inn. Rooms are individually decorated, with most colored in shades of beige and accented with country antiques that are comfortable rather than fussy. Feather beds and down comforters and pillows add a luxurious touch. Watch the sunrise from the wraparound porch, or sleep in, snuggled beneath a down comforter. You can hunker down by the big stone fireplace on rainy days. ✉ *211 Beach Ave., Kennebunk 04046,* ☎ *207/967–3850,* ℻ *207/967–4719,* ⱲⱭⒷ *www.beachhseinn.com. 35 rooms. Cable TV, in-room VCRs, some in-room hot tubs, beach, boating, bicycles; no smoking. AE, MC, V. CP.*

$$$$ ⊡ **Captain Lord Mansion.** Of all the mansions in Kennebunkport's historic district that have been converted to inns, the 1812 Captain Lord Mansion is the most stately and sumptuously appointed. Distinctive architecture, including a suspended elliptical staircase, gas fireplaces in all rooms, and near–museum quality accoutrements, make for a formal but not stuffy setting. Six rooms have whirlpool tubs. The extravagant suite has two fireplaces, a double whirlpool, a hydro-massage body spa, a TV/VCR and stereo system, and a king-size canopy bed. ✉ *Pleasant and Green Sts. (Box 800, 04046),* ☎ *207/967–3141,* ℻ *207/967–3172,* ⱲⱭⒷ *www.captainlord.com. 15 rooms, 1 suite. In-room data ports, Internet, meeting rooms; no room TVs, no kids under 12, no smoking. D, MC, V. BP.*

$$$$ ⊡ **The Seaside.** This handsome seaside property has been in the hands of the Severance family since 1667. The modern motel units, all with sliding-glass doors that open onto private decks or patios (half with ocean views), are appropriate for families; so are the cottages with one to four bedrooms. ✉ *80 Beach Ave., Kennebunk 04046,* ☎ *207/967–4461 or 866/300–6750,* ℻ *207/967–1135,* ⱲⱭⒷ *www.kennebunkbeach.com. 22 rooms, 11 cottages. Refrigerators, cable TV, beach, playground, laundry service; no pets, no smoking. AE, MC, V. Cottages closed Nov.–May. CP.*

$$$$ ⊡ **White Barn Inn.** For a romantic overnight stay, you need look no
★   further than the exclusive White Barn Inn, known for its attentive, pampering service. No detail has been overlooked in the meticulously appointed rooms, from plush bedding and reading lamps to robes and slippers. Rooms are in the main inn and adjacent buildings. Some have fireplaces, hot tubs, and luxurious baths with steam showers. The ample breakfast includes quiche and freshly baked pastries. The inn is within walking distance of Dock Square and the beach. ✉ *37 Beach Ave. (Box 560C, Kennebunkport 04046),* ☎ *207/967–2321,* ℻ *207/ 967–1100,* ⱲⱭⒷ *www.whitebarninn.com. 16 rooms, 9 suites. Restaurant, in-room data ports, cable TV, in-room VCRs, pool, bicycles, piano bar, dry cleaning, laundry, concierge, Internet, meeting room; no smoking, no kids under 12. AE, MC, V. BP.*

$$$$ ⊡ **The Yachtsman.** Relaxing in one of the handsome rooms—in muted shades of beige, brown, and black—in this riverfront hotel feels like you're aboard an elegant yacht. Down comforters cover the king-size beds, and nautical artwork adorns the walls. French doors open onto

private patios overlooking the marina. A hearty Continental breakfast and afternoon tea are served on the riverfront patio. The shops and restaurants of Dock Square are just a short walk away. ✉ *Ocean Ave. (Box 2609, Kennebunkport 04046),* ☎ *207/967–2511,* FAX *207/967–5056,* WEB *www.yachtsmanlodge.com. 30 rooms. Refrigerators, boating, bicycles; no smoking. AE, MC, V. Closed early Dec.–Mar. CP.*

$$$–$$$$ 🏠 **Bufflehead Cove.** On the Kennebunk River at the end of a winding dirt road, this gray-shingle B&B amid quiet country fields and apple trees is only five minutes from Dock Square. Rooms in the main house have white wicker and flowers hand-painted on the walls. The Hideaway Suite, with a two-sided gas fireplace, king-size bed, and large whirlpool tub, overlooks the river. The Garden Studio has a fireplace and offers the most privacy. ✉ *18 Bufflehead Cove Rd. (Box 499, Kennebunk 04046),* ☎ FAX *207/967–3879,* WEB *www.buffleheadcove.com. 2 rooms, 3 suites, 1 cottage. Internet, dock, boating; no room phones, no TVs in some rooms, no kids, no smoking. D, MC, V. Closed Dec.–May. BP.*

$$–$$$ 🏠 **Rhumb Line.** Although the rooms are standard motel fare, the facilities set this family-friendly motor lodge apart. It's on the trolley line, making getting around Kennebunk-area sites easy. Lobster bakes (extra charge) are held nightly weekends late May–June and daily July–August. ✉ *41 Turbats Creek Rd. (Box 3067, Kennebunkport 04046),* ☎ *207/967–5457 or 800/337–4862,* FAX *207/967–4418,* WEB *www.rhumblinemaine.com. 56 rooms, 3 suites. Snack bar, refrigerators, cable TV, 3 pools (1 indoor), health club, hot tub, sauna, meeting rooms; no-smoking rooms. AE, D, MC, V. CP.*

$ 🏠 **St. Anthony's Franciscan Monastery Guest House.** Those in search of a quiet, contemplative retreat may want to choose one of the unadorned, motel-style rooms in a former dormitory on the grounds of a riverside monastery. The guest house is private yet within walking distance of Dock Square and the beach. The landscaped grounds, open to the public, have trails and shrines. The monks live in a Tudor mansion on the property, where Mass is said daily. This place is not recommended for those uncomfortable with Christian symbolism, although no religious participation is required. ✉ *28 Beach Ave., Kennebunkport 04043,* ☎ *207/967–2011. 60 rooms. Cable TV, saltwater pool; no room phones. No credit cards. Closed Sept. 10–June 10.*

Outdoor Activities and Sports

BEACHES

Kennebunk Beach has three parts: Gooch's Beach, Mother's Beach, and Kennebunk Beach. Beach Road, with its cottages and old Victorian boardinghouses, runs right behind them. Gooch's and Kennebunk attract teenagers; Mother's Beach, which has a small playground and tidal puddles for splashing, is popular with families. For parking permits (a fee is charged in summer), go to the **Kennebunk Town Office** (✉ 1 Summer St., ☎ 207/985–2102).

Three-mi-long **Goose Rocks,** a few minutes' drive north of town off Route 9, is a favorite of families with small children. You can pick up a parking permit ($5 a day, $15 a week) at the **Chamber of Commerce** (✉ 17 Western Ave., Lower Village, ☎ 207/967–0857).

BIKING

Cape-Able Bike Shop (✉ 83 Arundel Rd., Kennebunkport, ☎ 207/967–4382) rents bicycles.

BOATING AND FISHING

Cape Arundel Cruises (✉ Kennebunkport Marina, ☎ 207/967–5595) conducts scenic and theater cruises, deep-sea fishing, and whale-watching trips. **First Chance** (✉ 4-A Western Ave., Kennebunk, ☎ 207/967–

5507 or 800/967–2628) leads whale-watching cruises and guarantees sightings in season.

Shopping

The **Gallery on Chase Hill** (✉ 10 Chase Hill Rd., Kennebunk, ☎ 207/967–0049) presents original artwork by Maine and New England artists. **Mainely Quilts** (✉ 1 Temple St., Kennebunkport, ☎ 207/967–3571) sells a nice selection of quilts and teddy bears. **Marlow's Artisans Gallery** (✉ 39 Main St., Kennebunk, ☎ 207/985–2931) carries a large and eclectic collection of crafts. **Mast Cove Galleries** (✉ Mast Cove La., Kennebunkport, ☎ 207/967–3453) sells graphics, paintings, and sculpture by 105 artists. **Tom's of Maine Natural Living Store** (✉ 64 Main St., Kennebunk, ☎ 207/985–3874) sells all-natural personal-care products.

Old Orchard Beach

⑥ *15 mi north of Kennebunkport, 18 mi south of Portland.*

Old Orchard Beach, a few miles north of Biddeford on Route 9, is a 7-mi strip of sand beach with an amusement park that resembles a small Coney Island. Despite the summertime crowds and fried-food odors, the atmosphere can be captivating. During the 1940s and '50s, in the heyday of the Big Band era, the pier had a dance hall where stars of the time performed. Fire claimed the end of the pier, but booths with games and candy concessions still line both sides. Plans are under way to extend the pier and offer dinner-gaming cruises. In summer the town sponsors fireworks (usually on Thursday night). The many places to stay run the gamut from cheap motels to cottage colonies to full-service seasonal hotels. You won't find free parking anywhere in town, but there are ample lots. Amtrak has a seasonal stop here.

A world away from the beach scene is **Ocean Park** (☎ 207/934–9068), on the southwestern edge of town. This vacation community was founded in 1881 as a summer assembly, following the example of Chautauqua, New York. Today the community still hosts a variety of cultural happenings, including movies, concerts, workshops, and religious services. Most are presented in the Temple, which is on the National Register of Historic Places.

Ⓒ **Palace Playland** (✉ 1 Old Orchard St., ☎ 207/934–2001), open from Memorial Day to Labor Day, has rides, booths, and a roller coaster

Ⓒ that drops almost 50 ft. **Funtown/Splashtown** (✉ U.S. 1, Saco, ☎ 207/284–5139 or 800/878–2900) has more than 30 rides and amusements, including miniature golf, water slides, a wave pool, and Excalibur, a wooden roller coaster.

Dining and Lodging

$$–$$$$ ✗ **Joseph's by the Sea.** Big windows frame the ocean beyond the dunes at this fine restaurant, which offers outdoor dining in season. Appetizers may include goat cheese terrine and lobster potato pancake; try the grilled Tuscan swordfish or seared sea scallops for your main course. ✉ 55 W. Grand Ave., ☎ 207/934–5044. MC, V.

$$–$$$ ⌂ **Old Orchard Beach Inn.** Dating from 1730, this is Old Orchard Beach's oldest inn. It was saved from demolition in 1997 and was completely renovated. The spacious guest rooms are furnished with antiques, area rugs cover the pine floors, quilts brighten the beds, and lace curtains frame the windows. Many have views over the town of the shimmering Atlantic. ✉ 6 Portland Ave., 04064, ☎ 207/934–5834 or 877/700–6624, ℻ 207/934–0782, ⓦⓔⓑ www.oldorchardbeachinn.com. 17 rooms, 1 suite. In-room data ports, cable TV; no air-conditioning, no smoking. AE, D, MC, V. CP.

Nightlife and the Arts

In season, weekly concerts are held in Town Square every Monday and Tuesday night at 7. Fireworks light the sky Thursdays at 9:30 from late June through Labor Day. Concerts are held most Sunday evenings in Ocean Park.

Outdoor Activities and Sports

Ferry Beach State Park (⊠ Rte. 9, Saco, ☎ 207/283–0067) comprises 117 acres of beach, bike paths, and nature trails. The **Maine Audubon Society** (⊠ Rte. 9, Scarborough, ☎ 207/781–2330; 207/883–5100 from mid-June to Labor Day) operates guided canoe trips and rents canoes in Scarborough Marsh, the largest salt marsh in Maine. Programs at Maine Audubon's Falmouth headquarters (north of Portland) include nature walks and a discovery room for children.

York County Coast A to Z

To research prices, get advice from other travelers, and book travel arrangements, visit www.fodors.com.

AIR TRAVEL

Portland International Jetport is 35 mi northeast of Kennebunk.

BIKE TRAVEL

A bicycle can make it easy to get around the Kennebunks, but the lack of shoulders on some roads can be intimidating. Two good resources are the Bicycle Coalition of Maine and the Maine Department of Transportation.

➤ BIKE INFORMATION: **Bicycle Coalition of Maine** (⊠ Box 5275, Augusta 04332, ☎ 207/623–4511, WEB www.bikemaine.org). **Maine Dept. of Transportation Bike and Pedestrian Section** (WEB www.state.me.us/mdot/biketours.htm).

CAR TRAVEL

U.S. 1 from Kittery is the shopper's route north; other roads hug the coastline. Interstate 95 is usually faster for travelers headed to towns north of Ogunquit, but be forewarned that the Maine Turnpike/I–95 is in the midst of a widening project from Wells to Portland that will result in slowdowns and stops until completion in 2004. The renumbering of exits to coincide with mileage from the border, however, is expected to be completed by 2003.

Route 9 goes from Kennebunkport to Cape Porpoise and Goose Rocks. Parking is tight in Kennebunkport in peak season. Possibilities include the municipal lot next to the Congregational Church ($2 an hour from May to October) and 30 North Street (free year-round).

EMERGENCIES

➤ HOSPITALS AND EMERGENCY SERVICES: **Maine State Police** (⊠ Gray, ☎ 207/793–4500 or 800/482–0730). **Southern Maine Medical Center** (⊠ Rte. 111, Biddeford, ☎ 207/283–7000; 207/283–7100 emergency room). **York Hospital** (⊠ 15 Hospital Dr. York, ☎ 207/351–2157 or 800/283–7234).

LODGING

For home rentals in the Kennebunks, try Port Properties or Sand Dollar Real Estate Sales & Rentals. For rentals on the southern Maine coast, try Seaside Vacation Rentals. Garnsey Bros. rents condominiums and housekeeping cottages in Wells, Moody Beach, and Drakes Island. The Wight Agency specializes in waterfront rentals in Old Orchard.
➤ LODGING: **Garnsey Bros.** (⊠ 510 Webhannet Dr., Wells 04090, ☎ 207/646–8301, WEB www.garnsey.com). **Port Properties** (⊠ Box 799,

Kennebunkport 04046, ☎ 207/967–4400 or 800/443–7678, WEB www.portproperties.com). **Sand Dollar Real Estate Sales & Rentals** (⊠ 5 Dyke Rd., Goose Rocks Beach, Kennebunkport, 04046, ☎ 207/967–3421). **Seaside Vacation Rentals** (⊠ Box 2000, York 03909, ☎ 207/646–7671 or 207/363–1825, WEB www.seasiderentals.com). **The Wight Agency** (⊠ 125 W. Grand Ave., Old Orchard Beach 04064, ☎ 207/934–4576).

MEDIA

The *Biddeford Tribune* and the *Portland Press Herald*, the state's largest paper, are published daily. The *Maine Sunday Telegram* is the state's only Sunday paper. The *York County Coast Star* is published weekly.

WMEA 90.1 is the local National Public Radio affiliate. WCSH, channel 6, is the NBC affiliate. WMTW, channel 8, is the ABC affiliate. WGME, channel 13, is the CBS affiliate. WCBB, channel 10, or WMEA, channel 26, is the Maine Public Broadcasting affiliate.

TOURS

Gone With the Wind schedules guided kayak and windsurfing trips. Van tours of southern Maine are operated by Seacoast Tours. Routes include Portland, Ogunquit, Kittery and York, and Kennebunkport; tours are 1¼–4 hours. Intown Trolley conducts 45-minute sightseeing tours of the Kennebunks.
➤ TOUR OPERATORS: **Gone With the Wind** (⊠ Biddeford, ☎ 207/283–8446). **Intown Trolley** (⊠ Kennebunkport, ☎ 207/967–3686). **Seacoast Tours** (⊠ Perkins Cove, Ogunquit, ☎ 207/646–6326 or 800/328–8687).

TRAIN TRAVEL

Amtrak offers rail service from Boston to Portland, with stops in Wells and Saco and a seasonal stop in Old Orchard Beach.
➤ TRAIN INFORMATION: **Amtrak** (☎ 800/872–7245, WEB www. thedowneaster.com).

TRANSPORTATION AROUND YORK COUNTY COAST

Trolleys ($1–$3) serve several areas. A trolley circulates among the Yorks from late June to Labor Day. A trolley fleet serves the major tourist areas and beaches of Ogunquit in July and August. Trolleys circulate in Wells on weekends from Memorial Day to Columbus Day and daily from late June to Labor Day. Trolleys circulate through Kennebunkport to Kennebunk Beach from Memorial Day to Columbus Day; an all-day ticket is $8. Biddeford–Saco–Old Orchard Beach Transit operates a trolley that circulates through Old Orchard Beach and a bus service from Old Orchard to Portland with stops in Scarborough and at the Maine Mall.

VISITOR INFORMATION

➤ TOURIST INFORMATION: **Gateway to Maine Chamber of Commerce** (⊠ 191 State Rd., Kittery 03904, ☎ 207/439–7574 or 800/639–9645, WEB www.gatewaytomaine.org). **Kennebunk-Kennebunkport Chamber of Commerce** (⊠ Box 740, Kennebunk 04043, ☎ 207/967–0857, WEB www.visitthekennebunks.com). **Maine Tourism Association & Visitor Information Center** (⊠ U.S. 1 and I–95, Kittery 03904, ☎ 207/439–1319). **Ogunquit Chamber of Commerce** (⊠ U.S. 1 [Box 2289, Ogunquit 03907], ☎ 207/646–2939, WEB www.ogunquit.org). **Old Orchard Beach Chamber of Commerce** (⊠ 1st St. [Box 600, Old Orchard Beach 04064], ☎ 207/934–2500 or 800/365–9386, WEB www.oldorchardbeachmaine.com). **Wells Chamber of Commerce** (⊠ Box 356, Wells 04090, ☎ 207/646–2451, WEB www.wellschamber.org).

The **Yorks Chamber of Commerce** (✉ 571 U.S. 1, York 03903, ☎ 207/363–4422 or 800/639–2442, WEB www.yorkme.org).

PORTLAND TO WALDOBORO

This south–mid-coast area provides an overview of Maine: a little bit of urban life, a little more coastline, and a nice dollop of history and architecture. Maine's largest city, Portland, holds some pleasant surprises, including the Old Port, among the finest urban renovation projects on the East Coast. Freeport, north of Portland, was made famous by its L.L. Bean store, whose success led to the opening of scores of other clothing stores and outlets. Brunswick is best known for Bowdoin College. Bath has been a shipbuilding center since 1607; the Maine Maritime Museum preserves its history. Wiscasset contains many antiques shops and galleries.

The Boothbays—the coastal areas of Boothbay Harbor, East Boothbay, Linekin Neck, Southport Island, and the inland town of Boothbay—attract hordes of vacationing families and flotillas of pleasure craft. The Pemaquid peninsula juts into the Atlantic south of Damariscotta and just east of the Boothbays. Near Pemaquid Beach you can view the objects unearthed at the Colonial Pemaquid Restoration, including the remains of an old customs house, a tavern, a jail, a forge, and homes.

Portland

105 mi northeast of Boston; 320 mi northeast of New York City; 215 mi southwest of St. Stephen, New Brunswick.

Portland's role as a cultural and economic center for the region has given the gentrifying city of 65,000 plenty of attractions that make it well worth a day or two of exploration. Its restored Old Port balances modern commercial enterprise and salty waterfront character in an area bustling with restaurants, shops, and galleries. Water tours of the harbor and excursions to islands of Casco Bay depart from the piers of Commercial Street. Downtown Portland, in a funk for years, is now a burgeoning arts district connected to the Old Port by a revitalized Congress Street, where L.L. Bean operates a factory store.

Portland's first home was built on the peninsula now known as Munjoy Hill in 1632. The British burned the city in 1775, when residents refused to surrender arms, but it was rebuilt and became a major trading center. Much of Portland was destroyed on July 4 in the Great Fire of 1866, when a boy threw a celebration firecracker into a pile of wood shavings; 1,500 buildings burned to the ground. Poet Henry Wadsworth Longfellow said at the time that his city reminded him of the ruins of Pompeii. The Great Fire started not far from where people now wander the streets of the Old Port.

Congress Street runs the length of the peninsular city from alongside the Western Promenade in the southwest to the Eastern Promenade on Munjoy Hill in the northeast, passing through the small downtown area. A few blocks southeast of downtown, the bustling Old Port sprawls along the waterfront. Below Munjoy Hill is India Street, where the Great Fire of 1866 started.

❼ The **Portland Observatory** on Munjoy Hill was built in 1807 by Capt. Lemuel Moody, a retired sea captain. It is the last remaining signal tower in the country and is held in place by 122 tons of ballast. After visiting the small museum at the base, you can climb to the Orb deck and take in views of Portland, the islands, and inland to the White Mountains. ⊠ *138 Congress St.,* ☎ *207/774–5561.* ☜ *$3.* ⊙ *Memorial Day–Columbus Day, daily 10–5.*

★ **❽** The Italianate-style Morse-Libby Mansion, known as **Victoria Mansion,** was built between 1858 and 1860 and is widely regarded as the most sumptuously ornamented dwelling of its period remaining in the country. Architect Henry Austin designed the house for hotelier Ruggles Morse and his wife, Olive; the interior design—everything from the plasterwork to the furniture (much of it original)—is the only surviving commission of New York designer Gustave Herter. Inside the elegant brownstone exterior of this National Historic Landmark are colorful frescoed walls and ceilings, ornate marble mantelpieces, gilded gas chandeliers, a magnificent 6- by 25-ft stained-glass ceiling window, and a freestanding mahogany staircase; guided tours cover all the details. ⊠ *109 Danforth St.,* ☎ *207/772–4841,* WEB *www.victoriamansion.org.* ☜ *$8.* ⊙ *May–Oct., Tues.–Sat. 10–4, Sun. 1–5.*

🖐 **❾** Touching is okay at the relatively small but fun **Children's Museum of Maine,** where kids can pretend they are fishing for lobster or are shopkeepers or computer experts. The majority of the museum's exhibits, many of which have a Maine theme, are best for children 10 and younger. Camera Obscura, an exhibit about optics, provides fascinating panoramic views of the city. ⊠ *142 Free St.,* ☎ *207/828–1234,* WEB *www.kitetails.com.* ☜ *Museum $5; Camera Obscura only, $3.* ⊙ *Memorial Day–Labor Day, Mon.–Sat. 10–5, Sun. noon–5; early Sept.–Memorial Day, Tues.–Sat. 10–5, Sun. noon–5.*

★ **❿** The **Portland Museum of Art,** Maine's largest public art institution, has a number of strong collections, including fine seascapes and landscapes by Winslow Homer, John Marin, Andrew Wyeth, Edward Hopper, Marsden Hartley, and other painters. Homer's *Pulling the Dory* and *Weatherbeaten,* two quintessential Maine-coast images, are here; the museum owns 17 paintings by Homer. The Joan Whitney Payson Collection of Impressionist and Postimpressionist art includes works by Monet, Picasso, and Renoir. Harry N. Cobb, an associate of I. M. Pei, designed the strikingly modern Charles Shipman Payson building. The renovated McLellan-Sweat House is expected to open in fall 2002 with additional galleries housing the museum's 19th-century collection and decorative art as well as interactive educational stations. ⊠ *7 Congress Sq.,* ☎ *207/775–6148; 800/639–4067 recorded information,* WEB *www.portlandmuseum.org.* ☜ *$6, free Fri. 5–9.* ⊙ *Memorial Day–Columbus Day, Mon.–Wed. and weekends 10–5; Thurs.–Fri. 10–9; Columbus Day–Memorial Day, closed Mon.*

⓫ The **Wadsworth Longfellow House,** the boyhood home of the poet and the first brick house in Portland, is particularly interesting because most of the furnishings are original to the house. The late-Colonial-style structure, built in 1785, sits back from the street and has a small portico over its entrance and four chimneys surmounting the hip roof. The house is part of the Center for Maine History, which includes the adjacent Maine History Gallery and a research library; the gift shop has a good selection of books about Maine. ⊠ *489 Congress St.,* ☎ *207/774–1822,* WEB *www.mainehistory.org.* ☜ *$6, Center $4.* ⊙ *House and Maine History Gallery June–Oct., daily 10–5; library Tues.–Sat., 10–3; last tour at 4.*

★ **⓬** The **Old Port** bridges the gap between the city's 19th-century commercial activities and those of today. Like the Customs House, the brick buildings and warehouses of the Old Port were built following the Great Fire of 1866 and were intended to last for ages. When the city's economy slumped in the mid-20th century, however, the Old Port declined

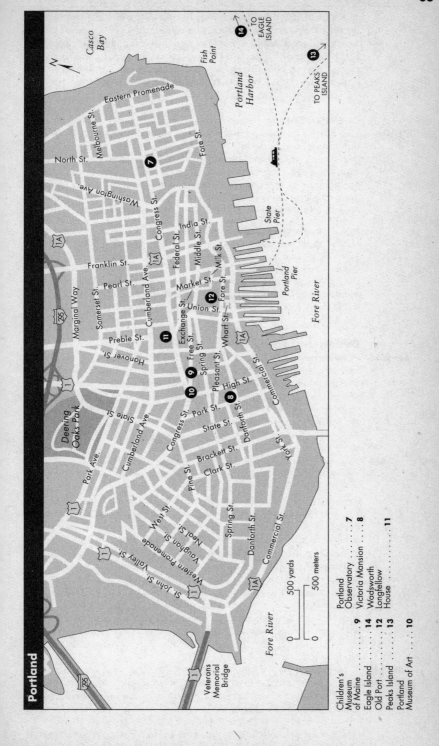

33

Portland

Casco Bay

Fish Point

N

Eastern Promenade

Melbourne St.

North St.

Washington Ave.

Congress St.

Fore St.

India St.

Federal St.

Middle St.

Milk St.

Franklin St.

1A

Marginal Way

Pearl St.

Somerset St.

Cumberland Ave.

Market St.

Fore St.

Wharf St.

Exchange St.

Union St.

1A

Preble St.

Hanover St.

Free St.

Spring St.

Pleasant St.

High St.

Deering Oaks Park

State St.

Congress St.

Park St.

State St.

Commercial St.

Brackett St.

Pine St.

Clark St.

Danforth St.

York St.

Park Ave.

Cumberland Ave.

West St.

Neal St.

Vaughan St.

Spring St.

Danforth St.

Commercial St.

St. John St.

Valley St.

Western Promenade

Veterans Memorial Bridge

95

1

1A

Fore River

Portland Harbor

TO EAGLE ISLAND

TO PEAKS ISLAND

State Pier

Portland Pier

Fore River

Portland Pier

7 8 9 10 11 12 13 14

0 500 yards

0 500 meters

Children's Museum of Maine 9
Eagle Island 14
Old Port 12
Peaks Island 13
Portland Museum of Art 10

Portland Observatory 7
Victoria Mansion 8
Wadsworth Longfellow House 11

and seemed slated for demolition. Then artists and craftspeople began opening shops in the late 1960s, and restaurants, boutiques, and bookstores followed. Allow a couple of hours to wander at leisure on Market, Exchange, Middle, and Fore streets. You can park your car at the city garage on Fore Street (between Exchange and Union streets) or opposite the U.S. Customs House at the corner of Fore and Pearl streets.

OFF THE BEATEN PATH

CAPE ELIZABETH – This upscale Portland suburb juts out into the Atlantic. Take Route 77 south and east from Portland and follow signs to Two Lights State Park, home to Two Lights, one of the cape's three lighthouses. You can wander through World War II bunkers and picnic on the rocky coast. Stay on Two Lights Road to the end, where you'll find another lighthouse, privately owned, and the Lobster Shack, a seafood-in-the-rough restaurant. Return to the center of Cape Elizabeth and turn right on Shore Road, which winds along the coast to Portland.

Historic **Portland Head Light,** familiar to many from photographs and Edward Hopper's painting, was commissioned by George Washington in 1791. Besides a harbor view, its park has walking paths and picnic facilities. The keeper's house is now the Museum at Portland Head Light. The lighthouse is about 2 mi from the town center in Fort Williams Park. *Museum:* ⊠ *1000 Shore Rd., Cape Elizabeth,* ☎ *207/799–2661.* ⊠ *$2.* ☉ *June–Oct., daily 10–4; Apr.–May and Nov.–Dec., weekends 10–4.*

Dining and Lodging

$$–$$$$
★

✕ **Street and Co.** Fish and seafood are the specialties here, and you won't find any better or fresher. You enter through the kitchen, with all its wonderful aromas, and dine, amid dried herbs and shelves of staples, at one of a dozen copper-topped tables (so your waiter can place a skillet of steaming seafood directly in front of you). Some good choices are lobster diavolo for two, scallops in Pernod and cream, and sole Française. A vegetarian dish is the only alternative to seafood. ⊠ *33 Wharf St.,* ☎ *207/775–0887. AE, MC, V. No lunch.*

$$$
✕ **Aubergine.** This casual bistro and wine bar has staked out a prime downtown location, near both L.L. Bean and the Portland Museum of Art. The French-inspired menu changes daily but might list appetizers such as creamy onion soup with fresh tarragon or duck liver pâté and entrées such as roasted Atlantic scallops with tomato Choron or duck breast with mixed peppercorns. Wines by the glass are chosen to complement the dishes. ⊠ *555 Congress St.,* ☎ *207/874–0680. MC, V. Closed Sun.–Mon. No lunch.*

$$$
✕ **Hugos.** Chef-owner Rob Evans has turned Hugos, always a popular eatery, into one of the city's best restaurants. The subdued yet elegant dining room is a perfect background for Evans' masterful, creative cuisine. The menu, which may include pistachio-crusted lobster or pan-fried Deer Isle scallops, changes weekly. For a splurge, ask for the Chef's Menu, in which Evans will send out multiple courses of his choosing. ⊠ *88 Middle St.,* ☎ *207/774–8538. AE, MC, V. Closed Sun.–Mon. No lunch.*

$$–$$$
★

✕ **Fore Street.** Two of Maine's best chefs, Sam Hayward and Dana Street, opened this restaurant in a renovated, cavernous warehouse on the edge of the Old Port. Every table in the two-level main dining room has a view of the enormous brick oven and hearth and the open kitchen, where creative entrées such as roasted Maine lobster, apple-wood-grilled Atlantic swordfish loin, and wood oven–braised cassoulet are prepared. ⊠ *288 Fore St.,* ☎ *207/775–2717. AE, MC, V. No lunch.*

$$–$$$ ✕ **Walter's Cafe.** Brick walls and wood floors in this popular two-story restaurant capture the 19th-century spirit of Old Port. Begin with lobster bisque or deep-fried lemongrass shrimp sticks; then move on to a shrimp and andouille bake. ⊠ *15 Exchange St.,* ☎ *207/871–9258. AE, MC, V. Closed Sun.–Mon. No lunch.*

$–$$$ ✕ **Ri-Ra.** Whether you're in the mood for a pint of beer and corned beef and cabbage or a crock of mussels and whole roasted rainbow trout, Ri-Ra's delivers. Settle into a comfy couch in the downstairs pub or take a table in the upstairs dining room, where walls of windows overlook the busy ferry terminal. ⊠ *72 Commercial St.,* ☎ *207/761–4446. AE, MC, V.*

$–$$ ✕ **Portland Public Market.** Nibble your way through this handsome, airy market where 20 locally owned businesses sell fresh foods, organic produce, and imported specialty items, including fresh baked goods, soups, smoked seafood, rotisserie chicken, aged cheeses, and free-range meats. The market is open Monday–Saturday 9–7, Sunday 10–5; some vendors open at 7. ⊠ *25 Preble St.,* ☎ *207/228–2000.*

$$$$ ✕▥ **Inn by the Sea.** This all-suites inn welcomes families and dogs. All the spacious suites include kitchens and overlook the Atlantic, and it's just a short walk down a private boardwalk to sandy Crescent Beach, a popular family spot. The Audubon dining room ($$$–$$$$), open to nonguests, serves fine seafood and regional dishes. Dogs are welcomed with a room-service pet menu, evening turndown treats, and oversize beach towels. Its shingle-style design, typical of turn-of-the-20th-century New England shorefront cottages and hotels, includes a varied roofline punctuated by turretlike features and gables, balconies, a covered porch supported by columns, an open deck, and big windows. ⊠ *40 Bowery Beach Rd., Cape Elizabeth 04107 (7 mi south of Portland),* ☎ *207/799–3134 or 800/888–4287,* FAX *207/799–4779,* WEB *www.innbythesea.com. 25 suites, 18 cottages. Restaurant, in-room data ports, kitchens, microwaves, refrigerators, cable TV, in-room VCRs, pool, tennis court, croquet, lobby lounge, baby-sitting, dry cleaning, Internet, meeting rooms; no smoking. AE, D, MC, V.*

$$$$ ▥ **Black Point Inn.** Toward the tip of the peninsula that juts into the ocean at Prouts Neck stands this stylish, tastefully updated old-fashioned resort with spectacular views up and down the Maine coast. The extensive grounds contain beaches, trails, and sports facilities, including use of tennis courts and golf course of the nearby country club. The Cliff Walk runs along the Atlantic headlands that Winslow Homer (his studio is nearby) often painted. The inn is 12 mi south of Portland and about 10 mi north of Old Orchard Beach by road. ⊠ *510 Black Point Rd., Scarborough 04074,* ☎ *207/883–2500 or 800/258–0003,* FAX *207/883–9976,* WEB *www.blackpointinn.com. 73 rooms, 12 suites. Restaurant, bar, 2 pools (1 indoor), hot tub, golf privileges, croquet, volleyball, boating, bicycles. AE, D, MC, V. MAP.*

$$$$ ▥ **Inn on Carleton.** After a day of exploring Portland's museums and shops, you'll find a quiet retreat at this elegant brick town house on the city's Western Promenade. Built in 1869, it is furnished throughout with period antiques as well as artwork by contemporary Maine artists. A restored trompe l'oeil painting by Charles Schumacher greets you at the entryway, and more of his work is displayed in the back dining room. ⊠ *46 Carleton St., 04102,* ☎ *207/775–1910 or 800/639–1779,* FAX *207/761–0956,* WEB *www.innoncarleton.com. 6 rooms. Internet; no room phones, no room TVs, no kids under 16, no smoking. D, MC, V. BP.*

$$$$ ▥ **Portland Regency Hotel.** The only major hotel in the center of the Old Port, the brick Regency building was Portland's armory in the late 19th century. Most rooms have four-poster beds, tall standing mirrors, floral curtains, and love seats. You can walk to shops, restaurants, and

museums from the hotel. ✉ *20 Milk St., 04101,* ☎ *207/774–4200 or 800/727–3436,* FAX *207/775–2150,* WEB *www.theregency.com. 87 rooms, 8 suites. Restaurant, in-room data ports, minibars, cable TV, hot tub, massage, sauna, steam room, health club, dry cleaning, Internet, business services, meeting rooms; no-smoking rooms. AE, D, DC, MC, V.*

$$$–$$$$ ⊡ **Pomegranate Inn.** The classic architecture of this handsome inn in the architecturally rich Western Promenade area gives no hint of the surprises within. Vivid hand-painted walls, floors, and woodwork combine with contemporary artwork, and the result is both stimulating and comforting. Rooms are individually decorated, and five have fireplaces. Room 8, in the carriage house, has a private garden terrace. ✉ *49 Neal St., 04102,* ☎ *207/772–1006 or 800/356–0408,* FAX *207/ 773–4426,* WEB *www.pomegranateinn.com. 7 rooms, 1 suite. In-room data ports; no kids under 16, no smoking. AE, D, DC, MC, V. BP.*

$$$ ⊡ **Inn at St. John.** This gem of a small hotel was built by railroad tycoon John Deering in 1897. Victorian accents flavor the rooms, which have a mix of traditional and antique furnishings—no two are alike. It's an uphill walk to downtown attractions from here. ✉ *939 Congress St., 04102,* ☎ *207/773–6481 or 800/636–9127,* FAX *207/756–7629,* WEB *www.innatstjohn.com. 37 rooms, 22 with bath. Some refrigerators, some microwaves, cable TV with movies, in-room data ports; no-smoking rooms. D, DC, MC, V. CP.*

Nightlife and the Arts

NIGHTLIFE

Asylum (✉ 121 Center St., ☎ 207/772–8274) oozes with live entertainment and dancing on two levels and a sports bar; it books local and regional rock, pop, and hip-hop groups. **Brian Boru** (✉ 57 Center St., ☎ 207/780–1506) is an Irish pub with occasional entertainment, ranging from Celtic to reggae, and an outside deck. For laughs, head to **Comedy Connection** (✉ 6 Custom Wharf, ☎ 207/774–5554). **Gritty's** (✉ 396 Fore St., ☎ 207/772–2739) brews fine ales and serves British pub fare and seafood dishes. The **Pavilion** (✉ 199 Middle St., ☎ 207/773–6422) houses one of Portland's most popular dance clubs. **Stone Coast Brewery** (✉ 14 York St., ☎ 207/773–2337) is a brewpub with billiards and occasional live entertainment. For live blues every night of the week, head to the **Big Easy Blues Club** (✉ 55 Market St., ☎ 207/871–8817).

THE ARTS

Cumberland County Civic Center (✉ 1 Civic Center Sq., ☎ 207/775–3458) hosts concerts, sporting events, and family shows. **Portland City Hall's Merrill Auditorium** (✉ 20 Myrtle St., ☎ 207/874–8200) hosts events by the Portland Symphony Orchestra, Portland Concert Association, Portland Opera Repertory Theater, and the site of numerous theatrical and musical events. On most Tuesdays from mid-June to September, organ recitals ($5 donation) are given on the auditorium's huge 1912 Kotzschmar Memorial Organ. **Portland Performing Arts Center** (✉ 25A Forest Ave., ☎ 207/761–0591) presents music, dance, and theater performances. **Portland Stage Company** (✉ 25-A Forest Ave., ☎ 207/774–0465) mounts productions year-round at the Portland Performing Arts Center. Rock concerts and other events are frequently staged at the **State Theatre** (✉ 609 Congress St., Arts District, ☎ 207/773–2337).

Outdoor Activities and Sports

BALLOON RIDES

Balloon Rides (✉ 17 Freeman St., ☎ 207/772–4730) operates scenic flights over southern Maine.

BASEBALL

The Class AA **Portland Sea Dogs** (☎ 207/879–9500), a farm team of the Florida Marlins, play at Hadlock Field (✉ 271 Park Ave.). Tickets cost $4–$6.

BEACHES

Crescent Beach State Park (✉ Rte. 77, Cape Elizabeth, ☎ 207/767–3625), about 8 mi south of Portland, has a sand beach, picnic tables, a seasonal snack bar, and a bathhouse. Popular with families with young children, it charges a nominal fee for admittance.

BOAT TRIPS

For tours of the harbor, Casco Bay, and the scenic nearby islands, try **Bay View Cruises** (✉ Fisherman's Wharf, ☎ 207/761–0496). **Casco Bay Lines,** (✉ Maine State Pier, Waterfront, ☎ 207/774–7871) provides narrated cruises and transportation to Casco Bay Islands. **Eagle Island Tours** (✉ Long Wharf, ☎ 207/774–6498) conducts daily cruises to Eagle Island and seal-watching cruises. **Old Port Mariner Fleet** (✉ Long Wharf, ☎ 207/775–0727 or 800/437–3270) leads scenic cruises and whale-watching and fishing trips.

HOCKEY

The **Portland Pirates,** the farm team of the Washington Capitals, play home games at the Cumberland County Civic Center (✉ 85 Free St., ☎ 207/828–4665). Tickets cost $10–$14.

Shopping

For a city this size, you'll find a plethora of locally owned stores and art and crafts galleries, particularly those in or near the Old Port; trendy Exchange Street is great for browsing.

ART AND ANTIQUES

Abacus (✉ 44 Exchange St., old port, ☎ 207/772–4880), an appealing crafts gallery, has unusual gift items in glass, wood, and textiles, plus fine modern jewelry. **Greenhut Galleries** (✉ 146 Middle St., ☎ 207/772–2693) shows contemporary art and sculpture by Maine artists. **F. O. Bailey Antiquarians** (✉ 141 Middle St., ☎ 207/774–1479), Portland's largest retail showroom, carries antique and reproduction furniture and jewelry, paintings, rugs, and china. **Institute for Contemporary Art** (✉ 522 Congress St., ☎ 207/879–5742), at the Maine College of Art, showcases contemporary artwork from around the world. The **Pine Tree Shop & Bayview Gallery** (✉ 75 Market St., ☎ 207/773–3007 or 800/244–3007) has original art and prints by prominent Maine painters. Representing 100 American artists, the spacious **Stein Gallery** (✉ 195 Middle St., ☎ 207/772–9072) showcases decorative and sculptural contemporary glass.

BOOKS

Carlson and Turner (✉ 241 Congress St., ☎ 207/773–4200) is an antiquarian-book dealer with an estimated 70,000 titles.

CLOTHING

Family-owned **Casco Bay Wool Works** (✉ 10 Moulton St., ☎ 207/879–9665) sells beautiful handcrafted wool capes, shawls, blankets, and scarves.

FURNITURE

Made locally, the handsome cherrywood pieces at **Green Design Furniture** (✉ 267 Commercial St., ☎ 207/775–4234; 800/853–4234 orders) have a classic feel—somewhat Asian, somewhat Mission; a unique system of joinery enables easy assembly after shipping.

MALL

Maine Mall (⊠ 364 Maine Mall Rd., South Portland, ☎ 207/774–0303), 5 mi south of Portland, has 145 stores, including Sears, Filene's, JC Penney, and Macy's.

Casco Bay Islands

The islands of Casco Bay are also known as the Calendar Islands because an early explorer mistakenly thought there was one for each day of the year (in reality there are only 140). These islands range from ledges visible only at low tide to populous Peaks Island, which is a suburb of Portland. Some islands are uninhabited, others support year-round communities as well as stores and restaurants. Fort Gorges commands Hog Island Ledge, and Eagle Island is the site of Arctic explorer Admiral Peary's home. The brightly painted ferries of Casco Bay Lines are the islands' lifeline. There is frequent service to the most-populated ones, including Peaks, Long, Little Diamond, and Great Diamond. A ride on the bay is a great way to experience the Maine coast.

⑬ Peaks Island, nearest to Portland, is the most developed of the Calendar Islands, but you can still commune with the wind and the sea, explore an old fort, and ramble along the alternately rocky and sandy shore. The trip to the island by boat is particularly enjoyable at or near sunset. Order a lobster sandwich or cold beer on the outdoor deck of **Jones' Landing** restaurant, steps from the dock. A circle trip without stops takes about 90 minutes. On the far side of the island you can stop on the rugged shoreline and have lunch. A small museum with Civil War artifacts, open in summer, is maintained in the **Fifth Maine Regiment** building. When the Civil War broke out in 1861, Maine was asked to raise only a single regiment to fight, but the state raised 10 and sent the 5th Maine Regiment into the war's first battle, at Bull Run.

⑭ Eagle Island, owned by the state and open to the public for day trips in summer, was the home of Admiral Robert E. Peary, the American explorer of the North Pole. Peary built a stone-and-wood house on the 17-acre island as a summer retreat in 1904 but made it his permanent residence. Filled with Peary's stuffed Arctic birds, the quartz he brought home and set into the fieldstone fireplace, and other objects, the house remains as it was when Peary lived in it. A boat ride here offers a classic Maine experience as you pass by forested islands, and the island has a rocky beach and some trails to explore. The *Kristy K.* and *Fish Hawk* depart from Long Wharf in Portland (you can also visit the island from Freeport) and make four-hour narrated tours; tours of Portland Head Light and seal-watching cruises are also conducted. ⊠ *Long Wharf,* ☎ *207/774–6498.* ☞ *$8–$15, depending on tour.* ☉ *Departures late May–Labor Day, daily beginning 10 AM.*

Freeport

⑮ *17 mi northeast of Portland, 10 mi southwest of Brunswick.*

Freeport, on U.S. 1, has charming backstreets lined with historic buildings and old clapboard houses, and the pretty little harbor on the Harraseeket River in South Freeport, 3 mi from downtown, is a relaxing place to linger. Most people, however, come here simply to shop— L. L. Bean is the store that put Freeport on the map, and plenty of outlets and some specialty stores have settled here. Still, if you choose, you can stay awhile and sample both parts of the Freeport experience: shopping along the town streets and easy access to nearby historic sites and outdoor activities. The **Freeport Historical Society** mounts exhibits pertaining to the town's history. You can also pick up a walking map of the village here. ✉ *45 Main St.,* ☎ *207/865–0477.*

🔥 At the **Desert of Maine,** a 40-acre desert, a safari coach tours the sand dunes and you can walk nature trails, hunt for gemstones, and watch sand artists at work. Poor agricultural practices in the late 18th century combined with massive land clearing and overgrazing uncovered this desert, which was actually formed by a glacier during the last Ice Age. ✉ *I–95, Exit 19,* ☎ *207/865–6962,* WEB *www.desertofmaine.com.* 🎫 *$7.50.* ☉ *Early May–mid-Oct., daily.*

Dining and Lodging

$–$$$ ✕ **Harraseeket Lunch & Lobster Co.** Seafood baskets and lobster dinners are what this bare-bones place beside the town landing in South Freeport is all about. You can eat outside on picnic tables in good weather. ✉ *On the pier, end of Main St.,* ☎ *207/865–4888. Reservations not accepted. No credit cards. Closed mid-Oct.–Apr.*

$$$–$$$$ ✕🏨 **Harraseeket Inn.** Despite modern appointments such as elevators and whirlpool baths in some rooms, this 1850 Greek Revival home provides a pleasantly old-fashioned country-inn experience just a few minutes' walk from L. L. Bean. Guest rooms have print fabrics and reproductions of Federal quarter-canopy beds. The formal Maine Dining Room ($$$–$$$$) specializes in contemporary American regional cuisine such as lamb ragout ravioli and pan-roasted halibut with potato chowder. The casual Broad Arrow Tavern ($–$$$) serves heartier fare. ✉ *162 Main St., 04032,* ☎ *207/865–9377 or 800/342–6423,* FAX *207/ 865–1684,* WEB *www.stayfreeport.com. 82 rooms, 2 suites. 2 restaurants, in-room data ports, some microwaves, some refrigerators, cable TV, indoor pool, croquet, meeting room, some pets allowed (fee); no-smoking rooms. AE, D, DC, MC, V. BP.*

$$$ 🏨 **Atlantic Seal Bed & Breakfast.** The nautical theme of this 1850 waterfront Cape Cod home complements the pleasant water views from all three of its rooms. Owner Capt. Thomas Ring provides homemade quilts, antiques, and down comforters for each room; he also leads boat trips. ✉ *25 Main St. (Box 146, South Freeport 04078),* ☎ *207/865– 6112; 877/285–7325 seasonal. 2 rooms, 1 suite. Cable TV, in-room VCRs, boating, mountain biking; no smoking. AE, MC, V. BP.*

$$ 🏨 **Isaac Randall House.** On a 5-acre lot within walking distance of downtown shops, this circa-1829 inn is a quiet retreat. Victorian antiques and country pieces fill the rooms. A red caboose in the backyard has been turned into a room that's ideal for families. Two rooms are in the town's former police station, now moved to the property. ✉ *10 Independence Dr., 04032,* ☎ *207/865–9295 or 800/865–9295,* FAX *207/865– 9003,* WEB *www.isaacrandall.com. 11 rooms, 1 suite. Some in-room data ports, some microwaves, some refrigerators, cable TV in some rooms, ice-skating, playground, baby-sitting, some pets allowed; no smoking. AE, D, MC, V. BP.*

$ 🏨 **Maine Idyll Motor Court.** The third and fourth generations of the Marsteller family operate this simple 1932 cottage colony. The tidy white cabins are shaded by towering pines and popular with families. Wood floors and paneling enrich the rustic interior of each cabin. ✉ *325 Rte. 1, 04032,* ☎ *207/865–4201. 20 1- to 3-bedroom cottages. Refrigerators, some microwaves, cable TV in some rooms, 2 playgrounds, some pets allowed; no air-conditioning in some rooms, no-smoking rooms. No credit cards. Closed mid-Nov.–mid-Apr. CP.*

Outdoor Activities and Sports

Atlantic Seal Cruises (✉ South Freeport, ☎ 207/865–6112 or 877/285– 7325 seasonal) operates day trips to Eagle Island and Seguin Island lighthouse and evening seal and osprey watches.

L.L. Bean's year-round **Outdoor Discovery Schools** (✉ Freeport, ☎ 888/ 552–3261) include half- and one-day classes, as well as longer trips that teach canoeing, kayaking, fly-fishing, cross-country skiing, and other sports. Classes are for all skill levels; it's best to sign up several months in advance if possible.

STATE PARKS

Wolfe's Neck Woods State Park has 5 mi of good hiking trails along Casco Bay, the Harraseeket River, and a fringe salt marsh. Naturalists lead walks. The park has picnic tables and grills but no camping. ✉ *Wolfe's Neck Rd. (follow Bow St. opposite L.L. Bean off U.S. 1),* ☎ *207/865–4465.* ☜ *$2 Memorial Day–Labor Day, $1 off-season.*

Bradbury Mountain State Park has moderate trails to the top of Bradbury Mountain, which has views of the sea. A picnic area and shelter, a ball field, a playground, and 41 campsites are among the facilities. ✉ *Rte. 9, Pownal (I–95, 5 mi from Freeport-Durham exit),* ☎ *207/ 688–4712.* ☜ *$2 Memorial Day–Labor Day, $1 off-season.*

Shopping

The ***Freeport Visitors Guide*** (☎ 207/865–1212; 800/865–1994 for a copy) lists the more than 100 shops and factory outlet stores that can be found on Main Street, Bow Street, and elsewhere, including such big-name designers as Coach, Brooks Brothers, Polo Ralph Lauren, and Cole-Haan. Don't overlook the specialty stores, such as crafts galleries and shops selling unique items.

Cuddledown of Maine (✉ 237 U.S. 1, ☎ 207/865–1713) has a selection of down comforters, pillows, and luxurious bedding. Head upstairs for discounted merchandise. Kids get their chance to shop at the educational toy store **Play and Learn** (✉ 140 Main St., ☎ 207/865– 6434). **Thos. Moser Cabinetmakers** (✉ 149 Main St., ☎ 207/865–4519) sells high-quality handmade furniture with clean, classic lines.

Founded in 1912 as a mail-order merchandiser of products for hunters, guides, and anglers, **L.L. Bean** (✉ 95 Main St. [U.S. 1], ☎ 800/341– 4341) attracts 3½ million shoppers a year to its giant store (open 24 hours a day) in the heart of Freeport's shopping district. You can still find the original hunting boots, along with cotton, wool, and silk sweaters; camping and ski equipment; comforters; and hundreds of other items for the home, car, boat, or campsite. The **L.L. Bean Factory Store** (✉ Depot St., ☎ 800/341–4341) has seconds and discontinued merchandise at discount prices. **L.L. Bean Kids** (✉ 8 Nathan Nye St., ☎ 800/341–4341) specializes in children's merchandise and has a climbing wall and other activities that appeal to kids.

Brunswick

⓰ *10 mi north of Freeport.*

Lovely brick and clapboard homes and structures are the highlights of the town's Federal Street Historic District, which includes Federal Street and Park Row and the stately campus of Bowdoin College. Pleasant Street, in the center of town, is the business district. Harriet Beecher Stowe wrote *Uncle Tom's Cabin* while living in Brunswick.

The 110-acre campus of **Bowdoin College** (✉ Maine, Bath, and College Sts., off east end of Pleasant St.) holds an enclave of distinguished architecture, gardens, and grassy quadrangles, along with several museums. Nathaniel Hawthorne, Civil War hero Joshua L. Chamberlain, and the poet Henry Wadsworth Longfellow attended Bowdoin.

Bowdoin's imposing neo-Gothic Hubbard Hall holds the **Peary–MacMillan Arctic Museum,** with photographs, navigational instruments, and artifacts from the first successful expedition to the North Pole, in 1909, by two of Bowdoin's most famous alumni, Admiral Robert E. Peary and Donald B. MacMillan. Changing exhibits document conditions in the Arctic. ☎ *207/725–3416.* 🖼 *Free.* ⊙ *Tues.–Sat. 10–5, Sun. 2–5.*

The **Bowdoin College Museum of Art,** in a splendid Renaissance Revival–style building designed by Charles F. McKim in 1894, displays small but good collections that encompass Assyrian and classical art and works by Dutch, Italian, French, and Flemish old masters; a superb gathering of Colonial and Federal paintings, notably Gilbert Stuart portraits of Madison and Jefferson; and a Winslow Homer Gallery of engravings, etchings, and memorabilia (open in summer only). The museum's collection also includes 19th- and 20th-century American painting and sculpture, with works by Mary Cassatt, Andrew Wyeth, and Robert Rauschenberg. ⊠ *Walker Art Bldg.,* ☎ *207/725–3275.* 🖼 *Free.* ⊙ *Tues.–Sat. 10–5, Sun. 2–5.*

The **General Joshua L. Chamberlain Museum** displays memorabilia and documents the life of Maine's most celebrated Civil War hero. The general, who played an instrumental role in the Union army's victory at Gettysburg, was elected governor in 1867. From 1871 to 1883 he served as president of Bowdoin College. ⊠ *226 Main St.,* ☎ *207/729–6606.* 🖼 *$4.* ⊙ *Late May–mid-Oct., Tues.–Sat. 10–4.*

OFF THE
BEATEN PATH

THE HARPSWELLS – A side trip from Bath or Brunswick on Route 123 or Route 24 takes you to the peninsulas and islands known collectively as the Harpswells. Small coves along Harpswell Neck shelter the boats of lobstermen, and summer cottages are tucked away amid the birch and spruce trees. Along Route 123, signs with blue herons mark the studios and galleries of the Harpswell Craft Guild. For lunch, follow the signs off Route 123 to **Dolphin Marina** restaurant (⊠ end of Basin Point Rd., off Ash Point Rd.) and try the delicious fish stew and a blueberry muffin.

Dining and Lodging

$$ ✕ **The Great Impasta.** You can match your favorite pasta and sauce to create your own dish at this storefront restaurant, a good choice for lunch, tea, or dinner. The seafood lasagna is tasty, too. ⊠ *42 Maine St.,* ☎ *207/729–5858. Reservations not accepted. D, DC, MC, V.*

$ ✕ **Fat Boy Drive-In.** Put your lights on for service at this old-fashioned drive-in restaurant renowned for its BLTs made with Canadian bacon, frappés (try the blueberry), and onion rings. ⊠ *Bath Rd.,* ☎ *207/729–9431. No credit cards. Closed mid-Oct.–mid-Mar.*

$$$ 🏨 **Captain Daniel Stone Inn.** This Federal-style inn overlooks the Androscoggin River and Route 1. No two rooms are furnished identically, but all contain executive-style comforts and many have whirlpool baths, queen-size beds, and pullout sofas. A guest parlor, a breakfast room, and excellent service in the Narcissa Stone Restaurant (no lunch on Saturday) make this an upscale escape from college-town funkiness. ⊠ *10 Water St., 04011,* ☎ *877/573–5151 or* ☎ FAX *207/725–9898,* WEB *www.someplacesdifferent.com. 30 rooms, 4 suites. Restaurant, cable TV; no-smoking rooms. AE, D, DC, MC, V. CP.*

$$–$$$ 🏨 **Captain's Watch Bed and Breakfast and Sail Charter.** Built in 1862 and originally known as the Union Hotel, the Captain's Watch is the oldest surviving hotel on the Maine coast. Although much smaller than originally built, this National Historic Register property retains its distinctive octagonal cupola and a homey, old-fashioned feel. Two guest

rooms share access to the cupola. Others have less-inspired but still-pleasant water views. You can arrange to go on a day sail aboard the inn's 37-ft sloop, *Symbion.* ⊠ *926 Cundy's Harbor Rd., Harpswell 04079,* ☎ *207/725–0979. 4 rooms. Internet; no TV in some rooms, no air-conditioning, no room phones, no kids under 10, no smoking. MC, V for deposit only. BP.*

Nightlife and the Arts

Bowdoin Summer Music Festival (☎ 207/725–3322 information; 207/725–3895 tickets) is a six-week concert series featuring performances by students, faculty, and prestigious guest artists. **Maine State Music Theater** (⊠ Pickard Theater, Bowdoin College, ☎ 207/725–8769) stages musicals from mid-June to September. **Theater Project of Brunswick** (⊠ 14 School St., ☎ 207/729–8584) performs semiprofessional, children's, and community theater.

Outdoor Activities and Sports

H2Outfitters (⊠ Rte. 24, Orr's Island, ☎ 207/833–5257 or 800/205–2925) provides sea-kayaking instruction and rentals and conducts day and overnight trips.

Shopping

ICON Contemporary Art (⊠ 19 Mason St., ☎ 207/725–8157) specializes in modern art. **Wyler Craft Gallery** (⊠ 150 Maine St., ☎ 207/729–1321) carries crafts, jewelry, and clothing.

Tontine Fine Candies (⊠ Tontine Mall, 149 Maine St., ☎ 207/729–4462) sells chocolates and other goodies. A **farmers' market** takes place on Tuesday and Friday from May to October, on the town mall between Maine Street and Park Row.

Bath

⑰ *11 mi northeast of Brunswick, 38 mi northeast of Portland.*

Bath has been a shipbuilding center since 1607, so it's appropriate that a museum here explores the state's rich maritime heritage. These days the Bath Iron Works turns out guided-missile frigates for the U.S. Navy and merchant container ships. On Front and Centre streets in the heart of Bath's historic district, amid 19th-century Victorian homes, antiques shops and intriguing specialty shops invite browsing. It's a good idea to avoid Bath and U.S. 1 on weekdays 3:15–4:30 PM, when BIW's major shift change occurs. The massive exodus can tie up traffic for miles.

★ At the **Maine Maritime Museum,** displays in the Maritime History Building and in the buildings of the former Percy & Small shipyard examine the world of shipbuilding and the relationship between Mainers and the sea. The history building contains themed exhibits with maritime paintings, ship models, journals, photographs, artifacts, and videos. From May to November, one-hour tours (call for times) of the shipyard explain how wooden ships were built; at other times you can visit the buildings on your own. You can also watch boatbuilders wield their tools on classic Maine boats in the boat shop and learn about lobstering in a special exhibit building. In summer, boat tours sail the scenic Kennebec River (extra charge); a number of boats, including the 142-ft Grand Banks fishing schooner *Sherman Zwicker,* are on display when in port. The museum has a gift shop and bookstore, and you can picnic on the grounds. ⊠ *243 Washington St.,* WEB *www.bathmaine.com.* 🎟 *$9.50; tickets valid for 2 consecutive days.* ☉ *Daily 9:30–5.*
Sagadahoc Preservation (☎ 207/443–2174) conducts guided walking tours of private homes and historic buildings from mid-June to early-September. Call for schedule and fees.

Reid State Park (☎ 207/371–2303), on Georgetown Island, off Route 127, has 1½ mi of sand on three beaches. Facilities include bathhouses, picnic tables, fireplaces, and a snack bar. Parking lots fill by 11 AM on summer Sundays and holidays.

OFF THE BEATEN PATH	**POPHAM** – Follow Route 209 south from Bath to Popham, the site of the short-lived 1607 Popham Colony, where the *Virginia,* the first English ship built in the Northeast, was launched. Benedict Arnold set off from Popham in 1775 on his ill-fated march against the British in Québec. Granite-walled **Ft. Popham** (⊠ Phippsburg, ☎ 207/389–1335) was built in 1861. **Popham State Park,** at the end of Route 209, has a sand beach, a marsh area, bathhouses, and picnic tables.

Dining and Lodging

$$$ ★ ✕ **Robinhood Free Meetinghouse.** Chef Michael Gagne, one of Maine's best, prepares his classic and creative multiethnic cuisine in this 1855 Greek Revival–style meetinghouse with cream-color walls, pine floorboards, cherry Shaker-style chairs, and white table linens. You might begin with the artichoke strudel; veal saltimbocca and confit of duck are two entrées. Finish up with Gagne's signature Obsession in Three Chocolates. ⊠ *210 Robinhood Rd., Georgetown,* ☎ *207/371–2188. AE, D, MC, V. Closed some weeknights mid-Oct.–mid-May. No lunch.*

$$–$$$ ✕ **Kristina's Restaurant & Bakery.** This restaurant in a frame house with a front deck prepares some of the finest pies, pastries, and cakes on the coast. The satisfying new American cuisine served for dinner usually includes fresh seafood and grilled meats. All meals can be packed to go. ⊠ *160 Centre St.,* ☎ *207/442–8577. D, MC, V. Closed Jan. No dinner Sun. Call ahead in winter.*

$$$$ 🏨 **Sebasco Harbor Resort.** This family resort sprawls over 575 oceanfront acres at the foot of the Phippsburg peninsula. The owners have retained the resort's old-fashioned feel while updating and renovating the facilities. Rooms in the Main Inn were renovated in 2002. The antique furnishings remain, but the rooms have been spruced up with new drapes, carpeting, and bedspreads. Lighthouse rooms have the best views and location and were renovated in 1998. A new all-suites building is slated to open in spring 2003. The suites will have kitchenettes, living areas, and decks with ocean views over the gardens. ⊠ *Rte. 217 (Box 75, Sebasco Estates 04565),* ☎ *207/389–1161 or 800/225–3819,* FAX *207/389–2004,* WEB *www.sebasco.com. 115 rooms, 23 cottages. 3 restaurants, cable TV, in-room data ports, saltwater pool, hair salon, sauna, 9-hole golf course, 3-hole golf course, 2 tennis courts, bowling, health club, Ping-Pong, dock, boating, bicycles, video game room, shop, recreation room, lounge, children's programs, playground, Internet, meeting rooms, airport shuttle; no air-conditioning, no-smoking rooms. AE, D, MC, V. Closed Nov.–mid-May. MAP available.*

$$$–$$$$ 🏨 **The Inn at Bath.** Filled with antiques, this handsome 1810 Greek Revival inn in the town's historic district makes a convenient and comfortable base for exploring Bath on foot. Five rooms have woodburning fireplaces, and two have two-person whirlpool tubs. ⊠ *969 Washington St., 04530,* ☎ *207/443–4294 or 800/423–0964,* FAX *207/ 443–4295,* WEB *www.innatbath.com. 8 rooms, 1 suite. Cable TV, in-room VCRs, in-room data ports, Internet, meeting rooms, some pets allowed; no smoking. AE, D, MC, V. BP.*

$$$–$$$$ 🏨 **1774 Inn.** On the National Register of Historic Places, the 1774 Inn is a pre-Revolutionary mansion with handsome interior detailing and magnificent antiques. The inn, on a bend in the Kennebec River, has large corner guest rooms in the main house, two with fireplaces. In the attached ell is a room with a deck overlooking the river. A four-bedroom cottage on the river is available for longer stays. ⊠ *44 Parker*

Head Rd., Phippsburg Center 04562, ☎ 207/389–1774, FAX 207/389–9076. 7 rooms, 1 cottage. No kids under 12, no smoking. MC, V. BP.

$$–$$$$ 🏠 **Popham Beach Bed & Breakfast.** Housed in a former Coast Guard station, this casual bed-and-breakfast sits right on Popham Beach. Rooms are comfortably but not fancifully furnished. The nicest are the Library, with two walls lined with books, and the Bunkroom; both have queen-size beds and overlook the beach. ⊠ 4 Riverview Ave., Phippsburg 04562, ☎ 207/389–2409, FAX 207/389–2379,, WEB www.pophambeachbandb.com. 4 rooms, 3 with bath; 1 suite. No air-conditioning, no in-room phones, no room TVs, no kids under 15, no smoking. MC, V. BP.

Nightlife and the Arts

Chocolate Church Arts Center (⊠ 804 Washington St., ☎ 207/442–8455) hosts folk, jazz, and classical concerts, theater productions, and performances for children. The gallery exhibits works in various media by Maine artists.

Shopping

The **Montsweag Flea Market** (⊠ U.S. 1 between Bath and Wiscasset, ☎ 207/443–2809) is a roadside attraction with trash and treasures. It's open on weekends from May to October and also on Wednesday (for antiques) and Friday during the summer. **West Island Gallery** (⊠ 37 Bay Point Rd., Georgetown, ☎ 207/443–9625) carries contemporary Maine art and quality crafts.

Wiscasset

⑱   10 mi north of Bath, 46 mi northeast of Portland.

Settled in 1663 on the banks of the Sheepscot River, Wiscasset fittingly bills itself as Maine's Prettiest Village. Stroll through town and you'll pass by elegant sea captains' homes (many now antiques shops or galleries), old cemeteries, churches, and public buildings. Unfortunately, Route 1 doubles as Main Street, and traffic often slows to a crawl and backs up for miles.

The **Nickels-Sortwell House,** maintained by the Society for the Preservation of New England Antiquities, is an outstanding example of Federal architecture. ⊠ 12 Main St., ☎ 207/882–6218. 🎟 $5. ☉ June–mid-Oct., Wed.–Sun. 11–5; tours on the hr 11–4.

The 1807 **Castle Tucker** is known for its extravagant architecture, Victorian appointments, and freestanding elliptical staircase. It's run by the Society for the Preservation of New England Antiquities. ⊠ Lee and High Sts., ☎ 207/882–7364. 🎟 $5. ☉ June–mid-Oct., Wed.–Sun. 11–5; tours on the hr 11–4.

★   The 1852 **Musical Wonder House,** formerly a sea captain's home, houses a private collection of thousands of antique music boxes from around the world. ⊠ 18 High St., ☎ 207/882–7163 or 800/336–3725, WEB www.musicalwonderhouse.com. 🎟 $2; ½-hr presentation on main floor $10; 1-hr full downstairs presentation $18; 3-hr tour of entire house $30 by reservation only, minimum 2 people. ☉ Memorial Day–mid-Oct., daily 10–5; last tour usually at 4; call ahead for 3-hr tours.

Dining and Lodging

$–$$$ ✕ **Le Garage.** The best tables at this automotive garage turned casual restaurant are on the glassed-in porch overlooking the Sheepscot River and Wiscasset's harbor. Entrées include homemade chicken pie, sea scallops au gratin, charbroiled lamb and vegetable kebabs, and pastas and salads. ⊠ Water St., ☎ 207/882–5409. MC, V. Closed Jan.

$$ ⊞ **Marston House.** Two carriage-house rooms provide a quiet retreat from the bustle of Main Street but are just a stone's throw from the action. Both have private entrances and fireplaces and are simply furnished with Shaker- and Colonial-style pieces. The rooms can be joined by opening a door between them. A hearty Continental breakfast is delivered to your room. ⊠ *101 Main St. (Box 517, 04578),* ☎ *207/882–6010 or 800/852–4137,* ℻ *207/882–6965. 2 rooms. Fans. AE, MC, V. Closed Nov.–Apr. CP.*

Shopping

The Wiscasset area rivals Searsport as a destination for antiquing. Shops line Wiscasset's main and side streets and extend over the bridge into Edgecomb. The **Butterstamp Workshop** (⊠ 55 Middle St., ☎ 207/882–7825) carries handcrafted folk-art designs from antique molds. The **Maine Art Gallery** (⊠ Warren St., ☎ 207/882–7511) presents the works of local artists. **Marston House American Antiques** (⊠ 101 Main St., ☎ 207/882–6010) specializes in 18th- and 19th-century painted furniture and "smalls" (small objects), homespun textiles, and antique garden accessories and tools. The **Wiscasset Bay Gallery** (⊠ Main St., ☎ 207/882–7682) displays a fine collection of the works from 19th- and 20th-century American and European artists. **Treats** (⊠ Main St., ☎ 207/882–6192) dishes up sandwiches, cheeses, bread, and other goodies for a picnic at Waterfront Park.

Boothbay

⑲ *10 mi southeast of Wiscasset, 60 mi northeast of Portland, 50 mi southwest of Camden.*

When Portlanders want a break from city life, many come north to the Boothbay region, which comprises Boothbay proper, East Boothbay, and Boothbay Harbor. This part of the shoreline is a craggy stretch of inlets where pleasure craft anchor alongside trawlers and lobster boats. Commercial Street, Wharf Street, the By-Way, and Townsend Avenue are filled with shops, galleries, and ice cream parlors. You can browse for hours in the trinket and T-shirt shops, crafts galleries, clothing stores, and boutiques that line the streets around the harbor. Excursion boats leave from the piers off Commercial Street. From the harbor, you can catch a boat to Monhegan Island.

☾ At the **Boothbay Railway Village,** about 1 mi north of Boothbay, you can ride 1½ mi on a narrow-gauge steam train through a re-creation of a century-old New England village. Among the 24 buildings is a museum with more than 50 antique automobiles and trucks. ⊠ *Rte. 27,* ☎ *207/633–4727,* 🌐 *www.railwayvillage.org.* 🎟 *$7.* ☉ *Memorial Day weekend and early June–Columbus Day, daily 9:30–5; special Halloween and Christmas schedules.*

☾ The **Department of Marine Resources Aquarium** has a shark you can pet, touch tanks, and rare blue and multiclawed lobsters. ⊠ *194 McKown Point Rd., West Boothbay Harbor,* ☎ *207/633–9559.* 🎟 *$3.* ☉ *Memorial Day–late Sept., daily 10–5.*

Dining and Lodging

$$–$$$$ ✕ **Christopher's Boathouse.** You can't beat the harbor view or the stylish food at this restaurant in a renovated boathouse where you can watch the chefs at work. The lobster and mango bisque with spicy lobster wontons is noteworthy. Some main-course options are lobster succotash and Asian-spiced tuna steak with Caribbean salsa; finish off with the raspberry almond flan. ⊠ *25 Union St., Boothbay Harbor,* ☎ *207/633–6565. DC, MC, V. Closed Mar., and Mon.–Wed. Jan.–Feb.*

$–$$ ✕ **Lobstermen's Co-op.** Crustacean lovers and landlubbers alike will find something to satisfy their cravings at this dockside working lobster pound. Lobster, steamers, hamburgers, and sandwiches are on the menu. Eat indoors or outside to watch the lobstermen at work. ⊠ *Atlantic Ave., Boothbay Harbor,* ☎ *207/633–4900. D, MC, V. Closed mid-Oct.–mid-May.*

$$$ ⊞ **Admiral's Quarters Inn.** This renovated 1830 sea captain's house is ideally situated for exploring Boothbay Harbor by foot. All rooms have fireplaces, and some have private decks overlooking the harbor. On rainy days you can relax by the woodstove in the solarium. ⊠ *71 Commercial St., Boothbay Harbor 04538,* ☎ *207/633–2474 or 800/ 644–1878,* ℻ *207/633–5904,* ⟦WEB⟧ *www.admiralsquartersinn.com. 2 rooms, 5 suites. Cable TV, Internet; no kids under 12, no smoking. D, MC, V. Closed Dec.–mid-Feb. BP.*

$$$ ⊞ **Spruce Point Inn.** Escape the hubbub of Boothbay Harbor at this sprawling resort, which is a short shuttle ride from town, yet a world away. Guest rooms in the main inn are comfortable but not fancy, and most have ocean views, fireplaces, and whirlpool baths. The nearby fog horn blows in inclement weather. ⊠ *Atlantic Ave. (Box 237, Boothbay Harbor 04538),* ☎ *207/633–4152 or 800/553–0289,* ℻ *207/ 633–7138,* ⟦WEB⟧ *www.sprucepointinn.com. 21 rooms, 41 suites, 7 cottages. Restaurant, cable TV, some microwaves, pool, saltwater pool, massage, spa, 2 tennis courts, gym, dock, lounge, meeting rooms, children's programs. AE, D, DC, MC, V. Closed mid-Oct.–late May.*

$$–$$$ ⊞ **Hodgdon Island Inn.** Every room in this 1810 inn, which is within walking distance of a lobster pound and a botanical garden, has a view of the water; two rooms open onto a shared deck. Inside, artwork from New England and the Caribbean graces the walls. ⊠ *374 Barters Island Rd., 04571,* ☎ *207/633–7474,* ℻ *207/733–0571,* ⟦WEB⟧ *www. hodgdonislandinn.com. 6 rooms. Fans; no air-conditioning, no room phones, no room TVs, pool, no smoking. D, MC, V. BP.*

$$–$$$ ⊞ **Welch House.** This 1873 sea captain's house sits high on a hill, a few minutes' walk from the center of town. Antiques, artwork, and bric-a-brac from the owner's worldwide travels adorn the rooms. From the shared third-floor deck, you can take in the 180-degree views of the harbor. ⊠ *36 McKown St., 04538,* ☎ *207/633–3431 or 800/ 279–7313,* ⟦WEB⟧ *www.welchhouse.com. 16 rooms. Cable TV; no air-conditioning in some rooms, no in-room phones, no kids under 8, no smoking indoors. MC, V. Closed Dec.–Mar. BP.*

Outdoor Activities and Sports

BOAT TRIPS

Balmy Day Cruises (⊠ Pier 8, 62 Commercial St., Boothbay Harbor, ☎ 207/633–2284 or 800/298–2284) operates day boat trips to Monhegan Island and tours of the harbor. **Boothbay Whale Watch** (⊠ Pier 6, ☎ 207/633–3500 or 800/942–5363) conducts whale-watching tours and evening sunset-nature cruises. **Cap'n Fish's Boat Trips** (⊠ Pier 1, Boothbay Harbor, ☎ 207/633–3244 or 800/636–3244) runs regional sightseeing cruises, including puffin-watching excursions, lobster-hauling and whale-watching rides, and trips to Damariscove Harbor, Pemaquid Point, and up the Kennebec River to Bath.

KAYAKING

Tidal Transit Ocean Kayak Co. (☎ 207/633–7140) offers guided tours and rentals.

Shopping

Gleason Fine Art (✉ 7 Oak St., ☎ 207/633–6849) showcases fine art—regional and national, early 19th century and contemporary. **House of Logan** (✉ 20 Townsend Ave., ☎ 207/633–2293) stocks upscale casual and fancy attire for men and women. **McKown Square Quilts** (✉ 14-B Boothbay House Hill Rd., ☎ 207/633–2007) displays quilts and fiber art in seven rooms. Beautiful housewares and attractive children's clothes can be found at the **Village Store & Children's Shop** (✉ 34 Townsend Ave., ☎ 207/633–2293).

Highly reputable **Edgecomb Potters** (✉ 727 Boothbay Rd., ☎ 207/882–6802) sells stylish glazed porcelain pottery and other crafts at rather high prices; some discontinued items or seconds are discounted. There's a store in Freeport if you miss this one. **Sheepscot River Pottery** (✉ U.S. 1, ☎ 207/882–9410) displays hand-painted pottery and a large collection of American-made crafts, including jewelry, kitchenware, furniture, and home accessories.

Pemaquid Peninsula

20 *8 mi southeast of Wiscasset.*

A detour off U.S. 1 via Routes 130 and 32 leads to the Pemaquid Peninsula and a satisfying microcosm of coastal Maine. Art galleries, country stores, antiques and crafts shops, and lobster shacks dot the country roads that meander to the tip of the point, where you'll find a much-photographed lighthouse perched on an unforgiving rock ledge, as well as a pleasant beach. Exploring here reaps many rewards, including views of salt ponds, the ocean, and boat-clogged harbors. The twin towns of Damariscotta and Newcastle anchor the region, but small fishing villages such as Pemaquid, New Harbor, and Round Pond give the peninsula its purely Maine flavor.

At what is now the **Colonial Pemaquid Restoration,** on a small peninsula jutting into the Pemaquid River, English mariners established a fishing and trading settlement in the early 17th century. The excavations at Ft. William Henry, begun in the mid-1960s, have turned up thousands of artifacts from the Colonial settlement, including the remains of an old customs house, a tavern, a jail, a forge, and homes. Some items are from even earlier Native American settlements. The state operates a museum displaying many of the artifacts. ✉ *Off Rte. 130, New Harbor,* ☎ *207/677–2423.* ▣ *$2.* ☉ *Memorial Day–Labor Day, daily 9:30–5.*

★ Route 130 terminates at the **Pemaquid Point Light,** which looks as though it sprouted from the ragged, tilted chunk of granite that it commands. The former lighthouse keeper's cottage is now the Fishermen's Museum, with photographs, models, and artifacts that explore commercial fishing in Maine. Here, too, is the Pemaquid Art Gallery, which mounts exhibitions from July to Labor Day. ✉ *Museum: Rte. 130,* ☎ *207/677–2494.* ▣ *$1.* ☉ *Memorial Day–Columbus Day, Mon.–Sat. 10–5, Sun. 11–5.*

Dining and Lodging

$$ ✕ **Round Pond Lobstermen's Co-op.** Lobster doesn't get much rougher,
★ any fresher, or any cheaper than what's served at this no-frills dockside takeout. The best deal is the dinner special: a 1-pound lobster, steamers, and corn-on-the-cob, with a bag of chips. Regulars often bring beer, wine, bread, and salads. Settle in at a picnic table and breathe in the fresh salt air while you drink in the view over dreamy Round Pond

Harbor. ⊠ *Round Pond Harbor, off Rte. 32, Round Pond,* ☎ *207/ 529–5725. MC, V.*

$$$–$$$$ ✕🖼 **The Bradley Inn.** Within walking distance of Pemaquid Point Lighthouse, this former rooming house for summer rusticators alternated between abandonment and operation as a B&B until complete renovation in the 1990s. It now houses one of the best dining rooms in the state. The menu ($$$–$$$$; closed Mon.–Wed. Nov.–Mar.) changes nightly and emphasizes fresh and local foods. Guest rooms are comfortable and uncluttered; some have fireplaces and rooms on the third floor have ocean views. ⊠ *3063 Bristol Rd., New Harbor 04554,* ☎ *207/677–2105 or 800/942–5560,* ℻ *207/677–3367,* 🕸 *www.bradleyinn.com. 12 rooms, 4 suites. Restaurant, fans, bicycles, boccie, croquet, lounge, baby-sitting, Internet, meeting rooms; no air-conditioning, no TVs in some rooms, no smoking. AE, MC, V. BP.*

$$$–$$$$ ✕🖼 **Newcastle Inn.** A riverside location and an excellent dining room highlight this classic country inn. All the rooms are filled with country pieces and antiques; some rooms have fireplaces and whirlpool baths. Breakfast is served on the back deck in fine weather. The four-course dinners ($$$$) at the inn, open to the public by reservation, emphasize local seafood. ⊠ *60 River Rd., Newcastle 04553,* ☎ *207/563–5685 or 800/832–8669,* ℻ *207/563–6877,* 🕸 *www.newcastleinn.com. 11 rooms, 4 suites. Restaurant, pub; no air-conditioning in some rooms, no room phones, no room TVs, no kids under 12, no smoking. AE, MC, V. BP.*

$$ 🖼 **Mill Pond Inn.** A quiet residential street holds this circa-1780 inn, which is on a mill pond across the street from Damariscotta Lake. Loons, otters, and bald eagles reside on the lake, and you can arrange a trip with the owner, a Registered Maine Guide, on the inn's 17-ft antique lapstrake boat. The rooms are warm and inviting, though you may find it hard to tear yourself away from the hammocks-for-two overlooking the pond. ⊠ *50 Main St., off Rte. 215 N, Nobleboro 04555,* ☎ *207/563–8014,* 🕸 *www.millpondinn.com. 6 rooms, 1 suite. Horseshoes, boating, bicycles, pub; no air-conditioning, no room phones, no room TVs, no kids under 12, no smoking. No credit cards. BP.*

$–$$ 🖼 **Hotel Pemaquid.** This 1888 inn is less than 500 ft from the lighthouse at Pemaquid Point. The main building is Victorian in style; cottages and bungalow units have a more contemporary feel; and the carriage-house suite is ideal for honeymooners or others seeking a romantic retreat. ⊠ *3098 Bristol Rd. (Rte. 130), New Harbor 04554,* ☎ *207/677–2312,* 🕸 *www.hotelpemaquid.com. 21 rooms, 17 with bath; 4 suites; 3 cottages; 1 apartment. No air-conditioning, no room phones, no room TVs, no-smoking rooms. No credit cards. Closed mid-Oct.–mid-May.*

Nightlife and the Arts

Round Top Center for the Arts (⊠ Business Rte. 1, Damariscotta, ☎ 207/563–1507) has a gallery with rotating exhibits and a performance hall where classical, folk, operatic, and jazz concerts are held.

Outdoor Activities and Sports

Pemaquid Beach Park (⊠ off Rte. 130, New Harbor, ☎ 207/677–2754) has a sand beach, a snack bar, changing facilities, and picnic tables overlooking John's Bay.

Shopping

Of the villages on and near the Pemaquid Peninsula, downtown Damariscotta has boutiques, a book shop, clothing stores, and galleries. New Harbor and Round Pond have crafts and antiques shops as well as artisans' studios. Antiques shops dot the main thoroughfares in the region.

If gardening is your passion, **Bramble's** (✉ Main St., Damariscotta, ☎ 207/563–2800) is the place for tools, sculpture, pots, artwork, and topiary. **Granite Hill Store** (✉ Backshore Rd., Round Pond, ☎ 207/529–5864) has penny candy, kitchen goodies, baskets, and cards on the first floor, antiques and books on the second, and an ice cream window on the side. The work of more than 50 Maine artisans is displayed in the 15 rooms of the **Pemaquid Craft Co-op** (✉ 2545 Bristol Rd., New Harbor, ☎ 207/677–2077). You never know what you'll find at **Reny's** (✉ Main St., Damariscotta, ☎ 207/563–5757)—perhaps merchandise from L. L. Bean or a designer coat. This bargain chain has outlets in many Maine towns, but this is its hometown, and there are two outlets: one for clothes, the other for everything else. The **Stable Gallery** (✉ Water St., Damariscotta, ☎ 207/563–1991) is a barn with fine Maine crafts, paintings, and prints by more than 100 artisans.

Waldoboro

㉑ *10 mi northeast of Damariscotta.*

Veer off U.S. 1 onto Main Street or down Route 220 or 32, and you'll discover a seafaring town with a proud shipbuilding past. The town's Main Street is lined with houses and businesses representing numerous architectural styles, including Cape Cod, Queen Anne, Stick, Greek Revival, and Italianate.

The **Waldoborough Historical Society Museum** comprises the one-room Boggs Schoolhouse, built in 1857; the Town Pound, built in 1819; and a barn and museum filled with artifacts and antiques, including hooked rugs, old toys, tools, clothing, and housewares. ✉ *Rte. 220,* ☎ *no phone.* ▨ *Free.* ◷ *July–Labor Day, daily 1–4:30.*

One of the three oldest churches in Maine, the **Old German Church** was built in 1772 on the eastern side of the Medomak River, then moved across the ice to its present site in 1794. Inside you'll find box pews and a 9-ft-tall chalice pulpit. ✉ *Rte. 32,* ☎ *207/832–5639.* ◷ *July–Aug., daily 1–3.*

The **Fawcett's Toy Museum** delights adults and children with collectible toys, from Betty Boop and Charlie Brown to Mickey Mouse and Popeye, and original comic art. ✉ *3506 Rte. 1,* ☎ *207/832–7398.* ▨ *$3.* ◷ *Memorial Day–Columbus Day, Thurs.–Mon. 10–4; Columbus Day–Dec. 24, weekends noon–3:30.*

Dining and Lodging

$–$$$ ✕ **Pine Cone Cafe.** Paintings by local artist Eric Hopkins hang on the
★ walls of this cozy restaurant, which serves up hearty soups, salads, and a mix of home-style and creative entrées. Try the corn-fried soft-shell crab tower or turkey potpie; the crème brûlée is a good choice for dessert. In favorable weather ask for a table on the back deck overlooking the river. ✉ *13 Friendship St.,* ☎ *207/832–6337. MC, V.*

$–$$ ✕ **Moody's Diner.** Settle into one of the well-worn wooden booths or snag a counter stool at this old-style diner for home-cooking fare. Breakfast is served all day; don't miss the legendary walnut pie. ✉ *Rte. 1,* ☎ *207/832–5362. D, MC, V.*

$ ▥ **Roaring Lion.** Tin walls and ceilings and other Victorian-era architectural details highlight this friendly B&B. Special diets are accommodated. During summer, a used-book sale is held in the barn on Saturday mornings. ✉ *995 Main St., 04572,* ☎ *207/832–4038,* ℻ *207/832–7892,* WEB *www.roaringlion.com. 4 rooms, 1 with bath. No air-conditioning, no room phones, no room TVs, no smoking. No credit cards. BP.*

Nightlife and the Arts

The **Waldo Theatre** (✉ 916 Main St., ☎ 207/832–6060), a Greek Revival–style cinema with an Art Deco interior, stages concerts, plays, lectures, and other performances.

Shopping

Glockenspiel Imports (✉ U.S. 1, ☎ 207/832–8000) sells traditional German lace. For a taste of authentic German sauerkraut, visit **Morse's Sauerkraut** (✉ 3856 Washington Rd./Rte. 220 N, ☎ 207/832–5569). The **Waldoboro 5 & 10/Fernald's General Store** (✉ 17 Friendship St., ☎ 207/832–4624) is the oldest continually operated five-and-ten in the country. It has an old-fashioned soda fountain, which serves sandwiches, soups, and ice cream; there's even a penny candy counter.

Portland to Waldoboro A to Z

To research prices, get advice from other travelers, and book travel arrangements, visit www.fodors.com.

BIKE TRAVEL

The craggy fingers of land that dominate this part of the coast are fun for experienced cyclists to explore. The lack of shoulders on most roads combined with heavy tourist traffic can be intimidating. Two good resources are the Bicycle Coalition of Maine and the Maine Department of Transportation, which include information on trails and bike shops around the state.

➤ BIKE INFORMATION: **Bicycle Coalition of Maine** (✉ Box 5275, Augusta, ☎ 207/623–4511, WEB www.bikemaine.org). **Maine Dept. of Transportation Bike and Pedestrian Section** (WEB www.state.me.us/mdot/biketours.htm).

BOAT AND FERRY TRAVEL

Casco Bay Lines provides ferry service from Portland to the islands of Casco Bay.

➤ BOAT AND FERRY INFORMATION: **Casco Bay Lines** (☎ 207/774–7871, WEB www.cascobaylines.com).

BUS TRAVEL TO AND FROM PORTLAND

Greater Portland's Metro runs seven bus routes in Portland, South Portland, and Westbrook. The fare is $1; exact change ($1 bills accepted) is required. Buses run from 5:30 AM to 11:45 PM.

➤ BUS INFORMATION: **Greater Portland's Metro** (☎ 207/774–0351).

CAR TRAVEL

Congress Street leads from I–295 into the heart of Portland; the Gateway Garage on High Street, off Congress, is a convenient place to leave your car downtown. North of Portland, U.S. 1 brings you to Freeport's Main Street, which continues on to Brunswick and Bath. East of Wiscasset you can take Route 27 south to the Boothbays, where Route 96 is a good choice for further exploration. To visit the Pemaquid region, take Route 129 off Business Route 1 in Damariscotta; then pick up Route 130 and follow it down to Pemaquid Point. Return to Waldoboro and U.S. 1 on Route 32 from New Harbor.

In Portland, metered on-street parking is available at 25¢ per half hour, with a two-hour maximum. Parking lots and garages can be found near the Portland Public Market, downtown, in the Old Port, and on the waterfront; most charge $1 per hour or $8–$12 per day. If you're shopping or dining, remember to ask local vendors if they participate in the Park & Shop program, which provides an hour of free shopping for each participating vendor visited.

EMERGENCIES

➤ HOSPITALS: **Maine Medical Center** (✉ 22 Bramhall St., Portland, ☎ 207/871–0111). **Mid Coast Hospital** (✉ 123 Medical Center Dr., Brunswick, ☎ 207/729–0181). **Miles Memorial Hospital** (✉ Bristol Rd., Damariscotta, ☎ 207/563–1234). **St. Andrews Hospital** (✉ 3 St. Andrews La., Boothbay Harbor, ☎ 207/633–2121).

LODGING

Your Island Connection manages vacation home rentals in Great, Orr's, and Bailey islands, near Brunswick. A Summer Place and Cottage Connection of Maine rent cottages and condos in the Boothbay region. For rentals in the Pemaquid area, contact Newcastle Square Rentals.

➤ LODGING: **A Summer Place** (✉ Box 165, West Boothbay Harbor 04575, ☎ 207/633–4889, WEB www.asummahplace.com). **Cottage Connection of Maine** (✉ Box 662, Boothbay Harbor 04538, ☎ 207/ 633–6545 or 800/823–9501, WEB www.cottageconnection.com). **Newcastle Square Rentals** (✉ 18 Main St., Damariscotta 04543, ☎ 207/ 563–6500, WEB www.cheneycompanies.com). **Your Island Connection** (✉ Box 300, Bailey Island 04003, ☎ 207/833–7705, WEB www.mainerentals.com).

MAIL AND SHIPPING

➤ MAIL AND SHIPPING: **U.S. Post Office** (✉ 125 Forest Ave., Portland, ☎ 207/871–8461), open weekdays 7:30–7, Saturday 7:30–5. **U.S. Post Office Station A** (✉ 622 Congress St., Portland, ☎ 207/871–8449), open weekdays 8:30–5, Saturday 9–noon. **U.S. Post Office and postal store** (✉ 400 Congress St., Portland, ☎ 207/871–8464), open weekdays 8–7, Saturday 9–1.

MEDIA

The *Portland Press Herald* is published Monday–Saturday; the *Maine Sunday Telegram* is published on Sunday. The *Times Record,* which covers the Bath-Brunswick region, publishes Monday–Friday, with an entertainment section on Thursday. A number of weekly newspapers provides local coverage and entertainment listings. These include the *Coastal Journal* (Brunswick through Waldoboro), *Wiscasset Newspaper, Boothbay Register, Lincoln County News* (Wiscasset through Waldoboro), and *Lincoln County Weekly* (Wiscasset through Waldoboro). Two magazines, *Portland Monthly* and the bimonthly *Port City Life,* cover Portland.

WMEA 90.1 is the local National Public Radio affiliate. WCSH, channel 6, is the NBC affiliate; WMTW, channel 8, is the ABC affiliate; and WGME, channel 13, is the CBS affiliate. Channel 10 is the Maine Public Broadcasting affiliate.

OUTDOOR ACTIVITIES AND SPORTS

BOATING

For boat rentals, *see* town listings. The Maine Professional Guides Association represents kayaking guides.

➤ CONTACT: **Maine Professional Guides Association** (✉ Box 847, Augusta 04332, ☎ 207/549–5631, WEB www.maineguides.org).

TOURS

BUS TOURS

In Portland, the informative trolley tours of Mainely Tours cover the city's historical and architectural highlights from Memorial Day through October. Other tours combine a city tour with a bay cruise or a trip to four lighthouses.

➤ Tour Operator: **Mainely Tours** (✉ 5½ Moulton St., ☎ 207/774‑0808).

WALKING TOURS

Greater Portland Landmarks conducts 1½-hour walking tours of the city from July through September; tours begin at the Convention and Visitors Bureau and cost $8. Sagadahoc Preservation leads walking tours of historic homes and buildings in Bath on Tuesday and Thursday afternoons from mid-June to September. Tours begin at the Winter Street Church and cost $10; reservations are recommended.
➤ Tour Operators: **Convention and Visitors Bureau** (☎ 207/772–5800). **Greater Portland Landmarks** (✉ 165 State St., ☎ 207/774–5561). **Sagadahoc Preservation** (✉ 165 State St., ☎ 207/443–2174). **Winter Street Church Center** (✉ 880 Washington St.).

VISITOR INFORMATION
➤ Contacts: **Boothbay Harbor Region Chamber of Commerce** (✉ Box 356, Boothbay Harbor 04538, ☎ 207/633–2353, WEB www.boothbayharbor.com). **Chamber of Commerce of the Bath/Brunswick Region** (✉ 45 Front St., Bath 04530, ☎ 207/443–9751; ✉ 59 Pleasant St., Brunswick 04011, ☎ 207/725–8797, WEB www.midcoastmaine.com). **Convention and Visitors Bureau of Greater Portland** (✉ 305 Commercial St., Portland 04101, ☎ 207/772–5800 or 877/833–1374, WEB www.visitportland.com). **Damariscotta Region Chamber of Commerce** (✉ Box 13, Damariscotta 04543, ☎ 207/563–8340, WEB www.damariscottaregion.com). **Freeport Merchants Association** (✉ 23 Depot St., Freeport 04032, ☎ 207/865–1212 or 877/865–1212, WEB www.freeportusa.com). **Greater Portland Chamber of Commerce** (✉ 145 Middle St., Portland 04101, ☎ 207/772–2811, WEB www.portlandregion.com). **Maine Tourism Association** (✉ U.S. 1 [I–95, Exit 17], Yarmouth 04347, ☎ 207/846–0833, WEB www.mainetourism.com).

PENOBSCOT BAY

Purists hold that the Maine coast begins at Penobscot Bay, where the vistas over the water are wider and bluer; the shore a jumble of broken granite boulders, cobblestones, and gravel punctuated by small sand beaches; and the water numbingly cold. Port Clyde, in the southwest, and Stonington, in the southeast, are the outer limits of Maine's largest bay, 35 mi apart across the bay waters but separated by a drive of almost 100 mi on scenic but slow two-lane highways. From Pemaquid Point at the western extremity of Muscongus Bay to Port Clyde at its eastern extent, it's less than 15 mi across the water, but it's 50 mi for the motorist, who must return north to U.S. 1 to reach the far shore. A relaxing sail on a windjammer is a great way to explore the area.

Thomaston, on the western edge of the region, has a fine collection of sea captains' homes. Rockland, the largest town on the bay, is a growing arts center, home of the Maine Lobster Festival, and the port of departure for trips to Vinalhaven, North Haven, and Matinicus islands. The Camden Hills, looming green over Camden's fashionable waterfront, turn bluer and fainter as you head toward Castine, the small town across the bay. In between Camden and Castine are Belfast and the antiques and flea market of Searsport. Deer Isle is connected to the mainland by a slender, high-arching bridge, but Isle au Haut, accessible from Deer Isle's fishing town of Stonington, can be reached by passenger ferry only: More than half of this steep, wooded island is wilderness, the most remote section of Acadia National Park.

The most promising shopping areas are Main Street in Rockland, Main and Bay View streets in Camden, and the Main Streets in Belfast, Blue Hill, and Stonington. Antiques shops are clustered in Searsport and scattered around the outskirts of villages, in farmhouses and barns. Yard sales abound in summer.

Thomaston

22 *10 mi northeast of Waldoboro, 72 mi northeast of Portland.*

The Maine State Prison that has loomed over Thomaston for decades has been replaced by a new facility in Warren. Plans call for the dreary monstrosity to be razed and replaced with a park. Prison aside, this is a delightful town, full of beautiful sea captains' homes and dotted with antiques and specialty shops. A National Historic District encompasses parts of High, Main, and Knox streets.

The **Montpelier: General Henry Knox Museum** was built in 1930 as a replica of the late-18th-century mansion of Major General Henry Knox, a general in the Revolutionary War and secretary of war in Washington's Cabinet. Antiques and Knox family possessions fill the interior. Architectural appointments include an oval room and a double staircase. ⊠ *U.S. 1 and Rte. 131,* ☎ *207/354–8062,* WEB *www. generalknoxmuseum.org.* ◻ *$5.* ⊙ *Memorial Day–late Sept., Tues.– Sat. 10–4, Sun. 1–4; tours on the hr and ½ hr 10–3.*

Dining

$$–$$$ ✕ **Thomaston Cafe & Bakery.** A changing selection of works by local artists adorns the walls of this small café. Entrées, prepared with locally grown and produced ingredients, may include seared fresh tuna on soba noodles, lobster ravioli with lobster sauce, or filet mignon with béarnaise sauce. ⊠ *154 Main St.,* ☎ *207/354–8589. MC, V. No dinner Sun.–Thurs.*

Shopping

The **Maine State Prison Showroom Outlet** (⊠ Main St., ☎ 207/354– 2535) carries crafts, furniture, and woodwork made by prisoners. Browse the well-chosen selections at **Personal Bookstore** (⊠ 144 Main St., ☎ 207/354–8058 or 800/391–8058), which also houses a gallery upstairs.

Tenants Harbor

23 *13 mi south of Thomaston.*

Tenants Harbor is a quintessential Maine fishing town, its harbor dominated by lobster boats, its shores rocky and slippery, its center full of clapboard houses, a church, and a general store. The fictional Dunnet Landing of Sarah Orne Jewett's classic *The Country of the Pointed Firs* (1896) is based on this region. It's a favorite with artists, too, and galleries and studios invite browsing.

The keeper's house at the **Marshall Point Lighthouse** has been turned into a museum containing memorabilia from the town of St. George (a few miles north of Tenants Harbor). The setting has inspired Jamie Wyeth and other artists. You can stroll the grounds and watch the boats go in and out of Port Clyde. ⊠ *Marshall Point Rd., Port Clyde,* ☎ *207/372–6450.* ◻ *Free.* ⊙ *June–Sept., weekdays 1–5, Sat. 10–5; May and Oct., weekends 1–5.*

Dining and Lodging

$$-$$$$ ╳⊡ **East Wind Inn & Meeting House.** Built as a sail loft in 1830, this comfortably old-fashioned inn has a dreamy view overlooking an island-studded harbor. Rooms in the main inn are plain and unadorned; those in the Meeting House (a converted sea captain's house) and the Wheeler Cottage have more comforts, including some with fireplaces. The inn's restaurant ($$–$$$) emphasizes local seafood. A take-out restaurant on the wharf serves lobster, clams, and lighter fare. ⊠ *Mechanic St., 04860,* ☎ *207/372–6366 or 800/241–8439,* FAX *207/372–6320,* WEB *www.eastwindinn.com. 18 rooms, 12 with bath; 3 suites; 4 apartments. 2 restaurants, cable TV in some rooms, some microwaves, meeting rooms, some pets allowed; no air-conditioning. AE, D, MC, V. Closed Dec.–Apr. BP.*

Shopping

Gallery-by-the-Sea (⊠ Port Clyde Village, Port Clyde, ☎ 207/372–8631) carries works by a dozen local artists, including Leo Brooks, Lawrence Goldsmith, and Emily Muir. **Port Clyde Arts & Crafts Society Gallery** (⊠ Rte. 131, Tenants Harbor, ☎ 207/372–0673) showcases members' works in a garden.

Monhegan Island

★ ㉔   *East of Pemaquid Peninsula, 10 mi south of Port Clyde.*

Remote Monhegan Island, with its high cliffs fronting the open sea, was known to Basque, Portuguese, and Breton fishermen well before Columbus "discovered" America. About a century ago Monhegan was discovered again by some of America's finest painters, including Rockwell Kent, Robert Henri, A. J. Hammond, and Edward Hopper, who sailed out to paint its meadows, savage cliffs, wild ocean views, and fishermen's shacks. Tourists followed, and today three excursion boats dock here. The village bustles with activity in summer, when many artists open their studios. You can escape the crowds on the island's 17 mi of hiking trails, which lead to the lighthouse and to the cliffs. Those who overnight here have a quieter experience, since lodging is limited. Bring a lunch if you're visiting during the day, as restaurants can have long waits at lunchtime.

The **Monhegan Museum,** in an 1824 lighthouse, and an adjacent, newly built assistant keeper's house have wonderful views of Manana Island and the Camden Hills in the distance. Inside, artworks and displays depict island life and local flora and birds. ⊠ *White Head Rd.,* ☎ *no phone.* ⊡ *Donations accepted.* ۞ *July–mid-Sept., daily 11:30–3:30.*

Lodging

$$$–$$$$ ⊡ **Island Inn.** This three-story inn, which dates from 1807, has a commanding presence on Monhegan's harbor. The waterside rooms are the nicest, with sunset views over the harbor and stark Manana Island. Some of the meadow-view rooms have the distinct disadvantage of being over kitchen vents. The property includes the main inn, the adjacent Pierce Cottage, a small bakery-café, and a dining room that serves breakfast, lunch, and dinner. ⊠ *1 Ocean Ave. (Box 128, 04852),* ☎ *207/596–0371,* FAX *207/594–5517 (seasonal),* WEB *www.islandinnmonhegan.com. 30 rooms, 15 with bath; 4 suites in 2 buildings. Restaurant, café; no air-conditioning, no room phones, no room TVs. MC, V. Closed Columbus Day–Memorial Day. BP.*

Outdoor Activities and Sports

Port Clyde, a fishing village at the end of Route 131, is the point of departure for the *Laura B.* (☎ 207/372–8848 schedules), the mail boat

Penobscot Bay

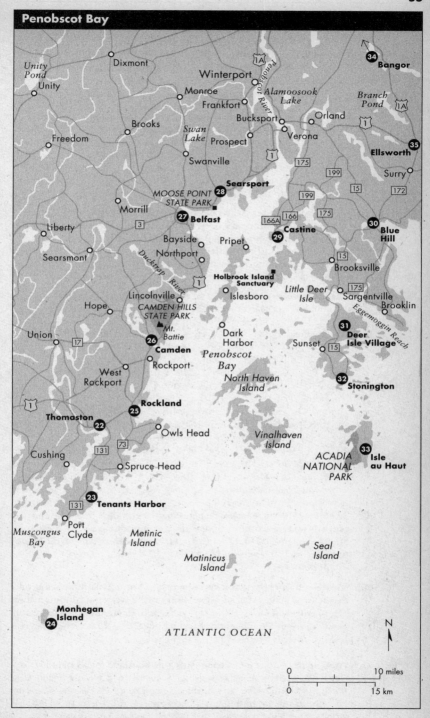

Unity Pond
Unity
Dixmont
Freedom
Brooks
Monroe
Frankfort
Winterport
1A
Alamoosook Lake
Bucksport
Orland
Branch Pond
1A
Prospect
Swanville
Verona
1
Ellsworth
35
Swan Lake
175
199
15
Surry
172
Searsport
28
MOOSE POINT STATE PARK
Morrill
27 Belfast
3
199
166 175
166A
Castine
29
30 Blue Hill
Liberty
Searsmont
Bayside
Pripet
Northport
1
Holbrook Island Sanctuary
15
Brooksville
175
Sargentville
Brooklin
Hope
Duckrap River
Lincolnville
CAMDEN HILLS STATE PARK
Islesboro
Little Deer Isle
Eggemoggin Reach
Union
17
Mt. Battie
26 Camden
Rockport
Dark Harbor
Penobscot Bay
Sunset
15
31 Deer Isle Village
West Rockport
North Haven Island
32 Stonington
1
Rockland
25
Thomaston
22
Owls Head
73
Vinalhaven Island
33 Isle au Haut
Cushing
131
Spruce Head
ACADIA NATIONAL PARK
23 Tenants Harbor
131
Port Clyde
Muscongus Bay
Metinic Island
Seal Island
Matinicus Island
Monhegan Island
24
ATLANTIC OCEAN
N
0   10 miles
0   15 km

that serves Monhegan Island. The **Balmy Days** (☎ 207/633–2284 or 800/298–2284) sails from Boothbay Harbor to Monhegan on daily trips in summer. **Hardy Boat Cruises** (☎ 207/677–2026 or 800/278–3346) leave daily from Shaw's Wharf in New Harbor.

Rockland

㉕ *4 mi northeast of Thomaston, 14 mi northeast of Tenants Harbor.*

Once a place to pass through on the way to tonier ports like Camden, Rockland now attracts attention on its own, thanks to the expansion of the Farnsworth Museum. Specialty shops and galleries line Main Street and the side streets, and restaurants and inns continue to open. A large fishing port and the commercial hub of this coastal area, with working boats moored alongside yachts and windjammers, Rockland still holds on to its working-class flavor, but it's fading.

Day trips to Vinalhaven and North Haven islands and distant Matinicus depart from the harbor, the outer portion of which is bisected by a nearly mile-long granite breakwater. At the end of the breakwater is a late-19th-century lighthouse, one of the best places in the area to watch the many windjammers sail in and out of Rockland Harbor. Owl's Head Lighthouse, off Route 73, is also a good vantage point.

★ The **Farnsworth Art Museum,** an excellent small museum of American art, contains works by Andrew, N. C., and Jamie Wyeth; Fitz Hugh Lane; George Bellows; Frank W. Benson; Edward Hopper; Louise Nevelson; and Fairfield Porter. The **Wyeth Center** is devoted to Maine-related works of the Wyeth family. Some works from the personal collection of Andrew and Betsy Wyeth include *The Patriot, Adrift, Maiden Hair, Dr. Syn, The Clearing,* and *Watch Cap.* Works by living Maine artists are shown in the **Jamien Morehouse Wing.** The **Farnsworth Homestead,** a handsome circa-1852 Greek Revival dwelling that is part of the museum, retains its original lavish Victorian furnishings. The museum also operates the **Olson House** (✉ Hathorn Point Rd., Cushing), which is depicted in Andrew Wyeth's famous painting *Christina's World.* ✉ *352 Main St.,* ☎ *207/596–6457,* WEB *www.farnsworthmuseum.org.* 🎫 *$9; Olson House only, $4.* ☉ *Museum Memorial Day–Columbus Day, daily 9–5; Columbus Day–Memorial Day, Tues.–Sat. 10–5, Sun. 1–5. Homestead Memorial Day–Columbus Day, daily 10–5. Olson House Memorial Day–Columbus Day, daily 11–4.*

☼ The **Shore Village Museum** displays many lighthouse and Coast Guard artifacts and has exhibits of maritime memorabilia. ✉ *104 Limerock St.,* ☎ *207/594–0311,* WEB *www.lighthouse.cc/shorevillage.* 🎫 *Donation suggested.* ☉ *June–mid-Oct., daily 10–4; mid-Oct.–June by chance or appointment.*

☼ **Owls Head Transportation Museum** displays antique aircraft, cars, and engines and stages special events every other weekend May–October. ✉ *117 Museum La., off Rte. 73, Owls Head (3 mi south of Rockland),* ☎ *207/594–4418,* WEB *www.ohtm.org.* 🎫 *$6.* ☉ *Apr.–Oct., daily 10–5; Nov.–Mar., daily 10–4.*

OFF THE BEATEN PATH   **VINALHAVEN –** You can take the ferry from Rockland to this island for a pleasant day of bicycling or walking. A number of parks are within walking distance of the ferry dock, including Armbrust Hill, the site of an abandoned quarry, and Lane's Island Preserve, a 40-acre site of moors, granite shoreline, tidal pools, and beach. You can learn about the island's quarrying history at the Historical Society Museum on High Street and even take a dip in the cool, clear waters of two quarries. Lawson's is 1 mi out on the North Haven Road; Booth Quarry is 1½ mi out East

Main Street. Neither has changing facilities, so go prepared. For ferry information, call **Maine State Ferry Service** (☎ 207/596–2202).

Dining and Lodging

$$–$$$ ✕ **Amalfi.** Delicious Mediterranean cuisine, a well-chosen and af-
★ fordable wine list, and excellent service have made this storefront Mediterranean bistro an immediate hit. The menu changes seasonally but may include the house paella with chorizo, chicken, shrimp, and mussels or duck risotto. ⊠ *421 Main St.,* ☎ *207/596–0012. D, MC, V. Closed Sun.–Mon.*

$$–$$$ ✕ **Café Miranda.** Expect to wait for a table at this cozy bistro, where the daily-changing menu reflects fresh, seasonal ingredients and the chef's creative renditions of both new American and traditional home-style foods. You can make a meal from the 20 or so appetizers, many roasted in the brick oven. The two dozen entrées may include crispy panfried soft-shell crabs with red bean ragout and yellow jasmine rice. The patio is a good choice on nice days. ⊠ *15 Oak St.,* ☎ *207/594–2034. MC, V. Closed Sun.–Mon. No lunch.*

$$–$$$ ✕ **Primo.** At this restaurant, James Beard Award–winning chef Melissa
★ Kelly and baker and pastry chef Price Kushner serve cuisine that combines fresh Maine ingredients with Mediterranean influences. The weekly changing menu may include wood-roasted black sea bass, local crab-stuffed turbot, or diver harvested–scallop and basil ravioli. ⊠ *2 S. Main St.,* ☎ *207/594–0770. Reservations essential. AE, D, DC, MC, V. Closed Tues.–Wed. No lunch.*

$$$$ ▦ **Samoset Resort.** On the Rockland-Rockport town line next to the breakwater, this sprawling ocean-side resort has excellent golf and fitness facilities. Most of the spacious rooms, decorated in deep green and burgundy tones, have views of Penobscot Bay over the fairways; all have patios or decks. ⊠ *220 Warrenton St., Rockport 04856,* ☎ *207/594–2511 or 800/341–1650,* FAX *207/594–0722,* WEB *www.samoset.com. 154 rooms, 24 suites. 3 restaurants, in-room data ports, some minibars, cable TV with movies and video games, 18-hole golf course, putting green, 4 tennis courts, pro shop, 2 pools (1 indoor), health club, hot tub, massage, sauna, dock, racquetball, lounge, baby-sitting, children's programs (ages 3–12), playground, dry cleaning, laundry service, concierge, Internet, business services, meeting rooms, airport shuttle; nosmoking rooms. AE, D, DC, MC, V.*

$$$–$$$$ ▦ **Berry Manor Inn.** Built in 1898 as the residence of Charles E. Berry,
★ a prominent Rockland merchant, this Victorian shingle-style inn has been carefully restored. The large guest rooms come elegantly furnished with antiques and reproduction pieces. All have fireplaces; TVs are available upon request. A guest pantry is stocked with sweets. ⊠ *81 Talbot Ave., 04841,* ☎ *207/596–7696 or 800/774–5692,* FAX *207/596–9958,* WEB *www.berrymanorinn.com. 8 rooms. In-room data ports, some inroom hot tubs, library, meeting room; no kids under 12, no smoking. AE, MC, V. BP.*

$$–$$$ ▦ **Limerock Inn.** You can walk to the Farnsworth and the Shore Vil-
★ lage museums from this magnificent Queen Anne–style Victorian on a quiet residential street. The meticulously decorated rooms include Island Cottage, with a whirlpool tub and doors that open onto a private deck overlooking a garden, and Grand Manan, which has a fireplace, a whirlpool tub, and a four-poster king-size bed. ⊠ *96 Limerock St., 04841,* ☎ *207/594–2257 or 800/546–3762,* FAX *207/594–1846,* WEB *www.limerockinn.com. 8 rooms. In-room data ports, bicycles, croquet; no air-conditioning, no room phones, no room TVs, no kids under 12, no smoking. D, MC, V. BP.*

Outdoor Activities and Sports

BOAT TRIPS

Bay Island Yacht Charters (⊠ 120 Tillison Ave., ☎ 207/596–5770 or 800/421–2492) operates bareboats and charters. The **Maine Windjammer Association** (⊠ Box 1144, Blue Hill 04614, ☎ 800/807–9463) represents the Rockland-based windjammers *American Eagle, Heritage, Isaac H. Evans, J&E Riggin, Nathaniel Bowditch, Stephen Taber,* and *Victory Chimes,* which sail on three- to eight-day cruises.

TOURS

Downeast Air Inc. (☎ 207/594–2171 or 800/594–2171) operates scenic flights and lighthouse tours.

Shopping

Archipelago (⊠ 386 Main St., ☎ 207/596–0701) carries work created by residents of Maine's islands. **Caldbeck Gallery** (⊠ 12 Elm St., ☎ 207/596–5935) displays contemporary Maine works by artists such as William Thon. **Harbor Square Gallery** (⊠ 374 Main St., ☎ 207/ 596–8700) has roomfuls of Maine-related arts and crafts.

Camden

26 *8 mi north of Rockland, 19 mi south of Belfast.*

"Where the mountains meet the sea," Camden's longtime publicity slogan, is an apt description, as you will discover when you look up from the harbor. The town is famous not only for geography but for its large fleet of windjammers—relics and replicas from the age of sailing. At just about any hour during the warm months you're likely to see at least one windjammer tied up in the harbor. The excursions, whether for an afternoon or a week, are best from June through September. Eggemoggin Reach is a famous cruising ground for yachts, as are the coves and inlets around Deer Isle and the Penobscot Bay waters between Camden and Castine. Busy downtown Camden has some of the best shopping in the region. The district's compact size makes it perfect for exploring on foot: shops, restaurants, and galleries line Main Street (U.S. 1) and Bayview, as well as side streets and alleys around the harbor.

Although their height may not be much more than 1,000 ft, the hills in **Camden Hills State Park** are lovely landmarks for miles along the low, rolling reaches of the Maine coast. The 5,500-acre park contains 20 mi of trails, including the easy Nature Trail up Mt. Battie. Hike or drive to the top for a magnificent view over Camden and island-studded Penobscot Bay. The 112-site camping area, open from mid-May to mid-October, has flush toilets and hot showers. The entrance is 2 mi north of Camden. ⊠ U.S. 1, ☎ 207/236–3109. ☞ *Trails and auto road up Mt. Battie $2.* ☉ *Daily dawn–dusk.*

Merryspring Horticultural Nature Park is a 66-acre retreat with herb, rose, rhododendron, hosta, and children's gardens as well as 4 mi of walking trails. ⊠ *Conway Rd., off U.S. 1,* ☎ 207/236–2239. ☞ *Free.* ☉ *Daily dawn–dusk.*

☺ **Kelmscott Farm** is a rare-breed animal farm (sheep, pigs, horses, poultry, goats, and cows) with displays, a nature trail, children's activities, a picnic area, heirloom gardens, and special events. ⊠ *Rte. 52, Lincolnville,* ☎ 207/763–4088 or 800/545–9363, WEB *www.kelmscott.org.* ☞ *$5.* ☉ *May–Oct., Tues.–Sun. 10–5; Nov.–Apr., Tues.–Sun. 10–3.*

Dining and Lodging

$–$$$ ✕ **Waterfront Restaurant.** A ringside seat on Camden Harbor can be had here; the best view is from the deck, open in warm weather. The fare is primarily seafood, but they also serve plenty of beef, chicken, and salads. Some lunchtime highlights are lobster and crabmeat rolls. ✉ *Bayview St.,* ☎ *207/236–3747. Reservations not accepted. AE, MC, V.*

$$–$$$ ✕⌷ **The Belmont.** Fresh flowers, gleaming woodwork, comfortable antiques, and Oriental rugs highlight this 19th-century Edwardian-style inn. Most rooms are spacious, and some have fireplaces. Adding to the experience is an elegant dining room, Marquis at the Belmont ($$–$$$$; closed Sun.), open to the public, where the menu might include grilled beef tenderloin with roasted pistachio blue-cheese butter. ✉ *6 Belmont Ave., 04843,* ☎ *207/230–1226 or 800/237–8053,* FAX *207/236–9872,* WEB *www.thebelmontinn.com. 6 rooms. Restaurant, bar; no air-conditioning in some rooms, no room TVs, no kids, no smoking. AE, MC, V. BP.*

$$–$$$ ✕⌷ **Hartstone Inn.** Michael and Mary Jo Salmon have turned this down-
★ town 1835 Mansard-style Victorian into an elegant and sophisticated retreat and culinary destination. No detail has been overlooked, from soft robes, down comforters, and chocolate truffles in the guest rooms to china, crystal, and silver in the dining room. The five-course, prix-fixe menu ($$$$; reservations essential; closed late Oct.–May, Mon.–Wed.; June–late Oct., Mon.–Tues.) changes daily. The inn hosts seasonal food festivals and off-season cooking classes. ✉ *42 Elm St., 04843,* ☎ *207/236–4259 or 800/788–4823,* FAX *207/235–9575,* WEB *www.hartstoneinn.com. 6 rooms, 4 suites. Restaurant, cable TV in some rooms, in-room data ports; no kids under 12, no smoking.*

$$–$$$ ✕⌷ **Whitehall Inn.** One of Camden's best-known inns, just north of town, is an 1843 white clapboard sea captain's home with a wide porch. The Millay Room, off the lobby, preserves memorabilia of the poet Edna St. Vincent Millay, who grew up in the area. The sparsely furnished rooms have dark-wood bedsteads, white bedspreads, and claw-foot tubs. The dining room ($$$), which serves traditional and creative American cuisine, is open to the public for dinner. ✉ *52 High St. (Box 558, 04843),* ☎ *207/236–3391 or 800/789–6565,* FAX *207/236–4427 (seasonal),* WEB *www.whitehall-inn.com. 50 rooms, 45 with bath. Restaurant, tennis court, shuffleboard; no phones in some rooms, no room TVs, no smoking. AE, MC, V. Closed mid-Oct.–mid-May. BP.*

$$–$$$ ✕⌷ **Youngtown Inn.** Inside this white Federal-style farmhouse are a French-inspired country retreat and a well-respected French restaurant ($$$). The country location guarantees quiet, and the inn is a short walk from the Fernald Neck Preserve on Lake Megunticook. Simple, airy rooms open to decks with views of the rolling countryside. Four have fireplaces. The restaurant, open to the public for dinner, serves entrées such as rack of lamb and breast of pheasant with foie gras mousse. ✉ *Rte. 52 at Youngtown Rd., Lincolnville 04849,* ☎ *207/763–4290 or 800/291–8438,* FAX *207/763–4078,* WEB *www.youngtowninn.com. 6 rooms, 1 suite. Restaurant, cable TV in some rooms; no room phones, no smoking. AE, MC, V. BP.*

$$$$ ⌷ **Inn at Ocean's Edge.** Perched on the ocean's edge, this shingle-style
★ inn looks as if it has been here for decades. In actuality, the original building dates from 1999 and the upper building from 2001. Both were built with modern-day comforts in mind. Every room has a king-size bed, an ocean view, a fireplace, and a whirlpool for two. ✉ *U.S. 1, Lincolnville (Box 704, Camden 04843),* ☎ *207/236–0945,* FAX *207/ 236–0609,* WEB *www.innatoceansedge.com. 26 rooms, 1 suite. In-room data ports, cable TV, in-room VCRs, gym, pub, meeting room; no kids under 14, no smoking. MC, V. BP.*

$$$ ⌷ **Victorian by the Sea.** It's less than 10 minutes from downtown Camden, but with a quiet waterside location well off U.S. 1, the Victorian Inn feels a world away. Most rooms and the wraparound porch have magnificent views over island-studded Penobscot Bay. Romantic touches

include canopy and brass beds, braided rugs, white wicker furniture, and floral wallpapers. Six guest rooms have fireplaces; four more fireplaces are in common rooms, including the glass-enclosed breakfast room. ⊠ *31 Sea View Dr., Lincolnville (Box 1385, Camden 04843),* ☎ *207/236–3785 or 800/382–9817,* FAX *207/236–0017,* WEB *www. victorianbythesea.com. 5 rooms, 2 suites. Fans; no air-conditioning in some rooms, no room phones, no room TVs, no kids under 12, no smoking. AE, MC, V. BP.*

$$-$$$ 🏠 **Camden Maine Stay.** This 1802 clapboard inn on the National Register of Historic Places is within walking distance of shops and restaurants. The grounds are classic and inviting, from the flowers lining the granite walk in summer to the snow-laden bushes in winter. Fresh and colorful, the rooms contain many pieces of Eastlake furniture; six have fireplaces. ⊠ *22 High St., 04842,* ☎ *207/236–9636,* FAX *207/236–0621,* WEB *www.camdenmainestay.com. 5 rooms, 3 suites. No room phones, no cable TV in some rooms, no kids under 10, no smoking. AE, MC, V. BP.*

Nightlife and the Arts

Bay Chamber Concerts (⊠ Rockport Opera House, 6 Central St., Rockport, ☎ 207/236–2823 or 888/707–2770) presents chamber music on Thursday and Friday night during July and August; concerts are given once a month from September to June. **Gilbert's Public House** (⊠ 12 Bay View St., ☎ 207/236–4320) has dancing and live entertainment. **Sea Dog Tavern & Brewery** (⊠ 43 Mechanic St., ☎ 207/236–6863), a popular brewpub in a converted woolen mill, hosts live bands playing blues, rock, and jazz. The **Whale's Tooth Pub** (⊠ U.S. 1, Lincolnville Beach, ☎ 207/236–3747) hosts live folk music on weekends.

Outdoor Activities and Sports

The *Betselma* (⊠ Camden Public Landing, ☎ 207/236–4446) operates one- and two-hour powerboat trips. **Brown Dog Bikes** (⊠ 46 Elm St., ☎ 207/236–6664) delivers rental bikes to area lodging. **Maine Sport** (⊠ U.S. 1, Rockport, ☎ 207/236–8797 or 800/722–0826), the best sports outfitter north of Freeport, rents bikes, camping and fishing gear, canoes, kayaks, cross-country skis, ice skates, and snowshoes. It also conducts skiing and kayaking clinics and trips. The **Maine Windjammer Association** (⊠ Box 1144, Blue Hill 04614, ☎ 800/807–9463) represents the Camden-based windjammers *Angelique, Grace Bailey, Lewis R. French, Mary Day,* and *Mercantile* and the Rockport-based *Timberwind.* Cruises last three to eight days.

Shopping

Center for Maine Contemporary Art (⊠ 162 Russell Ave., Rockport, ☎ 207/236–2875) specializes in contemporary Maine art. **Maine Gathering** (⊠ 21 Main St., ☎ 207/236–9004) sells a well-chosen selection of crafts, including Passamaquoddy and Penobscot baskets. **Maine's Massachusetts House Galleries** (⊠ U.S. 1, Lincolnville, ☎ 207/789–5705) display regional art, including bronzes, carvings, sculptures, and landscapes and seascapes in pencil, oil, and watercolor.

ABCD Books (⊠ 23 Bay View St., ☎ 207/236–3903 or 888/236–3903) has a discriminating selection of quality antiquarian and rare books. The **Owl and Turtle Bookshop** (⊠ 8 Bay View St., ☎ 207/236–4769) sells books, CDs, cassettes, and cards. The two-story shop has rooms devoted to marine and children's books. The **Pine Tree Shop & Bayview Gallery** (⊠ 33 Bay View St., ☎ 207/236–4534) specializes in original art, prints, and posters, almost all with Maine themes. **Stone Soup Books** (⊠ 35 Main St., second floor, ☎ no phone) stocks used contemporary fiction and is a great place to pick up a cache of books to read on inclement days. The **Windsor Chairmakers** (⊠ U.S. 1, Lincolnville,

☎ 207/789–5188 or 800/789–5188) sells custom-made handcrafted beds, chests, china cabinets, dining tables, highboys, and chairs.

Ski Areas

CAMDEN SNOW BOWL

The Maine coast isn't known for skiing, but this small, lively park has skiing, snowboarding, tubing, and tobogganing—plus magnificent views over Penobscot Bay. ⊠ *Hosmer Pond Rd. (Box 1207, 04843),* ☎ *207/236–3438.*

Downhill. The park has a 950-ft-vertical mountain, a small lodge with a cafeteria, a ski school, and ski and toboggan rentals. Camden Snow Bowl has 11 trails accessed by one double chair and two T-bars. It also has night skiing.

Other Activities. Camden Snow Bowl has a small lake that is cleared for ice-skating, a snow-tubing park, and a 400-ft toboggan run that shoots sledders out onto the lake. The North American Tobogganing Championships, a tongue-in-cheek event open to anyone, is held annually in early February

CROSS-COUNTRY SKIING

There are 16 km (10 mi) of cross-country skiing trails at **Camden Hills State Park** (⊠ U.S. 1, ☎ 207/236–9849). **Tanglewood 4-H Camp** (⊠ U.S. 1, ☎ 207/789–5868), about 5 mi away in Lincolnville, has 20 km (12½ mi) of trails.

Belfast

㉗ *19 mi north of Camden, 46 mi east of Augusta.*

Like many other Maine towns, Belfast has ridden the tides of affluence and depression since its glory days in the 1800s, when it was a shipbuilding center and home to many sea captains. Today it's high-tech, namely credit-card giant MBNA, that has helped rescue the city's economy. The upswing has brought the revival of the old-fashioned redbrick Victorian downtown and a lively waterfront, as well as affordable lodging and dining. The houses on Church Street are a veritable glossary of 19th-century architectural styles; pick up a map with a walking tour at the visitor center at the foot of Main Street.

The **Belfast & Moosehead Lake Railroad** (⊠ 44 Front St., ☎ 207/948–5500 or 800/392–5500, WEB www.belfastrailroad.com) operates a 90-minute trip from July to mid-October ($15) between Belfast and Waldo, providing views of Belfast Harbor, Lake Winnecook, and area towns. Narrators discuss the region's history and folklore.

Dining and Lodging

$$–$$$ ✕ **Spring Street Cafe.** Don't let the unassuming small Cape Cod–style house tucked on a side street fool you; this restaurant prepares such eclectic fare as Mediterranean halibut cake, Spring Street pad Thai, and Cuban-style roasted pork. Both small plates, ideal for those not too hungry, and large plates are served. ⊠ *38 Spring St.,* ☎ *207/338–4603. MC, V.*

$–$$ ✕ **Darby's.** Tin ceilings and an old-fashioned bar create a comfortable ambience for the creative casual fare served here. The eclectic menu lists hearty soups and sandwiches as well as dishes with an international flavor, such as Moroccan lamb and pad Thai. ⊠ *155 High St.,* ☎ *207/338–2339. AE, D, DC, MC, V.*

$$–$$$ ▥ **Jeweled Turret Inn.** Turrets, columns, gables, and magnificent woodwork embellish this inn, originally built in 1898 as the home of a local attorney. The inn is named for the jewel-like stained-glass windows in the stairway turret; the gem theme continues in the den, where the ornate rock fireplace is said to include rocks from every state in the Union. Elegant Victorian pieces furnish the rooms: The Opal room has a marble bath with whirlpool tub in addition to a French armoire and a four-poster. ⊠ *40 Pearl St., 04915,* ☎ *207/338–2304 or 800/696–2304,* WEB *www.jeweledturret.com. 7 rooms. No air-conditioning in some rooms, no room phones, no room TVs, no kids under 12, no smoking indoors. AE, MC, V. BP.*

$$–$$$ 🏠 **The White House.** This 1840–1842 landmark by Maine architect Calvin Ryder is considered one of the most sophisticated examples of Greek Revival architecture in New England. An eight-side cupola tops the house; inside are ornate plaster ceiling medallions, Italian marble fireplaces, an elliptical flying staircase, and intricate moldings. Crystal chandeliers, Oriental rugs, and antiques and reproduction pieces elegantly decorate the spacious rooms. You can relax in the English garden, in the gazebo, or under the enormous copper beech tree. ⊠ *1 Church St., 04915,* ☎ *207/338–1901 or 888/290–1901,* FAX *207/338–5161,* WEB *www.mainebb.com. 4 rooms, 2 suites. Some in-room hot tubs, some cable TV, some in-room VCRs, meeting room, some pets allowed; no kids under 12, no smoking. D, MC, V. BP.*

Outdoor Activities and Sports

KAYAKING

Belfast Kayak Tours (⊠ Belfast City Pier, ☎ 207/382–6204) provides fully outfitted trips and instruction.

PARKS

Belfast City Park (⊠ High St., 1 mi east of downtown) has a playground, tennis courts (lighted at night), a baseball diamond, and an outdoor swimming pool with lockers and showers. Use of the park is free.

Moose Point State Park (⊠ U.S. 1 between Belfast and Searsport, ☎ 207/548–2882) is ideal for easy hikes and picnics overlooking Penobscot Bay.

Shopping

Belfast's main and side streets house an eclectic selection of shops that mirror the city's economic base. Shoppers who prefer upscale boutiques rub elbows with those who bargain-hunt in thrift stores.

Visit the **Belfast Co-op** (⊠ 123 High St., ☎ 207/338–2352), the region's premier natural foods store, for healthful snacks and goodies. The Co-op also has a café with soups, sandwiches, and other fare. You can dine inside, outdoors on picnic tables, or have your order prepared to go. The **Green Store** (⊠ 71 Main St., ☎ 207/338–4045) sells environmentally friendly products, from lightbulbs to clothing. The **Gothic Cafe** (⊠ 108 Main St., ☎ 207/338–9901) sells melt-in-your-mouth pastries and to-die-for ice cream as well as architectural antiques.

Searsport

㉘ *11 mi northeast of Belfast, 57 mi east of Augusta.*

Searsport, Maine's second-largest deepwater port (after Portland), has a rich shipbuilding and seafaring history. In the 1880s, 10% of all captains under deepwater sail hailed from here. Many of the former sea captains' homes are now bed-and-breakfasts. They make an ideal base for exploring the multitude of antiques shops and flea markets lining U.S. 1 that have earned Searsport the title Maine's Antiques Capital.

★   The fine holdings within the nine historic and five modern buildings of the **Penobscot Marine Museum** provide fascinating documentation of the region's seafaring way of life. These buildings, including a still-active church and a sea captain's house, remain in their original spots in town. The museum's outstanding collection of marine art includes the largest collection of works by Thomas and James Buttersworth in the country. Also of note are photos of 284 local sea captains, a collection of China-trade articles, artifacts of the whaling industry (including lots of scrimshaw), navigational instruments, treasures collected by seafarers around the globe, and models of famous ships. The museum's newest building, a boat barn, opened in 2001 with exhibits of small craft. ☒ *5 U.S. 1, at Church St.,* ☎ *207/548–2529,* WEB *www.penobscotmarinemuseum.org.* ☒ *$8.* ☉ *Memorial Day–late Oct., Mon.–Sat. 10–5, Sun. noon–5; late Oct.–Memorial Day by appointment.*

Dining and Lodging

$$$ ✕ **The Rhumb Line.** The upscale restaurant in this 18th-century sea captain's home delivers fine dining, with formally attired waitstaff and excellent food. Pepper-glazed pork tenderloin, orange-glazed duck with potato pancakes, and horseradish-crusted salmon are typical entrées. ☒ *200 E. Main St. (U.S. 1),* ☎ *207/548–2600. MC, V. No lunch.*

$$ ⊞ **Brass Lantern.** This antiques-filled Victorian bed-and-breakfast is an elegant retreat after a day of shopping at nearby flea markets and antiques shops. Two rooms have water views. The multicourse breakfasts are served on china and crystal by candlelight in the tin-ceiling dining room. ☒ *81 W. Main St. (U.S. 1), 04874,* ☎ *207/548–0150 or 800/691–0150,* FAX *207/548–0304,* WEB *www.brasslanternmaine.com. 5 rooms. No air-conditioning, no room phones, no room TVs, no kids under 12, no smoking. D, MC, V. BP.*

$–$$ ⊞ **Homeport Inn.** This 1861 inn, a former sea captain's home, provides an opulent Victorian environment that might put you in the mood to rummage through the nearby antiques and treasure shops. The back rooms downstairs have private decks and views of the bay. Families often stay in the housekeeping cottages. ☒ *121 E. Main St. (U.S. 1),* ☎ *207/548–2259 or 800/742–5814,* WEB *www.bnbcity.com/inns/20015. 10 rooms, 7 with bath; 2 cottages. Some pets allowed; no air-conditioning, no room phones, no room TVs, no kids under 3, no smoking. AE, D, MC, V. BP.*

Shopping

Museum-quality model-ship kits can be found at **Bluejacket Shipcrafters** (☒ 160 E. Main St. [U.S. 1], ☎ 207/548–9970). Hundreds of teddy bears can be found at **Cranberry Hollow** (☒ 157 W. Main St. [U.S. 1], ☎ 207/548–2647); the owner also makes custom bears from old fur coats. **Pumpkin Patch Antiques** (☒ 15 W. Main St. [U.S. 1], ☎ 207/ 548–6047) displays such items as quilts, nautical memorabilia, and painted and wood furniture from about 20 dealers. It's open April through Thanksgiving or by appointment. More than 70 dealers show their wares in the two-story **Searsport Antique Mall** (☒ 149 E. Main St. [U.S. 1], ☎ 207/548–2640); look for everything from linens and silver to turn-of-the-20th-century oak.

Castine

29 *30 mi southeast of Searsport.*

Set on the tip of a peninsula, Castine is a quiet, peaceful place to escape most of the coastal crowds. The French, the British, the Dutch, and the Americans fought over the town from the 17th century to the War of 1812. Signs explaining this history are posted throughout town, making it ideal for a walking tour. Present-day Castine's many appealing attributes include its lively harbor front, Federal and Greek Revival houses, and town common; the two small museums and the ruins of a British fort are also worth exploring. For a nice stroll, park your car at the landing and walk up Main Street toward the white Trinitarian Federated Church, which has a tapering spire. Among the white clapboard buildings that ring the town common are the Ives House (once the summer home of the poet Robert Lowell), the Abbott School, and the Unitarian Church, capped by a whimsical belfry. The Maine Maritime Academy is also here, and its training ship often can be seen in port. You can pick up a map detailing the town's businesses, history, and historic sites at most local businesses.

The **Castine Historical Society Museum**'s changing exhibits relating to Castine's tumultuous history include the town's Bicentennial Quilt, created in 1996 to celebrate the town's 200th birthday. ⊠ *Town Common (Box 238, 04421),* ☎ *207/326–4118.* 🎫 *Free.* ⊙ *Tues.–Sat. 10–4, Sun. 1–4.*

Castine's **Soldiers and Sailors Monument** (⊠ Castine Town Common) honors the state's participation in the Civil War. The memorial was dedicated in May 1887 to the veterans of that conflict.

The **Wilson Museum** comprises four buildings. The main building houses anthropologist-geologist John Howard Wilson's collection of prehistoric artifacts from around the world, including rocks, minerals, and other intriguing objects. The **John Perkins House** is a restored Colonial house built in 1763 and enlarged in 1774 and 1783. The **Blacksmith Shop** holds demonstrations showing all the tricks of this old-time trade. Inside the **Hearse House** you can see the summer and winter hearses that serviced Castine more than a century ago. ⊠ *Perkins St.,* ☎ *207/677–2423.* 🎫 *Museum, Blacksmith Shop, and Hearse House free; John Perkins House $4.* ⊙ *Museum late May–late Sept., Tues.–Sun. 2–5. Guided tours of John Perkins House and demonstrations at Blacksmith Shop July–Aug., Sun. and Wed. 2–5. Hearse House, July–Aug., Sun. and Wed. 2–5*

Dining and Lodging

$–$$$ ✕ **Dennett's Wharf.** When you need a break from exploring Castine, this casual waterfront restaurant with indoor and outdoor tables serves a diverse menu, from burgers to lobster. ⊠ *15 Sea St.,* ☎ *207/326–9045. MC, V. Closed Columbus Day–May.*

$$–$$$ ✕🏠 **Manor Inn.** Bordering a 95-acre conservation forest with trails leading to the bay, this 1895 English manor–style inn provides a quiet retreat. Yoga classes are held in a fully equipped studio. Rooms are individually decorated, and four have fireplaces. The dining room ($$–$$$), which specializes in regional cuisine, is on the front porch and overlooks the expansive lawn and side gardens. The pub serves lighter fare. ⊠ *15 Manor Dr., off Battle Ave., 04421,* ☎ *207/326–4861 or 877/626–6746, FAX 207/326–0891, WEB www.manor-inn.com. 10 rooms, 2 suites. Restaurant, pub, some pets allowed (fee); no air-conditioning in some rooms, no room TVs, no-smoking rooms. AE, DC, MC, V. BP.*

$$ ✕🏠 **Castine Inn.** Upholstered easy chairs and fine prints and paintings
★ adorn this inn's airy and simply decorated rooms. The well-respected dining room ($$$–$$$$; closed Tues.), decorated with a wraparound mural of Castine, is open to the public for breakfast and dinner; the creative menu includes entrées such as oil-poached salmon. After dinner, unwind in the snug, English-style pub just off the lobby. ⊠ *33 Main St. (Box 41, 04421),* ☎ *207/326–4365, FAX 207/326–4570, WEB www.castineinn.com. 15 rooms, 4 suites. Restaurant, sauna, pub; no air-conditioning, no room phones, no room TVs, no kids under 8, no smoking. MC, V. Closed Nov.–late Apr. BP.*

Outdoor Activities and Sports

Castine Kayak Adventures (✉ Dennett's Wharf, ☎ 207/326–9045) operates tours with a registered Maine guide. The **Steam Launch Laurie Ellen** (✉ Dennett's Wharf, ☎ 207/326–9045 or 207/266–2841), the only wood-fired, steam-powered, USCG-inspected passenger steam launch in the country, conducts cruises around Castine Harbor and up the Bagaduce River.

Shopping

H.O.M.E. (✉ U.S. 1, Orland, ☎ 207/469–7961) is a cooperative crafts village with a crafts and pottery shop, weaving shop, flea market, market stand, and woodworking shop. **Leila Day Antiques** (✉ 53 Main St., ☎ 207/326–8786) specializes in antiques, quilts, folk art, and nautical accessories. **McGrath-Dunham Gallery** (✉ 9 Main St., ☎ 207/ 326–9175) carries paintings, sculpture, original prints, and pottery.

Blue Hill

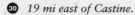 *19 mi east of Castine.*

Snugged between 943-ft Blue Hill Mountain and Blue Hill Bay, Blue Hill has a dramatic perch over the harbor that's popular with sailors and sea-kayakers. Originally known, for its granite quarries, copper mining, and shipbuilding, today the town flourishes with pottery and artisans. You'll find a plethora of galleries, small shops and studios, as well as bookstores and antiques shops. The Blue Hill Fair, held Labor Day weekend, is a traditional country fair with agricultural exhibits, food, and entertainment. It is renowned for its pottery and is a good spot for shopping and gallery hopping.

Jonathan Fisher was the first settled minister of Blue Hill. The **Parson Fisher House,** which he built from 1814 to 1820, provides a fascinating look at his many accomplishments and talents, which included writing and illustrating books and poetry, farming, painting, building furniture, and making a camera obscura. Also on view is a wooden clock he crafted while a student at Harvard; the face holds messages about time written in English, Greek, Latin, Hebrew, and French. ✉ *Rtes. 15/176,* ☎ *no phone.* ☞ *$3.* ☉ *July–mid-Sept., Mon.–Sat. 2–5.*

Dining and Lodging

$$$ ✕ **Arborvine.** Antiques, fireplaces, hardwood floors covered with Asian Oriental rugs, and candlelight set an inviting tone in each of the four dining rooms in this renovated, Cape Cod–style house. The menu emphasizes fresh native fish in season as well as entrées such as noisettes of lamb chasseur. A take-out lunch is available at the adjacent Moveable Feasts deli. ✉ *Main St.,* ☎ *207/374–2119. MC, V. Closed Mon.– Tues. No lunch.*

$$$–$$$$ ✿ **Blue Hill Inn.** Rambling and antiques-filled, this 1830 inn is a com-
★ forting place to relax after exploring nearby shops and galleries. Original pumpkin pine and painted floors set the tone for the mix of Empire and early Victorian pieces that fill the two parlors and guest rooms; five rooms have fireplaces. The Cape House Suite, with full kitchen and cable TV, is open all year. ✉ *40 Union St. (Box 403, 04614),* ☎ *207/374– 2844 or 800/826–7415,* 𝔽𝔸𝕏 *207/374–2829,* 𝖶𝖤𝖡 *www.bluehillinn.com. 11 rooms, 1 suite. Internet; no air-conditioning in some rooms, no room phones, no room TVs, no kids, no smoking. AE, MC, V. Closed Nov.–mid-May. BP.*

$$$–$$$$ ✿ **Oakland House.** An inn, dining hall, and cottages are tucked among the towering pines at this sprawling oceanfront property. Owner Jim Littlefield is a fourth-generation innkeeper. The Shore Oaks seaside inn, built in 1907 in the Arts and Crafts style, retains an elegant turn-of-the-20th-century ambience. Cottages, most with kitchenettes and fireplaces, are rustic but fully equipped. The inn has ½ mi of ocean shorefront on Eggemoggin Reach as well as a lake beach. ⊠ *435 Herrick Rd., Brooksville 04617,* ☎ *207/359–8521 or 800/359–7352,* FAX *207/359–9865,* WEB *www.oaklandhouse.com. 10 rooms, 7 with bath; 15 cottages. Dining room, some microwaves, lake, hiking, beaches, boating, recreation room, playground; no air-conditioning, no phones in some rooms, no TVs in some rooms, no-smoking rooms. MC, V. MAP.*

Nightlife and the Arts

Kneisel Hall Chamber Music Festival (⊠ Kneisel Hall, Rte. 15, ☎ 207/374–2811) has concerts on Sunday and Friday in summer.

Outdoor Activities and Sports

Holbrook Island Sanctuary (⊠ off Cape Rosier Rd., Brooksville, ☎ 207/326–4012) has a gravel beach with splendid views, a picnic area, and hiking trails.

Shopping

Big Chicken Barn (⊠ U.S. 1, Ellsworth, ☎ 207/374–2715) has three floors filled with books, antiques, and collectibles. **Handworks Gallery** (⊠ Main St., ☎ 207/374–5613) carries unusual crafts, jewelry, and clothing. **Leighton Gallery** (⊠ Parker Point Rd., ☎ 207/374–5001) shows oil paintings, lithographs, watercolors, and other contemporary art in the gallery, and sculpture in its garden. **Mark Bell Pottery** (⊠ Rte. 15, ☎ 207/374–5881) has received national acclaim for his porcelain bowls, bottles, and vases.

North Country Textiles (⊠ Main St., ☎ 207/374–2715) specializes in fine woven shawls, place mats, throws, baby blankets, and pillows in subtle patterns and color schemes. **Rackliffe Pottery** (⊠ Rte. 172, ☎ 207/374–2297) is famous for its vivid blue pottery, including plates, tea and coffee sets, pitchers, casseroles, and canisters. **Rowantrees Pottery** (⊠ Union St., ☎ 207/374–5535) has an extensive selection of styles and patterns in dinnerware, tea sets, vases, and decorative items.

En Route Scenic Route 15 south from Blue Hill passes through Brooksville and takes you over the graceful suspension bridge that crosses Eggemoggin Reach to Deer Isle. The turnout and picnic area at **Caterpillar Hill,** 1 mi south of the junction of Routes 15 and 175, commands a fabulous view of Penobscot Bay, hundreds of dark-green islands, and the Camden Hills across the bay.

Deer Isle Village

③ *16 mi south of Blue Hill.*

In Deer Isle Village, thick woods give way to tidal coves. Stacks of lobster traps populate the backyards of shingled houses, and dirt roads lead to summer cottages. The region is prized by craftsman and artists, and studios and galleries are plentiful.

Haystack Mountain School of Crafts attracts internationally renowned glassblowers, potters, sculptors, jewelers, blacksmiths, printmakers, and weavers to its summer institute. You can attend evening lectures or visit artists' studios (by appointment only). ⊠ *Rte. 15, south of Deer Isle Village (turn left at Gulf gas station and follow signs for 6 mi),* ☎ *207/348–2306.* ⊡ *Free.* ☉ *June–Sept.*

Dining and Lodging

$$$$ ✕🖾 **Pilgrim's Inn.** A deep-red, four-story gambrel-roof house, this inn
★ dates from about 1793 and overlooks a mill pond and harbor in Deer Isle Village. Wing chairs and Oriental rugs fill the library; a downstairs

taproom has a huge brick fireplace and pine furniture. Guest rooms are individually decorated. The dining room ($$$$; reservations essential; no lunch) is rustic yet elegant, with farm implements, French oil lamps, and tiny windows. The four-course menu changes nightly but might list rack of lamb or fresh seafood. ⊠ *20 Main. St. (Rte. 15A), 04627,* ☎ *207/348–6615 or 888/778–7505,* FAX *207/346–6615,* WEB *www. pilgrimsinn.com. 12 rooms, 3 seaside cottages. Restaurant, bicycles, some pets allowed; no air-conditioning, no in-room phones, no in-room TVs, no kids under 10 in inn, no smoking. AE, MC, V. Closed mid-Oct.–mid-May. BP, MAP.*

$$$–$$$$ ✕▣ **Goose Cove Lodge.** A country lane leads to this spectacular ocean-front property, where cottages and suites are scattered in the woodlands and on the shore along a sandy beach. At low tide, you can cross a sandbar to a nature preserve. Units vary in size; all but three have fireplaces. Dinner at the restaurant ($$–$$$; reservations essential) is superb, and the contemporary American fare includes at least one vegetarian entrée. On Monday night in July and August, there's a lobster feast on the beach. ⊠ *300 Goose Cove Rd. (Box 40, Sunset 04683),* ☎ *207/348–2508 or 800/728–1963,* FAX *207/348–2624,* WEB *www.goosecovelodge.com. 2 rooms, 7 suites, 13 cottages. 2 restaurants, hiking, beach, boating; no air-conditioning, no room phones, no room TVs, no smoking. D, MC, V. All but 3 units closed mid-Oct.–mid-May. BP.*

Shopping

Blue Heron Gallery & Studio (⊠ Rte. 15, ☎ 207/348–6051) sells the work of the Haystack Mountain School of Crafts faculty. **Harbor Farm** (⊠ 29 Little Deer Isle Rd., Little Deer Isle, ☎ 207/348–7737) carries wonderful products for the home, such as pottery, furniture, dinnerware, linens, and folk art. **Nervous Nellie's Jams and Jellies** (⊠ 598 Sunshine Rd., ☎ 800/777–6825) sells jams and jellies and operates a café. The outdoor sculpture garden is a hit with kids. **Old Deer Isle Parish House Antiques** (⊠ 7 Church St., ☎ 207/348–9964) is a place for poking around in jumbles of old kitchenware, glassware, books, and linens. **Turtle Gallery** (⊠ 61 N. Deer Isle Rd., ☎ 207/348–9977) shows contemporary painting and sculpture.

Stonington

㉜ *7 mi south of Deer Isle.*

Stonington's isolation at the tip of the Deer Isle peninsula has helped it retain its fishing-village flavor. This is changing now, as boutiques and galleries open in summer now line its main thoroughfare. Still, Stonington remains a working port town—the principal activity is at the waterfront, where fishing boats arrive with the day's catch. At night, the town can be rowdy. The high, sloped island that rises beyond the archipelago known as Merchants Row is Isle au Haut, which contains a remote section of Acadia National Park; it's accessible by mail boat from Stonington.

The tiny **Deer Isle Granite Museum** documents Stonington's quarrying tradition. The museum's centerpiece is an 8- by 15-ft working model of quarrying operations on Crotch Island and the town of Stonington in 1900. ⊠ *Main St.,* ☎ *207/367–6331.* ⬛ *Free.* ☉ *Memorial Day–Labor Day, Mon.–Sat. 10–5, Sun. 1–5.*

Dining and Lodging

$$–$$$ ✕ **Cafe Atlantic.** Whether you want ice cream, tasty boiled lobster, or a fancier meal, you'll find it at this harbor-front eatery. Country linens and antiques decorate the restaurant, which serves fresh seafood as well

as chicken and steak. For lobster in the rough, head to the deck over-hanging the water. ✉ *Main St.,* ☎ *207/367–6373. AE, D, MC, V. Closed Nov.–Apr.*

$$–$$$ ✕ **Lily's.** Local artwork embellishes the three dining rooms in this old Victorian house. The bistro-style menu emphasizes fresh, seasonal foods and may include entrées such as fresh salmon with a sesame butter sauce or curried chicken. The desserts are legendary. ✉ *Rte. 15,* ☎ *207/367–5936. MC, V. Closed weekends.*

$$ ⊡ **Inn on the Harbor.** From the front, this inn composed of four 100-year-old Victorian buildings is as plain and unadorned as Stonington itself. But out back it opens up, with an expansive deck over the harbor—a pleasant spot for a morning breakfast. Rooms on the harbor side have views, and some have fireplaces and private decks. Those on the street side lack the views and can be noisy at night. ✉ *Main St. (Box 69, 04681),* ☎ *207/367–2420 or 800/942–2420,* ℻ *207/367–5165,* 🕸 *www.innontheharbor.com. 14 rooms, 2 suites. Coffee shop, cable TV, in-room data ports; no air-conditioning, no kids under 12, no smoking inside. AE, D, MC, V. CP.*

The Arts

Stonington Opera House (✉ School St., ☎ 207/367–2788) hosts live theater, music, and dance events.

Outdoor Activities and Sports

The registered Maine guides of **Granite Island Guide Service** (☎ 207/367–2788) lead kayaking and canoe trips. **Old Quarry** (☎ 207/367–8977, 🕸 www.oldquarry.com) operates a charter and boat-taxi service; rents canoes, kayaks, and bicycles; and conducts guided kayak trips. Call for directions.

Shopping

The **Clown** (✉ Main St., ☎ 207/367–6348) has fine art, antiques, a good wine selection, and specialty foods. **Dockside Books & Gifts** (✉ W. Main St., ☎ 207/367–2652), on the harbor front, stocks an eclectic selection of books, crafts, and gifts. **Eastern Bay Gallery** (✉ Main St., ☎ 207/367–6368) carries contemporary Maine crafts; summer exhibits highlight the works of specific artists. **Firebird Gallery** (✉ W. Main St., ☎ 207/367–0955) sells fine contemporary crafts.

Isle au Haut

㉝   *14 mi south of Stonington.*

Isle au Haut thrusts its steeply ridged back out of the sea south of Stonington. Accessible only by passenger mail boat (☎ 207/367–5193), the island is worth visiting for the ferry ride itself, a half-hour cruise amid the tiny islands of Merchants Row, where you might see terns, guillemots, and harbor seals.

More than half the island is part of **Acadia National Park**: 17½ mi of trails extend through quiet spruce and birch woods, along beaches and seaside cliffs, and over the spine of the central mountain ridge. (For more information on the park, *see* Bar Harbor *and* Acadia National Park.) From mid-June to mid-September, the mail boat docks at **Duck Harbor** within the park. The small campground here, with five lean-tos, is open from mid-May to mid-October and fills up quickly. Reservations, which are essential, can be made after April 1 by writing to Acadia National Park (✉ Box 177, Bar Harbor 04609).

Lodging

$$$$ 🏠 **The Keeper's House.** Thick spruce forest surrounds this converted lighthouse keeper's house on a rock ledge. There is no electricity, but everyone receives a flashlight upon registering; you dine by candlelight and oil chandelier on seafood or chicken and read in the evening by kerosene lantern. Trails link the inn with Acadia National Park's Isle au Haut trail network, and you can walk to the village. The spacious rooms contain simple, painted-wood furniture and local crafts. A separate cottage, the Oil House, has no indoor plumbing. ✉ *Lighthouse Rd. (Box 26, 04645),* ☎ *207/367–2261,* WEB *www.keepershouse.com. 4 rooms without bath, 1 cottage. Dock, bicycles; no air-conditioning, no room phones, no room TVs. No credit cards. Closed Nov.–Apr. FAP.*

Penobscot Bay A to Z

To research prices, get advice from other travelers, and book travel arrangements, visit www.fodors.com.

BIKE TRAVEL

Like many parts of Maine, the roads in this region are narrow, winding and often without shoulders. As in most places on the Maine Coast, it's smart to stay off heavily traveled Route 1. Experienced cyclers should try the back roads around Camden to Belfast or explore the Blue Hill Peninsula region. Islesboro, Vinalhaven, and North Haven islands are popular day trips for cyclists, and traffic is light on both. You can take bicycles on the ferries at an extra fee. Be forewarned that island residents expect cyclists to obey the rules of the road.
➤ BIKE INFORMATION: **Brown Dog Bikes** (✉ 46 Elm. St., Camden, ☎ 207/236–6664, WEB www.browndogbike.com). **Maine Sport Outfitters** (✉ Rte. 1, Rockport, ☎ 207/236–7120 or 888/236–8797, WEB www.mainesport.com). **Old Quarry** (✉ R.R. 1, Box 700, Stonington, ☎ 207/367–8977, WEB www.oldquarry.com).

CAR TRAVEL

U.S. 1 follows the west coast of Penobscot Bay, linking Rockland, Rockport, Camden, Belfast, and Searsport. On the east side of the bay, Route 175 (south from U.S. 1) takes you to Route 166A (for Castine) and Route 15 (for Blue Hill, Deer Isle, and Stonington). A car is essential for exploring the bay area.

EMERGENCIES

➤ HOSPITALS: **Blue Hill Memorial Hospital** (✉ Water St., Blue Hill, ☎ 207/374–2836). **Island Medical Center** (✉ Airport Rd., Stonington, ☎ 207/367–2311). **Penobscot Bay Medical Center** (✉ U.S. 1, Rockport, ☎ 207/596–8000). **Waldo County General Hospital** (✉ 56 Northport Ave., Belfast, ☎ 207/338–2500).

LODGING

Camden Accommodations lists rental cottages and camps from Friendship to Searsport. For rentals on Monhegan Island, call Shining Sails. Coastal Cottage Rental Co. and Peninsula Property Rentals list properties on the Blue Hill Peninsula. For rentals in Stonington, try Island Vacation Rentals.
➤ LODGING: **Camden Accommodations** (✉ 43 Elm St., Camden 04614, ☎ 207/236–6090 or 800/344–4830, WEB www.camdenac.com). **Coastal Cottage Rental Company** (✉ Box 835, Blue Hill 04575, ☎ 207/374–3500, WEB www.vacationcottages.com). **Island Vacation Rentals** (✉ Box 446, Stonington 04681, ☎ 207/367–5095). **Peninsula Property Rentals** (✉ Box 611, Blue Hill 04614, ☎ 207/374–2428). **Shining Sails** (✉ Box 346, Monhegan 044852, ☎ 207/596–0041, WEB www.shiningsails.com).

MEDIA

Daily newspapers serving the region include the *Bangor Daily News,* published Monday–Friday; the *Portland Press Herald,* published Monday–Saturday; and the *Maine Sunday Telegram,* published on Sunday. The *Courier Gazette* (Rockland) is published thrice weekly.

WMEH 90.0 is the local National Public Radio affiliate. WCSH, channel 6, or WLBZ, channel 2, is the NBC affiliate. WMTW, channel 8, or WVII, channel 7, is the ABC affiliate. WGME, channel 13, or WABI, channel 5, is the CBS affiliate. WCBB, channel 10, or WMEB, channel 12, is the Maine Public Broadcasting affiliate.

OUTDOOR ACTIVITIES AND SPORTS

BOATING

For boat rentals, *see* individual listings by town. The Maine Windjammer Association represents 13 windjammers offering multiday sails along the Maine Coast. The Maine Professional Guides Association represents kayaking guides.

➤ CONTACTS: **Maine Windjammer Association** (✉ Box 1144, Blue Hill 04614, ☎ 800/807–9463, WEB www.sailmainecoast.com). **Maine Professional Guides Association** (✉ Box 847, Augusta 04332, ☎ 207/ 549–5631, WEB www.maineguides.org).

VISITOR INFORMATION

➤ CONTACTS: **Belfast Area Chamber of Commerce** (✉ 1 Main St. [Box 58, Belfast 04915], ☎ 207/338–5900, WEB www.belfastmaine.org). **Blue Hill Peninsula Chamber of Commerce** (✉ Box 520, Blue Hill 04614, ☎ 207/374–3242, WEB www.bluehillmaine.com). **Castine Town Office** (✉ Emerson Hall, Court St., Castine 04421, ☎ 207/326–4502). **Deer Isle–Stonington Chamber of Commerce** (✉ Box 459, Stonington 04681, ☎ 207/348–6124, WEB www.deerislemaine.com). **Rockland–Thomaston Area Chamber of Commerce** (✉ Box 508, Harbor Park, Rockland 04841, ☎ 207/596–0376 or 800/562–2529, WEB www. midcoast.com/~rtacc). **Rockport-Camden-Lincolnville Chamber of Commerce** (✉ Public Landing, Box 919, Camden 04843, ☎ 207/ 236–4404 or 800/223–5459, WEB www.camdenme.org). **Waldo County Regional Chamber of Commerce** (✉ School St., Unity 04988, ☎ 207/ 948–5050 or 800/870–9934, WEB palermo.org/wccc).

BANGOR TO MOUNT DESERT ISLAND

Just over an hour from the coast, along the Penobscot River, Bangor anchors northern and eastern Maine. Its plethora of cultural and shopping spots and its convenient access, via Bangor National Airport, make it an ideal starting point for visits to Maine's Great North Woods and Acadia National Park. Acadia is the informal name for the area east of Penobscot Bay that includes Mount Desert Island (pronounced "dessert") as well as Blue Hill Bay and Frenchman Bay. Mount Desert, 13 mi across, is Maine's largest island, and it encompasses most of Acadia National Park, an astonishingly beautiful preserve with rocky cliffs, crashing surf, and serene mountains and ponds. Maine's number one tourist attraction, it draws more than 4 million visitors a year. The 40,000 acres of woods and mountains, lake and shore, footpaths, carriage roads, and hiking trails that make up the park extend to other islands and some of the mainland. Outside the park, on Mount Desert's eastern shore, Bar Harbor has become a busy tourist town. Less commercial and congested are the smaller island towns, such as Southwest Harbor and Northeast Harbor, and the outlying islands.

Bangor

③④ *133 mi northeast of Portland, 46 mi north of Bar Harbor.*

Bangor is Maine's second largest city and the unofficial capital of northern Maine. The city rose to prominence in the 19th century, when its location on the Penobscot River and proximity to the North Woods helped it become the largest lumber port in the world. A 31-ft-tall statue honoring legendary lumberman Paul Bunyan stands in front of the Bangor Auditorium. Today the river is the focus of Bangor's economic redevelopment. Through 2004, the **National Folk Festival,** a free celebration of traditional arts, will take place in the revitalized riverfront and downtown. ☒ ☎ *800/916–6673,* WEB *www.nationalfolkfestival.com.* ☞ *Free.*

☺ The **Maine Discovery Museum,** opened in 2001, is the largest children's museum in the state. It has three floors of interactive and hands-on exhibits. Kids can explore Maine's ecosystem in Nature Trails, travel to foreign countries in Passport to the World, and walk through Maine's literary classics in Booktown, among other displays. ☒ *74 Main St.,* ☎ *207/262–7200,* WEB *www.mainediscoverymuseum.org.* ☞ *$5.50.* ☉ *Tues.–Thurs. and Sat. 9:30–5, Fri. 9:30–8, Sun. 11–5.*

Trained docents lead tours through the beautifully restored **Thomas A. Hill House,** an 1836 Greek Revival home listed on the National Register of Historic Places. ☒ *159 Union St.,* ☎ *207/942–5766.* ☞ *$5.* ☉ *June–Sept., Tues.–Sat. noon–4; Oct.–Dec., weekdays noon–4.*

The **Cole Land Transportation Museum** chronicles the history of transportation in Maine through historical photographs and more than 200 vehicles. ☒ *405 Perry Rd.,* ☎ *207/990–3600,* WEB *www.colemuseum.org.* ☞ *$5.* ☉ *May–mid-Nov., daily 9–5.*

Dining and Lodging

$–$$$$ ✕ **Ichiban.** A calming minimalistic interior, sushi bar, and traditional fare have earned this restaurant a dedicated local following. ☒ *226 3rd St., at Union St.,* ☎ *207/262–9308. MC, V. No lunch Sun.*

$$–$$$ ✕ **J. B. Parker's.** The extensive menu has everything from grilled polenta with a trio of sauces for vegetarians to veal Oscar with lobster, for those who can't decide between meat or fish. White-draped tables and deep red chairs fill the dining areas, local artwork covers the walls, and jazz or classical music is performed live on weekends. ☒ *167 Center St.,* ☎ *207/947–0167. MC, V. Closed Sun. No lunch Sat.*

$$–$$$ ✕ **Thistle's.** Paintings by local artists adorn the walls in this bright storefront restaurant. The diverse menu includes entrées such as Argentinian steak with chimichurri sauce, pickled ginger salmon picatta, and roast duckling. Musicians often perform during dinner. ☒ *175 Exchange St.,* ☎ *207/945–5480. MC, V. Closed Sun.*

$$–$$$$ ☷ **The Lucerne Inn.** Conveniently located midway between Bangor and Ellsworth, a good dining room, and views over Phillips Lake make this country inn a pleasant stop. Every room has a gas fireplace and whirlpool, and most have lake views. ☒ *Rte. 1A (R.R. 3, Box 540, Dedham 04429),* ☎ *207/843–5123 or 900/325–5123,* FAX *207/843–6138,* WEB *www.lucernneinn.com. 21 rooms, 4 suites. Restaurant, cable TV, pool, golf privileges, lounge, meeting rooms; no-smoking rooms. MC, V. CP.*

$$–$$$ ☷ **The Phenix Inn.** Inside a renovated 1873 National Historic Register property in downtown Bangor, this inn has comfortable but plain guest rooms; some overlook the Kenduskeag River. ☒ *20 Broad St., 04401,* ☎ *207/947–0411,* FAX *207/947–0255,* WEB *www.phenixinn.com. 29 rooms, 2 suites, 1 apartment. In-room data ports, cable TV, gym, some pets allowed; no-smoking rooms. AE, D, DC, MC, V. CP.*

The Arts

The **Bangor Symphony Orchestra** (⊠ 44 Central St., ☎ 207/942–
5555 or 800/639–3221) performs at the Bangor Opera House, from
September to April. The **Penobscot Theatre Company** (⊠ 183 Main
St., ☎ 207/942–3333) stages live classic and contemporary plays from
October to May. From mid-July to mid-August, it hosts the **Maine Shake-
speare Festival** on the riverfront.

Ellsworth

③⑤ *140 mi northeast of Portland, 28 mi south of Bangor.*

Ellsworth, the shire town of Hancock county, clogs with traffic during the summer months. Route 1 passes through an inviting downtown
lined with shops and a strip of shopping plazas and factory outlets, including L.L. Bean, between downtown and where Route 3 splits to
Mount Desert.

At the 130-acre **Stanwood Homestead Museum and Bird Sanctuary** you
can hike its trails and visit the 1850 Stanwood House Museum, a Cape
Cod–style house. Cordelia Stanwood, born in 1856, was one of Maine's
earliest ornithologists. ⊠ *Rte. 3,* ☎ *207/667–8460.* ☎ *Free; donations
accepted.* ☉ *Trails daily sunrise–sunset; museum mid-May–mid-Oct.,
daily 10–4.*

Between 1824 and 1828, Col. John Black built **Woodlawn,** an elegant
Georgian mansion. Inside are an especially fine elliptical flying staircase and period artifacts from the three generations of the Black family
who lived here. ⊠ *Rte. 172,* ☎ *207/667–8671.* ☎ *$5.* ☉ *June–mid-
Oct., Mon.–Sat. 10–4:30.*

The **Acadia Zoo** shelters about 45 species of wild and domestic animals, including reindeer, wolves, monkeys, and a moose in its pastures,
streams, and woods. A converted barn serves as a rain-forest habitat
for monkeys, birds, reptiles, and other Amazon creatures. ⊠ *446 Bar
Harbor Rd. (Rte. 3), Trenton,* ☎ *207/667–3244.* ☎ *$7.50.* ☉ *May–
Dec., daily 9:30–dusk.*

Outdoor Activities and Sports

BICYCLING

Bar Harbor Bicycle Shop (⊠ 193 Main St., Ellsworth, ☎ 207/667–6886,
WEB www.barharborbike.com) rents both recreational and high-per-
formance bikes by the half or full day.

Bar Harbor

③⑥ *160 mi northeast of Portland, 22 mi southeast of Ellsworth on Rte. 3.*

An upper-class resort town in the 19th century, Bar Harbor now serves
visitors to Acadia National Park with inns, motels, and restaurants.
Most of its grand mansions were destroyed in a fire that devastated
the island in 1947, but many surviving estates have been converted into
inns and restaurants. Motels abound, yet the town retains the beauty
of a commanding location on Frenchman Bay. Shops, restaurants, and
hotels are clustered along Main, Mount Desert, and Cottage streets.
Take a stroll down West Street, a National Historic District, where you
can see some of the grand cottages that survived the fire.

The **Bar Harbor Historical Society Museum** displays photographs of Bar
Harbor from the days when it catered to the very rich. Other exhibits
document the fire of 1947. ⊠ *33 Ledgelawn Ave.,* ☎ *207/288–3807
or 207/288–0000.* ☎ *Free.* ☉ *June–Oct., Mon.–Sat. 1–4 or by appointment.*

Mount Desert Island

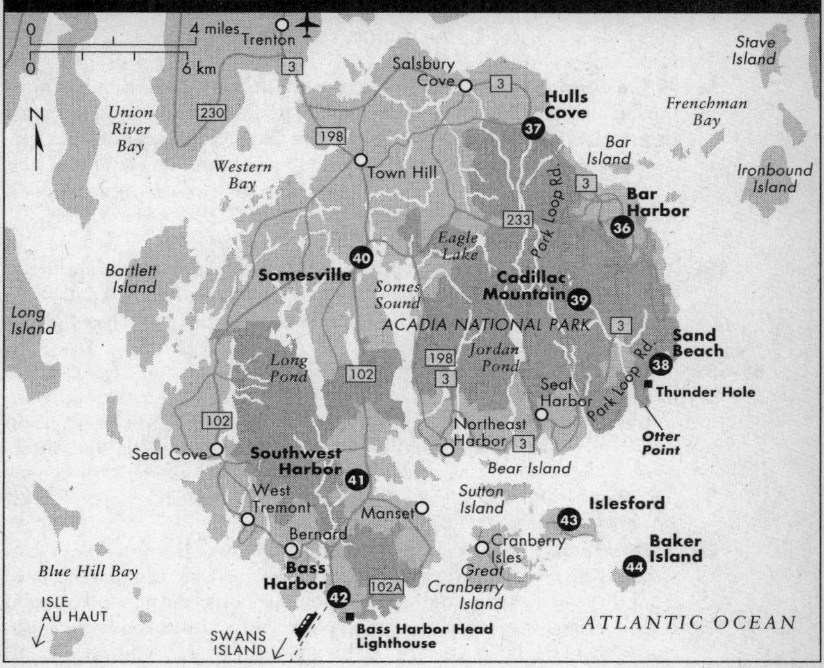

★ The **Abbe Museum,** with its collection of Native American artifacts, opened a new downtown museum in 2001. The museum's collections contain 50,000 objects spanning 10,000 years of Native American history, archaeology, and culture in Maine; many are on display in both permanent and changing exhibitions. A glass-walled archaeological laboratory allows you to observe staff and volunteers working with artifacts found during the museum's scientific excavations. The 1893 building, the former home of the YMCA, is eligible for the National Register of Historic Places. Its facade is an example of the eclectic Shingle Style often used for coastal summer homes at the turn of the 20th century. ✉ *26 Mount Desert St.,* ☎ *207/288–3519,* WEB *www.abbemuseum.org.* 🎟 *$4.50.* ⏲ *Memorial Day–mid-Oct., Sun.–Wed. 10–5, Thurs.–Sat. 10–9; mid-Oct.–Memorial Day, Thurs.–Sun. 10–5.*

☝ The small **Natural History Museum** at the College of the Atlantic has wildlife exhibits, a hands-on discovery room, interpretive programs, and a self-guided nature trail. ✉ *Rte. 3,* ☎ *207/288–5015.* 🎟 *$3.50.* ⏲ *Mid-June–Labor Day, Mon.–Sat. 10–5; Labor Day–mid-June, Thurs.–Fri. and Sun. 1–4, Sat. 10–4.*

Dining and Lodging

$$$$ ★ ✕ **George's.** Candles, flowers, and linens grace the tables, and art fills the walls of the four small dining rooms in this old house. Try the chargrilled swordfish with Mediterranean salsa over couscous or lobster strudel with chanterelle ragout from the prix-fixe menu. Jazz musicians perform nightly in peak season. ✉ *7 Stephen's La.,* ☎ *207/288–4505. AE, D, DC, MC, V. Closed Nov.–mid-June. No lunch.*

$$–$$$$ ★ ✕ **Havana.** Pumpkin-color walls, soft jazz, wood floors, and cloth-covered tables set the tone at this storefront restaurant on the fringe of downtown Bar Harbor. The Latin-influenced menu emphasizes local natural and organic ingredients and changes weekly. The menu may include crab-and-roasted-corn cakes or grilled swordfish, marinated in ginger and lime and finished with a scallion vinaigrette. ⊠ *318 Main St.,* ☎ *207/288–2822. Reservations essential. MC, V. Closed Sun.–Tues. late Oct.–mid-May.*

$$$ ✕ **The Burning Tree.** Fresh is the key word at this casual restaurant just
★   outside town. The ever-changing menu emphasizes seafood and organic produce and chicken; entrées include pan-sautéed monkfish, Cajun lobster, crab au gratin, chicken pot roast, and two or three vegetarian choices. Local contemporary art adorns the walls in the two dining rooms and on the porch. ⊠ *Rte. 3, Otter Creek,* ☎ *207/288–9331. D, MC, V. Closed Tues. and mid-Oct.–late May.*

$$$ ✕ **Mache.** It's the food that's bright at this small, dark bistro. The menu changes twice weekly but might include stew of braised fish and shellfish with organic veggies or crisp rendered duck breast with spiced plum–enriched juice. ⊠ *135 Cottage St.,* ☎ *207/388–0447. MC, V.*

$$–$$$ ✕ **Café This Way.** Jazz, unmatched tables and chairs, and a few couches provide a relaxing background for the creative, internationally inspired menu at this restaurant tucked in a backstreet. You might begin with crab cakes with tequila-lime sauce and then move on to cashew-crusted chicken over sautéed greens with sesame-ginger aioli or perhaps Thai seafood pot. Save room for the homemade desserts. ⊠ *14½ Mount Desert St.,* ☎ *207/288–4483. MC, V.*

$$ ✕ **Thrumcap.** Dark wood and gleaming hardwood floors exude elegance at this casual café and wine bar. You can mix and match plates from three price groupings. Menu choices include shrimp and boursin ravioli, grilled marinated quail with plum sauce, and coconut-fried lobster with black bean and tropical-fruit salsa. ⊠ *123 Cottage St.,* ☎ *207/288–3884. MC, V. Closed Sun. and Nov.–May.*

$$$–$$$$ ✕⛱ **Bar Harbor Inn.** This genteel inn dates from the 1880s. Rooms are spread out over three buildings on nicely landscaped waterfront property, just a short walk from town. Most rooms have balconies, hot tubs, fireplaces, and great views. Rooms in the Oceanfront Lodge have private decks or patios overlooking the ocean, while those in the Newport Lodge, behind it, are more simply furnished and smaller. The formal waterfront Reading Room ($$$–$$$$) serves mostly Continental fare but has such Maine specialties as lobster pie and a scrumptious Indian pudding. ⊠ *Newport Dr., 04609,* ☎ *207/288–3351 or 800/248–3351,* ℻ *207/288–5296,* 🌐 *www.barharborinn.com. 138 rooms, 15 suites. 2 restaurants, cable TV, pool, gym, business services, meeting room; no-smoking rooms. AE, D, DC, MC, V. CP.*

$$$$ ⛱ **Balance Rock Inn.** This grand summer cottage built in 1903 commands a prime, secluded waterfront location but is only two blocks from downtown. Rooms are spacious and meticulously furnished with reproduction pieces—four-poster and canopy beds in guest rooms, crystal chandeliers and a grand piano in common rooms. Some rooms have fireplaces, saunas, steam rooms, or porches; service is thoughtful. ⊠ *21 Albert Meadow, 04609,* ☎ *207/288–2610 or 800/753–0494,* ℻ *207/288–5534,* 🌐 *www.barharborvacations.com. 13 rooms, 1 suite, 3 apartments. In-room data ports, cable TV, in-room VCRs, pool, gym, bar, concierge. AE, D, MC, V. Closed late Oct.–early May. BP.*

$$$–$$$$ ⛱ **Nannau.** For a taste of 19th-century Bar Harbor, stay at this seaside 1904 estate, a National Register property secluded among towering evergreens just 1 mi from downtown Bar Harbor. The shingle-style house is comfortably furnished with period pieces and fabrics and wallpapers. All rooms have ocean views; two have fireplaces. The 4-acre property borders Compass Harbor and a section of Acadia National Park. ⊠ *396 Lower Main St. (Box 710, 04609),* ☎ *207/288–5575,* 🌐 *www.nannau.com. 3 rooms, 1 suite. No air-conditioning,*

no in-room TVs, no in-room phones, no smoking. MC, V. Closed Nov.–June. BP.

$$$–$$$$ 🖼 **Sunset on West.** Contemporary artwork fills this 1960 cottage over-
★   looking Bar Island and Frenchman's Bay. Some of the carefully appointed
rooms have porches, fireplaces, and whirlpool tubs; most have water
views. ✉ *115 West St., 04609,* ☎ *207/288–4242 or 877/406–4242,*
FAX *207/288–4545,* WEB *www.sunsetonwest.com. 2 rooms, 2 suites.
Cable TV, in-room VCRs; no kids under 16. MC, V. BP.*

$$$–$$$$ 🖼 **Ullikana.** Inside the stucco-and-timber walls of this traditional
★   Tudor cottage, the interior juxtaposes antiques with contemporary coun-
try pieces, vibrant color with French country wallpapers, and abstract
art with folk creations. The combination not only works—it shines.
Rooms are large, many have fireplaces, and some have decks. Break-
fast is an elaborate multicourse affair. The refurbished Yellow House
across the drive has six additional rooms decorated in traditional Old
Bar Harbor style. ✉ *16 The Field, 04609,* ☎ *207/288–9552,* FAX *207/
288–3682,* WEB *www.ullikana.com. 16 rooms. No air-conditioning in
some rooms, no kids, no smoking. MC, V. Closed Nov.–May. BP.*

$$ 🖼 **Cromwell Harbor Motel.** Less than 1 mi from downtown Bar Harbor is this clean and pleasant motel set amidst pretty gardens. You can
walk to a quiet section of Acadia National Park. ✉ *359 Main St., 04069,*
☎ *207/288–3201 or 800/544–3201,* WEB *www.cromwellharbor.com.
24 rooms. Cable TV, some refrigerators, some microwaves, pool; no-
smoking rooms. MC, V.*

$$ 🖼 **Seacroft Inn.** It's an easy walk to town or the Shore Path from this
rambling multigabled inn, which is a good choice for families. One room
has a fireplace, another a kitchen, yet another a private deck. A break-
fast basket is delivered to your room each morning. ✉ *18 Albert
Meadow, 04609,* ☎ *207/288–4669 or 800/824–9694. 3 rooms, 1
with bath; 1 suite; 1 studio; 1 efficiency. Cable TV, microwaves, re-
frigerators. MC, V. CP.*

Nightlife and the Arts

For dancing, try **Carmen Verandah** (✉ 119 Main St., upstairs, ☎ 207/
288–2766); the venue also hosts live blues, jazz, reggae, rock, and pop
bands. The art deco–style **Criterion Theater** (✉ 35 Cottage St., ☎ 207/
288–3441) stages concerts, movies, and theatrical performances.
Geddy's Pub (✉ 19 Main St., ☎ 207/288–5077) has live entertain-
ment early in the evening followed by a DJ spinning discs. At the **Lom-
poc Cafe & Brewpub** (✉ 30 Rodick St., ☎ 207/288–9513) you can
relax in a garden setting and play a game of boccie. Comfortable
chairs, pizza, and beer make the viewing easy at **Reel Pizza Cinerama**
(✉ 33-B Kennebec Pl., ☎ 207/288–3811).

Arcady Music Festival (☎ 207/288–3151) schedules concerts (primar-
ily classical) at locations around Mount Desert Island and at some off-
island sites, year-round. **Bar Harbor Music Festival** (✉ 59 Cottage St.,
☎ 207/288–5744) arranges jazz, chamber music, string-orchestra,
and pop concerts by young professionals from July to early August.

Outdoor Activities and Sports

BIKING

Acadia Bike & Canoe (✉ 48 Cottage St., ☎ 207/288–9605 or 800/526–
8615) rents and sells mountain bikes. **Bar Harbor Bicycle Shop** (✉ 141
Cottage St., ☎ 207/288–3886 or 800/824–2453) rents both recreational
and high-performance bikes by the half or full day.

BOATING

Acadia Bike & Canoe rents canoes and sea kayaks. **National Park Sea
Kayak Tours** (✉ 39 Cottage St., ☎ 207/288–0342 or 800/347–0940)
leads guided kayak tours. **Coastal Kayaking Tours** (✉ 48 Cottage St.,

☎ 207/288–9605 or 800/526–8615) conducts tours led by registered Maine guides. The four-mast schooner *Margaret Todd* (⊠ Bar Harbor Inn Pier, ☎ 207/288–4585) operates 1½- to 2-hour tours daily between mid-May and October.

STATE PARK

On Frenchman Bay but off Mount Desert Island, the 55-acre **Lamoine State Park** (⊠ Rte. 184, Lamoine, ☎ 207/667–4778) has a boat-launching ramp, a fishing pier, a children's playground, and a 61-site campground that's open mid-May–mid-October.

WHALE-WATCHING

Acadian Whale Watcher (⊠ Golden Anchor Pier, 52 West St., ☎ 207/288–9794 or 800/421–3307) runs 3½-hour whale-watching cruises from June to mid-October. **Bar Harbor Whale Watch Co.** (⊠ 1 West St., ☎ 207/288–3322 or 800/508–1499) operates the catamaran *Friendship V,* for whale-watching, and the *Katherine,* for lobster fishing and seal watching.

Shopping

Bar Harbor in summer is prime territory for browsing for gifts, T-shirts, and novelty items. For bargains, head for the outlets that line Route 3 in Ellsworth, which have good discounts on shoes, sportswear, cookware, and more.

The **Alone Moose–Fine Crafts** (⊠ 78 West St., ☎ 207/288–4229) has art glass and works in clay, pottery, wood, and fiberglass. Pick up a treat for your pet at **Bark Harbor** (⊠ 200 Main St., ☎ 207/288–0404), a specialty shop for pet owners. **Ben and Bill's Chocolate Emporium** (⊠ 66 Main St., ☎ 207/288–3281) is a chocolate lover's nirvana; the adventurous should try the lobster ice cream. **Birdsnest Gallery** (⊠ 12 Mount Desert St., ☎ 207/288–4054) sells fine art, paintings, and sculpture. The **Eclipse Gallery** (⊠ 12 Mount Desert St., ☎ 207/288–9048) carries handblown glass, ceramics, art photography, and wood furniture. **Island Artisans** (⊠ 99 Main St., ☎ 207/288–4214) sells basketry, pottery, fiber work, and jewelry created by Maine-based artisans. **Songs of the Sea** (⊠ 47 West St., ☎ 207/288–5653) specializes in folk music and sells handcrafted Irish, Scottish, and world instruments.

Acadia National Park

4 mi northwest of Bar Harbor (to Hulls Cove).

There is no one Acadia. The park holds some of the most spectacular and varied scenery on the eastern seaboard: a rugged coastline of surf-pounded granite and an interior graced by sculpted mountains, quiet ponds, and lush deciduous forests. Cadillac Mountain, the highest point of land on the eastern coast, dominates the park. Although it's rugged, Acadia National Park also has graceful stone bridges, horse-drawn carriages, and the elegant Jordan Point Tea House. The 27-mi Park Loop Road provides an excellent introduction, yet to truly appreciate the park you must get off the main road and experience it by walking, biking, or taking a carriage ride on the carriage trails, by hiking or perhaps sea kayaking. If you get off the beaten path, you'll find places in the park that you can have practically to yourself, despite the millions of visitors who descend in summer.

★ ❸❼ The popular **Hulls Cove** approach to Acadia National Park, northwest of Bar Harbor on Route 3, brings you to the start of the **Park Loop Road.** Even though it is often clogged with traffic in summer, the road provides the best introduction to the park. You can drive it in an hour, but allow at least half a day or more to explore the many sites along the route. At the start of the loop, the visitor center shows a free 15-minute orientation film. Acadia Rangers lead nature walks, children's programs, mountain hikes, photography programs, and evening talks. A schedule of programs is available here. You can also pick up the *Acadia Beaver Log* (the park's free newspaper detailing guided hikes and other ranger-led programs), books, maps of hiking trails and carriage roads, the schedule for naturalist-led tours, and cassettes for drive-it-yourself tours. Traveling south on the Park Loop Road, you'll reach a small ticket booth where you pay the $10-per-vehicle entrance fee, good for seven consecutive days. ⊠ *Visitor center, Park Loop Rd. off Rte. 3, ☎ 207/288–3338,* WEB *www.nps.gov/acad. ☉ Park daily. Visitor center mid-June–Aug., daily 8–6; mid-Apr.–mid-June and Sept.–Oct., daily 8–4:30.*

㊳ Sand Beach is a small stretch of pink sand backed by the mountains of Acadia and the odd lump of rock known as the Beehive. The **Ocean Trail,** which runs alongside the Park Loop Road from Sand Beach to the Otter Point parking area, is an easily accessible walk with some of the most awesome scenery in Maine: huge slabs of pink granite heaped at the ocean's edge, ocean views unobstructed to the horizon, and Thunder Hole, a natural seaside cave into which the ocean rushes and roars.

★ **㊴ Cadillac Mountain,** at 1,532 ft, is the highest point on the eastern seaboard. From the smooth, bald summit you have an awesome 360-degree view of the ocean, islands, jagged coastline, and woods and lakes of Acadia and its surroundings. You can drive or hike to the summit.

The original **Abbé Museum** (a larger museum opened in downtown Bar Harbor in 2001) displays Maine's Native American history with arrowheads, moccasins, tools, jewelry, and a well-documented collection of baskets. ⊠ *Sieur de Monts Spring exit from Rte. 3 or Acadia National Park Loop Rd., ☎ 207/288–3519.* ▦ *$2. ☉ July–Aug., daily 9–5; late May–June and Sept.–late Oct., daily 10–4.*

The **Wild Gardens of Acadia** present a miniature view of the plants that grow on Mount Desert Island. ⊠ *Rte. 3 at the Sieur de Monts Spring exit, ☎ 207/288–3400.* ▦ *Free.*

Dining and Lodging

$$–$$$ ✕ **Jordan Pond House.** Come for tea and the oversize popovers with homemade strawberry jam and ice cream, a century-old tradition at this restaurant overlooking Jordan Pond. If you choose to sit on the terrace or lawn, be forewarned that bees are more than a nuisance. The menu has both lunch and dinner items, including lobster stew, but these get mixed reviews. ⊠ *Park Loop Rd., ☎ 207/276–3316. AE, D, MC, V. Closed late Oct.–mid-May.*

$ ⚠ **Blackwoods and Seawall.** These two campgrounds with a total of 530 campsites, fill up quickly during the summer. Space at Seawall is a first-come, first-served basis, starting at 8 AM. Reservations for a May 1–October visit to Blackwoods can be made four months in advance. *Blackwoods:* ⊠ *Rte. 3, Otter Creek, ☎ 800/365–2267. ☉ Year-round. Seawall:* ⊠ *Rte. 102A, Southwest Harbor, ☎ 207/244–3600. Closed late Sept.–late May.*

Outdoor Activities and Sports

BIKING

The carriage roads that wind through the woods and fields of Acadia National Park are ideal for biking and jogging when the ground is dry and for cross-country skiing in winter. You can pick up trail maps at the Hulls Cove Visitor Center.

HIKING

Acadia National Park maintains nearly 200 mi of foot and carriage paths, from easy strolls along flatlands to rigorous climbs that involve ladders and hand holds on rock faces. Among the more rewarding hikes are the Precipice Trail to Champlain Mountain, the Great Head Loop, the Gorham Mountain Trail, and the path around Eagle Lake. The Hulls Cove Visitor Center has trail guides and maps and will help you match a trail with your interests and abilities.

Around Acadia

There's plenty to explore on Mount Desert Island beyond the 27-mi Park Loop Road. You can continue an auto tour of the island by heading west on Route 233 for the villages on Somes Sound, a true fjord—the only one on the East Coast—that almost bisects the island.

40 **Somesville,** the oldest settlement on the island (1621), is a carefully preserved New England village of white clapboard houses and churches, neat green lawns, and bits of blue water visible behind them.

41 **Southwest Harbor,** south from Somesville on Route 102, combines the salty character of a working port with the refinements of a summer resort community. From the town's Main Street (Route 102), turn left onto Clark Point Road to reach the harbor.

Mount Desert Oceanarium has exhibits in two locations on the fishing and sea life of the Gulf of Maine, a live-seal program, a lobster hatchery, and hands-on exhibits such as a touch tank. ⊠ *Clark Point Rd., Southwest Harbor,* ☎ *207/244–7330;* ⊠ *Rte. 3, Thomas Bay, Bar Harbor,* ☎ *207/288–5005.* ▣ *Call for admission fees (combination tickets available).* ☉ *Mid-May–late Oct., Mon.–Sat. 9–5.*

Wendell Gilley Museum of Bird Carving showcases bird carvings by Gilley, has carving demonstrations and workshops and natural-history programs, and exhibits wildlife art. ⊠ *4 Herrick Rd., Southwest Harbor,* ☎ *207/244–7555,* WEB *www.acadia.net/gilley.* ▣ *$3.50.* ☉ *July–Aug., Tues.–Sun. 10–5; June and Sept.–Oct., Tues.–Sun. 10–4; May and Nov.–Dec., Fri.–Sun. 10–4.*

42 **Bass Harbor,** 4 mi south of Southwest Harbor (follow Route 102A when Route 102 forks), is a tiny lobstering village with cottages for rent, inns, a restaurant, and a gift shop. You can visit the **Bass Harbor Head lighthouse,** which clings to a cliff at the eastern entrance to Blue Hill Bay. It was built in 1858. Also here is the **Maine State Ferry Service**'s car-and-passenger ferry (☎ 207/244–3254), which travels to Swans Island and Frenchboro.

Dining and Lodging

$–$$$ ✕ **Beal's Lobster Pier.** You can watch lobstermen bring in their catch at this working lobster pound. Order lobster at one take-out window and fried foods, burgers, and dessert at another. ⊠ *End of Clark Point Rd., Southwest Harbor,* ☎ *207/244–3202, 207/244–7178, or 800/244–7178. AE, MC, V. Closed mid-Oct.–mid-May.*

$–$$ ✕ **Seaweed Café.** This unpretentious restaurant serves natural and organic seafood with an Asian touch. Entrées include sushi, sashimi, and noodle dishes. ⊠ *Rte. 102, Southwest Harbor,* ☎ *207/244–0572. Reservations essential. No credit cards. Closed Sun.–Tues. No lunch.*

$$$ ⊡ **Claremont Hotel.** Built in 1884 and operated continuously as an inn, the Claremont calls up memories of the long, leisurely vacations of days gone by. The inn commands a view of Somes Sound. Croquet is played on the lawn, and cocktails and lunch are served at the Boat House in summer. Rooms are simply—some would say sparsely—decorated;

cottages are more rustic. The menu in the water-view dining room, open to the public for breakfast and dinner, changes weekly; reservations are essential, and a jacket is required for dinner. ⌂ *Off Clark Point Rd. (Box 137, Southwest Harbor 04679),* ☎ *207/244–5036 or 800/ 244–5036,* FAX *207/244–3512,* WEB *www.theclaremont.com. 30 rooms, 2 suites, 14 cottages. Restaurant, tennis court, dock, boating, bicycles, croquet; no air-conditioning, no phones in some rooms, no room TVs, no smoking. No credit cards. Hotel and restaurant closed mid-Oct.– mid-June; cottages closed Nov.–mid-May. BP, MAP.*

$$ ⌂ **Island House.** This sweet B&B on the quiet side of the island has four simple and bright rooms in the main house. The carriage-house suite comes complete with a sleeping loft and a kitchenette. ⌂ *121 Clark Point Rd. (Box 1006, Southwest Harbor 04679),* ☎ *207/244–5180,* WEB *www.acadia.net/islandhouse. 4 rooms, 1 suite. No air-condition- ing, no room phones, no room TVs, no kids under 5, no smoking. MC, V. BP.*

$–$$ ⌂ **Moorings Inn & Cottages.** Nothing is fancy here except the jaw-drop- ping view of Somes Sound. The main house dates to the late 18th cen- tury, its rooms decorated with antiques and country touches. The rooms in the attached motel wing lack the appointments of the main house but have sliding glass doors onto decks. The homey cottages have the most privacy and offer cooking facilities. Lookout Front has a fire- place, screened porch, and king-size bed. ⌂ *135 Shore Rd., Manset (Box 744, Southwest Harbor 04679),* ☎ *207/244–5523, 207/244–3210, or 800/596–5523,* WEB *www.mooringsinn.com. 13 rooms, 5 cottages, 1 apartment. Some refrigerators, some microwaves, dock, bicycling, boating; no air-conditioning, no room phones, no room TVs. No credit cards. Closed mid-Oct.–mid-May. CP.*

Outdoor Activities and Sports

BIKING

Southwest Cycle (⌂ Main St., Southwest Harbor, ☎ 207/244–5856) rents bicycles.

BOATING

Manset Yacht Service (⌂ Shore Rd., Manset, ☎ 207/244–4040) char- ters powerboats and sailboats. **Mansell Boat and Marine** (⌂ Rte. 102A, Manset, ☎ 207/244–5625) rents small powerboats and sailboats. **Na- tional Park Canoe and Kayak Rentals** (⌂ Pretty Marsh Rd., Somesville, at the head of Long Pond, ☎ 207/244–5854) rents canoes and kayaks. **Island Cruises** (⌂ Shore Rd., Bass Harbor, ☎ 207/244–5785) takes pas- sengers on a 40-ft lobster boat through the islands of Blue Hill Bay.

Shopping

E. L. Higgins (⌂ Bernard Rd., off Rte. 102, Bernard, ☎ 207/244– 3983) carries antique wicker, furniture, and glassware. **Marianne Clark Fine Antiques** (⌂ Main St., Southwest Harbor, ☎ 207/244–9247) sells formal and country furniture, American paintings, and accessories from the 18th and 19th centuries. **Port in a Storm Bookstore** (⌂ 1112 Main St., Somesville, ☎ 207/244–4114) stocks well-chosen inventory and is conducive to browsing, with soaring ceilings and comfy chairs.

Excursions to the Cranberry Isles

Off the southeast shore of Mount Desert Island at the entrance to Somes Sound, the five Cranberry Isles—Great Cranberry, Islesford (or Little Cranberry), Baker Island, Sutton Island, and Bear Island—escape the hubbub that engulfs Acadia National Park in summer. Sutton and Bear islands are privately owned. The **Beal & Bunker passenger ferry** (☎ 207/244–3575) serves Great Cranberry from Northeast Harbor. **Cranberry Cove Boating Company** (☎ 207/244–5882) serves Great

Cranberry, Sutton, and Islesford from Southwest Harbor. Baker Island is reached by the summer cruise boats of the **Islesford Ferry Company** (☎ 207/276–3717) from Northeast Harbor.

❹❸ **Islesford** comes closest to having a village: a collection of houses, a church, a fishermen's co-op, a market, and a post office near the ferry dock.

The **Islesford Historical Museum,** run by Acadia National Park, has displays of tools and documents relating to the island's history. ⊠ *Islesford,* ☎ *207/244–9224.* ⊡ *Free.* ☉ *Mid-June–late Sept., daily 10–noon and 12:30–4:30.*

❹❹ The 123-acre **Baker Island,** the most remote of the Cranberry Isles, looks almost black from a distance because of its thick spruce forest. The Islesford Ferry cruise boat from Northeast Harbor conducts a 4½-hour narrated tour, during which you are likely to see ospreys, harbor seals, and cormorants. Because Baker Island has no natural harbor, you take a fishing dory to get to shore.

Bangor to Mount Desert Island A to Z

To research prices, get advice from other travelers, and book travel arrangements, visit www.fodors.com.

BUS TRAVEL
The free Island Explorer shuttle services the entire island from mid-June through Labor Day. Concord Trailways operates shuttle service from Bangor airport to Bar Harbor with stops in Bangor and Ellsworth. Greyhound Bus Lines services Bangor. Vermont Transit services Bangor and Bar Harbor. Downeast Transportation operates buses from Ellsworth to various locations on Mount Desert, Bangor, the Schoodic Peninsula, and the Blue Hill Peninsula.
➤ BUS INFORMATION: Concord Trailways (☎ 207/942–8686 or 888/741–8686, ⓦⓔⓑ www.concordtrailways.com). Downeast Transportation (☎ 207/667–5796). Greyhound Bus Lines (☎ 800/231–2222, ⓦⓔⓑ www.greyhound.com). Island Explorer (☎ 207/667–5796). Vermont Transit (☎ 207/772–6587 or 800/451–3292, ⓦⓔⓑ www.vermonttransit.com).

CAR TRAVEL
Route 1A east connects Bangor to Route 1 in Ellsworth. Route 3 leads to Mount Desert Island. North of Bar Harbor, the scenic 27-mi Park Loop Road leaves Route 3 to circle the eastern quarter of Mount Desert Island, with one-way traffic from Sieur de Monts Spring to Seal Harbor and two-way traffic between Seal Harbor and Hulls Cove. Route 102, which serves the western half of Mount Desert, is reached from Route 3 just after it enters the island or from Route 233 west from Bar Harbor. All these island roads pass through the precincts of Acadia National Park.

EMERGENCIES
➤ HOSPITALS: **Eastern Maine Medical Center** (⊠ 489 State St., Bangor, ☎ 207/973–8000). **Maine Coast Memorial Hospital** (⊠ 50 Union St., Ellsworth, ☎ 207/667–5311). **Mount Desert Island Hospital** (⊠ 10 Wayman La., Bar Harbor, ☎ 207/288–5081). **Southwest Harbor Medical Center** (⊠ Herrick Rd., Southwest Harbor, ☎ 207/244–5513).

LODGING
Maine Island Properties lists private home rentals throughout the Acadia region. Mount Desert Properties specializes in private home rentals in the Mount Desert region. The Davis Agency has properties on the island as well as from Blue Hill to Hancock.

➤ LODGING: **The Davis Agency** (✉ 363 Main St., Southwest Harbor 04679, ☎ 207/244–3891, WEB www.daagy.com). **Maine Island Properties** (✉ Box 1025, Mount Desert 04660, ☎ 207/244–4348, WEB www.maineislandproperties.com). **Mount Desert Properties** (✉ Box 536, Bar Harbor 04609, ☎ 207/288–4523, WEB www.barharborvacationhome.com).

MEDIA

Daily newspapers serving the region include the *Bangor Daily News,* published Monday–Friday. Weekly papers include the *Bar Harbor Times, Ellsworth American,* and *Ellsworth Weekly.*

Community radio station WERU 89.9 FM in Blue Hill has eclectic programming. WMEH 90.0 is the local National Public Radio affiliate. WLBZ, channel 2, is the NBC affiliate. WVII, channel 7, is the ABC affiliate. WABI, channel 5, is the CBS affiliate. WMEB, channel 12, is the Maine Public Broadcasting affiliate.

OUTDOOR ACTIVITIES AND SPORTS
BOATING
For boat rentals, *see* listings by town. The Maine Professional Guides Association represents kayaking guides.
➤ CONTACT: **Maine Professional Guides Association** (✉ Box 847, Augusta 04332, ☎ 207/549–5631, WEB www.maineguides.org).

TOURS
Acadia National Park Tours operates a 2½-hour bus tour of Acadia National Park, narrated by a naturalist, from May to October, and 2½-hour narrated trolley tours. Bar Harbor Taxi and Tours conducts half-day historic and scenic tours of the area. Downeast Nature Tours leads personalized and small-group tours highlighting the island's flora and fauna.

Acadia Air, on Route 3 in Trenton, between Ellsworth and Bar Harbor at Hancock County Airport, rents aircraft and flies seven aerial sightseeing routes, from spring to fall. A Step Back in Time uses Victorian-costumed guides to lead walking tours that highlight the 1890s in Bar Harbor. Tours leave from 48 Cottage Street.
➤ CONTACTS: **A Step Back in Time** (☎ 207/288–9605). **Acadia Air** (☎ 207/667–5534). **Acadia National Park Tours** (☎ 207/288–3327). **Bar Harbor Taxi and Tours** (☎ 207/288–4020). **Downeast Nature Tours** (☎ 207/288–8128).

VISITOR INFORMATION
➤ CONTACTS: **Acadia National Park** (✉ Box 177, Bar Harbor 04609, ☎ 207/288–3338, WEB www.nps.gov/acad). **Bangor Convention and Visitors Bureau** (✉ 115 Main St., Bangor 04401, ☎ 207/947–5205 or 800/926–6673, WEB www.bangorcvb.org). **Bangor Region Chamber of Commerce** (✉ 519 Main St., Bangor 04401, ☎ 207/947–0307, WEB www.bangorregion.com). **Bar Harbor Chamber of Commerce** (✉ 93 Cottage St. [Box 158, Bar Harbor 04609], ☎ 207/288–3393, 207/288–5103, or 800/288–5103, WEB www.barharborinfo.com). **Southwest Harbor/Tremont Chamber of Commerce** (✉ Main St. [Box 1143, Southwest Harbor 04679], ☎ 207/244–9264 or 800/423–9264, WEB www.acadiachamber.com).

WAY DOWN EAST

East of Ellsworth on U.S. 1 is a different Maine, a place pretty much off the beaten path that seduces with a rugged, simple beauty. Red-hued blueberry barrens dot the landscape, and scraggly jack pines hug the highly accessible shoreline. The quiet pleasures include hiking, birding, and going on whale-watching and puffin cruises. Many artists live in the region; you can often purchase works directly from them.

Hancock

45 *9 mi east of Ellsworth.*

As you approach the small town of Hancock and the summer colony of cottages at Hancock Point, stunning views await, especially at sunset, over Frenchman Bay toward Mount Desert.

Dining and Lodging

$$$$ ✕▥ **Le Domaine.** Owner-chef Nicole L. Purslow whips up classic French haute cuisine ($$$–$$$$; closed Sun.–Mon.), the perfect accompaniments to which can be found amid the more than 5,000 bottles of French wine in the restaurant's cellar. Le Domaine is known primarily for its food, but its Provence-inspired guest rooms are also inviting; the two suites have fireplaces. Although the building fronts on U.S. 1, the rooms open to private decks overlooking the perennial gardens, private pond, and trails that meander the property's 100 acres, and the building is well insulated to block out road noise. ✉ U.S. 1 (HC 77, Box 496, 04640), ☎ 207/422–3395 or 800/554–8498, FAX 207/422–2316, WEB www.ledomaine.com. 5 rooms, 2 suites. Restaurant, in-room data ports, hiking, some pets allowed (fee); no room TVs. AE, D, MC, V. Closed late Oct.–mid-June. BP.

$$$ ✕▥ **Crocker House Inn.** Set amid tall fir trees, this century-old shingle-style cottage is a mere 200 yards from the water and holds comfortable rooms decorated with antiques and country furnishings. The accommodations in the Carriage House, which also has a TV room and a hot tub, are best for families. The inn's dining room ($$$), which serves New American cuisine, draws Maine residents from as far away as Bar Harbor. ✉ Hancock Point Rd. (HC 77, Box 171, 04640), ☎ 207/422–6806 or 877/715–6017, FAX 207/422–3105, WEB www.crockerhouse.com. 11 rooms. Restaurant, hot tub, bicycles, some pets allowed; no smoking. AE, D, MC, V. BP.

Nightlife and the Arts

Pierre Monteux School for Conductors (✉ off U.S. 1, ☎ 207/422–3931) presents orchestral and chamber concerts from mid-June through mid-August.

Shopping

Hog Bay Pottery (✉ 245 Hog Bay Rd., Franklin, ☎ 207/565–2282) sells pottery by Charles Grosjean and handwoven rugs by Susanne Grosjean. **Spring Woods Gallery** (✉ 40-A Willowbrook La., Sullivan, ☎ 207/422–3006) carries contemporary art by Paul and Ann Breeden and other artists, as well as Native American pottery, jewelry, and instruments. **Sullivan Harbor Farm** (✉ U.S. 1, Sullivan, ☎ 207/422–3735 or 800/422–4014) cold-smokes salmon in the traditional Scottish manner. **Sullivan Harbor Gallery** (✉ Town Office Building, U.S. 1, Sullivan, ☎ no phone) displays the work of local artisans.

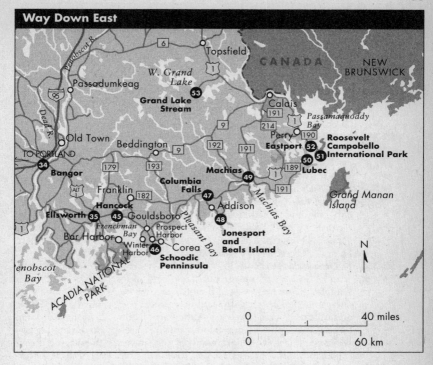

Way Down East

Schoodic Peninsula

46 *23 mi southeast of Hancock, 32 mi east of Ellsworth.*

The landscape of the Schoodic Peninsula makes it easy to understand why the overflow from Bar Harbor's wealthy summer population settled in Winter Harbor: the views over Frenchman's Bay to Mount Desert, the craggy coastline, and the towering evergreens. A drive through the community of Grindstone Neck shows what Bar Harbor might have been like before the Great Fire of 1947. Artists and craftspeople have opened galleries in and around Winter Harbor. No visit to Winter Harbor is complete without a stop at **Gerrish's Store** (⊠ Main St., ☎ 207/963–5575), which has an old-fashioned ice cream counter.

★ The Schoodic section of **Acadia National Park** (⊠ off Rte. 186, ☎ 207/288–3338), 2 mi east of Winter Harbor, has a scenic 6½-mi one-way loop that edges around the tip of the peninsula and yields views of Winter Harbor, Grindstone Neck, and Winter Harbor Lighthouse. At the tip of the point, huge slabs of pink granite lie jumbled along the shore, thrashed unmercifully by the crashing surf, and jack pines cling to life amid the rocks. The Fraser Point Day-Use Area at the beginning of the loop is an ideal place for a picnic. Work off your lunch with a hike up Schoodic Head for the panoramic views up and down the coast. Admission is free.

Prospect Harbor, on Route 186 northeast of Winter Harbor, is a small fishing village nearly untouched by tourism. There's little to do in **Corea,** at the tip of Route 195, other than watch the fishermen at work, pick your way over stone beaches, or gaze out to sea—and that's what makes it so special. **Petit Manan National Wildlife Refuge** (⊠ Pigeon Hill Rd. off Rte. 1, ☎ 207/546–2124) is a 2,166-acre refuge of fields, forest, and rocky shorefront on the peninsula east of Schoodic. You can explore the property on two walking trails; the wildlife viewing and bird-watching is renowned. Admission is free, parking is limited.

Dining and Lodging

$$$$ ✕ **Kitchen Garden.** This restaurant just off U.S. 1 in an old Cape Cod–style house is a wonderful surprise. The five-course, fixed-price menu emphasizes organic foods, home-grown produce, and Jamaican specialties. Bring your own wine or beer. ⊠ *335 Village Rd., Steuben,* ☎ *207/546–2708. Reservations essential. No credit cards. Closed July–Aug. Mon.–Tues. and Sept.–June. No lunch.*

$$–$$$ ✕ **Fisherman's Inn.** The menu at this popular establishment emphasizes local foods and wines. The house specialty is lobster pie, but beef, chicken, seafood, and Italian dishes also appear on the menu. ⊠ *7 Newman St., Winter Harbor,* ☎ *207/963–5585. AE, D, MC, V. Closed mid-Oct.–Memorial Day.*

$–$$ ✕ **West Bay Lobsters in the Rough.** Lobsters, steamers, corn-on-the-cob, coleslaw, baked beans, and homemade blueberry pie are among the dishes served. Eat at the outdoor tables or set up a picnic on nearby Schoodic Point. ⊠ *Rte. 186, Prospect Harbor,* ☎ *207/963–7021. AE, D, DC, MC, V. Closed Nov.–May.*

$$–$$$ ▤ **Oceanside Meadows.** Inspired by the ocean out the front door; fields,
★ woods, and a salt marsh out back; and moose, eagles, and other wildlife, the owners created the Institute for the Arts and Sciences, an environmental center with lectures, musical performances, art shows, and other events held weekly in the barn. Rooms, furnished with antiques, country pieces, and family treasures, are spread out among two white clapboard buildings; many have ocean views. Breakfast is an extravagant multicourse affair. ⊠ *Corea Rd. (Rte. 195), Prospect Harbor 04669,* ☎ *207/963–5557,* FAX *207/963–5928,* WEB *www.oceaninn.com. 12 rooms, 3 suites. Boating, croquet, hiking, horseshoes, beach, concert hall, Internet, meeting rooms, some pets allowed (fee); no air-conditioning, no room TVs, no-smoking rooms. AE, D, MC, V. Closed Nov.–Apr. BP.*

$$ ▤ **Black Duck.** This small bed-and-breakfast has comfortable public areas and guest rooms, tastefully decorated with antiques and art. Two tiny cottages perch on the harbor. ⊠ *Crowley Island Rd., Corea 04624,* ☎ *207/963–2689 or 877/963–2689,* FAX *207/963–7495,* WEB *www.blackduck.com. 2 rooms, 1 suite, 2 cottages. No air-conditioning, no room phones, no room TVs, no kids ages 1–8, no smoking. MC, V. Closed Nov.–Mar. BP.*

$ ▤ **The Pines.** This motel's location, right at the beginning of the Schoodic Point Loop, makes it a good value. The property includes a motel, cottages, and log cabins, all with hand-stitched quilts. ⊠ *17 Rte. 186, Winter Harbor 04693,* ☎ *207/963–2296,* WEB *www.ayuh.net. 3 rooms, 4 cottages, 2 cabins. Snack bar, cable TV, some kitchenettes, playground; no air-conditioning. MC, V.*

Outdoor Activities and Sports

Moose Look Guide Service (⊠ Rte. 186, Gouldsboro, ☎ 207/963–7720) provides kayak tours and rentals, rowboat and canoe rentals, and bike rentals; it also conducts guided fishing trips and all-terrain-vehicle tours.

Shopping

The wines sold at the **Bartlett Maine Estate Winery** (⊠ off Rte. 1, Gouldsboro, ☎ 207/546–2408) are produced from locally grown apples, pears, blueberries, and other fruit. **Lee Art Glass Studio** (⊠ Main St., Winter Harbor, ☎ 207/963–7004) carries fused-glass tableware and other items. **U.S. Bells** (⊠ Rte. 186, Prospect Harbor, ☎ 207/963–7184) produces hand-cast bronze wind and door bells. **Works of Hand**

(✉ 430 Main St., Winter Harbor, ☎ 207/963–2547) is a basket-making shop that also carries the works of local artisans.

Columbia Falls

47 *41 mi east of Ellsworth, 78 mi west of Calais.*

Columbia Falls, founded in the late 18th century, is a small, pretty village on the Pleasant River. Once a prosperous shipbuilding center, it still has a number of stately homes dating from that era.

★ Judge Thomas Ruggles, a wealthy lumber dealer, store owner, postmaster, and Justice of the Court of Sessions, built **Ruggles House** in 1818. The house's distinctive Federal architecture, flying staircase, Palladian window, and woodwork were crafted over a period of three years by Massachusetts wood-carver Alvah Peterson with a penknife. ✉ *Main St.,* ☎ *207/483–4637.* ⌑ *$3 donation requested.* ⊙ *June–mid-Oct., weekdays 9:30–4:30, Sun. 11–4:30.*

Lodging

$ 🏨 **Pleasant Bay Inn and Llama Keep.** This Cape Cod–style inn takes advantage of its riverfront location. You can stroll the nature paths on the property, which winds around a peninsula and out to Pleasant Bay; you can even take a llama with you for company. The rooms, all with water views, are decorated with antiques and have country touches. ✉ *386 West Side Rd. (Box 222, Addison 04606),* ☎ *207/483–4490,* FAX *207/483–4653. 3 rooms, 1 with bath; 1 suite. Some refrigerators; no air-conditioning, no phones in some rooms, no smoking, no TV in some rooms. MC, V. BP.*

Shopping

Columbia Falls Pottery (✉ Main St., ☎ 207/483–4075) stocks stoneware and a sampling of Maine foods.

Jonesport and Beals Island

48 *12 mi south of Columbia Falls, 20 mi southwest of Machias.*

Jonesport and Beals Island, two fishing communities joined by a bridge over the harbor, are less polished than the towns on the Schoodic Peninsula. The birding here is superb. **Norton of Jonesport** (☎ 207/497–5933) takes passengers on day trips to Machias Seal Island, where there's a large puffin colony.

Great Wass Island Preserve (☎ 207/729–5181) a 1,540-acre nature conservancy at the tip of Beals Island, protects rare plants, stunted pines, and raised peat bogs. Trails lead through the woods and emerge onto the undeveloped, raw coast, where you can make your way along the rocks and boulders before retreating into the forest. To get to the preserve from Jonesport, cross the bridge over Moosabec Reach to Beals Island. Go through Beals to Great Wass Island. Follow the road, which eventually becomes unpaved, to Black Duck Cove, about 3 mi from Beals, where there is a parking area on the left. Admission is free.

Dining and Lodging

$$–$$$$ ✕ **Seafarer's Wife and Old Salt Room.** These two restaurants share a central kitchen. Allow at least a couple of hours to dine at the Seafarer's Wife, where a five-course meal with main dishes such as a seafood platter and baked stuffed chicken is presented at a leisurely pace in a candlelit dining room. The casual Old Salt Room specializes in fresh fish and seafood. Bring your own wine—neither restaurant has a liquor license. ✉ *Rte. 187, Jonesport,* ☎ *207/497–2365. MC, V. Closed Jan.–Mar. No lunch.*

$$ 🖼 **Harbor House.** The two spacious rooms on the third floor of this
★   harbor-front building have big windows to take in the water view. Both
are tastefully furnished with Victorian touches such as cabbage rose
wallpaper and Oriental-style rugs, and both have separate sleeping and
sitting areas. An alcove is stocked with books, coffee, tea, and snacks.
Breakfast is served on the porch, and the owners will prepare a lob-
ster dinner if asked in advance. ⊠ *Sawyer Square (Box 468, Jonesport
04649),* ☎ *207/497–5417,* FAX *207/497–3211,* WEB *www.harborhs.com.
2 rooms. Cable TV, Internet; no air-conditioning, no room phones, no
kids under 12. MC, V. BP.*

$ 🖼 **Raspberry Shores.** This comfortably furnished Victorian sits on
Main Street, but its backyard slopes down to a small beach on Jones-
port Harbor. Rooms in the back of the house share the view, but the
nicest room is in the turret and right on the road, which can be noisy.
Owner Nan Ellis will prepare a Continental breakfast if you're taking
an early morning boat trip. ⊠ *Rte. 187 (Box 409, Jonesport 04649),*
☎ *207/497–2463 or 877/710–3268,* WEB *www.jonesportmaine.com. 3
rooms without bath. Beach, boating, bicycles, some pets allowed; no
air-conditioning, no room phones, no room TVs, no kids under 15,
no smoking. MC, V. Closed Nov.–Apr. BP.*

Machias

🔴 *20 mi northeast of Jonesport.*

Machias claims to be the site of the first naval battle of the Revolu-
tionary War. On June 12, 1775, despite being outnumbered and out-
armed, a small group of Machias men under the leadership of Jeremiah
O'Brien captured the armed British schooner *Margaretta* in a battle
now known as the Lexington of the Sea. The town's other claim to
fame is wild blueberries. The Machias Wild Blueberry Festival, held
annually during the third weekend in August, is a true community cel-
ebration complete with parade, crafts fair, concerts, and plenty of
blueberry dishes. Machias is the county seat of Washington County
and is home to a campus of the University of Maine.

★ The **Burnham Tavern Museum,** in a 1770 building, details the color-
ful history of Job Burnham, Mary O'Brien (his wife), and other early
residents of the area. It was here that the men of Machias laid the plans
that culminated in the capture of the *Margaretta*. ⊠ *Rte. 192,* ☎ *207/
255–4432.* 🎫 *$2.50.* ☉ *Mid-June–late Sept., weekdays 9–5; late Sept.–
mid-June, by appointment.*

Although small, the **Art Galleries at the University of Maine at Machias**
have a strong selection of paintings by John Marin and other Maine
artists. Two galleries showcase rotating exhibitions of works from the
permanent collection, the Marin Foundation collection, and visiting
shows. Don't miss the William Zorach sculpture just outside the front
door. ⊠ *Powers Hall, University of Maine at Machias, 9 O'Brien
Ave.,* ☎ *207/255–1200.* 🎫 *Free.* ☉ *Weekday afternoons or by ap-
pointment.*

Built by Nathan Gates in 1810, the **Gates House** houses the Machias-
port Historical Society. It contains an extensive collection of pho-
tographs, tools, period furniture, housewares, memorabilia, and a
genealogical library. ⊠ *Rte. 92, Machiasport,* ☎ *207/255–8461.* 🎫
$1. ☉ *Mid-June–early-Sept., Tues.–Fri. 12:30–4:30.*

The **O'Brien Cemetery** dates from the late 18th century; many of
Machias's earliest settlers and heroes are buried here. ⊠ *Bad Little Falls
Park off Rte. 92, Machias (walk through the park toward the water
and look for a stairway on your right, which leads to a path; follow*

it along the river until you see a white fence on a hill to your right; a small side path leads to the cemetery).

OFF THE BEATEN PATH — **JASPER BEACH**– No sand exists here, just smooth, heather-color jasper and rhyolite stones polished by the sea. ⊠ *Rte. 92, Buck's Harbor (9½ mi south of Machias).*

Dining and Lodging

$$–$$$ ✕ **Artist's Cafe.** The white-walled dining rooms in this old house provide a simple backdrop for artwork and creative food. The menu usually has a choice of four entrées such as a catch of the day, a rib-eye steak, and "The Mex," the house vegetarian dish. You might start with Horses Standing Still, handmade Thai dumplings filled with chicken and shrimp and served with a dipping sauce. ⊠ *3 Hill St.,* ☎ *207/255–8900. MC, V. Closed Sun.*

$$ ✕🏠 **Riverside Inn & Restaurant.** The Victorian era is captured in the furnishings and linens of this restored sea captain's home overlooking the East Machias River. Suites in the guest house have balconies, and one has a full kitchen. The restaurant ($$), open to the public for dinner Thursday–Saturday, is the best in the area, serving four-course feasts of contemporary American fare by candlelight. ⊠ *U.S. 1 (Box 373, 04630),* ☎ *207/255–4134,* 𝐅𝐀𝐗 *207/255–3580,* 𝐖𝐄𝐁 *www.riversideinn-maine.com. 2 rooms, 2 suites. Restaurant, cable TV; no air-conditioning, no room phones, no smoking. AE, MC, V. BP.*

Outdoor Activities and Sports

Machias Bay Boat Tours and Sea Kayaking (⊠ Buck's Harbor, Machiasport, ☎ 207/259–3338) operates day trips aboard the *Martha Ann* to see seals, islands and lighthouses, salmon aquaculture, and historical sites. Guided fishing and sea-kayaking trips are also conducted.

Lubec

⑤⓪ *28 mi east of Machias.*

Lubec is the first town in the United States to see the sunrise. Its rural beauty outshines this once thriving shipbuilding and sardine-packing site. Lubec is best appreciated by those who enjoy outdoor pleasures; there are few shops and little entertainment. It also makes a good base for day trips to Campobello Island.

★ **Quoddy Head State Park,** the easternmost point of land in the United States, is marked by candy-striped West Quoddy Head Light. The mystical 2-mi path along the cliffs here yields magnificent views of Canada's Grand Manan island. Whales can often be sighted offshore. The 483-acre park has a picnic area. ⊠ *S. Lubec Rd. off Rte. 189,* ☎ *no phone.* 🎫 *$1.* ☉ *Memorial Day–mid-Oct., daily 8–sunset; Apr.– Memorial Day and mid-Oct.–Dec., weekends 9–sunset.*

At **Cottage Garden** paths lead through perennial, rose, rock, water, herb, and vegetable gardens and through sections with woods, rhododendrons, dwarf conifers, and shrubs. ⊠ *S. Lubec Rd. off Rte. 189,* ☎ *207/733–2902.* 🎫 *Free.* ☉ *June–Aug., daily dawn–dusk.*

⑤① **Roosevelt Campobello International Park,** a joint project of the American and Canadian governments, has hiking trails and historical displays. Neatly manicured Campobello Island has always had a special appeal for the wealthy and famous. It was here that the Roosevelt family spent its summers. The 34-room **Roosevelt Cottage** was presented to Eleanor and Franklin as a wedding gift. The island can be reached by land only by crossing the International Bridge from Lubec. Stop at the information booth for an update on tides—specifically, when you will be able to walk out to East Quoddy Head Lighthouse—and details on walking and hiking trails. Once you've crossed the bridge, you're in the Atlantic time zone. ✉ *Rte. 774, Welshpool, Campobello Island, New Brunswick, Canada,* ☎ *506/752–2922.* ✆ *Free.* ☉ *House mid-May–mid-Oct., daily 10–6; grounds daily.*

Dining and Lodging

$–$$ ✕☷ **Home Port Inn.** Lubec's grandest accommodations are in this 1880 Colonial-style house atop a hill. The spacious rooms, some with water views, are furnished with antiques and family pieces. There are two sitting areas, and the living room has a fireplace and a television. The dining room ($$–$$$), the best in town, is open to the public for dinner. The menu emphasizes seafood. ✉ *45 Main St., 04652,* ☎ *207/ 733–2077 or 800/457–2077,* WEB *www.homeportinn.com. 7 rooms. Restaurant; no air-conditioning, no room phones, no room TVs, no smoking. AE, D, MC, V. Closed mid-Oct.–mid-June. CP.*

$ ☷ **Peacock House.** Four generations of the Peacock family lived in this 1860 Victorian before it was converted into an inn. A few of the simply furnished rooms have water views through lace-curtained windows. ✉ *27 Summer St., 04652,* ☎ FAX *207/733–2403 or 888/305–0036,* WEB *www.peacockhouse.com. 2 rooms, 3 suites. No air-conditioning in some rooms, no TV in some rooms, no room phones, no kids under 7. MC, V. Closed mid-Oct.–mid-May. BP.*

En Route The road to Eastport leads through the Pleasant Point Indian Reservation, where the **Waponahki Museum and Resource Center** explains the culture of the Passamaquoddy, or "People of the Dawn." Tools, baskets, beaded artifacts, historic photos, and arts and crafts are displayed. ✉ *Rte. 190, Perry,* ☎ *207/853–4001.* ✆ *Free.* ☉ *Weekdays 8:30–11 and noon–4.*

Eastport

52 *39 mi north of Lubec, 102 mi east of Ellsworth.*

Eastport is a small island connected to the mainland by a granite causeway. In the late 19th century, 14 sardine canneries operated in Eastport. The decline of that industry in the 20th century has left the city economically depressed, though a commercial port facility, growing aquaculture, and an increase in tourism bode well for the future. From the waterfront, you can take a ferry to Deer Island and Campobello.

The **National Historic Waterfront District** extends from the Customs House, down Water Street to Bank Square and the Peavey Library. Pick up a walking map at the **Chamber of Commerce** (✉ 78 Water St., ☎ 207/853–4644) and wander through streets lined with historic homes and buildings. You can also take the waterfront walkway to watch the fishing boats and freighters. The tides fluctuate as much as 28 ft, which explains the ladders and steep gangways necessary to access boats.

Raye's Mustard Mill is the only remaining mill in the United States producing stone-ground mustard. Historically, this mill served the sardine-packing industry. You can purchase mustards made on the premises at the mill's Pantry Store; Maine-made crafts and other foods are also for sale. ✉ *85 Washington St.,* ☎ *207/853–4451 or 800/853–1903.* ✆ *Free.* ☉ *Jan.–May, weekdays 8–5; June–Dec., daily 9–4:30. Tours on the hr Memorial Day–Labor Day; rest of yr subject to guide availability.*

The short hike to **Shakford Head** (✉ behind Washington County Technical College on Deep Cove Rd.) affords views over Passamaquoddy

Bay to Campobello. From here you can see the pens for Eastport's salmon-farming industry as well as the port facility.

Lodging

$–$$ Weston House. A Federal-style home built in 1810, this antiques-
★ filled inn overlooks Eastport and Passamaquoddy Bay from a prime in-town location. The family room, with a fireplace and a TV, is a casual place to plan the day's activities. An elegant multicourse breakfast is served in the formal dining room, and dinner is available by advance reservation. ⊠ *26 Boynton St., 04631,* ☎ *207/853–2907 or 800/853–2907,* FAX *207/853–0981. 4 rooms without bath. No air-conditioning, no room phones, no room TVs, no smoking. No credit cards. BP.*

Outdoor Activities and Sports

Harris Whale Watching (⊠ Harris Point Rd., ☎ 207/853–2940 or 207/853–4303) operates three-hour tours. **Tidal Trails** (⊠ Water St., ☎ 207/726–4799) conducts boat charters, natural-history tours, and guided bird-watching, canoeing, sea-kayaking, and saltwater-fishing trips.

Shopping

Dog Island Pottery (⊠ 224 Water St., ☎ 207/853–4775) stocks stoneware pottery and local crafts. The **Eastport Gallery** (⊠ 69 Water St., ☎ 207/853–4166) displays works by area artists. **45th Parallel** (⊠ U.S. 1, Perry, ☎ 207/853–9600) stocks a mix of antiques, crafts, and home furnishing. **Joe's Basket Shop** (⊠ Rte. 190, Pleasant Point, ☎ 207/853–2840) has fancy and coarse (work) baskets and jewelry made by the Passamaquoddy. **Quoddy Wigwam** (⊠ Rte. 1, Perry, ☎ 207/853–2488) sells handcrafted Maine moccasins.

Grand Lake Stream

53 *50 mi northwest of Eastport, 108 mi east of Bangor.*

This tiny community, on Grand Lake Stream between West Grand Lake and Big Lake, was once one of the largest tannery centers in the world. Today it's renowned for fishing, especially for land-locked salmon and smallmouth bass, and for the Grand Laker, a stable, square-ended wooden canoe built specifically for use on the big and often windy lakes in this region. Outdoors lovers will find lakes and rivers for swimming, boating, and fishing; trails for hiking; and plenty of places to spot wildlife. On the last full weekend of July, the town holds a juried folk arts festival, which attracts thousands of visitors.

The tiny **Grand Lake Stream Historical Society & Museum** is jam-packed with artifacts from the town's early days. Here you can learn more about the Grand Lake canoes, the town's tannery years, and its fishing heritage. ☎ *207/796–5562.* ⊠ *Donation accepted.* ⊙ *By chance or appointment.*

Lodging

$$$$ Leen's Lodge. Ten rustic cabins varying in size from one to four bedrooms are nestled on 23 wooded acres on West Grand Lake. All have woodstoves or fireplaces and big windows to take in the views. A country-style breakfast and a hearty, home-style dinner are served in a central lodge, where you'll also find a TV/VCR, card tables, books, and games. The lodge can arrange guided fishing trips, wildlife or photographic safaris, and other excursions. Boat rentals are available. ⊠ *Box 40, 04637,* ☎ *207/796–5575 or 800/995–3367,* WEB *www. leenslodge.com. 10 cabins. Some kitchenettes, hiking, beach, boating, recreation room, some pets allowed; no air-conditioning, no room phones, no room TVs. MC, V. Closed Nov.–Apr. MAP.*

$$$$ 🖥 **Weatherby's.** Nicknamed "the fishermen's resort," Weatherby's is ideal for those who want to be in the center of the action in Grand Lake Stream. Fifteen cottages, each with an open brick or Franklin fireplace, surround the main lodge, where you can take breakfast and dinner daily. Lunch is available upon request. The main lodge also has a library, television, and piano. ⊠ *Grand Lake Stream 04637,* ☎ *207/796–5558,* WEB *www.weatherbys.com. 15 cottages. No air-conditioning, no room phones, no room TVs. MC, V. Closed mid-Oct.–Apr. MAP.*

Outdoor Activities and Sports

The **Grand Lake Stream Guides Association** (⊠ Grand Lake Stream 04637) maintains more than 25 launch sites on area lakes. Guides lead fishing, family, boating, hiking, photographic, and wildlife trips.

Shopping

Shamel Boat & Canoe Works (⊠ Tough End Rd., ☎ 207/796–8199) specializes in building canoes.

Way Down East A to Z

To research prices, get advice from other travelers, and book travel arrangements, visit www.fodors.com.

BIKE TRAVEL

Narrow roads, most without shoulders, are the rule here, but you'll find some beautiful routes on the long fingers of land that stretch toward the ocean as well as on the inland side of Route 1, where you'll see plenty of lakes. Be aware that most land owned by logging companies is not open for bicycling.

BOAT AND FERRY TRAVEL

East Coast Ferries, Ltd. provides ferry service between Eastport and Deer Island and Deer Island and Campobello from late June to mid-September. Ferries run on Atlantic time, which is one hour earlier than Eastern time.

➤ BOAT AND FERRY INFORMATION: **East Coast Ferries, Ltd.** (☎ 506/747–2159, WEB www.eastcoastferries.nb.ca).

CAR TRAVEL

U.S. 1 is the primary coastal route, with smaller roads leading to the towns on the long fingers of land in this region. Route 182 is a pleasant inland route; Route 186 loops through the Schoodic Peninsula. The most direct route to Lubec is Route 189, but Route 191, between East Machias and West Lubec, is a scenic coastal drive.

LODGING

Black Duck Properties specializes in properties on the Schoodic Peninsula. Hearts of Maine has waterfront listings in the Machias region.
➤ LODGING: **Black Duck Properties** (⊠ Box 39, Corea 04624, ☎ 207/963–2689, WEB www.acadia.net/blackduck). **Hearts of Maine** (⊠ 10 High St., Machias 04564, ☎ 207/255–4210, WEB www.boldcoast.com/mainecottages).

MEDIA

The *Bangor Daily News* is published Monday–Friday. Weekly newspapers include *Calais Advertiser, Downeast Times* (Calais), *Downeast Coastal Press* (Cutler), *Machias Valley News Observer,* and the twice-monthly *Quoddy Tides* (Eastport).

WMEH 90.0 or WMED 89.7 is the local National Public Radio affiliate. WLBZ, channel 2, is the NBC affiliate. WVII, channel 7, is the

ABC affiliate. WABI, channel 5, is the CBS affiliate. WMEB, channel 12, or WMED, channel 13, is the Maine Public Broadcasting affiliate.

OUTDOOR ACTIVITIES AND SPORTS

BOATING

For boat rentals, *see* listings by town. The Maine Professional Guides Association represents kayaking guides.

➤ CONTACT: **Maine Professional Guides Association** (✉ Box 847, Augusta 04332, ☎ 207/549–5631, WEB www.maineguides.org).

FISHING

For information about fishing and licenses, contact the Maine Department of Inland Fisheries and Wildlife.

➤ CONTACT: **Maine Department of Inland Fisheries and Wildlife** (✉ 41 State House Station, Augusta 04333, ☎ 207/287–8000, WEB www.state.me.us/ifw).

TOURS

Quoddy Air has scenic flights. Scenic Island Tours leads tours of Eastport in a 1947 Dodge Woody bus.

➤ TOUR OPERATORS: **Quoddy Air** (✉ Eastport Municipal Airport, County Rd., Eastport, ☎ 207/853–0997). **Scenic Island Tours** (✉ 37 Washington St., Eastport, ☎ 207/853–2840).

VISITOR INFORMATION

➤ CONTACTS: **Downeast Coastal Chamber of Commerce** (✉ Box 331, Harrington 04643, ☎ 207/483–2131, WEB www.downeastcoastalchamber.org). **Eastport Area Chamber of Commerce** (✉ 72 Water St. [Box 254, Eastport 04631], ☎ 207/853–4644, WEB www.nemaine.com/eastportcc). **Grand Lake Stream Chamber of Commerce** (✉ Box 124, Grand Lake Stream 046337, ☎ 207/448–3000, WEB www.grandlakestream.com). **Lubec Area Chamber of Commerce** (✉ Box 123, Lubec 04652, ☎ 207/733–4522). **Machias Bay Area Chamber of Commerce** (✉ 378 Main St. [Box 606, Machias 04654], ☎ 207/255–4402, WEB www.nemaine.com/mbacc). **Quoddy Coastal Tourism Association of New Brunswick and Maine** (✉ Box 1171, St. Andrews, New Brunswick, Canada E0G 2X0, ☎ 800/377–9748). **Schoodic Peninsula Chamber of Commerce** (✉ Box 381, Winter Harbor 04693, ☎ 207/963–7658 or 800/231–3008, WEB www.acadia-schoodic.org).

WESTERN LAKES AND MOUNTAINS

Less than 20 mi northwest of Portland and the coast, the sparsely populated lake and mountain areas of western Maine stretch north along the New Hampshire border to Québec. In winter this is ski country; in summer the woods and waters draw vacationers.

The Sebago–Long Lake region bustles with activity in the summer. Harrison and the Waterfords are quieter. Bridgton attracts lake visitors in summer and skiers in winter, while Lovell is a dreamy escape. Kezar Lake, tucked away in a fold of the White Mountains, has long been a hideaway of the wealthy. Children's summer camps dot the region. Bethel, in the Androscoggin River valley, is a classic New England town, its town common lined with historic homes. The more rural Rangeley Lake area brings long stretches of pine, beech, spruce, and sky—and stylish inns and bed-and-breakfasts with access to golf, boating, fishing, and hiking. Snow sports, especially snowmobiling, are popular winter pastimes. Carrabassett Valley, just north of Kingfield, is home to Sugarloaf/USA, a major ski resort with a challenging golf course.

Sebago Lake

54 *17 mi northwest of Portland.*

Sebago Lake, which provides all the drinking water for Greater Portland, is Maine's best-known lake after Moosehead (☞ The North Woods). Many camps and year-round homes surround Sebago, which is popular with water-sports enthusiasts. At the north end of the lake, the **Songo Lock** (☎ 207/693–6231), which permits the passage of watercraft from Sebago Lake to Long Lake, is the lone surviving lock of the Cumberland and Oxford Canal. Built of wood and masonry, the original lock dates from 1830 and was expanded in 1911; today it sees heavy traffic in summer.

The 1,300-acre **Sebago Lake State Park** on the north shore of the lake provides swimming, picnicking, camping (250 sites), boating, and fishing (salmon and togue). ✉ *11 Park Access Rd., Casco,* ☎ *207/693–6613 May–mid-Oct.; 207/693–6231 mid-Oct.–Apr.* ▣ *$2.50.* ☉ *Daily 9–8.*

The **Jones Museum of Glass & Ceramics** houses more than 8,000 glass, pottery, stoneware, and porcelain objects from around the world. Also on the premises are a research library and gift shop. ✉ *35 Douglas Mountain Rd., off Rte. 107, Sebago,* ☎ *207/787–3370.* ▣ *$5.* ☉ *Mid-May–mid-Nov., Mon.–Sat. 10–5, Sun. 1–5; tours by appointment.*

OFF THE
BEATEN PATH

SABBATHDAY LAKE SHAKER MUSEUM – Established in the late 18th century, this is the last active Shaker community in the United States. Members continue to farm crops and herbs, and you can see the meetinghouse of 1794—a paradigm of Shaker design—and the ministry shop with 14 rooms of Shaker furniture, folk art, tools, farm implements, and crafts from the 18th to the early 20th century. There is also a small gift shop, but don't expect to find furniture or other large Shaker items. On the busy road out front, a farmer usually has summer and fall vegetables for sale. In autumn, he sells cider, apples, and pumpkins. ✉ *707 Shaker Rd. (Rte. 26), New Gloucester (20 mi north of Portland, 12 mi east of Naples),* ☎ *207/926–4597.* ▣ *Tour $6.* ☉ *Memorial Day–Columbus Day, Mon.–Sat. 10–4:30.*

Naples

55 *32 mi northwest of Portland.*

Naples occupies an enviable location between Long and Sebago lakes. On clear days, the view down Long Lake takes in the Presidential Range of the White Mountains, highlighted by often-snowcapped Mt. Washington. The Causeway, which divides Long Lake from Brandy Pond pulses with activity: Cruise and rental boats sail and motor on the lakes, moving between the two through a swing bridge; open-air cafés overflow and throngs of families parade along the sidewalk edging Long Lake. The town swells with seasonal residents and visitors in summer and all but shuts tight for winter.

☾ *Songo River Queen II,* a 92-ft stern-wheeler, takes passengers on hourlong cruises on Long Lake and longer voyages down the Songo River and through Songo Lock. ✉ *U.S. 302, Naples Causeway,* ☎ *207/693–6861.* ▣ *Long Lake cruise $8, Songo River ride $11.* ☉ *July–Labor Day, 5 cruises daily; call for spring and fall hrs.*

Western Maine

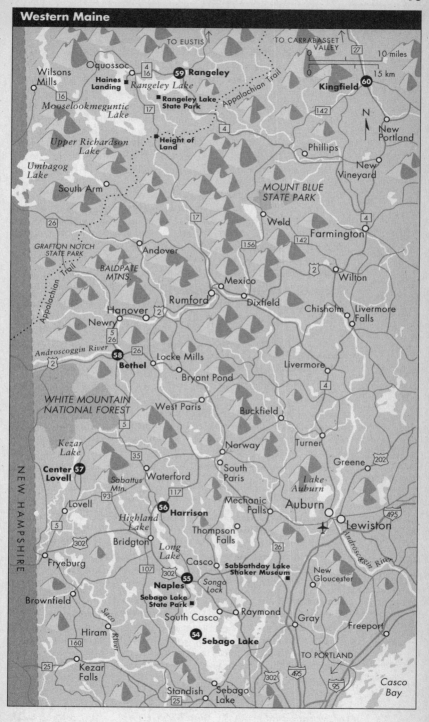

TO EUSTIS

TO CARRABASSET
VALLEY

0   10 miles
0   15 km

27

N

Wilsons
Mills

Oquossoc

4
16

59 **Rangeley**

Kingfield **60**

New
Portland

16

Haines
Landing

Rangeley Lake

Appalachian Trail

142

*Mooselookmeguntic
Lake*

17

Rangeley Lake
State Park

*Upper Richardson
Lake*

Height of
Land

4

Phillips

New
Vineyard

*Umbagog
Lake*

South Arm

MOUNT BLUE
STATE PARK

4

26

17

Weld

Farmington

GRAFTON NOTCH
STATE PARK

Andover

156

142

Wilton

BALDPATE
MTNS.

Mexico

2

Appalachian Trail

Rumford

Dixfield

Chisholm

Livermore
Falls

Hanover

2

Newry

5
26

Androscoggin River

26

58

Locke Mills

Livermore

2

Bethel

Bryant Pond

4

WHITE MOUNTAIN
NATIONAL FOREST

West Paris

Buckfield

5

*Kezar
Lake*

Norway

Turner

Greene

202

**Center
Lovell** **57**

35

Waterford

South
Paris

*Lake
Auburn*

*Sabattus
Mtn.*

117

Lovell

93

56 **Harrison**

Mechanic
Falls

Auburn

495

NEW HAMPSHIRE

5

*Highland
Lake*

Bridgton

Thompson
Falls

26

Lewiston

Fryeburg

302

107

*Long
Lake*

Casco

Sabbathday Lake
Shaker Museum

New
Gloucester

Androscoggin River

Brownfield

302

55

*Songo
Lock*

Freeport

Naples

Sebago Lake
State Park

Raymond

Gray

*Saco
River*

South Casco

Hiram

160

54 **Sebago Lake**

TO PORTLAND

25

Kezar
Falls

Standish

Sebago
Lake

302

495

95

*Casco
Bay*

25

Lodging

$$$$ ⌂ **Migis Lodge.** The lodge's pine-panel cottages, scattered among 100 shorefront acres, have fieldstone fireplaces and are handsomely furnished with braided rugs and handmade quilts. A warm, woodsy feeling pervades the main inn. The deck has views (marvelous at sunset) of Sebago Lake. All kinds of outdoor and indoor activities are included in the room rate, and canoes, kayaks, and sailboats are available. Three fancy meals are served daily in the main dining room. ⌂ *Migis Lodge Rd., off U.S. 302 (Box 40, South Casco 04077),* ☎ *207/655–4524,* FAX *207/655–2054,* WEB *www.migis.com. 29 cottages, 6 rooms. Dining room, cable TV, refrigerators, 2 tennis courts, gym, massage, spa, beach, boating, waterskiing, fishing, playground, recreation room, meeting rooms; no air-conditioning in some rooms. No credit cards. FAP.*

$$–$$$ ⌂ **Augustus Bove House.** Built as the Hotel Naples in the 1820s, this rambling brick B&B sits across from the Naples Causeway and has views down Long Lake. Rooms are furnished with antiques. ⌂ *Rte. 302 (R.R. 1, Box 501, 04055),* ☎ *207/693–6365 or 888/806–6249,* WEB *www.naplesmaine.com. 10 rooms, 8 with bath; 2 suites. Cable TV, in-room VCRs, some refrigerators, some microwaves, Internet; no smoking. AE, D, DC MC, V. BP.*

Outdoor Activities and Sports

U.S. 302 cuts through Naples, and in the center at the Naples Causeway are rental craft for fishing or cruising. Sebago, Long, and Rangeley lakes are popular areas for sailing and motorboating. For motorboat rentals, try **Mardon Marine** (⌂ U.S. 302, ☎ 207/693–6264). **Naples Marina** (⌂ U.S. 302 and Rte. 114, ☎ 207/693–6254) also rents motorboats. **Long Lake Marina** (⌂ U.S. 302, ☎ 207/693–3159) rents fishing boats and canoes.

Shopping

The **Cry of the Loon** (⌂ U.S. 302, South Casco, ☎ 207/655–5060) complex includes a gift shop: the Nest, a country home-furnishings shop, and the Barn, which carries specialty foods, nautical gifts, and other items.

Harrison

56 *10 mi north of Naples, 25 mi south of Bethel.*

Harrison anchors the northern end of Long Lake but is less commercial than Naples. The combination of woods, lakes, and views makes it a good choice for leaf-peepers. The nearby towns of North Waterford, South Waterford, and tiny Waterford, a National Historic District, are ideal for outdoors lovers who prefer to get away from the crowds.

Lodging

$$ ⌂ **Bear Mountain Inn.** After swimming at the private beach on Bear
★   Lake or hiking up Bear Mountain (across the street), it's nice to return to this rambling farmhouse inn, which the owner has meticulously decorated in a woodsy theme. The luxurious Great Grizzly Suite has a fireplace, whirlpool bath for two, and mesmerizing views, while the cozy Sugar Bear Cottage is a romantic retreat. Breakfast is served in the dining room, which has a fieldstone fireplace and lake views. ⌂ *Rte. 35, South Waterford 04084,* ☎ *207/583–4404,* FAX *207/583–2437,* WEB *www.bearmtninn.com. 8 rooms, 6 with bath; 1 suite; 1 cottage. Cable TV in some rooms, some in-room VCRs, Internet, badminton, croquet, horseshoes, volleyball, beach, boating, fishing, ice-skating, cross-country skiing, snowmobiling; no kids under 8, no smoking. MC, V. BP.*

$$ ⊡ **Harrison House.** When it was built in 1867, this house at the head of Long Lake was one of the most costly and elegant residences in town. Today it charms with feather beds, quilts, and a porch swing. The living room, dining room, and three guest rooms have lake views. All rooms have private baths, but four of the baths are adjacent to or across the hall from the rooms. ⊠ *16 Waterford Rd., 04040,* ☎ *207/583–6564. 5 rooms. No air-conditioning, no room phones, no room TVs, no smoking. AE, MC, V. BP.*

$$ ⊡ **Waterford Inne.** This gold-painted house on a hilltop provides a good home base for trips to lakes, ski trails, and antiques shops. The bedrooms have lots of nooks and crannies. The Nantucket, with a whale motif, and the Chesapeake, with a private porch and a fireplace, are the nicest. A converted woodshed holds five additional rooms, and though they have less character than the rooms in the inn, four have sunny decks. ⊠ *258 Chadbourne Rd. (Box 149, Waterford 04088),* ☎ FAX *207/583–4037. 7 rooms, 5 with bath; 1 suite. Ice-skating, cross-country skiing, some pets allowed (fee); no air-conditioning, no room phones, no room TVs, no smoking. AE. Closed Apr. BP.*

Nightlife and the Arts

From late June through Labor Day, **Deertrees Theater and Cultural Center** (⊠ Deertrees Rd. off Rte. 117, ☎ 207/583–6747) stages musicals, dramas, dance performances, shows for children, concerts, and other events in a theater listed on the National Register of Historic Places.

Outdoor Activities and Sports

For guided fishing trips, call **Carl Bois** (☎ 207/925–6262) in Lovell. **Mutiny Brook Stables** (⊠ Sweden Rd., South Waterford, ☎ 207/583–6650) outfits horseback tours in the Maine woods.

Center Lovell

⑤⑦ *17 mi northwest of Harrison, 28 mi south of Bethel.*

At Center Lovell you can barely glimpse the secluded Kezar Lake to the west, the retreat of wealthy and very private people. Sabattus Mountain, which rises behind Center Lovell, has a public hiking trail and stupendous views of the Presidential Range from the summit.

Dining and Lodging

$$$$ ✕⊡ **Quisisana.** This delightful cottage resort on Kezar Lake may inspire music lovers. After dinner, the staff—students and graduates of some of the country's finest music schools—perform everything from Broadway tunes to concert piano pieces at the music hall. One night dinner ($$$$) might be lobster and blueberry pie; the next it might be saddle of lamb with a black-olive tapenade or salmon-and-leek roulade. Most of the white-clapboard cottages have screened porches, pine-paneled living areas and fireplaces, and are simply furnished with wicker and country pieces. For most of the resort's season, a one-week stay beginning Saturday is required. ⊠ *Pleasant Point Rd., 04016,* ☎ *207/925–3500,* FAX *207/925–1004 in season,* WEB *www.quisisanaresort.com. 11 rooms in 2 lodges, 32 cottages. Restaurant, 3 tennis courts, windsurfing, boating, waterskiing, Ping-Pong, recreation room; no air-conditioning, no room phones, no room TVs, no smoking. No credit cards. Closed Sept.–mid-June. FAP.*

$–$$ ✕⊡ **Center Lovell Inn.** The current owners won this rambling old-fashioned country inn in an essay contest in 1993. The eclectic furnishings blend mid-19th and mid-20th centuries in a pleasing, homey style. The best tables for dining ($$$–$$$$) are on the wraparound porch, which has sunset views over Kezar Lake and the White Mountains. Entrées may include pan-seared muscovy duck, fillet of bison, or fresh swordfish. Rooms are upstairs and in the adjacent Harmon House. ⊠ *Rte. 5 (Box 261, 04016),* ☎ *207/925–1575 or 800/777–2698,* WEB *www. centerlovellinn.com. 6 rooms, 4 with bath; 1 suite. Restaurant; no air-conditioning, no room phones, no room TVs, no smoking. D, MC, V. Closed Nov.–late Dec. and Apr.–mid-May.*

Outdoor Activities and Sports

BOATING AND FISHING

For guided fishing trips, call **Carl Bois** (☎ 207/925–6262) in Lovell. **Kezar Lake Marina** (⊠ West Lovell Rd. at The Narrows, Lovell, ☎ 207/925–3000) rents boats.

CANOEING

Two scenic canoeing routes on the Saco River (near Fryeburg) are the gentle stretch from Swan's Falls to East Brownfield (19 mi) and from East Brownfield to Hiram (14 mi). For rentals, try **Saco River Canoe and Kayak** (⊠ Rte. 5, Fryeburg, ☎ 207/935–2369).

DOGSLEDDING

Winter Journeys (☎ 207/928–2026) in Lovell operates day and multi-tiday dogsledding trips.

Bethel

⑤⑧ *28 mi north of Lovell, 66 mi north of Portland.*

Bethel is pure New England, a town with white clapboard houses and white-steeple churches and a mountain vista at the end of every street. In winter, this is ski country: Sunday River ski area in Newry is only a few miles north.

A stroll in Bethel should begin at the Bethel Historical Society's **Regional History Center.** The center's campus comprises two buildings, the 1821 O'Neil Robinson House and the 1813 Dr. Moses Mason House; both are listed on the National Register of Historic Places. The Robinson House has exhibits pertaining to the region's history and a small gift shop. The Moses Mason House has nine period rooms and a front hall and stairway wall decorated with murals by Rufus Porter. Pick up materials here for a walking tour of Bethel Hill Village, most of which is on the National Register of Historic Places. ⊠ *14 Broad St.,* ☎ *207/ 824–2908 or 800/824–2910,* WEB *www.bethelhistorical.org.* 🖃 *$3.* ☺ *O'Neil Robinson House July–Aug. and Dec., Tues.–Sun. 1–4; Sept.– Oct. and Jan.–June, Tues.–Fri. 1–4. Moses Mason House July–Aug., Tues.–Sun. 1–4; Sept.–June by appointment.*

The **Major Gideon's House** on Broad Street has a columned-front portico typical of the Greek Revival style. The severe white **West Parish Congregational Church** (1847), with an unadorned triangular pediment and a steeple supported on open columns, is on Church Street, around the common from the Major Gideon Hastings House. The campus of **Gould Academy** (⊠ Church St., ☎ 207/824–7777), a preparatory school, opened its doors in 1835; the dominant style of the school buildings is Georgian.

Dining and Lodging

$$$　✕🏠 **Gideon Hastings House.** Lace curtains, gleaming hardwood floors, and tin ceilings welcome you to this historic inn and restaurant. The two spacious guest rooms can be connected as a family suite. The restaurant's menu ($$–$$$; closed Tues.) ranges from pizzas to entrées such as filet mignon and chicken stuffed with goat cheese, artichoke hearts, and sun-dried tomatoes. ⊠ *22 Broad St., 04217,* ☎ *207/824–3496,* WEB *www.gideonhastingshouse.com. 2 rooms with shared bath, 2 suites.*

Restaurant, in-room data ports, in-room VCRs, boccie, bar; no air-conditioning. MC, V. BP.

$$ ✕ 🖼 **L'Auberge.** Built as a barn in the late 1850s, L'Auberge has evolved into a casual inn with a French country accent and one of the area's best restaurants. The inn is on 5 acres just off the Bethel Common. The menu ($$$; closed Tues.–Wed.) changes seasonally but might include hors d'oeuvres such as pâté de campagne or escargots and entrées such as sea bass Provençal or caramelized duck breast. ✉ *24 Mill Hill Rd., 04217,* ☎ *207/824–2774 or 800/760–2774,* WEB *www.laubergecountryinn.com. 6 rooms, 1 apartment. Restaurant, baby-sitting, Internet, some pets allowed; no air-conditioning, no room TVs, no room phones. AE, D, MC, V. BP.*

$$ ✕ 🖼 **Victoria Inn.** It's hard to miss this turreted inn, with its beige-, mauve-, and teal-painted exterior and attached carriage house topped with a cupola. Inside, Victorian details include ceiling rosettes, stained-glass windows, elaborate fireplace mantels, and gleaming oak trim. Guest rooms vary in size; most are furnished with reproductions of antiques. The restaurant, open to the public for dinner ($$–$$$; closed Mon.), has three rooms, one with a wraparound mural of Italian scenes. Choose from entrées such as lobster ravioli and filet mignon. ✉ *32 Main St. (Box 249, 04217),* ☎ *207/824–8060 or 888/774–1235,* FAX *207/824–3926,* WEB *www.victoria-inn.com. 15 rooms. Restaurant, cable TV, in-room data ports; no smoking. AE, MC, V. BP.*

$–$$ ✕ 🖼 **Briar Lea.** At this Georgian-style inn, you can snuggle under a down comforter at night in rooms decorated in a warm and inviting country style. The dining room ($$–$$$; no lunch) is open to the public for breakfast and dinner. Entrées may include pork chops, rainbow trout, and crispy roast duck. A children's menu is available. ✉ *150 Mayville Rd. (Rte. 2), 04217,* ☎ *207/824–4717 or 877/311–1299,* FAX *207/ 824–7121,* WEB *www.briarlearestaurant.com. 6 rooms. Restaurant, cable TV, some pets allowed (fee); no-smoking. AE, D, MC, V. Call ahead Nov.–late Dec., Apr.–May. BP.*

$$$ 🖼 **Jordan Grand Resort Hotel.** A hit with Sunday River skiers, this condominium hotel provides ski-in, ski-out access to the Jordan Bowl trails. The outdoor pool is heated. Room rates include lift tickets. ✉ *1 Grand Cir., off Skiway Rd. and U.S. 2 (Box 450, Newry 04217),* ☎ *207/824– 5000 or 800/543–2754,* FAX *207/824–5399. 195 condominiums. 2 restaurants, some kitchenettes, café, pool, health club, baby-sitting, meeting room. AE, D, MC, V.*

$$$ 🖼 **Sunday River Inn.** This homey chalet on the Sunday River ski-area access road has private rooms for families and dorm rooms (bring your sleeping bag) for groups and students, all within easy access of the slopes. A hearty breakfast and dinner are served buffet-style, and a stone hearth dominates the comfortable living room. The inn operates an excellent ski-touring center; rates include touring ticket. ✉ *213 Skiway Rd., Newry 04261,* ☎ *207/824–2410,* FAX *207/824–3181,* WEB *www. sundayriverinn.com. 19 rooms, 3 with private bath; 5 dorms with shared bath. Hot tub, sauna, cross-country skiing, downhill skiing; no air-conditioning, no room TVs, no room phones, no smoking. AE, D, MC, V. Closed Apr.–late Nov. MAP.*

Nightlife and the Arts

For a quiet evening, head to the piano bar at the **Bethel Inn and Country Club** (✉ Village Common, ☎ 207/824–2175). At Sunday River, the **Bumps Pub** (✉ Whitecap Lodge, ☎ 207/824–5269) has après-ski and evening entertainment. Tuesday night is comedy night, ski movies are shown on Wednesday, and rock/pop bands play on weekends and holidays. **Sunday River Brewing Company** (✉ U.S. 2, ☎ 207/824–4253) has pub fare and live entertainment—usually progressive rock bands—

on weekends. The **Sudbury Inn** (✉ 151 Main St., ☎ 207/824–2174) draws the après-ski crowd with mostly live blues.

Outdoor Activities and Sports

CANOEING

Bethel Outdoor Adventures (✉ 121 Mayville Rd., ☎ 207/824–4224) rents canoes, kayaks, bikes, and snowmobiles.

DOGSLEDDING

Mahoosuc Guide Service (✉ Bear River Rd., Newry, ☎ 207/824–2073) leads day and multiday dogsledding expeditions on the Maine–New Hampshire border.

HIKING

Telemark Inn & Llama Treks (✉ King's Hwy., Mason Township, ☎ 207/836–2703) operates one- to six-day llama-supported hiking trips in the White Mountain National Forest.

HORSEBACK RIDING

Sparrowhawk Mountain Ranch (✉ 600 Fleming Rd., ☎ 207/836–2528) leads one-hour to day-long trail rides and also has an indoor arena.

SNOWMOBILING

Sun Valley Sports (✉ 129 Sunday River Rd., ☎ 207/824–7533 or 877/851–7533, WEB www.sunvalleysports.com) rents snowmobiles and gives tours. It also operates fly-fishing trips, canoe and kayak rentals, and moose and wildlife safaris.

NATIONAL FORESTS AND PARKS

At **Grafton Notch State Park** (✉ Rte. 26, 14 mi north of Bethel, ☎ 207/824–2912) you can take an easy nature walk to Mother Walker Falls or Moose Cave and see the spectacular Screw Auger Falls, or you can hike to the summit of Old Speck Mountain, the state's third-highest peak. If you have the stamina and the equipment, you can pick up the Appalachian Trail here, hike over Saddleback Mountain, and continue on to Katahdin. The **Maine Appalachian Trail Club** (✉ Box 283, Augusta 04330) publishes a map and trail guide.

White Mountain National Forest straddles New Hampshire and Maine. Although the highest peaks are on the New Hampshire side, the Maine section has magnificent rugged terrain, camping and picnic areas, and hiking from hour-long nature loops to a 5½-hour scramble up Speckled Mountain. ✉ *Evans Notch Visitor Center, 18 Mayville Rd., 04217,* ☎ *207/824–2134.* ⊡ *Parking pass (good 1–7 days) $5.* ☉ *Center early May–mid-Oct., daily 8–5; mid-Oct.–early May, daily 8:30–4:30.*

Shopping

Bonnema Potters (✉ 146 Lower Main St., ☎ 207/824–2821) sells plates, lamps, tiles, and vases in colorful modern designs. The **Lyons' Den** (✉ U.S. 2, Hanover, ☎ 207/364–8634), a great barn of a place near Bethel, stocks antique glass, china, tools, prints, rugs, hand-wrought iron, and some furniture. **Mt. Mann Jewelers** (✉ 57 Main St., ☎ 207/824–3030) carries contemporary jewelry with unusual gems.

Ski Areas

SUNDAY RIVER

What was once a sleepy little ski area with minimal facilities has evolved into a sprawling resort that attracts skiers from as far away as Europe. Spread throughout the valley are three base areas, two condominium hotels, trailside condominiums, town houses, and a ski dorm. Sunday River is home to the Maine Handicapped Skiing program, which provides lessons and services for skiers with disabilities. ✉ *Sunday River Rd. off U.S. 2, Newry (Box 450, Bethel 04217),* ☎ *207/824–3000; 207/824–5200 snow conditions; 800/543–2754 reservations.*

Downhill. White Heat has gained fame as the steepest, longest, widest lift-served trail in the East; but skiers of all abilities will find plenty of suitable terrain, from a 5-km (3-mi) beginner run to steep glades, in-your-face bumps, and terrain parks. The area has 127 trails, the majority of them in the intermediate range. Expert and advanced runs are grouped from the peaks, and most beginner slopes are near the base. Trails spreading down from eight peaks have a total vertical descent of 2,340 ft and are served by nine quads, four triples, and two double chairlifts and three surface lifts.

Other activities. The Entertainment Center at White Cap has a lighted halfpipe, a lighted ice-skating rink, a tubing area, a teen center, and a nightclub with live music.

Child care. Three licensed day-care centers accommodate children ages 6 weeks–6 years. Coaching for children ages 3–18 is available in the Children's Center at the South Ridge base area.

Summer and year-round activities. Within the housing complexes are indoor pools, outdoor heated pools, saunas, hot tubs, and four tennis courts. In summer, a mountain park attracts families with hiking and mountain biking.

CROSS-COUNTRY SKIING

Bethel Inn Touring Center (⊠ Village Common, ☎ 207/824–6276) has 40 km (25 mi) of trails and provides ski and snowshoe rentals and lessons. **Carter's Cross-Country Ski Center** (⊠ 786 Intervale Rd., ☎ 207/539–4848) has 50 km (31 mi) for all levels of skiers; a center in Oxford has 35 km (22 mi) of trails for novice and intermediate skiing. Both centers provide lessons and snowshoe, ski, and sled rentals. **Sunday River Cross-Country Ski Center** (⊠ 23 Skiway Rd., Newry, ☎ 207/824–2410), based at the Sunday River Inn, has 40 km (25 mi) of trails; all are tracked and most have skating lanes. A special trail is designated for skiing with dogs. Lessons and rentals are available.

En Route The routes north from Bethel to the Rangeley district are all scenic, particularly in the autumn when the maples are aflame with color. In the town of Newry, make a short detour to the **Artist's Bridge** (turn off Route 26 onto Sunday River Road and drive about 3 mi), the most painted and photographed of Maine's eight covered bridges. Route 26 continues north to the gorges and waterfalls of **Grafton Notch State Park.** Past the park, Route 26 continues to Errol, New Hampshire, where Route 16 will return you east around the north shore of Mooselookmeguntic Lake, through Oquossoc, and into Rangeley.

A more direct route (if marginally less scenic) from Bethel to Rangeley still allows a stop in Newry. Follow U.S. 2 north and east from Bethel to the twin towns of Rumford and Mexico, where Route 17 continues north to Oquossoc, about an hour's drive. The high point of this route is **Height of Land,** with its unforgettable views of mountains ranges and the island-studded blue mass of Mooselookmeguntic Lake. At **Haines Landing** on Mooselookmeguntic Lake, you can stand at 1,400 ft above sea level and face the same magnificent scenery you admired at 2,400 ft from Height of Land on Route 17.

Rangeley

 67 mi north of Bethel.

Rangeley, north of Rangeley Lake on Route 4/16, has long lured anglers and winter-sports enthusiasts to its more than 40 lakes and ponds and 450 square mi of woodlands. Equally popular in summer or winter, Rangeley has a rough, wilderness feel to it. Lodgings are in the woods, around the lake, and along the golf course.

The **Wilhelm Reich Museum** interprets the life and work of controversial physician-scientist Wilhelm Reich (1897–1957), who believed that a force called orgone energy was the source of neurosis. The Orgone Energy Observatory, designed for Reich in 1948, exhibits biographical materials, inventions, and the equipment used in his experiments. Also on view are Reich's library, personal memorabilia, and artwork. Trails lace the 175-acre grounds, and the observatory deck has magnificent views of the countryside. ⊠ *Dodge Pond Rd.*, ☎ *207/864–3443*, WEB *www.rangeleymaine.com/wilhelmreich.* ☒ *$4.* ☉ *July–Aug., Wed.–Sun. 1–5; Sept., Sun. 1–5.*

OFF THE
BEATEN PATH
SANDY RIVER & RANGELEY LAKES RAILROAD – You can ride a mile through the woods along a narrow-gauge railroad on a century-old train drawn by a replica of the *Sandy River No. 4* locomotive. ⊠ *Bridge Hill Rd., Phillips (20 mi southeast of Rangeley)*, ☎ *207/778–3621*, WEB *www.srrl-rr.org.* ☒ *$3.* ☉ *June–Oct., 1st and 3rd Sun. each month; rides hourly 11–3.*

Dining and Lodging

$$–$$$ ✕ **Gingerbread House.** A big fieldstone fireplace, well-spaced tables, and an antique marble soda fountain, all with views of the woods beyond, make for comfortable surroundings at this gingerbread-trim house, which is open for breakfast, lunch, and dinner. Soups, salads, and sandwiches at lunch give way to entrées such as shrimp scampi, roasted cranberry-maple chicken, and Maine crab cakes. ⊠ *Rtes. 17 and 4, Oquossoc*, ☎ *207/864–3602. AE, D, MC, V. Closed Mon. No dinner Sun.*

$$–$$$ ✕ **Porter House Restaurant.** This popular restaurant, seemingly in the middle of nowhere, draws diners from Rangeley, Kingfield, and Canada with its good service, excellent food, and casual surroundings. Of the 1908 farmhouse's four dining rooms, the front one downstairs, which has a fireplace, is the most intimate and elegant. The broad Continental-style menu includes entrées for diners with light appetites. On the heavier side are porterhouse steak and roast duckling. ⊠ *Rte. 27, Eustis (20 mi north of Rangeley)*, ☎ *207/246–7932. Reservations essential. AE, D, MC, V. Closed Mon.–Tues.*

$$ ✕🔲 **Country Club Inn.** Built in the 1920s on the Mingo Springs Golf Course, this retreat has a secluded hilltop location and sweeping lake and mountain views. Fieldstone fireplaces anchor both ends of the inn's living room. Rooms downstairs in the main building and in the 1950s motel-style wing are cheerfully if minimally decorated. The glassed-in dining room ($$–$$$)—open to nonguests by reservation only—has linen-draped tables set well apart. The menu lists entrées such as veal Gruyère and roast duck Montmorency. ⊠ *1 Country Club Rd., 04970*, ☎ *207/864–3831*, WEB *www.countryclubinnrangeley.com. 19 rooms. Restaurant, cable TV, 18-hole golf course, pool, bar; no air-conditioning, no-smoking rooms. AE, MC, V. Closed Apr.–mid-May and mid-Oct.–late Dec. BP, MAP.*

$$ ✕🔲 **Rangeley Inn and Motor Lodge.** From Main Street you see only the three-story blue inn building (circa 1907), but behind it is a motel wing with views of Haley Pond, a lawn, and a garden. Some of the inn's sizable rooms have iron-and-brass beds and subdued wallpaper, some have claw-foot tubs, and others have whirlpool tubs. The dining room ($$$–$$$$) has Continental-style choices, including chicken in creamy champagne sauce and filet mignon; the tavern serves casual fare such as soups, sandwiches, steaks, and ribs. You can choose to in-

clude breakfast and dinner in the rate. ✉ *51 Main St. (Box 160, 04970),* ☎ *207/864–3341 or 800/666–3687,* FAX *207/864–3634,* WEB *www.rangeleyinn.com. 36 inn rooms, 15 motel rooms, 2 cabins. Restaurant, cable TV, some microwaves, some refrigerators, bar, Internet, meeting rooms, some pets allowed (fee); no air-conditioning. AE, D, MC, V.*

$$$$ **Grant's Kennebago Camps.** People have been roughing it in comfort at this traditional sporting camp on Kennebago Lake for more than 85 years, lured by the mountain views, excellent fly-fishing, and hearty home-cooked meals. The wilderness setting is nothing less than spectacular. The cabins, whose screened porches overlook the lake, have woodstoves and are finished in knotty pine. Meals are served in the cheerful waterfront dining room. ✉ *Off Rte. 16 (Box 786, 04970),* ☎ *207/864–3608 or 800/633–4815,* WEB *www.grantscamps.com. 18 cabins. Dining room, lake, windsurfing, boating, fishing, mountain bikes, hiking, playground, some pets allowed (fee); no air-conditioning, no room phones, no room TVs. D, MC, V. Closed Oct.–mid-May. FAP.*

$$–$$$ **Hunter Cove on Rangeley Lake.** These rustic lakeside cabins, which sleep from two to six people, provide all the comforts of home. The interiors are unfinished knotty pine and include kitchens, full baths, and comfortable if plain living rooms. Cabin No. 1 has a fieldstone fireplace, and others have wood-burning stoves. Cabin Nos. 5 and 8 have hot tubs. If you visit in summer, you can take advantage of a sand swimming beach, boat rentals, and a nearby golf course. In winter, snowmobile right to your door or ski nearby (cross-country and downhill). ✉ *334 Mingo Loop Rd.,* ☎ *207/864–3383,* WEB *www.huntercove.com. 8 cabins. Cable TV, in-room VCRs, microwaves, beach, boating, some pets allowed (fee). AE.*

Nightlife and the Arts

Rangeley Friends of the Arts (✉ Box 333, 04970, ☎ no phone) sponsors musical theater, fiddlers' contests, rock and jazz, classical, and other summer fare, mostly at Lakeside Park.

Outdoor Activities and Sports

BOATING

Rangeley and Mooselookmeguntic lakes are good for canoeing, sailing, and motorboating. For fishing and paddleboat rentals, call **Oquossoc Cove Marina** (✉ Oquossoc, ☎ 207/864–3463). **Dockside Sports Center** (✉ Town Cove, ☎ 207/864–2424) rents boats, canoes, and other crafts. **River's Edge Sports** (✉ Rte. 4/16, Oquossoc, ☎ 207/864–5582) rents canoes.

FISHING

Fishing for brook trout and salmon is at its best in May, June, and September; the Rangeley area is especially popular with fly-fishers. **Westwind Charters and Guide Service** (☎ 207/864–5437) provides fishing guides and services.

SNOWMOBILING

More than 100 mi of maintained trails link lakes and towns to wilderness camps in the Rangeley area. The **Maine Snowmobile Association** has information about Maine's nearly 8,000-mi trail system.

STATE PARK

On the south shore of Rangeley Lake, **Rangeley Lake State Park** (✉ off Rte. 17, ☎ 207/864–3858) has superb lakeside scenery, swimming, picnic tables, a boat ramp, showers, and 50 campsites.

Ski Areas

SADDLEBACK SKI AND SUMMER LAKE PRESERVE

A down-home atmosphere prevails at Saddleback, where the quiet and the absence of crowds, even on holiday weekends, draw return visitors—many of them families. The Appalachian Trail crosses Saddleback's summit ridge. ⊠ *Saddleback Rd. off Rte. 4 (Box 490, 04970),* ☎ *207/864–5671; 207/864–3380 snow conditions; 207/864–5364 reservations,* WEB *www.saddlebackskiarea.com.*

Downhill. The terrain is short and concentrated at the top of the mountain, accessible only by a T-bar. The middle of the mountain is mainly intermediate, with a few meandering easy trails; the beginner or novice slopes are toward the bottom. Two double chairlifts and three T-bars carry skiers to the 41 trails on the 1,830-ft mount.

Cross-country. Forty kilometers (25 miles) of groomed cross-country trails spread out from the base area and circle Saddleback Lake and several ponds and rivers.

Child care. The nursery takes children ages 6 weeks–8 years. Ski classes and programs for kids of different levels and ages are offered.

Summer activities. Hiking is the big sport in warm weather.

Kingfield

⑥ *33 mi east of Rangeley, 15 mi west of Phillips.*

In the shadows of Mt. Abraham and Sugarloaf Mountain, Kingfield has everything a "real" New England town should have: a general store, historic inns, and a white clapboard church. Sugarloaf/USA has golf and tennis in summer.

The **Stanley Museum** houses a collection of original Stanley Steamer cars built by the Stanley twins, Kingfield's most famous natives. ⊠ *40 School St.,* ☎ *207/265–2729.* ⊡ *$2.* ⊙ *May–Oct., Tues.–Sun. 10–4; Nov.–Apr., weekdays 1–4.*

Nowetah's American Indian Museum displays an extensive collection of baskets as well as artifacts from native peoples of North and South America. This small museum is part of a store. ⊠ *Rte. 27, New Portland,* ☎ *207/628–4981.* ⊡ *Free.* ⊙ *Daily 10–5.*

Dining and Lodging

$–$$$ ✕ **Gepetto's.** Gepetto's combines efficient service with a diverse menu including homemade soups, hearty salads, burgers, pizza, vegetarian pasta, and fresh seafood. Hanging plants brighten the pine-paneled dining rooms, and big windows let you watch skiers as they schuss the slopes or walk through the village. ⊠ *Sugarloaf Base Village, Carrabassett Valley,* ☎ *207/237–2953. MC, V.*

$–$$ ✕⊡ **Sugarloaf Inn.** Guest rooms at this country inn could use a face-lift, but you can't beat the ski-on access to Sugarloaf/USA. Rooms range from king-size on the fourth floor to dorm-style (bunk beds) on the ground floor. A greenhouse section of the Seasons Restaurant ($$–$$$) affords views of the slopes. At breakfast the sunlight pours into the dining room, and at dinner you can watch the snow-grooming machines prepare your favorite run. The in-house brewpub is a comfortable après-ski spot. ⊠ *Sugarloaf Access Rd. (R.R. 1, Box 5000, Carrabassett Valley 04947),* ☎ *207/237–6814 or 800/843–5623,* FAX *207/237–3773,* WEB *www.sugarloaf.com. 38 rooms, 4 dorm-style rooms. Restaurant, cable TV, golf privileges, pool, health club, cross-country skiing, downhill skiing, pub, video game room, meeting room; no smoking. AE, D, MC, V.*

$ ✕⊡ **One and Three Stanley Avenue.** These sister properties, a fine-dining restaurant and a simple B&B, are in adjacent Victorian houses. The quiet neighborhood is a few minutes' walk from downtown Kingfield and about a 20-minute drive from Sugarloaf/USA. Both are decorated with period furnishings. The restaurant ($$$–$$$$; closed May–mid-Nov.) specializes in creative Continental fare and emphasizes fresh Maine ingredients. ⊠ *3 Stanley Ave. (Box 169, 04947),* ☎ *207/265–5541,* WEB *www.stanleyavenue.com. 6 rooms, 3 with bath. Restaurant; no air-conditioning, no room phones, no smoking. MC, V. BP.*

$–$$$ ⌂ **Grand Summit.** New England ambience and European-style service are combined at this six-story brick hotel at the base of the lifts at Sugarloaf/USA. Oak and redwood paneling in the main rooms is enhanced by contemporary furnishings. Valet parking, ski tuning, and lockers are available. ⊠ *R.R. 1, Box 2299, Carrabassett Valley 04947,* ☎ *207/237–4205 or 800/527–9879,* FAX *207/237–2874,* WEB *www.sugarloaf.com. 100 rooms, 19 suites. Restaurant, cable TV with video games, some microwaves, some refrigerators, hot tub, massage, sauna, spa, video game room, meeting room; no-smoking rooms. AE, D, DC, MC, V.*

Nightlife and the Arts

Monday is blues night at the **Bag & Kettle** (☎ 207/237–2451), which is the best choice for pizza and burgers. A microbrewery on the access road, the **Sugarloaf Brewing Company** (☎ 207/237–2211) pulls in revelers who come for après-ski brewskies. **Widowmaker Lounge** (☎ 207/237–6845) frequently presents live entertainment in the base lodge.

Outdoor Activities and Sports

T.A.D. Dog Sled Services (⊠ Rte. 27, Carrabassett Valley, ☎ 207/246–4461) conducts short 1½-mi rides near Sugarloaf/USA; sleds accommodate up to two adults and two children.

Ski Areas

SUGARLOAF/USA

Abundant natural snow, a huge mountain, and the only above-treeline skiing in the East have made Sugarloaf one of Maine's best-known ski areas. Two slope-side hotels and hundreds of slope-side condominiums provide ski-in, ski-out access, and the base village has restaurants and shops. Once you are here, a car is unnecessary—a shuttle connects all mountain operations. Summer is much quieter than winter, but you can bike, hike, golf, and fish. ⊠ *Sugarloaf Access Rd. (R.R. 1, Box 5000, Carrabassett Valley 04947),* ☎ *207/237–2000; 207/237–6808 snow conditions; 800/843–5623 reservations.*

Downhill. With a vertical of 2,820 ft, Sugarloaf is taller than any other New England ski peak except Killington in Vermont. The advanced terrain begins with the steep snowfields on top, wide open and treeless. Coming down the face of the mountain, black-diamond runs are everywhere, often blending into easier terrain. Many intermediate trails can be found down the front face, and a couple more come off the summit. Easier runs are predominantly toward the bottom, with a few long, winding runs that twist and turn from higher elevations. The mountain has three terrain parks and a halfpipe. Serving the resort's 129 trails are two high-speed quad, two quad, one triple, and eight double chairlifts and one T-bar.

Cross-country. The Sugarloaf Ski Outdoor Center has 105 km (62 mi) of cross-country trails that loop and wind through the valley. Trails connect to the resort.

Other activities. Snowshoeing and ice skating are available at the Outdoor Center. On Wednesday and Saturday nights, you can take a Sno-Cat to **Bullwinkles,** a mid-mountain restaurant, for a multicourse dining adventure (☎ 207/237–2000; $85 per person, reservations essential).

Child care. A nursery takes children ages 10 weeks–5 years. Children's ski programs begin at age 3. A night nursery is open on Thursday and Saturday 6–10 PM by reservation. Instruction is provided on a half-day or full-day basis for children ages 4–14.

Summer and year-round activities. The resort has a superb 18-hole, Robert Trent Jones, Jr.–designed golf course and six tennis courts for public use in warmer months. The Original Golf School operates from late June to late October. You can get advice on planning mountain biking and hiking trips, and the resort has canoe and bike rentals and can arrange fly-fishing instruction. The **Sugarloaf Sports and Fitness Club** (☏ 207/237–6946) has an indoor pool, six indoor and outdoor hot tubs, racquetball courts, full fitness and spa facilities, and a beauty salon. Use of club facilities is included in all lodging packages. The **Anti-Gravity Center** (☏ 207/237–5566) has a climbing wall, weight room, basketball court, trampolines, and indoor skate park.

Western Lakes and Mountains A to Z

To research prices, get advice from other travelers, and book travel arrangements, visit www.fodors.com.

AIR TRAVEL

Mountain Air Service provides air access to remote areas, scenic flights, and charter-fishing trips. Naples Seaplane Service operates charter and scenic flights over the lakes region.
➤ AIRLINES AND CONTACTS: **Mountain Air Service** (✉ Rangeley, ☏ 207/864–5307). **Naples Seaplane Service** (✉ Rte. 302, Naples Causeway, Naples, ☏ 207/693–5138).

BIKE TRAVEL

Numerous back roads provide plenty of mountain biking. As in other parts of the state, few roads have shoulders.
➤ BIKE INFORMATION: **Bethel Outdoor Adventures** (✉ 121 Mayville Rd., Bethel, ☏ 207/824–4224 or 800/533–3607, WEB www.BethelOutdoorAdventure.com). **Rangeley Mountain Bike Touring** (✉ 53 Main St. Rangeley, ☏ 207/864–5799). **Ride On!** (✉ Village Center, Sugarloaf Resort, Carrabassett Valley, ☏ 207/237–6986).

BUS TRAVEL

The Mountain Express is a free shuttle bus that operates between Bethel village and Sunday River. The Sunday River Trolley links hotels and condos at the ski resort with lifts and lodges. Sunday River's Jordan Shuttle vans operate between the Jordan Grand and South Ridge Base Lodge during the day and the White Cap Base Lodge in the evening.

CAR TRAVEL

A car is essential to tour the western lakes and mountains. To travel from town to town in the order described in this section, drive U.S. 302 to Naples, then Route 35 to Harrison and the Waterfords. Take the Sweden Road, an ideal pick for autumn due to its vistas of the White Mountains, across to Lovell and pick up Route 5 to Bethel. From there, take Route 26 to U.S. 2 to Route 17 to Oquossoc, then head east on Route 16 through Rangeley to Kingfield.

EMERGENCIES

➤ HOSPITALS: **Bethel Family Health Center** (✉ 42 Railroad St., Bethel, ☏ 207/824–2193 or 800/287–2292). **Mt. Abram Regional Health Center** (✉ Depot St., Kingfield, ☏ 207/265–4555). **Northern Cumberland Memorial Hospital** (✉ S. High St., Bridgton, ☏ 207/647–8841).

Rangeley Regional Health Center (⊠ Main St., Rangeley, ☎ 207/864–3303).

LODGING

Krainin Real Estate specializes in lakefront rentals in the Sebago area. In the Bethel area, try Maine Street Realty. Morton & Furbish has extensive rental listings in the Rangeley Lakes region.

➤ LODGING: **Krainin Real Estate** (⊠ Rte. 302, South Casco, ☎ 207/655–3811 or 800/639–2321, WEB www.krainin.com). **Maine Street Realty** (⊠ 57 Main St., Bethel, ☎ 800/824–2141, WEB www.mainestreetrealty.com). **Morton & Furbish** (⊠ Rangeley, ☎ 207/864–5777 or 888/218–4882, WEB www.rangeleyrentals.com). **Sugarloaf Area Reservations Service** (☎ 207/235–2100 or 800/843–2732).

MEDIA

The *Portland Press Herald* is published Monday–Saturday; the *Maine Sunday Telegram* is published on Sunday. The *Lewiston Sun Journal* is published daily. Weekly newspapers include the *Bethel Citizen*, *Bridgton News, Irregular* (Kingfield), and *Suburban News* (Windham).

WMEA 90.1 is the public broadcasting affiliate for the Sebago Lakes region. WCSH, channel 6, is the NBC affiliate. WMTW, channel 8, is the ABC affiliate. WGME, channel 13, is the CBS affiliate. WCBB, channel 10, is the Maine Public Broadcasting affiliate.

OUTDOOR ACTIVITIES AND SPORTS

FISHING

For information about fishing and licenses, contact the Maine Department of Inland Fisheries and Wildlife.

➤ CONTACT: **Maine Department of Inland Fisheries and Wildlife** (⊠ 41 State House Station, Augusta 04333, ☎ 207/287–8000, WEB www.state.me.us/ifw).

SKIING

Sunday River is one of the state's largest alpine areas. Family-friendly Mt. Abram also has night skiing. Saddleback delivers a back-to-basics ski experience. You can cross-country ski at Nordic centers with groomed trails or go on a backcountry excursion. For information on cross-country ski centers, shops, and lodging packages, contact the Maine Nordic Ski Council. For information on alpine skiing, contact Ski Maine.

➤ CONTACTS: **Maine Nordic Ski Council** (⊠ Box 645, Bethel 04217, ☎ 207/824–3694 or 800/754–9263, WEB www.mnsc.com). **Ski Maine** (⊠ Box 7566, Portland 04112, ☎ 207/622–6983; 207/761–3774; 888/624–6345 snow conditions; WEB www.skimaine.com).

VISITOR INFORMATION

Bethel's Chamber of Commerce has a reservations service. For reservations at Sugarloaf/USA, contact Sugarloaf Area Reservations Service.

➤ CONTACTS: **Bethel Area Chamber of Commerce** (⊠ 30 Cross St. [Box 439, Bethel 04217], ☎ 207/824–2282, WEB www.bethelmaine.com). **Bethel's Chamber of Commerce Reservation Service** (☎ 207/824–3585 or 800/442–5826). **Greater Bridgton–Lakes Region Chamber of Commerce** (⊠ U.S. 302 [Box 236, Bridgton 04009], ☎ 207/647–3472, WEB www.mainelakeschamber.com). **Greater Windham Chamber of Commerce** (⊠ U.S. 302 [Box 1015, Windham 04062], ☎ 207/892–8265, WEB windhamchamber.sebagolake.org). **Maine Tourism Association Welcome Center** (⊠ U.S. 2 [Box 1084, Bethel 04217], ☎ 207/824–4582). **Naples Business Association** (⊠ Box 412, Naples 04055, ☎ 207/693–3285 summer). **Rangeley Lakes Region Chamber of Com-**

merce (⊠ Main St. [Box 317, Rangeley 04970], ☏ 207/864–5571 or 800/685–2537, WEB www.rangeleymaine.com). **Sugarloaf Area Chamber of Commerce** (⊠ R.R. 1, Box 2151, Kingfield 04947, ☏ 207/235–2100).

THE NORTH WOODS

Maine's North Woods, the vast area in the north-central section of the state, is best experienced by canoe or raft, hiking trail, or on a fishing trip. Some great theaters for these activities are Moosehead Lake, Baxter State Park, and the Allagash Wilderness Waterway—as well as the summer resort town of Greenville. Maine's largest lake, Moosehead supplies more in the way of rustic camps, restaurants, guides, and outfitters than any other northern locale. Its 420 mi of shorefront, three-quarters of which is owned by paper manufacturers, is virtually uninhabited.

Greenville

⑥ *160 mi northeast of Portland, 71 mi northwest of Bangor.*

Greenville, the largest town on Moosehead Lake, is an outdoors lover's paradise. Boating, fishing, and hiking are popular in summer; snowmobiling and skiing in winter. The town has the greatest selection of shops, restaurants, and inns in the region, though many of these are closed mid-October–mid-June.

The **Greenville Historical Society** leads guided tours of the Eveleth-Crafts-Sheridan House, a late-19th-century Victorian mansion filled with period antiques. Special exhibits and displays change annually. A small lumberman's museum and a fine exhibit of Native American artifacts dating from 9,000 BC to the 1700s are in the Carriage House. ⊠ *Pritham Ave.,* ☏ *207/695–2909,* WEB *www.mooseheadhistory.org.* ▣ *$2.* ☉ *Mid-June–Sept., Wed.–Fri. 1–4.*

Moosehead Marine Museum has exhibits on the local logging industry and the steamship era on Moosehead Lake, plus photographs of the Mount Kineo Hotel. ⊠ *Main St.,* ☏ *207/695–2716.* ▣ *$3.* ☉ *Late May–early Oct., daily 10–4.*

The Moosehead Marine Museum runs three- and five-hour trips on Moosehead Lake aboard the ★*Katahdin,* a 1914 steamship (now diesel). The 115-ft ship, also called *The Kate,* carried passengers to Kineo until 1942 and then was used in the logging industry until 1975. ⊠ *Main St. (boarding on shoreline by museum),* ☏ *207/695–2716,* WEB *www.katahdincruises.com.* ▣ *$20–$26.* ☉ *July–Columbus Day.*

OFF THE
BEATEN PATH

KINEO – Once a thriving summer resort, the original Mount Kineo Hotel (built in 1830 and torn down in the 1940s) was accessed primarily by steamship. Today Kineo makes a pleasant day trip. You can take the Kineo Shuttle, which departs from the State Dock in Rockwood (☏ 207/534–8812), or rent a motorboat in Rockwood and make the journey across the lake in about 15 minutes. You can hike the Kineo's summit for awesome views down the lake. A map is available at the Moosehead Area Chamber of Commerce.

Dining and Lodging

$$$$ ✕▣ **Blair Hill Inn.** Beautiful gardens and a hilltop location with marvelous views over the lake distinguish this 1891 estate. Guest rooms are spacious, and four have fireplaces. A restaurant, open to the public by reservation, serves a five-course dinner ($$$$) from late May to

The North Woods

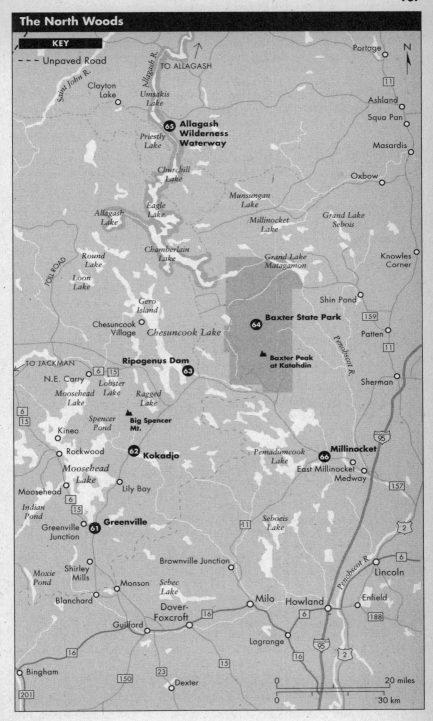

KEY

- - - Unpaved Road

TO ALLAGASH

Portage

N

Saint John R.

Allagash R.

Clayton Lake

Umsakis Lake

Ashland

Squa Pan

11

65 Allagash Wilderness Waterway

Priestly Lake

Masardis

Churchill Lake

Munsungan Lake

Oxbow

Eagle Lake

Millinocket Lake

Grand Lake Sebois

Allagash Lake

Chamberlain Lake

Grand Lake Matagamon

Knowles Corner

TOLL ROAD

Round Lake

Loon Lake

Gero Island

Shin Pond

159

64 Baxter State Park

Patten

Chesuncook Village

Chesuncook Lake

Penobscot R.

11

TO JACKMAN

Ripogenus Dam

N.E. Carry

6 15

63

▲ Baxter Peak at Katahdin

Sherman

Lobster Lake

Moosehead Lake

Ragged Lake

6 15

Spencer Pond

▲ **Big Spencer Mt.**

95

Kineo

62 Kokadjo

Pemadumcook Lake

66 Millinocket

Rockwood

East Millinocket

Medway

Moosehead Lake

Lily Bay

157

Moosehead

6

Indian Pond

15

Seboeis Lake

2

61 Greenville

Greenville Junction

11

6

Moxie Pond

Shirley Mills

Brownville Junction

Lincoln

Monson

Sebec Lake

Penobscot R.

Enfield

Blanchard

Dover-Foxcroft

Milo

Howland

188

16

6

Guilford

Lagrange

95

16

16

2

150

23

15

201

Bingham

Dexter

0   20 miles

0   30 km

mid-October on Friday and Saturday nights. Arrive early to enjoy cocktails on the wraparound porch. The inn hosts a music series from June through September and cooking school weekends in the off-season. ⊠ *Lily Bay Rd. (Box 1288, 04441),* ☎ *207/695–0224,* ℻ *207/ 695–4324,* WEB *www.blairhill.com, 8 rooms, 2 suites. Restaurant, cable TV in some rooms, outdoor hot tub, gym, Internet; no air-conditioning, no room phones, no kids under 10, no smoking. D, MC, V. BP.*

$$$ ✕⊡ **Greenville Inn.** The ornate cherry and mahogany paneling, Oriental rugs, and lead glass create an aura of masculine ease in this 1985 former lumber baron's mansion. Some rooms and cottages have lake views as does the restaurant ($$$; reservations essential; closed Nov.– Apr.; no lunch). Revised daily, the menu reflects the owners' Austrian background with choices such as spicy maple-glazed salmon fillets with potato pancakes and pork tenderloin with paprika sauce and spaetzle. ⊠ *Norris St. (Box 1194, 04441),* ☎ *207/695–2206 or 888/695– 6000,* ℻ *207/695–0335,* WEB *www.greenvilleinn.com. 4 rooms, 1 suite in main inn; 1 suite in carriage house; 6 cottages. Restaurant, cable TV in some rooms; no air-conditioning, no room phones, no kids under 8. D, MC, V. CP.*

$$$$ ⊡ **Attean Lake Lodge.** The Holden family has owned and operated this island lodge about an hour and a half northwest of Greenville since 1900. Log cabins, which sleep from two to six people, provide a secluded environment. Look for lobster, beef, and veal at the substantial meals; cookouts and picnic lunches add variety. ⊠ *Off Rte. 201, Birch Island (Box 457, Jackman 04945),* ☎ *207/668–3792,* ℻ *207/ 668–4016,* WEB *www.atteanlodge.com. 18 cabins. Beach, boating, recreation room, library. AE, MC, V. Closed Oct.–May. FAP.*

$$$$ ⊡ **Little Lyford Pond Camps.** When you want to get away from everything—electricity, plumbing, phones—this remote and rustic wilderness retreat with llamas and sheep, dogs, and chickens casts a magical spell. Gulf Hagas is a half-day hike, moose are abundant, and the fly-fishing is excellent. Cabins have woodstoves, gas lanterns, and small libraries. The home-cooked fare is vegetarian oriented with some fish and poultry. Winter access is by cross-country ski. ⊠ *(Box 340, 04441),* ☎ *207/695–3288,* WEB *www.littlelyford.com. 9 cottages. Ponds, sauna (winter), boating, fishing, hiking, cross-country skiing, some pets allowed (fee); no air-conditioning, no room TVs, no phones, no smoking. No credit cards. Closed Apr. and Nov.–early Dec. FAP.*

$$$–$$$$ ⊡ **Lodge at Moosehead Lake.** All rooms in this grand manor overlooking Moosehead Lake have fireplaces and hand-carved four-poster beds; some have lake views. The carriage-house suites open on to private patios. The dining room, where breakfast is served, has a spectacular view of the water. Four-course, prix-fixe dinners are occasionally available; entrées may include pan-seared salmon with citrus. ⊠ *Lily Bay Rd. (Box 1167, 04441),* ☎ *207/695–4400,* ℻ *207/695–2281,* WEB *www.lodgeatmooseheadlake.com. 5 rooms, 3 suites. Dining room, cable TV, in-room VCRs, hot tubs, snowmobiling, lobby lounge; no kids under 14, no smoking. D, MC, V. Closed late Oct.–late Dec. and mid-Mar.–mid-May.*

$$ ⊡ **Lakeview House.** You get nearly the same sweeping views over Moosehead Lake at this small, minimally decorated B&B as you do from the more exclusive and expensive Lodge at Moosehead Lake. ⊠ *358 Lily Bay Rd. (Box 1102, 04441),* ☎ *207/695–2229,* ℻ *207/695– 8951,* WEB *www.lakeviewhouse.com. 2 rooms, 1 suite. Cable TV, some pets allowed; no room phones, no smoking. Call ahead in winter. BP.*

$ ⊡ **Chalet Moosehead.** Fifty yards off Route 6/15 and right on Moosehead Lake, this property has suites (with two double beds, a living room, and a kitchenette), motel rooms, and cabins, all with picture windows to capture the view. The attractive grounds include a private beach and dock. Some rooms have balconies overlooking the lake. ⊠ *Rte. 6/15 (Box 327, Greenville Junction 04442),* ☎ *207/695–2950 or 800/290–3645,* WEB *www.mooseheadlodging.com. 19 rooms, 8 efficiencies. Cable TV, some in-room hot tubs, some kitchenettes, some refrigerators, dock, beach, boating, horseshoes, snowmobiling, some pets allowed (fee); no air-conditioning, no-smoking rooms. AE, D, MC, V.*

Outdoor Activities and Sports

Beaver Cove Marina (☎ 207/695–3526) rents boats and snowmobiles. **Big Lake Marina** (☎ 207/695–4487) is a full-service marina with boat rentals. **Moose Country Safaris and Dogsled Trips** (☎ 207/876–4907) leads moose safaris, dogsled trips, and canoe and kayak trips. **Northwoods Outfitters** (☎ 207/695–3288) outfits a variety of sports and offers tours, moose safaris, dogsledding, and trail advice.

FISHING

Togue, landlocked salmon, and brook and lake trout lure thousands of anglers to the region from ice-out in mid-May until September; the hardiest return in winter to ice-fish. Call for current **information** (☎ 207/695–3756 or 800/322–9844) on water levels.

RAFTING

The Kennebec and Dead rivers and the west branch of the Penobscot River provide thrilling white-water rafting (guides are strongly recommended). These rivers are dam-controlled, so trips run rain or shine daily from May to October (day and multiday trips are conducted). Most guided raft trips on the Kennebec and Dead rivers leave from the Forks, southwest of Moosehead Lake, on Route 201; Penobscot River trips leave from either Greenville or Millinocket. Many rafting outfitters operate resort facilities in their base towns. **Raft Maine** (☎ 800/723–8633) has lodging and rafting packages and information about outfitters.

STATE PARK

Lily Bay State Park (⊠ Lily Bay Rd., ☎ 207/695–2700; ⌛ $2), 8 mi northeast of Greenville, has a good swimming beach, two boat-launching ramps, and two campgrounds with 91 sites.

Shopping

Indian Hill Trading Post (⊠ Rte. 6/15, ☎ 207/695–2104) stocks just about anything you might need for a North Woods vacation, including sporting and camping equipment, canoes, and fishing licenses; there's even an adjacent grocery store. You enter **Moosehead Traders** (⊠ Moosehead Center Mall, Rte. 6/15, ☎ 207/695–3806) through an antler archway; inside are books, clothing, and antiques and artifacts.

Ski Areas

BIG SQUAW MOUNTAIN RESORT

At this remote but pretty resort overlooking Moosehead Lake, the emphasis is on affordable family skiing—prices are downright cheap compared with those at other in-state areas. ⊠ *Rte. 6/15 (Box D, 04441),* ☎ *207/695–1000.*

Downhill. Trails are laid out according to difficulty, with the easy slopes toward the bottom, intermediate trails weaving from midpoint, and steeper runs high up off the 1,750-vertical-ft peak. The 22 trails are served by one triple and one double chairlift and two surface lifts.

Child care. The nursery takes children from infants through age six. The ski school has daily lessons and racing classes for children of all ages.

Kokadjo

⓺² *22 mi northeast of Greenville.*

Kokadjo, population "not many," has a sign that reads KEEP MAINE GREEN. "This is God's country. Why set it on fire and make it look like hell?" This is the last outpost before you enter the North Woods. As you leave Kokadjo, bear left at the fork and follow signs to Baxter State Park. A drive of 5 mi along this road (now dirt) brings you to the Sias Hill checkpoint, where from June to November a fee may be charged to travel the next 40 mi. Access is through a forest where you're likely to encounter logging trucks (which have the right of way), logging equipment, and work in progress. Drive carefully; sightings of moose, deer, and even bear are common.

Ripogenus Dam

⓺³ *20 mi northeast of Kokadjo, 25 mins southeast of Chesuncook Village by floatplane.*

Ripogenus Dam and the granite-walled Ripogenus Gorge are on Ripogenus Lake, east of Chesuncook Lake. The gorge is the jumping-off point for the famous 12-mi West Branch of the Penobscot River whitewater rafting trip and the most popular put-in point for Allagash canoe trips. The Penobscot River drops more than 70 ft per mi through the gorge, giving rafters a hold-on-for-your-life ride. The best spot to watch the Penobscot rafters is from Pray's Big Eddy Wilderness Campground, overlooking the rock-choked Crib Works Rapid (a Class V rapid). To get here, follow the main road northeast and turn left on Telos Road; the campground is about 10 yards after the bridge.

En Route From Pray's Big Eddy Wilderness Campground, take the main road (here called the Golden Road for the amount of money it took the Great Northern Paper Company to build it) southeast toward Millinocket. The road soon becomes paved. After you drive over the one-lane Abol Bridge and pass through the Debsconeag checkpoint, bear left to reach Togue Pond Gatehouse, the southern entrance to Baxter State Park.

Baxter State Park

★ ⓺⁴ *24 mi northwest of Millinocket.*

Few places in Maine are as remote or as beautiful as Baxter State Park and the Allagash Wilderness Waterway. Baxter, a gift from Governor Percival Baxter, is the jewel in the crown of northern Maine, a 204,733-acre wilderness area that surrounds Katahdin, Maine's highest mountain (5,267 ft at Baxter Peak) and the terminus of the Appalachian Trail. There are 46 mountain peaks and ridges, 18 of which exceed an elevation of 3,000 ft. Day-use parking areas fill quickly in season; it's best to arrive early, before 8 AM. The park is intersected by more than 180 mi of trails. No pets, domestic animals, oversize vehicles, cell phones, radios, all-terrain vehicles, motorboats, or motorcycles are allowed in the park, and there are no pay phones, gas stations, stores, or running water or electricity. The one visitor center is at Togue Pond, for which Millinocket is the nearest gateway. ⊠ *Mailing address: 64 Balsam Dr., Millinocket 04462,* ☎ *207/723–5140.* ☞ *$8 per vehicle; free to Maine residents.*

OFF THE
BEATEN PATH   **LUMBERMAN'S MUSEUM** – This museum comprises 10 buildings filled with exhibits depicting the history of logging, including models, dioramas, and equipment. ⊠ *Shin Pond Rd. (Rte. 159), Patten (22 mi east of*

Baxter State Park), ☎ *207/528–2650,* WEB *www.lumbermensmuseum. org.* 🎫 *$5.* ⊘ *July–Aug., Fri.–Sun. 10–4; Memorial Day–June and Sept.–Columbus Day, Tues.–Sun. 10–4.*

Lodging

$ ⚠ **Baxter State Park Authority.** Camping spaces at the 10 campgrounds here can be reserved only by mail or in person. Reservations can be made beginning the first working day in January—some sites are fully booked for midsummer weekends soon after that. The state also maintains primitive backcountry sites. ✉ *64 Balsam Dr., Millinocket 04462,* ☎ *207/723–5140.*

Outdoor Activities and Sports

Katahdin, in Baxter State Park, draws thousands of hikers every year for the daylong climb to the summit and the stunning views of woods, mountains, and lakes from the hair-raising Knife Edge Trail along its ridge. The crowds can be formidable on clear summer days, so if you crave solitude, tackle one of the 45 other mountains in the park, all of which are accessible from a 150-mi network of trails. South Turner can be climbed in a morning (if you're fit)—it has a great view of Katahdin across the valley. On the way you'll pass Sandy Stream Pond, where moose are often seen at dusk. The Owl, the Brothers, and Doubletop Mountain are good day hikes.

Allagash Wilderness Waterway

65 *22 mi north of Ripogenus Dam.*

The Allagash is a spectacular 92-mi corridor of lakes and rivers that cuts across 170,000 acres of wilderness, beginning at the northwest corner of Baxter State Park and running north to the town of Allagash, 10 mi from the Canadian border. For information, contact the **Allagash Wilderness Waterway** (✉ 106 Hogan Rd., Bangor 04401, ☎ 207/ 941–4014).

Outdoor Activities and Sports

The Allagash rapids are ranked Class I and Class II (very easy and easy), but that doesn't mean the river is a piece of cake; river conditions vary greatly with the depth and volume of water, and even a Class I rapid can hang your canoe up on a rock, capsize you, or spin you around. On the lakes, strong winds can halt your progress for days. The Allagash should not be undertaken lightly or without planning; the complete 92-mi course requires 7 to 10 days. The canoeing season along the Allagash is from mid-May to October, although it's wise to remember that the black-fly season ends about July 1. The best bet for a novice is to go with a guide; a good outfitter will help plan your route and provide your craft and transportation.

Millinocket

66 *19 mi southeast of Baxter State Park, 70 mi north of Bangor, 90 mi northwest of Greenville.*

Millinocket, a paper-mill town with a population of 7,000, is a gateway to Baxter State Park and Maine's North Woods. Most visitors to this region come to hike, camp, canoe or raft, not to explore Millinocket itself. Although it has a smattering of motels and restaurants, Millinocket is the place to stock up on supplies, fill your gas tank, or grab a hot meal or shower before heading into the wilderness. Numerous rafting and canoeing outfitters and guides are based here.

KATAHDIN IRON WORKS – For a worthwhile day trip from Millinocket, take Route 11 and head southwest to a trailhead 5 mi north of Brownville Junction. Drive the gravel road 6 mi to Katahdin Iron Works, the site of a mining operation that employed nearly 200 workers in the mid-1800s; a deteriorated kiln, a stone furnace, and a charcoal-storage building are all that remain. From here, a hiking trail leads over fairly rugged terrain to **Gulf Hagas,** with natural chasms, cliffs, a 3½-mi gorge, waterfalls, pools, exotic flora, and rock formations.

Lodging

$$$$ 🖬 **Bradford Camps.** It's tempting to laze the day away on the front porch of these rustic lakefront log cabins (no electricity) or by the massive field-stone fireplace in the main lodge. But alas, you have miles of trails, woods, and roads to explore, rivers and lakes to fish and canoe, and even the Allagash is close enough for a day trip. Rates include three hearty, home-style meals. Floatplane transportation is available from Millinocket and other locations. ⊠ *Box 729, Ashland 04732,* ☎ *207/746–7777 May–Nov.; 207/439–6364 Dec.–Apr.,* WEB *www.bradfordcamps.com. 8 cabins. Dining room, lake, hiking, boating; no air-conditioning, no room phones, no room TVs. Closed late Nov.–May.*

$$$$ 🖬 **Libby Camps.** Matt Libby, along with his wife, Ellen, represent the fifth generation of Libbys to run this sporting camp on Millinocket Lake, the headwaters of the Allagash and Aroostook rivers. Skylights brighten the well-kept cabins, where handmade quilts cover the beds and wood-stoves keep the chill at bay (there's no electricity). The main lodge is open and airy with a magnificent central stone fireplace. Rates include all meals as well as use of sea kayaks, canoes, and sail and motor boats. ⊠ *Box 810, Ashland 04732,* ☎ *207/435–8274,* FAX *207/435–3230,* WEB *www.libbycamps.com. 8 cabins, 10 rustic outpost cabins. Hiking, beach, boating, fishing; no air-conditioning, no room phones, no room TVs. MC, V. Closed late Nov.–Apr. FAP.*

$ 🖬 **Big Moose Inn.** There's nothing fancy about this old-fashioned inn and the cabins and campsites nestled between Ambejesus and Millinocket lakes, just 8 mi from the entrance to Baxter State Park. The inn has a big stone-and-brick fireplace decorated with a moose trophy and snow-shoes; inn rooms are comfortably furnished with country pieces. The popular dining room, open for dinner Wednesday–Saturday, empha-sizes seafood. Canoes and a store are other amenities. ⊠ *Baxter State Park Rd. (Box 98, 04462),* ☎ *207/723–8391,* FAX *207/723–8199,* WEB *www.bigmoosecabins.com. 11 rooms without bath, 11 cabins, 44 campsites. Restaurant, boating, fishing, hiking, snowmobiling; no air-conditioning, no room phones, no room TVs. MC, V. Closed late Nov.–May. CP.*

$ 🖬 **Gateway Inn.** After roughing it in the woods, this motel just off I–95 provides clean facilities. Book a room with a deck facing Katahdin for the best views. ⊠ *Rte. 157 (Box 637, Medway 04460),* ☎ *207/746–3193,* FAX *207/746–3430,* WEB *www.medwaygateway.com. 30 rooms, 8 efficiencies. Cable TV, some kitchenettes, gym, indoor pool, hot tub, sauna, snowmobiling, meeting room, some pets allowed; no-smoking rooms. AE, D, MC, V. CP.*

Outdoor Activities and Sports

Katahdin Outfitters (⊠ Baxter State Park Rd., ☎ 800/862–2663 or 207/723–5700) outfits canoeing expeditions. **New England Outdoor Center** (☎ 207/723–5438 or 800/766–7238) rents snowmobiles and of-fers guided trips.

The North Woods A to Z

To research prices, get advice from other travelers, and book travel arrangements, visit www.fodors.com.

AIR TRAVEL

Charter flights, usually by seaplane, from Bangor, Greenville, or Millinocket to smaller towns and remote lake and forest areas can be arranged with a number of flying services, which will transport you and your gear and help you find a guide.

➤ AIRLINES AND CONTACTS: **Currier's Flying Service** (⊠ Greenville Junction, ☎ 207/695–2778). **Folsom's Air Service** (⊠ Greenville, ☎ 207/695–2821). **Katahdin Air Service** (⊠ Millinocket, ☎ 207/723–8378). **Scotty's Flying Service** (⊠ Shin Pond, ☎ 207/528–2626).

AIRPORTS

Bangor International Airport is the closest airport (☞ Maine A to Z).

BIKE TRAVEL

Mountain biking is popular in the Greenville area, but no bikes are allowed on logging roads. Expect to pay $20–$25 for a rental bicycle.

➤ BIKE INFORMATION: **Northwoods Outfitters** (⊠ Main St., Greenville, ☎ 207/695–3288, WEB www.maineoutfitter.com).

CAR TRAVEL

A car is essential to negotiate this vast region but may not be useful to someone spending a vacation entirely at a wilderness camp. Public roads are scarce in the north country, but lumber companies maintain private roads that are often open to the public (sometimes by permit only). When driving on a logging road, always give lumber-company trucks the right of way. Be aware that loggers often take the middle of the road and will neither move over nor slow down for you.

I–95 provides the quickest access to the North Woods. U.S. 201 is the major route to Jackman and to Québec. Route 15 connects Jackman to Greenville and Bangor. The Golden Road is a private, paper company–operated road that links Greenville to Millinocket. Be sure to have a full tank of gas before heading on the many private roads in the region.

EMERGENCIES

➤ HOSPITALS: **Charles A. Dean Memorial Hospital** (⊠ Pritham Ave., Greenville, ☎ 207/695–2223 or 800/260–4000). **Mayo Regional Hospital** (⊠ 75 W. Main St., Dover-Foxcroft, ☎ 207/564–8401). **Millinocket Regional Hospital** (⊠ 200 Somerset St., Millinocket, ☎ 207/723–5161).

LODGING
CAMPING

Reservations for state park campsites (excluding Baxter State Park) can be made through the Bureau of Parks and Lands, which can also tell you if you need a camping permit and where to obtain one. Maine Sporting Camp Association publishes a list of its members, with details on the facilities available at each camp.

The Maine Campground Owners Association publishes a helpful annual directory of its members. The Maine Forest Service, Department of Conservation will direct you to the nearest place to get a fire permit. Maine Tourism Association publishes a listing of private campsites and cottage rentals. North Maine Woods maintains 500 primitive campsites on commercial forest land.

➤ CONTACTS: **Bureau of Parks and Lands** (✉ State House Station 22, Augusta 04333, ☏ 207/287–3821; 800/332–1501 in Maine). **Maine Campground Owners Association** (✉ 655 Main St., Lewiston 04240, ☏ 207/782–5874, WEB www.campmaine.com). **Maine Forest Service, Department of Conservation** (✉ State House Station 22, Augusta 04333, ☏ 207/287–2791). **Maine Sporting Camp Association** (✉ Box 119, Millinocket 04462, WEB www.mainesportingcamps.com). **Maine Tourism Association** (✉ 325-B Water St., Hallowell 04347, ☏ 207/623–0363; 800/533–9595 outside Maine). **North Maine Woods** (✉ 41 Main St. [Box 425, Ashland 04732], ☏ 207/435–6213, WEB www.northmainewoods.org).

MEDIA

The *Bangor Daily News* is published Monday–Friday. Weekly newspapers include *Katahdin Times* (Millinocket) and *Moosehead Messenger* (Greenville).

WMEH 90.0, a public broadcasting affiliate, reaches southern portions of the North Woods region. WLBZ, channel 2, is the NBC affiliate. WVII, channel 7, is the ABC affiliate. WABI, channel 5, is the CBS affiliate. WMEB, channel 12, is the Maine Public Broadcasting affiliate.

OUTDOOR ACTIVITIES AND SPORTS

CANOEING

Most canoe rental operations will arrange transportation, help plan your route, and provide a guide. Transport to wilderness lakes can be arranged through the flying services listed under Air Travel.

The Bureau of Parks and Lands (☞ Lodging) provides information on independent Allagash canoeing and camping. Allagash Canoe Trips operates guided trips on the Allagash Waterway, plus the Moose, Penobscot, and St. John rivers. Canoe Maine with Gil Gilpatrick conducts fully outfitted canoeing trips on Maine rivers. Mahoosuc Guide Service runs guided trips on the Penobscot, Allagash, and Moose rivers.

Northwoods Outfitters rents equipment and leads trips on regional lakes and rivers, including the Allagash and the West Branch of the Penobscot. North Woods Ways is a Maine Master guide service on the state's rivers and lakes. Sunrise International outfits trips on eastern and northern Maine waterways and other locations. Willard Jalbert Camps has been leading guided Allagash trips since the late 1800s. North Maine Woods has maps, a canoeing guide for the St. John River, and lists of outfitters, camps, and campsites.

➤ CONTACTS: **Allagash Canoe Trips** (✉ Box 713, Greenville 04441, ☏ 207/695–3668). **Canoe Maine with Gil Gilpatrick** (✉ Box 461, Skowhegan 04976, ☏ 207/453–6959). **Mahoosuc Guide Service** (✉ Bear River Rd., Newry 04261, ☏ 207/824–2073). **North Maine Woods** (✉ Box 425, Ashland 04732, ☏ 207/435–6213). **Northwoods Outfitters** (✉ Maine St. [Box 160, Greenville 04441], ☏ 207/695–3288). **North Woods Ways** (✉ R.R. 2, Box 159A, Guilford 04443, ☏ 207/997–3723). **Sunrise International** (✉ 4 Union Pl., Suite 21, Bangor 04401, ☏ 207/942–9300 or 800/980–2300). **Willard Jalbert Camps** (✉ 6 Winchester St., Presque Isle 04769, ☏ 207/764–0494).

FISHING

For information about fishing and licenses, contact the Maine Department of Inland Fisheries and Wildlife. Guides are available through most wilderness camps, sporting goods stores, and canoe outfitters. For assistance in finding a guide, contact Maine Professional Guides Association or North Maine Woods (☞ Canoeing).

➤ CONTACTS: **Maine Department of Inland Fisheries and Wildlife** (✉ 41 State House Station, Augusta 04333, ☎ 207/287–8000, WEB www.state.me.us/ifw). **Maine Professional Guides Association** (✉ Box 336, Augusta 04332, ☎ 207/622–6241, WEB www.maineguides.org).

HORSEBACK RIDING

North Woods Riding Adventures, owned by registered Maine guides Judy Cross-Strehlke and Bob Strehlke, conducts one-day, two-day, and week-long pack trips (10 people maximum) through parts of Piscataquis County. A popular two-day trip explores the Whitecap–Barren Mountain Range, near Katahdin Iron Works.
➤ CONTACT: **North Woods Riding Adventures** (✉ 64 Garland Line Rd., Dover-Foxcroft 04426, ☎ 207/564–3451).

RAFTING

Raft Maine is an association of white-water outfitters licensed to lead trips down the Kennebec and Dead rivers and the West Branch of the Penobscot River. Rafting season begins May 1 and continues through mid-October.
➤ CONTACT: **Raft Maine** (☎ 800/723–8633, WEB www.raftmaine.com).
➤ CONTACT: **Maine Snowmobile Association** (✉ Box 77, Augusta 04332, ☎ 207/622–6983; 207/626–5717 trail conditions; WEB www.mesnow.com).

VISITOR INFORMATION

➤ CONTACTS: **Baxter State Park Authority** (✉ 64 Balsam Dr., Millinocket 04462, ☎ 207/723–5140). **Katahdin Area Chamber of Commerce** (✉ 1029 Central St., Millinocket 04462, ☎ 207/723–4443, WEB www.katahdinmaine.com). **Moosehead Lake Region Chamber of Commerce** (✉ Rte. 6/15 [Box 581, Greenville 04441], ☎ 207/695–2702, WEB www.mooseheadlake.org).

MAINE A TO Z

To research prices, get advice from other travelers, and book travel arrangements, visit www.fodors.com.

AIR TRAVEL

Regional flying services, operating from regional and municipal airports, provide access to remote lakes and wilderness areas as well as to Penobscot Bay islands.

AIRPORTS

Portland International Jetport is served by Air Nova, American, Business Express, Continental, Delta, Northwest, TWA, United, and US Airways. Bangor International Airport is served by Business Express, Continental, Delta/Comair, and US Airways. Hancock County Airport, 8 mi northwest of Bar Harbor, is served by US Airways Express. Knox County Regional Airport, in Owls Head, 3 mi south of Rockland, has flights to Boston and Bar Harbor on US Airways Express.
➤ AIRPORT INFORMATION: **Portland International Jetport** (✉ Westbrook St. off Rte. 9, ☎ 207/774–7301, WEB www.portlandjetport.org). **Bangor International Airport** (✉ Godfrey Blvd., ☎ 207/947–0384, WEB www.flybangor.com.org). **Hancock County Airport** (✉ Rte. 3, Trenton, ☎ 207/667–7329, WEB www.bhairport.co). **Knox County Regional Airport** (✉ off Rte. 73, ☎ 207/594–4131, WEB knoxcounty.midcoast.com).

BIKE TRAVEL

For information on bicycling in Maine and a list of companies operating tours, contact the Bicycle Coalition of Maine. The Maine De-

partment of Transportation Web site has information on bike tours.
➤ CONTACTS: **Bicycle Coalition of Maine** (⊠ Box 5275, Augusta, ☎
207/623–4511, WEB www.bikemaine.org). **Maine Department of
Transportation Bike and Pedestrian Section** (WEB www.state.me.
us/mdot/biketours.htm).

BOAT AND FERRY TRAVEL

Northumberland/Bay Ferries operates the Cat, a high-speed car-ferry
service on a catamaran, between Yarmouth, Nova Scotia, and Bar Harbor from mid-May to mid-October. The crossing takes three hours, and
the Cat has everything from a casino to sightseeing decks. Prince of
Fundy Cruises operates a car ferry from May to October between Portland and Yarmouth, Nova Scotia. Maine State Ferry Service provides
service from Rockland, Lincolnville, and Bass Harbor to islands in Penobscot and Blue Hill bays. East Coast Ferries operates between Deer Island, New Brunswick, and Eastport.
➤ BOAT AND FERRY INFORMATION: **East Coast Ferries** (☎ 506/747–
2159). **Maine State Ferry Service** (☎ 207/596–2202 or 800/491–4883,
WEB www.state.me.us/mdot/opt/ferry/ferry.htm). **Northumberland/Bay
Ferries** (☎ 888/249–7245, WEB www.nfl-bay.com). **Prince of Fundy
Cruises** (☎ 800/341–7540; 800/482–0955 in Maine; WEB www.
scotiaprince.com).

BUS TRAVEL

Concord Trailways provides service to Bangor, Bath, Belfast, Brunswick,
Camden/Rockport, Damariscotta, Lincolnville, Orono, Portland, Rockland, Searsport, Waldoboro, and Wiscasset. Greyhound Bus Lines
serves Augusta, Bangor, Bath, Belfast, Brunswick, Camden, Damariscotta,
Lewiston, Lincolnville, Orono, Portland, Rockland, Searsport, Waldoboro, Waterville, and Wiscasset. Vermont Transit provides service
to Augusta, Bangor, Bar Harbor, Brunswick, Caribou, Ellsworth, Houlton, Lewiston, Old Orchard Beach, Portland, and Waterville.
➤ BUS INFORMATION: **Concord Trailways** (☎ 800/639–3317, WEB
www.concordtrailways.com). **Greyhound Bus Lines** (☎ 800/231–
2222, WEB www.greyhound.com). **Vermont Transit** (☎ 207/772–6587
or 800/451–3292, WEB www.vermonttransit.com).

CAR RENTAL

➤ MAJOR AGENCIES: **Alamo** (⊠ 1000 Westbrook St., Portland, ☎ 207/
775–0855; 800/327–9633 in Portland). **Avis** (⊠ Portland International
Jetport, Portland, ☎ 207/874–7500; ⊠ Bangor International Airport,
Bangor, ☎ 207/947–8383 or 800/831–2847, WEB www.avis.com). **Budget** (⊠ 1128 Westbrook St., Portland, ☎ 800/527–7000; ⊠ Bangor International Airport, Bangor, ☎ 207/945–9429 or 800/527–0700, WEB
www.budgetmaine.com). **Hertz** (⊠ 1049 Westbrook St., Portland International Jetport, Portland, ☎ 207/774–4544; ⊠ Bangor International
Airport, Bangor, ☎ 207/942–5519 or 800/654–3131, WEB www.hertz.
com). **National** (⊠ Portland International Jetport, Portland, ☎ 207/773–
0036; ⊠ Bangor International Airport, Bangor, ☎ 207/947–0158 or
800/227–7368, WEB www.nationalcar.com).

CAR TRAVEL

Interstate 95 is the fastest route to and through the state from coastal
New Hampshire and points south, turning inland at Brunswick and
going on to Bangor and the Canadian border. U.S. 1, more leisurely
and scenic, is the principal coastal highway from New Hampshire to
Canada. U.S. 302 is the primary access to the Sebago Lake region, while
Route 26 leads to the western mountains and Route 27 leads to the
Rangeley and Sugarloaf regions. U.S. 201 is the fastest route to Québec,
and Route 9 is the inland route from Bangor to Calais.

The maximum speed limit is 65 mph, unless otherwise posted, on I–95 and the Maine Turnpike. For condition and updates on construction on the Maine Turnpike, contact the Maine Turnpike ·Authority. Local municipalities post speed limits on roads within their jurisdictions. State law requires drivers to stop for pedestrians. Drivers can make right turns on red if no sign prohibits such turns. Note that Maine law requires drivers to turn on their lights when windshield wipers are operating.

In many areas a car is the only practical means of travel. The *Maine Map and Travel Guide,* available for a small fee from the Maine Tourism Association, is useful for driving throughout the state; it has directories, mileage charts, and enlarged maps of city areas. DeLorme's *Maine Atlas & Gazetteer,* sold at local bookstores, includes enlarged, detailed maps of every part of the state.

➤ CONTACT: **Maine Turnpike Authority** (☎ 800/698–7747), WEB www.maineturnpike.com.

LODGING

CAMPING

Reservations for state park campsites (excluding Baxter State Park) can be made from January until August 23 through the Bureau of Parks and Lands. Make reservations as far ahead as possible (at least seven days in advance), because sites go quickly. The Maine Campground Owners Association has a statewide listing of private campgrounds.

➤ CONTACTS: **Bureau of Parks and Lands** (☎ 207/287–3824; 800/332–1501 in Maine). **Maine Campground Owners Association** (✉ 655 Main St., Lewiston 04240, ☎ 207/782–5874, FAX 207/782–4497, WEB www.campmaine.com).

OUTDOOR ACTIVITIES AND SPORTS

BIRDING

The Maine Audubon Society provides information on birding in Maine and hosts field trips for novice to expert birders.

➤ CONTACT: **Maine Audubon Society** (✉ 20 Gilsland Farm Rd., Falmouth 04105, ☎ 207/781–6180, WEB www.maineaudubon.org).

FISHING

For information about fishing and licenses, contact the Maine Department of Inland Fisheries and Wildlife. The Maine Professional Guides Association maintains and mails out listings of its members and their specialties.

➤ CONTACTS: **Maine Department of Inland Fisheries and Wildlife** (✉ 41 State House Station, Augusta 04333, ☎ 207/287–8000, WEB www.state.me.us/ifw). **Maine Professional Guides Association** (✉ Box 847, Augusta 04332, ☎ 207/549–5631, WEB www.maineguides.org).

KAYAKING

A number of outfitters provide sea-kayaking instruction as well as tours along the Maine coast.

➤ CONTACTS: **Maine Island Kayak Co.** (✉ 70 Luther St., Peaks Island, 04018, ☎ 207/766–2373 or 800/796–2376). **Maine Sport Outfitters** (✉ U.S. 1, Rockport 04856, ☎ 207/236–8797 or 800/722–0826). **Sunrise County Canoe & Kayak** (✉ Cathance Lake, Grove Post 04657, ☎ 207/454–7708 or 800/980–2300).

PARKS AND PUBLIC LANDS

The Bureau of Parks and Public Lands publishes the brochure "Outdoors in Maine," a listing of state parks, public reserved lands, state historic trails, boat access sites, snowmobile trails, and all-terrain-vehicle trails.

➤ CONTACT: **Bureau of Parks and Public Lands** (✉ 22 State House Station, Augusta 04333, ☎ 207/287–3821, WEB www.state.me.us/doc/parks).

RAFTING

Raft Maine provides information on white-water rafting on the Kennebec, Penobscot, and Dead rivers.
➤ CONTACT: **Raft Maine** (✉ Box 3, Bethel 04217, ☎ 800/723–8633, WEB www.raftmaine.com).

SKIING

For information on alpine skiing, contact Ski Maine. For information on cross-country ski centers, shops, and lodging packages, contact the Maine Nordic Ski Council.
➤ CONTACTS: **Maine Nordic Ski Council** (✉ Box 645, Bethel 04217, ☎ 207/824–3694 or 800/754–9263, WEB www.mnsc.com). **Ski Maine** (✉ Box 7566, Portland 04112, ☎ 207/622–6983; 207/761–3774; 888/624–6345 snow conditions; WEB www.skimaine.com).

SNOWMOBILING

The Maine Snowmobile Association distributes an excellent statewide trail map of about 8,000 mi of trails.
➤ CONTACT: **Maine Snowmobile Association** (✉ Box 77, Augusta 04332, ☎ 207/622–6983; 207/626–5717 trail conditions; WEB www.mesnow.com).

SPORTING CAMPS

Maine Sporting Camp Association publishes a directory of sporting camps throughout the state.
➤ CONTACT: **Maine Sporting Camp Association** (✉ Box 89, Jay 04249, WEB www.mainesportingcamps.com).

WINDJAMMING

The Maine Windjammer Association represents 13 schooners offering multiday cruises along the Maine coast.
➤ CONTACT: **Maine Windjammer Association** (✉ Box 1144, Blue Hill 04614, ☎ 800/807–9463, WEB www.sailmainecoast.com).

TRAIN TRAVEL

Amtrak's Downeaster operates between Boston and Portland with stops in Saco and Wells year-round and in Old Orchard Beach in the summer. At press time, Acadian Railway is scheduled to begin operating luxury excursion trains in Maine's North Woods in spring 2002. Trains will depart from New York, Boston, Portland, and Montreal, and many excursions will travel from Maine to the Canadian Maritimes with stops in Greenville.
➤ TRAIN INFORMATION: **Acadian Railway** (☎ 800/659–7602, WEB www.AcadianRailway.com). **Amtrak** (☎ 800/872–7245, WEB www.amtrak.com or www.thedowneaster.com).

VISITOR INFORMATION

The Maine Tourism Association operates a welcome center on U.S. 2 in Bethel. State of Maine Visitor Information Centers are on Union Street in Calais, Route 203 in Fryeburg, I–95 and U.S. 1 in Kittery, and on U.S. 1 in Yarmouth, I–95, Exit 17. For a brochure describing eight art museums along the Maine coast, write the Maine Art Museum Trail. The Maine Crafts Association publishes a "Guide to Crafts and Culture." "The Maine Archives and Museums Directory" lists museums, historical societies, archives, and historic sites statewide. Call the Maine Garden and Landscape Trail for a map and guide. The Web site, www.mainemusic.org, lists music-related events around the state.

➤ CONTACTS: **The Maine Archives and Museums Directory** (✉ 60 Community Dr., Augusta 04330, ☎ 800/452–8786, WEB www. mainemuseums.org). **Maine Art Museum Trail** (✉ 75 Russell St., Lewiston 04240 ☎ 800/782–6497, WEB www.maineartmuseums.org). **Maine Crafts Association** (✉ 15 Walton St., Portland 04103, WEB www.mainecrafts.maine.com). **Maine Garden and Landscape Trail** (✉ ☎ 800/782–6497). **Maine Innkeepers Association** (✉ 305 Commercial St., Portland 04101, ☎ 207/773–7670, WEB www.maineinns.com). **Maine Office of Tourism** (✉ 33 Stone St., Augusta 04333, ☎ 888/624–6345, WEB www.visitmaine.com). **Maine Tourism Association** (✉ 325-B Water St. [Box 2300, Hallowell 04347], ☎ 207/623–0363 or 888/624–6345, WEB www.mainetourism.com).

3 VERMONT

Southern Vermont has manicured landscapes, immaculate villages, and summer theaters, as well as a surprisingly large chunk of wilderness in the Green Mountain National Forest. Central Vermont is home to the state's largest ski resort, Killington, along with the rolling farmland vistas of the lower Lake Champlain valley. Up north, Vermont attractions include the state's largest city, cosmopolitan and collegiate Burlington; the nation's smallest state capital, Montpelier; the legendary slopes of Stowe; and the leafy back roads of the Northeast Kingdom.

E VERYWHERE YOU LOOK IN VERMONT, the evidence is clear: this is not the state it was 30 years ago. That may be true for the rest of New England as well, but the contrasts between the present and recent past seem all the more sharply drawn in the Green Mountain State, if only because an aura of timelessness has always been at the heart of the Vermont image. Vermont was where all the quirks and virtues outsiders associate with up-country New England were supposed to reside. It was where the Yankees were Yankee-est and where cows outnumbered people.

Updated by
Kay and Bill
Scheller

Not that you should be alarmed if you haven't been here in a while; Vermont hasn't become southern California, or even, for that matter, southern New Hampshire. The state's population, which increased from 335,000 to only 390,000 from 1860 to 1960, began to climb sharply as interstate highways and resort development made their impact. By 1990 the state had 563,000 residents; today, a population of approximately 600,000 indicates some leveling off in the rate of growth. This is still the most rural state in the Union (meaning that it has the smallest percentage of citizens living in statistically defined metropolitan areas), and it still turns out most of New England's milk, even though people finally outnumber cows. Vermont remains a place where cars occasionally have to stop while a dairy farmer walks his herd across a secondary road; and up in Essex County, in what George Aiken dubbed the Northeast Kingdom, there are townships with zero population. And the kind of scrupulous, straightforward, plainspoken politics practiced by Governor (later Senator) Aiken for 50 years has not become outmoded in a state that still turns out on town-meeting day.

How has Vermont changed? In strictly physical terms, the most obvious transformations have taken place in and around the two major cities, Burlington and Rutland, and near the larger ski resorts, such as Stowe, Killington, Stratton, and Mt. Snow. Burlington's Church Street, once a paradigm of all the sleepy redbrick shopping thoroughfares in northern New England, is now a pedestrian mall with chic bistros; outside the city, suburban development has supplanted farms in towns where someone's trip to Burlington might once have been an item in a weekly newspaper. As for the ski areas, it's no longer enough simply to have the latest in chairlift technology. Slope-side hotels and condos have boomed, especially in the southern part of the state, turning ski areas into big-time resort destinations. And once-sleepy Manchester has become one of New England's factory-outlet meccas.

The real metamorphosis in the Green Mountains, however, has to do more with style, with the personality of the place, than with development. The past couple of decades have seen a tremendous influx of outsiders—not only skiers and "leaf peepers" but people who have come to stay year-round—and many of them are determined either to freshen the local scene with their own idiosyncrasies or to make Vermont even more like Vermont than they found it. On the one hand, this translates into the fact that Vermont is the only state represented in Washington by an independent socialist congressman; on the other, it means that sheep farming has been reintroduced to the state, largely to provide a high-quality product for the hand-weaving industry.

This ties in with another local phenomenon, one best described as Made in Vermont. Once upon a time, maple syrup and sharp cheddar cheese were the products that carried Vermont's name to the world. The market niche that they created has since been widened by Vermonters—a great many of them refugees from more hectic arenas of commerce—

Vermont

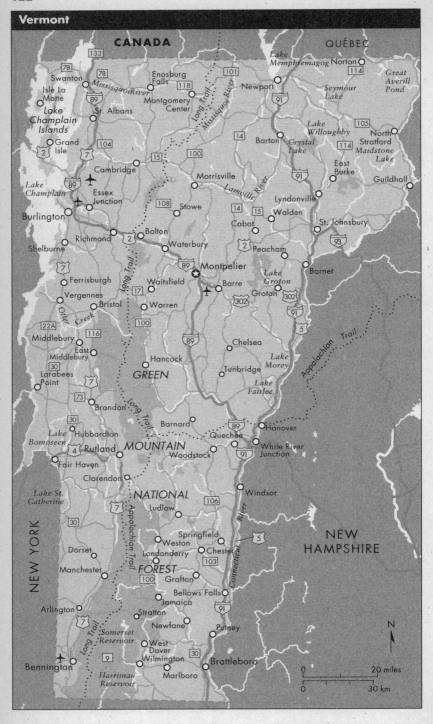

CANADA

QUÉBEC

Lake Memphremagog Norton

Swanton Enosburg Falls Newport Seymour Lake Great Averill Pond

Isle La Motte Missisquoi River Montgomery Center

St. Albans Lake Willoughby North Stratford

Lake Champlain Islands Barton Crystal Lake Maidstone Lake

Grand Isle Cambridge Morrisville East Burke Guildhall

Lamoille River

Lake Champlain Essex Junction Stowe Lyndonville

Burlington Cabot Walden St. Johnsbury

Shelburne Richmond Bolton Waterbury Peacham Barnet

Ferrisburgh Montpelier Lake Groton

Long Trail Waitsfield Barre Groton

Vergennes Warren

Bristol Chelsea

Middlebury Hancock Lake Morey

East Middlebury GREEN Tunbridge Lake Fairlee

Larabees Point Appalachian Trail

Brandon Barnard Hanover

Lake Bomoseen Hubbardton Quechee White River Junction

Rutland MOUNTAIN Woodstock

Fair Haven Clarendon

Lake St. Catherine NATIONAL Windsor

Ludlow

NEW YORK Springfield NEW HAMPSHIRE

Dorset Weston Chester

Londonderry

Manchester FOREST Grafton

Arlington Bellows Falls

Stratton Jamaica

Newfane Putney

Somerset Reservoir West Dover Wilmington

Bennington Marlboro Brattleboro

Harriman Reservoir

Connecticut River

Long Trail

N

0 20 miles

0 30 km

who now sell a plethora of goods with the ineffable cachet of Vermont manufacture, from Vermont wood toys and Vermont apple wines to Vermont chocolates and even Vermont vodka. The most successful Made in Vermont product is Ben & Jerry's ice cream, which absorbs a significant portion of Vermont's milk output.

The character and appearance of the landscape are what most readily ignite preservationists' passions in Vermont. Farming may be changing—sheep, goats, llamas, emus, and even elk graze the Green Mountain foothills—but farms are farms, valued for their open-space counterpoint to Vermont forests and villages. The Vermont Land Trust has saved thousands of acres of farmland through the purchase of development rights; meanwhile, vast tracts of northern woodlands have been preserved for wildlife habitat, recreation, and low-impact forestry. The challenge is to bring Vermont into the 21st century while making sure it still looks like Vermont. The model might be an old farmhouse, with fiber-optic cables hidden in its walls.

Pleasures and Pastimes

Dining

Over the past few years, Vermont chefs have been working hard to fulfill two distinct responsibilities. One is the need to honor the traditions of Yankee cooking—the realm of pot roast and Indian pudding, sticky buns, and homemade corn relish. Two is to satisfy the sophisticated palate of travelers and residents, who seek ethnic cuisines, lighter adaptations of classics, and new American treatments of seasonal ingredients that now characterize urban menus.

The more ambitious restaurants and inn kitchens have not only managed to balance these two gastronomic imperatives but also have succeeded in combining them. The trick is to take an innovative approach with Vermont game and local produce, introduce fresh herbs and other seasonings, and change menus to suit the season. Look for imaginative approaches to native New England foods such as fiddlehead ferns (available only for a short time in the spring), maple syrup (Vermont is the largest U.S. producer), dairy products (especially cheese), native fruits and berries, "new Vermont" products such as salsa and salad dressings, and venison, quail, pheasant, and other game.

Your chances of finding a table for dinner vary with the season: many restaurants have lengthy waits during peak seasons (when it's always a good idea to make a reservation) and then shut down during the slow months of April and November. Some of the best dining is found at country inns.

CATEGORY	COST*
$$$$	over $25
$$$	$17–$25
$$	$9–$16
$	under $9

*per person, for a main-course dinner

Lodging

Vermont's largest hotels are in Burlington and near the major ski resorts. Burlington has a dearth of inns and bed-and-breakfasts, though chain hotels provide dependable accommodations. Elsewhere you'll find inns, B&Bs, and small motels. The many lovely and sometimes quite luxurious inns and B&Bs provide what many people consider the quintessential Vermont lodging experience. Rates are highest during foliage season, from late September to mid-October, and lowest in late spring and November, when many properties close. Many of the larger hotels offer package rates.

CATEGORY	COST*
$$$$	over $180
$$$	$130–$180
$$	$80–$130
$	under $80

All prices are for a standard double room during peak season and not including tax or gratuities. Some inns add a 15% service charge.

National Forests

The two sections of the 355,000-acre Green Mountain National Forest (GMNF) are central and southern Vermont's primary stronghold of woodland and high mountain terrain. Like all other national forests, it contains sections on which timber leases are sometimes granted, but it's possible to travel through much of this preserve without seeing significant evidence of human intrusion. In addition to the paved public highways that traverse the GMNF, many of the occasional logging roads are maintained for public use, and although unpaved, these are kept in good condition during snow-free times of the year.

The Forest Service maintains a number of picnic areas and primitive campgrounds; complete information is available from the Forest Supervisor. Fishing, subject to state laws and seasonal closings and limits, is allowed throughout the GMNF. Canoeing, cross-country skiing, and hiking are also popular; the Appalachian and Long trails run the length of the forest. Snowmobiles and other forms of motorized transportation, such as all-terrain vehicles, are permitted on marked trails, except within roadless areas designated as wilderness.

Outdoor Activities and Sports

BIKING

Vermont, especially the often deserted roads of the Northeast Kingdom, is great bicycle-touring country. Many companies lead weekend tours and weeklong trips throughout the state. If you'd like to go it on your own, most chambers of commerce have brochures highlighting good cycling routes in their area, including *Vermont Life* magazine's "Bicycle Vermont" map and guide, and many bookstores sell *25 Bicycle Tours in Vermont* by John Freidin.

FISHING

Central Vermont is the heart of the state's warm-water lake and pond fishing. Harriman and Somerset reservoirs have both warm- and cold-water species; Harriman has a greater variety. Lake Dunmore produced the state-record rainbow trout; Lakes Bomoseen and St. Catherine are good for rainbows and largemouth bass. In the east, Lakes Fairlee and Morey hold bass, perch, and chain pickerel, while the lower part of the Connecticut River contains smallmouth bass, walleye, and perch; shad are returning via the fish ladders at Vernon and Bellows Falls.

In northern Vermont, rainbow and brown trout inhabit the Missisquoi, Lamoille, Winooski, and Willoughby rivers. Lakes Seymour, Willoughby, and Memphremagog and Great Averill Pond in the Northeast Kingdom are good for salmon and lake trout. The Dog River near Montpelier has one of the best wild populations of brown trout in the state, and landlocked Atlantic salmon are returning to the Clyde River following removal of a controversial dam.

Lake Champlain, stocked annually with salmon and lake trout, has become the state's ice-fishing capital; walleye, bass, pike, and channel catfish are also taken. Ice fishing is also popular on Lake Memphremagog.

SKIING

The Green Mountains run through the middle of Vermont like a bumpy spine, visible from almost every point in the state; generous accumulations of snow make the mountains an ideal site for skiing. Increased snowmaking capacity and improved, high-tech computerized equipment at many areas virtually assure a good day on the slopes. Vermont has 26 alpine ski resorts with nearly 1,000 trails and some 5,000 acres of skiable terrain. Combined, the resorts operate nearly 200 lifts and have the capacity to carry some 215,000 skiers per hour. Though grooming is sophisticated at all Vermont areas, conditions usually run to a typically Eastern hard pack, with powder a rare luxury and ice a bugbear after January thaw. The best advice for skiing in Vermont is to keep your skis well tuned.

Route 100 is also known as Skier's Highway, passing by 13 of the state's ski areas. Vermont's major resorts are Stowe, Jay Peak, Sugarbush, Killington, Okemo, Mt. Snow, and Stratton. Midsize, less-hectic areas to consider include Ascutney, Bromley, Smugglers' Notch, Pico, Mad River Glen, Burke Mountain, and Bolton Valley Holiday Resort.

Exploring Vermont

Vermont can be divided into three regions. The southern part of the state, flanked by Bennington on the west and Brattleboro on the east, played an important role in Vermont's Revolutionary War–era drive to independence (yes, there was once a Republic of Vermont) and its eventual statehood. The central part is characterized by rugged mountains and the gently rolling dairy lands near Lake Champlain. Northern Vermont is the site of the state's capital, Montpelier, and its largest city, Burlington, yet it is also home to Vermont's most rural area, the Northeast Kingdom.

Numbers in the text correspond to numbers in the margin and on the Southern Vermont, Central Vermont, and Northern Vermont maps.

Great Itineraries

There are many ways to take advantage of Vermont's beauty—skiing or hiking its mountains, biking or driving its back roads, fishing or sailing its waters, shopping for local products, visiting its museums and sights, or simply finding the perfect inn and never leaving the front porch. Distances in Vermont are relatively short, yet the mountains and many back roads will slow a traveler's pace. You can see a representative north–south section of Vermont in a few days; if you have up to a week you can hit the highlights around the state.

IF YOU HAVE 3 DAYS

Spend a few hours in historic **Bennington** ⑤ in the southern part of Vermont; then travel north to see Hildene and stay in 🖫 **Manchester** ⑦. On your second day take Route 100 through Weston and travel north through the Green Mountains to Route 125, where you turn west to explore 🖫 **Middlebury** ㉖. On day three, enter the Champlain Valley, which has views of the Adirondack Mountains to the west. Stop at Shelburne Farms and carry on to **Burlington** ㊲; catch the sunset from the waterfront and take a walk on Church Street.

IF YOU HAVE 5 TO 7 DAYS

You can make several side trips off Route 100 and also visit the Northeast Kingdom on a trip of this length. Visit **Bennington** ⑤ and 🖫 **Manchester** ⑦ on day one. Spend your second day walking around the small towns of **Chester** ⑫ and 🖫 **Grafton** ⑬. On day three head north to explore **Woodstock** ㉑ and 🖫 **Quechee** ⑳, stopping at either the Billings Farm Museum and Marsh-Billings-Rockefeller National Historical Park or the Vermont Institute of Natural Science. Head leisurely on your fourth day toward ⛰ **Middlebury** ㉖, along one of Vermont's most inspiring mountain drives, Route 125 west of Route 100. Between Hancock and Middlebury, you'll pass nature trails and the picnic spot at Texas Falls Recreation Area, then traverse a moderately steep mountain pass. Spend day five in ⛰ **Burlington** ㉗. On day six head east to **Waterbury** ㉛ and then north to ⛰ **Stowe** ㉝ and Mt. Mansfield for a full day. Begin your last day with a few hours in **Montpelier** ㉚ on your way to **Peacham** ㊽, **St. Johnsbury** ㊼, ⛰ **Lake Willoughby** ㊺, and the serenity and back roads of the Northeast Kingdom. Especially noteworthy are U.S. 5, Route 5A, and Route 14.

When to Tour Vermont

The number of visitors and the rates for lodging reach their peaks along with the color of the leaves during foliage season, from late September to mid-October. But if you have never seen a kaleidoscope of autumn colors, it is worth braving the slow-moving traffic and paying the extra money. In summer the state is lush and green. Winter, of course, is high season at Vermont's ski resorts. Rates are lowest in late spring and November, although many properties close during these times.

SOUTHERN VERMONT

The Vermont tradition of independence and rebellion began in southern Vermont. Many towns founded in the early 18th century as frontier outposts or fortifications were later important as trading centers. In the western region the Green Mountain Boys fought off both the British and the claims of land-hungry New Yorkers—some say their descendants are still fighting. In the 19th century, as many towns turned to manufacturing, the farmers here retreated to hillier regions and, as the modern ski and summer-home booms got under way, retreated even farther.

The first thing you'll notice upon entering the state is the conspicuous lack of billboards along the highways and roads. The foresight back in the 1960s to prohibit them has made for a refreshing absence of aggressive visual clutter that allows unencumbered views of working farmland, fresh-as-paint villages, and quiet back roads—but does not hide the reality of abandoned dairy barns, bustling ski resorts, and strip-mall sprawl. Reaching Vermont via the well-settled districts around Brattleboro and Bennington, you'll discover beautifully desolate woodlands nestled between these gateways. Much of the Green Mountain National Forest's southern section occupies rugged uplands where homesteads and farms once thrived more than 400 years ago.

The towns are listed in counterclockwise order, beginning in the east, south of the junction of I–91 and Route 9 in Brattleboro, and following the southern boundary of the state toward Bennington, then north up to Manchester and Weston and south back to Newfane.

Brattleboro

❶ *60 mi south of White River Junction.*

Its downtown bustling with activity, Brattleboro, with about 13,000 inhabitants, is the center of commerce for southeastern Vermont. This town at the confluence of the West and Connecticut rivers originated as a frontier scouting post and became a thriving industrial center and resort town in the 1800s. Since the late 1960s the area has drawn political activists and a raft of earnest counterculturists.

Southern Vermont

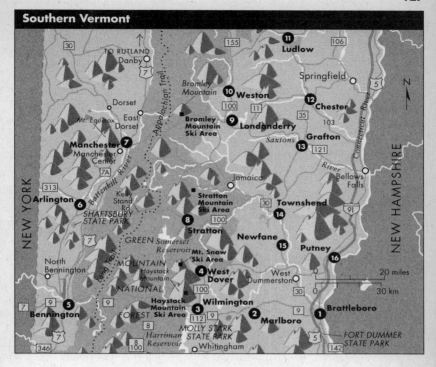

The **Brattleboro Museum and Art Center,** housed in historic Union Station, presents changing exhibits created by locally, nationally, and internationally renowned artists. Each year the museum focuses on a unifying theme, which provides a structure for that year's exhibits and programs. ⊠ *Vernon and Main Sts.,* ☎ *802/257–0124,* WEB *www.brattleboromuseum.org.* ⌦ *$3.* ☉ *May–Dec., Tues.–Sun. noon–6.*

Dining and Lodging

$$$ ✕ **Peter Havens.** In a town better known for tofu than toniness, this chic little bistro knows just what to do with a filet mignon—serve it with Roquefort walnut butter, of course. Look for the house-cured gravlax made with lemon vodka and fresh seasonal seafood, which even includes a spring fling with soft-shell crabs. The wine list is superb. ⊠ *32 Elliot St.,* ☎ *802/257–3333. MC, V. Closed Sun.–Mon. No lunch.*

$$ ✕ **Sarkis Market.** Gail Sarkis's Lebanese grandmother gave her many of the recipes she uses to create Middle Eastern delicacies such as falafel, stuffed grape leaves, hummus, and *kibbe*—a layered meat loaf stuffed with ground lamb, pine nuts, and onions. Undecided about what to order? Go for the combination plate and finish with homemade baklava. ⊠ *50 Elliot St.,* ☎ *802/258–4906. AE, MC, V. Call for hrs.*

$–$$ ✕ **Top of the Hill Grill.** Hickory-smoked ribs and beef brisket, apple smoked turkey, and pulled pork are a few of the "divinely inspired" favorites at this barbecue just out of town. Those looking to cross the border can try the tortilla roll-ups and fajitas. Larger parties can opt for "family-style" dinners. Homemade pecan pie is the dessert of choice. You can sit indoors in the informal dining with big windows, but the best seats are outdoors at picnic tables overlooking the West River. ⊠ *632 Putney Rd.,* ☎ *802/258–9178. No credit cards. Closed Oct.–Apr.*

$ ✕ **Common Ground.** The political posters and concert fliers that line the staircase here attest to Vermont's progressive element. The stairs lead to loftlike, rough-hewn dining rooms. Owned cooperatively by the staff and volunteer-run, this mostly organic vegetarian restaurant serves cashew burgers, veggie stir-fries, curries, hot soup and stew, and a humble bowl of brown rice. All the desserts, including a chocolate cake with peanut butter frosting, are made without white sugar. Sunday brunch is served 11–2. ⊠ *25 Elliot St.,* ☎ *802/257–0855. No credit cards. Closed Mon.–Wed. No lunch Thurs.–Sat.*

$$ ✕▥ **Latchis Hotel.** Front rooms at this 1938 downtown Art Deco landmark overlook busy—and often noisy—Main Street. All the rooms are furnished comfortably, many with their original restored 1930s furniture; the suites are a bargain. Muffins are delivered to your room late in the evening or early in the morning, and you can catch a movie under the zodiac ceiling of the adjoining Latchis Theater. The hotel's restaurant, ($$) the Lucca Brasserie and Bistro, serves lunch on weekends and dinner nightly. ⊠ *50 Main`St., 05301,* ☎ *802/254–6300,* FAX *802/254–6304,* WEB *www.brattleboro.com/latchis. 30 rooms, 3 suites. Restaurant, cable TV, pub. AE, MC, V. CP.*

$$$–$$$$ ▥ **Forty Putney Road.** Owners Mimi and Rob Hamlin's French-style home provides elegant yet comfortable accommodations. Rooms are furnished with antiques; the suite has a gas fireplace. A separate cottage with a full kitchen sleeps four. In warm weather, breakfast is served on the patio of the formally landscaped grounds, which lead to the shores of the West River. The inn is a popular spot to celebrate Civil Unions. ⊠ *40 Putney Rd., 05301,* ☎ *802/254–6268 or 800/941–2413,* FAX *802/258–2673,* WEB *www.putney.net/40putneyrd. 3 rooms, 1 suite, 1 cottage. In-room VCRs, pub, some pets allowed. AE, D, MC, V. BP.*

Nightlife and the Arts

Common Ground (⊠ 25 Elliot St., ☎ 802/257–0855) hosts live music, mostly from local bands. **Mole's Eye Cafe** (⊠ 4 High St., ☎ 802/257–0771) hosts an open-mike night every Thursday and live bands Friday and Saturday.

Outdoor Activities and Sports

BIKING

Brattleboro Bicycle Shop (⊠ 165 Main St., ☎ 802/254–8644 or 800/272–8245) rents and repairs hybrid bikes. **Burrows Specialized Sports** (⊠ 105 Main St., ☎ 802/254–9430) services bikes, skis, and snowboards and rents skis and snowshoes.

CANOEING

Vermont Canoe Touring Center (⊠ U.S. 5, ☎ 802/257–5008) conducts guided and self-guided tours, rents canoes and kayaks, and provides a shuttle service.

SKATING

Nelson Withington Skating Rink (⊠ Memorial Park, 4 Guilford St., ☎ 802/257–2311) rents skates.

STATE PARK

The hiking trails at **Fort Dummer State Park** (⊠ S. Main St., 2 mi south of Brattleboro, ☎ 802/254–2610) afford views of the Connecticut River valley; campsites are available.

Shopping

The **Book Cellar** (⊠ 120 Main St., ☎ 802/254–6026) stocks two floors with a variety of local titles. You can watch **Tom and Sally's Homemade Chocolates** being made just around the corner from their shop (⊠ 55 Elliot St., ☎ 802/258–3065), which also sells the famous chocolate Vermont Meadow Muffins. **Vermont Artisan Designs** (⊠ 106 Main St., ☏ 802/257–7044) displays ceramics, glass, wood, clothing, jewelry, and furniture.

Marlboro

❷ *10 mi west of Brattleboro.*

Tiny Marlboro draws musicians and audiences from around the world each summer to the Marlboro Music Festival, founded by Rudolf Serkin and joined for many years by Pablo Casals. **Marlboro College,** high on a hill off Route 9, is the center of musical activity. The college's white-frame buildings have outstanding views of the valley below, and the campus is studded with apple trees.

The **Southern Vermont Natural History Museum** houses one of New England's largest collections of mounted birds, specimens of three extinct birds, and a complete collection of mammals native to the Northeast. The museum also has weather displays and live hawk and owl exhibits. ⊠ *Rte. 9,* ☏ *802/464–0048.* ⚏ *$3.* ☉ *Memorial Day–late Oct., daily 10–5; late Oct.–Memorial Day, weekends 10–4, weather permitting.*

Nightlife and the Arts

The **Marlboro Music Festival** (⊠ Marlboro Music Center, Marlboro College, ☏ 802/254–2394; 215/569–4690 Sept.–June) presents chamber music at weekend concerts from mid-July to mid-August. The **New England Bach Festival** (☏ 802/257–4523) is held at Marlboro College in October.

Wilmington

❸ *8 mi west of Marlboro.*

Wilmington is the shopping and dining center for the Mt. Snow ski area (☞ West Dover) to the north. Main Street has a cohesive assemblage of 18th- and 19th-century buildings, many of them listed on the National Register of Historic Places. For a town stroll, pick up a self-guided tour map from the **Mount Snow Valley Chamber of Commerce** (⊠ W. Main St./Rte. 9, ☏ 802/464–8092 or 877/887–6884, ⓌⒺⒷ www.visitvermont.com).

North River Winery, which occupies a converted farmhouse and barn, produces fruit wines such as Green Mountain Apple and Vermont Pear. ⊠ *Rte. 112, 6 mi south of Wilmington, Jacksonville,* ☏ *802/368–7557.* ⚏ *Free.* ☉ *Daily 10–5; tours late May–Dec.*

OFF THE BEATEN PATH | **SCENIC TOUR –** To begin a scenic (though well-traveled) 35-mi circular tour with panoramic views of the region's mountains, farmland, and abundant cow population, drive west on Route 9 to the intersection with Route 8. Turn south and continue to the junction with Route 100; follow Route 100 through Whitingham (the birthplace of the Mormon prophet Brigham Young), and stay with the road as it turns north again and takes you back to Route 9.

Dining and Lodging

$$$–$$$$ | ✕ **Le Petit Chef.** Chef Betty Hillman prepares a tasty selection of French-inspired dishes in her cozy white-clapboard farmhouse restaurant. Appetizers include her hallmark Bird's Nest, a shoestring-potato basket filled with savory delicacies. The rack of lamb served table-side for two is a stand-out. Desserts are all made in-house and include crunch meringue pie and strawberry-rhubarb shortcake. ⊠ *Rte. 100, 05363,* ☏ *802/464–8437. Reservations essential. AE, D, MC, V. Closed Tues.*

$$$–$$$$ ⊞ **White House of Wilmington.** The grand staircase in this Federal-style mansion leads to rooms with antique bathrooms and brass wall sconces; some rooms have fireplaces and lofts. You'll also find a cross-country ski touring and snowshoeing center, a tubing hill, and 12 km (7 mi) of groomed trails. You can dine at the restaurant for a fixed price of $35. ⊠ *178 Rte. 9 E, 05363,* ☎ *802/464–2135 or 800/541–2135,* FAX *802/464–5222,* WEB *www.whitehouseinn.com. 25 rooms. Restaurant, 2 pools (1 indoor), some in-room hot tubs, sauna, cross-country skiing, pub; no-smoking rooms, no kids under 8. AE, D, MC, V. BP.*

$$$ ⊞ **Trail's End, A Country Inn.** This cozy four-season lodge is set on 10 acres 4 mi from Mt. Snow. The inn's centerpiece is its cathedral-ceiling living room with catwalk loft seating and a 21-ft fieldstone fireplace. Guest rooms are comfortable; some have fireplaces. Dinner is served during the holiday season only. Cross-country ski trails are nearby. ⊠ *5 Trail's End La., 05363,* ☎ *802/464–2727 or 800/859–2585,* FAX *802/464–5532,* WEB *www.trailsendvt.com. 13 rooms, 2 suites. Some refrigerators, some microwaves, tennis court, pool, pond, fishing; no kids under 6. AE, D, MC, V. BP.*

Nightlife and the Arts

A year-round roster of music, theater, film, and fine art is presented at the **Memorial Hall Center for the Arts** (⊠ 14 W. Main St., ☎ 802/464–8411). In addition to steak and Mexican specialties, the standard fare on weekends at **Poncho's Wreck** (⊠ S. Main St., ☎ 802/464–9320) is acoustic jazz or mellow rock. **Sitzmark** (⊠ Rte. 100, ☎ 802/464–3384) hosts rock bands on weekends.

Outdoor Activities and Sports

SLEIGH RIDES

Adams Farm (⊠ 15 Higley Hill Rd., ☎ 802/464–3762) has three double-traverse sleighs drawn by Belgian draft horses. Rides include a narrated tour and hot chocolate. The farm store sells more than 200 handmade quilts and sweaters. An indoor petting farm is open Wednesday–Sunday from November to April, and an outdoor version is open daily the rest of the year.

STATE PARK

Molly Stark State Park (⊠ Rte. 9, east of Wilmington, ☎ 802/464–5460) has campsites and a hiking trail that leads to a vista from a fire tower on Mt. Olga.

WATER SPORTS

Lake Whitingham (Harriman Reservoir), just west of Wilmington, is the largest lake in the state, with good fishing. Boat-launch areas are at Wards Cove, Whitingham, Mountain Mills, and the Ox Bow. **Green Mountain Flagship Company** (⊠ Rte. 9, 2 mi west of Wilmington, ☎ 802/464–2975) runs a cruise boat on Lake Whitingham and rents canoes, kayaks, surf bikes, and sailboats from May to late October.

Shopping

Quaigh Design Centre (⊠ W. Main St./Rte. 9, ☎ 802/464–2780) sells New England crafts, artwork from Britain and New England—including works by Vermont woodcut artists Sabra Field and Mary Azarian—and Scottish woolens and tartans. **Wilmington Flea Market** (⊠ Rtes. 9 and 100 S, ☎ 802/464–3345) sells antiques on weekends from Memorial Day to mid-October.

West Dover

❹ *6 mi north of Wilmington.*

The Congregational church in small West Dover, a classic New England town, dates from the 1700s. The year-round population of about 1,000 swells on winter weekends as skiers flock to Mt. Snow/Haystack Ski Resort. The many condos, lodges, and inns at the base of the mountain accommodate them.

Dining and Lodging

$$$$ ✕🖬 **Inn at Saw Mill Farm.** One of Vermont's two Relais & Châteaux
★ inns (the other is the Pitcher Inn), this inn has all the upscale amenities expected at these properties. English chintzes, antiques, and dark wood set a comfortable tone in the common room. Each of the guest rooms is individually decorated, and many have sitting areas and fireplaces. The 22 landscaped acres are perfect for hiking. The restaurant's ($$$$) seasonal menu might include potato-crusted black sea bass with wild mushrooms and orzo or a grilled veal chop with wild mushroom risotto and rosemary sauce. The wine selection, with more than 30,000 bottles, is superb. ⊠ *Rte. 100 and Crosstown Rd., 05356,* ☎ *800/493–1133 or 802/464–8131,* FAX *802/464–1130,* WEB *www. vermontdirect.com/sawmill. 21 rooms. Restaurant, tennis court, pool, fishing; no room phones, no room TVs, no kids under 6. AE, DC, MC, V. Closed Easter–late May. MAP.*

$$$ ✕🖬 **Doveberry Inn.** After a day's skiing, this handsome country inn just a few minutes from the slopes provides a welcome haven. You can warm up by the fireplace in the living room with a glass of wine from the bar. Guest rooms are cheerful and bright; one room has a fireplace. The restaurant ($$$; closed Tues.) serves northern Italian specialties such as wood-grilled veal chop with wild mushrooms and pan-seared salmon with herbed risotto in intimate, candlelit dining rooms. ⊠ *Rte. 100, 05356,* ☎ *802/464–5652 or 800/722–3204,* FAX *802/464– 6229,* WEB *www.doveberryinn.com. 8 rooms. Restaurant, some in-room VCRs, bar; no kids under 8. AE, MC, V. BP.*

$$ ✕🖬 **Deerhill Inn and Restaurant.** A huge fireplace at this English-style
★ country inn dominates the living room, and English hand-painted yellow wallpaper, a garden-scene mural, and collections of antique plates accent the dining rooms. Several guest rooms have hand-painted murals and fireplaces. The three spacious balcony rooms have great views. The restaurant's ($$$–$$$$; closed Wed. in summer, Tues.–Wed. in winter) upscale comfort food might include a veal medallion with wild mushrooms in a lemon cream sauce or a black-pepper sirloin steak. ⊠ *Valley View Rd. (Box 136, 05356),* ☎ *802/464–3100 or 800/993–3379,* FAX *802/464–5474,* WEB *www.deerhill.com. 15 rooms, 2 suites. Restaurant, some cable TV, pool; no-smoking rooms, no kids under 8. AE, MC, V. BP, MAP.*

Nightlife and the Arts

Deacon's Den Tavern (⊠ Rte. 100, ☎ 802/464–9361) hosts bands on weekends from Thanksgiving through Easter. The **Snow Barn** (⊠ near the base of Mt. Snow, ☎ 802/464–1100 ext. 4693) has live music several nights a week.

Ski Areas

MT. SNOW/HAYSTACK SKI RESORT

One of the state's premier family resorts has a full roster of year-round activities. Since it opened in the 1950s as one of Vermont's first ski areas, the almost 800-acre facility has grown to encompass the Grand Summit Hotel and Crown Club (☎ 800/451–4211), a 201-room slope-side condo, hotel, and conference center; a golf course; a 45-mi mountain-biking park; and an extensive network of hiking trails. One lift ticket lets you ski at Mt. Snow and at nearby Haystack. A free shuttle connects the two ski areas. Haystack is open on weekends and holidays only. ✉ *400 Mountain Rd., Mt. Snow 05356,* ☎ *802/464–3333; 800/ 245–7669 lodging; 802/464–2151 snow conditions,* WEB *www. mountsnow.com.*

Downhill. Mt. Snow has five separate mountain faces. More than half of the 132 trails down its 1,700-ft vertical summit are intermediate, wide, and sunny. Most of the beginner slopes are toward the bottom; most of the expert terrain is on the North Face, where there's excellent fall-line skiing. The trails are served by 23 lifts, including three high-speed quads, one regular quad, 10 triple chairs, four double chairs, and three Magic Carpets (similar to an escalator). Snowmaking covers 85% of the terrain. The ski school's Perfect Turn instruction program is designed to help skiers of all ages and abilities.

Child care. The well-organized child-care center (reservations essential) takes children ages 6 weeks–6 years. The center has age-appropriate toys and balances indoor play—including arts and crafts—with trips outdoors. The Pre-ski program is for 3-year-olds, and a Perfect Kids program for ages 4–12 teaches skiing and snowboarding.

Summer activities. Mt. Snow offers two- to seven-day Grand Summer Vacation packages with activities, including golf at the 18-hole Mt. Snow Golf Course, mountain biking on ski trails and forest roads, and use of the health club, with a pool, hot tubs, and spa. The Summit Local triple chairlift transports riders to the 3,600-ft peak. Swimming, boating, and a children's water-play pool are available at the resort's Snow Lake. A hiking center, in-line skating park, climbing wall, and BMX track provide other summer fun.

CROSS-COUNTRY SKIING/SNOWSHOEING

Three cross-country-trail areas within 4 mi of Mt. Snow/Haystack provide more than 150 km (90 mi) of varied terrain. The **Hermitage** (✉ Coldbrook Rd., Wilmington, ☎ 802/464–3511) has 50 km (30 mi) of groomed trails. **Timber Creek** (✉ Rte. 100, north of the Mt. Snow entrance, ☎ 802/464–0999) is appealingly small with 16 km (10 mi) of thoughtfully groomed trails. The groomed trails at the **White House of Wilmington** (✉ Rtes. 9 and 100, ☎ 802/464–2135) cover 50 km (30 mi).

Snowmobile Tours

At **Sitzmark** (✉ East Dover Rd., Wilmington, ☎ 802/464–3384) guides lead snowmobile tours across a golf course and through 50 acres of woods and fields.

Bennington

❺ *21 mi west of Wilmington.*

Bennington, college town and commercial focus of Vermont's southwest corner, lies at the edge of the Green Mountain National Forest. It has retained much of the industrial character it developed in the 19th century, when paper mills, gristmills, and potteries formed the city's economic base. It was in Bennington, at the Catamount Tavern, that Ethan Allen organized the Green Mountain Boys, who helped capture Ft. Ticonderoga in 1775. Here also, in 1777, American general John Stark urged his militia to attack the British-paid Hessian troops across the New York border: "There are the redcoats; they will be ours or tonight Molly Stark sleeps a widow!"

A brochure available at the Chamber of Commerce describes a self-guided walking tour of **Old Bennington,** a National Register Historic District west of downtown. Impressive white-column Greek Revival and sturdy Federal-style brick homes stand around the village green. In the graveyard of the **Old First Church,** at Church Street and Monument Avenue, the tombstone of the poet Robert Frost proclaims, "I had a lover's quarrel with the world."

The **Bennington Battle Monument,** a 306-ft stone obelisk with an elevator to the top, commemorates General Stark's victory over the British, who attempted to capture Bennington's stockpile of supplies. The battle, which took place near Walloomsac Heights in New York State on August 16, 1777, helped bring about the surrender two months later of the British commander "Gentleman Johnny" Burgoyne at Saratoga in New York. ⊠ *15 Monument Ave.,* ☎ *802/447–0550.* ▦ *$1.50.* ☉ *Mid-Apr.–Oct., daily 9–5.*

The **Bennington Museum**'s rich collections include vestiges of rural life, a percentage of which are packed into towering glass cases. The decorative arts are well represented; one room is devoted to early Bennington pottery. Two rooms cover the history of American glass and contain fine Tiffany specimens. The museum displays the largest public collection of the work of Grandma Moses (1860–1961), the popular self-taught folk artist who lived and painted in the area. Among the 30 paintings and assorted memorabilia are her only self-portrait and the famous painted caboose window. Also here are the only surviving automobile of Bennington's Martin company, a 1925 Wasp, and the Bennington Flag, one of the oldest versions of the Stars and Stripes in existence. ⊠ *W. Main St./Rte. 9,* ☎ *802/447–1571,* WEB *www.benningtonmuseum.com.* ▦ *$6.* ☉ *Nov.–May, daily 9–5; June–Oct., daily 9–6.*

Built in 1865 and once home to two Vermont governors, the **Park-McCullough House** is a 35-room classic French Empire–style mansion furnished with period pieces. Several restored flower gardens grace the landscaped grounds, and a stable houses a collection of antique carriages. Call for details on the summer concert series, Victorian Christmas, and other special events. ⊠ *Corner of Park and West Sts., North Bennington,* ☎ *802/442–5441,* WEB *www.park/mccullough.org.* ▦ *$6.* ☉ *Mid-May–mid-Oct., Thurs.–Mon. 10–4; last tour at 3.*

Contemporary stone sculpture and white-frame neo-Colonial dorms surrounded by acres of cornfields punctuate the green meadows of **Bennington College**'s placid campus. The small liberal arts college, one of the most expensive to attend in the country, is noted for its progressive program in the arts. ⊠ *Rte. 67A, off U.S. 7 (look for stone entrance gate),* ☎ *800/833–6845 tour information.*

Dining and Lodging

$ ✕ **Blue Benn Diner.** Breakfast is served all day in this authentic diner, where the eats include turkey hash and breakfast burritos, with scrambled eggs, sausage, and chilies, plus pancakes of all imaginable varieties. The menu lists many vegetarian selections. Lines may be long, especially on weekends. ⊠ *U.S. 7 N,* ☎ *802/442–5140. Reservations not accepted. No credit cards. No dinner Sat.–Tues.*

$$$–$$$$ ▦ **South Shire Inn.** Canopy beds in lushly carpeted rooms, ornate plaster moldings, and a dark mahogany fireplace in the library re-create the grandeur of the Victorian past; fireplaces in some rooms add warmth. The South Shire is in a quiet residential neighborhood within walking distance of the bus depot and downtown stores. Breakfast is served in the dining room. ⊠ *124 Elm St., 05201,* ☎ *802/447–3839,*

FAX *802/442–3547,* WEB *www.southshire.com. 9 rooms. Cable TV, some in-room hot tubs; no kids under 12. AE, MC, V. BP.*

$–$$ 🏠 **Molly Stark Inn.** Tidy blue-plaid wallpaper, gleaming hardwood floors, antique furnishings, and a wood-burning stove in a brick alcove of the sitting room add country charm to this 1860 Queen Anne Victorian. Molly's Room, at the back of the building, gets less noise from Route 9; the attic suite is the most spacious. Three cottages have fireplaces and are more secluded. ⊠ *1067 E. Main St./Rte. 9, 05201,* ☎ *802/442–9631 or 800/356–3076,* FAX *802/442–5224,* WEB *www.mollystarkinn.com. 9 rooms. Some cable TV, some in-room hot tubs; no air-conditioning in some rooms, no kids under 10. AE, D, MC, V. BP.*

Nightlife and the Arts

The **Bennington Center for the Arts** (⊠ Rte. 9 at Gypsy La., ☎ 802/442–7158) hosts cultural events, including exhibitions by local and nationally recognized artists, and of wildlife and Native American art. The **Oldcastle Theatre Co.** (☎ 802/447–0564) at the Bennington Center for the Arts, whose season runs from May through October, is one of the Northeast's finest regional theaters.

Outdoor Activities and Sports

Cutting Edge (⊠ 160 Benmont Ave., ☎ 802/442–8664) rents and repairs bicycles and also sells and rents snowboards and cross-country skis. It has one of Vermont's few skateboarding parks, open Monday–Saturday 10–6, and Sunday noon–6.

HIKING

Four miles east of Bennington, the **Long Trail** crosses Route 9 and runs south to the top of Harmon Hill. Allot two or three hours for this hike.

STATE PARKS

Lake Shaftsbury State Park (⊠ Rte. 7A, 10½ mi north of Bennington, ☎ 802/375–9978) is one of a few parks in Vermont with group camping. It has a swimming beach, nature trails, boat and canoe rentals, and a snack bar. **Woodford State Park** (⊠ Rte. 9, 10 mi east of Bennington, ☎ 802/447–7169) has an activities center on Adams Reservoir, campsites, a playground, boat and canoe rentals, and nature trails.

Shopping

The **Apple Barn and Country Bake Shop** (⊠ U.S. 7 S, ☎ 802/447–7780) sells home-baked goodies, fresh cider, Vermont cheeses, and maple syrup. The showroom at the **Bennington Potters Yard** (⊠ 324 County St., ☎ 802/447–7531 or 800/205–8033) stocks first-quality pottery and antiques in addition to seconds from the famed Bennington Potters. On the free tour you can follow the clay through production and hear about the Potters Yard, in business for five decades. Tours begin at 10 and 2 in spring, summer, and fall. **Hawkins House Craftsmarket** (⊠ 262 North St./U.S. 7, ☎ 802/447–0488) showcases jewelry, wooden ware, glass, pottery, rugs, and clothing from more than 450 craftspeople.

Arlington

❻ *15 mi north of Bennington.*

Don't be surprised to see familiar-looking (if considerably aged) faces among the roughly 2,200 people of Arlington. The illustrator Norman Rockwell lived here from 1939 to 1953, and many of the models for his portraits of small-town life were his neighbors. First settled in 1763, Arlington was called Tory Hollow for its Loyalist sympathies— even though a number of the Green Mountain Boys lived here, too.

Smaller than Bennington and more down-to-earth than upper-crust Manchester to the north, Arlington exudes a certain Rockwellian folksiness. Dorothy Canfield Fisher, a novelist popular in the 1930s and 1940s, also lived here.

Although no original paintings are displayed at the **Norman Rockwell Exhibition,** the rooms are crammed with reproductions of the illustrator's works, arranged in every way conceivable: chronologically, by subject matter, and juxtaposed with photos of the models—several of whom work here. ⊠ *Main St./Rte. 7A,* ☎ *802/375–6423,* WEB *www.normanrockwellexhibit.com.* ⌧ *$2.* ☉ *May–Oct., daily 9–5; Nov.–Dec. and Feb.–Apr., daily 10–4.*

Dining and Lodging

$$$$ ✕🏠 **West Mountain Inn.** Spectacular views, labyrinthine gardens, and
★ pet llamas are hallmarks of this inn, built in the 1840s on 150 acres as an elegant summer retreat. The children's room, brightly painted with life-size Disney characters, is stocked with games, stuffed animals, and a TV with VCR. Six-course prix-fixe dinners ($$$$) highlighting updated Continental cuisine are served in a low-beam candlelit dining room. Request a table by the window. ⊠ *West Mountain Inn Rd., 05250,* ☎ *802/375–6516,* FAX *802/375–6553,* WEB *www.westmountaininn.com. 18 rooms, 6 suites. Restaurant, some microwaves, hiking, cross-country skiing, bar, meeting room; no phones in some rooms. AE, D, MC, V. MAP.*

$$–$$$$ ✕🏠 **Arlington Inn.** Greek Revival columns at this 1848 home lend it
★ an imposing presence, but the atmosphere is hardly forbidding. Victorian-style wallpaper and original moldings and wainscoting are highlights. King-size rooms have fireplaces and two-person hot tubs. The five rooms in the carriage house have country-French and Queen Anne furnishings. The restaurant serves regional American dishes ($$$–$$$$). The grounds have a garden, gazebo, pond, and waterfall. ⊠ *Rte. 7A, 05250,* ☎ *802/375–6532 or 800/443–9442,* FAX *802/375–6534,* WEB *www.arlingtoninn.com. 13 rooms, 5 suites. Restaurant, cable TV, meeting rooms. AE, D, MC, V. BP.*

$$ 🏠 **Hill Farm Inn.** This homey inn on the Battenkill River has the feel of the country farmhouse it used to be. The fireplace in the informal living room, the sturdy antiques, and the spinning wheel in the upstairs hallway all convey a relaxed, friendly environment. The Battenkill Suite has a beamed cathedral ceiling, and from its porch you can see Mt. Equinox. The rooms in the 1790 guest house are private; the charming one- and two-bedroom cabins are open from spring through fall. ⊠ *458 Hill Farm Rd., off Rte. 7A, 05250,* ☎ *802/375–2269 or 800/882–2545,* FAX *802/375–9918,* WEB *www.hillfarminn.com. 5 rooms, 6 suites, 4 cabins. Some kitchenettes, some refrigerators, in-room VCRs; no air-conditioning in some rooms. D, MC, V. BP.*

Outdoor Activities and Sports

Battenkill Canoe, Ltd./Vermont Canoe Trips (⊠ Rte. 7A, ☎ 802/362–2800 or 800/421–5268) rents canoes and runs inn-to-inn tours and day trips on the Battenkill.

Shopping

Equinox Valley Nursery (⊠ Rte. 7A between Arlington and Manchester, ☎ 802/362–2610) is known for its perennials (more than 1,000 varieties). The nursery has 17 greenhouses and a conservatory, sells 150 varieties of herbs, and carries many Vermont-made products in the large gift shop.

Manchester

★ **❼** *9 mi northeast of Arlington.*

Manchester, where Ira Allen proposed financing Vermont's participation in the American Revolution by confiscating Tory estates, has been a popular summer retreat since the mid-19th century. Manchester Village's tree-shaded marble sidewalks and stately old homes reflect the luxurious resort lifestyle of a century ago. Manchester Center's upscale factory outlets appeal to the affluent 20th-century ski crowd drawn by nearby Bromley and Stratton mountains. Warning: shoppers come in droves at times, giving the place the feel of a crowded mall on the weekend before Christmas. If you're coming here from Arlington, take pretty Route 7A, which passes directly by a number of sights.

★ **Hildene,** the summer home of Abraham Lincoln's son and onetime Pullman company chairman Robert Todd Lincoln, is a beautifully preserved 412-acre estate. The 24-room mansion, with its Georgian Revival symmetry, welcoming central hallway, and grand curved staircase, is unusual in that its rooms are not roped off. When the 1,000-pipe Aeolian organ is played, the music reverberates as though from the mansion's very bones. Tours include a short film on the owner's life and a walk through the elaborate formal gardens. When snow conditions permit, you can cross-country ski on the property, which has views of nearby mountains. ⊠ *Rte. 7A,* ☎ *802/362–1788,* WEB *www.hildene.org.* ✍ *$8.* ☉ *Mid-May–Oct., daily 9:30–5:30; visitor center daily 9–5:30. Tours on the ½ hr (first tour at 9:30, last tour at 4). Candlelight tours Dec. 27–29 at 5 PM.*

The **American Museum of Fly Fishing,** which houses the largest collection of fly-fishing equipment in the world, displays more than 1,500 rods, 800 reels, 30,000 flies, and the tackle of famous people such as Winslow Homer, Bing Crosby, and Jimmy Carter. Its library of 2,500 books is open by appointment. ⊠ *Rte. 7A at Seminary Ave.,* ☎ *802/362–3300,* WEB *www.amff.com.* ✍ *$3.* ☉ *Mon.–Sat. 10–4.*

The **Southern Vermont Arts Center** showcases rotating exhibits and its permanent collection of more than 700 pieces of 19th- and 20th-century American art in a 12,500-square-ft museum. The center's original building, a graceful Georgian mansion on 375 acres, is the frequent site of concerts, performances, and film screenings. In summer and fall, a restaurant with magnificent views opens for business. ⊠ *West Rd.,* ☎ *802/362–1405,* WEB *www.svac.org.* ✍ *$6.* ☉ *May–Oct., Tues.–Sat. 10–5, Sun. noon–5; Nov.–Apr., Mon.–Sat. 10–5.*

You may want to keep your eye on the temperature gauge of your car as you drive the 5-mi toll road to the top of 3,825-ft **Mt. Equinox.** Along the way you'll see the Battenkill trout stream and the surrounding Vermont countryside. Picnic tables line the drive, and you can look down both sides of the mountain from a notch known as the Saddle. ⊠ *Off Rte. 7A, south of Manchester,* ☎ *802/362–1114.* ✍ *Car and driver $6, each additional adult $2.* ☉ *May–Oct., daily 8 AM–10 PM.*

Green Mountain Railroad operates **Vermont Valley Flyer,** a vintage passenger coach that travels along the Battenkill River to Arlington (with fall excursions extending to North Bennington). It departs from the junction of Routes 11 and 30. ☎ *802/463–3069 or 800/707–3530,* WEB *www.rails-vt.com.* ✍ *$14.* ☉ *July 4–Sept. 1 and mid-Sept.–mid-Oct., Wed.–Mon. Train departs several times daily; call for schedule.*

Dining and Lodging

$$$$ ✕ **Chantecleer.** Intimate dining rooms have been created in a former dairy barn with a large fieldstone fireplace. The menu reflects the chef's Swiss background: appetizers include *Bündnerfleisch* (air-dried Swiss beef) and frogs' legs in garlic butter; rack of lamb, whole Dover sole filleted table-side, and veal chops highlight the entrées. The restaurant is 5 mi north of Manchester. ✉ *Rte. 7A, East Dorset,* ☏ *802/362–1616. Reservations essential. AE, DC, MC, V. Closed Tues. in summer; Mon.–Tues. in winter; and late Oct.–Thanksgiving and mid-Apr.–mid-May. No lunch.*

$$–$$$ ✕ **Bistro Henry's.** This airy restaurant on the outskirts of town attracts a devoted clientele for authentic Mediterranean fare. The menu lists fresh fish, seasonal game, and eclectic dishes such as rare tuna with wasabi and soy. The wine list is extensive. ✉ *Rte. 11/30,* ☏ *802/362–4982. AE, D, DC, MC, V. Closed Mon. No lunch.*

$$$$ ✕▥ **The Equinox.** Even before Abe Lincoln's family began summering here, this grand white-column resort was a local fixture. The spacious, sunny rooms are furnished with antique reproductions. The main hotel houses rooms and Presidential Suites; the Orvis Inn has one- and two-bedroom suites; and more rooms are in the Town House. Richly upholstered settees and fireplace in the Marsh Tavern create a plush traditional ambience. Men are requested to wear jackets in the elegant Colonnade restaurant ($$$–$$$$). The Sunday brunch is spectacular. ✉ *3567 Main St./Rte. 7A, Manchester Village 05254,* ☏ *802/362–4700 or 800/362–4747,* ℻ *802/362–1595,* ⓌⒺⒷ *www.equinoxresort.com. 163 rooms, 14 suites. 3 restaurants, 18-hole golf course, 3 tennis courts, 2 pools (1 indoor), health club, sauna, steam room, fishing, mountain bikes, croquet, horseback riding, cross-country skiing, ice-skating, snowmobiling, bar, meeting rooms; no smoking rooms. AE, D, DC, MC, V. MAP.*

$–$$$ ✕▥ **Barrows House.** This 200-year-old Federal-style inn and minire-
★   sort 8 mi from Bromley has guest rooms in eight buildings spread over 11 acres. Some have gas or wood-burning fireplaces and afford great privacy. Dinner ($$$)—served in the spacious main dining room, the greenhouse room, and the tavern—includes perennial favorites such as rack of lamb as well as nightly specials, which might include native grilled trout. ✉ *Rte. 30 (Box 98, Dorset 05251),* ☏ *802/867–4455 or 800/639–1620,* ℻ *802/867–0132,* ⓌⒺⒷ *www.barrowshouse.com. 18 rooms, 10 suites. Restaurant, cable TV, 2 tennis courts, pool, sauna, bicycles, cross-country skiing, some pets allowed. AE, D, DC, MC, V. BP, MAP.*

$$$$ ▥ **Inn at Ormsby Hill.** Once a stop on the Underground Railroad, this
★   1774 Federal-style building has guest rooms furnished with antiques and canopied or four-poster beds and fireplaces. Some have mountain views. Breakfasts are in the conservatory—entrées may include baked, stuffed French toast with an apricot brandy sauce. ✉ *1842 Main St./Rte. 7A, 05255,* ☏ *802/362–1163 or 800/670–2841,* ℻ *802/362–5176,* ⓌⒺⒷ *www.ormsbyhill.com. 10 rooms. In-room hot tubs; no kids. D, MC, V. BP.*

$$$–$$$$ ▥ **Wilburton Inn.** Overlooking the Battenkill Valley, this turn-of-the-20th-century Tudor mansion has 11 lovingly furnished bedrooms and suites, and richly paneled common rooms decorated with part of the owners' vast art collection. Five guest buildings are spread over the grounds, dotted with sculpture. Eight rooms have private decks with mountain views. A buffet breakfast is served in the Terrace Room, and dinner is served in the handsome Billiard Room. One note: weddings take place here most summer weekends. ✉ *River Rd., 05254,* ☏ *802/362–2500 or 800/648–4944,* ℻ *802/362–1107,* ⓌⒺⒷ *www.*

wilburton.com. 30 rooms, 4 suites. Restaurant, some cable TV, some microwaves, 3 tennis courts, pool. AE, MC, V. BP.

$$–$$$$ ☒ **1811 House.** At this mansion once owned by President Lincoln's
★ granddaughter, you can experience life in an English country home without crossing the Atlantic. Three acres of lawn are landscaped in the English floral style. Rooms contain period antiques; six have fireplaces and eight have four-poster beds. Bathrooms are old-fashioned but serviceable. Three rooms in the cottage have fireplaces and modern baths. ⊠ *Rte. 7A (Box 39, 05254),* ☎ *802/362–1811 or 800/432–1811,* FAX *802/362–2443,* WEB *www.1811house.com. 13 rooms, 1 suite. Pub, video game room; no kids under 16. AE, D, MC, V. BP.*

$–$$ ☒ **Aspen Motel.** A rare find in this area, the immaculate, family-owned Aspen is set well back from the highway and moderately priced. The spacious, tastefully decorated rooms have Colonial-style furnishings; a common room has a fireplace. ⊠ *Rte. 7A N, 05255,* ☎ *802/362–2450,* FAX *802/362–1348,* WEB *www.thisisvermont.com/aspen. 24 rooms, 1 cottage. Pool, some refrigerators, playground. AE, D, MC, V.*

Nightlife and the Arts

The two pre–Revolutionary War barns of the **Dorset Playhouse** (⊠ off town green, Dorset, ☎ 802/867–5777) host a community group in winter and a resident professional troupe in summer. The **Marsh Tavern** (☎ 802/362–4700) at the Equinox hosts cabaret music and jazz from Wednesday to Sunday in summer and on weekends in winter. **Mulligan's** (⊠ Rte. 7A, ☎ 802/362–3663) is a popular hangout in Manchester Village, especially for the après-ski set.

Outdoor Activities and Sports

BIKING

The 20-mi Dorset–Manchester trail runs from Manchester Village north on West Street to Route 30, turns west at the Dorset village green onto West Road, and heads back south to Manchester. **Battenkill Sports** (⊠ 1240 Depot St. [U.S. 7, Exit 4], ☎ 802/362–2734 or 800/340–2734) rents and repairs bikes and provides maps and route suggestions.

FISHING

Battenkill Anglers (⊠ 6204 Main St., Manchester Center, ☎ 802/362–3184) teaches the art and science of fly-fishing in both private and group lessons. The **Orvis Co.** (⊠ Rte. 7A, Manchester Center, ☎ 800/235–9763) hosts a nationally known fly-fishing school on the Battenkill, the state's most famous trout stream, with 2½-day courses given weekly between April and October.

HIKING

One of the most popular segments of Vermont's **Long Trail** starts at Route 11/30 west of Peru Notch and goes to the top of Bromley Mountain. The round-trip trek takes about four hours.

The **Mountain Goat** (⊠ 4676 Main St., ☎ 802/362–5159) sells hiking, backpacking, and climbing equipment and rents snowshoes and cross-country and telemark skis. The shop also conducts rock- and ice-climbing clinics.

STATE PARK

Emerald Lake State Park (⊠ U.S. 7, North Dorset, ☎ 802/362–1655), 9 mi north of Manchester, has campsites, a marked nature trail, an on-site naturalist, boat and canoe rentals, and a snack bar.

Shopping

ART AND ANTIQUES

Carriage Trade (⊠ Rte. 7A north of Manchester Center, ☎ 802/362–1125) contains room after room of Early American antiques and has a fine collection of ceramics. **Danby Antiques Center** (⊠ ⅛ mi off U.S. 7, Danby, ☎ 802/293–5990), 13 mi north of Manchester, has 11 rooms and a barn filled with furniture and accessories, folk art, textiles, and stoneware. Vermont-based artists display their oils, watercolors, and sculptures at **Gallery North Star** (⊠ Rte. 7A, ☎ 802/362–4541). The **Peel Gallery of Fine Art** (⊠ Peel Gallery Rd., Danby, ☎ 802/293–5230), which has celebrated its third decade in business, represents 40 professional American artists. **Tilting at Windmills Gallery** (⊠ Rte. 11/30, ☎ 802/362–3022) exhibits the works of well-known artists such as Douglas Flackman of the Hudson River School.

BOOKS

Northshire Bookstore (⊠ 4869 Main St., ☎ 802/362–2200 or 800/437–3700), a community bookstore for more than 20 years, carries many travel and children's books and sponsors readings year-round.

CLOTHING AND SPECIALTY ITEMS

Alfred Baier (⊠ Butternut La., ☎ 802/362–3371) makes and sells pipes in his studio-workshop. **Orvis Fly Fishing Outlet** (⊠ Union St., ☎ 802/362–6455) sells discounted fishing supplies in what was Orvis's shop in the 1800s.

FISHING GEAR

Orvis Retail Store (⊠ Rte. 7A, ☎ 802/362–3750), one of the largest suppliers of fishing gear in the Northeast, also carries clothing, gifts, and hunting supplies.

MALLS AND MARKETPLACES

Manchester Designer Outlets (⊠ U.S. 7 and Rte. 11/30, ☎ 802/362–3736 or 800/955–7467) has such big-city names as Joan & David, Baccarat, Coach, Ralph Lauren, and Cole-Haan. At **Manchester Square** (⊠ Rte. 11/30 and Richville Rd.) you'll find outlet stores for Giorgio Armani, Yves Delorme/Palais Royal, Vermont Toy Chest, Brooks Brothers, Levi Strauss, Escada, and more.

Ski Areas

BROMLEY MOUNTAIN

The first trails at Bromley were cut in 1936. The area has a comfortable red-clapboard base lodge, built when the ski area first opened; it was later expanded. Many families appreciate the resort's conviviality, with its large ski shop and a condominium village adjacent to the slopes. A reduced-price, two-day lift pass is available, as is a snowboard park-only lift ticket. Kids six and under ski free when accompanied by an adult. Eighty percent of the area is covered by snowmaking. ⊠ *Rte. 11 (Box 1130, Manchester Center 05255),* ☎ *802/824–5522 information and snow conditions; 800/865–4786 lodging,* WEB *www.bromley.com.*

Downhill. Most ski areas are laid out to face the north or east, but Bromley faces south, making it one of the warmer spots to ski in New England. Its 43 trails are equally divided into beginner, intermediate, and advanced terrain; the last is serviced by the Blue Ribbon quad chairlift on the east side. The vertical drop is 1,334 ft. Four double chairlifts, two quad lifts, a J-bar, and two surface lifts for beginners provide transportation. The high-speed quad lift takes skiers from the base to the summit in just six minutes.

Child care. Bromley is one of the region's best places to bring children. Besides a nursery for children ages 6 weeks–4 years, ski instruction is provided for children ages 3–12.

Summer activities. The area becomes a veritable playground in summer. At the DevalKart and the Alpine Slide, passengers ride up on a chairlift and come down on wheeled sleds (or ride back down on the chair). There's also a helium-filled, parachute-harnessed tethered balloon; a climbing wall; kiddie bumper cars; and a huge trampoline.

CROSS-COUNTRY SKIING

The **Meadowbrook Inn** (⊠ Rte. 11, Landgrove, ☎ 802/824–6444 or 800/498–6445) maintains 21 km (16 mi) of marked trails for cross-country skiing and snowshoeing. The inn, which has eight guest rooms and a restaurant, has rental gear and provides lessons.

Stratton

⑧   *18 mi southeast of Manchester.*

Stratton, home to the famous Stratton Mountain Resort, has a self-contained town center with shops, restaurants, and lodgings clustered at the base of the slopes. There's plenty of activity year-round between skiing and summer sports.

Lodging

$$–$$$$ 🖬 **Stratton Mountain Inn and Village Lodge.** This complex not only comprises the largest inn on the mountain but is the only slope-side hotel at Stratton. The inn is within walking distance of the lifts. Ski packages that include lift tickets bring down room rates. ⊠ *Middle Ridge Rd., 05155,* ☎ *802/297–2500; 877/887–3767 lodging;* FAX *802/297–1778,* WEB *www.strattonmountain.com;. 120 rooms, 91 lodge units. Restaurant, minibars, microwaves, refrigerators, golf course, 2 tennis courts, outdoor pool (summer only), hot tub, sauna, cross-country skiing, downhill skiing, lounge, video game room, meeting rooms; no air-conditioning in some rooms, no-smoking rooms. AE, DC, MC, V. BP mid-Apr.–mid–Dec.*

$–$$ 🖬 **Red Fox Inn.** Tom and Cindy Logan's "white house," just 4 mi from Stratton and 8 mi from Bromley, provides pleasant and comfortable accommodations. Each room has a private bath, and the suite has a fireplace and hot tub. Dinner is served nightly in the restaurant next door; a full roster of entertainment in the Tavern includes Irish and folk music as well as rock and roll. A special 50%-off room rate is offered Sunday–Thursday. ⊠ *Winhall Hollow Rd., Bondville 05340,* ☎ *802/297–2488,* FAX *802/297–02156,* WEB *www.redfoxxinn.com. 9 rooms. Restaurant, bar, some pets allowed. MC, V.*

Nightlife and the Arts

Popular **Mulligan's** (⊠ Mountain Rd., ☎ 802/297–9293) hosts bands or DJs in the late afternoon and on weekends. The **Red Fox Inn** (⊠ Winhall Hollow Rd., Bondville, ☎ 802/297–2488) hosts Irish music Tuesday night in winter; live folk music on Sunday night; an open mike on Thursday night; and rock and roll at other times.

Ski Areas

STRATTON MOUNTAIN

Since its creation in 1961, Stratton has undergone physical transformations and upgrades, yet the area's sophisticated character has been retained. It is a popular destination for affluent families and young professionals from the New York–southern Connecticut corridor. An entire village, with a covered parking structure for 700 cars, is at the base of the mountain. Adjacent to the base lodge are a condo-hotel, restaurants, and about 25 shops lining a pedestrian mall. Stratton is 4 mi up its own access road off Route 30 in Bondville, about 30 minutes from Manchester's popular shopping zone. ⊠ *R.R. 1, Box 145, Stratton Mountain 05155,* ☎ *802/297–2200; 800/843–6867; 802/297–4211 snow conditions; 800/787–2886 lodging,* WEB *www.stratton.com.*

Downhill. Stratton's skiing is in three sectors. The first is the lower mountain directly in front of the base lodge-village-condo complex; several lifts reach mid-mountain from this entry point, and practically all skiing is beginner or low-intermediate. Above that, the upper mountain, with a vertical drop of 2,000 ft, has a high-speed, 12-passenger gondola, Starship XII. Down the face are the expert trails, and on either side are intermediate cruising runs with a smattering of wide beginner slopes. The third sector, the Sun Bowl, is off to one side with two high-speed, six-passenger lifts and two expert trails, a full base lodge, and plenty of intermediate terrain. Snowmaking covers 85% of the terrain. Stratton hosts the U.S. Open Snowboarding championships; its snowboard park has a 380-ft halfpipe. A Ski Learning Park provides its own Park Packages for novice skiers. In all, Stratton has 11 lifts that service 90 trails and 90 acres of glades.

Cross-country. The resort has more than 30 km (18 mi) of cross-country skiing and two Nordic centers: Sun Bowl and Country Club.

Child care. The day-care center takes children from ages 6 weeks–5 years for indoor activities and outdoor excursions. There is a ski school for children ages 4–12. A junior racing program and special instruction groups are geared toward more experienced young skiers.

Summer and year-round activities. Stratton has 15 outdoor tennis courts, 27 holes of golf, horseback riding, mountain biking and hiking accessed by a gondola to the summit, and instructional programs in tennis and golf. The sports center, open year-round, contains two indoor tennis courts, three racquetball courts, a 25-meter indoor swimming pool, a hot tub, a steam room, a fitness facility with Nautilus equipment, and a restaurant. Stratton also hosts summer entertainment and family activities, including a skating park and climbing wall.

Londonderry

⑨ *12 mi north of Stratton.*

Within 20 minutes of Stratton and Bromley and Magic mountains, Londonderry is a major shopping center, with lodgings convenient to ski areas yet tucked away from on-site hustle and bustle.

Dining and Lodging

$–$$ ✕🏠 **Swiss Inn & Restaurant.** Guest rooms are large and comfortable at this relaxing and homey onetime dairy farm, which also houses a popular Swiss-German restaurant ($$–$$$). Among the specialties are raclette and Wiener schnitzel. Continental fare includes shrimp à la Marseilles. A lighter tavern menu is also available. ⊠ *249 Rte. 11, 05148,* ☎ *802/824–3442 or 800/847–9477,* ᖴᴬˣ *802/824–3957,* ᴡᴇʙ *www. swissinn.com. 19 rooms. Cable TV, tennis court, pool, pond, lounge. MC, V. BP.*

$$$ 🏠 **Londonderry Inn.** This inn is particularly inviting for groups and families with small children. Rooms, with patchwork quilts, hand-hooked rugs, and teddy bears, are spacious and comfortable, and many can be used as suites to accommodate larger parties. The rambling inn, an 1826 farmhouse on 9 acres, is a state-awarded "Green" hotel, which recognizes it as an environmentally sensitive lodging. ⊠ *Rte. 100, South Londonderry 05155,* ☎ *802/824–5226,* ᖴᴬˣ *802/824–3146,* ᴡᴇʙ *www.londonderryinn.com. 24 rooms. Pool, cross-country skiing, cinema. AE, D, MC, V. BP.*

Shopping

J. J. Hapgood Store (⊠ off Rte. 11, Peru, ☎ 802/824–5911) is an old-fashioned country store, complete with a potbellied stove.

Weston

⑩ *5 mi north of Londonderry.*

Although perhaps best known for the Vermont Country Store, Weston is famed as one of the first Vermont towns to have discovered its own intrinsic loveliness—and marketability. With its summer theater, pretty town green, and Victorian bandstand, as well as an assortment of shops offering variety without modern sprawl, the little village really lives up to its vaunted image.

The **Mill Museum,** down the road from the Vermont Country Store, has numerous hands-on displays depicting the engineering and mechanics of one of the town's mills. The many old tools on view kept towns like Weston running smoothly in their early days. ⊠ *Rte. 100,* ☏ *802/824–3119.* 🖼 *Donations accepted.* ⊘ *July–Aug., Wed.–Sun. 1–4; Sept.–mid-Oct., weekends 1–4.*

Dining and Lodging

$$$–$$$$ ✕🖼 **Inn at Weston.** Country elegance best describes this 1848 village inn and adjoining Coleman House. Some rooms and suites have fireplaces. The restaurant ($$$–$$$$; closed Mon.) serves contemporary regional cuisine amid candlelight. Vermont cheddar cheese and Granny Smith apple omelets are popular at breakfast. ⊠ *Rte. 100 (Box 66, 05161),* ☏ *802/824–6789,* 🖷 *802/824–3073,* ᴡᴇʙ *www.innweston.com. 13 rooms. Restaurant, some in-room hot tubs, pub; no TV in some rooms, no kids under 12. AE, DC, MC, V. BP.*

$–$$ 🖼 **Colonial House Inn & Motel.** You'll find warmth and charm at this family-friendly complex just 2 mi south of the village. Relax on comfortable furniture in the large living room or enjoy the sun in the solarium. Homey, country furnishings adorn both of the two inn rooms and the motel units. The complimentary breakfast includes fresh goodies from the on-site bakery; a family-style dinner is served Friday and Saturday nights. ⊠ *287 Rte. 100, 05161,* ☏ *802/824–6286 or 800/639–5033,* 🖷 *802/824–3934,* ᴡᴇʙ *www.cohoinn.com. 9 motel units, 2 inn rooms with shared bath. Cable TV. D, MC, V. BP.*

Nightlife and the Arts

The members of the **Weston Playhouse** (⊠ Village Green, off Rte. 100, ☏ 802/824–5288), the oldest professional theater in Vermont, produce Broadway plays, musicals, and other works. Their season runs from late June to early September.

The **Kinhaven Music School** (⊠ Lawrence Hill Rd., ☏ 802/824–3365) stages free student concerts on Friday at 4 PM and Sunday at 2:30 in July and August.

Shopping

The **Vermont Country Store** (⊠ Rte. 100, ☏ 802/824–3184, ᴡᴇʙ www.vtcountrystore.com) sets aside one room of its old-fashioned emporium for Vermont Common Crackers and bins of fudge and other candy. For years the retail store and its mail-order catalog have carried nearly forgotten items such as Lilac Vegetal aftershave, Monkey Brand black tooth powder, Flexible Flyer sleds, and tiny wax bottles of colored syrup, but have also sold plenty of practical items such as sturdy outdoor clothing and even a manual typewriter. Nostalgia-evoking implements dangle from the store's walls and ceiling. (There's another store on Route 103 in Rockingham.)

Drury House Antiques (⊠ Village Green, ☏ 802/824–4395) specializes in antique clocks, fly rods, and other fishing-related objects. The **Todd Gallery** (⊠ 614 Main St., ☏ 802/824–5606) exhibits paintings, prints, and sculptures by Vermont artists and craftspeople.

Ludlow

⑪ *9 mi northeast of Weston.*

Ludlow was once a nondescript factory town that just happened to have a major ski area—Okemo—on its outskirts. Today the old General Electric plant is gone, its premises recycled into a rambling, block-long complex of shops and restaurants, and the town seems much more integrated into the ski scene. A beautiful, often-photographed historic church overlooks the town green.

Dining and Lodging

$–$$$ ✕ **Pot Belly Pub.** Après-ski fun seekers pile into this popular restaurant-nightspot for house specialties such as Belly burgers, smoked ribs, steaks, applejack pork, and fresh seafood. Live entertainment—from jazz and rhythm-and-blues to swing—keeps patrons warm on winter weekends. ⊠ *130 Main St.,* ☎ *802/228–8989. AE, DC, MC, V.*

$$–$$$$ ✕⌂ **Governor's Inn.** This 19th-century Victorian country home on the village green is a welcome retreat for those looking for gracious accommodations and creative, contemporary fare. The second- and third-floor guest rooms are decorated with antique furnishings; the third-floor rooms, including the suite, have gas-lit fire stoves. Chef–co-owner Kathy Kubec prepares prix-fixe, six-course dinners Thursday–Sunday ($$$$; reservations essential). An elegant breakfast is served at individual tables for two. ⊠ *86 Main St., 05149,* ☎ *802/228–8830 or 800/468–3766,* FAX *802/228–2961,* WEB *www.thegovernorsinn.com. 9 rooms. Some cable TV; no kids under 12. AE, D, MC, V. BP.*

$$$–$$$$ ⌂ **Andrie Rose Inn.** Many of the antiques-filled rooms at this 1829 inn and adjacent buildings have whirlpool tubs and mountain views. Two-person luxury suites have whirlpool tubs, fireplaces, and steam showers for two. Full-floor condo suites in the 1883 Victorian Town House sleep up to 12, and two family suites have fireplaces and kitchens. Candlelight breakfast is included in standard rooms; a breakfast basket is delivered to the luxury suites. A four-course dinner with a seasonal menu is served Friday and Saturday. ⊠ *13 Pleasant St., 05149,* ☎ *802/223–4846 or 800/223–4846,* FAX *802/228–7910,* WEB *www.andrieroseinn.com. 9 rooms, 14 suites. Restaurant, some cable TV, some refrigerators, some microwaves, bicycles, bar; no air-conditioning in some rooms, no phones in some rooms. AE, V. BP.*

$$$–$$$$ ⌂ **Okemo Mountain Lodge.** The one-bedroom contemporary country condominiums clustered around the base of Okemo's ski lifts come with fireplaces and decks. The restaurant is open for breakfast and lunch only. The Okemo Mountain Lodging Service rents one- to five-bedroom units in the Kettle Brook, Winterplace, and Solitude slope-side condominiums. Ski-and-stay packages are available for three or more non-holiday nights. ⊠ *77 Okemo Ridge Rd., off Rte. 103, 05149,* ☎ *802/228–5571, 802/228–4041, or 800/786–5366,* FAX *802/228–2079,* WEB *www.okemo.com. 55 rooms. Restaurant, kitchens, in-room VCRs, cross-country skiing, downhill skiing, bar. AE, MC, V.*

Outdoor Activities and Sports

Cavendish Trail Horse Rides (⊠ 20 Mile Stream Rd., Proctorsville, ☎ 802/226–7821) operates horse-drawn sleigh rides in snowy weather, wagon rides at other times, and guided trail rides from mid-May to mid-October.

Ski Areas

OKEMO MOUNTAIN RESORT

An ideal ski area for families with children, family-owned Okemo has evolved into a major year-round resort. The main attraction is a long, broad, gentle slope with two beginner lifts just above the base lodge.

All the facilities at the bottom of the mountain are close together, so family members can regroup easily during the ski day. The resort offers numerous ski and snowboarding packages. ⊠ *77 Okemo Ridge Rd./Rte. 100,* ☎ *802/228–4041; 800/786–5366 lodging; 802/228–5222 snow conditions,* WEB *www.okemo.com.*

Downhill. Above the broad beginner's slope at the base, the upper part of Okemo has a varied network of trails: long, winding, easy trails for beginners; straight fall-line runs for experts; and curving, cruising slopes for intermediates. Fifty percent of the trails have an intermediate rating; 25% are rated novice, and 25% are rated for experts. The 98 trails are served by an efficient lift system of 14 lifts, including seven quads, three triple chairlifts, and four surface lifts; 95% are covered by snowmaking. From the summit to the base lodge, the vertical drop is 2,150 ft, the highest in southern Vermont. Okemo has a self-contained snowboarding area serviced by a surface lift; the mile-long park has two halfpipes, including the 400-ft-long Super Pipe. There's also a snowboard park for beginners.

Cross-country skiing/snowshoeing. The **Okemo Valley Nordic Center** (⊠ Fox La., ☎ 802/228–1396) has 28 km (16 mi) of groomed cross-country trails and 10 km (6 mi) of dedicated snowshoe trails and rents equipment.

Child care. The area's nursery, for children ages 6 weeks–8 years, has many indoor activities and supervised outings. The MiniStar Ski Program is for children ages 3–4; the SnowStar program is for kids ages 4–7. Nursery reservations are essential. Okemo also runs a Kids' Night Out evening child-care program on Saturdays during the regular season and certain holiday weeks.

Summer activities. The Okemo Valley Golf Club has an 18-hole, par-71, 6,000-yard course. Seven target greens, a putting green, a golf academy, and an indoor putting green, swing stations, and a simulator provide plenty of ways to improve your game.

Chester

🕐 *11 mi east of Weston.*

Gingerbread Victorians frame Chester's town green. The local pharmacy on Main Street has been in continuous operation since the 1860s. The stone village on North Street on the outskirts of town, two rows of buildings constructed from quarried stone, was built by two brothers and is said to have been used during the Civil War as a station on the Underground Railroad.

In Chester's restored 1852 train station you can board the **Green Mountain Flyer** for a 26-mi, two-hour round-trip journey to Bellows Falls, on the Connecticut River at the eastern edge of the state. The cars that date from the golden age of railroading travel past covered bridges and along the Brockway Mills gorge. The fall foliage trips are spectacular. ⊠ *Rte. 103,* ☎ *802/463–3069 or 800/707–3530,* WEB *www.rails-vt.com.* 🎫 *$11 in summer, $12 in fall.* ☺ *Late June–mid-Sept., Tues.–Sun.; mid-Sept.–late-Oct., daily. Train departs several times daily; call for schedule.*

Dining and Lodging

$$–$$$ ✕ **Raspberries and Thyme.** Breakfast specials, homemade soups, a large selection of salads, homemade desserts, and a menu listing more than 40 sandwiches make this one of the area's most popular spots for casual dining. ⊠ *On the Green,* ☎ *802/875–4486. AE, D, MC, V. No dinner Tues.*

$$–$$$ ⊞ **Chester House Inn.** All of the rooms in this handsomely restored 1780 historic inn on the Green have private baths. Five have fireplaces, and three have hot tubs or steam showers. Breakfast and dinner are served in the elegant Keeping Room, which has a fireplace. ✉ *266 Main St., 05143,* ☎ *802/875–2205 or 888/875–2205,* FAX *802/875–6602,* WEB *www.chesterhouseinn.com. 7 rooms. Restaurant, some in-room hot tubs, bar. D, DC, MC, V.*

$$ ⊞ **Fullerton Inn.** Guest rooms with country quilts and lace curtains vary in size and amenities at this three-story, wooden 19th-century building with a big porch. Some favorites are the bright corner rooms and Nos. 8 and 10, which share a private porch. The restaurant serves breakfast Tuesday–Saturday in winter and Monday–Saturday in summer. Dinner is served every night except Wednesday. A shuttle bus to local attractions and ski areas stops in front of the inn. ✉ *40 Common, on the Green, 05143,* ☎ *802/875–2444,* FAX *802/875–6414,* WEB *www.fullertoninn.com. 21 rooms, 3 suites. Restaurant, lounge, shop; no kids under 13. AE, D, MC, V. BP.*

Outdoor Activities and Sports

A 26-mi **driving or biking loop** out of Chester follows the Williams River along Route 103 to Pleasant Valley Road north of Bellows Falls. At Saxtons River, turn west onto Route 121 and follow along the river to connect with Route 35. When the two routes separate, follow Route 35 north back to Chester.

Shopping

The **National Survey Charthouse** (✉ Main St., ☎ 802/875–2121) is a pleasant place for a rainy-day browse, especially for map lovers. More than 125 dealers sell antiques and country crafts at **Stone House Village Antiques Center** (✉ Rte. 103 S, ☎ 802/875–4477).

Grafton

★ ⑬ *8 mi south of Chester.*

Like many Vermont villages its size, Grafton enjoyed its heyday as an agricultural community well before the Civil War, when its citizens grazed some 10,000 sheep and spun their wool into sturdy yarn for locally woven fabric. Unlike most other out-of-the-way country towns, though, Grafton was born again, following a long decline, by preservationists determined to revitalize not only its centerpiece, the Old Tavern, but many other commercial and residential structures in the village center. Beginning in 1963, the Windham Foundation—Vermont's second-largest private foundation—commenced the rehabilitation of Grafton. The **Historical Society** documents the town's renewal. ✉ *Townshend Rd.,* ☎ *802/843–2584 visitor center information.* ⊡ *$1.* ⊙ *June–late Sept., weekends 1:30–4; late Sept.–Oct., daily 1:30–4.*

Dining and Lodging

$$$$ ✕⊞ **Old Tavern at Grafton.** White-column porches on both stories wrap around the main building of this commanding 1801 inn. The main building has 11 rooms; the rest are dispersed among six other buildings in town. Two dining rooms ($$$), one with formal Georgian furniture, the other with rustic paneling and low beams, serve inspired Continental fare. The inn runs the nearby Grafton Ponds Cross-Country Ski Center. ✉ *Rte. 121, 05146,* ☎ *802/843–2231 or 800/843–1801,* FAX *802/843–2245,* WEB *www.old-tavern.com. 48 rooms, 7 suites. Restaurant, café, tennis court, pond, mountain bikes, paddle tennis, cross-country skiing, ice-skating, bar, Internet, meeting rooms. AE, MC, V. Closed Apr. BP.*

Shopping

Gallery North Star (⊠ Townshend Rd., ☎ 802/843–2465) exhibits the oils, watercolors, lithographs, and sculptures of Vermont-based artists.

Townshend

⑭ *9 mi south of Grafton.*

One of a string of pretty villages along the banks of the West River, Townshend embodies the Vermont ideal of a lovely town green presided over by a gracefully proportioned church spire. The spire belongs to the 1790 Congregational Meeting House, one of the state's oldest houses of worship. Just north on Route 30 is the Scott Bridge (closed to traffic), the state's longest single-span covered bridge.

At **Townshend State Park,** you'll find a sandy beach and a trailhead for the rigorous, 2.7-mi hike to the top of Bald Mountain. Campsites are available. ⊠ *Rte. 30 N,* ☎ *802/365–7500.*

Dining and Lodging

$ ✕ **Townshend Dam Diner.** Folks come from miles around to enjoy traditional fare such as Mom's meat loaf, chili, and roast beef croquettes, as well as Townshend-raised bison burgers, and creative daily specials. Breakfast, served all day every day, includes such tasty treats as raspberry chocolate-chip walnut pancakes and homemade French toast. ⊠ *Rte. 30,* ☎ *802/874–4107. No credit cards. Closed Tues.*

$$$$ ✕▥ **Windham Hill Inn.** Period antiques, Oriental carpets, and locally made furniture are hallmarks of this 1825 brick farmhouse and white barn annex house. Most rooms have fireplaces; all have magnificent views of the West River valley. A prix-fixe four-course candlelight dinner ($$$; à la carte menu also available) is served in the Frog Pond Dining Room. ⊠ *311 Lawrence Dr., West Townshend 05359,* ☎ *800/ 944–4080,* 🖷 *802/874–4702,* 🕸 *www.windhamhill.com. 21 rooms. Restaurant, tennis court, pool, hiking, cross-country skiing, ice-skating; no kids under 12. BP.*

$ ▥ **Boardman House.** This handsome Greek Revival home on the town green combines modern comfort with the relaxed charm of a 19th-century farmhouse. The uncluttered guest rooms are furnished with Shaker-style furniture, colorful duvets, and paintings. Both the breakfast room and front hall have trompe l'oeil floors. ⊠ *On the Green, 05353,* ☎ *802/ 365–4086,* 🕸 *www.southvermont.com/townshend/boardmanhouse. 5 rooms, 1 suite. Some cable TV, sauna. No credit cards. BP.*

Outdoor Activities and Sports

You can rent canoes, kayaks, tubes, cross-country skis, and snowshoes at **Townshend Outdoors** (⊠ Rte. 30, ☎ 802/365–7309).

Shopping

The **Big Black Bear Shop** at Mary Meyer Stuffed Toys Factory, the state's oldest stuffed toy company, offers discounts of up to 70% on bear-related products (⊠ Rte. 30, ☎ 888/758–2327).

Newfane

⑮ *15 mi south of Grafton.*

With a village green surrounded by pristine white buildings, Newfane is sometimes described as the quintessential New England small town. The 1839 First Congregational Church and the Windham County Court House, with 17 green-shuttered windows and a rounded cupola, are often open. The building with the four-pointed spire is Union Hall, built in 1832.

Dining and Lodging

$$–$$$ ✕⊡ **Four Columns.** Rooms in this white-columned, 1834 Greek Revival mansion are decorated with a mix of antiques and turn-of-the-20th-century reproductions. Most of the suites have cathedral ceilings; all have double whirlpool baths and gas fireplaces. Two third-floor suites in the old section afford the most privacy. The elegant restaurant ($$$–$$$$; closed Tues.) serves new American cuisine. ⊠ *West St. (Box 278, 05345),* ☎ *802/365–7713 or 800/787–6633,* FAX *802/365–0022,* WEB *www.fourcolumnsinn.com. 9 rooms, 6 suites. Restaurant, pool, hiking, bar, Internet, some pets allowed (fee). AE, D, DC, MC, V. CP.*

Shopping

The **Newfane Country Store** (⊠ Rte. 30, ☎ 802/365–7916) carries many quilts (which can also be custom ordered), homemade fudge, and other Vermont foods, gifts, and crafts. Collectibles dealers from across the state sell their wares at the **Newfane Flea Market** (⊠ Rte. 30, ☎ 802/365–7771), held every weekend during summer and fall. Corncob-smoked ham and bacon and Vermont cheeses are just a few of the delectable goodies at **Lawrence's Smoke House** (⊠ Rte. 30, ☎ 802/ 365–7372).

Putney

⑯ *7 mi east of Newfane, 9 mi north of Brattleboro.*

Putney, a Connecticut River valley town just upriver from Brattleboro, was a prime destination for many of the converts to alternative rural lifestyles who swarmed into Vermont during the late 1960s and early '70s. Those who remain maintain a tradition of progressive schools, artisanship, and organic farming.

◔ **Harlow's Sugar House** (⊠ U.S. 5, ☎ 802/387–5852), 2 mi north of Putney, has a working cider mill and sugarhouse, as well as berry picking in summer and apple picking in autumn. You can buy cider, maple syrup, and other items in the gift shop.

Tours are given of the **Green Mountain Spinnery,** a factory-shop that sells yarn, knitting accessories, and patterns. ⊠ *Depot Rd. at Exit 4 off I–91,* ☎ 802/387–4528 or 800/321–9665. ☉ *Tours at 1:30 on the 1st and 3rd Tues. of month.*

Dining and Lodging

$$–$$$ ✕⊡ **Putney Inn.** The inn's main building dates from the 1790s and was later part of a seminary—the present-day pub was the chapel. Two fireplaces dominate the lobby. The spacious, modern rooms in an adjacent building have Queen Anne mahogany reproductions and are 100 yards from the banks of the Connecticut River. The restaurant ($$$) serves regionally inspired cuisine—seafood, New England potpies, a wild-game mixed grill, and burgers with Vermont cheddar—marked by innovative flourishes. ⊠ *Depot Rd., 05346,* ☎ *802/387–5517 or 800/653–5517,* FAX *802/387–5211,* WEB *www.putneyinn.com. 25 rooms. Restaurant, lounge, meeting rooms, some pets allowed (fee). AE, D, MC, V. BP.*

$$$ ⊡ **Hickory Ridge House Bed and Breakfast.** On the National Register of Historic Places, this 1808 Federal-style mansion with Palladian windows and a parlor with a Rumford fireplace has large, comfortable guest rooms filled with antiques and country furnishings. Five rooms have wood-burning fireplaces and private baths. A two-bedroom cottage, with a full kitchen and fireplace, can be rented as a unit or the rooms can be rented separately. ⊠ *53 Hickory Ridge Rd., 05346,* ☎ *802/387–5709 or 800/380–9218,* FAX *802/387–4328,*

WEB *www.hickoryridgehouse.com. 6 rooms, 1 cottage. Hiking, cross-country skiing. AE, MC, V. BP.*

Shopping
Allen Bros. (⊠ U.S. 5 north of Putney, ☎ 802/722–3395) bakes apple pies, makes cider doughnuts, and sells Vermont foods and products.

Southern Vermont A to Z

To research prices, get advice from other travelers, and book travel arrangements, visit www.fodors.com.

BUS TRAVEL
Vermont Transit links Bennington, Manchester, and Brattleboro.
➤ Bus Information: **Vermont Transit** (☎ 800/552–8737).

CAR TRAVEL
In the south the principal east–west highway is Route 9, the Molly Stark Trail, from Brattleboro to Bennington. The most important north–south roads are U.S. 7; the more scenic Route 7A; Route 100, which runs through the state's center; I–91; and U.S. 5, which runs along the state's eastern border. Route 30 from Brattleboro to Manchester is a scenic drive.

EMERGENCIES
➤ Hospitals: **Brattleboro Memorial Hospital** (⊠ 9 Belmont Ave., Brattleboro, ☎ 802/257–0341). **Southwestern Vermont Medical Center** (⊠ 100 Hospital Dr., Bennington, ☎ 802/442–6361).

VISITOR INFORMATION
➤ Contacts: **Bennington Area Chamber of Commerce** (⊠ Veterans Memorial Dr., Bennington 05201, ☎ 802/447–3311 or 800/229–0252, WEB www.bennington.com). **Brattleboro Area Chamber of Commerce** (⊠ 180 Main St., Brattleboro 05301, ☎ 802/254–4565, WEB www.brattleboro.com). **Chamber of Commerce, Manchester and the Mountains** (⊠ 5046 Main St., Manchester 05255, ☎ 802/362–2100, WEB www.manchestervermont.net). **Mt. Snow Valley Chamber of Commerce** (⊠ W. Main St. [Box 3, Wilmington 05363], ☎ 802/464–8092 or 877/887–6884, WEB www.visitvermont.com).

CENTRAL VERMONT

Central Vermont's economy once centered on the mills and railroad yards of Rutland and the marble quarries that honeycomb nearby towns. Vermont's "second city" is still a busy commercial hub, but today, as in much of the rest of the state, it's tourism that drives the economic engine. The center of the dynamo is the massive ski-and-stay infrastructure around Killington, the East's largest downhill resort.

However, Central Vermont has more to discover than high-speed chairlifts and slope-side condos. The protected (except for occasional logging) lands of the Green Mountain National Forest surround the spine of Vermont's central range; off to the west, the rolling dairy land of the southern Lake Champlain valley is one of the truly undiscovered corners of the state. To the east, in the Connecticut River valley, are towns as diverse as Calvin Coolidge's Plymouth, a Yankee Brigadoon, and busy, polished-to-perfection Woodstock, where upscale shops are just a short walk from America's newest national park.

The coverage of towns begins with Windsor, on U.S. 5 near I–91 at the state's eastern edge; winds westward toward U.S. 7; then continues north before heading over the spine of the Green Mountains.

Windsor

⓱ *50 mi north of Brattleboro, 42 mi east of Rutland.*

Windsor justly bills itself as the birthplace of Vermont. An interpretive exhibit on Vermont's constitution, the first in the United States to prohibit slavery and establish a system of public schools, is housed in the **Old Constitution House.** The site, where in 1777 grant holders declared Vermont an independent republic, contains 18th- and 19th-century furnishings, American paintings and prints, and Vermont-made tools, toys, and kitchenware. ✉ *N. Main St.,* ☎ *802/828–3211.* ⬜ *$1.* ☉ *Late May–mid-Oct., Wed.–Sun. 11–5.*

The firm of Robbins & Lawrence became famous for applying the "American system" (the use of interchangeable parts) to the manufacture of rifles. Although the company no longer exists, the **American Precision Museum** extols the Yankee ingenuity that created a major machine-tool industry here in the 19th century. The museum contains the largest collection of historically significant machine tools in the country and presents changing exhibits. ✉ *196 Main St.,* ☎ *802/674–6628.* ⬜ *$5.* ☉ *Memorial Day–Nov. 1, daily 10–5.*

The mission of the **Vermont State Craft Gallery,** in the restored 1846 Windsor House, is to advance the appreciation of Vermont crafts through education and exhibition. The center presents crafts exhibitions and operates a small museum. ✉ *54 Main St.,* ☎ *802/674–6729.* ☉ *Mon.–Sat. 10–5, Sun. 1–5.*

Glass blowers demonstrate their art at **Simon Pearce** (✉ U.S. 5, ☎ 802/674–6280 or 800/774–5277), where there's also a retail shop.

At 460 ft, the **Cornish–Windsor Covered Bridge** off U.S. 5, which spans the Connecticut River between Windsor and Cornish, New Hampshire, is the longest in the state.

Dining and Lodging

$$–$$$ ✕ **Windsor Station.** This converted main-line railroad station serves such entrées as chicken Kiev, filet mignon, and prime rib. The booths, with their curtained brass railings, were created from the high-back railroad benches of the depot. ✉ *Depot Ave.,* ☎ *802/674–2052. AE, MC, V. Closed Mon. in fall and winter. No lunch.*

$$–$$$$ ✕⬜ **Juniper Hill Inn.** An expanse of green lawn with Adirondack chairs and a garden of perennials sweeps up to the portico of this turn-of-the-20th-century Greek Revival mansion. Eleven of the antiques-furnished bedrooms have fireplaces. Four-course dinners ($$$$; reservations essential) are served in the candlelit dining room at 7 PM. Tuesday–Saturday may include sautéed scallops with glazed garlic and champagne sauce. ✉ *153 Pembroke Rd., 05089,* ☎ *802/674–5273 or 800/359–2541,* ℻ *802/674–2041,* ⬛ *www.juniperhillinn.com. 16 rooms. Restaurant, pool, hiking, meeting room; no kids under 12. AE, D, MC, V. BP.*

Nightlife and the Arts

Destiny (✉ U.S. 5, Windsor, ☎ 802/674–6671) hosts rock bands most days and has a DJ on Sunday.

Brownsville

⓲ *5 mi southwest of Windsor.*

Brownsville, a small village at the foot of Ascutney Mountain, has everything a village needs: a country store, post office, town hall, and historic grange building. The Ascutney Mountain ski area is a self-contained four-season resort.

Central Vermont

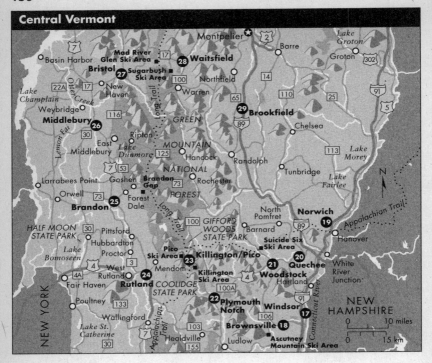

Lodging

$$–$$$$ 🏨 **Ascutney Mountain Resort Hotel.** One of the big attractions of this five-building resort hotel–condo complex is the ski lift outside the main door. The comfortable, well-maintained suites come in different configurations and sizes—some with fireplaces and decks. Slope-side multilevel condos have three bedrooms, three baths, and private entrances. The Ascutney Harvest Inn, within the complex, serves Continental cuisine. ⊠ *Hotel Rd., off Rte. 44 (Box 699, 05037),* ☎ *802/484–7711 or 800/243–0011,* ℻ *802/484–3117. 212 units. 3 restaurants, some kitchens, 2 pools (1 indoor), hot tub, health club, racquetball, ice-skating. AE, MC, V.*

$–$$ 🏨 **Mill Brook.** This Victorian farmhouse, built in 1880, is directly across from the Ascutney ski slopes. Making après-ski idleness easy are the four sitting rooms, decorated with antiques and contemporary furnishings. The honeymoon suite has a separate dressing room with a claw-foot bathtub; the other suites are perfect for families. Rates include afternoon tea. ⊠ *Rte. 44 (Box 410, 05037),* ☎ *802/484–7283,* 🌐 *www.millbrookbb.com. 2 rooms, 3 suites. Hot tub, some pets allowed (fee). AE, MC, V. BP.*

Nightlife and the Arts

Crow's Nest Club (⊠ Ascutney Mountain Resort Hotel, Hotel Rd., off Rte. 44, ☎ 802/484–7711) hosts live blues, country, rock and folk on weekends.

Ski Areas

ASCUTNEY MOUNTAIN RESORT

The Plausteiner family, whose patriarch, John, was instrumental in operations at Mt. Snow and White Face Mountain, in Lake Placid, New York, purchased this resort in the mid-1990s and since then has been continually making improvements. The self-contained resort has a 10-

acre Learning Park with its own chairlift and surface lift, 95% snow-making coverage, and a Sports and Fitness Center. The five buildings of the resort village include ski-in, ski-out hotel suites and condominium units. ⊠ *Rte. 44, off I–91 (Box 699, Brownsville 05037),* ☎ *802/484–7711; 800/243–0011 lodging.*

Downhill. Fifty-six trails with varying terrain are serviced by six lifts, including a mile-long North Peak Express high-speed quad, three triple chairs, one double chair, and a surface lift. Beginner and novice skiers stay toward the base, while intermediates enjoy the band that wraps the midsection. For experts, tougher black-diamond runs top the mountain. One disadvantage to Ascutney is that there is no easy way down from the summit, so novice skiers should not make the trip. Ascutney is popular with families because it provides some of the least-expensive junior lift tickets in the region.

Cross-country skiing. The resort has 32 km (19 mi) of groomed cross-country trails and offers rentals.

Child care. Day care is available for children from ages 6 weeks–6 years, with learn-to-ski options and rental equipment for toddlers and up. There are half- and full-day instruction programs for children ages 3–12; a Mini-Olympians program for ages 4–6; and a Young Olympians program for ages 7–12.

Summer and year-round activities. Ascutney Mountain Resort Hotel has a sports-and-fitness center with full-size indoor and outdoor pools, a hot tub, racquetball, aerobics facilities and classes, weight training, and massage. Summer activities include mountain biking, hiking, and tennis.

Norwich

⑲ *6 mi north of White River Junction, 22 mi north of Brownsville.*

Norwich, comprised of beautifully kept 18th- and 19th-century homes surrounding a handsome green, is home to Dartmouth College and an excellent science museum.

★☾ Numerous hands-on exhibits at the **Montshire Museum of Science** explore space, nature, and technology; there are also living habitats, aquariums, and many children's programs. A maze of trails wind through 100 acres of pristine woodland. An ideal destination for a rainy day, this is one of the finest museums in New England. ⊠ *1 Montshire Rd.,* ☎ *802/649–2200,* WEB *www.montshire.org.* ⊠ *$6.50.* ☉ *Daily 10–5.*

Shopping

The shelves at **King Arthur Flour Baker's Store** (⊠ 135 Rte. 5 S, ☎ 802/649–3881) are stocked with all the tools and ingredients in the company's Baker's Catalogue, including mixes and flours, and local products. The bakery has a viewing area.

Quechee

⑳ *11 mi south of Norwich, 6 mi west of White River Junction.*

Quechee is perched astride the Ottauquechee River. Quechee Gorge, 165 ft deep, is impressive though sometimes overrun by tourists. You can see the mile-long gorge, carved by a glacier, from U.S. 4, but many people picnic nearby or scramble down one of several descents for a closer look.

More than a decade ago Simon Pearce set up **Simon Pearce,** an eponymous glassblowing factory in an old mill by a waterfall here, using the water power to drive his furnace. Today the glassblowing factory is at the heart of a handsome, upscale shopping complex that also houses a weaver (demonstrations Tuesday–Sunday) and a pottery studio. You can watch the glassblowers at work daily and then purchase their wares in the gift shop or enjoy food served on seconds in the restaurant, which overlooks the waterfall. ⊠ *The Mill, Main St.,* ☎ *802/295–2711,* WEB *www.simonpearceglass.com.* ⊙ *Store daily 9–9.*

Dining and Lodging

$$–$$$ ✕ **Simon Pearce.** Candlelight, sparkling glassware from the studio downstairs, contemporary dinnerware, exposed brick, and large windows that overlook the roaring Ottauquechee River create an ideal setting for contemporary American cuisine. Sesame-crusted tuna with noodle cakes and wasabi as well as roast duck with mango chutney sauce are house specialties; the wine cellar holds several hundred vintages. ⊠ *Main St.,* ☎ *802/295–1470. AE, D, DC, MC, V.*

$$$ ✕🏠 **Quechee Inn at Marshland Farm.** Each room in this handsomely restored 1793 country home is decorated with Queen Anne–style furnishings and period antiques. Activities include cross-country skiing on groomed ski trails, bike and canoe rentals, a fly-fishing school, and privileges at the Quechee Country Club. The dining room's ($$$) creative dishes include entrées such as duck confit and seared sesame tuna. ⊠ *Clubhouse Rd., 05059,* ☎ *802/295–3133 or 800/235–3133,* FAX *802/295–6587,* WEB *www.quecheeinn.com. 22 rooms, 2 suites. Restaurant, golf privileges, fishing, bicycles, cross-country skiing, meeting room. AE, D, DC, MC, V. BP.*

$$–$$$ ✕🏠 **Parker House.** The peach-and-blue rooms of this 1857 Victorian mansion are named for former residents: Emily has a marble fireplace and Joseph has a view of the Ottauquechee River. The elegant dining room ($$$) prepares sophisticated American comfort cuisine such as loin of venison with a port and balsamic vinegar sauce. You also have access to the Quechee Country Club's facilities. ⊠ *1792 Quechee Main St. (Box 0780, 05059),* ☎ *802/295–6077,* FAX *802/296–6696,* WEB *www.theparkerhouseinn.com. 7 rooms. Restaurant, golf privileges; no air-conditioning in some rooms. AE, MC, V. BP.*

Outdoor Activities and Sports

FISHING

The **Vermont Fly Fishing School/Wilderness Trails** (⊠ Quechee Inn, Clubhouse Rd., ☎ 802/295–7620) leads workshops, rents fishing gear and mountain bikes, and arranges canoe and kayak trips. In winter, the company conducts cross-country and snowshoe treks.

POLO

Quechee Polo Club (⊠ Dewey's Mill Rd., ½ mi north of U.S. 4, ☎ 802/295–7152) draws hundreds of spectators on summer Saturdays to its matches near the Quechee Gorge. Admission is $3 per person or $6 per carload.

Shopping

The 40 dealers at the **Hartland Antiques Center** (⊠ U.S. 4, ☎ 802/457–4745) stock furniture, paper items, china, glass, and collectibles. More than 350 dealers sell their wares at the **Quechee Gorge Village** (⊠ U.S. 4, ☎ 802/295–1550 or 800/438–5565), an antiques and crafts mall in an immense reconstructed barn that also houses a country store and a classic diner. A merry-go-round and a small-scale working railroad operate when weather permits.

Ottauquechee Valley Winery (⊠ 5967 Woodstock Rd./U.S. 4, ☎ 802/295–9463), in a historic 1870s barn complex, has a tasting room and sells fruit wines, such as apple and blueberry.

Scotland by the Yard (✉ U.S. 4, ☎ 802/295–5351 or 800/295–5351) is the place to shop for all things Scottish, from kilts to Harris tweed jackets and tartan ties.

Woodstock

★ ㉑ *4 mi west of Quechee.*

Perfectly preserved Federal-style houses surround Woodstock's tree-lined village green, and streams flow around the town center, which is anchored by a covered bridge. The town owes much of its pristine appearance to the Rockefeller family's interest in historic preservation and land conservation. Woodstock's history of conservation dates from the 19th century: town native George Perkins Marsh, a congressman and diplomat, wrote the pioneering book *Man and Nature* in 1864 and was closely involved in the creation of the Smithsonian Institution in Washington, D.C.

☯ The **Billings Farm and Museum,** on the grounds of George Perkins Marsh's boyhood home, was founded by Frederick Billings in 1870 as a model of conservation and is one of the oldest dairy farms in the country. Billings, a lawyer and businessman, put into practice Marsh's ideas about the long-term effects of farming and grazing. Exhibits in the reconstructed Queen Anne farmhouse, school, general store, workshop, and former Marsh homestead demonstrate the lives and skills of early Vermont settlers. ✉ *Rte. 12, ½ mi north of Woodstock,* ☎ *802/457–2355,* WEB *www.billingsfarm.org.* ☜ *$8.* ☉ *May–late Oct., daily 10–5; call for Thanksgiving and Dec. weekend schedules.*

The 500-acre **Marsh-Billings-Rockefeller National Historical Park,** which opened in 1998, is Vermont's only national park and the nation's first to focus on conservation and stewardship of natural resources. The park encompasses the forest lands planned by Frederick Billings according to the principles of George Perkins Marsh, as well as Billings' mansion, gardens, and carriage roads. The entire property was the gift of Laurance S. Rockefeller, who lived here with his late wife, Mary, Frederick Billings' granddaughter. It is adjacent to the Billings Farm and Museum. The residential complex is accessible by guided tour only, but you can explore the extensive network of carriage roads and trails on your own. ✉ *Rte. 12,* ☎ *802/457–3368,* WEB *www.nps.marsh-billings.com.* ☜ *Tour $6.* ☉ *Memorial Day–Oct., daily for guided tours only (call for schedules); grounds daily dawn–dusk.*

Period furnishings of the Woodstock Historical Society fill the white clapboard **Dana House,** built circa 1807. Exhibits include the town charter, furniture, maps, and locally minted silver. The converted barn houses the Woodstock Works exhibit, an economic portrait of the town. ✉ *26 Elm St.,* ☎ *802/457–1822.* ☜ *$2.* ☉ *Mid-May–mid-Oct., Mon.–Sat. 10–4, Sun. noon–4; mid-Oct.–mid-May, by appointment only.*

The Raptor Center of the ☯ **Vermont Institute of Natural Science** (VINS) houses 23 species of birds of prey, among them bald eagles, peregrine falcons, and 3-ounce saw-whet owls. There are also ravens, turkey vultures, and snowy owls. All the caged birds have been found injured and unable to survive in the wild. This nonprofit, environmental research and education center is on a 77-acre nature preserve with walking trails. ✉ *Church Hill Rd.,* ☎ *802/457–2779,* WEB *www.vinsweb.org.* ☜ *$7.* ☉ *Mon.–Sat. 10–4.*

Dining and Lodging

$$$–$$$$ ✕ **Prince & the Pauper.** Modern French and American fare with a Ver-
★   mont accent is the focus of this candlelit Colonial restaurant. The
          grilled duck breast might have an Asian five-spice sauce; lamb and pork
          sausage in puff pastry comes with a honey-mustard sauce. A three-course
          prix-fixe menu is available for $38; a less-expensive bistro menu is avail-
          able in the lounge. ⊠ *24 Elm St.,* ☎ *802/457–1818. AE, D, MC, V.*
          No lunch.

$–$$ ✕ **Pane & Salute.** Regional Italian breads are a specialty, but this
          restaurant serves a lot more. Try the Tuscan pizzas and pasta entrées
          such as penne with spinach, pine nuts, raisins, and garlic. Add a glass
          of Chianti and *mangia bene.* Desserts include meringues with whipped
          cream and raspberry sauce. Sunday brunch is served from 10 to 2. ⊠
          61 Central St., ☎ *802/457–4882. D, MC, V. Closed Tues.–Wed.*

$$$$ ✕🖭 **Jackson House Inn.** European antiques, Oriental rugs, and French-
★   cut crystal fill the formal parlor and cozy library at this inn. One wing
          houses suites with gas fireplaces, down duvets, and thermal massage
          tubs; the other wing has the restaurant ($$$$), whose focal point is a
          granite, open-hearth fireplace. Herb-crusted cod with an artichoke
          ragout and lamb shanks braised in red wine and port typify the lighter,
          contemporary cuisine. You can choose from a prix-fixe, three-course
          menu or the five-course chef's tasting menu ($65). ⊠ *114-3 Senior La.,*
          05091, ☎ *802/457–2065 or 800/448–1890,* 🅵🅰🆇 *802/457–9290,* 🆆🅴🅱
          www.jacksonhouse.com. 9 rooms, 6 suites. Restaurant, gym, sauna,
          Internet, meeting room; no kids under 14. AE, MC, V. BP.

$$$$ ✕🖭 **Woodstock Inn and Resort.** Resort entrepreneur Laurance Rock-
          efeller, long a Woodstock resident, made this elegant country inn a flag-
          ship property of his Rockresorts chain. Rooms are spacious, serene,
          and set well back from Woodstock's often noisy main street. Dinner
          ($$$–$$$$), served by candlelight, highlights classic American and nou-
          velle New England. Lighter fare is served in the more casual café. You
          can ski free midweek at the inn-owned Suicide Six. ⊠ *14 The Green,*
          U.S. 4, 05091, ☎ *802/457–1100 or 800/448–7900,* 🅵🅰🆇 *802/457–6699,*
          🆆🅴🅱 *www.woodstockinn.com. 144 rooms, 7 suites. 2 restaurants, 2 18-*
          hole golf courses, 12 tennis courts, 2 pools (1 indoor), health club, sauna,
          croquet, racquetball, squash, cross-country skiing, meeting room. AE,
          MC, V. MAP.

$$$–$$$$ ✕🖭 **Kedron Valley Inn.** Two 19th-century buildings, including the 13-
★   room Main House, and a 1968 log structure make up this inn on 15
          acres. Many of the rooms have a fireplace or a Franklin stove, two have
          decks, one has a veranda, and another has a terrace overlooking a stream.
          The motel units in back are decorated with country antiques and re-
          productions. In the restaurant ($$$–$$$$), the chef creates French mas-
          terpieces such as fillet of Norwegian salmon stuffed with herb seafood
          mousse in puff pastry. ⊠ *Rte. 106, 05071,* ☎ *802/457–1473 or 800/*
          836–1193, 🅵🅰🆇 *802/457–4469,* 🆆🅴🅱 *www.kedronvalleyinn.com. 21*
          rooms, 7 suites. Restaurant, pond, beach, bar, meeting room, some pets
          allowed (fee); no air-conditioning in some rooms. AE, D, MC, V.
          Closed Apr. and 10 days before Thanksgiving. BP, MAP.

$$$$ 🖭 **Twin Farms.** At the center of this exclusive 300-acre resort—Ver-
          mont's most sumptuous and most expensive—stands the 1795 farm-
          house where writers Sinclair Lewis and Dorothy Thompson lived.
          Twin Farms' rooms and cottages are fantasy environments, drawing
          their inspiration from Moorish, Scandinavian, Japanese, and Adiron-
          dack design. There are fireplaces throughout, along with museum-qual-
          ity artworks. The rich contemporary cuisine emphasizes local ingredients.
          ⊠ *Stage Rd., off Rte. 12, 8 mi north of Woodstock (Box 115, Barnard*
          05031), ☎ *802/234–9999 or 800/894–6327,* 🅵🅰🆇 *802/234–9990,* 🆆🅴🅱
          www.twinfarms.com. 6 rooms, 9 cottages. Dining room, Japanese

baths, gym, spa, boating, bicycles, ice-skating, cross-country skiing, downhill skiing, recreation room, meeting room; no kids. AE, DC, MC, V. FAP.

$$–$$$ 🏨 **Shire Motel.** Some rooms in this immaculate motel have decks overlooking the Ottauquechee River and the Billings Farm. All have four-poster beds and wing chairs; the suites have hot tubs and fireplaces. Complimentary coffee is served each morning. ✉ *46 Pleasant St., 05091,* ☎ *802/457–2211,* FAX *802/457–5836,* WEB *www.shiremotel.com. 33 rooms, 3 suites. Refrigerators. AE, D, MC, V.*

$$–$$$ 🏨 **Winslow House.** Jeff and Kathy Bendis take great pride in their beau-
★ tifully restored 200-year-old farmhouse, which has hardwood and wide pine flooring, fine architectural details, and lovely but simple antique furnishings. The two guest rooms on the first floor include a suite with a private sitting room and a day bed; the three second-floor accommodations include two suites with private sitting rooms and a spacious room with a cathedral ceiling and private balcony. Breakfast is served by candlelight. ✉ *492 Woodstock Rd./U.S. 4, 05091,* ☎ *802/457–1820,* WEB *www.thewinslowhousevt.com. 2 rooms, 3 suites. Refrigerators, some pets allowed; no kids under 8. MC, V. BP.*

$$ 🏨 **Deer Brook Inn B&B.** Each spacious, immaculate guest room at this 1820 Colonial-style farmhouse has comfortable, unpretentious furnishings. The quilts are handmade by the inn's owner, Rosemary McGinty, who will bring her two golden retrievers out to meet you on request. The Deer Brook is 5 mi from downtown Woodstock and 10 mi from Killington. ✉ *535 U.S. 4, 05091,* ☎ *802/672–3713,* WEB *www.bbhost.com/deerbrookinn. 4 rooms, 1 suite. AE, MC, V. BP.*

Outdoor Activities and Sports

BIKING

Cyclery Plus (✉ 36 U.S. 4 W, West Woodstock, ☎ 802/457–3377) rents, sells, and services bikes and also distributes a free touring map of local rides.

GOLF

Robert Trent Jones, Sr. designed the 18-hole, par-69 course at **Woodstock Country Club** (✉ South St., ☎ 802/457–2114), which is run by the Woodstock Inn. Greens fees are $32–$75; cart rentals are $38.

HORSEBACK RIDING

Kedron Valley Stables (✉ Rte. 106, South Woodstock, ☎ 802/457–2734 or 800/225–6301) gives lessons and conducts guided trail rides and excursions in a sleigh and a wagon. The stable also organizes year-round, inn-to-inn four-day riding packages.

STATE PARK

Coolidge State Park (✉ Rte. 100A, 2 mi north of Rte. 100, ☎ 802/672–3612) abuts Coolidge State Forest and has campsites (log lean-tos from the 1930s).

Shopping

The **Marketplace at Bridgewater Mills** (✉ U.S. 4, west of Woodstock, ☎ 802/672–3332) houses shops and attractions in a three-story converted woolen mill. There's an antiques and crafts center, a bookstore, Miranda Thomas pottery, and handsome Charles Shackleton furniture. Sample Vermont stocks foods and gifts.

Stephen Huneck Studio (✉ 49 Central St., ☎ 802/457–3206) invites canines and humans to visit the artist's gallery, filled with whimsical animal carvings, prints, and furniture. **Taftsville Country Store** (✉ U.S. 4, Taftsville, ☎ 802/457–1135 or 800/854–0013) sells an excellent selection of Vermont cheeses, moderately priced wines, and Vermont specialty foods. The **Village Butcher** (✉ Elm St., ☎ 802/457–2756) is an emporium of Vermont comestibles. **Who Is Sylvia?** (⊠ 26 Central St., ☎ 802/457–1110), in the old firehouse, sells vintage clothing and antique linens, lace, and jewelry.

Sugarbush Farm Inc. (⊠ 591 Sugarbush Farm Rd., ☎ 802/457–1757 or 800/281–1757) taps 5,000 maple trees to make syrup each spring. You can purchase syrup here and take a self-guided tour at any time of the year. The farm also makes excellent cheeses. The road can be messy, so call for conditions and directions.

Ski Areas

SUICIDE SIX

The site of the first ski tow in the United States (1934), this resort is owned and operated by the Woodstock Inn and Resort. The inn's package plans are remarkably inexpensive, considering the high quality of the accommodations. ⊠ *Pomfret Rd., 05091,* ☎ *802/457–6661; 800/448–7900 lodging; 802/457–6666 snow conditions.*

Downhill. Despite Suicide Six's short vertical of only 650 ft, the skiing is challenging. There are steep runs down the mountain's face, intermediate trails that wind around the hill, and glade skiing. Beginner terrain is mostly toward the bottom. Two double chairlifts and one surface lift service the 23 trails and slopes. The resort also has a snowboard area with a halfpipe. Snowmaking covers 50% of the area's terrain.

Child care. The ski area has no nursery, but baby-sitting can be arranged through the Woodstock Inn if you're a guest. Lessons for children are given by the ski-school staff, and there's a children's ski-and-play park for kids ages three to seven.

Summer and year-round activities. Outdoor tennis courts, lighted paddle courts, croquet, and an 18-hole golf course are open in summer. The **Woodstock Health and Fitness Center** (☎ 802/457–6656), open year-round, has an indoor lap pool; indoor tennis, squash, and racquetball courts; whirlpool, steam, sauna, and massage rooms; and exercise and aerobics rooms.

CROSS-COUNTRY

The **Woodstock Ski Touring Center** (☎ 802/457–6674), headquartered at the Woodstock Country Club (⊠ Rte. 106), has 60 km (37 mi) of trails. Equipment and lessons are available.

Plymouth Notch

㉒ *14 mi southwest of Woodstock.*

U.S. president Calvin Coolidge was born and buried in Plymouth Notch, a town that shares his character: low-key and quiet. The perfectly preserved 19th-century buildings of the **Plymouth Notch Historic District** look more like a large farm than a town; in addition to the homestead there's the general store once run by Coolidge's father, a visitor center, a cheese factory (with tasty cheeses for sale), and a one-room schoolhouse. Coolidge's grave is in the cemetery across Route 100A. The Aldrich House, which mounts changing historical exhibits, is open on some weekdays during the off-season. ⊠ *Rte. 100A, 6 mi south of U.S. 4, east of Rte. 100,* ☎ *802/672–3773.* ☞ *$5.* ☼ *Late May–mid-Oct., daily 9:30–5.*

Killington/Pico

㉓ *11 mi (Pico) and 15 mi (Killington) east of Rutland.*

The intersection of U.S. 4 and Route 100 is the heart of central Vermont's ski country, with the Killington, Pico, and Okemo resorts nearby. Unfortunate strip development characterizes the Killington access road, but the views from the top of the mountain are worth the drive.

Dining and Lodging

$$$$
★ ✕ **Hemingway's.** With a national reputation, Hemingway's is as good as dining gets in central Vermont. Among the house specialties are the cream of garlic soup and a seasonal kaleidoscope of dishes based on native game, fresh seafood, and prime meats. Weekends, diners can opt for the prix-fixe, three- to six-course menu or the four-course wine-tasting menu. An à la carte menu is available during the week. Request seating in either the formal, vaulted dining room or the intimate wine cellar. ⊠ *U.S. 4,* ☏ *802/422–3886. AE, D, DC, MC, V. Closed most Mon.–Tues., early Nov., and mid-Apr.–mid-May. No lunch.*

$$$$
★ ✕⊞ **Red Clover Inn.** Elegant accommodations and fine dining ($$$–$$$$) are the attractions at this romantic 1840s hideaway on 13 mountain acres 5 mi from Killington. Among the antiques-filled rooms in the inn and carriage house are three with fireplaces and whirlpool tubs for two. Many rooms have mountain views. A four-course candlelight dinner, with choice of menu, is served Monday–Saturday evenings. *Wine Spectator* magazine cited the inn's wine list as one of the world's most outstanding. ⊠ *7 Woodward Rd., Mendon 05701,* ☏ *802/775–2290 or 800/752–0571,* 𝖥𝖠𝖷 *802/773–0594,* 𝖶𝖤𝖡 *www. redcloverinn.com. 14 rooms. Dining room, cable TV in some rooms, pool, hiking, meeting rooms, some pets allowed (fee); no kids under 12. D, MC, V. Closed Apr.–Memorial Day. BP, MAP.*

$$$
✕⊞ **Birch Ridge Inn.** A slate-covered carriageway leads to one of Killington's newest inns, a former executive retreat that has been converted into an upscale getaway. Rooms range in styles from Colonial and Shaker to Mission, and all have a sitting area. Six rooms have gas fireplaces, and four of these also have whirlpool baths. In the intimate dining room ($$$$), you can choose either a four-course meal or an à la carte menu ($$$–$$$$), which includes dishes such as pan-seared duckling breast. ⊠ *Butler Rd., at Killington Rd., 05751,* ☏ *802/422–4293 or 800/435–8566,* 𝖥𝖠𝖷 *802/422–3406,* 𝖶𝖤𝖡 *www.birchridge.com. 10 rooms. Restaurant, lounge; no air-conditioning in some rooms, no kids under 12. AE, MC, V. BP, MAP.*

$$$
✕⊞ **Summit Lodge.** Three miles from Killington Peak, this rustic two-story country lodge caters to a varied crowd of ski enthusiasts, who are warmly met by the lodge's mascots—a pair of Saint Bernards. Country appointments and antiques blend with modern conveniences to create relaxing surroundings. The restaurant ($$–$$$) serves Continental specialties such as rack of lamb and chicken Birmingham—a boneless breast of chicken with spinach, garlic, feta cheese, and sundried tomatoes. ⊠ *Killington Rd., 05751,* ☏ *802/422–3535 or 800/635–6343,* 𝖥𝖠𝖷 *802/422–3536,* 𝖶𝖤𝖡 *www.summitlodgevermont.com. 43 rooms, 2 suites. Restaurant, pool, pond, hot tub, massage, sauna, ice-skating, bar, nightclub, video game room, meeting rooms; no-smoking rooms. AE, DC, MC, V. BP; MAP only certain vacation/holiday periods.*

$$–$$$$
⊞ **Cortina Inn & Resort.** Close to the ski resort, this large lodge provides comfortable accommodations and a host of year-round activities. The contemporary country rooms have private balconies or terraces; deluxe rooms have mountain or garden views. Two-room family suites have bunk beds. Amenities include guided snowmobile, fly-fishing, and mountain-biking tours. ⊠ *U.S. 4, Killington 05751,* ☏ *802/773–3333 or 800/451–6108,* 𝖥𝖠𝖷 *802/775–6948,* 𝖶𝖤𝖡 *www. cortinainn.com. 89 rooms, 7 suites. 2 restaurants, some cable TV, 8 tennis courts, indoor pool, health club, hot tub, sauna, horseback*

riding, ice-skating, sleigh rides, some pets allowed (fee). AE, D, DC, MC, V. BP.

$$–$$$ ☒ **Mountain Meadows Lodge.** Simple but comfortable accommodations and a plethora of activities for both kids and adults make this lakefront resort a perfect family getaway. Mountain Meadow Munchkins provides child care. Dinner is served Friday and Saturday nights, and a light menu is available Sunday–Thursday. ☒ *285 Thundering Brook Rd., 05751,* ☎ *802/775–1010 or 800/370–4567,* FAX *802/773–4459,* WEB *www.mtmeadowslodge.com. 20 rooms, 1 suite. Restaurant, pool, lake, sauna, boating, fishing, hiking, cross-country skiing, tobogganing, recreation room, children's programs. AE, D, MC, V. Closed mid-Oct.–mid-Nov. BP, MAP.*

Nightlife and the Arts

The pub at the **Inn at Long Trail** (☒ U.S. 4, ☎ 802/775–7181) hosts Irish music on weekends. The **Pickle Barrel** (☒ Killington Rd., ☎ 802/422–3035), a favorite with the après-ski crowd, presents pop and rock acts and can get pretty rowdy. Dance to blues and rock at the **Wobbly Barn** (☒ Killington Rd., ☎ 802/422–3392), open only during ski season.

Outdoor Activities and Sports

FISHING

Gifford Woods State Park's Kent Pond (☒ Rte. 100, ½ mi north of U.S. 4, ☎ 802/775–5354) is a terrific fishing hole; campsites are available.

GOLF

The 18-hole, par-71 **Green Mountain National Golf Course** (☒ Rte. 100 N, Shelburne, ☎ 802/422–4653) has earned accolades as one of the state's best. Greens fees are $52 midweek and $57 weekends in May and June; $57 midweek and $62 weekends from late June through fall. Cart rental is $18 per person. At its namesake resort, **Killington Golf Course** (☒ 4763 Killington Rd., 05751, ☎ 802/422–6700) has a challenging 18-hole course. Greens fees are $51; carts run for $16.

ICE-SKATING

Cortina Inn has an ice-skating rink and runs sleigh rides; you can also skate on Summit Pond.

Ski Areas

KILLINGTON

"Megamountain," "Beast of the East," and plain "huge" are apt descriptions of Killington. The American Skiing Company operates Killington and its neighbor, Pico, and over the past several years has improved lifts, snowmaking capabilities, and lodging options. The resort has the longest ski season in the East as well as the country's most extensive snowmaking system. Killington's après-ski activities are plentiful and have been rated best in the East by the national ski magazines. With a single call to Killington's hot line or a visit to its Web site, skiers can plan an entire vacation: choose accommodations; book air or railroad transportation; and arrange for rental equipment and ski lessons. Killington ticket holders can also ski at Pico: a shuttle connects the two areas. ☒ *4763 Killington Rd., 05751,* ☎ *802/422–6200; 800/621–6867 lodging; 802/422–3261 snow conditions,* WEB *www.killington.com.*

Downhill. It would probably take several weeks to test all 200 trails on the seven mountains of the Killington complex, even though all except Pico interconnect. About 70% of the 1,182 acres of skiing terrain can be covered with machine-made snow. Transporting skiers to the peaks of this complex are 32 lifts, including two gondolas, 12 quads (including six high-speed express quads), six triples, and a Magic Carpet. The K-1 Express Gondola goes to the area's highest elevation, at 4,241 ft off Killington Peak, and a vertical drop of 3,050 ft to the base of the Skyeship, the world's fastest and first heated eight-passenger lift. The Skyeship base station has a rotisserie, food court, and a coffee bar. The skiing includes everything from Outer Limits, one of the steepest and most challenging mogul trails anywhere in the country, to the 6½-mi Great Eastern Trail. In the Fusion Zones, underbrush and low branches have been cleared away to provide tree skiing. Killington's Superpipe is one of the best-rated in the East. Two alpine parks and a 420 ft-long superpipe are set-up for snowboarders.

Child care. Nursery care is available for children ages 6 weeks–6 years old. Instruction programs are available for youngsters from ages 3–8; those from 6 to 12 can join an all-day program.

Summer activities. The Killington-Pico complex has a host of activities including an alpine slide, a golf course, a "Bungee Thing" ride, two water slides, a skateboard park, and a swimming pool. The resort rents mountain bikes and advises hikers. The **K1 Express Gondola** (☎ 802/ 422–6200) takes you up the mountain on the Killington Skyeship.

PICO SKI RESORT

Although it's only 5 mi down the road from Killington, Pico—one of the state's first ski areas—has long been a favorite among people looking for old New England–style skiing, with lots of glades and winding and narrow trails. A village square lies at the base, with condo-hotel, restaurants, and shops. ⊠ *Rte. 4, Killington 05751,* ☎ *802/422–3333; 800/621–6867 lodging; 802/422–3261 snow conditions.*

Downhill. Many of the 48 trails are advanced to expert, with two intermediate bail-out trails for the timid. The rest of the mountain's 2,000 ft of vertical terrain is mostly intermediate or easier. The mountain has seven lifts including two high-speed quads, two triples, and three double chairs and has 75% snowmaking coverage. Snowboarding is permitted everywhere on Pico, and there is a Terrain Park. For instruction of any kind, head to the Alpine Learning Center.

Child care. Pico's nursery takes children ages 6 months–6 years and provides indoor activities and outdoor play. The ski school has full- and half-day instruction programs for children ages 3–12.

Summer and year-round activities. A sports center (☎ 802/773–1786) at the base of the mountain has fitness facilities, a 75-ft pool, whirlpool tub, saunas, and a massage room. You can also take advantage of activities at Killington.

CROSS-COUNTRY SKIING

Mountain Meadows (⊠ Thundering Brook Rd., ☎ 802/775–7077 or 800/221–0598) has 57 km (34½ mi) of groomed trails and 10 km (6 mi) of marked outlying trails. You can also access 500 acres of backcountry skiing. **Mountain Top Inn and Resort** (☎ 802/483–6089 or 800/ 445–2100) is mammoth, with 120 km (72 mi) of trails, 80 km (49 mi) of which are groomed.

Rutland

 15 mi southwest of Killington, 32 mi south of Middlebury, 31 mi west of Woodstock, 47 mi west of White River Junction.

On and around U.S. 7 in Rutland are strips of shopping centers and a seemingly endless row of traffic lights, although the mansions of the marble magnates who made the town famous still command whatever attention can be safely diverted from the traffic. Rutland's compact downtown, one of only a handful of urban centers in Vermont, has experienced a modest revival and is worth an hour's stroll. The area's traditional economic ties to railroading and marble, the latter an industry that became part of such illustrious structures as the central research building of the New York Public Library in New York City, have been rapidly eclipsed by the growth of the Pico and Killington ski areas to the east. If you're planning to visit more than one of the area's attractions, ask about the "One Great Day" admission at the Vermont Marble Exhibit, New England Maple Museum, or Wilson Castle.

The **Chaffee Center for the Visual Arts** (⊠ 16 S. Main St., ☎ 802/775–0356) exhibits and sells the output of more than 250 Vermont artists who work in various media. It's closed Tuesday.

The highlight of the Rutland area, the **Vermont Marble Exhibit** includes a sculptor-in-residence who transforms stone into finished works of art or commerce (you can choose first-hand the marble for a custom-built kitchen counter). The gallery illustrates the many industrial and artistic applications of marble—such as the hall of presidents and a replica of Leonardo da Vinci's *Last Supper* in marble—and depicts the industry's history via exhibits and a video. Factory seconds and foreign and domestic marble items are for sale. ⊠ *62 Main St., Proctor (4 mi north of Rutland, off Rte. 3)*, ☎ *802/459–2300 or 800/427–1396.* ▢ *$6.* ◷ *Mid-May–Oct., daily 9–5:30.*

A 32-room mansion built in 1888 by a doctor, **Wilson Castle** comes complete with turrets, towers, stained glass, and 13 fireplaces. It's magnificently furnished with European and Asian objets d'art. Head west out of Rutland on Route 4A and follow signs. ⊠ *West Proctor Rd., Proctor*, ☎ *802/773–3284,* ⊞ *www.wilsoncastle.com.* ▢ *$7.* ◷ *Late May–mid-Oct., daily 9–5:30.*

Dining and Lodging

$–$$$ ✗ **The Palms.** When this Rutland landmark opened its doors on Palm Sunday in 1933 it was the first restaurant in the state to serve pizza. It's still owned by the same family. The menu is primarily southern Italian, with specialties such as fried mozzarella; antipasto Neapolitan (with provolone, pepperoni, mild peppers, anchovies, and house dressing); and the chef's personal creation, veal à la Palms—veal scallops topped with mushrooms, two kinds of cheese, and a special tomato sauce. Dessert choices are fairly pedestrian. ⊠ *36 Strongs St.*, ☎ *802/773–2367. AE, MC, V. Closed Sun. No lunch.*

$$$$ 🏨 **Mountain Top Inn and Resort.** On 500 acres overlooking Chittenden Reservoir and the Green Mountain National Forest, this is a year-round outdoor enthusiast's inn. There's an equestrian center and golf school, and activities include swimming and canoeing. A tip: opt for the more-expensive deluxe rooms, which are larger and have spectacular views. ⊠ *195 Mountaintop Rd., Chittenden 05737*, ☎ *802/483–2311 or 800/445–2100,* ⅲ *802/483–6373,* ⊞ *www.mountaintopinn.com. 35 rooms, 6 cottages, 6 chalets. Restaurant, driving range, pool, beach, boating, fishing, horseback riding, cross-country skiing, ice-skating, sleigh rides. AE, MC, V. Closed late Oct.–late Dec. and mid-Mar.–mid-May. BP, MAP.*

$$–$$$ 🏨 **Inn at Rutland.** One alternative to Rutland's chain motel accommodations is this renovated Victorian mansion. The ornate oak staircase lined with heavy embossed gold and leather wainscoting leads to rooms that blend modern bathrooms with late-19th-century touches such as elaborate ceiling moldings and frosted glass. The two large common rooms, one with a fireplace, have views of surrounding mountains and valleys. The meal plan varies. Afternoon tea is served daily. ⊠ *70 N. Main St., 05701*, ☎ *802/773–0575 or 800/808–0575,* ⅲ *802/775–3506,* ⊞ *www.innatrutland.com. 11 rooms. Cable TV, library. AE, D, MC, V.*

Nightlife and the Arts

Crossroads Arts Council (⊠ 39 E. Center St., ☎ 802/775–5413) presents music, opera, dance, jazz, and theater year-round at venues throughout the region.

Outdoor Activities and Sports

Half Moon State Park's principal attraction is Half Moon Pond (⊠ Town Rd., 3½ mi off Rte. 30, west of Hubbardton, ☎ 802/273–2848). The park has nature trails, campsites, and boat and canoe rentals.

Shopping

Tuttle Antiquarian Books (⊠ 28 S. Main St., ☎ 802/773–8229) stocks rare and out-of-print books, genealogies, local histories, and miniature books; you also find a large collection of books on Asia.

Brandon

🟤 *15 mi northwest of Rutland.*

Straddling busy U.S. 7, Brandon nevertheless has broad side streets lined with gracious Victorian houses, lodging at the landmark Brandon Inn or at smaller B&Bs, and ready access to the mountain scenery and recreation of nearby Brandon Gap.

The **Stephen A. Douglas Birthplace** commemorates the "Little Giant" (he stood only 5 ft, 2 inches tall), best known for his debates with Abraham Lincoln in 1858. Douglas, who became a U.S. representative and senator from Illinois, was born here on April 23, 1813. His boyhood home and a monument to his memory are just north of the village, next to the Baptist church. ⊠ *U.S. 7.* ☎ *802/247–6569 or 802/247–6332.* 🏛 *Donations welcome.* ⊘ *By appointment.*

Maple syrup is Vermont's signature product, and the **New England Maple Museum and Gift Shop** explains the history and process of turning maple sap into syrup with murals, exhibits, and a slide show. ⊠ *U.S. 7, Pittsford (9 mi south of Brandon),* ☎ *802/483–9414.* 🏛 *Museum $2.50.* ⊘ *Late May–Oct., daily 8:30–5:30; Nov.–Dec. and mid-Mar.–late May, daily 10–4.*

Dining and Lodging

$$$$ ✕🏠 **Blueberry Hill Inn.** In the Green Mountain National Forest and 5½ mi off a mountain pass on a dirt road, the inn has lush gardens and a pond with a wood-fired sauna on its bank. Many rooms have views of the mountains; all are furnished with antiques and quilts. The restaurant prepares a four-course ($$$$) dinner nightly, with dishes such as venison fillet with cherry sauce. The ski-touring center has 80 km (50 mi) of trails. ⊠ *1307 Goshen–Ripkin Rd., Goshen 05733,* ☎ *802/247–6735 or 800/448–0707,* 🖷 *802/247–3983,* ⓦ *www.blueberryhillinn.com. 12 rooms. Restaurant, sauna, mountain bikes, hiking, volleyball, cross-country skiing, some pets allowed. MC, V. MAP.*

$$$ ✕🏠 **Lilac Inn.** The bridal suite at this Greek Revival mansion has a pewter canopy bed, whirlpool bath for two, and fireplace. The other rooms, all furnished and with claw-foot tubs and handheld European shower heads, are also charming. The elegant dining room ($$$), overlooking the gardens, serves dishes such as fig-mango pork short ribs and green tea–encrusted yellowfin tuna. The inn is a popular spot for weddings on summer weekends. ⊠ *53 Park St./Rte. 73, 05733,* ☎ *802/247–5463 or 800/221–0720,* 🖷 *802/247–5499,* ⓦ *www.lilacinn.com. 9 rooms. Restaurant, meeting rooms, some pets allowed (fee); no kids under 12. AE, MC, V. BP.*

$$–$$$$ [icon] **The Brandon Inn.** Built in 1786, this National Register of Historic Places inn in the center of town has the state's oldest elevator (circa 1901), comfortable and spacious guest rooms, and Victorian-furnished common rooms that feel like they've been frozen in time. Moderately priced fare, including the house-special barbecued spareribs, are served in the elegant, multipillared dining room. ⊠ *20 Park St., 05733,* ☎ *800/639–8685,* FAX *802/247–5768,* WEB *www.brandoninn.com. 35 rooms. Restaurant, pool, recreation room. AE, D, MC, V. BP.*

Outdoor Activities and Sports

Moosalamoo (☎ 800/448–0707) is the name given by a partnership of public and private entities to a 20,000-acre chunk of Green Mountain National Forest land (along with several private holdings) just northeast of Brandon. More than 60 mi of trails take hikers, mountain bikers, and cross-country skiers through some of Vermont's most gorgeous mountain terrain. Attractions include Branbury State Park, on the shores of Lake Dunmore; secluded Silver Lake; and sections of both the Long Trail and Catamount Trail (the latter is a Massachusetts-to-Québec ski trail). Both the Blueberry Hill Inn and **Churchill House Inn** (☎ 802/247–3078) have direct public access to trails.

GOLF

Neshobe Golf Club (⊠ Rte. 73, east of Brandon, ☎ 802/247–3611) has 18 holes of par-72 golf on a bent-grass course totaling nearly 6,500 yards. The Green Mountain views are terrific. Several local inns offer golf packages.

HIKING

About 8 mi east of Brandon on Route 73, a trail that takes an hour to hike starts at Brandon Gap and climbs steeply up **Mt. Horrid.** South of Lake Dunmore on Route 53, a large turnout marks a trail (a hike of about two hours) to the **Falls of Lana.** Four trails—two short ones of less than 1 mi each and two longer ones—lead to the old abandoned Revolutionary War fortifications at **Mt. Independence**; to reach them, take the first left turn off Route 73 west of Orwell and go right at the fork. The road will turn to gravel and once again will fork; take a sharp left-hand turn toward a small marina. The parking lot is on the left at the top of the hill.

Shopping

The **Warren Kimble Gallery & Studio** (⊠ off Rte. 73 E, ☎ 802/247–3026 or 800/954–6253) is the workplace, gallery, and gift shop of the nationally renowned folk artist.

Middlebury

★ ㉖   *17 mi north of Brandon, 34 mi south of Burlington.*

In the late 1800s Middlebury was the largest Vermont community west of the Green Mountains: an industrial center of river-powered wool, grain, and marble mills. This is Robert Frost country; Vermont's late poet laureate spent 23 summers at a farm east of Middlebury. Otter Creek, the state's longest river, traverses the town center. Still a cultural and economic hub amid the Champlain Valley's serene pastoral patchwork, the town and countryside invite a day of exploration.

Smack in the middle of town, **Middlebury College** (☎ 802/443–5000), founded in 1800, was conceived as a more godly alternative to the worldly University of Vermont. The college has no religious affiliation today, however. The early 19th-century stone buildings contrast provocatively with the postmodern architecture of the Center for the Arts and the sports center. Music, theater, and dance performances take place throughout the year at the **Wright Memorial Theatre** and **Center for the Arts.**

The **Middlebury College Museum of Art** has a permanent collection of paintings, photography, works on paper, and sculpture. ⊠ *Center for the Arts, Rte. 30,* ☎ *802/443–5007.* ☞ *Free.* ☉ *Mid-Jan.–mid Dec., Tues.–Fri. 10–5, weekends noon–5.*

The **Vermont Folklife Center** exhibits photography, antiques, folk paintings, manuscripts, and other artifacts and contemporary works that examine Vermont life. The center is in the basement of the restored 1801 home of Gamaliel Painter, the founder of Middlebury College. ⊠ *3 Court St.,* ☎ *802/388–4964.* ☞ *Donations accepted.* ☉ *Gallery May–Dec., Tues.–Sat. 11–4. Oral history archive weekdays 10–4.*

The **Henry Sheldon Museum of Vermont History,** an 1829 marble merchant's house, is the oldest community museum in the country. The period rooms contain Vermont-made textiles, furniture, toys, clothes, kitchen tools, and paintings. ⊠ *1 Park St.,* ☎ *802/388–2117.* ☞ *$4.* ☉ *Mon.–Sat. 10–5.*

More than a crafts store, the **Vermont State Craft Center at Frog Hollow** mounts changing exhibitions and displays exquisite work in wood, glass, metal, clay, and fiber by more than 250 Vermont artisans. The center, which overlooks Otter Creek, sponsors classes taught by some of those artists. Burlington and Manchester also have centers. ⊠ *1 Mill St.,* ☎ *802/388–3177,* WEB *www.froghollow.org.* ☉ *Call for hrs.*

The Morgan horse—the official state animal—has an even temper, good stamina, and slightly truncated legs in proportion to its body. The University of Vermont's **UVM Morgan Horse Farm,** about 2½ mi west of Middlebury, is a breeding and training center where in summer you can tour the stables and paddocks. ⊠ *74 Battell Dr., off Horse Farm Rd. (follow signs off Rte. 23), Weybridge,* ☎ *802/388–2011.* ☞ *$4.* ☉ *May–Oct., daily 9–5 (last tour at 4).*

About 10 mi east of town on Route 125 (1 mi west of Middlebury College's Bread Loaf campus), the easy ¾-mi **Robert Frost Interpretive Trail** winds through quiet woodland. Plaques along the way bear quotations from Frost's poems. A picnic area is across the road from the trailhead.

OFF THE BEATEN PATH

FORT TICONDEROGA FERRY – Established in 1759, the Fort Ti cable ferry crosses Lake Champlain between Shoreham and Fort Ticonderoga, New York, at one of the oldest ferry crossings in North America in just six minutes. ⊠ *4675 Rte. 74 W,18 mi southwest of Middlebury, Shoreham* ☎ *802/897–7999.* ☞ *Cars, pickups, and vans with driver and passenger $7; pedestrians $1.* ☉ *May–last Sun. of Oct.*

Dining and Lodging

$$–$$$ ✕ **Fire & Ice.** A 55-item salad bar (with peel-and-eat shrimp), prime rib, steak, fish, and a house specialty—homemade mashed potatoes— are all choices at this family-friendly spot. Although large, the space is divided into several rooms (each with a different theme) and has numerous intimate nooks and crannies for diners who seek privacy. Families may want to request a table next to the "children's corner," which is outfitted with cushions and a VCR. Sunday dinner begins at 1. ⊠ *26 Seymour St.,* ☎ *802/388–7166 or 800/367–7166. AE, D, DC, MC, V. No lunch Mon.*

$$–$$$ ✕ **Roland's Place.** Chef Roland Gaujac prepares classic French and
★ American dishes in a 1796 house. Some dishes use locally raised lamb,
turkey, and venison; other entrées include shrimp with chipotle and
roasted garlic vinaigrette on fried ravioli. A prix-fixe menu is available,
and a special menu served daily from 5 to 6 lists numerous à la carte
dishes. ⊠ *U.S. 7, New Haven,* ☎ *802/453–6309. AE, D, DC, MC, V.
Hrs vary; call ahead.*

$ ✕ **Baba's Market & Deli.** Authentic Lebanese dishes are the specialty
in this cheerful, informal spot near the college. Among the standouts
are kibbe, stuffed grape leaves, moussaka, and pizza prepared in a wood-
fired oven. ⊠ *54 College St.,* ☎ *802/388–6408. MC, V.*

$$–$$$$ ⊡ **Middlebury Inn.** Since 1827 gracious New England–style hospital-
ity has been the hallmark of this three-story brick Georgian inn. The
property also encompasses a contemporary motel with Early Ameri-
can–style furnishings and the Victorian-era Porter House Mansion. Com-
plimentary afternoon tea is served daily between 3 and 4 except
holidays. In nice weather, you can have lunch on the wicker-furnished
porch. Rooms facing the lovely town green can be noisy if the win-
dow is open. ⊠ *14 Courthouse Sq., 05753,* ☎ *802/388–4961 or 800/
842–4666,* FAX *802/388–4563,* WEB *www.middleburyinn.com. 75 rooms.
Restaurant, some pets allowed; no smoking rooms. AE, D, MC, V. CP,
MAP.*

$$–$$$ ⊡ **Swift House Inn.** The Georgian home of a 19th-century governor
★ contains white-panel wainscoting, mahogany, and marble fireplaces.
The rooms—most with Oriental rugs and nine with fireplaces—have
period reproductions such as canopy beds, curtains with swags, and
claw-foot tubs. Some bathrooms have double whirlpool tubs. Rooms
in the gatehouse suffer from street noise but are charming; a carriage
house holds six luxury accommodations. ⊠ *25 Stewart La., 05753,*
☎ *802/388–9925,* FAX *802/388–9927,* WEB *www.swifthouseinn.com. 21
rooms, 1 suite. Sauna, steam room, pub, meeting room; no smoking
rooms. AE, D, DC, MC, V. CP.*

$ ⊡ **Lemon Fair.** This unfussy, family-friendly bed-and-breakfast was tiny
Bridport's first church before it was moved to its present location over-
looking the town green in 1819. Furnishings are Early American and the
grounds are spacious. The common room is a cozy spot in which to curl
up by the fireplace. The inn is just 8 mi from downtown Middlebury.
The owners live next door and will rent out the entire house. ⊠ *Crown
Point Rd., Bridport 05734,* ☎ *802/758–9238,* FAX *802/758–2135,* WEB
www.lemonfair.com. 3 rooms, 1 suite. Pool. No credit cards. BP.

Outdoor Activities and Sports
The **Bike Center** (⊠ 74 Main St., ☎ 802/388–6666) has ski and bike
sales, rentals, and repairs.

HIKING
On Route 116, about 5½ mi north of East Middlebury, a U.S. Forest
Service sign marks a dirt road that forks to the right and leads to the
start of the two- to three-hour hike to **Abbey Pond,** which has a beaver
lodge and dam as well as a view of Robert Frost Mountain.

Shopping
Historic Marble Works (⊠ Maple St., ☎ 802/388–3701), a renovated
marble manufacturing facility, is a collection of unique shops set amid
quarrying equipment and factory buildings. **Danforth Pewterers** (☎
802/388–0098) sells handcrafted pewter vases, lamps, and tableware.
De Pasquale's (☎ 802/388–3385) prepares subs and fresh fried-fish
platters for takeout and sells imported Italian groceries and wines. **Holy
Cow** (⊠ 44 Main St., ☎ 802/388–6737) is where Woody Jackson sells
his Holstein cattle–inspired T-shirts, memorabilia, and paintings.

Bristol

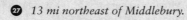 *13 mi northeast of Middlebury.*

At the northeastern threshold of the Green Mountain National Forest, where the rolling farmlands of the Champlain Valley meet the foothills of Vermont's main mountain chain, Bristol has a redbrick 19th-century Main Street that reflects the town's prosperous heyday as the center of a number of wood-products industries. Almost overshadowing the still-busy little downtown are the brooding heights of the Bristol Cliffs Wilderness Area, a section of national forest that has been assured permanent status as a primitive, roadless tract.

Dining

$$$–$$$$ ✕ **Mary's at Baldwin Creek.** This restaurant and B&B in a 1790 farmhouse provides a truly inspired culinary experience. The innovative fare includes a superb garlic soup and Vermont rack of lamb with a rosemary-mustard sauce. Farmhouse dinners on Wednesday in summer highlight Vermont products. A café menu is also available. Four rooms above the restaurant have simple, comfortable furnishings. ⊠ *Rte. 116,* ☎ *802/453–2432. AE, DC, MC, V. Closed Mon.–Tues. No lunch.*

Outdoor Activities and Sports

A challenging 32-mi bicycle ride starts in Bristol. Take North Street from the traffic light in town and continue north to Monkton Ridge and on to Hinesburg. To return, follow Route 116 south through Starksboro and back to Bristol.

Shopping

Folkheart (⊠ 18 Main St., ☎ 802/453–4101) carries unusual jewelry, toys, and crafts from around the world.

En Route From Bristol, Route 17 winds eastward up and over the **Appalachian Gap,** one of Vermont's most panoramic mountain passes. The views from the top and on the way down the other side toward the ski town of Waitsfield are a just reward for the challenging drive.

Waitsfield

❷⑧ *20 mi east of Bristol, 55 mi north of Rutland, 32 mi northeast of Middlebury, 19 mi southwest of Montpelier.*

Although close to Sugarbush and Mad River Glen ski areas, the Mad River valley towns of Waitsfield and Warren are decidedly low-key. The gently carved ridges cradling the valley and the swell of pastures and fields lining the river seem to keep further notions of ski-resort sprawl at bay. With a map from the Sugarbush Chamber of Commerce you can investigate back roads off Route 100 that have exhilarating valley views.

Dining and Lodging

$$$–$$$$ ✕ **Spotted Cow.** Jay and Renate Young attract a steady clientele to their intimate dining room decorated with contemporary furnishings and warm woods. Lunch items include a fresh spinach salad with fried oysters and Bermuda codfish cakes. For dinner, try a ragout of seafood in puff pastry or the house specialty: sautéed medallions of New Zealand venison finished in lingonberry crème fraîche. Sunday brunch is served 10:30–3. ⊠ *Bridge St.,* ☎ *802/496–5151. MC, V. Closed Mon.*

$$–$$$ ✕ **American Flatbread.** For ideologically and gastronomically sound pizza, you won't find a better place in the Green Mountains than this modest haven between Waitsfield and Warren. Organic flour and produce fuel mind and body, and Vermont hardwood fuels the earth-and-stone oven. The "punctuated equilibrium flatbread," made with olive-pepper goat cheese and rosemary, is a dream, as are more traditional pizzas. It's open Monday–Thursday 7:30 AM–8 PM for takeout, Friday and Saturday 5:30–9:30 for dinner. ⊠ *Rte. 100,* ☎ *802/496–8856. Reservations not accepted. MC, V. Closed Sun.*

$$–$$$ ✕ **Common Man.** *Pescespada de merida* (grilled New England swordfish steak) and ravioli *alla calabrese* share the menu with French classics such as braised rabbit, *entrecôte maison* (sirloin steak with an herb and garlic butter sauce), rack of lamb, and roast duck. The restaurant, a local institution since 1972, is housed in a mid-1800s barn with hand-hewn rafters and crystal chandeliers. Dinner is served by candlelight. ⊠ *German Flats Rd., Warren,* ☎ *802/583–2800. AE, D, MC, V. Closed Mon. Easter–Christmas. No lunch.*

$$$$ ✕🖩 **Pitcher Inn.** Each guest room at this Relais & Châteaux property
★ has its own motif. A curved ceiling in the Mallard gives the illusion of a duck blind, and the windows are etched and frosted in the likeness of the banks of a marsh. All rooms have stereos; nine have fireplaces and six have steam showers. The formal dining room ($$$–$$$$) specializes in local produce and wild game; you can also dine in the private wine cellar. ⊠ *275 Main St. (Box 347, Warren 05674),* ☎ *802/ 496–6350 or 888/867–4824,* FAX *802/496–6354,* WEB *www. pitcherinn.com. 9 rooms, 2 suites. Restaurant, in-room data ports, hot tub, billiards; no kids under 16 (except in suites). AE, MC, V. BP.*

$$ ✕🖩 **Tucker Hill Lodge.** Guest rooms in this country inn, convenient to both Sugarbush and Wild Cat, are adorned in country-casual furnishings. There are fireplaces in three guest rooms and in the living room, dining room, and pub. The menu at the Steak Place ($$–$$$$) includes a 24-ounce steak and barbecue ribs, as well as fish and vegetarian choices. Lighter fare is served in the pub area for late-night patrons. Dinner can be included in the room rate if desired. ⊠ *65 Marble Hill Rd./Rte. 17, 05673,* ☎ *802/496–3983 or 800/543–7841,* FAX *802/496–9837,* WEB *www.tuckerhill.com. 18 rooms, 6 suites. Restaurant, in-room data ports, tennis court, pool, hiking, bar, meeting rooms; no air-conditioning in some rooms. AE, MC, V. CP.*

$$–$$$$ 🖩 **Inn at the Round Barn Farm.** A Shaker-style round barn (one of only eight in the state) dominates the farm's 215 acres. The inn's guest rooms, inside an 1806 farmhouse, are sumptuous, with eyelet-trimmed sheets, elaborate four-poster beds, rich-colored wallpapers, and brass wall lamps for easy bedtime reading. Seven have fireplaces, four have whirlpool tubs, and five have steam showers. The inn also arranges snowshoe packages and tours. ⊠ *1661 E. Warren Rd., 05673,* ☎ *802/496– 2276,* FAX *802/496–8832,* WEB *www.innatroundbarn.com. 12 rooms. In-door pool, cross-country skiing, library, recreation room. AE, D, MC, V. BP.*

Nightlife and the Arts

The Back Room at **Chez Henri** (⊠ Sugarbush Village, ☎ 802/583–2600) has a pool table and is popular with the après-ski and late-night dance crowds. Local bands play music at **Gallagher's** (⊠ Rtes. 100 and 17, ☎ 802/496–8800).

The **Green Mountain Cultural Center** (⊠ Inn at the Round Barn Farm, E. Warren Rd., ☎ 802/496–7722), a nonprofit organization, brings concerts and art exhibits, as well as educational workshops, to the Mad River valley. The **Valley Players** (⊠ Rte. 100, ☎ 802/496–9612) present musicals, dramas, follies, and holiday shows.

Outdoor Activities and Sports

BIKING

The popular 14-mi Waitsfield–Warren loop begins when you cross the covered bridge in Waitsfield. Keep right on East Warren Road to the four-way intersection in East Warren; continue straight and then bear right, riding down Brook Road to the village of Warren. Return by turning right (north) on Route 100 back toward Waitsfield.

Clearwater Sports (⊠ Rte. 100, ☎ 802/496–2708) rents canoes, kayaks, and camping equipment and leads guided river trips and whitewater instruction in the warm months; in the winter, the store leads snowshoe tours and rents telemark equipment, snowshoes, and one-person Mad River Rocket sleds.

GOLF

Great views and challenging play are the trademarks of the Robert Trent Jones–designed 18-hole, par-72 course at **Sugarbush Resort** (⊠ Golf Course Rd., ☎ 802/583–6727). The greens fee runs from $32 to $52; a cart (sometimes mandatory) costs $17.

SLEIGH RIDES

The 100-year-old sleigh of the **Lareau Farm Country Inn** (⊠ Rte. 100, ☎ 802/496–4949 or 800/833–0766) cruises along the banks of the Mad River.

Shopping

ART AND ANTIQUES

Cabin Fever Quilts (⊠ Rte. 100, ☎ 802/496–2287), which shares a building with Luminosity Stained Glass Studios, sells fine handmade quilts. **Luminosity Stained Glass Studios** (☎ 802/496–2231), inside the converted Old Church on Route 100, specializes in stained glass, custom lighting, and art glass.

CRAFTS

All Things Bright and Beautiful (⊠ Bridge St., ☎ 802/496–3997) is a 12-room Victorian house jammed to the rafters with stuffed animals of all shapes, sizes, and colors as well as folk art, prints, and collectibles. **Warren Village Pottery** (⊠ Main St., Warren, ☎ 802/496–4162) sells handcrafted wares from its retail shop and specializes in functional stoneware pottery.

Ski Areas

MAD RIVER GLEN

The hundreds of shareholders who own Mad River Glen are dedicated, knowledgeable skiers devoted to keeping skiing what it used to be— a pristine alpine experience. Mad River's unkempt aura attracts rugged individualists looking for less-polished terrain: the area was developed in the late 1940s and has changed relatively little since then. It remains one of only a handful of resorts in the country that ban snowboarding. Skiers can use their tickets at nearby Sugarbush; a free shuttle bus runs between the two areas. ⊠ *Rte. 17, 05673, ☎ 802/ 496–3551; 800/850–6742 cooperative office; 802/496–2001 snow conditions,* WEB *www.madriverglen.com.*

Downhill. Mad River is steep, with natural slopes that follow the contours of the mountain. The terrain changes constantly on the 45 interconnected trails, of which 30% are beginner, 30% are intermediate, and 40% are expert. Intermediate and novice terrain is regularly groomed. Five lifts, including a single 1940s chairlift that may be the only lift of its vintage still carrying skiers, service the mountain's 2,037-ft vertical drop. Most of Mad River's trails (85%) are covered only by natural snow.

Telemark/snowshoe. The "Mecca of Free-Heel Skiing" sponsors telemark programs through the season and each March hosts the North America Telemark Organization, which attracts up to 1,200 skiers. There is a $5 fee to use the snowshoe trails, and rentals are available.

Child care. The nursery is for infants to 6 years. The ski school runs classes for little ones ages 4 to 12. Junior racing is available weekends and during holidays.

SUGARBUSH

In the Warren-Waitsfield ski world, Sugarbush is Mad River Glen's alter ego. The Slide Brook Express quad connects the two mountains, Sugarbush South and Sugarbush North. A computer-controlled system for snowmaking has increased coverage to nearly 70%. At the base of the mountain is a village with condominiums, restaurants, shops, bars, and a sports center. Skiers can use their tickets at nearby Mad River Glen; a free shuttle bus runs between the two areas. ✉ *Sugarbush Access Rd., accessible from Rte. 100 or Rte. 17 (Box 350, Warren 05674),* ☎ *802/583–6300; 800/537–8427 lodging; 802/583–7669 snow conditions,* WEB *www.sugarbush.com.*

Downhill. Sugarbush is two distinct, connected mountain complexes. The Sugarbush South area is what old-timers recall as Sugarbush Mountain: with a vertical of 2,400 ft, it is known for formidable steeps toward the top and in front of the main base lodge. Sugarbush North offers what South has in short supply—beginner runs. North also has steep fall-line pitches and intermediate cruisers off its 2,650 vertical ft. There are 115 trails in all: 23% beginner, 48% intermediate, 29% expert. The resort has 18 lifts: seven quads (including four high-speed versions), three triples, four doubles, and four surface lifts.

Child care. The Sugarbush Day School accepts children ages 6 weeks–6 years; older children have indoor play areas and can go on outdoor excursions. There's half- and full-day instruction available for children ages 4–11. Kids have their own Magic Carpet lift. Sugarbear Forest, a terrain garden, has fun bumps and jumps.

Summer and year-round activities. The **Sugarbush Mountain Biking & Technical Hiking Center** (☎ 802/583–6572) has bike rentals and miles of terrain; it provides guided tours and instruction. Open year-round, the **Sugarbush Health and Racquet Club** (☎ 802/583–6700), near the ski lifts, has Nautilus and Universal equipment; tennis, squash, and racquetball courts; a whirlpool, a sauna, and steam rooms; one indoor pool; and a 30-ft-high climbing wall.

CROSS-COUNTRY SKIING

Blueberry Lake Cross-Country Ski Area (✉ Plunkton Rd., Warren, ☎ 802/496–6687) has 30 km (18 mi) of groomed trails through thickly wooded glades. **Ole's** (✉ Airport Rd., Warren, ☎ 802/496–3430) runs a cross-country center and small restaurant out of the tiny Warren airport; it has 50 km (37 mi) of groomed European-style trails that span out into the surrounding woods from the landing strips.

Brookfield

㉙ *26 mi southeast of Waitsfield, 15 mi south of Montpelier.*

The residents of secluded Brookfield have voted several times to keep the town's roads unpaved and even turned down an offered I–89 exit when the interstate highway was being built in the '60s. Route 14 east of town is a scenic road. Crossing the nation's only **floating bridge** (✉ Rte. 65 between Rtes. 12 and 14) feels like driving on water. The bridge, supported by nearly 400 barrels, sits at water level. It's the scene of the annual ice-harvest festival in January, though it's closed to traffic in winter.

Dining and Lodging

$$$ ✕ **Ariel's.** Reserve a seat on the porch overlooking the lake (summer and fall), and put yourself in the capable hands of Culinary Institute of America–trained chef Lee Duberman, who prepares eclectic treats such as sautéed breast and confit leg of duck as well as seared fillet of salmon. Husband-sommelier Ricard Fink recommends selections from the wine cellar. The full menu is offered Friday and Saturday; a pub menu is served Wednesday, Thursday, and Sunday. ✉ *Main St.,* ☎ *802/ 276–3939. D, MC, V. Closed Mon.–Tues.*

$$–$$$ ⊞ **Green Trails Inn.** The enormous fieldstone fireplace that dominates
★ the living and dining area of this historic inn overlooking Sunset Lake is symbolic of the stalwart hospitality of new innkeepers Nina Gaby and Craig Smith. Comfortably elegant rooms in two buildings have antiques and Oriental rugs. The suite has a fireplace, and two rooms have whirlpool tubs. Dinner is prepared on request. ✉ *Main St., 05036,* ☎ *802/276–3412 or 800/243–3412,* ⓦⓔⓑ *www.greentrailsinn.com. 13 rooms, 9 with bath. Dining room, lake, boating, cross-country skiing, ski shop, sleigh rides. D, MC, V. BP.*

Central Vermont A to Z

To research prices, get advice from other travelers, and book travel arrangements, visit www.fodors.com.

BUS TRAVEL

Vermont Transit links Rutland, White River Junction, Burlington, and many smaller towns.

➤ Bus Information: **Vermont Transit** (☎ 800/552–8737).

CAR TRAVEL

The major east–west road is U.S. 4, which stretches from White River Junction in the east to Fair Haven in the west. Route 125 connects Middlebury on U.S. 7 with Hancock on Route 100; Route 100 splits the region in half along the eastern edge of the Green Mountains. Route 17 travels east–west from Waitsfield over the Appalachian Gap through Bristol and down to the shores of Lake Champlain. Interstate–91 and the parallel U.S. 5 follow the state's eastern border; U.S. 7 and Route 30 are the north–south highways in the west. Interstate–89 links White River Junction with Montpelier to the north.

EMERGENCIES

➤ Hospitals: **Porter Hospital** (✉ South St., Middlebury, ☎ 802/388–7901). **Rutland Medical Center** (✉ 160 Allen St., Rutland, ☎ 802/775–7111; 800/649–2187 in Vermont).

LODGING

Sugarbush Reservations and the Woodstock Area Chamber of Commerce provide lodging referral services.

➤ Reservation Services: **Sugarbush Reservations** (☎ 800/537–8427). **Woodstock Area Chamber of Commerce** (☎ 802/457–3555 or 888/496–6378).

TOURS

Country Inns Along the Trail arranges self-guided and guided hiking and skiing trips and provides self-guided biking trips from inn to inn in Vermont. The Vermont Icelandic Horse Farm conducts year-round guided riding expeditions on easy-to-ride Icelandic horses. Full-day, half-day, and hourly rides as well as weekend tours and inn-to-inn treks are available.

➤ Tour Operators: **Country Inns Along the Trail** (✉ 834 Van Cortland Rd., Brandon 05733, ☎ 802/247–3300 or 800/838–3301).

Vermont Icelandic Horse Farm (⊠ N. Fayston Rd., Waitsfield 05673, ☎ 802/496–7141).

VISITOR INFORMATION
➤ TOURIST INFORMATION: **Addison County Chamber of Commerce** (⊠ 2 Court St., Middlebury 05753, ☎ 802/388–7951 or 800/733–8376, WEB www.midvermont.com). **Quechee Chamber of Commerce** (⊠ 1789 Quechee St. [Box 106, Quechee 05059], ☎ 802/295–7900 or 800/295–5451, WEB www.quechee.com). **Rutland Region Chamber of Commerce** (⊠ 256 N. Main St., Rutland 05701, ☎ 802/773–2747 or 800/756–8880, WEB www.rutlandvermont.com). **Sugarbush Chamber of Commerce** (⊠ Rte. 100 [Box 173, Waitsfield 05673], ☎ 802/496–3409 or 800/828–4748, WEB www.madrivervalley.com). **Woodstock Area Chamber of Commerce** (⊠ 18 Central St. [Box 486, Woodstock 05091], ☎ 802/457–3555 or 888/496–6378, WEB www.woodstockvt.com).

NORTHERN VERMONT

Vermont's northernmost region reveals the state's greatest contrasts. To the west, along Lake Champlain, Burlington and its Chittenden County suburbs have grown so rapidly that rural wags now say that Burlington's greatest advantage is that it's "close to Vermont." The north country also harbors Vermont's tiny capital, Montpelier, and its highest mountain, Mt. Mansfield, site of the famous Stowe ski slopes. To the northeast of Burlington and Montpelier spreads a sparsely populated and heavily wooded territory, the domain of loggers as much as farmers, where French spills out of the radio and the last snows melt toward the first of June.

You'll find plenty to do in the region's cities (Burlington, Montpelier, St. Johnsbury, and Barre), in the bustling resort area of Stowe, in the Lake Champlain Islands, and—if you like the outdoors—in the wilds of the Northeast Kingdom.

The coverage of towns in this area begins in the state capital, Montpelier; moves west toward Waterbury, Stowe, and Burlington; then goes north through the Lake Champlain Islands, east along the boundary with Canada toward Jay Peak and Newport, and south into the heart of the Northeast Kingdom before completing the circle in Barre.

Montpelier

30 *38 mi southeast of Burlington, 115 mi north of Brattleboro.*

With only about 8,000 residents, Montpelier is the country's least populous state capital. The intersection of State and Main streets is the city hub, bustling with the activity of state and city workers during the day. It's a pleasant place to spend an afternoon shopping and browsing; in true small-town Vermont fashion, though, the streets become deserted at night.

The **Vermont State House**—with a gleaming gold dome and columns of Barre granite 6 ft in diameter—is impressive for a city this size. The goddess of agriculture tops the dome. The Greek Revival building dates from 1836, although it was rebuilt after a fire in 1859; the latter year's Victorian style was adhered to in a lavish 1994 restoration. Interior paintings and exhibits make much of Vermont's sterling Civil War record. ⊠ *115 State St.,* ☎ *802/828–2228.* 🖾 *Donation.* ☉ *Weekdays 8–4; tours July–mid-Oct., weekdays every ½ hr 10–3:30 (last tour at 3:30), Sat. 11–3 (last tour at 2:30). Self-guided tours available when building is open.*

Perhaps you're wondering what the last panther shot in Vermont looked like? Why New England bridges are covered? What a niddy-noddy is? Or what Christmas was like for a Bethel boy in 1879? ("I skated on my new skates. In the morning Papa and I set up a stove for Gramper.") The **Vermont Museum,** on the ground floor of the Vermont Historical Society offices in Montpelier, satisfies the curious with intriguing and informative exhibits. At press time it was scheduled to reopen, after extensive renovations, in late 2002. ⊠ *109 State St.,* ☎ *802/ 828–2291,* WEB *www.state.vt.us/vhs.* 🖾 *$3.* ☉ *Call for hrs.*

Dining and Lodging

$$–$$$ ✕ **Chef's Table.** Nearly everyone working here is a student at the New
★ England Culinary Institute. Although this is a training ground, the quality and inventiveness are anything but beginner's luck. The menu changes daily. Dining is more formal than that of the sister operation downstairs, the Main Street Bar and Grill (open daily for lunch and dinner). A 15% gratuity is added to the bill. ⊠ *118 Main St.,* ☎ *802/ 229–9202; 802/223–3188 grill. AE, D, DC, MC, V. Closed Sun. No lunch Sat.*

$$ ✕ **River Run Restaurant.** Mississippi-raised chef Jimmy Kennedy has brought outstanding Southern fare to the shores of the Winooski River. Fried catfish, hush puppies, collard greens, and whiskey cake are just a few of the surprises awaiting diners at this tiny restaurant housed in a former speakeasy. Try the buttermilk biscuits at breakfast. ⊠ *Main St., Plainfield,* ☎ *802/454–1246. No credit cards. BYOB. Closed Mon.–Tues.*

$$ ✕ **Sarducci's.** Legislative lunches have been a lot more leisurely ever since Sarducci's came along to fill the trattoria void in Vermont's capital. These bright, cheerful rooms alongside the Winooski River are a great spot for pizza fresh from wood-fired ovens, wonderfully textured homemade Italian breads, and imaginative pasta dishes such as pasta pugliese, which marries penne with basil, black olives, roasted eggplant, Portobello mushrooms, and sun-dried tomatoes. ⊠ *3 Main St.,* ☎ *802/ 223–0229. Reservations not accepted. AE, MC, V. No lunch Sun.*

$$–$$$ 🖾 **Inn at Montpelier.** This inn built in the early 1800s was renovated with the business traveler in mind, but the architectural detailing, antique four-poster beds, Windsor chairs, and classical guitar on the stereo attract the leisure trade as well. The formal sitting room has a wide wraparound Colonial Revival porch, perfect for reading a book or watching the townsfolk stroll by. The rooms in the annex, also a 19th-century building, are equally spiffy. ⊠ *147 Main St., 05602,* ☎ *802/223–2727,* FAX *802/223–0722,* WEB *www.innatmontpelier.com. 19 rooms. Meeting room. AE, D, DC, MC, V. CP.*

Waterbury

③ *12 mi northwest of Montpelier.*

The face of Waterbury's compact downtown is changing as coffee shops, restaurants, and galleries begin to move into the brick buildings that once housed tired-looking furniture and hardware stores. But the anchor here remains the huge state office complex that was formerly a hospital. The little red train station comes to life only when Amtrak's *Vermonter* stops in town, once a day in each direction. The principal draws for visitors, however, are north of I–89, along Route 100.

Ben & Jerry's Ice Cream Factory is the Valhalla for ice cream lovers. Ben and Jerry began selling ice cream from a renovated gas station in Burlington in the 1970s. Famous for their social and environmental consciousness, the boys do good works while living off the butterfat

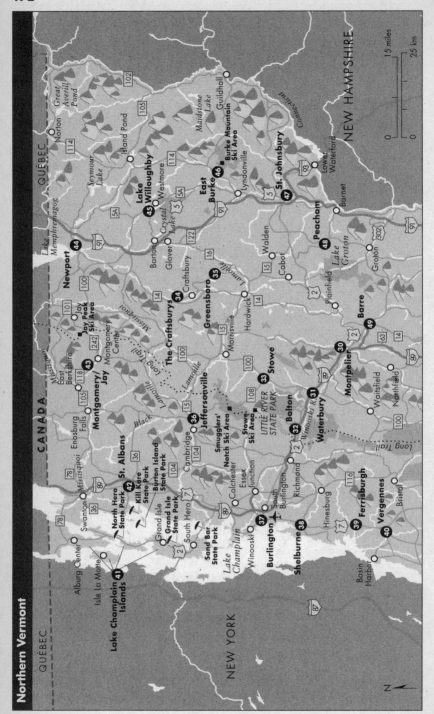

Northern Vermont

of the land. The tour only skims the surface of the behind-the-scenes goings-on at the plant—a flaw forgiven when the free samples are dished out. ⊠ *Rte. 100, 1 mi north of I–89,* ☎ *802/846–1500; 802/882–1260 recorded information,* WEB *www.benjerry.com;.* 🎟 *Tour $2.* ☉ *June, daily 9–5; July–late Aug., daily 9–8; late Aug.–Oct., daily 9–6; Nov.– May, daily 10–5. Tours every ½ hr in winter, more frequent in summer. Gift and scoop shops stay open an hr later.*

Dining and Lodging

$$–$$$$ ✕ **Mist Grill Cafe, Bakery, Roastery.** The fare is best described as country bistro at this casual contemporary restaurant in a renovated gristmill overlooking Thatcher Brook Falls. The menu includes handmade breakfast treats and a ploughman's lunch. Grilled rib steak and pork loin are served Thursday–Saturday evenings, and Sunday "supper" dishes up traditional comfort foods. ⊠ *92 Stowe St.,* ☎ *802/244–2233. AE, MC, V. Closed Mon.*

$–$$ ✕🏨 **Thatcher Brook Inn.** Twin gazebos poised on both ends of the front porch of this sprawling 1899 inn define its space on busy Route 100. Three buildings hold comfortable guest rooms of all sizes, with modern bathroom fixtures and Laura Ashley–style floral wallpaper. Some rooms have fireplaces and whirlpool tubs. The pine-paneled tavern is a popular socializing spot, and classic French cuisine ($$–$$$) is served in the dining room. ⊠ *Rte. 100, 05676,* ☎ *802/244–5911 or 800/292– 5911,* FAX *802/244–1294,* WEB *www.thatcherbrook.com. 21 rooms, 1 suite. Restaurant, some cable TV, pub; no air-conditioning in some rooms. AE, D, DC, MC, V. BP.*

$–$$ 🏨 **Old Stagecoach Inn.** Unwind in the spacious, comfortable rooms at this former-stagecoach stop, now a beautifully restored inn. Antiques embellish all of the individually decorated rooms. The suites, in a separate section, are perfect if you're traveling with kids or pets. An elegant breakfast buffet is served daily. A two-minute walk takes you to restaurants and shops. ⊠ *18 N. Main St., 05676,* ☎ *800/262–2206,* WEB *www.oldstagecoach.com. 8 rooms, 7 with bath; 3 suites. Bar. AE, D, MC, V.*

Outdoor Activities and Sports

Mt. Mansfield State Forest and Little River State Park (⊠ U.S. 2, 1½ mi west of Waterbury, ☎ 802/244–7103) have extensive trail systems for hiking, including one that reaches the headquarters of the Civilian Conservation Corps unit that was stationed here in the 1930s. At Little River State Park, you'll find campsites and trails leading to Mt. Mansfield and Camel's Hump.

Shopping

The **Cold Hollow Cider Mill** (⊠ Rte. 100, 3 mi north of I–89, ☎ 802/ 244–8771 or 800/327–7537) sells cider, baked goods, Vermont produce, and specialty foods. Tastes of fresh-pressed cider are served while you watch how it is made. **Green Mountain Chocolate Complex** (⊠ Rte. 100, 2½ mi north of I–89, ☎ 802/244–1139) houses specialty shops including the Cabot Cheese Annex Store (☎ 802/244–6334) and the Shimmering Glass Studio and Gallery (☎ 802/244–8134). The **Red Hen Baking Company** (⊠ Rte. 100 S, ☎ 802/244–0966) bakes wonderful artisan breads. The **Vermont Clay Studio & Gallery** (⊠ Rte. 100, ☎ 802/244–1126) displays works by artists from around the country.

Bolton

32 *8 mi northwest of Waterbury, 20 mi northwest of Montpelier, 20 mi southeast of Burlington.*

There isn't much to the town of Bolton itself, but Bolton Valley Holiday Resort bustles with activity.

Dining and Lodging

$$–$$$ ✕🛏 **Black Bear Inn.** Teddy bears in all shapes and sizes decorate this mountaintop inn near the Bolton resort and overlooking the Green Mountains. Twelve rooms have glass-door fire stoves and balconies, and six have private hot tubs. Owner-chef Ken Richardson, a graduate of the Culinary Institute of America, serves dishes ($$–$$$) such as grilled Atlantic salmon with a maple-Dijon mustard glaze. ⊠ *Bolton Access Rd., 05477,* ☎ *802/434–2126; 800/395–6335 outside Vermont;* FAX *802/434–5161,* WEB *www.blkbearinn.com;. 24 rooms. Restaurant, pool, outdoor hot tub, kennel. MC, V. BP, MAP.*

$$$ 🛏 **Bolton Resort Hotel and Condominiums.** This slope-side complex includes functional, contemporary rooms, all with mountain views and most with balconies. Studios and suites with kitchens and fireplaces are available, as are condominiums. You can use the resort's sports center, including a pool, sauna, and indoor tennis courts. Ski packages are available. ⊠ *Mountain Rd., 05477,* ☎ *802/434–3444 or 877/926–5866,* FAX *802/434–2131,* WEB *www.boltonvalleyvt.com. 60 rooms, 50 suites, 100 condominiums. AE, MC, V.*

Ski Areas

BOLTON VALLEY HOLIDAY RESORT

Although the area continues to struggle through difficult financial times, a face-lift in 2000 put Bolton well on the way to its goal of becoming a four-season destination. The minivillage at the base of the mountain encompasses a hotel, several restaurants, a wine and cheese shop, and a sports shop. The major attraction, however, is the downhill ski facility. ⊠ *Bolton Access Rd., 05477,* ☎ *802/434–3444 or 877/926–5866,* WEB *www.boltonvalley.com.*

Downhill. Bolton's six lifts include a quad chair, four double chairs, and a surface lift, which service 52 trails covering 157 acres of skiable terrain. The majority of the trails are rated for intermediates; the longest is the 2½-mi Cobrass Run. The vertical drop is 1,625 ft. The resort has 60% snowmaking coverage and provides top-to-bottom night skiing Monday–Saturday until 10 PM. There's a 1,500-ft terrain park for snowboarders.

Cross-country skiing. A Nordic center has cross-country ski, telemark, and snowshoe rentals and lessons. The resort has 35 km (22 mi) of groomed trails and 65 km (40 mi) of natural trails, including some where dogs are permitted. Naturalist-led snowshoe tours are scheduled daily.

Child care. The licensed Honey Bear Child Care Center provides care for children 6 weeks–6 years of age. There are ski programs for ages 3–15.

Summer and year-round activities. The resort has a mountain bike center that rents bikes; indoor and outdoor tennis courts; and hiking trails. A chairlift transports hikers to the top of the mountain but not down. The sports center, open year-round, houses the indoor tennis courts and a pool, sauna, whirlpool, and weight room.

Stowe

★ ③③ *16 mi northeast of Bolton, 22 mi northwest of Montpelier, 36 mi east of Burlington.*

Ever since the Civilian Conservation Corps cut the first downhill trails on Mt. Mansfield, ever since Austrian instructors first told weekenders to "bend mit der knees," Stowe has been the spiritual home of Vermont skiing. The village itself is tiny, just a few blocks of shops and restaurants clustered around a snow-white church spire—but it serves as the anchor for the Mountain Road, which leads north past more places to dine, stay, and shop on its way to those fabled slopes.

To many, Stowe rings a bell as the place where the von Trapp family, of *Sound of Music* fame, chose to settle after fleeing Austria. Set amid acres of pastures that fall away and allow for wide-angle panoramas of the mountains beyond, the **Trapp Family Lodge** (⊠ Luce Hill Rd., ☎ 802/253–8511 or 800/826–7000) is the site of a popular outdoor music series in summer and an extensive cross-country ski-trail network in winter. The **Vermont Ski Museum** (⊠ One South Main St., ☎ 802/253–9911) has exhibits documenting the history of skiing in Vermont.

For more than a century the history of Stowe has been determined by the town's proximity to **Mt. Mansfield**, at 4,393 ft the highest elevation in the state. As early as 1858, the intrepid were trooping to the area to view the mountain, which has a shape that suggests the profile of the face of a man lying on his back. If hiking to the top isn't your idea of a good time, in summer you can take the 4½-mi toll road to the top for a short scenic walk and a magnificent view. ⊠ *Mountain Rd., 7 mi from Rte. 100,* ☎ *802/253–3000.* ⊠ *Toll road $14.* ☉ *Mid-May–mid-Oct., daily 10–5.*

Mt. Mansfield's upper reaches are accessible by the eight-seat **gondola** that continuously shuttles up to the area of "the Chin" and the **Cliff House Restaurant** (☎ 802/253–3000 ext. 237), where lunch is served daily 11–2:30. ⊠ *Mountain Rd., 8 mi off Rte. 100,* ☎ *802/253–3000.* ⊠ *Gondola $14.* ☉ *Mid-June–mid-Oct., daily 10–5; early Dec.–late Apr., daily 8–4 for skiers.*

Dining and Lodging

$$–$$$ ✕ **Chelsea Grill.** Stowe's newest "in" dinner spot blends the accoutrements of a traditional Vermont country restaurant with the glitz and ambition of a big-city dining room. The chef describes his cuisine as "refined country comfort food," with such appetizers as a deviled fried-oyster salad with smoked bacon and lemon parsley vinaigrette, and entrées such as grilled rack of lamb with roasted peppers and pan-roasted sea bass with citrus couscous. Homemade desserts are every bit as creative. ⊠ *18 Edson Hill Rd.,* ☎ *802/253–3075. MC, V.*

$$–$$$ ✕ **Mes Amis.** At this small bistro, locals queue up for house special-
★ ties such as fresh oysters, lobster bisque, braised lamb shanks, roast duck (secret recipe), and bananas Foster. You can dine in the candlelit dining room or outside on the patio, especially on a warm summer's night. ⊠ *311 Mountain Rd.,* ☎ *802/253–8669. D, MC, V. Closed Mon.*

$–$$ ✕ **Miguel's Stowe Away.** Miguel's serves up all the Tex-Mex standards along with tasty surprises such as coconut-fried shrimp, chicken Santa Fe, and a maple flan. Steaks and burgers round out the gringo menu. The cozy front room has a pool table (no quarters required) and a bar stocked with frosty Corona beer. Miguel's has an outpost on the Sugarbush Access Road in Warren (☎ 802/583–3858). ⊠ *3148 Mountain Rd.,* ☎ *802/53–7574 or 800/245–1240. AE, D, MC, V. No lunch.*

$$$$ ✕🖫 **Topnotch at Stowe Resort and Spa.** One of the state's poshest resorts occupies 120 acres overlooking Mt. Mansfield. Floor-to-ceiling windows, a freestanding circular stone fireplace, and cathedral ceilings distinguish the lobby. Country-decorated rooms have thick carpeting and accents such as painted barn-board walls or Italian prints. The large European spa provides 20 massage-treatment rooms and fitness programs. Maxwell's restaurant serves contemporary Continental cuisine. ⊠ *Mountain Rd., 05672,* ☎ *802/253–8585 or 800/451–8686,* 𝖥𝖠𝖷 *802/253–9263,* 𝖶𝖤𝖡 *www.topnotch-resort.com. 77 rooms, 13 suites, 30 town* houses. 2 restaurants, 10 tennis courts (4 indoor), 2 pools (1 indoor), massage, sauna, spa, horseback riding, cross-country skiing, sleigh rides, bar, video game room; no-smoking rooms. AE, D, DC, MC, V. MAP.

$$$–$$$$ ✕▥ **Edson Hill Manor.** At this French-Canadian–style manor atop 225
★ acres of rolling hills Oriental rugs accent the dark wide-board floors, and a huge stone fireplace in the living room provides a cozy ambience. Guest rooms have fireplaces, canopy beds, and down comforters. The dining room ($$$–$$$$; closed Sun.–Thurs. Apr.–May; no lunch) has walls of windows, wildflower paintings, and vines climbing to the ceiling. The contemporary cuisine might include rack of lamb or pan-seared salmon. ⊠ 1500 Edson Hill Rd., 05672, ☎ 802/253–7371 or 800/621–0284, FAX 802/253–4036, WEB www.stowevt.com. 25 rooms. Restaurant, some cable TV, pool, hiking, horseback riding, cross-country skiing, sleigh rides, meeting room; no air-conditioning in some rooms. D, MC, V. BP, MAP.

$$$$ ▥ **Stone Hill Inn.** The amenities of a fine hotel and the intimacy of a B&B characterize this adult-oriented inn just off the Mountain Road. Each elegantly decorated (and soundproof) guest room has a king-size bed, sitting area, and two-person whirlpool bath in front of a fireplace. Common areas include a sitting room and a game room, and the 10 acres of grounds are beautifully landscaped with gardens and waterfalls. ⊠ 89 Houston Farm Rd., 05672, ☎ 802/253–6282, FAX 802/253–7415, WEB www.stonehillinn.com. 9 rooms. Golf privileges, outdoor hot tub, hiking, tobogganing, recreation room. AE, D, DC, MC, V. BP.

$$$–$$$$ ▥ **Stoweflake Mountain Resort and Spa.** You'll find scenic mountain views and accommodations here, from comfortable, country-inn rooms to luxurious suites with fireplaces, wet bars, refrigerators, and balconies. This full-service resort also has one- to three-bedroom fully equipped town houses and hosts Stowe's annual Hot Air Balloon Festival. ⊠ 1746 Mountain Rd. (Box 369, 05672), ☎ 802/253–7355, FAX 802/253–6858, WEB www.stoweflake.com. 94 rooms, 30 town houses. 2 restaurants, some kitchenettes, some microwaves, driving range, putting green, 2 tennis courts, pool, hair salon, sauna, spa, bicycles, sleigh rides, recreation room, business services, meeting rooms. AE, D, DC, MC, V. BP, MAP.

$$ ▥ **Inn at Turner Mill.** Families will feel particularly welcome at this simple inn tucked well off the main road. Accommodations range from a one-bedroom unit to a two-bedroom apartment with two private baths, full kitchen, and fireplace. The inn is close to the ski area, a short walk from a swimming hole, and just across the road from miles of hiking trails. You can rent snowshoes here or purchase a pass to a nearby health club. ⊠ 56 Turner Mill La., 05672, ☎ 802/253–2062 or 800/992–0016, WEB www.turnermill.com. 5 units. Some kitchens. AE, MC, V. BP.

$–$$ ▥ **Sunset Motor Inn.** Strategically set among northern Vermont's big-three ski areas, this family-owned, family-friendly motel has clean and comfortable accommodations. Rooms numbered 70–87 are larger and have whirlpool baths and refrigerators; the best are the ones facing the back of the motel. There's a restaurant next door. ⊠ Junction of Rtes. 15 and 100, Morrisville 05661, ☎ 802/888–4956 or 800/544–2347, FAX 802/888–3698, WEB www.sunsetmotorinn.com. 55 rooms. Pool, some refrigerators; no-smoking rooms. AE, D, MC, V. CP.

Nightlife and the Arts

NIGHTLIFE

The **Matterhorn Night Club** (⊠ Mountain Rd., ☎ 802/253–8198) hosts live music and dancing Thursday–Saturday nights and a DJ Sunday evenings. Live weekend entertainment takes place at **Stoweflake**

Mountain Resort and Spa (☎ 802/253–7355). Entertainers perform at the **Topnotch at Stowe** (☎ 802/253–8585) lounge on weekends.

Stowe Performing Arts (☎ 802/253–7792) sponsors a series of classical and jazz concerts during July in the Trapp Family Lodge meadow. **Stowe Theater Guild** (✉ Town Hall Theater, Main St., ☎ 802/253–3961 summer only) performs musicals in July and August.

Outdoor Activities and Sports

A **recreational path** begins behind the Community Church in the center of town and meanders for 5⅓ mi along the river valley, with many entry points along the way. Whether you're on foot, skis, bike, or in-line skates, it's a tranquil spot to enjoy the outdoors.

The junction of Routes 100 and 108 is the start of a 21-mi tour with scenic views of Mt. Mansfield; the course takes you along Route 100 to Stagecoach Road, to Morristown, over to Morrisville, and south on Randolph Road. The **Mountain Sports and Bike Shop** (✉ Mountain Rd., ☎ 802/253–7919; 800/682–4534 outside Stowe area) supplies equipment and rents bicycles.

Umiak Outdoor Outfitters (✉ 849 S. Main St./Rte. 100, just south of Stowe Village, ☎ 802/253–2317) specializes in canoes and kayaks, rents them for day trips, and leads overnight excursions. The store also operates a rental outpost at Lake Elmore State Park in Elmore, on the Winooski River off Route 2 in Waterbury, at North Beach in Burlington, and on the Lamoille River in Jeffersonville.

The **Fly Rod Shop** (✉ Rte. 100, 3 mi south of Stowe, ☎ 802/253–7346 or 800/535–9763) provides a guiding service; gives fly-tying, casting, and rod-building classes in winter; rents fly tackle; and sells equipment, including classic and collectible firearms.

Stowe Country Club (✉ Mountain Rd., ☎ 802/253–4893) has a scenic 18-hole, par-72 course; a driving range; and a putting green. Greens fee is $35–$65; cart rental is $16.

An ascent of **Mt. Mansfield** makes for a scenic day hike. Trails lead from Route 108 (the Mountain Road) to the summit ridge, where they meet the north-to-south Long Trail. An option is to take the gondola at Stowe to the top and walk down along a ski trail. Views from the summit take in New Hampshire's White Mountains, New York's Adirondacks across Lake Champlain, and southern Québec. The Green Mountain Club has a trail guide.

For the two-hour climb to **Stowe Pinnacle,** go 1½ mi south of Stowe on Route 100 and turn east on Gold Brook Road opposite the Nichols Farm Lodge; turn left at the first intersection, continue straight at an intersection by a covered bridge, turn right after almost 2 mi, and travel 2⅓ mi to a parking lot on the left. The trail crosses an abandoned pasture and takes a short, steep climb to views of the Green Mountains and Stowe Valley.

Jackson Arena (✉ Park St., ☎ 802/253–6148 or 802/253–4402) is a public ice-skating rink, with skate rentals available.

Charlie Horse Sleigh and Carriage Rides (✉ Mountain Rd., ☎ 802/253–2215) operates rides daily from 11 to 7; reservations are suggested for evening rides.

Topnotch at Stowe Resort and Spa has 10 outdoor and 4 indoor courts. Public courts are at Stowe's elementary school.

Shopping

Mountain Road is lined with shops from town up toward the ski area.

Ski Areas

To be precise, the name of the village is Stowe and the name of the mountain is Mt. Mansfield, but to generations of skiers, the area, the complex, and the region are just plain Stowe. The resort is a classic that dates from the 1930s. Even today the area's mystique attracts as many serious skiers as social skiers. Improved snowmaking, new lifts, and free shuttle buses that gather skiers from lodges, inns, and motels along Mountain Road have added convenience to the Stowe experience. Yet the traditions remain: the Winter Carnival in January, the Sugar Slalom in April, ski weeks all winter. Three base lodges provide the essentials, including two on-mountain restaurants. A 10-year expansion plan scheduled to begin in 2003 will include base lodges, a hotel, retail shops, and a golf course. ✉ *5781 Mountain Rd., 05672, ☎ 802/253–3000; 800/253–4754 lodging; 802/253–3600 snow conditions.*

Downhill. Mt. Mansfield, with an elevation of 4,395 ft and a vertical drop of 2,360 ft, is one of the giants among Eastern ski mountains and the highest in Vermont. The mountain's symmetrical shape allows skiers of all abilities long, satisfying runs from the summit. The famous Front Four (National, Liftline, Starr, and Goat) are the intimidating centerpieces for tough, expert runs, yet there is plenty of mellow intermediate skiing, with 59% of the runs rated at that level. One long beginner trail, the Toll Road Trail, is 3⅔ mi. Mansfield's satellite sector is a network of intermediate trails and one expert trail off a basin served by a gondola. Spruce Peak, separate from the main mountain, is a teaching hill and a pleasant experience for intermediates and beginners. In addition to the high-speed, eight-passenger gondola, Stowe has 11 lifts, including a quad, one triple, and six double chairlifts, plus one handle tow, to service its 48 trails. Night-skiing trails are accessed by the gondola. The resort has 73% snowmaking coverage. Snowboard facilities include a halfpipe and two terrain parks—one for beginners, at Spruce Peak, and one for experts, on the Mt. Mansfield side.

Cross-country. The resort has 35 km (22 mi) of groomed cross-country trails and 40 km (24 mi) of backcountry trails. Four interconnecting cross-country ski areas have more than 150 km (90 mi) of groomed trails within the town of Stowe.

Child care. The child-care center takes children ages 6 weeks–6 years, with kids' ski-school programs for ages 6 to 12. A center on Spruce Peak is headquarters for programs for children ages 3–12, including a program for teenagers 13–17.

Summer activities. The resort provides hiking, in-line skating, an alpine slide, gondola rides, and an 18-hole golf course.

The Craftsburys

③④ *27 mi northeast of Stowe.*

The three villages of the Craftsburys—Craftsbury Common, Craftsbury, and East Craftsbury—are among Vermont's finest and oldest towns. Handsome white houses and barns, the requisite common, and terrific views make them well worth the drive. Craftsbury General Store in Craftsbury Village is a great place to stock up on picnic supplies and local information. The rolling farmland hints at the way Vermont used to be: the area's sheer distance from civilization and its rugged weather have kept most of the state's development farther south.

Dining and Lodging

$$$$ ✕🛏 **Inn on the Common.** All rooms at this Federal-style complex contain antique reproductions and contemporary furnishings; deluxe rooms have seating areas and fireplaces. Cocktails are served in the cozy library, and five-course dinners ($$$$; reservations essential) are served in the dining room overlooking the gardens. You have access to the facilities at the Craftsbury Sports Center and Albany's Wellness Barn. Cross-country ski trails connect with those at the Craftsbury Nordic Center. ⊠ *On the common, 05827,* ☎ *802/586–9619 or 800/521–2233,* FAX *802/586–2249,* WEB *www.innonthecommon.com. 15 rooms, 1 suite. Dining room, tennis court, pool, cross-country skiing, lounge, library. AE, MC, V. MAP.*

$$$–$$$$ 🛏 **Craftsbury Outdoor Center.** This outdoors enthusiast's haven has standard accommodations and sporting packages. Cross-country skiing is terrific on 135 km (80 mi) of trails (85 km [50 mi] groomed); the rest of the year, sculling and running camps are held. You can ski, mountain bike, and canoe at day-use rates; equipment rental is available. Meals are served buffet-style. ⊠ *Lost Nation Rd. (Box 31, 05827),* ☎ *802/586–7767 or 800/729–7751,* FAX *802/586–7768,* WEB *www.craftsbury.com. 49 rooms, 10 with bath; 4 cottages; 2 efficiencies. Dining room, boating, mountain bikes, cross-country skiing, meeting room. MC, V.*

$ 🛏 **Craftsbury Bed & Breakfast.** Craftsbury's longest-operating traditional B&B is a lovely place to unwind. Owner Margaret Ramsdell creates an air of peaceful informality at her farmhouse, right down to the absence of a TV. Common rooms include a spacious country kitchen with a woodstove and a living room. In summer, relax on lawn chairs in the big yard; in winter, ski on the property's cross-country ski trails, which are part of a 105-km (65-mi) network. ⊠ *Wylie Hill, 05827,* ☎ *802/586–2206,* WEB *www.scenesofvermont.com/craftsburybb. 6 rooms with shared bath. MC, V. BP.*

Greensboro

③⑤ *10 mi southeast of Craftsbury Common.*

Greensboro, tucked along the southern shore of Caspian Lake, has been a summer resort for literati, academics, and old-money types for more than a century. It exudes an unpretentious, genteel character of such places with a small village center where most of the people running about their errands seem to know each other. A town beach is right off the main street.

Lodging

$$$$ 🛏 **Highland Lodge.** Tranquillity reigns at this 1860 house overlooking a pristine lake. The lodge's 120 acres of rambling woods and pastures are laced with hiking and skiing trails (ski rentals available). Comfortable guest rooms have Early American–style furnishings; most

have views of the lake. The one- to three-bedroom cottages are more private (four with gas stoves stay open in winter). The traditional dinner menu might include entrées such as roasted leg of lamb. ⊠ *1608 Craftsbury Rd., 05841,* ☎ *802/533–2647,* FAX *802/533–7494,* WEB *www.highlandlodge.com. 11 rooms, 11 cottages. Restaurant, tennis court, lake, boating, hiking, cross-country skiing, recreation room; no air-conditioning. D, MC, V. Closed mid-Mar.–late May and mid-Oct.– mid-Dec. MAP.*

Shopping

The **Miller's Thumb** (⊠ Main St., ☎ 802/533–2960 or 800/680–7886) sells Italian pottery, Vermont furniture, crafts and antiques, and April Cornell clothing and linens. **Willey's Store** (⊠ Main St., ☎ 802/533– 2621), with wooden floors and tin ceilings, warrants exploration. Foodstuffs, baskets, candy, kitchen paraphernalia, and more are packed to the rafters.

Jeffersonville

36 *36 mi west of Greensboro, 18 mi north of Stowe, 28 mi northeast of Burlington.*

Mt. Mansfield and Madonna Peak tower over Jeffersonville, whose activities are closely linked with those of Smugglers' Notch Ski Resort.

Boyden Valley Winery (⊠ junction of Rtes. 15 and 104, Cambridge, ☎ 802/644–8151) conducts tours of its microwinery and showcases an excellent selection of Vermont specialty products and local handicrafts, including fine furniture. The winery is closed Monday in summer and Monday–Thursday in winter.

Lodging

$$$$ 🏨 **Smugglers' Notch Resort.** Most of the condos at this large year-round resort have fireplaces and decks. The resort is known for its many family programs. Rates include lift tickets and ski lessons in season, and kids six weeks to two years of age get free care if parents stay three or more nights. ⊠ *Rte. 108, 05464,* ☎ *802/644–8851 or 800/451–8752,* FAX *802/644–1230,* WEB *www.smugs.com. 502 condominiums. 3 restaurants, 6 tennis courts, pool, gym, hot tub, sauna, downhill skiing, iceskating, bar, recreation room, baby-sitting, children's programs (ages 3–17), playground. AE, DC, MC, V.*

$–$$ 🏨 **Mannsview Inn.** Bette and Kelley Mann operate what may be Vermont's only B&B, canoe touring center, and antiques center. Decorated with a Victorian accents, the inn furnishes its charming guest rooms with antiques, high poster beds, whirlpool baths, and fireplaces. An antique pool table fills one side of the living room, and breakfast is served in a glassed-in room overlooking the mountains. ⊠ *Rte. 108, 05464,* ☎ *802/644–8321 or 888/937–6266,* FAX *802/644–2006,* WEB *www.mannsview.com. 6 rooms. Outdoor hot tub. AE, D, MC, V. BP.*

$ 🏨 **Deer Run Motor Inn.** This comfortable two-story motel may be the north country's best bargain. Although it's right on busy Route 15, the rooms are set well back (second-floor rooms with queen-size beds face the rear), and each has a coffeemaker, deck, and sliding glass doors. Other amenities include a swing set and grills. ⊠ *80 Deer Run Loop, 05464,* ☎ *802/644–8866 or 800/354–2728,* WEB *www.deerrunmotorinn.com. 25 units. Picnic area, cable TV, pool, some pets allowed (fee); no-smoking rooms. AE, D, MC, V.*

Outdoor Activities and Sports

Applecheek Farm (⊠ 567 McFarlane Rd., Hyde Park, ☎ 802/888–4482) runs daytime and evening (by lantern) hay and sleigh rides, llama treks, and farm tours. **Green River Canoe & Kayak** (☎ 802/644–8336 or 802/644–8714), at the junction of Route 15 and 108 behind Jana's Restaurant, rents canoes and kayaks on the Lamoille River and leads guided canoe trips to Boyden Valley Winery. **Northern Vermont Llamas** (✉ 766 Lapland Rd., Waterville, ☎ 802/644–2257) conducts half- and full-day treks from May through October along the cross-country ski trails of Smugglers' Notch. The llamas carry everything, including snacks and lunches. Advance reservations are essential.

Smugglers' Notch Canoe Touring (✉ Rte. 108, ☎ 802/644–8321 or 888/937–6266) provides canoes, kayaks, and shuttle service on the Lamoille River from Mannsview Inn. Tubing is also available. **Smugglers' Notch State Park** (✉ Rte. 108, 10 mi north of Mt. Mansfield, ☎ 802/253–4014) is good for picnicking and hiking on wild terrain among large boulders. **Vermont Horse Park** (✉ Rte. 108, ☎ 802/644–5347) leads rides on authentic horse-drawn sleighs as well as trail rides when weather permits.

Shopping
ANTIQUES

The **Buggy Man** (✉ Rte. 15, 7 mi east of Jeffersonville, ☎ 802/635–2110) sells American furniture and collectibles including horse-drawn vehicles. **Mel Siegel** (✉ Rte. 15, 7 mi east of Jeffersonville, ☎ 802/635–7838) specializes in 19th-century American furniture and glassware. **Smugglers Notch Antique Center** (✉ Rte. 108, ☎ 802/644–8321) sells antiques and collectibles of 60 dealers in a rambling barn.

CLOTHING

The **Forget-Me-Not Shop.** (✉ Rte. 15, 6½ mi east of Jeffersonville, ☎ 802/635–2335) sells men's and women's designer clothing, military surplus, and jewelry at incredibly low prices. **Johnson Woolen Mills** (✉ Main St., Johnson, 9 mi east of Jeffersonville, ☎ 802/635–2271) is an authentic factory store with deals on woolen blankets, yard goods, and the famous Johnson outerwear.

CRAFTS

Vermont Rug Makers (✉ Rte. 100C, East Johnson, 10 mi east of Jeffersonville, ☎ 802/635–2434) weaves imaginative rugs and tapestries from fabrics, wools, and exotic materials. Its International Gallery displays rugs and tapestries from countries throughout the world. The shop has a branch on Main Street in Stowe.

Ski Areas
SMUGGLERS' NOTCH RESORT

This sprawling resort complex consistently wins accolades for its family programs. Its children's ski school is one of the best in the country—possibly *the* best. But skiers of all levels come here (Smugglers' was the first ski area in the East to designate a triple-black-diamond run—the Black Hole). All the essentials are available in the village at the base of the Morse Mountain lifts, including lodgings, restaurants, and several shops. ✉ *Rte. 108, 05464,* ☎ *802/644–8851 or 800/451–8752,* WEB *www.smuggs.com.*

Downhill. Smugglers' has three mountains. The highest, Madonna, with a vertical drop of 2,610 ft, is in the center and connects with a trail network to Sterling (1,500-ft vertical). The third mountain, Morse (1,150-ft vertical), is adjacent to Smugglers' "village" of shops, restaurants, and lodgings; it's connected to the other peaks by trails and a shuttle bus. The wild, craggy landscape lends a pristine wilderness feel to the skiing experience on the two higher mountains. The tops of each of the mountains have expert terrain—a couple of double-black diamonds make Madonna memorable. Intermediate trails fill the lower sections. Morse has many beginner and advanced beginner trails. Smugglers' 70 trails are served by eight lifts, including six chairs and two surface lifts. Top-to-bottom snowmaking on all three mountains allows for 62% coverage. Several terrain parks are provided for snowboarders, including Prohibition Park, at 3,500 ft one of the longest in Vermont. Night skiing and snowboarding classes are given at the new Learning and Fun Park.

Cross-country/snowshoeing. The area has 27 km (18 mi) of groomed and tracked cross-country trails and 20 km (12 mi) of snowshoe trails.

Other activities. The self-contained village has ice-skating and sleigh rides. The numerous snowshoeing programs include family walks and backcountry trips. The FunZone at SmuggsCentral has an indoor pool, playground, slides, miniature golf, a hot tub, ice-skating rink, and Nordic Center. A Teen Center is open from 5 PM until midnight.

Child care. The state-of-the-art Alice's Wonderland Child Care Center accepts children ages 6 weeks–6 years. Ski camps for kids ages 3–17 provide excellent instruction, plus movies, games, and other activities.

Summer and year-round activities. Smugglers' has a full roster of summertime programs, including a pool, complete with waterfalls and water slides; the Giant Rapid River Ride (the longest water ride in the state); lawn games; and mountain biking and hiking programs. It also has an indoor sports center, the FunZone. Horseback riding is available in summer and fall.

Burlington

★ ③⑦ *31 mi southwest of Jeffersonville, 76 mi south of Montréal, 349 mi north of New York City, 223 mi northwest of Boston.*

Cited in survey after survey as one of America's most livable small cities, Burlington has the vibrant character of a college town in which a lot of the graduates have stayed behind to put down roots. The largest population center in Vermont, the city was founded in 1763 and is now the center of a rapidly growing suburban area. It has held its own against highway malls by cleverly positioning itself in the "festival marketplace" retail style, as well as by trading on its incomparable location on Lake Champlain. The Church Street Marketplace—a pedestrian mall of boutiques, restaurants, sidewalk cafés, crafts vendors, and street performers—is an animated downtown focal point. The Burlington area's eclectic population includes many transplants from larger urban areas as well as roughly 20,000 students from the area's four colleges. For years it was the only city in America with a socialist mayor—now the nation's sole socialist congressional representative.

Crouched on the shores of Lake Champlain, which shimmers in the shadows of the Adirondacks to the west, Burlington's revitalized waterfront teems with outdoors enthusiasts who stroll along its recreation path and ply the waters in sailboats and motor craft in summer. A 500-passenger, three-level cruise vessel, **Shoreline Cruise's *The Spirit of Ethan Allen III,*** takes people on narrated cruises and on dinner and sunset sailings that drift by the Adirondacks and the Green Mountains. ⊠ *Burlington Boat House, College St. at Battery St.,* ☎ *802/862-8300.* ⊡ *$9.95.* ⊙ *Cruises late May–mid-Oct., daily 10–9.*

Part of the waterfront's revitalization and still a work in progress, the **Center for Lake Champlain** was closed at this writing for renovations and scheduled to reopen in June 2003. Check the Web site for updates. ✉ *1 College St.,* ☎ *802/864–1848,* WEB *www.lakechamplaincenter.org.*

Crowning the hilltop above Burlington is the campus of the **University of Vermont** (☎ 802/656–3480), known simply as UVM for the abbreviation of its Latin name, Universitas Viridis Montis—the University of the Green Mountains. With more than 10,000 students, UVM is the state's principal institution of higher learning. The most architecturally interesting buildings face the Green, which contains some of the grandest surviving specimens of the elm trees that once shaded virtually every street in Burlington, as well as a statue of UVM founder Ira Allen, Ethan's brother. The **Robert Hull Fleming Art Museum** (✉ Colchester Ave., ☎ 802/656–0750), just behind the Ira Allen Chapel, houses American portraits and landscapes, including works by Sargent, Homer, and Bierstadt; two Corots and a Fragonard; and an Egyptian mummy. Contemporary Vermont works are also exhibited.

Burlington's **Intervale** encompasses 700 acres of open land along the Winooski River. You can rent canoes, bike the 2-mi trail (which connects with Burlington's 10-mi Cycle the City loop), take a river tour, or hike the trails. Gardener's Supply Company (✉ 128 Intervale Rd., ☎ 802/660–3505, WEB www.gardeners.com), a major direct-mail gardening company, with greenhouses and outdoor display gardens, oversees the project. The company also provides maps, information, and a schedule of the many seasonal events held there. One of the earliest residents of the Intervale was Ethan Allen, Vermont's Revolutionary-era guerrilla fighter, who remains a captivating figure. Exhibits at the **Ethan Allen Homestead** visitor center answer questions about his flamboyant life. The house contains such frontier hallmarks as rough saw-cut boards and an open hearth for cooking. A re-created Colonial kitchen garden resembles the one the Allens would have had. After the tour and multimedia presentation, you can stretch your legs on scenic trails along the Winooski River. ✉ *North Ave. off Rte. 127, north of Burlington,* ☎ *802/865–4556,* WEB *www.sover.net/~eahome.com.* ✇ *$5.* ⊙ *Call for schedule.*

OFF THE BEATEN PATH

GREEN MOUNTAIN AUDUBON NATURE CENTER – This is a wonderful place to discover Vermont's outdoor wonders. The center's 300 acres of diverse habitats are a sanctuary for all things wild, and the 5 mi of trails provide an opportunity to explore the workings of differing natural communities. Events include dusk walks, wildflower and birding rambles, nature workshops, and educational activities for kids and adults. The center is 18 mi southeast of Burlington. ✉ *Huntington–Richmond Rd., Richmond,* ☎ *802/434–3068.* ✇ *Donations accepted.* ⊙ *Grounds daily dawn–dusk, center Mon.–Sat. 8–4.*

Dining and Lodging

$$–$$$ ✕ **Leunig's Bistro.** Church Street's café delivers alfresco dining, bistro cuisine, and live jazz Tuesday–Thursday evenings. Favorite entrées include herb-crusted rack of lamb and pine nut chicken breast with a red grape white wine sauce. A prix-fixe dinner for two for $30, served Sunday–Thursday 5–6, is one of the city's best bargains. ✉ *115 Church St.,* ☎ *802/863–3759. AE, D, DC, MC, V.*

$$–$$$ ✕ **NECI Commons.** The initials stand for New England Culinary Institute, the respected Montpelier academy whose students and teachers run this all-under-one-roof café, bakery, market, restaurant, and bar. The deli counter can get a little pricey, but everything is fresh and tasty. It's open daily for lunch and dinner and on Sunday for brunch. Mornings, homemade pastries and muffins are served in the market area. ✉ *25 Church St.,* ☎ *802/862–6324. AE, D, MC, V.*

$$–$$$ ✕ **Trattoria Delia.** Didn't manage to rent that villa in Umbria this year?
★ The next best thing, if your travels bring you to Burlington, is this superb Italian country eatery just around the corner from City Hall Park. Local game and produce are the stars, as in roast rabbit marinated in herbs, wine, and olive oil. The chef's passion for the truly homemade extends to wild boar sausage, salami, and fresh mozzarella. Wood-grilled items are a specialty. ⊠ *152 St. Paul St.,* ☎ *802/864–5253. AE, D, DC, MC, V. No lunch.*

$$ ✕ **Junior's.** New York–style pizza and freshly made calzones share the menu with spaghetti and meatballs, shrimp *fra diavola*, and penne àla vodka with prosciutto, onions, and mushrooms at this pizzeria. Weekend reservations are recommended for dinner seating in the second floor, white-tableclothed dining room. ⊠ *6 Roosevelt Hwy., Colchester,* ☎ *802/655–5555. AE, MC, V.*

$$ ✕ **Old Heidelberg German Restaurant.** This chef-owned restaurant, graciously appointed with linens and fresh flowers, serves such tasty Teutonic standards as sauerbraten, pork and veal schnitzels, and homemade bratwurst; hearty homemade goulash and potato soups round out the luncheon and appetizer menus. German cuisine is the original "comfort food"—perfect for a cold northern Vermont winter night. German beers and wines are available. ⊠ *1016 Shelburne Rd./Rte. 7,* ☎ *802/ 865–4423. AE, D, DC, MC, V. Closed Mon.*

$$ ✕ **Parima Thai Restaurant.** Chef's specials such as crispy roasted duck in tamarind sauce and seafood *phuket* (shrimp, mussels, cod, and squid sautéed in basil sauce) join a menu of traditional Thai including curries and pad Thai (stir-fried noodles with shrimp or chicken). This handsomely appointed restaurant has one of the most elegant bars in town and a seasonal patio. Lunch is served weekdays. ⊠ *185 Pearl St.,* ☎ *802/864–7917. AE, D, DC, MC, V.*

$–$$ ✕ **Ri Ra.** Brought to Burlington from Ireland in pieces and reassembled on-site, this Irish pub serves classic fare such as bangers and mash and fish-and-chips, along with burgers and fish. The luncheon buffet serves traditional Irish carvery. ⊠ *123 Church St.,* ☎ *802/860–9401. MC, V.*

$$$$ ✕🏠 **Inn at Essex.** About 10 mi from downtown Burlington—next to Essex Outlet Fair—is a state-of-the-art inn and conference center dressed in country clothing. Rooms have flowered wallpaper and reproduction period desks; 30 have fireplaces. The two restaurants ($$$– $$$$) are run by the New England Culinary Institute. Butlers serve dishes such as sweet dumpling squash with ginger-garlic basmati rice. Five-onion soup and daily flatbread pizza specials are among the highlights at the Tavern. ⊠ *70 Essex Way, off Rte. 15, Essex Junction 05452,* ☎ *802/878–1100 or 800/727–4295,* ℻ *802/878–0063,* 🕸 *www.innatessex.com. 120 rooms. 2 restaurants, pool, billiards, bar, library, business services, meeting rooms. AE, D, DC, MC, V. CP.*

$$–$$$$ 🏠 **Willard Street Inn.** High in the historic hill section of Burlington,
★ this grand house with an exterior marble staircase and English gardens incorporates elements of Queen Anne and Colonial–Georgian Revival styles. The stately foyer, paneled in cherry, leads to a more formal sitting room with velvet drapes. The solarium is bright and sunny with marble floors, many plants, and big velvet couches for contemplating views of Lake Champlain. All the rooms have down comforters and phones; some have lake views and canopied beds. Orange French toast is among the breakfast favorites. ⊠ *349 S. Willard St., 05401,* ☎ *802/651–8710 or 800/577–8712,* ℻ *802/651–8714,* 🕸 *www.willardstreetinn.com. 14 rooms. AE, D, MC, V. BP.*

Nightlife and the Arts

NIGHTLIFE

The music at the **Club Metronome** (✉ 188 Main St., ☎ 802/865–4563) ranges from cutting-edge sounds to funk, blues, and reggae. National and local musicians come to **Higher Ground** (✉ 1 Main St., Winooski, ☎ 802/654–8888). The band Phish got its start at **Nectar's** (✉ 188 Main St., ☎ 802/658–4771). This place is always jumping to the sounds of local bands and never charges a cover. **Red Square Bar and Grill** (✉ 136 Church St., ☎ 802/859–8909) hosts a Sunday gospel brunch from late January through early March and live music, including funk, jazz, and other eclectic selections, Monday–Saturday. Food is served on the garden patio in nice weather. **Ri Ra** (✉ 123 Church St., ☎ 802/860–9401) hosts live entertainment with an Irish flair. **Vermont Pub and Brewery** (✉ 144 College St., ☎ 802/865–0500) makes its own beer and fruit seltzers and is arguably the most popular spot in town. Folk musicians play here regularly.

THE ARTS

City Hall's **Burlington City Arts** (☎ 802/865–7166; 802/865–9163 24-hr Artsline) has up-to-date arts-related information. The **Fire House Art Gallery** (✉ 135 Church St., ☎ 802/865–7165) exhibits works by local artists. **Flynn Theatre for the Performing Arts** (✉ 153 Main St., ☎ 802/652–4500 information; 802/863–5966 tickets; WEB www.flynncenter.org), a grandiose old structure, is the cultural heart of Burlington; it schedules the Vermont Symphony Orchestra, theater, dance, big-name musicians, and lectures. The **Lyric Theater** (☎ 802/658–1484) stages musical productions in the fall and spring at the Flynn Theatre. **St. Michael's Playhouse** (✉ St. Michael's College, Rte. 15, Colchester, ☎ 802/654–2281 box office; 802/654–2617 administrative office) performs in the McCarthy Arts Center Theater. The **UVM Lane Series** (☎ 802/656–4455 programs and times; 802/656–3085 box office) sponsors classical as well as folk music concerts in the Flynn Theatre, Ira Allen Chapel, and the UVM Recital Hall. The **Vermont Symphony Orchestra** (☎ 802/874–5741) performs throughout the state year-round and at the Flynn from October through May.

Outdoor Activities and Sports

BEACHES

The **North Beaches** are on the northern edge of Burlington: North Beach Park (✉ off North Ave., ☎ 802/864–0123), Bayside Beach (✉ Rte. 127 near Malletts Bay), and Leddy Beach (✉ Leddy Park Rd., off North Ave.), which is popular for sailboarding.

BIKING

Burlington's 10-mi Cycle the City loop runs along the waterfront, connecting several city parks and beaches. It also passes the Community Boathouse and runs within several blocks of downtown restaurants and shops. **North Star Cyclery** (✉ 100 Main St., ☎ 802/863–3832) rents bicycles and provides maps of bicycle routes. **Ski Rack** (✉ 81 Main St., ☎ 802/658–3313 or 800/882–4530) rents and services bikes and provides maps.

WATER SPORTS

Burlington Community Boathouse (✉ foot of College St., Burlington Harbor, ☎ 802/865–3377) rents Jet Skis, sailboards, sailboats from 13 ft to 40 ft, and motorboats (some captained); the boathouse also gives lessons. **Malletts Bay Marina** (✉ 228 Lakeshore Dr., Colchester, ☎ 802/862–4072) has facilities for mooring, sells gasoline, and repairs boats. **Marble Island Resort** (✉ Colchester, ☎ 802/864–6800) has a marina and a 9-hole golf course. **Point Bay Marina** (✉ 1401 Thompson's Point Rd., Charlotte, ☎ 802/425–2431) provides full service and repairs.

Shopping

ANTIQUES

Architectural Salvage Warehouse (⊠ 53 Main St., ☎ 802/658–5011) is a great place to hunt for claw-foot tubs, stained-glass windows, mantels, andirons, and other similar items. The large rhinoceros head bursting out of the **Conant Custom Brass** (⊠ 270 Pine St., ☎ 802/658–4482) storefront may tempt you in to see the custom work, including decorative lighting and bathroom fixtures.

CRAFTS

In addition to its popular pottery, **Bennington Potters North** (⊠ 127 College St., ☎ 802/863–2221 or 800/205–8033) stocks interesting gifts, glassware, furniture, and other housewares. **Vermont State Craft Center** (⊠ 85 Church St., ☎ 802/863–6458) displays contemporary and traditional crafts by more than 200 Vermont artisans. **Yankee Pride** (⊠ Champlain Mill, E. Canal St., Winooski, ☎ 802/655–0500) has a large inventory of quilting fabrics and supplies as well as Vermont-made quilts.

MALLS AND MARKETPLACES

The remodeled **Burlington Square Mall** (⊠ Church St., ☎ 802/658–2545) has a Starbucks, a large Filene's department store, and a few dozen other shops. The **Champlain Mill** (⊠ U.S. 2/7, northeast of Burlington, ☎ 802/655–9477), a former woolen mill on the banks of the Winooski River, holds three floors of stores, including several clothing shops and restaurants. **Church Street Marketplace** (⊠ Main St. to Pearl St., ☎ 802/863–1648), a pedestrian thoroughfare, is lined with boutiques, cafés, and street vendors. Look for bargains at the rapidly growing **Essex Outlet Fair** (⊠ junction of Rtes. 15 and 289, Essex, ☎ 802/878–2851), with such outlets as Brooks Brothers, Polo Ralph Lauren, and Levi's, among others. **University Mall** (⊠ Dorset St., ☎ 802/863–1066), housing Sears, Bon Ton, and JCPenney, continues to expand.

Shelburne

38 *5 mi south of Burlington.*

Once a village surrounded by small farms and lakeshore estates, Shelburne is now largely a bedroom community for Burlington. It's distinguished by one of the nation's premier repositories of Americana and by a tycoon's gilded-age fiefdom that has become a model farm and agricultural education center.

A few miles south of Burlington, the Champlain Valley gives way to fertile farmland, affording stunning views of the rugged Adirondacks across the lake. You can trace much of New England's history simply by wandering the 45 acres and 37 buildings of the **Shelburne Museum.** The outstanding 80,000-object collection of Americana consists of 18th- and 19th-century period homes and furniture, fine and folk art, farm tools, more than 200 carriages and sleighs, Audubon prints, an old-fashioned jail, and even a private railroad car from the days of steam. The museum also has an assortment of duck decoys, an old stone cottage, a display of early toys, and the *Ticonderoga*, an old side-wheel steamship, grounded amid lawn and trees. ⊠ *U.S. 7,* ☎ *802/985–3346 or 802/985–3344,* WEB *www.shelburnemuseum.org.* ☜ *$17.50 for 2 consecutive days.* ☉ *Mid-May–late Oct., daily 10–5; late Apr.–mid-May, daily 1–4.*

★☺ Founded in the 1880s as a private estate, the 1,400-acre **Shelburne Farms** is an educational and cultural resource center with, among other things, a working dairy farm, a Children's Farmyard, and a spot for watching the farm's famous cheddar cheese being made. Frederick Law Olmsted, co-creator of New York's Central Park, designed the magnificent grounds overlooking Lake Champlain. For an additional charge of $5, you can tour the 1891 breeding barn. ⊠ *West of U.S. 7 at Harbor and Bay Rds.,* ☎ *802/985–8686,* WEB *www.shelburnefarms. org.* ▨ *Day pass $6, tour an additional $5.* ☉ *Visitor center and shop daily 10–5; tours mid-May–mid-Oct. (last tour at 3:30); mid-Oct.–mid-May, walking trails open, weather permitting.*

☺ On the 25-minute tour of the **Vermont Teddy Bear Company,** you'll hear more puns than you ever thought possible and learn how a few homemade bears, sold from a cart on Church Street, have turned into a multimillion-dollar business. A children's play tent is set up outdoors in summer, and you can wander the beautiful 57-acre property. ⊠ *2236 Shelburne Rd.,* ☎ *802/985–3001.* ▨ *Tour $2.* ☉ *Tours Mon.–Sat. 9:30– 5, Sun. 10:30–4; store Mon.–Sat. 9–6, Sun. 10–5.*

At the 6-acre **Vermont Wildflower Farm,** the display along the flowering pathways changes constantly: violets in the spring, daisies and black-eyed Susans for summer, and, for fall, flowers with colors that rival those of the trees' foliage. You can buy wildflower seeds, crafts, and books here. ⊠ *U.S. 7, Charlotte, 5 mi south of the Shelburne Museum,* ☎ *802/425–3641,* WEB *www.americanmeadows.com.* ▨ *$3.* ☉ *Early May–late Oct., daily 10–5.*

Dining and Lodging

$$$ ✕ **Café Shelburne Français.** This popular restaurant serves creative
★ French bistro cuisine. Some specialties are sweetbreads in a port wine and mushroom sauce in puff pastry and homemade fettuccine with prunes. Desserts such as the sweet chocolate layered terrine and maple-syrup mousse with orange terrine are fabulous. ⊠ *U.S. 7,* ☎ *802/985– 3939. AE, MC, V. Closed Sun.–Mon. No lunch.*

$–$$ ✕ **La Villa Mediterranean.** Made-to-order pasta dishes, pizza (in three sizes), grilled items such as salmon and lamb chops, and an assortment of tasty appetizers make this family-friendly restaurant a popular choice for lunch and dinner. The large, open dining room seats 60 at candlelit, linen-covered tables. Diners can watch chefs prepare their meals near the open kitchen. ⊠ *Rte. 7, Tenneybrook Square,* ☎ *802/ 985–2596. MC, V. Closed Sun.*

$$–$$$$ ✕▥ **Inn at Shelburne Farms.** This turn-of-the-20th-century Tudor-
★ style inn, once the home of William Seward and Lila Vanderbilt Webb, overlooks Lake Champlain, the distant Adirondacks, and the sea of pastures that make up this 1,400-acre working farm. Each room is different, from the wallpaper to the period antiques. The dining room ($$$– $$$$) defines elegance, and Sunday brunch (not served in May) is one of the area's best. ⊠ *Harbor Rd., 05482,* ☎ *802/985–8498,* FAX *802/ 985–8123,* WEB *www.shelburnefarms.org. 24 rooms, 17 with bath. Restaurant, tennis court, lake, boating, fishing, billiards, hiking. AE, D, DC, MC, V. Closed mid-Oct.–mid-May.*

$$–$$$$ ▥ **Heart of the Village Inn.** Each of the elegantly furnished rooms at this handsomely restored 1886 B&B across from Town Hall (and within walking distance of the Café Shelburne Français) provides coziness and comfort. Four rooms and a suite in the carriage barn are more spacious and have modern accommodations. ⊠ *5347 Shelburne Rd./Rte. 7, 05482,* ☎ *802/985–2800 or 877/808–7031,* FAX *802/985– 2870,* WEB *www.heartofthevillage.com. 8 rooms, 1 suite. Cable TV. AE, MC, V. BP.*

Outdoor Activities and Sports

A moderately easy 18½-mi bike trail begins at the blinker on U.S. 7 in Shelburne and follows Mt. Philo Road, Hinesburg Road, Route 116, and Irish Hill Road.

Shopping

When you enter **Shelburne Country Store** (⊠ Village Green, off U.S. 7, ☎ 802/985–3657) you'll step back in time. Walk past the potbellied stove and take in the aroma emanating from the fudge neatly piled behind huge antique glass cases. The store specializes in candles, weather vanes, glassware, and local foods.

Ferrisburg

③⑨ *9 mi south of Shelburne.*

A bedroom community for nearby Burlington, rural Ferrisburg is home to one of Vermont's oldest resorts, a museum, a fine restaurant, and Button Bay and Kingsland Bay state parks.

Rokeby Museum, the onetime home of 19th-century author and illustrator Rowland E. Robinson, was once a stop on the Underground Railroad. Today the National Historic Landmark is preserved as a time capsule, incorporating more than 200 years of family treasures. The property includes eight historic outbuildings and hiking trails. Guided tours are given at 11, 12:30, and 2. ⊠ *Rte. 7,* ☎ *802/877–3406.* ☞ *$4.* ☺ *Mid-May–mid-Oct., Thurs.–Sun.*

Dining

$$–$$$ ✗ **Starry Night Cafe.** Since it opened, this chic restaurant housed in an old cider mill has become one of the hottest spots around, increasing in size to meet growing demand. Appetizers include house specials such as honey-chili glazed shrimp and gazpacho. Among the entrées are lobster-stuffed sole, pan-seared scallops, and grilled New York steak. ⊠ *5467 Rte. 7,* ☎ *802/877–0316. MC, V.*

Shopping

Dakin Farm (⊠ Rte. 7, ☎ 800/993–2546) sells cob-smoked ham, aged cheddar cheese, and other specialty foods; come in for free samples. The **Ferrisburg Artisans' Guild** (⊠ 303 Cherry St./Rte. 7, ☎ 802/877–3668), next to the Starry Night Cafe, provides work space for potters, sculptors, and furniture makers and exhibits the works of local craftspeople.

Vergennes

④⓪ *3 mi south of Ferrisburg.*

Vermont's oldest city, founded in 1788, is also the third oldest in New England. The downtown area is a compact district of Victorian homes and public buildings. Main Street slopes down to Otter Creek Falls, where cannonballs were made during the War of 1812. The statue of Thomas MacDonough on the Green immortalizes the victor of the Battle of Plattsburgh in 1814.

OFF THE
BEATEN PATH

LAKE CHAMPLAIN MARITIME MUSEUM – A replica of Benedict Arnold's Revolutionary War gunboat is part of this museum, which documents centuries of activity on the historically significant lake. The museum commemorates the days when steamships sailed along the coast of northern Vermont carrying logs, livestock, and merchandise bound for New York City. Among the 13 exhibit areas is a blacksmith's shop. A one-room stone schoolhouse built in the early 19th century houses historic maps, nautical prints, and maritime objects. Also on-site are a nautical archaeology center, a conservation laboratory, and a restaurant. ⊠ *Basin Harbor Rd., Basin Harbor (14 mi west of Bristol, 7 mi west of Vergennes),* ☎ *802/475–2022.* ☞ *$8.* ☉ *May–mid-Oct., daily 10–5.*

Dining and Lodging

$$$–$$$$ ✕ **Christophe's on the Green.** Amid simple elegance—high ceilings, crisp linens, fresh flowers—inside an old hotel in the center of town, this restaurant serves classic, artfully prepared French cuisine. Among the specialties are braised rabbit and Cornish hen in a phyllo pastry. The three-course fixed-price dinner for $45 is an excellent value. ⊠ *5 Green St.,* ☎ *802/877–3414. MC, V. Closed mid-Oct.–mid-May and Sun.–Mon.*

$$$–$$$$ ✕🏠 **Basin Harbor Club.** On 700 acres overlooking Lake Champlain ★ this family resort provides luxurious accommodations, a full roster of amenities including an 18-hole golf course, boating (with a 40-ft tour boat), and daylong children's programs. Some rooms have fireplaces, decks, or porches. The restaurant menu ($$–$$$) is classic American, the wine list excellent. Coats and ties are required in common areas after 6 PM from mid-June through Labor Day. ⊠ *Basin Harbor Rd., Vergennes 05491,* ☎ *802/475–2311 or 800/622–4000,* 𝔽𝔸𝕏 *802/475– 6545,* 𝕎𝔼𝔹 *www.basinharbor.com. 36 rooms, 2 suites in 3 guest houses, 77 cottages. 2 restaurants, 18-hole golf course, 5 tennis courts, pool, health club, boating, bicycles, children's programs (ages 3–15). MC, V. Closed mid-Oct.–mid-May. FAP July–Aug.; BP spring and fall.*

$$–$$$ 🏠 **Whitford House.** Antiques and original art adorn the walls of this late-18th-century country farmhouse on 37 acres of meadowlands. All three bedrooms in the main house have spectacular views of rolling dairy lands and the distant Adirondacks. The guest cottage, which sleeps four, has a microwave, refrigerator, and wet bar. Dinner is prepared by request. ⊠ *912 Grandey Rd., Addison 05491,* ☎ *802/758–2704 or 800/746–2704,* 𝔽𝔸𝕏 *802/758–2089,* 𝕎𝔼𝔹 *www.whitfordhouseinn.com. 3 rooms, 1 cottage. Library, some pets allowed. MC, V. BP.*

Shopping

Kennedy Brothers Marketplace (⊠ Rte. 22A, ☎ 802/877–2975), in a renovated creamery, displays the wares of craftspeople, woodworkers, and antiques and collectibles dealers.

Lake Champlain Islands

❹① *43 mi from Vergennes, 20 mi northwest of Shelburne, 15 mi northwest of Burlington.*

South Hero, North Hero, Isle La Motte, and the Alburg peninsula compose the elongated archipelago that stretches southward from the Canadian border. Because of their temperate climate, the islands hold several apple orchards and numerous state parks and are a center of water recreation in summer and ice fishing in winter. A scenic drive through the islands on U.S. 2 begins at I–89 and travels north to Alburg Center; Route 78 takes you back to the mainland.

Snow Farm Vineyard and Winery has self-guided tours, a tasting room, and free concerts on the lawn for 10 Thursday evenings, beginning in mid-June. ⊠ *190 W. Shore Rd., South Hero,* ☎ *802/372–9463.* ☞ *Free.* ☉ *May–Dec., daily 10–5; tours at 11 and 2.*

Hyde Log Cabin, built in 1783 on South Hero, is often cited as the country's oldest surviving log cabin. ⊠ *U.S. 2, Grand Isle,* ☎ *802/828–3051.* ☞ *$3.* ☉ *July 4–Labor Day, Thurs.–Mon. 11–5.*

The **Royal Lipizzaner Stallions,** descendants of the noble white horses bred in Austria since the 16th century, perform intricate dressage maneuvers at their summer home on the islands. ✉ *U.S. 2, North Hero,* ☎ *802/372–5683.* 🎦 *Barn visits free between performances; shows $15 adults, $8 children.* ⊙ *Mid-July–late Aug., Thurs.–Fri. at 6 PM, weekends at 2:30 PM.*

St. Anne's Shrine marks the site where French soldiers and Jesuits put ashore in 1665 and built a fort, creating Vermont's first European settlement. The state's first Roman Catholic Mass was celebrated here on July 26, 1666. ✉ *W. Shore Rd., Isle La Motte,* ☎ *802/928–3362.* 🎦 *Free.* ⊙ *Mid-May–mid-Oct., daily 9–7.*

On the mainland east of the Alburg Peninsula, the **Missisquoi National Wildlife Refuge** (✉ off Rte. 78, Swanton, 36 mi north of Burlington, ☎ 802/868–4781) consists of 6,300 acres of federally protected wetlands, meadows, and woods. It's a beautiful area for bird-watching, canoeing, or walking nature trails.

Dining and Lodging

$$–$$$ ✕ **Ruthcliffe Lodge & Restaurant.** Good food and splendid scenery make this off-the-beaten-path motel and restaurant overlooking Lake Champlain worth the drive. Owner-chef Mark Infante specializes in Italian pasta, fish, and meat dishes; save room for the homemade desserts. Fixed-price dinners include soup, salad, bread, and coffee or tea. Seven of the nine motel rooms overlook the lake. ✉ *Old Quarry Rd., Isle La Motte,* ☎ *802/928–3200. MC, V. Closed Columbus Day–mid-May. No lunch mid-May–June and Sept.–Columbus Day.*

$$–$$$$ 🏨 **North Hero House Inn and Restaurant.** A classic country inn, North Hero House overlooks Lake Champlain and has four buildings, including the 1891 Colonial Revival main house with nine guest rooms, the restaurant, a pub room, library, and sitting room. Many rooms have water views, and each is decorated with country furnishings and antiques. Dinner is served in the informal glass greenhouse or Colonial-style dining room, or on the glassed-in veranda. Friday evenings in summer there's a lobster bake on the beach. ✉ *U.S. 2, North Hero 05474,* ☎ *802/ 372–4732 or 888/525–3644,* 𝖥𝖠𝖷 *802/372–3218,* 𝖶𝖤𝖡 *www.northherohouse.com. 26 rooms. Restaurant, hot tub, boating, pub, library, meeting rooms; no air-conditioning in some rooms. AE, MC, V. CP.*

$$–$$$ 🏨 **Shore Acres Inn and Restaurant.** This lakefront motel well off the main road has clean, comfortable rooms overlooking the water and ½ mi of private lakeshore. Breakfast and dinner are served in the restaurant overlooking the lake. You have free access to a 9-hole, par-3 golf course. ✉ *U.S. 2, North Hero 05474,* ☎ *802/372–8722,* 𝖶𝖤𝖡 *www.shoreacres.com. 23 rooms. Restaurant, 9-hole golf course, 2 tennis courts. AE, MC, V. Closed Nov.–Apr.; 4 rooms in annex open year-round.*

Outdoor Activities and Sports

BIKING

Bike Shed Rentals (✉ W. Shore Rd., Isle La Motte, ☎ 802/928–3440) rents bikes of all sizes and shapes. **Hero's Welcome** (✉ U.S. 2, North Hero, ☎ 802/372–4161 or 800/372–4376) rents bikes for adults and children.

BOATING

Apple Island Resort (✉ U.S. 2, South Hero, ☎ 802/372–3922) rents sailboats, rowboats, canoes, and motorboats. **Henry's Sportsman's Cottages** (✉ 218 Poor Farm Rd., Alburg, ☎ 802/796–3616) rents motorboats. **Hero's Welcome** (✉ U.S. 2, North Hero, ☎ 802/372–4161 or 800/372–4376) has canoes and kayaks for rent. **Sea Trek Charters** (✉ Tudhope Sailing Center, U.S. 2, Grand Isle, ☎ 802/372–5391) on South Hero Island conducts full-day fishing and sightseeing trips aboard a 25-ft cruiser.

STATE PARKS

Alburg Dunes State Park, one of the state's newest parks, has a sandy beach and some fine examples of rare flora and fauna along the hiking trails. ⊠ *Off U.S. 2, Alburg,* ☎ *802/796–4170.* ☒ *$2.50.* ☉ *Late May–Labor Day, daily dawn–dusk.*

Grand Isle State Park has a fitness trail, hiking trails, and boat rentals. ⊠ *U.S. 2, Grand Isle,* ☎ *802/372–4300.* ☒ *$2.* ☉ *Late May–Labor Day, daily dawn–dusk.*

North Hero State Park's 400 acres hold a swimming beach, nature trail, and campsites. You can rent rowboats and canoes. ⊠ *North Hero,* ☎ *802/372–8727.* ☒ *$2.* ☉ *Late May–Labor Day, daily dawn–dusk.*

Sand Bar State Park, with one of Vermont's best swimming beaches, has a snack bar, changing room, and boat rental concession. ⊠ *U.S. 2, South Hero,* ☎ *802/893–2825.* ☒ *$2 weekdays, $3 weekends.* ☉ *Late May–Labor Day, daily dawn–dusk.*

Shopping

Open July–December, **Allenholm Farm** (⊠ 111 South St., South Hero, ☎ 802/372–5566) has a farm store that stocks local produce.

St. Albans

❷ *18 mi south of Alburg Center.*

Don't let the suburban sprawl on the outskirts of St. Albans fool you. The city's compact Victorian downtown, built during its heyday as a bustling railroad center, is alive with shops, restaurants, and cafés. St. Albans' centerpiece is Taylor Park, a broad green space graced with an ornate bronze fountain and lined with churches and an array of imposing 19th-century municipal buildings. St. Albans was the scene of the northernmost action of the Civil War, an 1864 robbery of the city's banks by a band of Confederate soldiers disguised as civilians. The **St. Albans Historical Museum** is inside an 1861 three-story brick house (⊠ Church St., ☎ 802/527–7933).

Dining and Lodging

$$–$$$ ✕ **Jeff's Maine Seafood.** Long one of the area's best spots for seafood, this deli has an attractive adjoining dining room and serves appetizers such as crispy salmon potato cakes topped with sour cream and caviar and entrées including sautéed sea scallops, plum tomatoes, and scallions in an artichoke Parmesan sauce over linguine. Meat and poultry are also on the menu. A Light Fare menu is available Tuesday, Wednesday, and Thursday evenings. ⊠ *65 N. Main St.,* ☎ *802/524–6135. AE, DC, MC, V. Closed Sun. No dinner Mon.*

$–$$$ ✕ **Chow! Bella.** This narrow, handsomely decorated Victorian parlor of the former St. Albans Opera House complements chef-owner Connie Jacobs Warden's culinary creations. Pastas, individual flatbreads such as Bella Greek Shrimp with tomatoes, calamata olives and spinach, and Black Angus New York strip steak with Gorgonzola Berkshire shiitake sauce are all worth sampling. For dessert, try the baklava cheesecake or Italian walnut tort. ⊠ *28 N. Main St.,* ☎ *802/524–1405. AE, D, MC, V. Closed Sun. No dinner Mon.*

$ ✕ **Kept Writer Book Shop & Café.** Pairing soft classical music and the aroma of freshly brewed coffee with a fine selection of used tomes, this bookstore and café exudes warmth. The menu includes such light fare as sandwich croissants and *spanakopita* (spinach pie), locally baked goodies, and moderately priced wine and beer. It's a cozy retreat perfect for curling up with a good book or the newspaper. ⊠ *5 Lake St.,* ☎ *802/527–6242. MC, V. Closed Mon.*

$$$$ ⌂ **The Tyler Place Family Resort.** Even newborns are kept busy at this family resort on 165 acres overlooking Lake Champlain. The staff provides an ongoing roster of children's programs and daily activities for all ages. Accommodations include two-bedroom family suites in the inn and cottages with two to four bedrooms, decorated with simple country furnishings including colorful quilts, unfussy antiques, and handcrafts. Parents can dine *sans enfants* by candlelight. ⌂ *Old Dock Rd./Rte 7, Highgate Springs 05460,* ☎ *802/868–4000,* FAX *802/868–5621,* WEB *www.tylerplace.com. 29 cabins, 12 suites. Pool, aerobics, boating, biking. One-week minimum stay; $89/child for ages 2½–16. D, MC, V. Closed mid-Sept.–late May. FAP.*

$$ ⌂ **Highgate Manor.** Breakfast is served on the grand veranda overlooking the perennial gardens of this imposing 1850s Victorian mansion just a few minutes from St. Albans. Rooms are decorated with Victorian furnishings with touches such as antique iron bedsteads, claw-foot bathtubs, wicker furniture, antique armoires, and plush settees. Three of the five guest rooms have private baths; one has a gas stove. The Lovers' Suite has a fireplace and huge jetted claw-foot tub. The manor is a popular spot for weddings, parties, and civil union celebrations. ⌂ *464 Highgate Rd./Rte. 207, Highgate Falls 05459,* ☎ *802/868–5610,* FAX *802/868–5610,* WEB *www.highgatemanor.com. 4 rooms, 2 with bath; 1 suite. Library. MC, V. BP.*

Shopping
Rail City Market (⌂ 8 S. Main St.) sells an excellent selection of natural foods, teas, spices and coffees, and body creams and soaps.

Montgomery/Jay

㊸   *51 mi northeast of Burlington.*

Montgomery is a small village near the Canadian border and Jay Peak ski resort. Amid the surrounding countryside are seven historic covered bridges. **Kilgore's Store** (⌂ Main St., Montgomery Center, ☎ 802/326–3058), an old-time country store with an antique soda fountain, is a great place to stock up on picnic supplies, eat a hearty bowl of soup and an overstuffed sandwich, and check out local crafts.

Lodging
$$$ ⌂ **Hotel Jay & Jay Peak Condominiums.** Cheerful simplicity and convenience make this a popular skiers' retreat. Rooms on the southwest side have a view of Jay Peak, and those on the north overlook the valley; upper floors have balconies. The studio to three-bedroom condominiums (most slope-side) have fireplaces, modern kitchens, and washers and dryers. In winter, a minimum two-night stay is required. The meal plan varies during the year; breakfast and dinner are included in ski season. ⌂ *Rte. 242, 05859,* ☎ *802/988–2611; 800/451–4449 outside Vermont;* FAX *802/988–4049,* WEB *www.jaypeakresort.com;. 48 rooms, 94 condominiums. Restaurant, 2 tennis courts, pool, hot tub, sauna, downhill skiing, bar, recreation room, children's programs. AE, D, DC, MC, V. CP, MAP.*

$$ ⌂ **Black Lantern.** Built in 1803 as a stagecoach stop, the inn has been providing bed and board ever since. Though the feeling is country, touches of sophistication abound. All the suites have whirlpools and fireplaces. An outdoor hot tub, sheltered by a gazebo, overlooks the mountains. The restaurant menu includes pan-seared salmon dishes and rack of lamb. ⌂ *Rte. 118, Montgomery Village 05470,* ☎ *802/326–4507 or 800/255–8661,* FAX *802/326–4077,* WEB *www.blacklantern.com. 9 rooms, 6 suites. Restaurant, some cable TV, hot tub, some pets allowed (fee). AE, D, DC, MC, V. BP.*

$$ ⓘ **Inn on Trout River.** Guest rooms at this 100-year-old inn are decorated in either English country cottage style or country Victorian, and all have down quilts and flannel sheets in winter. The back lawn rambles down to the river, and llama treks are available for groups. The restaurant specializes in American and Continental fare with a heart-healthy emphasis. ✉ *Main St., Montgomery Center 05471,* ☎ *802/326–4391 or 800/338–7049,* ℻ *802/326–3194,* 🖥 *www.troutinn.com. 9 rooms, 1 suite. Restaurant, pub, library. AE, D, MC, V. BP, MAP.*

Ski Areas

JAY PEAK

Sticking up out of the flat farmland, Jay averages 351 inches of snowfall a year—more than any other Vermont ski area. Its proximity to Québec attracts Montréalers and discourages eastern seaboarders; hence, the prices are moderate and the lift lines shorter than at other resorts. The area is renowned for its glade skiing, powder, and long season. ✉ *Rte. 242, Jay 05859,* ☎ *802/988–2611; 800/451–4449 outside VT,* 🖥 *www.jaypeakresort.com.*

Downhill. Jay Peak is in fact two mountains with 75 trails, the highest reaching nearly 4,000 ft with a vertical drop of 2,153 ft. The area is served by seven lifts, including Vermont's only tramway, which transports skiers to the top of the mountain in just seven minutes, and the longest detachable quad in the East. The area also has a quad, a triple, and a double chairlift and two T-bars. The smaller mountain has more straight-fall-line, expert terrain, and the tram-side peak has many curving and meandering trails perfectly suited for intermediate and beginning skiers. Jay, highly rated for gladed skiing by major skiing publications, has 19 gladed trails. The longest trail, Ullr's Dream, is 3 mi. Every morning at 9 AM the ski school conducts a free tour, from the tram down one trail. Jay has 75% snowmaking coverage. The area has a halfpipe and snowboard terrain for snowboarders.

Cross-country. A touring center at the base of the mountain has 20 km (12 mi) of groomed cross-country trails. There is a $5 trail fee. A network of 200 km (124 mi) of trails is in the vicinity.

Other activities. Snowshoes and snowmobiles can be rented, and guided walks are led by a naturalist. Telemark rentals and instruction are available.

Child care. The child-care center for youngsters ages 3 to 5 is open from 9 AM to 9 PM. If you're staying at Hotel Jay and the Jay Peak Condominiums, you receive this nursery care free, as well as free skiing for children ages 6 and under, evening care, and supervised dining at the hotel. Infant care is available on a fee basis with advanced reservations. Children ages 5–10 can participate in a daylong Mountain Explorers program, which includes lunch; a MINIrider program for snowboarders ages 5–10 is also available.

Summer activities. Jay Peak runs tram rides to the summit from mid-June through September ($10) and rents mountain bikes.

CROSS-COUNTRY SKIING

Hazen's Notch Cross Country Ski Center and B&B (✉ Rte. 58, ☎ 802/326–4708), delightfully remote at any time of the year, has 50 km (31 mi) of marked and groomed trails and rents equipment and snowshoes.

En Route   The descent from Jay Peak on Route 101 leads to Route 100, which can be the beginning of a scenic loop tour of Routes 14, 5, 58, and back to 100, or it can take you east to the city of Newport on Lake Memphremagog. You will encounter some of the most unspoiled areas in all Vermont on the drive south from Newport on either U.S. 5 or

I–91 (I–91 is faster, but U.S. 5 is prettier). This region, the Northeast Kingdom, is named for the remoteness and stalwart independence that have helped preserve its rural nature.

Newport

44 *20 mi east of Jay Peak.*

From its rough-and-tumble days as a logging town, Newport passed through a long stretch of doldrums and decline before discovering that revitalization lay in taking advantage of its splendid location on the southern shores of Lake Memphremagog, Vermont's second-largest lake (only the southern 3 mi of the lake lie within the state; the northern 30 mi are in Canada). Only a block from the waterfront, downtown's main street has evolved into a busy shopping district. The waterfront city dock has a handsome public boathouse where tours of the lake begin. One of the best ways to explore the lake on both sides of the border is aboard the 49-passenger *Stardust Princess,* which sails from the city dock from mid-May through Labor Day. ⊠ *Newport City Dock,* ☎ *802/334–6617.*

Dining and Lodging

$–$$$ ✕ **The East Side.** With an outdoor deck that overlooks the lake, this popular spot serves American fare such as beef stew and prime rib and specialties such as Crab Chicken—a boneless breast of chicken stuffed with crabmeat and topped with lobster sauce. Homemade soups and desserts also share the menu, and daily specials include overstuffed sandwiches. ⊠ *Lake St.,* ☎ *802/334–2340. D, MC, V.*

$–$$ 🏨 **Newport City Motel.** Rooms at this reasonably priced, two-story motel, a short distance from the center of town, are clean, modern, and nicely furnished. ⊠ *444 E. Main St., 05855,* ☎ *800/338–6558,* fAX *802/334–6557. 64 rooms, 1 suite. Indoor pool, exercise equipment, hot tub, video game room, laundry service. AE, D, DC, MC, V.*

Outdoor Activities and Sports

The **Great Outdoors of Newport** (⊠ 177 Main St., ☎ 802/334–2831) rents boats, kayaks, and canoes, as well as cross-country skis and snowshoes. The store sells fishing supplies and bicycles.

Shopping

Bogner Haus Factory Outlet (⊠ 150 Main St., ☎ 802/334–0135) sells first-quality men's and women's skiwear and golf apparel as well as snowboarding and active wear.

Lake Willoughby

45 *30 mi southeast of Montgomery (summer route; 50 mi by winter route), 28 mi north of St. Johnsbury.*

Flanking the eastern and western shores of Lake Willoughby, the cliffs of surrounding Mts. Pisgah and Hor drop to water's edge, giving this glacially carved, 500-ft-deep lake a striking resemblance to a Norwegian fjord. The beautiful lake is popular for summer and winter recreation, and the trails to the top of Mt. Pisgah reward hikers with glorious views.

The **Bread and Puppet Museum** is a ramshackle barn that houses a surrealistic collection of props used in past performances by the world-renowned Bread and Puppet Theater. The troupe, whose members live communally on the surrounding farm, have been performing social and political commentary with the towering (they're supported by people on stilts), eerily expressive puppets for about 30 years. ⊠ *Rte. 122,*

Glover, 1 mi east of Rte. 16, ☎ 802/525–3031. ✉ Donations accepted.
⊙ June–Oct., daily 9–5; other times by appointment.

Lodging

$$$ 🖃 **WilloughVale Inn.** At the northern end of Lake Willoughby, this hand-some inn, with wraparound veranda, has eight spacious, nicely furnished rooms overlooking the lake. The dining room is open for dinner Thursday–Saturday in winter, Thursday–Monday in summer. The shore-front housekeeping cottages have fireplaces, screened porches, and private docks and sleep up to four persons. Cottages rent by the week in July and August. ⊠ *Rte. 5A, Westmore 05860, ☎ 802/525–4123 or 800/594–9102, ℻ 802/525–4514, ₩ₑʙ www.willoughvale.com. 8 rooms, 4 cottages. Dining room, boating. AE, MC, V. CP.*

East Burke

46 *17 mi south of Lake Willoughby.*

A jam-packed general store, a post office, and a couple of great places to eat are in the center of East Burke, near the Burke Mountain ski area. A major attraction is the 100 mi of old logging, fire, and country roads, which are good for self-guided hiking, mountain biking, cross-country skiing, and snowshoeing. The **Kingdom Trails Association** (⊠ Box 204, East Burke 05832, ☎ 802/626–0737, ₩ₑʙ www.kingdomtrails. org) manages the trails and provides information.

Dining and Lodging

$$–$$$ ✗ **River Garden Café.** You can eat outdoors on the enclosed porch or the patio and view the perennial gardens that rim the grounds, or dine inside the bright and cheerful café. The fare includes lamb tenderloin, warm artichoke dip, bruschetta, pastas, and fresh fish. A lighter menu is served nightly. ⊠ *Rte. 114, East Burke, ☎ 802/626–3514. AE, D, MC, V. Closed Mon., Nov., and 1 wk in Apr.*

$$$ ✗🖃 **Inn at Mountain View Farm.** The renovated 1890 creamery on a hilltop amid 440 acres of hills and meadows has second-floor guest rooms handsomely furnished with antiques and handmade quilts. Cross-country ski, snowshoe, hiking, and mountain-biking trails are right at the doorstep. Darling's Country Bistro ($$–$$$; no lunch Thurs.–Sun.) serves hearty fare such as beef carbonnade with caramelized onions as well as fish and vegetarian dishes. ⊠ *Darling Hill Rd. (Box 355, 05832), ☎ 802/626–9924 or 800/572–4509, ₩ₑʙ www.innmtnview. com. 15 rooms. Restaurant, hiking, cross-country skiing, sleigh rides, meeting room; no air-conditioning in some rooms. AE, MC, V. Closed Apr. and Nov. BP.*

$$ ✗🖃 **Wildflower Inn.** The hilltop views are breathtaking at this ram-
★ bling, family-oriented complex of old farm buildings on 500 acres. Guest rooms in the restored Federal-style main house and three other build-ings are furnished with reproductions and contemporary furnishings. Rooms in the carriage house have kitchenettes and bunk beds. The restau-rant ($$–$$$) serves dishes such as a seasonal tricolor peppercorn-cognac breast of duck and blackened prime rib. ⊠ *2059 Darling Hill Rd., west of East Burke, Lyndonville 05851, ☎ 802/626–8310 or 800/627–8310, ℻ 802/626–3039, ₩ₑʙ www.wildflowerinn.com. 10 rooms, 11 suites. Restaurant, tennis court, pool, hot tub, sauna, fishing, soccer, ice-skating, skiing, sleigh rides, snowmobiling, recreation rooms, meeting room; no air-conditioning in some rooms. MC, V. Closed Apr. and Nov. BP.*

$ ✗🖃 **Old Cutter Inn.** Inside this small converted farmhouse only ½ mi from the Burke Mountain base lodge are quaint inn rooms in the main building and comfortable, if less charming, accommodations in an annex. The restaurant ($$–$$$) serves fare that reflects the Swiss chef-owner's heritage, as well as superb, good-value Continental cuisine including osso buco, chateaubriand, and veal piccata. ✉ *143 Pinkham Rd., 05832,* ☎ *802/626–5152 or 800/295–1943,* WEB *www.pbpub.com/cutter.htm. 9 rooms, 5 with bath; 1 suite. Restaurant, pool, hiking, bicycles, cross-country skiing, bar. D, MC, V. Restaurant closed Wed., Apr., and Nov. MAP.*

Outdoor Activities and Sports

Village Sport Shop (✉ 4 Broad St., Lyndonville, ☎ 802/626–8448) rents canoes, kayaks, bikes, rollerblades, paddleboats, snowshoes, and cross-country and downhill skis.

Shopping

Bailey's & Burke, Inc. (✉ Rte. 114, ☎ 802/626–9250) sells baked goods, pizza and sandwiches, wine, clothing, and sundries.

Ski Areas

BURKE MOUNTAIN

This low-key, moderately priced resort has plenty of terrain for beginners, but intermediate skiers, experts, racers, telemarkers, and snowboarders will find time-honored narrow New England trails. Many packages at Burke are significantly less expensive than those at other Vermont areas. ✉ *Mountain Rd., East Burke 05832,* ☎ *802/626–3322; 802/626–1390 snow conditions; 802/748–6137 reservations,* WEB *www.skiburke.com.*

Downhill. With a 2,000-ft vertical drop and 43 trails and glades, Burke is something of a sleeper among the larger Eastern ski areas. It has greatly increased its snowmaking capability (76%), which is enhanced by the mountain's northern location and exposure, assuring plenty of natural snow. A 5-acre snowboard park (with a halfpipe and snowmaking capabilities) invites all levels. Burke has one quad, one double chairlift, and two surface lifts. Lift lines, even on weekends and holidays, are light to nonexistent.

Child care. In the Children's Center, the nursery takes children ages 6 months–6 years on weekends and holidays. SKIwee and MINIriders lessons through the ski school are available to children ages 4–16.

Summer activities. Hiking, biking (rentals are available), and a children's swing are summer options.

CROSS-COUNTRY SKIING

Burke Ski Touring Center (☎ 802/626–8338) has 80 km (50 mi) of trails (65 km [39 mi] groomed); some lead to high points with scenic views. There's a snack bar at the center.

St. Johnsbury

🜨 *16 mi south of East Burke, 39 mi northeast of Montpelier.*

St. Johnsbury is the southern gateway to the Northeast Kingdom. Though the town was chartered in 1786, its identity was not firmly established until 1830, when Thaddeus Fairbanks invented the platform scale, a device that revolutionized weighing methods that had been in use since the beginning of recorded history. Because of the Fairbanks family's philanthropic efforts, the city, with its distinctly 19th-century industrial feel, has a strong cultural and architectural imprint.

Opened in 1891, the **Fairbanks Museum and Planetarium** attests to the Fairbanks family's inquisitiveness about all things scientific. The red-brick building in the squat Romanesque Revival architectural style of H. H. Richardson houses Vermont plants and animals, as well as ethnographic and natural history collections from around the globe.

There's also a 50-seat planetarium and a hands-on exhibit room for kids. On the third Saturday in September, the museum sponsors the Festival of Traditional Crafts, with demonstrations of early American household and farm skills such as candle and soap making. ⊠ *Main and Prospect Sts.,* ☎ *802/748–2372,* WEB *www.fairbanksmuseum.org.* 🖾 *Museum $5, planetarium $3.* ☉ *Mon.–Sat. 9–4, Sun. 1–5. Planetarium shows July–Aug., daily at 11 and 1:30; Sept.–June, weekends at 1:30.*

★ The **St. Johnsbury Athenaeum,** with its dark rich paneling, polished Victorian woodwork, and ornate circular staircases that rise to the gallery around the perimeter, is one of the oldest art galleries in the country. The gallery at the back of the building specializes in Hudson River School paintings and has the overwhelming *Domes of Yosemite* by Albert Bierstadt. ⊠ *1171 Main St.,* ☎ *802/748–8291,* WEB *www.stjathenaeum.org.* 🖾 *Free.* ☉ *Mon. and Wed. 10–8, Tues. and Thurs.–Fri. 10–5:30, Sat. 9:30–4.*

Take a tour of the world's oldest and largest maple candy factory at **Maple Grove Maple Museum and Factory.** Be sure to visit the museum, where a film shows how maple syrup is made. ⊠ *1052 Portland St., Rte 2,* ☎ *802/748–5141,* WEB *www.maplegrove.com.* 🖾 *Tour $1.* ☉ *Daily 8–3.*

Dog Mountain is artist–dog lover Stephen Huneck's art gallery (works are for sale) and sculpture garden, complete with a chapel where humans and their canine companions can meditate. ⊠ *Off Spaulding Rd.,* ☎ *802/748–2700 or 800/449–2580,* WEB *www.huneck.com.* 🖾 *Free.* ☉ *June–Oct., Mon.–Sat. 10–5, Sun. 11–4, and by appointment.*

OFF THE
BEATEN PATH

CABOT CREAMERY – The biggest cheese producer in the state, a dairy cooperative, has a visitor center with an audiovisual presentation about the dairy and cheese industry. You can taste samples, purchase cheese, and tour the plant. The center is midway between Barre and St. Johnsbury. ⊠ *2870 Main St./Rte. 215, 3 mi north of U.S. 2, Cabot,* ☎ *802/563–3393; 800/639–4031 orders only.* 🖾 *$1.* ☉ *June–Oct., daily 9–5; Nov.–Dec. and Feb.–May, Mon.–Sat. 9–4; call ahead to check cheese-making days.*

Dining and Lodging

$$$$ ✕🖾 **Rabbit Hill Inn.** Many of the elegant rooms at this classic, white-
★ columned inn have fireplaces and views of the Connecticut River and New Hampshire's White Mountains. The intimate candlelit dining room serves a five-course fixed-price dinner ($$$$) featuring contemporary new American and regional dishes such as grilled venison loin with cranberry juniper orange glaze. Meat and fish are smoked on the premises. ⊠ *Rte. 18, Lower Waterford, 11 mi south of St. Johnsbury, 05848,* ☎ *802/748–5168 or 800/762–8669,* FAX *802/748–8342,* WEB *www.rabbithillinn.com. 19 rooms. Restaurant, some in-room hot tubs, hiking, cross-country skiing, pub; no kids under 13. AE, MC, V. Closed 1st 3 wks in Apr., 1st 2 wks in Nov. MAP.*

$$ 🖾 **Emergo Farm.** Bebo and Lori Webster rent out three guest rooms in their 1890, 15-room farmhouse on a 240-acre dairy farm that has been in the Webster family for five generations. Lori collects antiques, which are liberally sprinkled throughout the house and in the second-floor guest rooms. One room has its own bath. The other two, which share a bath, have a kitchen and can be rented out as a suite to sleep up to six. The view from the hilltop picnic grove is spectacular. ⊠ *261 Webster Hill Rd., Danville 05828,* ☎ *802/684–2215. 3 rooms, 1 with bath. BP.*

Shopping

The **Trout River Brewing Co.** (⌂ 58 Broad St., Lyndonville, ☎ 802/626–9396 or 888/296–2739) brews all-natural premium ales and lagers and has six styles on tap daily. The tasting room is open Wednesday–Sunday 11 AM–6 PM.

Peacham

48   *10 mi southwest of St. Johnsbury.*

Tiny Peacham's stunning scenery and 18th-century charm have made it a favorite with urban refugees, artists seeking solitude and inspiration, and movie directors looking for the quintessential New England village. *Ethan Frome*, starring Liam Neeson, was filmed here.

Gourmet soups and hearty lamb and barley stew are among the seasonally changing take-out specialties at the **Peacham Store** (⌂ Main St., ☎ 802/592–3310). You can browse through the locally made crafts while waiting for your order. Next door, the **Peacham Corner Guild** sells local handcrafts.

Barre

49   *7 mi southeast of Montpelier, 35 mi southwest of St. Johnsbury.*

Barre has been famous as the source of Vermont granite ever since two men began working the quarries in the early 1800s; the number of immigrant laborers attracted to the industry made the city prominent in the early years of the American labor movement. Downtown, at the corner of Maple and North Main, look for the statue of a representative Italian stonecutter of a century ago. On Route 14, just north of Barre, stop at Hope Cemetery to see spectacular examples of carving.

The attractions of the **Rock of Ages granite quarry** range from the awe-inspiring (the quarry resembles the Grand Canyon in miniature) to the mildly ghoulish (you can consult a directory of tombstone dealers throughout the country). You might recognize the sheer walls of the quarry from *Batman and Robin,* the film starring George Clooney and Arnold Schwarzenegger. At the crafts center, skilled artisans sculpt monuments; at the quarries themselves, 25-ton blocks of stone are cut from sheer 475-ft walls by workers who clearly earn their pay. ⌂ *Exit 6 off I–89, follow Rte. 63,* ☎ *802/476–3119.* ⊡ *Tour of active quarry $4, craftsman center and self-guided tour free.* ☉ *Visitor center May–Oct., Mon.–Sat. 8:30–5, Sun. noon–5; narrated tours every 45 mins 9:15–3 weekdays June–mid-Oct.*

Dining and Lodging

$–$$ ✕ **A Single Pebble.** Chef and co-owner Steve Bogart has been cooking creative, authentic Asian dishes for more than 30 years. He prepares traditional clay-pot dishes as well as wok specialties such as sesame catfish and kung po chicken. The dry fried green beans (sautéed with flecks of pork, black beans, preserved vegetables, and garlic) is a house specialty. All dishes can be made without meat. ⌂ *135 Barre–Montpelier Rd.,* ☎ *802/476–9700. Reservations essential. D, MC, V. Closed Sun.–Mon. No lunch.*

$$ ✕⌂ **Autumn Harvest Inn.** You'll be tempted to spend the whole day on the porch that graces the front of this casual inn, built in 1790. It sits atop a knoll overlooking a 46-acre workhorse farm and the surrounding valley. Rooms are functional and uncluttered, with an emphasis on comfort and simplicity. One suite has a fireplace. Prime rib and veal dishes are among the highlights of the seasonal country menu at the restaurant ($$–$$$; no lunch), where dinner is served by candlelight Tuesday–Saturday (Wednesday–Saturday in winter). ⊠ *118 Clark Rd., Williamstown 05679,* ☎ *802/433–1355,* FAX *802/433– 5501,* WEB *www.central-vt.com/web/autumn. 18 rooms. Restaurant, pond, horseback riding, cross-country skiing, sleigh rides, bar, some pets allowed. AE, MC, V. MAP.*

Northern Vermont A to Z

To research prices, get advice from other travelers, and book travel ar- rangements, visit www.fodors.com.

BOAT AND FERRY TRAVEL

Lake Champlain Ferries, in operation since 1826, operates three ferry crossings during the summer months and one—between Grand Isle and Plattsburgh, New York—in winter through thick lake ice. Ferries leave from the King Street Dock in Burlington, Charlotte, and Grand Isle. This is a convenient means of getting to and from New York State, as well as a pleasant way to spend an afternoon.

➤ BOAT AND FERRY INFORMATION: **Lake Champlain Ferries** (☎ 802/864– 9804).

BUS TRAVEL

Vermont Transit links Burlington, Waterbury, Montpelier, St. Johns- bury, and Newport.

➤ BUS INFORMATION: **Vermont Transit** (☎ 800/231–2222 or 802/864– 6811).

CAR TRAVEL

In north-central Vermont, I–89 heads west from Montpelier to Burling- ton and continues north to Canada. Interstate 91 is the principal north–south route in the east, and Route 100 runs north–south through the center of the state. North of I–89, Routes 104 and 15 provide a major east–west transverse. From Barton, near Lake Willoughby, U.S. 5 and Route 122 south are beautiful drives. Strip-mall drudge bogs down the section of U.S. 5 around Lyndonville.

EMERGENCIES

➤ HOSPITALS AND EMERGENCY SERVICES: **Copley Hospital** (⊠ Washington Hwy., Morrisville, ☎ 802/999–4231). **Fletcher Allen Health Care** (⊠ 111 Colchester Ave., Burlington, ☎ 802/847–2434), 24-hour emergency health care information. **Northeastern Vermont Regional Hospital** (⊠ Hospital Dr., St. Johnsbury, ☎ 802/748–8141).

OUTDOOR ACTIVITIES AND SPORTS
HIKING
The Green Mountain Club maintains the Long Trail—the north–south border-to-border footpath that runs the length of the spine of the Green Mountains—as well as other trails nearby. The club headquar- ters sells maps and guides, and experts dispense advice.

➤ CONTACT: **Green Mountain Club** (⊠ Rte. 100, Waterbury, ☎ 802/ 244–7037).

TOURS

P.O.M.G. Bike Tours of Vermont leads weekend and five-day adult camp- ing-bike tours. True North Kayak Tours operates a guided tour of Lake Champlain and a natural-history tour and will arrange a custom mul- tiday trip. The company also coordinates special trips for kids.

➤ TOUR OPERATORS: **P.O.M.G. Bike Tours of Vermont** (⊠ Richmond, ☎ 802/434–2270). **True North Kayak Tours** (⊠ 53 Nash Pl., Burling- ton, ☎ 802/860–1910).

TRAIN TRAVEL

The *Champlain Flyer* transports passengers between Burlington and Charlotte—with a stop in Shelburne—in just 25 minutes. Fare is $1 one-way, and $2 round-trip. The *Champlain Valley Weekender* runs between Middlebury and Burlington, with stops in Vergennes and Shelburne. The views from the coach cars, which date from the 1930s, are of Lake Champlain, the valley farmlands, and surrounding mountains.

➤ TRAIN INFORMATION: *Champlain Flyer* (☎ 802/951–4010). *Champlain Valley Weekender* (☎ 802/463–3069 or 800/707–3530).

VISITOR INFORMATION

➤ TOURIST INFORMATION: **Lake Champlain Islands Chamber of Commerce** (✉ 3537 Rte. 2, Suite 100 [Box 213, North Hero 05474], ☎ 802/372–5683, WEB www.Champlain Islands.com). **Lake Champlain Regional Chamber of Commerce** (✉ 60 Main St., Suite 100, Burlington 05401, ☎ 802/863–3489 or 877/686–5253, WEB www.vermont.org). **Northeast Kingdom Chamber of Commerce** (✉ 357 Western Ave., St. Johnsbury 05819, ☎ 802/748–3678 or 800/639–6379, WEB www. vermontnekchamber.org). **Northeast Kingdom Travel and Tourism Association** (✉ Box 465, Barton 05822, ☎ 802/525–4386 or 888/884–8001, WEB www.travelthekingdom.com). **Smugglers' Notch Area Chamber of Commerce** (✉ Box 364, Jeffersonville 05464, ☎ 802/644–2239, WEB www.smugnotch.com). The **Stowe Area Association** (✉ Main St. [Box 1320, Stowe 05672], ☎ 802/253–7321 or 877/603–8693, WEB www.stoweinfo.com). **Vermont North Country Chamber of Commerce** (✉ The Causeway, Newport 05855, ☎ 802/334–7782 or 800/635–4643, WEB www.vtnorthcountry.com).

VERMONT A TO Z

To research prices, get advice from other travelers, and book travel arrangements, visit www.fodors.com.

AIRPORTS AND TRANSFERS

Continental, Delta, United, Jet Blue, and US Airways fly into Burlington International Airport (BTV). Rutland State Airport (RUT) has daily service to and from Boston on US Airways Express. West of Bennington and convenient to southern Vermont, Albany International Airport (ALB) in New York State is served by 10 major U.S. carriers.

➤ AIRPORT INFORMATION: **Albany International Airport** (✉ 737 Albany Shaker Rd., Albany, ☎ 518/869–3021, WEB www.albanyairport.com). **Burlington International Airport** (✉ Airport Dr., 4 mi east of Burlington off U.S. 2, ☎ 802/863–2874). **Rutland State Airport** (✉ 1002 Airport Rd., North Clarendon, ☎ 802/747–7101).

AIRPORT TRANSFERS

Aircraft charters are available at Burlington International Airport from Heritage Flight Services. Mansfield Heliflight provides helicopter transportation throughout New England. Chittenden Country Transportation Authority buses connect Burlington International Airport with downtown Burlington. Buses leave the airport for the downtown depot at Cherry and Church streets at 10 minutes after and 20 minutes before each hour, 6:15 AM–10:30 PM; they leave downtown at 15 minutes before and 5 minutes after the hour.

➤ SHUTTLES: **Chittenden Country Transportation Authority** (☎ 802/864–0211). **Heritage Flight Services** (☎ 802/863–3626 or 800/782–0773, WEB www.heritageflgt.com). **Mansfield Heliflight** (✉ Milton, ☎ 802/893–1003 or 800/872–0884, WEB www.mansfieldheliflight.com).

BIKE TRAVEL

Vermont is a popular destination for cyclists, who find villages and towns—with their inns, B&Bs, and restaurants—spaced closely enough for comfortable traveling. Secondary roads in the western part of the state, in the relatively gentle terrain of the Champlain Valley and islands, are best for cyclists who prefer not to be challenged by steep hills. Roads that follow the major east–west river valleys—the Winooski, Lamoille and Missisquoi—are similarly forgiving. For cyclists in top shape, hundreds of miles of twisting blacktop and gravel roads crisscross the Green Mountains. Especially challenging are Middlebury, Lincoln and Brandon gaps in north-central Vermont, and punishing Smugglers' Notch north of Stowe.

In general, touring bikes with 10 or more gears are preferable; for gravel roads, hybrid or mountain bikes are recommended. Several of the larger ski areas, such as Killington, Smugglers' Notch, and Jay Peak, as well as the Green Mountain National Forest maintain mountain bike trails.

BUS TRAVEL

Bonanza Bus Lines connects New York City and Providence with Bennington. Service is twice daily (morning and afternoon) from each city. Vermont Transit connects Bennington, Brattleboro, Burlington, Rutland, and other Vermont cities and towns with Boston, Springfield, Albany, New York, Montréal, and cities in New Hampshire. Local service in Burlington and surrounding communities is provided by Chittenden County Transportation Authority.

➤ BUS INFORMATION: **Bonanza Bus Lines** (☎ 800/556–3815). **Chittenden Country Transportation Authority** (☎ 802/864–0211). **Vermont Transit** (☎ 800/552–8737).

CAR TRAVEL

Interstate 91, which stretches from Connecticut and Massachusetts in the south to Québec in the north, reaches most points along Vermont's eastern border. Interstate–89, from New Hampshire to the east and Québec to the north, crosses central Vermont from White River Junction to Burlington. Southwestern Vermont can be reached by U.S. 7 from Massachusetts and U.S. 4 from New York.

The official speed limit in Vermont is 50 mph, unless otherwise posted; on the interstates it's 65 mph. Right turns are permitted on a red light unless otherwise indicated. You can get a state map, which has mileage charts and enlarged maps of major downtown areas, free from the Vermont Department of Tourism and Marketing. The *Vermont Atlas and Gazetteer,* sold in many bookstores, shows nearly every road in the state and is great for driving on the back roads.

CHILDREN IN VERMONT

Popular attractions such as the Shelburne Museum, Shelburne Farms, Montshire Museum of Science, Billings Farm and Museum, and Southern Vermont Art Center frequently host events for children; inquire directly or check local newspapers. Larger, family-oriented resorts such as the Basin Harbor Club, Tyler Place, Smugglers' Notch, and Mountain Meadows Lodge have ongoing children's programs with full supervision.

BABY-SITTING

Baby-sitting agencies are uncommon in Vermont. Instead, parents generally rely on services provided or arranged by hotels and resorts. Rates generally run $8–$10 per hour, more if more than one child is involved.

EMERGENCIES

➤ EMERGENCY SERVICES: **Ambulance, fire, police** (☎ 911). **Vermont Poison Control Center** (✉ Burlington, ☎ 802/847–3456). **Vermont State Police** (☎ 800/525–5555).

LODGING

The Vermont Chamber of Commerce (☞ Visitor Information) publishes the *Vermont Travelers' Guidebook*, which is an extensive list of lodgings, and additional guides to country inns and vacation rentals. The Vermont Department of Tourism and Marketing (☞ Visitor Information) has a brochure that lists lodgings at working farms.

CAMPING

Call Vermont's Department of Forests, Parks, and Recreation for a copy of the "Vermont Campground Guide," which lists state parks and other public and private camping facilities. Call the following numbers from the second Tuesday in January through May 1; after that, call the individual parks. Between Labor Day and January, reservations are not accepted.

➤ CONTACTS: **Department of Forests, Parks, and Recreation** (☎ 802/241–3655; ☎ 802/885–8891 or 800/299–3071 in southeastern Vermont; ☎ 802/483–2001 or 800/658–1622 in southwestern Vermont; ☎ 802/879–5674 or 800/252–2363 in northwestern Vermont; ☎ 802/479–4280 or 800/658–6934 in northeastern Vermont).

MEDIA

Vermont's largest newspaper, available throughout the state, is the *Burlington Free Press*, a member of the Gannett chain. For upcoming event and performances, see its Thursday "Weekend" section. The *Rutland Herald*, winner of a 2001 Pulitzer Prize for editorial writing, carries *New York Times* wire service stories and is also available throughout much of the state. *Seven Days* is a Burlington-based, free alternative weekly with wide distribution and extensive arts and entertainment listings.

Vermont's two leading magazines are *Vermont Life*, published quarterly by the state, and the privately owned *Vermont*, a bimonthly that covers political as well as lifestyle issues and has a more upscale slant. *Yankee*, published 10 times yearly in Dublin, New Hampshire, covers all New England and has events listings for each state.

Vermont television stations include affiliates of CBS (WCAX, channel 7); NBC (WPTZ, channel 5); ABC (WVNY, channel 22); and Fox (channel 44). Vermont Public Television is on channel 33 throughout much of the state. Vermont Public Radio (VPR) broadcasts local and National Public Radio (NPR) programs through the state; frequency is 107.9 through much of northern Vermont; check local newspaper listings for frequencies elsewhere. Northern Vermont listeners can also pick up the excellent programming of the Canadian Broadcasting Company (CBC) at frequency 93.5.

OUTDOOR ACTIVITIES AND SPORTS

A hot line has tips on peak viewing locations and times and up-to-date snow conditions.

➤ CONTACT: **Foliage and Snow Hot Line** (☎ 802/828–3239).

CANOEING

Umiak Outdoor Outfitters has shuttles to nearby rivers for day excursions and customized overnight trips. Vermont Canoe Trippers/Battenkill Canoe, Ltd. organizes canoe tours (some are inn-to-inn) and fishing trips.

➤ CONTACTS: **Umiak Outdoor Outfitters** (✉ 849 S. Main St., Stowe, ☎ 802/253–2317). **Vermont Canoe Trippers/Battenkill Canoe, Ltd.** (✉ River Rd., off Rte. 7A, Arlington, ☎ 802/362–2800).

FISHING

For information about fishing, including licenses, call the Vermont Fish and Wildlife Department. Strictly Trout will arrange a fly-fishing trip on any Vermont stream or river, including the Battenkill.
➤ CONTACTS: **Strictly Trout** (☎ 802/869–3116). **Vermont Fish and Wildlife Department** (☎ 802/241–3700, WEB www.anr.state.vt.us/fur/furhome).

HIKING

The Green Mountain Club publishes hiking maps and guides. The club also manages the Long Trail, the north–south trail that traverses the entire state.
➤ CONTACT: **Green Mountain Club** (✉ Rte. 100, Waterbury, ☎ 802/244–7037, WEB www.greenmountainclub.org).

HORSEBACK RIDING

Kedron Valley Stables has one- to six-day riding tours with lodging in country inns.
➤ CONTACT: **Kedron Valley Stables** (✉ South Woodstock, ☎ 802/457–1480 or 800/225–6301).

SKIING

For information, contact Ski Vermont/Vermont Ski Area Association.
➤ CONTACT: **Ski Vermont/Vermont Ski Area Association** (✉ 26 State St. [Box 368, Montpelier 05601], ☎ 802/223–2439, WEB www.skivermont.com).

STATE PARKS

Vermont state parks open during the last week in May and close after the Labor Day or Columbus Day weekend, depending on location. Day-use charges are $2.50 per person for ages 14 and up, $2 for ages 4–13; children under 4 are free. Call individual parks or the Department of Forests, Parks, and Recreation for information.
➤ CONTACT: **Department of Forests, Parks, and Recreation** (☎ 802/241–3655, WEB www.vtstateparks.com).

TOURS

Bicycle Holidays helps you plan your own inn-to-inn tour by providing route directions and booking your accommodations. Vermont Bicycle Touring leads numerous tours in the state and the region. New England Hiking Holidays leads guided walks with lodging in country inns. North Wind Hiking and Walking Tours conducts guided walking tours through Vermont's countryside.
➤ TOUR OPERATORS: **Bicycle Holidays** (✉ Munger St., Middlebury, ☎ 802/388–2453 or 800/292–5388). **New England Hiking Holidays** (✉ North Conway, NH, ☎ 603/356–9696 or 800/869–0949). **North Wind Hiking and Walking Tours** (✉ Waitsfield, ☎ 802/496–5771 or 800/496–5771). **Vermont Bicycle Touring** (✉ Monkton Rd., Bristol, ☎ 802/453–4811 or 800/245–3868).

TRAIN TRAVEL

Amtrak's *Vermonter* is a daytime service linking Washington, D.C., with Brattleboro, Bellows Falls, White River Junction, Montpelier, Waterbury, Essex Junction, and St. Albans. The *Adirondack,* which runs from Washington, D.C., to Montréal, serves Albany, Ft. Edward (near Glens Falls), Ft. Ticonderoga, and Plattsburgh, allowing relatively convenient access to western Vermont. The *Ethan Allen Express* connects New York City with Fair Haven and Rutland.

➤ Train Information: **Amtrak** (☎ 800/872–7245, WEB www.amtrak. com).

VISITOR INFORMATION

➤ Tourist Information: **Forest Supervisor, Green Mountain National Forest** (✉ 231 N. Main St., Rutland 05701, ☎ 802/747–6700). **Vermont Chamber of Commerce** (✉ Box 37, Montpelier 05601, ☎ 802/223–3443). **Vermont Department of Tourism and Marketing** (✉ 134 State St., Montpelier 05602, ☎ 802/828–3237 or 800/837–6668). There are **state information centers** on the Massachusetts border at I–91, the New Hampshire border at I–89, the New York border at Route 4A, and the Canadian border at I–89.

4 NEW HAMPSHIRE

Ocean, mountains, lakes—New Hampshire has them all. The engaging coastal city of Portsmouth is a gateway to smaller towns with sandy beaches. The Lakes Region is a summer and fall haven for fishing, swimming, and boating. The White Mountains attract people who come to gaze on Mt. Washington; the East's tallest peak, to ski and snowboard, to hike, and to shop at North Conway's outlet stores. Western and central New Hampshire have a string of cities along I–93 as well as unspoiled historical villages.

By Paula J. Flanders

Updated and revised by Andrew Collins

CRUSTY, AUTONOMOUS NEW HAMPSHIRE is often defined more by what it is not than by what it is. It lacks Vermont's folksy charm, and its coast isn't nearly as grand as that of Maine. Its politics tend toward conservative (with a distinctly libertarian slant), unlike the decidedly more liberal Massachusetts. It was the first colony to declare independence from Great Britain, the first to adopt a state constitution, and the first to require that constitution to be referred to the people for approval.

From the start, New Hampshire residents took their hard-won freedoms seriously. Twenty years after the Revolutionary War's Battle of Bennington, New Hampshire native Gen. John Stark, who led the troops to that crucial victory, wrote a letter to be read at the reunion he was too ill to attend. In it, he reminded his men, "Live free or die; death is not the worst of evils." The first half of that sentiment is now the Granite State's motto. Nothing symbolizes those freedoms more than voting, not only for government officials but also on issues during an annual town meeting. And residents truly relish their role as host of the nation's earliest presidential primary.

New Hampshire's independent spirit, mountain peaks, clear air, and sparkling lakes have attracted trailblazers and artists for centuries. The first hiker to reach the top of Mt. Washington was Darby Field, in 1642. The first summer home appeared on one of the state's many lakes in 1763. Ralph Waldo Emerson, Henry David Thoreau, Nathaniel Hawthorne, and Louisa May Alcott all visited and wrote about the state, sparking a strong literary tradition that continues today. Filmmaker Ken Burns, writer J. D. Salinger, and poet Donald Hall all make their homes here.

Portsmouth has several theater groups, both cutting-edge and mainstream. New Hampshire's oldest professional troupe, Tamworth's Barnstormers, claims the son of a president as its founder. Shops throughout the state often display the work of local artisans. On back roads and in small towns, you can find makers of fine furniture, glassblowers, potters, weavers, and woodworkers. The League of New Hampshire Craftsmen operates eight stores and runs the nation's oldest crafts fair each year in early August.

The state's diverse terrain makes it popular with everyone from avid adventurers to young families looking for easy access to nature. You can ski, snowboard, hike, and fish as well as explore on snowmobiles, sailboats, and mountain bikes. Rock climbing and snowshoeing are popular, too. Natives have no objection to others' enjoying the state's beauty as long as they leave some money behind. New Hampshire has long resisted both sales and income taxes, so tourism adds much-needed revenue to the government coffers.

With a few of its cities consistently rated among the most livable in the nation, New Hampshire has seen considerable growth over the past decade or two. Longtime residents worry that the state will soon take on two personalities: one of rapidly growing cities to the southeast and the other of quiet villages to the west and north. Although the influx of newcomers has brought change, the independent nature of the people and the state's natural beauty remain constant.

Pleasures and Pastimes

Dining

New Hampshire prides itself on seafood—not just lobster but also salmon pie, steamed mussels, fried clams, and seared tuna. Across the state you'll

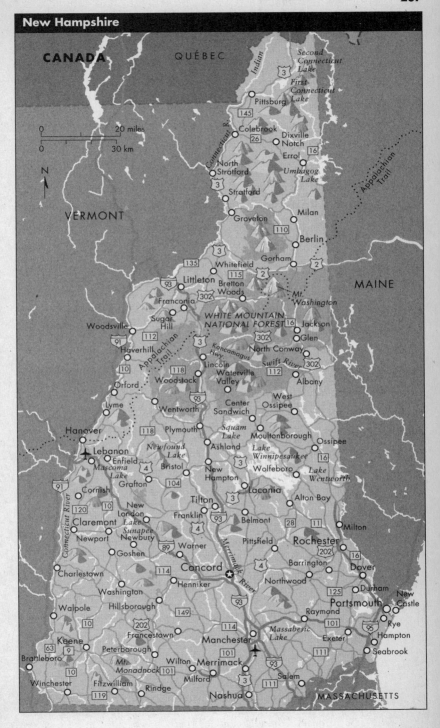

New Hampshire

find country taverns with upscale Continental and American menus, many of them embracing regional ingredients and cutting-edge preparations. Alongside a growing number of contemporary eateries are such state traditions as greasy-spoon diners, pizzerias, and pubs that serve hearty comfort fare.

CATEGORY	COST*
$$$$	over $25
$$$	$17–$25
$$	$9–$16
$	under $9

*per person, for a main-course dinner

Lodging

In the mid-19th century, wealthy Bostonians took imposing country homes during the summer months. Many of these houses have been converted into handsome inns. The smallest have only a couple of rooms and are typically done in period style. The largest contain 30 or more rooms and have in-room fireplaces and even hot tubs. Pampering amenities increase each year at some of these inns, which, along with bed-and-breakfasts, dominate New Hampshire's lodging scene. You'll also find a great many well-kept, often family-owned motor lodges—particularly in the White Mountains and Lakes regions. A few of the grand old resorts still stand, with their world-class cooking staffs and tradition of top-notch service. In the Merrimack River valley, as well as along major highways, chain hotels and motels prevail.

CATEGORY	COST
$$$$	over $180
$$$	$130–$180
$$	$80–$130
$	under $80

*All prices are for a standard double room during peak season and not including tax or gratuities. Some inns add a 15% service charge.

National and State Parks and Forests

The awesome White Mountain National Forest covers 770,000 acres in northern New Hampshire, and Mt. Washington Park crowns the Northeast's highest peak. You can camp, picnic, hike, fish, swim, bike, and ski at numerous other park and recreation areas, including Franconia Notch, Crawford Notch, and Mt. Sunapee. Rhododendron State Park, in Fitzwilliam in the Monadnock region, has a singular collection of wild rhododendrons.

Outdoor Activities and Sports

BEACHES AND LAKES

New Hampshire makes the most of its 18-mi coastline with several good beaches, among them Hampton Beach and Wallis Sands in Rye. For warmer, fresh waters, head to pristine Lake Winnipesaukee, Lake Sunapee, Squam Lake, and Newfound Lake.

BIKING

A safe, scenic route along New Hampshire's seacoast is the bike path along Route 1A, for which you can park at Odiorne Point and follow the road 14 mi south to Seabrook. (Some bikers begin at Prescott Park in Portsmouth and take Route 1B into New Castle, but beware of the traffic.) Another pretty route is from Newington Town Hall to the Great Bay Estuary. White Mountains routes are detailed in "The White Mountain Ride Guide," sold at area sports and bookshops. There's also a bike path in Franconia Notch State Park at the Lafayette Campground and a mountain-biking center, Great Glen Trails, at the base of Mt. Washington. Many ski areas have lift-serviced mountain biking in summer.

FISHING

Brook and rainbow trout, salmon, smallmouth bass, pickerel, and horned pout are just some of the species that swim in the fresh waters of the Lakes, Sunapee, and Monadnock regions. In winter, ice fishing from huts known as "ice bobs" is common throughout the state. Alton Bay has an "Ice Out" salmon derby in spring. Between April and October, deep-sea anglers take to the ocean for cod, mackerel, and bluefish.

SKIING AND SNOW SPORTS

Scandinavian settlers who came to New Hampshire's high, handsome, rugged peaks in the late 1800s brought their skis with them. Skiing got its modern start here in the 1920s with the cutting of trails on Cannon Mountain. You can now ski or snowboard at nearly 20 areas, from the old, established slopes (Cannon, Cranmore, Wildcat) to more contemporary ones (Attitash, Loon, Waterville Valley). Packages assembled by the ski areas allow you to sample different resorts.

Shopping

The absence of sales tax makes New Hampshire a hugely popular shopping destination. Outside the outlet meccas of North Conway and Tilton, this pastime revolves around antiques and local crafts, though in the southern Lakes Region and Hampton Beach, tacky souvenirs are the norm.

Summertime fairs, such as the one operated by the League of New Hampshire Craftsmen at Mt. Sunapee State Park, are a good way to see the best arts and crafts. Look for pottery, jewelry, and wooden boxes. Antiques shops appear in clusters along U.S. 4, between Route 125 and Concord; along Route 119, from Fitzwilliam to Hinsdale; along Route 101, from Marlborough to Wilton; and in the towns of North Conway, North Hampton, Hopkinton, Hollis, and Amherst. In the Lakes Region, most shops are along the eastern side of Winnipesaukee, near Wolfeboro. Many stores are in barns and homes along back roads; quite a few are open by chance or by appointment. Depression glass, silverware, and china abound, with high-quality furniture becoming scarcer and more expensive.

Exploring New Hampshire

The main attraction of southern New Hampshire's coast are historical Portsmouth and bustling Hampton Beach; several somewhat quieter communities such as Durham and Exeter are a bit farther inland. The east-central Lakes Region has good hiking trails, antiques shops, and, of course, water sports. To hike, ski, and photograph vibrant foliage, head to the north's White Mountains. The southwest is hemmed in to the east by the central Merrimack Valley, which has a string of fast-growing communities along I–93 and U.S. 3.

Numbers in the text and in the margin correspond to numbers on the maps: New Hampshire Coast, New Hampshire Lakes, The White Mountains, Dartmouth–Lake Sunapee, and Monadnock Region and Central New Hampshire.

Great Itineraries

Some people come to New Hampshire to hike or ski the mountains, fish and sail the lakes, or cycle along the back roads. Others prefer to drive through scenic towns, visiting museums and shops. Although New Hampshire is a small state, roads curve around lakes and mountains, making distances longer than they appear. You can get a taste of the coast, lake, and mountain areas in three to five days; eight days gives you time to make a comprehensive loop.

IF YOU HAVE 3 DAYS

Drive along Route 1A to see the coast or take a boat tour of the Isles of Shoals before exploring **Portsmouth** ①. The next day visit **Wolfeboro** ㉒, on the eastern edge of Lake Winnipesaukee, good for an overnight stop. The following morning drive across the scenic **Kancamagus Highway** ㊲ (Route 112) from Conway to **Lincoln** ㉕ to see the granite ledges and sparkling streams of the White Mountains.

IF YOU HAVE 5 DAYS

After visiting **Portsmouth** ① and **Wolfeboro** ㉒, explore Squam and Ossipee lakes and the charming towns near them: **Moultonborough** ⑱, **Center Harbor** ⑮, and **Tamworth** ⑲. Spend your third night in the White Mountains town of **Jackson** ㉝. After crossing the **Kancamagus Highway** ㊲ (Route 112) to **Lincoln** ㉕, tour the western part of the White Mountain National Forest via Route 112 to Route 118. Take Route 25A and then Route 10 south through the upper Connecticut River valley to **Hanover** ㊺, home of Dartmouth College, for an overnight. Follow I–89 back by way of **Newbury** ㊸ and the Lake Sunapee region.

IF YOU HAVE 8 DAYS

Spend your first two nights in **Portsmouth** ①, allowing a chance to visit Strawbery Banke Museum and soak up the city's history as well as explore the short, scenic shoreline. Then follow the five-day itinerary above as far as **Hanover** ㊺. From here, visit the Shaker Community at **Enfield** ㊹; then take either Route 12A along the Connecticut River or Route 10 south to **Keene** ㊾. Route 119 leads east to Rhododendron State Park in **Fitzwilliam** ㊿.

When to Tour New Hampshire

In summer, people flock to seaside beaches, mountain trails, and lake boat ramps. In the cities, festivals showcase music, theater, and crafts. Fall brings leaf-peepers, especially to the White Mountains and along the Kancamagus Highway (Route 112). Skiers take to the slopes in winter, when Christmas lights and carnivals brighten the long, dark nights. Spring's unpredictable weather—along with April's mud and late May's black flies—tends to deter visitors. Still, the season has its joys, not the least of which is the appearance of the state flower, the purple lilac, from mid-May to early June.

THE COAST

New Hampshire's 18-mi stretch of coastline packs in a wealth of scenery and diversions. The honky-tonk of Hampton Beach gets plenty of attention, good and bad, but first-timers are often surprised by the significant chunk of shoreline that remains pristine—especially through the town of Rye. This tour begins in the regional hub, Portsmouth; cuts down the coast to the beaches; branches inland to the quintessential prep school town of Exeter; and then runs back up north through Dover, Durham (home to the University of New Hampshire), and Rochester. From here it's a short drive to the Lakes Region.

Portsmouth

★ ❶ *47 mi southeast of Concord; 50 mi southwest of Portland, Maine; 56 mi north of Boston.*

Settled in 1623 as Strawbery Banke, Portsmouth became a prosperous port before the Revolutionary War, and like similarly wealthy Newport, Rhode Island, it harbored many Tory sympathizers throughout the campaign. Filled with grand residential architecture spanning the 18th through early 20th centuries, this city of 23,000 has numerous house-museums, including the collection of buildings that make up the Strawberry Banke Museum. With hip eateries, quirky shops, swank cocktail bars, respected theaters, and jumping live-music venues, this sheltered harbor city is a hot destination. Downtown, especially around elegant Market Square, buzzes with conviviality.

The **Portsmouth Harbour Trail** passes more than 70 18th- and 19th-century structures downtown, through the South End, and along State and Congress streets. You can purchase a tour map ($2.50) at the information kiosk in Market Square, at the chamber of commerce, and at several house-museums. Guided walks are conducted late spring to early fall ☎ 603/436–3988 *for guided tour,* WEB *www.seacoastnh.com/harbour-trail.* 🎟 *$7 for guided tour.* ☉ *May–mid-Oct., Thurs.–Mon.*

The **Portsmouth Black Heritage Trail** (☎ 603/431–2768, WEB www.seacoastnh.com/blackhistory) is a self-guided walk that visits sites important to African-American history in Portsmouth. Included are the **New Hampshire Gazette Printing Office,** where skilled slave Primus Fowle operated the paper's printing press for some 50 years beginning in 1756, and the city's 1866 **Election Hall,** outside of which the city's black citizens held annual celebrations of the Emancipation Proclamation.

The yellow, hip-roof **John Paul Jones House** was a boardinghouse when the Revolutionary War hero lived here while supervising shipbuilding for the Continental Navy. The 1758 structure, now the headquarters of the Portsmouth Historical Society, contains furniture, costumes, glass, guns, portraits, and documents from the late 18th century. ✉ *43 Middle St.,* ☎ *603/436–8420,* WEB *www.seacoastnh.com/touring/jpjhouse.html.* 🎟 *$4.* ☉ *June–mid-Oct., Mon.–Sat. 10–4, Sun. noon–4.*

The period interior of the **Moffatt-Ladd House,** built in 1763, tells the story of Portsmouth's merchant class through portraits, letters, and fine furnishings. The Colonial Revival garden includes a horse chestnut tree planted by Gen. William Whipple when he returned home after signing the Declaration of Independence in 1776. ✉ *154 Market St.,* ☎ *603/436–8221.* 🎟 *$5, garden tour $1.* ☉ *Mid-June–mid-Oct., Mon.–Sat. 11–5, Sun. 1–5.*

NEED A BREAK?

Drop by **Annabelle's Natural Ice Cream** (✉ 49 Ceres St., ☎ 603/436–3400) for a dish of Ghirardelli chocolate chip or Almond Joy ice cream. **Cafe Brioche** (✉ 14 Market Sq., ☎ 603/430–9225) serves coffee, thick deli sandwiches, and fresh-baked pastries.

★ The first English settlers named the area around today's Portsmouth for the wild strawberries abundant along the shores of the Piscataqua River. **Strawbery Banke Museum,** the city's largest and most-impressive museum, now uses the name. The 10-acre compound has 46 buildings that date from 1695 to 1820 as well as period gardens, exhibits, and craftspeople. Ten furnished homes represent 300 years of history in one continuously occupied neighborhood. Half the interior of the Drisco House, built in 1795, depicts its history as a Colonial dry-goods store, while the living room and kitchen are decorated as they were in the 1950s, showing how buildings are adapted. The Shapiro House has been restored to reflect the life of the Russian Jewish immigrant family who lived in the home in the early 1900s. Perhaps the most opulent house, done in decadent Victorian style, is the 1860 Goodwin Mansion, former home of Gov. Ichabod Goodwin.

✉ *Marcy St.,* ☎ *603/433–1100,* WEB *www.strawberybanke.org.* 🎫 *$12.*
🕓 *May–Oct., daily 10–5; Nov.–Dec. and Feb.–Apr., Wed.–Sat. 10–2.*

Picnicking is popular in **Prescott Park,** on the waterfront between
Strawbery Banke Museum and the Piscataqua River. A large formal
garden with fountains is perfect for whiling away an afternoon. The
park also contains Point of Graves, Portsmouth's oldest burial ground,
and two 17th-century warehouses.

🦆 Nineteen hands-on exhibits, geared toward kids under 11, at the **Children's Museum of Portsmouth** explore lobstering, sound and music,
computers, space travel, and other subjects. Some programs require
reservations. ✉ *280 Marcy St.,* ☎ *603/436–3853,* WEB *www.
childrens-museum.org.* 🎫 *$5.* 🕓 *Tues.–Sat. 10–5, Sun. 1–5; also
Mon. 10–5 in summer and during school vacations.*

The **Wentworth-Coolidge State Historic Mansion,** a National Historic
Landmark that's now part of Little Harbor State Park, was originally
the residence of Benning Wentworth, New Hampshire's first royal
governor (1753–70). Notable among its period furnishings is the
carved pine mantelpiece in the council chamber. Wentworth's imported lilac trees bloom each May. The visitor center stages lectures
and exhibits. ✉ *Little Harbor Rd., near South Street Cemetery,* ☎ *603/
436–6607.* 🎫 *$2.50.* 🕓 *Grounds daily; mansion June–Sept., Tues. and
Thurs.–Sat. 10–3, Sun. 1–6.*

Docked at the **Port of Portsmouth Maritime Museum** in Albacore Park
is the USS *Albacore,* built here in 1953. You can board this prototype
submarine, which was a floating laboratory assigned to test an innovative hull design, dive brakes, and sonar systems for the navy. The
nearby Memorial Garden and its reflecting pool are dedicated to those
who have lost their lives in submarine service. ✉ *600 Market St.,* ☎
603/436–3680. 🎫 *$5.* 🕓 *Daily 9:30–5:30.*

The **Redhook Ale Brewery,** visible from the Spaulding Turnpike, conducts tours that end with a beer tasting. If you don't have time to tour,
you can stop in the Cataqua Public House to sample the fresh ales and
have a bite to eat (open daily, lunch and dinner). ✉ *Pease International
Tradeport, 35 Corporate Dr.,* ☎ *603/430–8600,* WEB *www.redhook.com.*
🎫 *$1.* 🕓 *Tours weekdays at 2, weekends at 2 and 4.*

Dining and Lodging

$$$–$$$$ ✕ **Dunfey's Aboard the *John Wanamaker.*** Portsmouth's floating
restaurant, on a restored 1920s tugboat, prepares such creative deli-
cacies as tandoori game hen, marinated in buttermilk, chilies, ginger,
garlic, and cilantro, and then slow-roasted and served with a turmeric-
pomodoro sauce, sautéed spinach, and polenta. You can enjoy the bistro-
like main dining room or unwind in the Wheelhouse Bar. The upper-level
deck is a favorite on starry summer nights for light meals, a glass of
wine, or dessert and cappuccino. Reservations are a good idea on
weekends. ✉ *1 Harbour Pl.,* ☎ *603/433–3111. AE, MC, V. Closed
Mon. No lunch winter.*

$$$–$$$$ ✕ **The Library.** Most of this 1785 mansion, a former luxury hotel, has
been converted to condominiums, but the restaurant retains hand-carved
mahogany paneling, a marble-top bar, and bookcases on every wall.
Although the kitchen churns out such light dishes as sesame-encrusted
tuna with a soy reduction, the mainstays are traditional dishes like char-
grilled rib chop and pan-seared rack of lamb with a blackberry sauce.
The check arrives between the pages of a vintage best-seller. Order an
ale in the English-style pub. Sunday brunch is a big to-do. ✉ *401 State
St.,* ☎ *603/431–5202. Reservations essential. AE, D, DC, MC, V.*

$$–$$$$ ✕ **Lou's Upstairs Grill.** Movers and shakers favor this snazzy spot for power lunches and after-work cocktails. The space is dramatic—with tall windows and a bold red, white, and gray color scheme—and the kitchen reinterprets conventional American recipes. The surf-and-turf here pairs tournedos of beef tenderloin with seared sea scallops over basmati rice with horseradish cream. The fried chicken comes lightly crisped with sour-cream mashed potatoes. ✉ *100 Market St.,* ☎ *603/766–4745. AE, D, MC, V.*

$$–$$$ ✕ **Blue Mermaid World Grill.** The chefs at Blue Mermaid prepare globally influenced fare on a wood-burning grill. Specialties include lobster-and-shrimp pad thai; pan-seared cod with a coconut cream sauce and plantain chips; and polenta lasagna layered with cilantro, adobo, goat cheese, and roasted tomatoes. In summer you can eat on a deck that overlooks the historical Hill neighborhood. Entertainers perform (outdoors in summer) on Friday and Saturday. ✉ *409 Hanover St.,* ☎ *603/427–2583. AE, D, DC, MC, V.*

$$–$$$ ✕ **Jumping Jay's.** A wildly popular spot downtown, this offbeat, dimly lit eatery presents a changing menu of world-beat cooking, and nary a red-meat platter is served. Try the steamed Prince Edward Island mussels with a spicy lemongrass and saffron sauce, the lobster risotto, or the Chilean sea bass with a ginger-orange marinade. Singles often gather at the central bar for dinner and schmoozing. ✉ *150 Congress St.,* ☎ *603/766–3474. D, MC, V. No lunch.*

$$–$$$ ✕ **Porto Bello Ristorante Italiano.** In the second-story dining room of
★ this family-run Neapolitan restaurant overlooking the harbor, you can savor daily antipasto specials ranging from grilled calamari to fresh mozzarella. Pastas include spinach gnocchi and lobster tails over fettuccine. Veal *carciofi*—a 6-ounce cutlet served with artichokes—is a specialty. ✉ *67 Bow St.,* ☎ *603/431–2989. AE, D, MC, V. Closed Mon.–Tues. No lunch.*

$–$$ ✕ **Muddy River Smokehouse.** Red-check tablecloths and murals of trees and meadows evoke an outdoor summer barbecue joint—even when the weather turns cold. Roll up your sleeves and dig into corn bread and molasses baked beans as well as blackened catfish or a burger. Devotees swear by the Pig City platter of grilled ribs, smoked sweet sausage, and pulled pork. ✉ *21 Congress St.,* ☎ *603/430–9582. AE, MC, V.*

$–$$ ✕ **Poco's.** Sure, Poco's boisterous downstairs bar and spacious out-
★ side deck have earned it a reputation as a collegiate hangout, but the upstairs dining room turns out exceptional Southwestern and pan-Latin cuisine—and at great prices. Avocado-wrapped fried oysters with chipotle tartar sauce and lobster quesadilla with Brie, caramelized onions, and roasted corn–tomato salsa are among the better choices. Most tables have great views of the Piscataqua River. ✉ *37 Bow St.,* ☎ *603/431–5967. AE, D, MC, V.*

$$$–$$$$ 🏨 **Sheraton Harborside Portsmouth Hotel.** Portsmouth's only luxury hotel, this five-story redbrick building is within easy walking distance of shops and attractions. Many rooms have large windows overlooking Portsmouth Harbor and the Piscataqua River. Suites have full kitchens and living rooms. The Harbor's Edge Restaurant serves a popular Sunday brunch. ✉ *250 Market St., 03801,* ☎ *603/431–2300 or 800/325–3535,* ℻ *603/431–7805,* 🌐 *www.sheratonportsmouth.com. 179 rooms, 24 suites. 2 restaurants, room service, in-room data ports, some kitchens, indoor pool, health club, sauna, bar, nightclub, business services, meeting rooms. AE, D, DC, MC, V.*

$$$ 🏨 **Sise Inn.** Each room at this 1880s Queen Anne–style town house is decorated in Victorian style, with designer fabrics, antiques, and reproductions. Some rooms have fireplaces, and about half are in a 1980s addition that blends well with the older section. It's close to Market Square. ✉ *40 Court St., 03801,* ☎ *877/747–3466,* ☎ ℻ *603/433–*

1200, WEB *www.someplacesdifferent.com/sise.htm. 26 rooms, 8 suites. Some in-room hot tubs, in-room VCRs, laundry service, meeting rooms. AE, DC, MC, V. CP.*

$$-$$$ 🏠 **Wren's Nest Village Inn.** With standard rooms, suites, efficiencies, and cottages, the Wren's Nest draws lots of families and groups of friends; many regulars rent for weeks at a time. Guest quarters are clean, well maintained, and decorated with nautical artwork, and the 4 acres of lawns and gardens are attractive. It's a 10-minute drive south of downtown Portsmouth and convenient to Rye and the beaches. ⊠ *3548 Lafayette Rd. (U.S. 1), 03801,* ☎ *603/436–2481,* WEB *www.portsmouthnh. com/wrensnest. 35 units. Some in-room hot tubs, some kitchens, refrigerators, some in-room VCRs, volleyball. AE, D, MC, V.*

$$ 🏠 **Inn at Christian Shore.** Perennial gardens surround this handsome, yellow-clapboard Federal house, which is equidistant to downtown and the Maritime Museum. Original beam ceilings and rough-hewn hardwood floors reveal the building's rich history, and an eclectic mix of pre-Columbian, African, and European art makes a distinctive statement. The breakfast is memorable—the frittata-like Spanish tortillas are a specialty. ⊠ *335 Maplewood Ave., 03801,* ☎ *603/431–6770,* WEB *www.portsmouthnh.com/christianshore. 5 rooms. No room phones, no room TVs, no kids, no-smoking rooms. MC, V. BP.*

$$ 🏠 **Martin Hill Inn.** Within walking distance of the historic district and the waterfront, this inn consists of extensive gardens around a building from 1815 and another from 1850. The quiet rooms are furnished with antiques and decorated in formal Colonial or country-Victorian styles. The Greenhouse Suite has a solarium. ⊠ *404 Islington St., 03801,* ☎ *603/436–2287,* WEB *www.portsmouthnh.com/martinhillinn. 4 rooms, 3 suites. No room phones, no room TVs, no-smoking rooms. MC, V. BP.*

Nightlife and the Arts

NIGHTLIFE

The late-night coffeehouse **Breaking New Grounds** (⊠ 16 Market St., ☎ 603/436–9555) buzzes with a festive vibe and a mixed-age clientele. **King Tiki** (⊠ 2 Bow St., ☎ 603/430–5228), a bar-restaurant that oozes Polynesian kitsch, delights scenesters, poseurs, and other revelers with karaoke nights, retro music, and goofy drinks.

The **Portsmouth Gas Light Co.** (⊠ 64 Market St., ☎ 603/430–9122), a brick-oven pizzeria and restaurant, hosts local rock bands in its lounge or courtyard. People come from as far away as Boston and Portland to hang out at the **Press Room** (⊠ 77 Daniel St., ☎ 603/431–5186), which showcases folk, jazz, blues, and bluegrass performers.

THE ARTS

Beloved for its acoustics, the 1878 **Music Hall** (⊠ 28 Chestnut St., ☎ 603/436–2400 or 603/436–9900 film line) brings the best touring events to the seacoast—from classical and pop concerts to dance and theater. The hall also hosts art-house film series. From September through June the **Players' Ring** (⊠ 105 Marcy St., ☎ 603/436–8123) stages more than 15 original and well-known plays and performances by local theater groups.

The **Pontine Movement Theatre** (⊠ 135 McDonough St., ☎ 603/436–6660) presents dance performances in a renovated warehouse. The company also tours throughout northern New England. The **Prescott Park Arts Festival** (⊠ 105 Marcy St., ☎ 603/436–2848) presents theater, dance, and musical events outdoors June–August. The **Seacoast Repertory Theatre** (⊠ 125 Bow St., ☎ 603/433–4472 or 800/639–7650) has a year-round schedule of musicals, classic dramas, and works by up-and-coming playwrights, as well as a youth theater.

Outdoor Activities and Sports

Just inland from Portsmouth, the **Great Bay Estuarine Research Reserve** is one of southeastern New Hampshire's most precious assets. Amid its 4,471 acres of tidal waters, mudflats, and about 48 mi of inland shoreline, you can spot blue herons, ospreys, and snowy egrets, particularly during spring and fall migrations. Winter eagles also live here. The best public access is via the **Sandy Point Discovery Center** (⊠ 89 Depot Rd., off Rte. 101, Stratham, ☎ 603/778–0015, WEB www.greatbay.org). The facility has year-round interpretive programs, indoor and outdoor exhibits, a library and bookshop, and a 1,700-ft boardwalk as well as other trails through mudflats and upland forest. The center, about 15 mi southeast of Durham and 6 mi west of Exit 3 from I–95 in Portsmouth, also distributes maps and information. ⊠ *Information: New Hampshire Fish & Game Dept., 37 Concord Rd., Durham 03824,* ☎ *603/868–1095.* ⊠ *Free.* ⊙ *Daily dawn–dusk.*

Portsmouth doesn't have sandy stretches, but the **Seacoast Trolley** (☎ 603/431–6975 or 800/828–3762, WEB www.locallink.com/seacoast-trolley), which operates from mid-June through Labor Day, departs from Market Square on the hour (daily 10–5) for Portsmouth sights and area beaches. The **Urban Forestry Center** (⊠ 45 Elwyn Rd., ☎ 603/431–6774) has gardens and marked trails appropriate for short hikes on its 180 acres.

Shopping

Market Square, in the center of town, has gift and clothing boutiques, book and card shops, and exquisite crafts stores. **Byrne & Carlson** (⊠ 121 State St., ☎ 888/559–9778) produces handmade chocolates in the finest European tradition. **Kumminz Gallery** (⊠ 65 Daniel St., ☎ 603/433–6488) carries pottery, jewelry, and fiber art by New Hampshire artisans. **N. W. Barrett** (⊠ 53 Market St., ☎ 603/431–4262) specializes in leather, jewelry, pottery, and fiber and other arts and crafts. It also sells furniture, including affordable steam-bent oak pieces and one-of-a-kind lamps and rocking chairs.

Pierce Gallery (⊠ 105 Market St., ☎ 603/436–1988) has prints and paintings of the Maine and New Hampshire coasts. The **Portsmouth Bookshop** (⊠ 1–7 Islington St., ☎ 603/433–4406) carries old and rare books and maps. At **Salamandra Glass Studios** (⊠ 67 Bow St., ☎ 603/436–1038), you'll find hand-blown glass vases, bowls, and other items.

Isles of Shoals

❷ *10 mi southeast of Portsmouth, by ferry.*

Many of these nine small, rocky islands (eight at high tide) retain the earthy names—Hog and Smuttynose, to cite but two—given them by transient 17th-century fishermen. A history of piracy, murder, and ghosts surrounds the archipelago, long populated by an independent lot who, according to one writer, hadn't the sense to winter on the mainland. Not all the islands lie within the state's border: after an ownership dispute, five went to Maine and four to New Hampshire.

Celia Thaxter, a native islander, romanticized these islands with her poetry in *Among the Isles of Shoals* (1873) and celebrated her garden in *An Island Garden* (1894; now reissued with the original color illustrations by Childe Hassam). In the late 19th century, **Appledore Island** became an offshore retreat for Thaxter's coterie of writers, musicians, and artists. The island is now used by the Marine Laboratory of Cornell University. **Star Island** contains a nondenominational conference center and is open to those on guided tours.

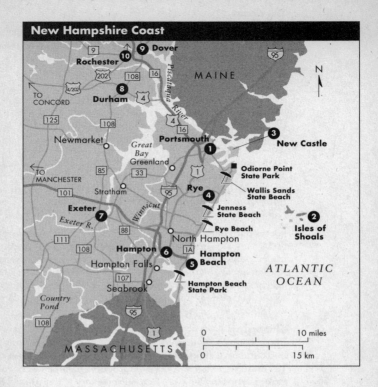

New Hampshire Coast

New Castle

③ *3 mi southeast of Portsmouth.*

Though it consists of a single square mile of land, the small island of New Castle was once known as Great Island. The narrow roads lined with pre-Revolutionary houses and upscale condos and homes make the island, which is accessible from the mainland by car, perfect for a stroll.

Wentworth by the Sea, the last of the state's great seaside resorts, is impossible to miss as you approach New Castle on Route 1B. Empty these days, it was the site of the signing of the Russo-Japanese Treaty in 1905, a fact that attracts many Japanese tourists. The current owners and the town have reached an agreement to bring this grand hotel back to life; renovations were under way at press time.

Ft. Constitution was built in 1631 and then rebuilt in 1666 as Ft. William and Mary, a British stronghold overlooking Portsmouth Harbor. The fort earned notoriety in 1774, when patriots raided it in one of Revolutionary America's first overtly defiant acts against King George III. The rebels later used the captured munitions against the British at the Battle of Bunker Hill. Panels throughout the fort explain its history. ⊠ *Rte. 1B at the Coast Guard Station,* ☎ *603/436–1552.* ⚐ *Free.* ☉ *Mid-June–Labor Day, daily 9–5; Labor Day–mid-June, weekends 9–5.*

Rye

④ *8 mi south of Portsmouth.*

In 1623 the first Europeans established a settlement at Odiorne Point in what is now the largely undeveloped and picturesque town of Rye, making it the birthplace of New Hampshire. Today the area's main draws are a lovely state park, oceanfront beaches, and the views from Route 1A.

★ ☕ **Odiorne Point State Park** encompasses more than 330 acres of protected land, on the site where David Thompson established the first permanent European site in what is now New Hampshire. Stroll several nature trails with interpretive panels describing the park's military history or simply enjoy the vistas of the nearby Isles of Shoals. The rocky shore's tidal pools shelter crabs, periwinkles, and sea anemones. Throughout the year, the Seacoast Science Center conducts guided walks and interpretive programs and has exhibits on the area's natural history. Displays trace the social history of Odiorne Point back to the Ice Age, and the tidal-pool touch tank and 1,000-gallon Gulf of Maine deepwater aquarium are popular with kids. Day camp is offered for grades K–8 throughout the summer and during school vacations. ⊠ *570 Ocean Blvd. (Rte. 1A), north of Wallis Sands, Rye State Beach,* ☎ *603/436–8043 science center; 603/436–1552 park,* ⟨WEB⟩ *www.seacentr.org.* ⟨⟩ *Science center $1 (guided walks and some interpretive programs $4); park Memorial Day–Columbus Day and weekends $3.* ☉ *Science center daily 10–5, park daily 8 AM–dusk.*

Dining and Lodging

$$–$$$ ✕ **Saunders at Rye Harbor.** Folks have been lazing about on the waterfront deck at sunset or over lunch since this place opened in the 1920s. Fresh-caught lobster, broiled scallops with a butter-and-crumb topping, and baked-stuffed shrimp are among the specialties. ⊠ *175 Harbor Rd.,* ☎ *603/964–6466. AE, MC, V. Closed Tues.*

$$–$$$ ✕ **Wildflowers Cafe.** You might think that this weathered bungalow near Jenness Beach is just another vacation hideaway rather than a sun-filled eatery serving memorable home-cooking. For breakfast, try the scallops, bacon, spinach, and poached eggs topped with hollandaise sauce. The savory smoked-cheddar cheesecake with tomato, thyme, and roasted–red pepper coulis makes a wonderful dinner entrée. Owner Roberta Daly bakes all her own breads and desserts. ⊠ *2197 Ocean Blvd.,* ☎ *603/964–5132. MC, V. No dinner Mon.–Tues.*

$$–$$$$ ⌂ **Rock Ledge Manor.** Built out on a point, this mid-19th-century gambrel-roof house with a wraparound porch once anchored a resort colony. Rooms have water views, brass-and-iron beds, and marble-top dressers; the family suite has a balcony. Owners Stan and Stella Smith serve breakfast in the sunny dining room overlooking the Atlantic. ⊠ *1413 Ocean Blvd., 03870,* ☎ *603/431–1413,* ⟨WEB⟩ *www.rockledgemanor.com. 2 rooms, 1 suite. Dining room; no room phones, no room TVs, no kids under 11, no smoking. No credit cards. BP.*

Outdoor Activities and Sports

BEACHES
Good for swimming and sunning, **Jenness State Beach,** on Route 1A, is a favorite with locals. The facilities include a bathhouse, lifeguards, and metered parking. **Wallis Sands State Beach,** on Route 1A, is a swimmers' beach with bright white sands and a bathhouse. There's plenty of parking; rates are $8 on weekends, $5 weekdays in summer.

FISHING
For a full- or half-day deep-sea angling charter, try **Atlantic Fishing Fleet** (⊠ Rye Harbor, ☎ 603/964–5220 or 800/942–5364).

Shopping
Although Rye isn't known for its shopping, **Antiques at Rye Center** (⊠ 655 Wallis Rd., ☎ 603/964–8999) is worth searching out for well-presented antiques from hand-painted porcelain to early toys.

En Route On Route 1A as it winds south through Rye to North Hampton, you'll pass a group of late-19th- and early 20th-century mansions known as **Millionaires' Row.** Because of the way the road curves, the drive south along this route is especially breathtaking.

Hampton Beach

❺ *8 mi south of Rye.*

Hampton Beach, from Route 27 to where Route 1A crosses the causeway, is an authentic seaside amusement center—the domain of fried-dough stands, loud music, arcade games, palm readers, parasailing, and bronzed bodies. An estimated 150,000 people visit the town and its free public beach on the Fourth of July, and it draws plenty of people until late September, when things close up. The 3-mi boardwalk, where kids can play games and see how saltwater taffy is made, looks as if it were snatched out of the 1940s; in fact, the whole community remains remarkably free of modern franchises. Free outdoor concerts are held on many a summer evening, and once a week there's a fireworks display. Talent shows and karaoke performances take place in the Seashell Stage, right on the beach.

Each summer locals hold a children's festival in August and celebrate the end of the season with a huge seafood feast on the weekend after Labor Day. For a quieter time, stop by for a sunrise stroll, when only seagulls and the occasional jogger interrupt the serenity.

Away from the beach crowds, you'll find **Fuller Gardens,** a late-1920s estate garden (the mansion was razed in 1961) designed in the Colonial Revival style by landscape architect Arthur Shurtleff, with a 1938 addition by the Olmsted brothers. With 2,000 rosebushes, a hosta garden, an annual display garden, a tropical conservatory, and a Japanese garden, it blooms all summer long. The Fuller Foundation is currently restoring the grounds according to original blueprints. ⊠ *10 Willow Ave., North Hampton,* ☎ *603/964–5414,* WEB *www.fullergardens.org.* 🎫 *$6.* ☉ *Mid-May–mid-Oct., daily 10–6.*

Dining and Lodging

$$$–$$$$ ✕ **Ron's Landing at Rocky Bend.** Amid the motels lining Ocean Boulevard is this casually elegant restaurant. Pan-seared ahi over mixed greens with a Thai peanut dressing makes a tempting starter. For an entrée, try the oven-roasted salmon with a hoisin (soybeans, garlic, and chili peppers) glaze, a Fra Angelico cream sauce, slivered almonds, and sliced apple or the baked haddock stuffed with scallops and lobster and served with lemon-dill butter. From many tables you can enjoy a sweeping Atlantic view. ⊠ *379 Ocean Blvd.,* ☎ *603/929–2122. AE, D, DC, MC, V. No lunch Mon.–Sat.*

$$–$$$$ ✕🏨 **Ashworth by the Sea.** This family-owned hotel was built across the street from Hampton Beach in 1912, though furnishings vary from period to contemporary. Most rooms have decks, though you should request a beachside room for an ocean view; otherwise you'll look out onto the pool or street. The Ashworth Dining Room ($$–$$$) serves steaks, poultry, and seafood. Of the seven lobster variations, the lobster meat wrapped in haddock with a crawfish-sherry sauce stands out. ⊠ *295 Ocean Blvd., 03842,* ☎ *603/926–6762 or 800/345–6736,* FAX *603/926–2002,* WEB *www.ashworthhotel.com. 105 rooms. 3 restaurants, pool. AE, D, DC, MC, V.*

$$$ 🏨 **D. W.'s Oceanside Inn.** The square front and simple awnings of this inn look much the same as those on all the other buildings lining Ocean Boulevard. Individually decorated rooms have carefully selected antiques and collectibles. You can curl up with a book by the

fireplace in the living room or watch the waves from the second-floor veranda. Should Hampton Beach's crush of people and noise begin to overwhelm, you'll appreciate the soundproofing. A separate three-bedroom cottage sleeps up to six guests and has a kitchen. ✉ 365 Ocean Blvd., 03842, ☎ FAX 603/926–3542, WEB www.oceansideinn.com. 9 rooms, 1 cottage. In-room safes, some kitchens; no kids, no-smoking rooms. AE, D, MC, V. Closed mid-Oct.–mid-May. BP.

Nightlife

Despite its name, the **Hampton Beach Casino Ballroom** (✉ 169 Ocean Blvd., ☎ 603/929–4100) isn't a gambling establishment but rather a late-19th-century, 2,000-seat performance venue that has hosted everyone from Janis Joplin to Jerry Seinfeld to Barenaked Ladies. Performances are scheduled weekly from April through October.

Outdoor Activities and Sports

BEACHES

Hampton Beach State Park (✉ Rte. 1A, ☎ 603/926–3784) is a quiet stretch of sand that shares its name with the town. The park, on the southwestern edge of town at the mouth of the Hampton River, has picnic tables, a store (seasonal), parking ($8 on summer weekends, $5 weekdays in summer), and a bathhouse.

FISHING AND WHALE-WATCHING

Several companies conduct whale-watching excursions as well as half-day, full-day, and nighttime cruises. Most leave from the Hampton State Pier on Route 1A. **Al Gauron Deep Sea Fishing** (☎ 603/926–2469) maintains a fleet of four boats for whale-watching cruises and fishing charters. **Eastman Fishing Fleet** (✉ Seabrook, ☎ 603/474–3461) offers whale-watching and fishing cruises, with evening and morning charters. **Smith & Gilmore** (☎ 603/926–3503) conducts deep-sea fishing expeditions and whale-watching trips.

Hampton

❻ *3 mi northwest of Hampton Beach, 11 mi southwest of Portsmouth, 45 mi north of Boston.*

One of New Hampshire's first towns, Hampton was settled in 1638. Its name in the 17th century was Winnacunnet, which means "beautiful place of pines." Today busy U.S. 1 defines its center and makes it a crossroads for anyone traveling along the seacoast. Hampton's early hub was **Meeting House Green,** where 42 stones represent the founding families. It's still a tranquil place surrounded by pine trees.

Tuck Museum, across from Meeting House Green, contains displays on the town's early history. The grounds also include a 19th-century schoolhouse, a farm museum, and a fire-fighting museum. ✉ 40 Park Ave., ☎ 603/929–0781; 603/926–2543 appointments. 🎟 Free. ☀ June–Sept., Tues.–Fri. and Sun. 1–4 PM and by appointment.

At 400-acre **Applecrest Farm Orchards** you can pick your own apples and berries or buy fresh fruit pies and cookies. Fall brings cider pressing, hay rides, pumpkins, and music on weekends. In winter a cross-country ski trail traverses the orchard. ✉ 133 Rte. 88, Hampton Falls, ☎ 603/926–3721, WEB www.applecrest.com. ☀ Daily 9–5.

Lodging

$$–$$$ 🏨 **Hampton Falls Inn.** Intricate Burmese wall hangings and leather furniture fill the lobby of this modern motel only 3½ mi from Hampton Beach. The bright, airy rooms and minisuites are large, and many have a view of the neighboring farm. An enclosed porch looks out over the woods and fields. ✉ 11 Lafayette Rd., 03844, ☎ 603/926–9545

or 800/356–1729, FAX 603/926–4155, WEB *www.hamptonfallsinn.com.*
33 rooms, 15 suites. Restaurant, minibars, some microwaves, some re-
frigerators, indoor pool, hot tub, meeting room. AE, D, DC, MC, V.

$$ 🖥 **Victoria Inn.** Easygoing innkeepers Ron and Marina Mansfield run
this romantic B&B half a mile from Hampton Beach. The 1875 struc-
ture, built as a carriage house, is decorated with plush Victorian an-
tiques and fabrics. The wraparound porch and the gazebo are great
spots to relax with a book on a warm summer afternoon. The dining
room overlooks the former summer home of President Franklin Pierce.
✉ *430 High St., 03842,* ☎ *603/929–1437 or 800/291–2672,* FAX *603/*
929–0747, WEB *www.thevictoriainn.com. 3 rooms, 2 suites. Dining*
room, bicycles. AE, MC, V. BP.

$ ⛺ **Tidewater Campground.** This camping area has 200 sites, a large
playground, a pool, a game room, and a basketball court. ✉ *160*
Lafayette Rd., 03842, ☎ *603/926–5474. MC, V. Closed mid-Oct.–mid-*
May.

Shopping

Antiques shops line U.S. 1 (Lafayette Rd.) in Hampton and neighbor-
ing Hampton Falls. The more than 50 dealers at **Antiques at Hamp-
ton Falls** (✉ Lafayette Rd., ☎ 603/926–1971) have all types of antiques
and collectibles. **Antiques New Hampshire** (✉ Lafayette Rd., ☎ 603/
926–9603) is a group shop with 35 dealers and a range of items. **An-
tiques One** (✉ 80 Lafayette Rd., ☎ 603/926–5332) carries everything
but furniture, including books and maps. The prodigious **Barn Antiques
at Hampton Falls** (✉ 44 Lafayette Rd., ☎ 603/926–9003) is known
for American and European furniture.

Exeter

❼ *9 mi northwest of Hampton, 52 mi north of Boston, 47 mi southeast*
of Concord.

In Exeter's center, contemporary shops mix well with the buildings of
the esteemed Phillips Exeter Academy, which opened in 1783, and other
equally historical structures. During the Revolutionary War, Exeter was
the state capital, and it was here amid intense patriotic fervor that the
first state constitution and the first Declaration of Independence from
Great Britain were put to paper. These days Exeter shares more in ap-
pearance and personality with Boston's blue-blooded satellite com-
munities than the rest of New Hampshire—indeed, plenty of locals
commute to Beantown.

The **American Independence Museum,** adjacent to Phillips Exeter
Academy in the Ladd-Gilman House, celebrates the birth of our na-
tion. The story of the Revolution unfolds during each guided tour, on
which you'll see drafts of the U.S. Constitution and the first Purple Heart.
Other items include letters and documents written by George Wash-
ington and the household furnishings of John Taylor Gilman, one of
New Hampshire's early governors. The museum also hosts a Revolu-
tionary War Festival in June. ✉ *1 Governor's La.,* ☎ *603/772–2622,*
WEB *www.independencemuseum.org.* 🎫 *$5.* ☉ *May–Oct., Wed.–Sun.*
noon–5 (last tour at 4).

Dining and Lodging

$$–$$$ ✕ **Tavern at River's Edge.** A convivial downtown gathering spot on
the Exeter River, this tavern pulls in parents of prep school kids, UNH
students, and suburban yuppies. It may be informal, but the kitchen
turns out surprisingly sophisticated chow. You might start with sautéed
ragout of Portobello and shiitake mushrooms, sun-dried tomatoes,
roasted shallots, garlic, Madeira, and Asiago cheese. Move on to gin-

gered Atlantic salmon with lemon-and-jicama slaw, a crispy fried won-
ton, and a *ponzu* glaze. ⊠ *163 Water St.*, ☎ *603/772–7393. AE, D,
DC, MC, V. No lunch.*

$–$$ ✕ **Loaf and Ladle.** Chowders, soups, and stews as well as huge sand-
wiches on homemade bread are served cafeteria-style at this understated
eatery overlooking the river. Check the blackboard for the ever-changing rotation of specials, breads, and desserts, and don't miss the fresh
salad bar. ⊠ *9 Water St.*, ☎ *603/778–8955. Reservations not accepted. AE, D, DC, MC, V.*

$$–$$$ ✕⚏ **Inn and Conference Center of Exeter.** This brick Georgian-style
inn on the Phillips Exeter Academy campus has been the choice of visiting parents since it opened in the 1930s. It's furnished with antique
and reproduction pieces and possesses plenty of modern amenities.
Among the Terrace Restaurant's ($$–$$$$) specialties are mustard-glazed
American bison and pecan-encrusted Atlantic salmon with a pineap-
ple salsa. On Sunday, the line forms early for brunch. ⊠ *90 Front St.*,
03833, ☎ *603/772–5901 or 800/782–8444*, FAX *603/778–8757*, WEB
*www.someplacesdifferent.com/exeter.htm. 43 rooms, 3 suites. Restau-
rant, meeting rooms. AE, D, DC, MC, V.*

$$–$$$ ⚏ **Governor Jeremiah Smith House Inn.** Named for the Colonial gov-
ernor who eulogized George Washington, this dignified 1730s house
sits squarely in Exeter's impressive historic district, just a couple of blocks
from the river. Rooms capture the inn's spirit—period draperies, hand-
made quilts, wrought-iron sewing stands, gas stoves, canopy beds, and
oak antiques are typical. One efficiency is outfitted for longer stays.
Tea is served in the parlor each afternoon. ⊠ *41 Front St., 03833*, ☎
603/778–7770, WEB *www.portsmouthnh.com/jeremiahsmithinn. 8
rooms. No room phones, no TV in some rooms, no smoking. MC, V.
BP.*

$$–$$$ ⚏ **Inn by the Bandstand.** Common rooms in this 1809 Federal man-
sion are decorated in period style. Seven guest rooms have working fire-
places; some have marble baths and curtained four-poster beds. After
a day of sightseeing, you can relax with a glass of complimentary
sherry. ⊠ *4 Front St., 03833*, ☎ *603/772–6352 or 877/239–3837*, FAX
603/778–0212, WEB *www.innbythebandstand.com. 5 rooms, 4 suites.
In-room data ports, some in-room hot tubs, business services; no
smoking. AE, D, MC, V. CP.*

$ ⚠ **Exeter Elms Family Campground.** This 50-acre campground has 200
sites (some riverfront), a swimming pool, a playground, canoe rentals,
a video arcade, and a recreation program. ⊠ *188 Court St., 03833*,
☎ FAX *603/778–7631*, WEB *www.ucampnh.com/exeterelms. MC, V.
Closed mid-Sept.–mid-May.*

Shopping

A Picture's Worth a Thousand Words (⊠ 65 Water St., ☎ 603/778–
1991) stocks antique and contemporary prints, old maps, town his-
tories, and rare books. The **Travel and Nature Bookshop** (⊠ 59 Water
St., ☎ 603/772–5573) has a wide selection of travel books including
guides to New Hampshire hiking spots and other specialized titles. **Water
Street Books** (⊠ 125 Water St., ☎ 603/778–9731) carries new fiction
and nonfiction with an emphasis on New Hampshire authors.

Durham

8 *12 mi north of Exeter, 11 mi northwest of Portsmouth.*

Settled in 1635 and home of Gen. John Sullivan, a Revolutionary War
hero and three-time New Hampshire governor, Durham was where Sul-
livan and his band of rebel patriots stored the gunpowder they cap-
tured from Ft. William and Mary in New Castle. Easy access to Great

Bay via the Oyster River made Durham a maritime hub in the 19th century. Among the lures today are the water, farms that welcome visitors, and the University of New Hampshire (UNH), which occupies much of the town's center.

The **Art Gallery** at UNH occasionally exhibits items from a permanent collection of about 1,100 pieces but generally uses its space to host traveling exhibits. Noted items in the collection include 19th-century Japanese wood-block prints and American landscape paintings. ⊠ *Paul Creative Arts Center, 30 College Rd.,* ☎ *603/862–3712,* WEB *www.arts.unh.edu/gallery.html.* ⊡ *Free.* ☉ *Sept.–May, Mon.–Wed. 10–4, Thurs. 10–8, weekends 1–5.*

Emery Farm, which has been in the same family for 11 generations, sells fruits and vegetables in summer (including pick-your-own raspberries, strawberries, and blueberries), pumpkins in fall, and Christmas trees in December. The farm shop carries breads, pies, and local crafts. Children can pet the resident goats and sheep and attend the storytelling events that are often held on Tuesday mornings in July and August. ⊠ *U.S. 4, 1½ mi east of Rte. 108,* ☎ *603/742–8495.* ☉ *Late Apr.–Dec., daily 9–6.*

Several dozen American bison roam the **Little Bay Buffalo Farm.** The on-site Drowned Valley Trading Post sells bison-related gifts and top-quality bison meat. ⊠ *50 Langley Rd.,* ☎ *603/868–3300.* ☉ *Trading Post daily 10–5, observation area daily 10 AM–dusk.*

Dining and Lodging

$$$–$$$$ ✕⬚ **Three Chimneys Inn.** This stately yellow structure has graced a hill overlooking the Oyster River since 1649. Rooms in the house and the 1795 barn are named after plants from the gardens and filled with Georgian- and Federal-style antiques and reproductions, canopy or four-poster beds with Edwardian drapes, and Oriental rugs; half have fireplaces. Specialties in the Maples dining room ($$$–$$$$) include mussel salad and braised bison short ribs with blackberries, blue cheese, watercress, and caramelized-onion mash. The comfy Frost Sawyer Tavern ($–$$) serves simpler fare as does the outdoor conservatory, which is open spring through fall. ⊠ *17 Newmarket Rd., 03824,* ☎ *603/868–7800 or 888/399–9777,* FAX *603/868–2964,* WEB *www.threechimneysinn.com. 23 rooms. 3 restaurants, in-room data ports, some in-room hot tubs, business services, meeting room; no smoking. AE, D, MC, V. BP.*

$$–$$$ ✕⬚ **New England Conference Center and Hotel.** In a wooded area on the UNH campus, this contemporary hotel is large enough to be a full-service conference center but quiet enough to seem like a retreat. The Acorns Restaurant ($$–$$$) specializes in American regional cuisine and is a favorite place for Sunday brunch. A signature dish is blackened red snapper with pineapple chutney. ⊠ *15 Strafford Ave., 03824,* ☎ *603/862–2801 or 800/909–6931,* FAX *603/862–4897,* WEB *www.necc.unh.edu. 115 rooms. 2 restaurants, in-room data ports, health club, bar, Internet, business services, meeting rooms. AE, DC, MC, V.*

Nightlife and the Arts

Students and local yupsters head to the **Stone Church** (⊠ 5 Granite St., Newmarket, ☎ 603/659–6321)—in an authentic 1835 former Methodist church—to listen to live rock, jazz, blues, and folk.

The **Celebrity Series** (☎ 603/862–2290) at UNH brings music, theater, and dance to several venues. The **UNH Department of Theater and Dance** (⊠ Paul Creative Arts Center, 30 College Rd., ☎ 603/862–2919) produces a variety of shows. UNH's **Whittemore Center Arena** (⊠ 128 Main St., ☎ 603/862–4000) hosts everything from Boston Pops concerts to home shows, plus college sports.

Outdoor Activities and Sports

You can take a picnic to or hike several trails at 130-acre **Wagon Hill Farm** (⊠ U.S. 4 across from Emery Farm, ☎ no phone), overlooking the Oyster River. The old farm wagon on the top of a hill is one of the most-photographed spots in New England. Park next to the farmhouse and follow walking trails to the wagon and through the woods to the picnic area by the water. Sledding and cross-country skiing are winter activities.

Dover

❾ *6 mi northeast of Durham.*

Dover Point was settled in 1623 by fishermen who worked Great Bay. By the end of the century, the town center had moved inland to its present location. The falls on the Cocheco River made Dover a prolific textile-mill town. Many of the brick mill buildings have been converted to restaurants and shops.

The **Woodman Institute** consists of three buildings: the 1675 William Damm Garrison House, the 1813 J. P. Hale House (home to abolitionist Senator John P. Hale from 1840 to 1873), and the 1818 Woodman House. Exhibits focus on early American cooking utensils, clothing, furniture, New Hampshire's involvement in the Civil War, and natural history. ⊠ *182–190 Central Ave.,* ☎ *603/742–1038,* WEB *www.seacoastnh.com/woodman.* ⊡ *$3.* ☉ *Apr.–Nov., Wed.–Sun. 12:30–4:30; Dec.–Jan., weekends 12:30–4:30.*

Dining

$$–$$$ ✕ **Firehouse One.** A fire station was transformed to create this dramatic bi-level eatery complete with exposed brick, pressed-tin walls, and a vaulted ceiling. Through tall, arched windows you can admire the vintage mills of downtown Dover. The main restaurant serves jazzed-up comfort fare, from chicken satay with Thai sesame-peanut sauce to grilled Delmonico rib-eye rubbed with cracked black pepper and served with roasted-corn salsa. On the upper level, Garrison City Tavern has dancing and one of the state's longest granite bars. ⊠ *1 Orchard St.,* ☎ *603/749–2220. AE, D, MC, V.*

$–$$$ ✕ **Newick's Seafood Restaurant.** Newick's, which also has locations in Hampton and Merrimack, might serve the best lobster roll on the New England coast, but regulars cherish the scallop pies and onion rings, too. This oversize shack serves seafood in heaping portions. Picture windows allow terrific views over Great Bay. ⊠ *431 Dover Point Rd.,* ☎ *603/742–3205. AE, D, MC, V.*

Shopping

Downtown Dover Crafts (⊠ 464 Central Ave., ☎ 603/749–4952) showcases country-style crafts by local artisans who are part of a collective. **Just the Thing!** (⊠ 451 Central Ave., ☎ 603/742–9040) carries an engaging mix of vintage collectibles and contemporary handicrafts. You can watch artisans work at **Salmon Falls Stoneware** (⊠ Oak Street Engine House, ☎ 603/749–1467 or 800/621–2030), which is known for its salt-glaze stoneware made using a method favored by early American potters. **Tuttle's Red Barn** (⊠ 151 Dover Point Rd., ☎ 603/742–4313) carries jams, pickles, and other farm products.

Rochester

 10 mi north of Dover, 22 mi northwest of Portsmouth, 21 mi south of Wakefield.

This old mill factory city on the Cocheco River may not be as quaint as the state's coastal communities and lake hamlets, but it's an excellent base for exploring either region and has plenty of fine Victorian architecture. Stroll around the central intersection at Main, Wakefield, and Congress streets to get a feel for the town's heritage, or drive up along the mighty Salmon Falls River, which once powered the town's many manufacturers—everything from shoes to carbonated beverages to bricks has been produced here.

Dining and Lodging

$$–$$$ ✕⌂ **Governor's Inn.** Just north of downtown, this pair of neighboring, early 20th-century Georgian-style mansions are the former homes of state governors (and brothers) Huntley and Roland Spaulding. Guests now make their way about the homes' stately marble fireplaces, elliptical staircases, garden patios, and lavishly furnished bedrooms. The restaurant ($$–$$$; closed Mon.) presents an often-changing menu of regional American dishes such as Cajun rabbit roasted with an andouille–and–corn bread stuffing. ✉ *78 Wakefield St., 03867,* ☎ *603/332–0107,* FAX *603/335–1985,* WEB *www.governorsinn.com. 16 rooms, 4 suites. Restaurant, in-room data ports, some kitchenettes, bar; no-smoking rooms. D, MC, V.*

The Coast A to Z

To research prices, get advice from other travelers, and book travel arrangements, visit www.fodors.com.

AIRPORTS

Manchester Airport is a one-hour drive from the coastal region (☞ New Hampshire A to Z).

AIRPORT TRANSFERS

Hampton Shuttle links the region's towns to both Manchester Airport and Boston's Logan Airport.

➤ INFORMATION: **Hampton Shuttle** (☎ 603/659–9893 or 800/225–6426).

BUS TRAVEL

C&J Trailways, Concord Trailways, and Vermont Transit provide bus service to and from the coast. UNH Wildcat Transit provides limited service to coastal-area towns.

➤ BUS INFORMATION: **C&J Trailways** (☎ 603/430–1100 or 800/258–7111). **Concord Trailways** (☎ 603/228–3300 or 800/639–3317). **UNH Wildcat Transit** (☎ 603/862–2328). **Vermont Transit** (☎ 800/552–8737).

CAR TRAVEL

The main (and fastest) route to New Hampshire's coast from other states is I–95, which runs from the Massachusetts border to that of Maine. Coastal Route 1A has views of water, beaches, and summer estates. The more convenient U.S. 1 travels inland. The Spaulding Turnpike (Route 16) and U.S. 4 connect Portsmouth with Dover, Durham, and Rochester. Route 108 links Durham and Exeter.

EMERGENCIES

➤ EMERGENCY SERVICES: **Exeter Hospital** (✉ 10 Buzell Ave., Exeter, ☎ 603/778–7311). **New Hampshire State Police** (☎ 603/271–3636 or 800/

852–3411). **Portsmouth Regional Hospital** (✉ 333 Borthwick Ave., Portsmouth, ☎ 603/436–5110).

➤ PHARMACY: **Rite Aid** (✉ 800 Islington St., Portsmouth, ☎ 603/436–2454).

OUTDOORS AND SPORTS

FISHING

Many companies offer rentals and charters for deep-sea fishing and cruises. For information about fishing and licenses, call the New Hampshire Fish and Game Department.

➤ CONTACT: **New Hampshire Fish and Game Department** (☎ 603/271–3211).

HIKING

An excellent 1-mi trail reaches the summit of Blue Job Mountain, where a fire tower has a good view. The trailhead is on Crown Point Road, off Route 202A, 13 mi northwest of Dover. The New Hampshire Division of Parks and Recreation maintains the Rockingham Recreation Trail, which wends 27 mi from Newfields, just north of Exeter, to Manchester and is open to hikers, bikers, snowmobilers, and cross-country skiers.

➤ CONTACT: **New Hampshire Division of Parks and Recreation** (☎ 603/271–3556).

TOURS

Portsmouth Livery Company gives narrated horse-and-carriage tours through Colonial Portsmouth and Strawbery Banke. The Isles of Shoals Steamship Company runs island cruises, river trips, foliage excursions, and whale-watching expeditions from April to January out of Portsmouth. Capt. Jeremy Bell hosts these voyages aboard the M/V *Thomas Laighton,* a replica of a Victorian steamship, and the smaller and more modern M/V *Oceanic.* Lunch and light snacks are available on board, or you can bring your own. Some trips include a stop at Star Island and include a walking tour.

New Hampshire Seacoast Cruises conducts naturalist-led whale-watching tours and narrated Isles of Shoals cruises aboard the 150-passenger M/V *Granite State* from May to October out of Rye Harbor State Marina. From May to October, Portsmouth Harbor Cruises operates tours of Portsmouth Harbor, trips to the Isles of Shoals, foliage trips on the Cocheco River, and sunset cruises aboard the M/V *Heritage.*

➤ TOUR-OPERATOR RECOMMENDATIONS: **Isles of Shoals Steamship Company** (✉ Barker Wharf, 315 Market St., Portsmouth, ☎ 603/431–5500 or 800/441–4620). **New Hampshire Seacoast Cruises** (✉ Rye Harbor State Marina, Rte. 1A, Rye, ☎ 603/964–5545 or 800/964–5545). **Portsmouth Harbor Cruises** (✉ Ceres Street Dock, Portsmouth, ☎ 603/436–8084 or 800/776–0915). **Portsmouth Livery Company** (✉ Market Sq., ☎ 603/427–0044).

VISITOR INFORMATION

➤ TOURIST INFORMATION: **Exeter Area Chamber of Commerce** (✉ 120 Water St., Exeter 03833, ☎ 603/772–2411, WEB www.exeterarea.org). **Greater Dover Chamber of Commerce** (✉ 299 Central Ave., Dover 03820, ☎ 603/742–2218, WEB www.dovernh.org). **Greater Portsmouth Chamber of Commerce** (✉ 500 Market St., Portsmouth 03802, ☎ 603/436–1118, WEB www.portcity.org). **Hampton Beach Area Chamber of Commerce** (✉ 409 Lafayette Rd., Hampton 03842, ☎ 603/926–8718, WEB www.hamptonbeaches.com).

➤ WEB SITE: WEB www.seacoastnh.com.

LAKES REGION

Lake Winnipesaukee, a Native American name for "smile of the great spirit," is the largest of the dozens of lakes scattered across the eastern half of central New Hampshire. With about 240 mi of shoreline full of inlets and coves, it's the largest in the state. Some claim Winnipesaukee has an island for each day of the year, but the total actually falls well short: 274.

In contrast to Winnipesaukee's summer-long bustle, the more secluded Squam Lake has a dearth of public-access points. Its tranquillity no doubt attracted the producers of *On Golden Pond*; several scenes of the Oscar-winning film were shot here. Nearby Lake Wentworth is named for the state's first royal governor, who, in building his country manor here, established North America's first summer resort.

Well-preserved Colonial and 19th-century villages are among the region's many landmarks, and you'll find hiking trails, good antiques shops, and myriad water-oriented activities. This tour begins at Laconia, just off I–93, and more or less circles Lake Winnipesaukee clockwise, with several side trips.

Laconia

⓫ *27 mi north of Concord, 94 mi north of Boston.*

The arrival in Laconia—then called Meredith Bridge—of the railroad in 1848 turned the once-sleepy hamlet into the Lakes Region's chief manufacturing hub. It acts today as the area's supply depot, a perfect role given its accessibility to both Winnisquam and Winnipesaukee lakes as well as I–93. Come here when you need to find a chain superstore or fast-food restaurant.

Belknap Mill (⊠ Mill Plaza, 25 Beacon St., ☎ 603/524–8813), the oldest unaltered, brick-built textile mill in the United States (1823), contains a knitting museum devoted to the textile industry and a year-round cultural center that sponsors concerts, workshops, exhibits, and a lecture series.

Dining and Lodging

$$–$$$ ✕ **Hickory Stick Farm.** The scent of duckling roasting (before being served with an herb stuffing and an orange-sherry sauce) frequently fills this restaurant inside a 200-year-old Cape. In fact, the duck dinners have become so renowned that the restaurant has developed a mail-order business for them. Other favorites from the mostly Continental and American menu include prime rib and vegetarian lasagna. ⊠ *66 Bean Hill Rd., Belmont (4 mi south of Laconia),* ☎ *603/524–3333. AE, D, MC, V. Closed Mon. No lunch Tues.–Sat.*

$$–$$$ ✕ **Le Chalet Rouge.** This yellow house with two small dining rooms recalls a country-French bistro. To start, try the house pâté, escargots, or steamed mussels. The steak au poivre is tender and well spiced, and the duckling is prepared with seasonal sauces: rhubarb in spring, raspberry in summer, orange in fall, creamy mustard in winter. ⊠ *385 W. Main St., Tilton (10 mi west of Laconia),* ☎ *603/286–4035. Reservations essential. MC, V. Closed Mon.–Tues. No lunch.*

$$ 🏨 **Ferry Point House.** Built in the 1800s as a summer retreat for the Pillsbury family of baking fame, this red Victorian farmhouse has superb views of Lake Winnisquam. White wicker furniture and hanging baskets of flowers grace the 60-ft veranda, and the gazebo by the water's edge is a pleasant place to lounge and listen for loons. A pedal boat and a rowboat await those eager to get in the water. The pretty rooms have

New Hampshire Lakes

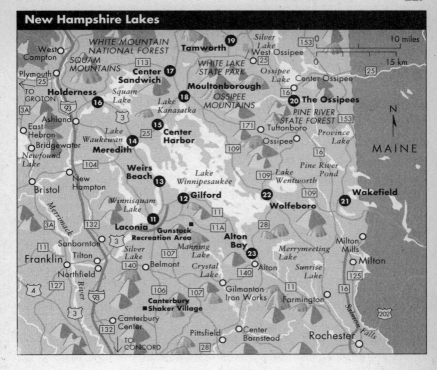

Oriental rugs and Victorian furniture. ⊠ *100 Lower Bay Rd., Sanbornton 03269,* ☎ *603/524–0087,* WEB *www.new-hampshire-inn.com. 6 rooms. Beach, boating, fishing; no room phones, no room TVs, no-smoking rooms. No credit cards. Closed Nov.–Mar. BP.*

Outdoor Activities and Sports

Bartlett Beach (⊠ Winnisquam Ave.) has a playground and picnic area. **Opechee Park** (⊠ N. Main St.) has dressing rooms, a baseball field, tennis courts, and picnic areas.

Shopping

The **Belknap Mall** (⊠ U.S. 3, ☎ 603/524–5651) has boutiques, crafts shops, and a New Hampshire State Liquor Store. The 53 stores at the **Lakes Region Factory Stores** (⊠ 120 Laconia Rd., I–93 Exit 20, Tilton, ☎ 888/746–7333) include Brooks Brothers, Eddie Bauer, Coach, Geoffrey Beene, and Black & Decker.

OFF THE BEATEN PATH

CANTERBURY SHAKER VILLAGE – Shaker furniture and inventions are well regarded, and this National Historic Landmark helps illuminate the world of the people who created them. Established as a religious community in 1792, the village flourished in the 1800s and practiced equality of the sexes and races, common ownership, celibacy, and pacifism. The last member of the community passed away in 1992. Shakers invented such household items as the clothespin and the flat broom and were known for the simplicity and integrity of their designs. Engaging 90-minute tours pass through some of the 694-acre property's 24 restored buildings, many of them still with original Shaker furnishings, and crafts demonstrations take place daily. The Creamery Restaurant serves lunch daily and candlelight dinners Friday–Saturday (reservations essential). A large shop sells fine Shaker reproductions. ⊠ *288 Shaker Rd., 15 mi south of Laconia via Rte. 106, Canterbury,* ☎ *603/783–9511 or*

866/783–9511, WEB *www.shakers.org.* ✉ *$10, good for 2 consecutive days.* ☺ *May–Oct., daily 10–5; Apr. and Nov.–Dec., weekends 10–4.*

Gilford

⑫ *4 mi northeast of Laconia.*

One of the larger public beaches on Lake Winnipesaukee is in Gilford. When the town was incorporated in 1812, the inhabitants asked the oldest resident to name it. A veteran of the Battle of the Guilford Courthouse, in North Carolina, he borrowed that town's name—though apparently he didn't know how to spell it. Quiet and peaceful, Gilford remains decidedly uncommercial.

Lodging

$$–$$$ 🏨 **B. Mae's Resort Inn.** All the rooms in this contemporary resort and conference center are large, if nondescript, and have a deck or patio; some are suites with kitchens. Close to the Gunstock ski area and within walking distance of Lake Winnipesaukee, B. Mae's is popular with skiers in winter and boaters in summer. ✉ *Rtes. 11 and 11B, 03246,* ☎ *603/293–7526 or 800/458–3877,* FAX *603/293–4340,* WEB *www.bmaesresort. com. 60 rooms, 24 suites. 2 restaurants, in-room data ports, in-room safes, some kitchens, some in-room VCRs, 2 pools (1 indoor), hot tub, gym, bar, recreation room. AE, D, DC, MC, V.*

$–$$ 🏨 **Gunstock Inn & Fitness Center.** The original building of this Colonial-style inn, just up the road from the Gunstock ski area, was constructed in the 1930s by Civilian Conservation Corps workers who cut the area's first ski trails. The inn has individually decorated rooms, some of which are large enough to accommodate families. Many rooms have views of the mountains and Lake Winnipesaukee. The snug tavern serves everything from seafood to burgers. In the fitness center, you can take water aerobics and body-toning classes free of charge. ✉ *580 Cherry Valley Rd., 03246,* ☎ *603/293–2021 or 800/654–0180,* FAX *603/293–2050,* WEB *www.gunstockinn.com. 23 rooms, 2 suites. Restaurant, some refrigerators, indoor pool, health club, sauna, steam room. AE, MC, V. BP.*

$ ⛺ **Gunstock Campground.** The campground at the Gunstock ski and recreation area has a pool and 300 tent and trailer sites as well as several cabins. ✉ *Rte. 11A (Box 1307, Laconia 03247),* ☎ *603/293–4341 or 800/486–7862. AE, D, MC, V.*

Nightlife and the Arts

The outdoor stage (with 2,500 covered seats) at **Meadowbrook Farm** (✉ 72 Meadowbrook La., off Rte. 11B, ☎ 603/293–4700 or 888/563–2369) hosts top music acts, from Nanci Griffith to 98°. The **New Hampshire Music Festival** (✉ 88 Belknap Mountain Rd., ☎ 603/524–1000) has performances by award-winning orchestras from early July to mid-August.

Outdoor Activities and Sports

Ellacoya State Beach (✉ Rte. 11, ☎ 603/293–7821) covers just 600 ft along the southwestern shore of Lake Winnipesaukee. In season, there's a bathhouse, picnic tables, and a fee ($3 from mid-May to Labor Day) for parking.

Shopping

Pepi Herrmann Crystal (✉ 3 Waterford Pl., ☎ 603/528–1020) sells hand-cut crystal chandeliers and stemware. You can take a tour and watch the artists at work.

Ski Area
GUNSTOCK USA

High above Lake Winnipesaukee, this all-purpose area dates from the 1930s. It once had the country's longest rope tow lift—an advantage that helped local downhill skier and Olympic silver medalist Penny Pitou perfect her craft. Gunstock allows patrons to return lift tickets for a cash refund for absolutely any reason within 75 minutes of purchase. Thrill Hill, a snowtubing park, has 10 runs, multipassenger tubes, and lift service. ⊠ *Rte. 11A (Box 1307, Laconia 03247)*, ☎ *603/293–4341 or 800/486–7862*, WEB *www.gunstock.com.*

Downhill. Clever trail cutting along with grooming and surface sculpting three times daily have made this otherwise pedestrian mountain good for intermediates. That's how most of the 44 trails are rated, with a few more challenging runs as well as designated sections for slow skiers and learners. Lower Ramrod trail is set up for snowboarding. Chairlifts include one quad, two triples, two doubles as well as two surface tows. At night, you'll find 15 lighted trails and five lifts in operation, making this the state's largest night-skiing facility.

Cross-country. Gunstock has 50 km (30 mi) of trails for skiing and snowshoeing. Some 15 km (9 mi) are for advanced skiers, and there are backcountry trails as well.

Child care. The nursery takes children ages 6 months and up; the ski school teaches children ages 3–14.

Summer activities. In summer, Gunstock has a swimming pool, a playground, hiking trails, mountain-bike rentals and trails, a skateboarding-blading park, guided horseback rides, pedal boats, and a campground.

Weirs Beach

13 *10 mi northwest of Gilford, 8 mi north of Laconia.*

Weirs Beach is Lake Winnipesaukee's center for arcade activity. Anyone who loves souvenir shops, fireworks, water slides, and hordes of children will feel right at home. Several cruise boats depart from the town dock.

The period cars of the **Winnipesaukee Scenic Railroad** carry you along the lakeshore on one- or two-hour rides; boarding is at Weirs Beach or Meredith. Special trips that include certain meals are also available. ⊠ *U.S. 3, Weirs Beach*, ☎ *603/279–5253 or 603/745–2135*, WEB *www.hoborr.com.* ☎ *$9.95–$24.50.* ⊙ *July–mid-Sept., daily; Memorial Day–late June and mid-Sept.–mid-Oct. weekends only. Call for hrs and for special Santa trains in Dec.*

Day or night you can work your way through the miniature golf course, 20 lanes of bowling, and more than 500 games at **Funspot** (⊠ Rte. 11B, at U.S. 3, ☎ 603/366–4377). For a full aquatic experience, visit **Surf Coaster** (⊠ U.S. 3, ☎ 603/366–4991), which has seven slides, a wave pool, and a large area for young children. A giant **Water Slide** (⊠ U.S. 3, ☎ 603/366–5161) overlooks the lake.

Outdoor Activities and Sports
Thurston's Marina (⊠ U.S. 3 at the bridge, ☎ 603/366–4811 or 800/834–4812) rents pontoon boats, powerboats, and personal watercraft.

Meredith

⑭ *5 mi northwest of Weirs Beach, 41 mi north of Concord.*

Meredith, a one-time workaday mill town on U.S. 3 at Lake Winnipesaukee's western end, has watched its fortunes change for the better over the past decade or so. The opening and constant expansion of Inns at Mills Falls have attracted hundreds of visitors, and crafts shops and art galleries have sprung up. You can pick up area information at a kiosk across from the town docks.

At **Annalee's Doll Museum,** you can view a collection of the famous felt dolls and learn about the woman who created them. Annalee Davis Thorndike began making these poppets after her graduation from high school in 1933. They caught on with collectors, and the company has grown into an empire. ⊠ *Hemlock Dr. off Rte. 104,* ☎ *603/279–3333 or 800/433–6557,* WEB *www.annalee.com.* ☎ *Free.* ☉ *Memorial Day–mid-Oct.; call for hrs.*

Dining and Lodging

$$–$$$ ✕ **Mame's.** This 1820s tavern, once the home of the village doctor, now contains a warren of convivial dining rooms with exposed-brick walls, wooden beams, and wide-plank floors. Expect mostly American standbys of the seafood, steak, veal, and chicken variety; the mud pie is highly recommended. ⊠ *8 Plymouth St.,* ☎ *603/279–4631. AE, D, MC, V.*

$$–$$$$ ✕🏠 **Inns at Mill Falls.** Overlooking Lake Winnipesaukee and incor-
★ porating sections of the 19th-century Meredith Linen Mills, this complex has all the amenities of a full resort as well as warmth and personality. The central-most Inn at Mills Falls, which adjoins an 18-shop market, has a pool and 54 spacious rooms. The lakefront Inn at Bay Point has 24 rooms—most with balconies, some with fireplaces. The 23 rooms at the lake-view Chase House at Mill Falls all have fireplaces; some have balconies. The upscale Boathouse Grill ($$–$$$) serves such contemporary dishes as pan-seared almond-and-cornmeal-crusted trout with apple butter. The rustic-cabin motifs and the cedar-plank salmon will delight you at Camp ($$–$$$). For breakfast or lunch, try the Waterfall Cafe ($), which overlooks 40-ft cascades. Giuseppe's ($–$$), an Italian eatery, has live cabaret many nights. ⊠ *U.S. 3 at Rte. 25, 03253,* ☎ *603/279–7006 or 800/622–6455,* FAX *603/279–6797,* WEB *www.millsfalls.com. 101 rooms. 4 restaurants, some in-room hot tubs, indoor pool, sauna, beach, dock, boating, ice-skating, bar, shops, meeting rooms. AE, D, DC, MC, V.*

$ ⚠ **Clearwater Campground.** This wooded tent and RV campground on Lake Pemigewasset has 153 shady sites, several cabins, a large sandy beach, a recreation building, a playground, basketball and volleyball courts, and boat rentals and slips. ⊠ *26 Campground Rd., off Rte. 104, 03253,* ☎ *603/279–7761,* WEB *www.clearwatercampground.com. Closed mid-Oct.–mid-May.*

The Arts

The **Lakes Region Summer Theatre** (⊠ Interlakes Auditorium, Rte. 25, ☎ 603/279–9933) presents Broadway musicals.

Outdoor Activities and Sports

BEACHES

Wellington State Beach (⊠ off Rte. 3A, Bristol, 12 mi west of Meredith, ☎ 603/744–2197), on Newfound Lake's western shore, is beautiful. You can swim, picnic, hike along the ½-mi shoreline, or use the boat launch.

BOATING

Meredith Marina and Boating Center (⌧ Bayshore Dr., ☎ 603/279–7921) rents powerboats. **Wild Meadow Canoes & Kayaks** (⌧ Rte. 25 between Center Harbor and Meredith, ☎ 603/253–7536 or 800/427–7536) has canoes and kayaks for rent.

GOLF

Waukewan Golf Club (⌧ off U.S. 3 and Rte. 25, ☎ 603/279–6661) is an 18-hole, par-71 course. Greens fees are $22–$28.

Shopping

About 170 dealers operate out of the three-floor **Burlwood Antique Center** (⌧ U.S. 3, ☎ 603/279–6387), open May–October. The **Meredith League of New Hampshire Craftsmen** (⌧ 279 U.S. 3, ½ mi north of Rte. 104, ☎ 603/279–7920) sells works by area artisans. **Mill Falls Marketplace** (⌧ U.S. 3 at Rte. 25, ☎ 603/279–7006), part of the Inns at Mills Falls, contains shops with clothing, gifts, and books. The **Old Print Barn** (⌧ 1008 Winona Rd., ☎ 603/279–6479) carries rare prints—Currier & Ives, antique botanicals, and more—from around the world.

Center Harbor

⑮ *5 mi northeast of Meredith.*

In the middle of three bays at the northern end of Lake Winnipesaukee, the town of Center Harbor also borders Squam, Waukewan, and Winona lakes. This prime location, which takes in views of the White Mountains to the north, has long made it popular in summer, especially with boaters.

Outdoor Activities and Sports

Red Hill, a hiking trail on Bean Road off Route 25, northeast of Center Harbor, really does turn red in autumn. The reward at the end of the route is a view of Squam Lake and the mountains.

Shopping

Keepsake Quilting & Country Pleasures (⌧ Senter's Marketplace, Rte. 25B, ☎ 603/253–4026), reputedly America's largest quilt shop, contains 5,000 bolts of fabric, hundreds of quilting books, and countless supplies as well as handmade quilts.

Holderness

⑯ *8 mi northwest of Center Harbor, 8 mi northwest of Meredith.*

Routes 25B and 25 lead to the small, prim town of Holderness, between Squam and Little Squam lakes. *On Golden Pond,* starring Katharine Hepburn and Henry Fonda, was filmed on Squam, whose quiet beauty attracts nature lovers.

★ ☺ Trails at the 200-acre **Squam Lakes Natural Science Center** include a ¾-mi path that passes black bears, bobcats, otters, and other native wildlife in trailside enclosures. Educational events include the "Up Close to Animals" series in July and August, at which you can study a species in an intimate setting. The Gordon Children's Activity Center has interactive exhibits. A ride on a 28-ft pontoon boat is the best way to tour the lake and observe the loons. ⌧ Rtes. 113 and 25, ☎ 603/968–7194, WEB *www.nhnature.org.* ⏠ *$9, $7 May–June and Sept.–Oct.* ☉ *May–Oct., daily 9:30–4:30 (last entry at 3:30).*

Dining and Lodging

$$$$ ✕⌂ **Manor on Golden Pond.** Built in 1903, this dignified inn has 14 ★ acres of well-groomed grounds and a dock with canoes and pedal boats. You can stay in the main inn, the cottages, or, in summer and fall, the

carriage house. Sixteen rooms have wood-burning fireplaces; eight have two-person whirlpool baths. Three-, four-, or five-course prix-fixe dinners ($$$$; reservations essential) may include roasted breast and confit of Maine duck on a bed of creamy polenta served with glazed root vegetables and a port wine sauce. ⊠ *U.S. 3 and Shepard Hill Rd., 03245,* ☎ *603/968–3348 or 800/545–2141,* ꜰᴀx *603/968–2116,* ᴡᴇʙ *www.manorongoldenpond.com. 20 rooms, 3 cottages, 1 carriage house. Restaurant, in-room data ports, some in-room hot tubs, 2 tennis courts, pool, beach, boating, fishing, badminton, croquet, pub; no kids under 12. AE, MC, V. BP.*

$$–$$$ 🏨 **Glynn House Inn.** Jim and Gay Dunlop run this swanky, three-story, 1890s Queen Anne–style home with a turret and wraparound porch. Many rooms have fireplaces; the bi-level Honeymoon Suite has a whirlpool tub and fireplace downstairs and a four-poster bed and skylights above. Breakfast usually includes fresh-baked strudel. Squam Lake is minutes away. ⊠ *43 Highland St., Ashland 03217,* ☎ *603/968–3775 or 800/637–9599,* ꜰᴀx *603/968–3129,* ᴡᴇʙ *www.glynnhouse.com. 3 rooms, 6 suites. Some in-room hot tubs, in-room VCRs; no smoking. MC, V. BP.*

$$ 🏨 **Inn on Golden Pond.** This informal country home, built in 1879 and set on 50 wooded acres, is just up the road from Squam Lake. Rooms have hardwood floors, braided rugs, easy chairs, and calico-print bedspreads and curtains. The homemade jam at breakfast is made from rhubarb grown on the property. ⊠ *U.S. 3 (Box 680, 03245),* ☎ *603/968–7269,* ꜰᴀx *603/968–9226,* ᴡᴇʙ *www.innongoldenpond.com. 7 rooms, 1 suite. Hiking; no room phones, no room TVs, no kids under 12, no smoking. AE, MC, V. BP.*

$–$$ ⛺ **Yogi Bear's Jellystone Park.** This family-oriented camping resort has wooded, open, or riverfront sites; basic and deluxe cabins; and trailers. There's also a pool, a water playground, a hot tub, a miniature golf course, a basketball court, canoe and kayak rentals, and daily supervised activities. ⊠ *Rte. 132 (R.R. 1, Box 396, Ashland 03217),* ☎ *603/968–9000,* ᴡᴇʙ *www.jellystonenh.com. 275 sites, 43 cabins, 7 trailers.*

Outdoor Activities and Sports

White Mountain Country Club (⊠ N. Ashland Rd., Ashland, ☎ 603/536–2227) has an 18-hole, par-71 golf course. Greens fees are $28–$34.

Center Sandwich

★ ⑰ *12 mi northeast of Holderness.*

With Squam Lake to the west and the Sandwich Mountains to the north, Center Sandwich claims one of the prettiest settings of any Lakes Region community. So appealing are the town and its views that John Greenleaf Whittier used the Bearcamp River as the inspiration for his poem "Sunset on the Bearcamp." The town attracts artisans—crafts shops abound among its clutch of charming 18th- and 19th-century buildings.

The **Historical Society Museum** traces Center Sandwich's history through the faces of its inhabitants. Works by mid-19th-century portraitist and town son Albert Gallatin Hoit hang alongside a local photographer's exhibit portraying the town's mothers and daughters. The museum houses a replica country store and local furniture and other items. ⊠ *4 Maple St.,* ☎ *603/284–6269,* ᴡᴇʙ *www.sandwichnh.com/history.* 🖼 *Free.* ☉ *Late June–mid-Oct., Tues.–Sat. 11–5.*

Dining

$$–$$$ ✕ **Corner House Inn.** The restaurant, in a converted barn adorned with local arts and crafts, serves classic American fare. Before you get to the white-chocolate cheesecake with key-lime filling, try the chef's lobster-and-mushroom bisque or tasty garlic-and-horseradish-crusted rack of lamb. There's storytelling Thursday evening. ⊠ *Rtes. 109 and 113,* ☎ *603/284–6219 or 800/832–7829. AE, MC, V. Closed Mon. Nov.–May. No lunch.*

Moultonborough

⑱ *5 mi south of Center Sandwich.*

Moultonborough claims 6½ mi of shore on Lake Kanasatka, a large chunk of Lake Winnipesaukee, and even a small piece of Squam.

The **Old Country Store and Museum** (⊠ Moultonborough Corner, ☎ 603/476–5750) has been selling maple products, cheeses aged on-site, penny candy, and other items since 1781. Much of the equipment still used in the store is antique, and the museum (free) displays old farming and forging tools.

Castle in the Clouds is an odd, elaborate stone mansion built without nails; it has 16 rooms, 8 bathrooms, and doors made of lead. Construction began in 1911 and continued for three years. Owner Thomas Gustave Plant spent $7 million on this project and died penniless in 1946. A tour includes the mansion and the Castle Springs Microbrewery and spring-water facility on this 5,200-acre property; there's also hiking and pony and horseback rides. ⊠ *Rte. 171,* ☎ *603/476–2352 or 800/729–2468,* WEB *www.castlesprings.com.* ⌑ *With tour $12, without tour $6.* ☉ *Mid-May–late May, weekends 9–5; early June–early Sept., daily 9–5; early Sept.–late Oct., daily 9–4.*

The **Loon Center** at the **Frederick and Paula Anna Markus Wildlife Sanctuary** is the headquarters of the Loon Preservation Committee, an Audubon Society project. This bird, recognizable for its eerie calls and striking black-and-white coloring, resides on many New Hampshire lakes but is threatened by boat traffic, poor water quality, and habitat loss. The center presents changing exhibits about the birds. Two trails wind through the 200-acre property; vantage points on the Loon Nest Trail overlook the spot resident loons sometimes occupy in late spring and summer. ⊠ *Lees Mills Rd.,* ☎ *603/476–5666,* WEB *www.loon.org.* ⌑ *Free.* ☉ *July–Columbus Day, daily 9–5; Columbus Day–June, Mon.–Sat. 9–5.*

Dining

$$–$$$ ✕ **The Woodshed.** Farm implements and antiques hang on the walls of this enchanting, romantic 1860 barn. The fare is mostly traditional New England—sea scallops baked in butter and lamb chops with mint sauce—but the exceptionally fresh ingredients are sure to please. ⊠ *128 Lee Rd.,* ☎ *603/476–2311. AE, D, DC, MC, V. Closed Mon. No lunch.*

Tamworth

⑲ *12 mi northeast of Moultonborough, 20 mi southwest of North Conway.*

President Grover Cleveland summered in what remains a village of almost unreal quaintness—it's equally photogenic in verdant summer, during fall foliage, or under a blanket of snow. Cleveland's son, Francis, returned to stay and founded the acclaimed Barnstormers Theatre in 1931. Tamworth has a clutch of villages within its borders. At one of them—Chocorua—the view through the birches of Chocorua Lake has been so often photographed that you may experience déjà vu.

🐾 For 99 years, Dr. Edwin Remick and his father provided medical services to the Tamworth area and operated a family farm. At the **Remick Country Doctor Museum and Farm,** exhibits focus on the life of a country doctor and on the activities of the still-working farm. There are always hands-on activities, but try to visit when ice harvesting, stone-wall building, or the like is scheduled. ⊠ *58 Cleveland Hill Rd.,* ☎ *603/ 323–7591 or 800/686–6117,* WEB *www.remickmuseum.org.* 🎟 *Free.* ☉ *Nov.–June, weekdays 10–4; July–Oct., Mon.–Sat. 10–4.*

Dining and Lodging

$$$–$$$$ ✕🏠 **Tamworth Inn.** This 1833 Victorian inn is a great base both for
★   exploring the lakes and skiing in the White Mountains. Common rooms range from a beamed-ceiling pub to a dining room where tables are laid with white linen and crystal. Guest rooms have brass or antique beds, down comforters, and Caswell-Massey toiletries. The dining room ($$–$$$; closed Sun.–Mon. in summer and Sun.–Wed. in winter) serves seasonal cuisine with specialties such as grilled salmon brushed with olive oil and cracked black pepper and served with Yukon potato hash. ⊠ *Main St., 03886,* ☎ *603/323–7721 or 800/642– 7352,* FAX *603/323–2026,* WEB *www.tamworth.com. 16 rooms. Restaurant, some in-room hot tubs, pool, pub, some pets allowed (fee); no room phones, no room TVs, no smoking. AE, MC, V. Closed Apr. and 2 wks in Nov. BP, MAP.*

$–$$ 🏠 **Mt. Chocorua View House.** What began as a stagecoach stop has been operating as an inn almost continuously since 1845. Ideally located between the Lakes Region and the White Mountains, it draws many hikers and skiers. Guest rooms are welcoming with floral wallpapers, quilts, ceiling fans, and other personal touches. Common areas include a guest kitchen and a screened porch that might make hiking nearby Mt. Chocorua seem like too much work. ⊠ *Rte. 16 (Box 348, Chocorua 03817),* ☎ *603/323–8350 or 888/323–8350,* FAX *603/323– 3319,* WEB *www.mtchocorua.com. 6 rooms, 3 with bath; 1 suite. Gym; no room phones, no room TVs. AE, D, MC, V. BP.*

Nightlife and the Arts

The **Arts Council of Tamworth** (☎ 603/323–8104) produces concerts— soloists, string quartets, revues, children's programs—from September through June and an arts show in late July. **Barnstormers Summer Theatre** (⊠ Main St., ☎ 603/323–8500) has performances in July and August. The box office opens in June.

Outdoor Activities and Sports

The 72-acre stand of native pitch pine at **White Lake State Park** (⊠ Rte. 16, ☎ 603/323–7350) is a National Natural Landmark. The park has hiking trails, a sandy beach, trout fishing, canoe rentals, two camping areas, a picnic area, and swimming.

Shopping

The many theme rooms—a Christmas room, a bride's room, a children's room, among them—at the **Country Handcrafters & Chocorua Dam Ice Cream Shop** (⊠ Rte. 16, Chocorua, ☎ 603/323–8745) contain handcrafted items. When you're done shopping, try the ice cream, coffee, or tea and scones.

The Ossipees

20 *6 mi southeast of Tamworth, 21 mi south of North Conway.*

Route 16 between West Ossipee and Center Ossipee passes Ossipee Lake, known for fine fishing and swimming. Around these hamlets you'll find several antiques shops and galleries.

Dining

$$ ✗ **Jake's Seafood.** Oars and nautical trappings adorn the wood-paneled walls at this stop between West and Center Ossipee. The kitchen serves some of eastern New Hampshire's freshest and tastiest seafood, notably lobster pie, fried clams, and seafood casserole; other choices include steak, ribs, and chicken dishes. ⊠ *2055 Rte. 16,* ☎ *603/539–2805, MC, V. Closed Mon.–Wed.*

$–$$ ✗ **Yankee Smokehouse.** This down-home barbecue joint's logo depicting
★ two happy pigs foreshadows the gleeful enthusiasm with which patrons dive into the hefty sandwiches of sliced pork and smoked chicken and immense platters of baby back ribs and smoked sliced beef. Ample sides of slaw, beans, fries, and garlic toast complement the hearty fare. Born-and-bred Southerners have been known to come away impressed. ⊠ *Rtes. 16 and 25,* ☎ *603/539–7427. No credit cards. Closed Tues.–Wed.*

Shopping

Local craftspeople create much of the jewelry, turned wooden bowls, pewter goblets, and glassware sold at **Tramway Artisans** (⊠ Rte. 16, West Ossipee, ☎ 603/539–5700).

Wakefield

21 *21 mi south of West Ossipee, 43 mi north of Portsmouth, 64 mi northeast of Concord.*

East of Lake Winnipesaukee, seven laid-back villages combine to form Wakefield, a town with 10 lakes. Wakefield's 26-building historic district, just off Route 16 near the Maine border, consists of a church, houses, and an 18th-century inn. A few miles down Route 153 in Sanbornville you'll find Wakefield's present-day commercial district.

☉ The **Museum of Childhood** displays a one-room schoolhouse, a child's room and a kitchen from 1890, model trains, antique sleds, teddy bears, 3,500 dolls, and 44 furnished dollhouses. Special events are scheduled most Fridays. ⊠ *2784 Wakefield Rd.,* ☎ *603/522–8073.* ▦ *$3.* ☉ *Memorial Day–Labor Day, Mon. and Wed.–Sat. 11–4, Sun. 1–4.*

OFF THE BEATEN PATH	**NEW HAMPSHIRE FARM MUSEUM** – Roughly 10 mi south of Wakefield in northern Milton, a sleepy Colonial village that stretches along the Salmon Falls River, this facility houses more than 60,000 artifacts, retelling New Hampshire farm life from 1700 to the early 1900s. Take a guided tour through the Jones Farmhouse and then explore the Grand Barn—filled with vehicles and implements—the gardens, and the nature trails at your leisure. Special events demonstrating farm-related crafts take place throughout the season. ⊠ *Rte. 125/White Mountain Hwy.,* ☎ *603/652–7840,* ▦ *www.farmmuseum.org.* ▦ *$5.* ☉ *June–Oct., Wed.–Sun. 10–4.*

Lodging

$$ ▦ **Wakefield Inn.** The restoration of this 1804 stagecoach inn, a high-
★ light of Wakefield's historic district, has been handled with care. The dining-room windows retain the original panes and shutters, but the centerpiece is the freestanding spiral staircase, which rises three sto-

ries. The large rooms, named for famous guests or past owners, have wide-board pine floors, big sofas, and handmade quilts. In late fall and early spring, you can learn how to quilt as part of the weekend Quilting Package. ☒ *2723 Wakefield Rd., 03872,* ☎ *603/522–8272 or 800/245–0841,* WEB *www.wakefieldinn.com. 7 rooms. Dining room; no room phones, no room TVs, no kids under 10, no-smoking rooms. MC, V. BP.*

Wolfeboro

㉒ *21 mi south of West Ossipee, 28 mi northwest of Rochester, 49 mi northwest of Portsmouth.*

Quietly upscale and decidedly preppy Wolfeboro has been a resort since Royal Governor John Wentworth built his summer home on the shores of Lake Wentworth in 1768. The town center, bursting with tony boutiques, fringes Lake Winnipesaukee and sees about a tenfold population increase each summer. The century-old, white-clapboard buildings of the Brewster Academy prep school bracket the town's southern end. Expect none of the exuberant commercialism of Weirs Beach—Wolfeboro marches to a steady, relaxed beat, comfortable for all ages.

Uniforms, vehicles, and other artifacts at the **Wright Museum** illustrate the contributions of those on the home front to America's World War II effort. ☒ *77 Center St.,* ☎ *603/569–1212,* WEB *www. wrightmuseum.org.* ☒ *$6.* ☉ *May–Oct., Mon.–Sat. 10–4, Sun. noon–5; Nov.–Apr., Sat. 10–4, Sun. noon–4.*

NEED A
BREAK?   Brewster Academy students and summer folk converge upon groovy little **Lydia's** (☒ 30 N. Main St., ☎ 603/569–3991) for espressos, hearty sandwiches, homemade soups, bagels, and desserts.

The artisans at the **Hampshire Pewter Company** (☒ 43 Mill St., ☎ 603/ 569–4944 or 800/639–7704) use 16th-century techniques to make pewter tableware and accessories. Free tours are conducted at 9:30, 11, 1:30, and 3 most days, Memorial Day–Columbus Day, and by appointment at other times. The gift shop is open year-round.

Dining and Lodging

$$–$$$ ✕ **The Bittersweet.** This converted barn 2 mi north of downtown delights with its display of old quilts, pottery, sheet music, and china. Locals also love the nightly specials—the lobster pie is particularly popular. The upper level has antique tables and chairs and dining by candlelight. The lower-level lounge, with Victorian wicker furniture, serves lighter fare. ☒ *Rte. 28,* ☎ *603/569–3636. AE, D, MC, V. No dinner Sun. No lunch Mon.–Sat.*

$–$$$ ✕ **Wolfetrap Grill and Raw Bar.** The seafood at this festive shanty on Lake Winnipesaukee comes right from the adjacent fish market. You'll find all your favorites here, including a renowned clam boil for one that includes steamers, corn on the cob, onions, baked potatoes, sweet potatoes, sausage, and a hot dog. The raw bar has oysters and clams on the half shell. ☒ *19 Bay St.,* ☎ *603/569–1503. MC, V. Closed mid-Oct.–mid-May.*

$$$–$$$$ ✕🏠 **Wolfeboro Inn.** Built in the early 1800s, this white clapboard house has later additions with lake views. Rooms have polished cherry and pine furnishings, armoires, stenciled borders, and country quilts but could stand a little updating, especially the bathrooms and toiletries. Pub fare and more than 70 brands of beer are available at Wolfe's Tavern ($–$$), where fireplaces take the chill off cool evenings. The 1812 Steakhouse ($$–$$$) serves a popular slow-roasted prime rib. ☒ *90 N. Main St. (Box 1270, 03894),* ☎ *603/569–3016 or 800/451–2389,*

FAX 603/569–5375, WEB *www.wolfeboroinn.com. 41 rooms, 3 suites, 1 apartment. 2 restaurants, some refrigerators, beach, boating, bar, meeting room. AE, D, MC, V. CP.*

Outdoor Activities and Sports

BEACHES

Wentworth State Beach (⊠ Rte. 109, ☎ 603/569–3699) has good swimming, picnicking areas, ball fields, and a bathhouse.

BOATING

Winnipesaukee Kayak Company (⊠ 17 Bay St., ☎ 603/569–9926) gives kayak lessons and leads group excursions on the lake. **Wetwolfe Boat Rentals** (⊠ 17 Bay St., ☎ 603/569–1503) rents motorboats and personal watercraft.

GOLF

The Donald Ross–designed **Kingswood Golf Club** (⊠ Rte. 28, ☎ 603/569–3569) has an 18-hole, par-72 course; greens fees are $35.

HIKING

A short (¼-mi) hike to the 100-ft post-and-beam **Abenaki Tower,** followed by a more rigorous climb to the top, rewards you with a vast view of Lake Winnipesaukee and the Ossipee mountain range. The trailhead is a few miles north of town on Route 109.

WATER SPORTS

Scuba divers can explore a 130-ft-long cruise ship that sank in 30 ft of water off Glendale in 1895. **Dive Winnipesaukee Corp.** (⊠ 4 N. Main St., ☎ 603/569–8080) runs charters out to wrecks and offers rentals, repairs, scuba sales, and lessons in waterskiing and windsurfing.

Shopping

Architectural Attic (⊠ 49 Center St., Wolfeboro Falls, ☎ 603/569–8989) mixes an amazing array of antiques and housewares in with its architectural elements. You'll find an excellent regional-history section and plenty of children's titles at Wolfeboro's fine general-interest bookstore, the **Country Bookseller** (⊠ 9 Railroad Ave., ☎ 603/569–6030). **Made on Earth** (⊠ 33 Main St., ☎ 603/569–9100) carries New Age gifts, clothing, books, and crafts.

Alton Bay

㉓ *10 mi southwest of Wolfeboro, 20 mi southeast of Laconia.*

Lake Winnipesaukee's southern shore is alive with visitors from the moment the first flower blooms until the last maple sheds its leaves. Two mountain ridges hold 7 mi of the lake in Alton Bay, which is the name of both the inlet and the town at its tip. Cruise boats dock here, and small planes land here year-round, on both the water and the ice. There's a dance pavilion, along with miniature golf, a public beach, and a Victorian-style bandstand.

Mt. Major, 5 mi north of Alton Bay on Route 11, has a 2½-mi trail with views of Lake Winnipesaukee. At the top is a four-sided stone shelter built in 1925.

Dining

$$$$ ✕ **Crystal Quail.** This 12-seat restaurant, inside an 18th-century farmhouse, is worth the drive. The prix-fixe contemporary menu changes daily but might include saffron-garlic soup, a house pâté, quenelle-stuffed sole, or goose confit with apples and onions. ⊠ *202 Pitman Rd., Center Barnstead (12 mi south of Alton Bay),* ☎ 603/269–4151. *Reservations essential. No credit cards. BYOB. Closed Mon.–Tues. No lunch.*

Lakes Region A to Z

To research prices, get advice from other travelers, and book travel arrangements, visit www.fodors.com.

AIRPORTS AND TRANSFERS

Manchester Airport is about an hour to 90 minutes away by car (☞ New Hampshire A to Z).

AIRPORT TRANSFERS

Greater Laconia Transit Agency has door-to-door minibus service from Manchester Airport to anywhere within a 10-mi radius of Laconia. The cost is $110 one-way (for up to eight people).
➤ SHUTTLE: **Greater Laconia Transit Agency** (☎ 603/528–2496 or 800/294–2496).

BUS TRAVEL

Concord Trailways connects Boston's South Station and Logan Airport, via Concord and Manchester, with Center Harbor, Chocorua, Laconia, Meredith, Moultonborough, Plymouth, Tilton, and West Ossipee. Greater Laconia Transit Agency has regional bus service to Laconia, Ashland, Holderness, Tilton, Meredith, Plymouth, Belmont, and Franklin. In summer it also runs a trolley between Meredith and Weirs Beach.
➤ BUS INFORMATION: **Concord Trailways** (☎ 603/228–3300 or 800/639–3317). **Greater Laconia Transit Agency** (☎ 603/528–2496 or 800/294–2496).

CAR TRAVEL

On the western side of the Lakes Region, I–93 is the principal north–south artery. Exit 20 leads to U.S. 3 and Route 11 and the southwestern side of Lake Winnipesaukee. Take Exit 23 to Route 104 to Route 25 and the region's northwestern corner. From the coast, the Spaulding Turnpike (Route 16) heads to the White Mountains, with roads leading to the lakeside towns.

EMERGENCIES

➤ HOSPITAL: **Lakes Region General Hospital** (✉ 80 Highland St., Laconia, ☎ 603/524–3211).

LODGING

For longer stays in the Lakes Region consider renting a lakeside house or condominium. Among the agencies are Preferred Vacation Rental, Inc. and Strictly Rentals, Inc.

APARTMENT AND VILLA RENTALS

➤ LOCAL AGENTS: **Preferred Vacation Rentals, Inc.** (✉ Rte. 25 [Box 161, Center Harbor 03226], ☎ 603/253–7811, WEB www.preferredrentals.com). **Strictly Rentals, Inc.** (✉ 285 Rte. 25 [Box 695, Center Harbor 03226], ☎ 603/253–9800, WEB www.strictlyrentals.biz).

OUTDOORS AND SPORTS

The Lakes Region Association provides boating advice. The New Hampshire Fish and Game Department has information about fishing and licenses. The Alexandria headquarters of the Appalachian Mountain Club has trail information, as does the Laconia Office of the U.S. Forest Service.
➤ CONTACTS: **Appalachian Mountain Club** (☎ 617/523–0636). **Laconia Office of the U.S. Forest Service** (☎ 603/528–8721). The **Lakes Region Association** (☎ 603/744–8664 or 800/605–2537). **New Hampshire Fish and Game Department** (☎ 603/271–3211).

TOURS

The 230-ft M/S *Mount Washington* makes 2½-hour scenic cruises of Lake Winnipesaukee from Weirs Beach, mid-May–late October, with stops in Wolfeboro, Alton Bay, Center Harbor, and Meredith. Evening cruises include live music and a buffet dinner. The same company operates the M/V *Sophie C.,* which has been the area's floating post office for more than a century. The boat departs from Weirs Beach with mail and passengers Monday–Saturday, mid-June–Labor Day; call for stops. Additionally, the M/V *Doris E.* runs between Meredith and Weirs Beach throughout the summer.

From May to late October, Squam Lake Tours takes up to 24 passengers on a two-hour pontoon-boat tour of "Golden Pond." The company also operates guided fishing trips and private charters. Sky Bright operates airplane and helicopter tours and provides instruction on aerial photography.

➤ TOUR OPERATORS: **M/S *Mount Washington*** (☎ 603/366–5531 or 888/843–6686, WEB www.msmountwashington.com). **Sky Bright** (✉ Laconia Airport, Rte. 11, ☎ 800/639–6012, WEB www.skybright.com). **Squam Lake Tours** (☎ 603/968–7577, WEB www.squamlaketours.com).

VISITOR INFORMATION

➤ TOURIST INFORMATION: **Lakes Region Association** (✉ Rte. 104, just off I–93 Exit 23 [Box 430, New Hampton 03256], ☎ 603/744–8664 or 800/605–2537, WEB www.lakesregion.org). **Squam Lakes Area Chamber of Commerce** (✉ Box 665, Ashland 03217, ☎ 603/968–4494, WEB www.squamlakeschamber.com). **Wolfeboro Chamber of Commerce** (✉ 32 Central Ave. [Box 547, Wolfeboro 03894], ☎ 603/569–2200 or 800/516–5324, WEB www.wolfeboroonline.com/chamber).

THE WHITE MOUNTAINS

Sailors approaching East Coast harbors frequently mistake the pale peaks of the White Mountains—the highest range in the northeastern United States—for clouds. It was 1642 when explorer Darby Field could no longer contain his curiosity about one mountain in particular. He set off from his Exeter homestead and became the first man to climb what would eventually be called Mt. Washington. The 6,288-ft peak must have presented Field with formidable obstacles—its peak claims the highest wind velocity ever recorded and it can see snow every month of the year.

More than 350 years after Field's climb, curiosity about the mountains has not abated. Today, an auto road and a railway lead to the top of Mt. Washington, and people come here by the tens of thousands to hike and climb, to photograph the vistas, and to ski. The White Mountain National Forest consists of roughly 770,000 acres and includes the Presidential Range, whose peaks—like Mt. Washington—are all named after early presidents. Among the forest's scenic notches (deep mountain passes) are Pinkham, Franconia, and Crawford.

This tour begins in Waterville Valley, off I–93, and continues to North Woodstock. It then follows portions of the White Mountains Trail, a 100-mi loop designated as a National Scenic & Cultural Byway.

Waterville Valley

㉔ *60 mi north of Concord.*

In 1835, visitors began arriving in Waterville Valley, a 10-mi-long cul-de-sac cut by one of New England's several Mad rivers and circled by mountains. It was first a summer resort and then more of a ski area.

Although it's now a year-round getaway, Waterville Valley still has a small-town charm. There are inns, condos, restaurants, shops, conference facilities, a grocery store, and a post office.

Dining and Lodging

$–$$ ✕ **Chile Peppers.** Southwest-inspired Chile Peppers caters to skiers with fajitas, tacos, enchiladas, and other Tex-Mex staples. The food here may not be authentic Mexican, but it's well priced and filling. If you're solely into Tex, the lineup includes ribs, steak, seafood, and chicken. ⊠ *Town Square,* ☎ *603/236–4646. AE, DC, MC, V.*

$$$–$$$$ ▦ **Golden Eagle Lodge.** Waterville's premier condominium property— with its steep roof punctuated by dozens of gabled dormers—recalls the grand hotels of an earlier era. Rooms, however, are contemporary with upscale light-wood furniture and well-equipped kitchens; many have views of the surrounding peaks. The full-service complex has a two-story lobby and a capable front-desk staff. Guests have access to the White Mountain Athletic Club. ⊠ *6 Snow's Brook Rd. (Box 495, 03215),* ☎ *603/236–4600 or 888/703–2453,* 𝖥𝖠𝖷 *603/236–4947,* 𝖶𝖤𝖡 *www.goldeneaglelodge.com. 139 condominiums. Kitchenettes, indoor pool, sauna, recreation room. AE, D, DC, MC, V.*

$$–$$$ ▦ **Black Bear Lodge.** This family-oriented property has one-bedroom suites that sleep up to six and have full kitchens. Each unit is individually owned and decorated. Children's movies are shown at night in season, and there's bus service to the slopes. Guests can use the White Mountain Athletic Club. ⊠ *Village Rd. (Box 357, 03215),* ☎ *603/236–4501 or 800/349–2327,* 𝖥𝖠𝖷 *603/236–4114,* 𝖶𝖤𝖡 *www. black-bear-lodge.com. 107 suites. Kitchens, indoor-outdoor pool, hot tub, sauna, steam room, gym, recreation room. AE, D, DC, MC, V.*

$$–$$$ ▦ **Snowy Owl Inn.** You're treated to afternoon wine and cheese in the atrium lobby, which has a three-story fieldstone fireplace and many prints and watercolors of snowy owls. The fourth-floor bunk-bed lofts are ideal for families; first-floor rooms are suitable for couples seeking a quiet getaway. Four restaurants are within walking distance. Guests have access to the White Mountain Athletic Club. ⊠ *Village Rd. (Box 407, 03215),* ☎ *603/236–8383 or 800/766–9969,* 𝖥𝖠𝖷 *603/236–4890,* 𝖶𝖤𝖡 *www.snowyowlinn.com. 85 rooms. In-room data ports, some in-room hot tubs, some kitchens, some in-room VCRs, 2 pools (1 indoor), gym, meeting rooms. AE, D, DC, MC, V. BP.*

Outdoor Activities and Sports

The **White Mountain Athletic Club** (⊠ Rte. 49, ☎ 603/236–8303) has tennis, racquetball, and squash as well as a 25-meter indoor pool, a jogging track, exercise equipment, whirlpools, saunas, steam rooms, and a games room. The club is free to guests of many area lodgings.

Ski Area

WATERVILLE VALLEY

Former U.S. ski-team star Tom Corcoran designed this family-oriented resort. The lodgings and various amenities are about 1 mi from the slopes, but a shuttle renders a car unnecessary. ⊠ *1 Ski Area Rd. (Rte. 49) (Box 540, 03215),* ☎ *603/236–8311; 603/236–4144 snow conditions; 800/468–2553 lodging,* 𝖶𝖤𝖡 *www.waterville.com.*

Downhill. Mt. Tecumseh has been laid out with great care. This ski area has hosted more World Cup races than any other in the East, so most advanced skiers will be challenged. Most of the 52 trails are intermediate: straight down the fall line, wide, and agreeably long. A 7-acre tree-skiing area adds variety. Snowmaking coverage of 100% ensures good skiing even when nature doesn't cooperate. There's lift-service snow tubing and a snowboard terrain park that includes a timed boardercross course. The lifts serving the 2,020 ft of vertical rise

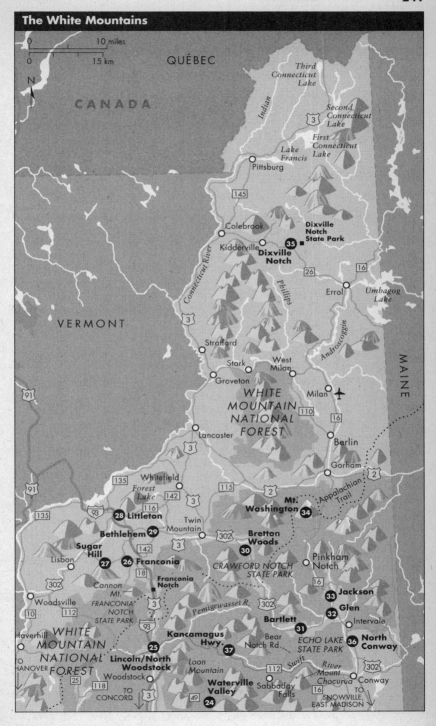

The White Mountains

include two high-speed detachable quads, two triple, three double, and four surface lifts.

Cross-country. The Waterville Valley cross-country network, with the ski center in the town square, has 105 km (65 mi) of trails. About two-thirds of them are groomed; the rest are backcountry.

Child care. The nursery takes children 6 months–4 years. SKIwee instruction accepts children ages 3–12. The Kinderpark, a children's slope, has a slow-running lift.

Summer activities. Hiking, mountain biking, tennis, and golf are popular activities. Mountain bikes are available for rent in the town square.

Lincoln/North Woodstock

㉕ *14 mi northwest of Waterville Valley, 63 mi north of Concord.*

Lincoln and North Woodstock, at the western end of the Kancamagus Highway (Route 112) or at Exit 32 off I–93, combine to make one of the state's liveliest resort areas. They appeal more to the social set and families than to couples seeking romantic retreats. Festivals, such as the New Hampshire Scottish Highland Games in mid-September, keep Lincoln swarming with people year-round; North Woodstock maintains more of a village feel.

☺ A ride on the **Hobo Railroad** yields scenic views of the Pemigewasset River and the White Mountain National Forest. The narrated excursions take 80 minutes. ⊠ *Kancamagus Hwy. (Rte. 112), Lincoln,* ☎ *603/745–2135,* WEB *www.hoborr.com.* ⊡ *$8.50.* ☉ *June–Labor Day, daily; May and Sept.–Oct., weekends; call for schedule.*

☺ At the **Whale's Tale Water Park,** you can float on an inner tube along a gentle river, careen down one of five water slides, take a trip in a multipassenger tube, or body-surf in the large wave pool. Whale Harbor and Orca Park Play Island contain water activities for small children and toddlers. ⊠ *U.S. 3, I–93 Exit 3, North Lincoln,* ☎ *603/745–8810,* WEB *www.whalestalewaterpark.com.* ⊡ *$20.* ☉ *Mid-June–Labor Day, daily 10–6.*

Dining and Lodging

$$–$$$ ✕🖭 **Woodstock Inn.** Run by the Rice family since 1982, this social but laid-back inn has rooms in four buildings. Rooms range from simple to romantic (with canopy beds and free champagne), and many accommodate groups. The restaurants include the elegant Clement Room Grill ($$–$$$), where the Mediterranean seafood sauté is a favorite, and the Woodstock Station ($), where the menu lists everything from meat loaf to fajitas. The Woodstock Inn Brewery ($) serves the same dishes as the Woodstock Station as well as six year-round brews and four seasonal ones. ⊠ *U.S. 3 (Box 118, North Woodstock 03262),* ☎ *603/745–3951 or 800/321–3985,* FAX *603/745–3701,* WEB *www.woodstockinnnh.com. 23 rooms, 19 with bath; 1 suite. 2 restaurants, some in-room hot tubs, refrigerators, outdoor hot tub, bar. AE, D, MC, V. BP.*

$$$–$$$$ 🖭 **Mountain Club on Loon.** This first-rate resort has an assortment of accommodations: suites that sleep as many as eight, studios with Murphy beds, and 117 units with kitchens. Many can be combined to form larger units. All rooms are within walking distance of the lifts, and condominiums are on or near the slopes. Entertainers perform in the lounge on most winter weekends. ⊠ *Kancamagus Hwy. (Rte. 112), Lincoln 03251,* ☎ *603/745–2244 or 800/229–7829,* FAX *603/745–2317,* WEB *www.mtnclubonloon.com. 234 units. Restaurant, some kitchens, 2 tennis courts, 2 pools (1 indoor), health club, massage, sauna, aerobics, racquetball, squash, bar, lounge, video game room. AE, D, MC, V.*

$$–$$$ ⊡ **Indian Head Resort.** Views across the 180 acres of this motel near the Loon and Cannon Mountain ski areas are of Indian Head Rock Profile and the Franconia Mountains. Cross-country ski trails and a mountain-bike trail from the resort connect to the Franconia Notch trail system. The Profile Room restaurant serves standard American fare. ⊠ *U.S. 3 (R.R. 1, Box 99, North Lincoln 03251),* ☎ *603/745–8000 or 800/343–8000,* FAX *603/745–8414,* WEB *www.indianheadresort.com. 100 rooms, 40 cottages. Restaurant, refrigerators, tennis court, 2 pools (1 indoor), lake, outdoor hot tub, sauna, fishing, bicycles, cross-country skiing, ice-skating, bar, recreation room. AE, D, DC, MC, V.*

Nightlife and the Arts

Skiers head to the **Granite Bar** (⊠ Kancamagus Hwy./Rte. 112, ☎ 603/745–5267) in the Mountain Club at the Loon Mountain resort. The **Olde Timbermill Pub** (⊠ Mill at Loon Mountain, Kancamagus Hwy./Rte. 112, ☎ 603/745–3603) has live dance music on weekends. The draws at the **Thunderbird Lounge** (⊠ Indian Head Resort, U.S. 3, North Lincoln, ☎ 603/745–8000) are nightly entertainment year-round and a large dance floor.

The **North Country Center for the Arts** (⊠ Papermill Theatre, Kancamagus Hwy./Rte. 112, Lincoln, ☎ 603/745–6032; 603/745–2141 box office) presents theater for children and adults and art exhibitions from July to September.

Outdoor Activities and Sports

At **Lost River in Kinsman Notch** (⊠ Kancamagus Hwy./Rte. 112, 6 mi west of North Woodstock, ☎ 603/745–8720 or 800/346–3687, WEB www.findlostriver.com) you can hike along the sheer granite river gorge and view such geological wonders as the Guillotine Rock and the Lemon Squeezer or pan for gemstones. A cafeteria, garden, and gift shop round out the amenities. It's open daily from mid-May to mid-October; admission is $8.50. **Pemi Valley Excursions** (⊠ Main St., I–93 Exit 32, Lincoln, ☎ 603/745–2744, WEB www.i93.com/pvsr) offers moose and wildlife bus tours June–October and guided snowmobile tours through the White Mountains in winter.

Shopping

The **Curious Cow** (⊠ Main St., North Woodstock, ☎ 603/745–9230) is a multidealer shop selling country crafts. **Millfront Marketplace, Mill at Loon Mountain** (⊠ Kancamagus Hwy./Rte. 112, Lincoln, ☎ 603/745–6261), a former paper factory, contains restaurants, boutiques, a bookstore, and a post office. **Sunburst Fashions** (⊠ 108 Main St., North Woodstock, ☎ 603/745–8745) stocks handcrafted gemstone jewelry and imported gifts.

Ski Area

LOON MOUNTAIN

A modern resort on the Kancamagus Highway (Route 112) and the Pemigewasset River, Loon Mountain opened in the 1960s and was greatly developed in the 1980s. In the base lodge and around the mountain are many food-service and lounge facilities. There's day and nighttime lift-service snow tubing on the lower slopes. Loon's Equestrian Center runs riverside horseback-riding trips. ⊠ *Kancamagus Hwy. (Rte. 112),* ☎ *603/745–8111; 603/745–8100 snow conditions; 800/227–4191 lodging,* WEB *www.loonmtn.com.*

Downhill. Wide, straight, and consistent intermediate trails prevail at Loon. Beginner trails and slopes are set apart. Most advanced runs are grouped on the North Peak section farther from the main mountain. Snowboarders have a halfpipe and their own park; an alpine garden with bumps and jumps provides thrills for skiers. The vertical is 2,100 ft; a four-passenger gondola, one high-speed detachable quad, two triple and three double chairlifts, and one surface lift serve the 44 trails and slopes.

Cross-country. The touring center at Loon Mountain has 35 km (22 mi) of cross-country trails.

Child care. The day-care center takes children from 6 weeks–8 years. The ski school runs several programs for children of different age groups. Children 5 and under ski free.

Summer activities. In summer and fall you can ride New Hampshire's longest gondola to the summit for panoramic mountain views. Among the daily activities at the summit are lumberjack shows, storytelling by a mountain man, and nature tours. You can also take self-guided walks to glacial caves or go horseback riding, mountain biking, and in-line skating and skateboarding in a state park.

Franconia

 16 mi northwest of Lincoln/North Woodstock.

Travelers have long passed through the White Mountains via Franconia Notch, and in the late 18th century a town evolved just to the north. It and the region's jagged rock formations and heavy coat of evergreens have stirred the imaginations of Washington Irving, Henry Wadsworth Longfellow, and Nathaniel Hawthorne, who penned a short story about the Old Man of the Mountain. The town remains enchanting, if sleepy, touched though it is by I–93 (a.k.a. the Franconia Notch Parkway) and modern ski resorts.

At **Frost Place,** Robert Frost's home from 1915 to 1920, the poet wrote one of his most-remembered works, "Stopping by Woods on a Snowy Evening." Two rooms host occasional readings and contain memorabilia and signed editions of his books. Outside, you can follow short trails marked with lines from Frost's poetry. ⊠ *Ridge Rd., off Rte. 116,* ☎ *603/823–5510.* ⚐ *$3.* ☉ *Memorial Day–June, weekends 1–5; July–Columbus Day, Wed.–Mon. 1–5.*

The **Old Man of the Mountain,** a rock-formation profile high above the notch, defines New Hampshire; you can't easily—and shouldn't—miss glimpsing this granite icon. Nathaniel Hawthorne wrote about it, New Hampshire resident Daniel Webster bragged about it, and P. T. Barnum tried to buy it. Stop at the posted turnouts from I–93 north- or southbound or along the shore of Profile Lake for the best views. There's also a small, free Old Man of the Mountain Museum administered by Franconia Notch State Park at the southbound viewing area (by the Cannon Mountain tram parking area); it's open daily 9–5.

The **Flume** is an 800-ft-long chasm with narrow walls that give the gorge's running water an eerie echo. The route through it has been built up with a series of boardwalks and stairways. The visitor center has exhibits on the region's history. ⊠ *Franconia Notch Pkwy., Exit 2,* ☎ *603/745–8391,* WEB *www.nhparks.state.nh.us/parkops/parks/franconia.html.* ⚐ *$8.* ☉ *Early May–late Oct., daily 9–5.*

Dining and Lodging

$$$ ✕🏠 **Franconia Inn.** At this 107-acre, family-friendly resort, you can play tennis, swim in the pool, hike, and even try soaring. The cross-country ski barn doubles as a horseback-riding center in the warmer months. Rooms have designer chintzes, canopy beds, and country furnishings; some have fireplaces. The restaurant ($$–$$$$) prepares standard American fare with upscale twists. Try the grilled black Angus beef with

sweet onion confit, Yukon gold mashed potatoes, and bourbon-pep-percorn demiglace. Meal plans are available. ✉ *1300 Easton Rd., 03580,* ☎ *603/823–5542 or 800/473–5299,* WEB *www.franconiainn.com. 29 rooms, 3 suites. Restaurant, some in-room hot tubs, some kitchenettes, 4 tennis courts, pool, hot tub, bicycles, badminton, croquet, hiking, horse-back riding, cross-country skiing, ice-skating, sleigh rides, bar. AE, MC, V. Closed Apr.–mid-May.*

$$ 🖬 **Horse and Hound Inn.** Off the beaten path yet convenient to the Cannon Mountain tram, this inn is on 8 acres surrounded by the White Mountain National Forest. Antiques and assorted collectibles add cheer, and the grounds are laced with 65 km (39 mi) of cross-country ski trails. ✉ *205 Wells Rd., 03580,* ☎ *603/823–5501 or 800/450–5501,* FAX *603/823–5501. 10 rooms, 8 with bath. Restaurant, cross-country skiing, bar, some pets allowed (fee); no room phones, no room TVs. AE, D, DC, MC, V. Closed Apr.–mid-May and mid-Oct.–Thanksgiving. BP, MAP.*

$ 🛆 **Lafayette Campground.** This campground has hiking and biking trails, 97 tent sites, showers, a camp store, a bike trail, and easy access to the Appalachian Trail. ✉ *U.S. 3 and I–93, Franconia Notch State Park, 03580,* ☎ *603/271–3628, 603/823–9513, or 877/647–2757 for reservations. MC, V.*

Nightlife

Hillwinds (✉ Main St., ☎ 603/823–5551), a restaurant and bar, has live entertainment on weekends.

Shopping

Stores in the **Franconia Marketplace** (✉ Main St., ☎ 603/823–5368) include the Grateful Bread Quality Bakery and Magoons Natural Foods.

Ski Areas

CANNON MOUNTAIN

The staff at this state-run facility in Franconia Notch State Park is attentive to skier services, family programs, snowmaking, and grooming. All this makes Cannon—one of the nation's first ski areas—a very sound value. **The New England Ski Museum** (☎ 603/823–7177, WEB www.skimuseum.org) sits at the base of the tramway and traces the history of the sport with displays of early gear as well as photos, books, and videos. Admission is free, and the museum is open daily noon–5 from late December through March and late May through mid-October. ✉ *Franconia Notch State Park, I–93 Exit 3, 03580,* ☎ *603/ 823–8800; 603/823–7771 snow conditions; 800/237–9007 lodging,* WEB *www.cannonmt.com.*

Downhill. Cannon's 42 trails present challenges—among them narrow, steep pitches off the peak of a 2,146 ft of vertical rise—rarely found in New Hampshire, particularly after a fresh fall of snow. The nicely contoured cruising trails are great for intermediates; beginners can head to the Brookside learning slope. There are also two glade-skiing trails—Turnpike and Banshee—and a lift-service tubing park. A 70-passenger tramway, two quads, three triples, and one surface lift all move you upward.

Cross-country. Nordic skiing is on a 13-km (8-mi) multiuse recreational path.

Child care. Cannon's Peabody Base Lodge takes children 1 and up. All-day and half-day SKIwee programs cater to kids 4–12, and season-long instruction can be arranged.

Summer activities. A multiuse recreational path runs parallel to the Franconia Notch Parkway (I–93). For $10 round-trip, the Cannon Mountain Aerial Tramway can transport you up 2,022 ft. It's an eight-minute ride to the top, where marked trails lead to an observation platform. The tram runs daily from mid-May through late October.

FRANCONIA VILLAGE CROSS-COUNTRY SKI CENTER

The ski center at the Franconia Inn has 65 km (39 mi) of groomed trails and 40 km (24 mi) of backcountry trails. One popular route leads to Bridal Veil Falls, a great spot for a picnic lunch. There are horse-drawn sleigh rides as well as ice-skating on a lighted rink. ⊠ *1300 Easton Rd., 03580,* ☎ *603/823–5542 or 800/473–5299,* 𝖥𝖠𝖷 *603/823–8078.*

Sugar Hill

❷ *6 mi west of Franconia.*

Sugar Hill, a village of 500 people, is deservedly famous for its spectacular sunsets and views of the Franconia Mountains, best seen from Sunset Hill, where a row of grand hotels and summer "cottages" once stood. Quiet country charm and good-quality B&Bs make Sugar Hill a romantic place.

Sugar Hill may be small, but the well-done **Sugar Hill Historical Museum** proves the town has a big history. Permanent and changing exhibits cover everything from settlement to the resort era to the present day. ⊠ *Rte. 117,* ☎ *603/823–5336.* ◻ *$2.* ☉ *July–mid-Oct., Thurs. and weekends 1–4.*

Dining and Lodging

$ ✕ **Polly's Pancake Parlor.** Originally a carriage shed built in 1830, this local institution was converted to a tearoom during the Depression, when the Dexters began serving all-you-can-eat pancakes, waffles, and French toast for 50¢. The prices have gone up some, but the descendants of the Dexters continue to serve pancakes and waffles made from grains ground on the property, their own country sausage, and pure maple syrup. ⊠ *Rte. 117,* ☎ *603/823–5575. D, MC, V. No dinner.*

$$–$$$$ ✕▦ **Sunset Hill House.** Since opening in 1882, this inn has been fa-
★ mous as one of the best places in New England to watch the sun go down. It's along a 1,700-ft ridge with views not just west toward the sun but also east out toward the Presidential Range. Many of the meticulously kept rooms have antiques dating from the inn's early years; gas fireplaces and decks grace the upper units. The restaurant ($$–$$$$) is highly acclaimed; try the pan-seared ostrich with a raspberry beurre blanc and then move on to roasted game hen with a lemon-spinach cream. A tavern ($–$$) serves lighter fare. ⊠ *Sunset Hill Rd., 03585,* ☎ *603/823–5522 or 800/786–4455,* 𝖶𝖤𝖡 *www.sunsethillhouse.com. 28 rooms. 2 restaurants, some in-room hot tubs, pool, mountain bikes, hiking, cross-country skiing, ice-skating, bar; no room TVs. AE, D, MC, V. BP, MAP.*

$$–$$$$ ✕▦ **Sugar Hill Inn.** The lawn's old carriage and the wraparound porch's wicker chairs put you in a nostalgic mood before you even enter this converted 1789 farmhouse. Antiques-filled guest quarters are in the main house or one of three cottages. Many rooms and suites have hand-stenciled walls and views of the Franconia Mountains; some have fireplaces. Bette Davis visited friends in this house—the room with the best vistas is named after her. The restaurant ($$$; reservations essential) serves such haute American fare as roasted duckling with a cranberry-orange glaze; the homemade desserts are always delicious. ⊠ *Rte. 117 (Box 954, 03585),* ☎ *603/823–5621 or 800/548–4748,* 𝖶𝖤𝖡 *www.sugarhillinn.com. 13 rooms, 5 suites. Restaurant, some in-room*

hot tubs, cross-country skiing, sleigh rides, pub; no room phones, no room TVs, no smoking. AE, MC, V. BP, MAP required during fall foliage season.

$$–$$$ ☷ **Foxglove.** Extensive gardens with hammocks are among the sybaritic delights at this rambling turn-of-the-20th-century home next to Lovers Lane. Common areas have a country French style and are furnished with antiques. Each guest room has a different motif. The Serengeti Room, for example, has animal-print linens, a chandelier with carnival glass shades, and black and brass bath fixtures. ⊠ *Rte. 117, 03585,* ☎ *603/823–8840 or 888/343–2220,* ᴀˣ *603/823–5755,* ᴡᴇʙ *www.foxgloveinn.com. 6 rooms. No room phones, no room TVs, no kids under 10, no smoking. BP.*

$$–$$$ ☷ **Hilltop.** Staying here is just like dropping by Grandma's. Rooms in the 1895 farmhouse have a quirky mix of antiques as well as handmade quilts and piles of pillows. Watch one of the hundreds of videos in the TV room or take in the sunset from one of the rockers on the porch. Roughly 20 acres of backcountry terrain is perfect for cross-country skiing. The large country breakfast includes homemade jams, pancakes made with homegrown berries, soufflés, and smoked meats. ⊠ *Rte. 117, 03585,* ☎ *603/823–5695 or 800/770–5695,* ᴀˣ *603/ 823–5518,* ᴡᴇʙ *www.hilltopinn.com. 3 rooms, 3 suites. Cross-country skiing, bar, library, some pets allowed; no room phones, no room TVs, no kids under 4, no-smoking rooms. D, MC, V. BP.*

Littleton

28 *9 mi northeast of Sugar Hill, 7 mi north of Franconia, 86 mi north of Concord.*

One of northern New Hampshire's largest towns is on a granite shelf along the Ammonoosuc River, whose swift current and drop of 235 ft enabled the community to flourish as a mill center in its early days. Later, the railroad came through, and Littleton grew into the region's commerce hub. In the minds of many, it's more a place to stock up on supplies than a bona fide destination, but few communities have worked harder at revitalization. Today, intriguing shops and eateries line the main street, whose tidy 19th- and early 20th-century buildings suggest a set in a Jimmy Stewart movie.

Just off Main Street, stop by the **Littleton Grist Mill** (⊠ 22 Mill St., ☎ 603/444–7478), a restored 1798 mill that contains a shop selling New England–made pottery, kitchenware, home accessories, and stoneground flour products. You'll also find original mill equipment on display.

NEED A BREAK? Beside the Littleton Grist Mill, the **Miller's Fare** (⊠ 16 Mill St., ☎ 603/ 444–2146) serves coffees, microbrews and wines, baked goods, sandwiches, and salads. In warm weather dine on a deck overlooking the Ammonoosuc River.

OFF THE BEATEN PATH **WHITEFIELD** – Like Dixville Notch and Bretton Woods, Whitefield became a prominent summer resort in the late 19th century, when wealthy industrialists flocked here to golf, ski, play polo, and hobnob. This rolling valley village tucked between two precipitous promontories may yet reclaim its vaunted past. The rambling, yellow-clapboard Mountain View Hotel has been fully refurbished. At this writing, the owners planned to open it as a hotel (with a 9-hole golf course, tennis courts, pools, and restaurants) in a year or two. Regardless, it's worth driving through the courtly Colonial Whitefield, 11 mi northeast of Littleton, and up Route

116 just beyond town to see this magnificent structure atop a bluff over-looking the Presidentials.

LANCASTER – About 8 mi north of Whitefield via U.S. 3, the affable seat of Coos County sits at the confluence of the Connecticut and Israel rivers, surrounded by low serrated peaks. Before becoming prosperous through commerce, Lancaster was an agricultural stronghold; at one time the only acceptable currency was the bushel of wheat. It's still an intimate mountain town. Like Littleton, though, it has restored much of its main street, which now has a dapper mix of Victorian homes, funky artisan and antiques shops, and prim churches and civic buildings. If you're peckish, pop inside the **Common Ground Cafe** (⊠ 55 Main St., ☎ 603/788–4379), a tiny bakery–espresso bar that serves sandwiches and snacks; it's inside a fine country clothier and shoe store called Simon the Tanner.

Dining and Lodging

$$–$$$ ✕⊡ **Beal House Inn.** Pencil-post beds, marble nightstands, and fluffy up-holstered chairs set a low-key, refined tone at this white 1833 Federal-style house. You can rent the two-bedroom suite—with a claw-foot tub, TV/VCR, kitchenette, and fireplace—by the night or the week. The cozy Flying Moose restaurant ($$–$$$) has an eclectic menu. From a classic escargots appetizer, you might move on to wood-grilled chicken in a spinach curry. Chef-owners José Luis and Catherine Pawelek prepare everything from scratch, including breakfast's specialty banana buttermilk pancakes. ⊠ 2 W. Main St., 03561, ☎ 603/444–2661 or 888/616–2325, FAX 603/444–6224, WEB www.bealhouseinn.com. 3 rooms, 5 suites. Restaurant, some kitchenettes, some in-room VCRs. MC, V. BP.

$ ⊡ **Thayer's Inn.** Although stately, this 1843 Greek Revival hotel, isn't
★ luxurious. The clean, well-kept rooms (some share a bath) are quaintly old-fashioned, with creaky floorboards, exposed pipes, vintage steam radiators, high ceilings, and comfy wing chairs. The friendly staff welcomes passersby for a look at a small third-floor room set up as it would have appeared in the 1840s or for a visit to the sixth-floor cupola, with its 360-degree views. There's no elevator—good to know if you planned to book an upper-floor room. ⊠ 111 Main St., 03561, ☎ 603/444–6469 or 800/634–8179, WEB www.thayersinn.com. 31 rooms, 7 suites. Some refrigerators, some in-room VCRs. MC, V.

Shopping

Potato Barn Antiques Center (⊠ U.S. 3, Northumberland, 6 mi north of Lancaster, ☎ 603/636–2611) has several dealers under one roof—specialties include vintage farm tools, clothing, and costume jewelry. In a restored mill on the Ammonoosuc River, the **Tannery Marketplace** (⊠ 111 Saranac St., ☎ 603/444–1200) contains an amazing array of architectural relics, antiques, collectibles, and estate leftovers. The **Village Book Store** (⊠ 81 Main St., ☎ 603/444–5263) has comprehensive selections of both nonfiction and fiction titles.

Bethlehem

29 *5 mi southeast of Littleton.*

In the days before antihistamines, hay-fever sufferers came by the bus load to Bethlehem, elevation 1,462 ft, whose crisp air has a blissfully low pollen count. Today this hamlet is notable for its distinctive arts and crafts, Victorian and Colonial homes, art deco movie theater, and shops and eateries on its main street.

Dining and Lodging

$$–$$$ ✕ **Tim-bir Alley.** For eight months of the year, this restaurant serves dinner in the Adair B&B's elegant dining rooms. The menu, which changes weekly, utilizes regional American ingredients in creative ways. Main dishes have included pork tenderloin with maple-balsamic glaze and apple-almond relish as well as sunflower-encrusted salmon with a smoked-tomato puree. Save room for such desserts as chocolate-glazed espresso cheesecake. The hours here change seasonally (and they're sometimes sporadic within a given season); it's best to call ahead. ⊠ *80 Guider La.,* ☎ *603/444–6142. No credit cards. No lunch.*

$$$–$$$$ ▣ **Adair.** In 1927 attorney Frank Hogan built this three-story Geor-
★ gian Revival home as a wedding present for his daughter, Dorothy Adair. Today it's a luxurious country inn, with walking paths that wind through gardens on 200 acres. Rooms, which have garden or mountain views, are furnished with period antiques and reproductions; many have fireplaces. One suite has a large two-person hot tub, a fireplace, a balcony, and a king-size sleigh bed. ⊠ *80 Guider La., 03574,* ☎ *603/444–2600 or 888/444–2600,* WEB *www.adairinn.com. 7 rooms, 2 suites, 1 cottage. Restaurant, some in-room hot tubs, tennis court, billiards; no room phones, no room TVs, no kids under 12, no smoking. AE, D, MC, V. BP.*

Outdoor Activities and Sports

The Society for the Protection of New Hampshire Forests owns two properties in Bethlehem open to visitors. **Bretzfelder Park** (⊠ Prospect St., ☎ 603/444–6228), a 77-acre nature and wildlife park, has a picnic shelter, hiking, and cross-country ski trails. The **Rocks Christmas Tree Farm** (⊠ 113 Glessner Rd., ☎ 603/444–6228) is a working Christmas-tree farm with walking trails, historical buildings, and educational programs.

Bretton Woods

30 *14 mi southeast of Bethlehem, 28 mi northeast of Lincoln/Woodstock.*

In the early 1900s private rail cars brought the elite from New York and Philadelphia to the Mount Washington Hotel, the jewel of Bretton Woods. The hotel was the site of a famous World Monetary Fund conference in 1944, which greatly affected the post–World War II economy. The area is also known for its cog railway and eponymous ski resort.

★ ☾ In 1858 Sylvester Marsh petitioned the state legislature for permission to build a steam railway up Mt. Washington. A politico retorted that he'd have better luck building a railroad to the moon. Just 11 years later, the **Mt. Washington Cog Railway** chugged up to the summit, and so it remains one of the state's most beloved attractions—a thrill in either direction. Allow three hours round-trip; call for schedule information. ⊠ *U.S. 302, 6 mi northeast of Bretton Woods,* ☎ *603/278–5404; 800/922–8825 outside New Hampshire;,* WEB *www.thecog.com.* ▨ *$49.* ☉ *Late Apr.–late May, weekends; late May–early Nov., daily.*

En Route Scenic U.S. 302 winds through the steep, wooded mountains on either side of spectacular Crawford Notch, southeast of Bretton Woods, and passes through **Crawford Notch State Park** (⊠ U.S. 302, Harts Location, ☎ 603/374–2272), where you can picnic and take a short hike to Arethusa Falls or the Silver and Flume cascades. The visitor center has a gift shop and a cafeteria; there's also a campground.

Dining and Lodging

$$–$$$$ ✕🏠 **Bretton Woods Mountain Resort.** Of Bretton Woods's three ho-
★ tels, the most famous is the leviathan 1902 Mount Washington, a
grand resort with a 900-ft-long veranda and full views of the Presi-
dentials. With stately public rooms and large, Victorian-style guest quar-
ters, the hotel retains an early 20th-century formality. A jacket and tie
are required in the dining room ($$$$), which serves such seasonal dishes
as lemon lobster ravioli with shrimp and scallops or roast pork with
onions and mushrooms. The mid-priced rooms at the 1896 Bretton Arms
Country Inn are less formal. On arrival, make reservations for its con-
temporary dining room ($$–$$$). Rooms at the more modern Bret-
ton Woods Motor Inn have balconies or patios. The Continental
cuisine at its Darby's Restaurant ($$) is served around a fireplace; the
bar is a skier hangout. For long stays, look into the 55 town homes.
✉ *U.S. 302, 03575,* ☎ *603/278–1000 or 800/258–0330,* FAX *603/
278–8838,* WEB *www.mtwashington.com. 339 units. 8 restaurants,
some in-room hot tubs, some kitchens, driving range, 27-hole golf course,
12 tennis courts, 2 pools (1 indoor), health club, hot tub, massage, sauna,
fishing, bicycles, hiking, horseback riding, cross-country skiing, downhill skiing, sleigh rides, 5 bars, recreation room, baby-sitting, children's programs (ages 5–12), meeting rooms. AE, D, MC, V. MAP.*

$ ⛺ **Dry River Campground.** This rustic campground in Crawford Notch
State Park has 30 tent sites and is a popular base for hiking the White
Mountain National Forest. ✉ *U.S. 302, Harts Location (Box 177, Twin
Mountain 03595),* ☎ *603/271–3628,* WEB *www.nhparks.state.nh.us/
parkops/parks/crawford.html. Closed mid-Dec.–mid-May.*

Ski Area

BRETTON WOODS

This expansive, well-run ski area has a tri-level base lodge, convenient
parking and drop-off areas, and an uncrowded setting. The views of
Mt. Washington alone are worth the visit; the scenery is especially beautiful from the Top o' Quad restaurant and from the former Cog Railway car atop West Mountain. ✉ *U.S. 302, 03575,* ☎ *603/278–3320;
603/278–3333 weather conditions; 800/232–2972 information; 800/
258–0330 lodging,* WEB *www.brettonwoods.com.*

Downhill. Although its 76 trails will appeal mostly to novice and intermediate skiers, steeper pitches near the top of the 1,500-ft vertical
and glade skiing will satisfy experts. Skiers and snowboarders can try
a terrain park with jumps and a halfpipe. The Accelerator halfpipe is
for snowboarders only. One high-speed detachable quad, one fixed-
grip quad, one triple, and three double chairlifts service the trails. The
area has night skiing and snowboarding on Friday, Saturday, and holidays. A limited lift-ticket policy helps keep lines short.

Cross-country. The large, full-service cross-country ski center has 100
km (62 mi) of groomed and double-track trails, many of them lift-
serviced. You can also rent snowshoes.

Child care. The nursery takes children ages 2 months–5 years. The ski
school has an all-day program for children ages 4 to 12. There's also
a snowboarding program for children 8–12. Rates include lifts, lessons,
equipment, lunch, and supervised play.

Bartlett

③① *18 mi southeast of Bretton Woods.*

With Bear Mountain to its south, Mt. Parker to its north, Mt. Cardi-
gan to its west, and the Saco River to its east, Bartlett, incorporated
in 1790, has an unforgettable setting. Lovely Bear Notch Road (closed

in winter) has the only midpoint access to the Kancamagus Highway (Route 112).

Lodging

$$–$$$$ ⊡ **Grand Summit Hotel & Conference Center.** The gables and curves of this resort mimic the slopes of nearby Attitash Bear Peak. Luxurious contemporary-style rooms have kitchenettes, VCRs, and stereos. The main dining room serves passable American fare; dishes at Crawford's Pub and Grill are lighter. ⊠ *U.S. 302 (Box 429, 03812),* ☎ *603/ 374–1900 or 888/554–1900,* ᴼᴬˣ *603/374–3040,* ᵂᴱᴮ *www.attitash.com. 143 rooms. 2 restaurants, room service, in-room data ports, some kitchens, in-room VCRs, pool, health club, hot tub, massage, steam room, downhill skiing, bar, recreation room, laundry facilities. AE, D, MC, V.*

$$–$$$ ⊡ **Attitash Mountain Village.** The style at this condo-motel complex is alpine contemporary, and the staff is young and enthusiastic. Units, some with fireplaces, accommodate from 2 to 14 people. The restaurant, with a varied and family-friendly menu, has unobstructed mountain views. ⊠ *U.S. 302, 03812,* ☎ *603/374–6501 or 800/862–1600,* ᴼᴬˣ *603/374–6509,* ᵂᴱᴮ *www.attitashmtvillage.com. 300 units. Restaurant, some in-room hot tubs, some kitchens, 2 tennis courts, 2 pools (1 indoor), sauna, fishing, mountain bikes, hiking, gym, cross-country skiing, downhill skiing, ice-skating, pub, recreation room, playground, laundry service, meeting rooms. AE, D, MC, V.*

Ski Area

ATTITASH BEAR PEAK

This high-profile resort, which hosts many special events, continues to expand and improve its infrastructure. Lodging at the base of the mountain is in condos and motel-style units. Attitash has a computerized lift-ticket system that allows skiers to pay as they run. Skiers can share the ticket, which is good for two years. ⊠ *U.S. 302 (Box 302, 03812),* ☎ *603/374–2368; 800/223–7669 snow conditions; 800/223– 7669 lodging,* ᵂᴱᴮ *www.attitash.com.*

Downhill. Enhanced with massive snowmaking (98%), the trails number 70 on two peaks, both with full-service base lodges. The bulk of the skiing and boarding is geared to intermediates and experts, with some steep pitches and glades. Beginners enjoy good terrain on the lower mountain and some runs from the top. At 500 ft, the Ground Zero halfpipe is New England's longest. The Attitash Adventure Center has a rental shop, lessons desk, and children's programs. Serving the 36 km (22 mi) of trails and the 1,750-ft vertical drop are two high-speed quads, one fixed-grip quad, three triple and three double chairlifts, and three surface tows.

Cross-country. The **Bear Notch Ski Touring Center** (☎ 603/374–2277) has more than 70 km (43 mi) of cross-country trails, more than 60 km (37 mi) of which are skate groomed and tracked. Backcountry skiing is unlimited, and there are 35 acres of tree skiing. Guests staying at the Grand Summit Hotel can rent equipment, get trail passes, and connect to the trails from the hotel door.

Child care. The Attitash Adventure Center nursery takes children ages 6 months to 5 years. Other programs accommodate children up to 16.

Summer activities. Attitash Bear Park has two dry alpine slides, four water slides, Buddy Bear's Playpool for children, horseback riding, lift-serviced mountain biking, and a driving range. A chairlift whisks passengers to the White Mountain Observation Tower, which delivers 270-degree views of the Whites.

Glen

③② *6 mi northeast of Bartlett; 89 mi northeast of Concord; 71 mi north-west of Portland, Maine.*

Glen is hardly more than a crossroads between North Conway and Jackson, but its central location has made it the home of a few noteworthy attractions and dining and lodging options.

🍽 That cluster of fluorescent buildings on Route 16 is **Story Land,** a theme park with life-size storybook and nursery-rhyme characters. The 16 rides and four shows include a flume ride, a Victorian-theme river-raft ride, and a farm-family variety show. In early spring and late fall, when only parts of the park are open, admission is reduced to $14. ⊠ *Rte. 16,* ☎ *603/383–4186,* WEB *www.storylandnh.com.* 🎟 *$19.* ☉ *Mid-June–Labor Day, daily 9–6; Memorial Day–mid-June and Labor Day–Columbus Day, weekends 10–5.*

🍽 **Heritage New Hampshire** uses theatrical sets, sound effects, and animation to render the state's history. You can "sail" on the *Reliance* from a village in 1634 England to the New World and then saunter along Portsmouth's streets in the late 1700s. Exhibits continue through the present day. ⊠ *Rte. 16,* ☎ *603/383–4186,* WEB *www.heritagenh.com.* 🎟 *$10.* ☉ *Memorial Day–mid-June, weekends 9–5; mid-June–mid-Oct., daily 9–5.*

Dining and Lodging

$–$$$ ✕ **Red Parka Pub.** Practically an institution, the Red Parka Pub has been in downtown Glen for more than two decades. The menu has everything a family could want, from an all-you-can-eat salad bar to scallop pie. The barbecued ribs are favorites, and you'll find hand-carved steaks of every type, from aged New York sirloin to prime rib. ⊠ *U.S. 302,* ☎ *603/383–4344. Reservations not accepted. AE, D, MC, V.*

$–$$ ✕ **Margarita Grill.** Après-ski and hiking types congregate in the dining room in cold weather and on the covered patio when it's warm for homemade salsas, wood-fired steaks, ribs, burgers, and a smattering of Tex-Mex and Cajun specialties. Unwind at the tequila bar after a day on the mountains. ⊠ *U.S. 302,* ☎ *603/383–6556. AE, D, MC, V.*

$$–$$$ ✕▨ **Bernerhof Inn.** With its hardwood floors, hooked rugs, and mix of antique and reproduction furniture, this hotel seems right at home in an alpine setting. The fanciest six rooms have brass beds and spa-size tubs; one suite has a Finnish sauna. The menu at the Rare Bear Bistro ($–$$$) includes Swiss specialties such as fondue and Wiener schnitzel as well as new American dishes—seared scallops with sage butter and butternut-squash sauce is a favorite. The Black Bear pub ($–$$) pours microbrews and serves sandwiches, pastas, bratwurst, and fish-and-chips. ⊠ *U.S. 302 (Box 240, 03838),* ☎ *603/383–9132 or 800/548–8007,* FAX *603/383–0809,* WEB *www.bernerhofinn.com. 7 rooms, 2 suites. Restaurant, some in-room hot tubs, pub; no smoking. AE, D, MC, V. BP.*

$$–$$$ ▨ **Storybook Resort Inn.** On a hillside near Attitash Bear Peak, this motor inn with large rooms is well suited to families. Copperfield's Restaurant serves gingerbread, sticky buns, omelets, and a children's menu. ⊠ *Intersection of U.S. 302 and Rte. 16 (Box 129, Glen Junction 03838),* ☎ *603/383–6800,* FAX *603/383–4678,* WEB *www.storybookresort.com. 78 rooms. Restaurant, picnic area, refrigerators, tennis court, 2 pools (1 indoor), wading pool, gym, sauna, Ping-Pong, bar, recreation room, playground, laundry facilities. AE, DC, MC, V.*

Jackson

★ ㉝ *5 mi north of Glen.*

Just off Route 16 via a red covered bridge, Jackson has retained its storybook New England character. Art and antiques shopping, tennis, golf, fishing, and hiking to waterfalls are among the draws. When the snow falls, Jackson becomes the state's cross-country skiing capital. Four downhill ski areas are nearby.

Dining and Lodging

$–$$$ ✕ **Red Fox Pub & Restaurant.** Some say this restaurant overlooking the Wentworth Golf Club gets its name from a wily fox with a penchant for stealing golf balls off the fairway. The wide-ranging menu has barbecue ribs and blue-cheese-and-bacon burgers as well as more substantial dishes such as seared sea scallops with an Asiago cream sauce. The Sunday jazz breakfast buffet draws raves. ⊠ *Rte. 16A,* ☎ *603/383–6659. AE, D, MC, V.*

$$$$ ✕🏨 **Inn at Thorn Hill.** Architect Stanford White designed this 1895 Victorian house, which is just steps from cross-country trails and Jackson village. The main inn's romantic touches include rose-motif wallpaper and such antiques as a blue-velvet fainting couch; many rooms have gas fireplaces. Carriage-house quarters are woodsy, and the cottages are secluded. The restaurant ($$$–$$$$; reservations essential) serves fine contemporary fare: the cider-and-chipotle-glazed shrimp with toasted barley and herbed-sausage risotto is a good bet. ⊠ *Thorn Hill Rd. (Box A, 03846),* ☎ *603/383–4242 or 800/289–8990,* ℻ *603/383–8062,* ⓦⓔⓑ *www.innatthornhill.com. 12 rooms, 4 suites, 3 cottages. Restaurant, some in-room hot tubs, some in-room VCRs, pool, hot tub, croquet, cross-country skiing, pub; no TV in some rooms, no smoking. AE, MC, V. BP, MAP.*

$$$–$$$$ ✕🏨 **Christmas Farm Inn.** Despite its wintery name, this 1778 inn is an all-season retreat. Rooms in the main building and the saltbox next door have Laura Ashley and Ralph Lauren prints. Suites have beamed ceilings and fireplaces. Standbys in the restaurant ($$$–$$$$) are grilled maple-glaze pork loin and tomato-fennel-saffron bouillabaisse. ⊠ *Rte. 16B (Box CC, 03846),* ☎ *603/383–4313 or 800/443–5837,* ℻ *603/383–6495,* ⓦⓔⓑ *www.christmasfarminn.com. 41 units. Restaurant, some in-room hot tubs, pool, health club, hot tub, massage, sauna, volleyball, cross-country skiing, pub, recreation room; no-smoking rooms. AE, MC, V. MAP.*

$$$–$$$$ ✕🏨 **Wentworth.** This pale-yellow 1869 Victorian charms with individually decorated rooms—many with fireplaces—accented with antiques. The dining room ($$–$$$) serves a five-course candlelight dinner with a menu that changes seasonally. Good choices are oven-poached lemon sole in a lobster-vanilla broth, and cider-glazed chicken skewers with thyme-whipped potatoes. ⊠ *Rte. 16A, 03846,* ☎ *603/383–9700 or 800/637–0013,* ℻ *603/383–4265,* ⓦⓔⓑ *www.thewentworth.com. 60 rooms in summer, 52 in winter. Restaurant, some in-room hot tubs, tennis court, pool, billiards, cross-country skiing, ice-skating, sleigh rides, bar. AE, D, DC, MC, V. MAP.*

$$$–$$$$ 🏨 **Ellis River House.** Most of the Victorian-style rooms in this unabashedly romantic inn on the Ellis River have fireplaces; some have balconies. In winter, a snow bridge across the river connects you with the Ellis River Trail and Jackson's cross-country trail system. ⊠ *Rte. 16 (Box 656, 03846),* ☎ *603/383–9339 or 800/233–8309,* ℻ *603/383–4142,* ⓦⓔⓑ *www.erhinn.com. 15 rooms, 3 suites, 1 cottage. Restaurant, some in-room hot tubs, pool, hot tub, sauna, billiards, cross-country skiing, pub; no kids under 12, no-smoking rooms. AE, D, DC, MC, V. BP.*

$$–$$$$ ⊡ **Inn at Jackson.** The builders of this 1902 Victorian, which overlooks the village, followed a design by Stanford White. Although the foyer's staircase is grand, everything else—from the braided rugs on the hardwood floors to the smattering of antiques—is unpretentious. The airy guest rooms have oversize windows; six have fireplaces. ⊠ *Thorn Hill Rd. (Box 807, 03846),* ☎ *603/383–4321 or 800/289–8600,* FAX *603/383–4085,* WEB *www.innatjackson.com. 14 rooms. Hot tub, cross-country skiing. AE, D, DC, MC, V. CP.*

$$–$$$$ ⊡ **Nordic Village Resort.** The light woods and white walls of these condos are as Scandinavian as the snowy views. Larger units have fireplaces and full kitchens. The 165-acre property is part of Luxury Mountain Getaways, which operates several upscale condos and hotels in the area. ⊠ *Rte. 16, 03846,* ☎ *603/383–9101 or 800/472–5207,* FAX *603/383–9823,* WEB *www.luxurymountaingetaways.com. 140 condominiums. Some in-room hot tubs, some kitchens, tennis court, 3 pools (1 indoor), hot tub, steam room, basketball, hiking, volleyball, cross-country skiing, ice-skating, sleigh rides. D, MC, V.*

$$–$$$ ⊡ **Eagle Mountain House.** With downhill slopes nearby and cross-country trails beginning at this 1879 country estate, skiing is the order of the day. Public areas are rustic but elegant, and the large guest rooms are furnished with late-Victorian pieces. On a warm day, you can nurse a drink in a rocking chair on the wraparound deck. ⊠ *Carter Notch Rd., 03846,* ☎ *603/383–9111 or 800/966–5779,* FAX *603/383–0854,* WEB *www.eaglemt.com. 93 rooms. 2 restaurants, 9-hole golf course, 2 tennis courts, pool, health club, hot tub, sauna, cross-country skiing, video game room, playground. AE, D, DC, MC, V.*

$$ ⊡ **Wildcat Inn & Tavern.** After a day of skiing, you can collapse on a comfy sofa by the fire at this 19th-century inn. The fragrance of home baking permeates into the suite-style guest rooms, which are full of knick-knacks and furniture of various periods. The tavern, where bands often perform, attracts skiers. In summer, dining is available in the garden. ⊠ *Rte. 16A, 03846,* ☎ *603/383–4245 or 800/228–4245,* FAX *603/383–6456,* WEB *www.wildcatinnandtavern.com. 6 rooms, 4 with bath; 7 suites; 1 cottage. 2 restaurants, some kitchenettes, in-room VCRs, bar. AE, MC, V. BP, MAP.*

$–$$ ⊡ **Briarcliff Motel.** This bright and clean motel is a short drive from outlet shopping and ½ mi south of North Conway Village along Route 16. Rooms have mini-refrigerators, coffeemakers, and utilitarian but perfectly pleasant furnishings. ⊠ *Rte. 16/U.S. 302 (Box 504, 03860),* ☎ *603/356–5584 or 800/338–4291,* WEB *www.briarcliffmotel.com. 18 rooms. Refrigerators, pool. AE, D, DC, MC. BP.*

Outdoor Activities and Sports

Nestlenook Farm (⊠ Dinsmore Rd., ☎ 603/383–9443) maintains an outdoor ice-skating rink with rentals, music, and a bonfire. Going snowshoeing or taking a sleigh ride are other winter options; in summer you can fly-fish or ride in a horse-drawn carriage.

Ski Areas

BLACK MOUNTAIN

Friendly, informal Black Mountain has a warming southern exposure. The Family Passport, which allows two adults and two juniors to ski at discounted rates, is a good value. Midweek rates here are usually the lowest in Mt. Washington valley. ⊠ *Rte. 16B, 03846,* ☎ *603/383–4490; 800/475–4669 snow conditions; 800/698–4490 lodging,* WEB *www.blackmt.com.*

Downhill. The 55 trails and six glades on the 1,100-vertical-ft mountain are evenly divided among beginner, intermediate, and expert.

There are triple and double chairlifts and two surface tows. In addition to trails, snowboarders can use two terrain parks and the half-pipe.

Child care. The nursery takes children 6 months–5 years. Kids 3–12 can take classes at the ski school.

JACKSON SKI TOURING FOUNDATION

One of the nation's top four cross-country skiing areas has 154 km (97 mi) of trails. About 96 km (60 mi) are track groomed and 85 km (53 mi) are skate groomed. There are roughly 63 km (39 mi) of marked backcountry trails. You can arrange lessons and rentals at the lodge, in the center of Jackson village. ⊠ *Main St., 03846,* ☎ *603/383–9355,* WEB *www.jacksonxc.org.*

Mt. Washington

★ ❸ *20 mi northwest of Jackson.*

In summer, you can drive to the top of Mt. Washington, the highest peak (6,288 ft) in the northeastern United States and home of a weather station that has recorded the world's highest winds. The Mt. Washington Auto Road, opened in 1861 and said to be the nation's first manufactured tourist attraction, begins at the Glen House, a gift shop and rest stop 15 mi north of Glen on Route 16. Allow two hours round-trip and check your brakes first. Cars with automatic transmissions that can't shift down into first gear aren't allowed on the road.

If you prefer not to drive on a curving, narrow road, take a guided tour in one of the "stages" (vans) that leave from Great Glen Trails Outdoors Center. In winter, they're refitted with snowmobile-like treads and can travel to just above the tree line. You have the option of cross-country skiing or snowshoeing down. (In summer, you can also take the Mt. Washington Cog Railway to the summit; ☞ Bretton Woods.)

Up top, visit the **Sherman Adams Summit Building,** which contains a museum of memorabilia from each of the three hotels that have stood on this spot and a display of native plant life and alpine flowers. Stand in the glassed-in viewing area to hear the wind roar. ☎ *603/466–3988,* WEB *www.mt-washington.com.* ☜ *Auto road $16 per car and driver, plus $6 for each adult passenger; van fare $22.* ☾ *Private cars, mid-May–late Oct.; van tours daily.*

Although not a town per se, scenic **Pinkham Notch** covers Mt. Washington's eastern side and includes several ravines, including Tuckerman Ravine, famous for spring skiing. The Appalachian Mountain Club maintains a large visitor center here on Route 16 that provides information to hikers and travelers and has guided hikes, outdoor skills workshops, a cafeteria, lodging, regional topography displays, and an outdoors shop.

Lodging

$–$$ 🏨 **Joe Dodge Lodge at Pinkham Notch.** The Appalachian Mountain Club operates this rustic lodge at the base of Mt. Washington. Accommodations range from single-sex bunk rooms (rented by the bunk) for as many as five people to private rooms—all have gleaming wood, cheerful quilts, and reading lights. The restaurant serves buffet breakfasts and lunches and family-style dinners. Packages include breakfast and dinner, plus skiing at Great Glen Trails and/or Wildcat Ski Area. ⊠ *Rte. 16 (Box 298, Gorham 03581),* ☎ *603/466–2727,* FAX *603/466–3871,* WEB *www.outdoors.org. 102 beds without bath. Restaurant, no room phones, no room TVs, no-smoking rooms. MC, V. MAP.*

Ski Areas

GREAT GLEN TRAILS OUTDOOR CENTER

A fire destroyed the center's large, sunny base lodge in spring 2001, but at this writing plans were under way to build an impressive 16,000-square-ft replacement. Cross-country skiers will use the center in winter, and hikers, mountain bikers, and backpackers will be able to take advantage of it in summer. Amenities will include a huge ski-gear and sports shop, food court, climbing wall, observation deck, and fieldstone fireplace. ⊠ *Rte. 16 (Box 300, Gorham 03581)*, ☎ *603/466–2333*, WEB *www.mt-washington.com/ggt.*

Cross-country. There are 40 km (24 mi) of cross-country trails—some with snowmaking—as well as access to more than 1,100 acres of backcountry. It's even possible to ski or snowshoe the lower half of the Mt. Washington Auto Road. Trees shelter most of the trails, so Mt. Washington's famous weather won't be a concern.

Summer activities. Great Glen Trails will put its extensive trail network to use for hiking, trail running, and mountain biking. The center will also have programs in canoeing, kayaking, and fly-fishing.

WILDCAT

Glade skiers favor Wildcat, with 28 acres of official tree skiing. Runs include some stunning double-black-diamond trails. Skiers who can hold a wedge should check out the 4-km-long (2½-mi-long) Polecat. Experts can zip down the Lynx. Views of Mt. Washington and Tuckerman Ravine are superb. The trails are classic New England—narrow and winding. ⊠ *Rte. 16, Pinkham Notch, Jackson 03846*, ☎ *603/466–3326; 888/754–9453 snow conditions; 800/255–6439 lodging*, WEB *www.skiwildcat.com.*

Downhill. Wildcat's expert runs deserve their designations and then some. Intermediates have mid-mountain–to–base trails, and beginners will find gentle terrain and a broad teaching slope. Snowboarders have several terrain parks and the run of the mountain. The 44 runs, with a 2,100-ft vertical drop, are served by one high-speed detachable quad and three triple chairlifts.

Child care. The child-care center takes children ages 2 months and up. Kids ages 5–12 can participate in SKIwee instruction on designated slopes.

Dixville Notch

㉟ *63 mi north of Mt. Washington, 66 mi northeast of Littleton, 149 mi north of Concord.*

Just 12 mi from the Canadian border, this tiny community is known for two things. It's the home of the Balsams Wilderness, one of New Hampshire's oldest and most celebrated resorts. And Dixville Notch and Harts Location are the first election districts in the nation to vote in the presidential primaries and general elections. At midnight on Election Day, the 30 or so Dixville Notch voters gather in the little meeting room beside a hotel service bar to cast their ballots and make national news.

One of the favorite pastimes in this area is spotting moose, those large, ungainly, yet elusive members of the deer family. Although you may catch sight of one or more yourself, **Northern Forest Moose Tours** (☎ 603/752–6060 or 800/992–7480) conducts bus tours of the region that have a 97% success rate for spotting moose.

OFF THE
BEATEN PATH

PITTSBURG – Well north of the White Mountains, in the great north woods, Pittsburg contains the four Connecticut Lakes and the springs that form the Connecticut River. The state's northern tip—a chunk of about 250 square mi—lies within the town's borders, the result of a dispute between the United States and Canada. The two countries couldn't decide on a border, so the region's inhabitants declared themselves independent of both countries in 1832. They named their nation the Indian Stream Republic, after the river that passes through the territory; its capital was Pittsburg. In 1835 the feisty, 40-man Indian Stream militia invaded Canada, with limited success. The Indian Stream War ended more by common consent than surrender; in 1842 the Webster-Ashburton Treaty fixed the international boundary. Indian Stream was incorporated as Pittsburg, New Hampshire's largest township.

Remote though it is, this frontier town teems with hunters, boaters, fishermen, hikers, and photographers from early summer through winter. Especially in the colder months, moose sightings are common. The town has more than a dozen lodges and several informal eateries. It's about a 90-minute drive from Littleton and 40-minute drive from Dixville Notch; add another 30 minutes to reach Fourth Connecticut Lake, nearly at the Canadian border. On your way, as you pass the village of Stewartson, note the sign along U.S. 3 marking the 45th Parallel, the point exactly midway between the Equator and the North Pole.

Dining and Lodging

$$$$
★

✕🏨 **The Balsams Wilderness.** Nestled in the pine groves of the north woods, this lavish grande dame has been rolling out the red carpet since 1866. It draws families, golf enthusiasts, skiers, and others for a varied slate of activities—from dancing to cooking demonstrations. The individually decorated rooms vary in size but are generally spacious and comfortably furnished; all have mountain views. In the dining room ($$–$$$$; jacket and tie), you might sample a chilled strawberry soup spiked with Grand Marnier, followed by poached salmon with golden caviar sauce. Rates, though steep, include breakfast and dinner and unlimited use of the facilities. ✉ *Rte. 26, 03576,* ☎ *603/255–3400; 800/255–0600; 800/255–0800 in New Hampshire;* FAX *603/255–4221,* WEB *www.thebalsams.com. 204 rooms. 3 restaurants, some in-room hot tubs, driving range, 18-hole golf course, 6 tennis courts, pool, gym, massage, boating, fishing, mountain bikes, hiking, cross-country skiing, downhill skiing, ice-skating, bar, shops, children's programs (ages 1–12), dry cleaning, laundry service, business services. AE, D, MC, V. Closed late Mar.–mid-May and mid-Oct.–mid-Dec. MAP winter, FAP spring–fall.*

$$$
🏨 **The Glen.** This rustic lodge with stick furniture, fieldstone, and cedar is on First Connecticut Lake and surrounded by log cabins, seven of which are right on the water. The cabins have efficiency kitchens and mini-refrigerators—not that you'll need either, because rates include meals in the lodge restaurant. ✉ *77 Glen Rd., 1 mi off U.S. 3, Pittsburg 03592,* ☎ *603/538–6500 or 800/445–4536,* WEB *theglen.org. 8 rooms, 10 cabins. Restaurant, kitchenettes, lake; no room phones, no room TVs. No credit cards. Closed mid-Oct.–mid-May. FAP.*

Outdoor Activities and Sports

Dixville Notch State Park (✉ Rte. 26, ☎ 603/323–2087), in the northernmost notch of the White Mountains, has picnic areas, a waterfall, and hiking trails.

Ski Area

THE BALSAMS WILDERNESS

Skiing was originally provided as an amenity for hotel guests at the Balsams, but the area has become popular with day-trippers as well.

⊠ *Rte. 26, 03576,* ☎ *603/255–3400; 603/255–3951 snow condi-tions; 800/255–0600; 800/255–0800 in New Hampshire;* FAX *603/255–4221.*

Downhill. Slopes with such names as Sanguinary, Umbagog, and Ma-galloway may sound tough, but they're only moderately difficult, lean-ing toward intermediate. There are 14 trails and four glades for every skill level from the top of the 1,000-ft vertical. One double chairlift and two T-bars carry you up the mountain. There's a halfpipe for snow-boarders.

Cross-country. The Balsams has 95 km (59 mi) of cross-country ski-ing, tracked and groomed for skating. Natural-history markers anno-tate some trails; you can also try telemark and backcountry skiing, and there are 29 km (18 mi) of snowshoeing trails.

Child care. The ski-lodge nursery takes children ages 6 months–5 years at no charge to hotel guests. Lessons are for kids 3 and up.

North Conway

36 *76 mi south of Dixville Notch, 7 mi south of Glen, 41 mi east of Lin-coln/North Woodstock.*

Before the arrival of the outlet stores, the town drew visitors for its in-spiring scenery, ski resorts, and access to White Mountain National Forest. Today, however, shopping is as big a sport as skiing, and busi-nesses line Route 16 for several miles.

The **Conway Scenic Railroad** operates trips of varying durations in vin-tage coaches pulled by steam or diesel engines. The views are fine in the dome observation coach on the 5½-hour trip through Crawford Notch. Lunch is served aboard the dining car on the Valley Train to Conway or Bartlett. The 1874 station displays lanterns, old tickets and timetables, and other railroad artifacts. Reserve early during foliage season for the dining excursions. ⊠ *Rte. 16/U.S. 302 (38 Norcross Cir.),* ☎ *603/356–5251 or 800/232–5251,* WEB *www.conwayscenic.com.* ☺ *$9.50–$46.* ☺ *Mid-Apr.–late Dec; call for times.*

At **Echo Lake State Park,** you needn't be a rock climber to catch views from the 700-ft White Horse and Cathedral ledges. From the top you'll see the entire valley, in which Echo Lake shines like a diamond. An unmarked trailhead another 7/10 mi on West Side Road leads to Diana's Baths, a series of waterfalls. ⊠ *Off U.S. 302,* ☎ *603/356–2672.* ☺ *$3.* ☺ *Late May–mid-June, weekends dawn–dusk; mid-June–early Sept., daily dawn–dusk.*

The **Hartmann Model Railroad Museum** houses 14 operating layouts (from G to Z scales), about 2,000 engines, and more than 5,000 cars and coaches. A café, a crafts store, a hobby shop, and an outdoor ride-on train are on-site. ⊠ *Rte. 16/U.S. 302 and Town Hall Rd., Intervale,* ☎ *603/356–9922,* WEB *www.hartmannrr.com.* ☺ *$6.* ☺ *Mid-June–mid-Oct., daily 9–5; mid-Oct.–mid-June, daily 10–5.*

The hands-on exhibits at the **Weather Discovery Center** teach how weather is monitored and how it affects us. The facility is a collabo-ration between the National and Atmospheric Administration Fore-cast Systems lab and the Mt. Washington Observatory at the summit of Mt. Washington. ⊠ *Rte. 16/U.S. 302, ⅓ mi north of rail tracks,* ☎ *603/356–2137,* WEB *www.mountwashington.org/discovery.* ☺ *$2.* ☺ *Fri.–Tues. 10–5.*

Dining and Lodging

$–$$ ✕ **Delaney's Hole in the Wall.** This casual restaurant has eclectic memorabilia that includes autographed baseballs and an early photo of skiing at Tuckerman Ravine hanging over the fireplace. Entrées range from fish-and-chips to fajitas to mussels and scallops sautéed with spiced sausage and Louisiana seasonings. ☒ *Rte. 16, ¼ mi north of North Conway,* ☎ *603/356–7776. D, MC, V.*

$–$$ ✕ **Muddy Moose.** Especially popular with younger singles and families, the Muddy Moose is inviting and rustic thanks to its fieldstone walls, exposed wood, and understated lighting. Dig into a Greek salad, grilled chicken Caesar wrap, char-grilled pork chops with a maple-cider glaze, or muddy moose pie. ☒ *Rte. 16, just south of North Conway,* ☎ *603/356–7696. AE, D, MC, V.*

$$$–$$$$ ✕🏠 **Snowvillage Inn.** Journalist Frank Simonds built the gambrel-
★ roof main house in 1916. To complement the inn's tome-jammed bookshelves, guest rooms are named for famous authors. The nicest of the rooms, with 12 windows that look out over the Presidential Range, is a tribute to Robert Frost. Two additional buildings—the carriage house and the chimney house—also have libraries. Menu highlights in the candlelit dining room ($$$; reservations essential) include grilled hanger steak with a roasted onion and Stilton sauce. For a different outdoors experience, reserve a place on an organized llama trek up Foss Mountain. Trips include a picnic with champagne. ☒ *Stuart Rd., 5 mi southeast of Conway (Box 68, Snowville 03849),* ☎ *603/447–2818 or 800/ 447–4345,* 𝖥𝖠𝖷 *603/447–5268,* WEB *www.snowvillageinn.com. 18 rooms. Restaurant, sauna, cross-country skiing; no room phones, no room TVs, no kids under 6, no smoking. AE, D, MC, V. BP, MAP.*

$$$–$$$$ ✕🏠 **White Mountain Hotel and Resort.** Rooms in this hotel at the base of Whitehorse Ledge have mountain views. Proximity to the White Mountain National Forest and Echo Lake State Park makes you feel farther away from the outlet malls than you actually are. Dinner at the Ledges restaurant ($$$) might include chicken saltimbocca or mustard-roasted rack of lamb with a jalapeño relish. ☒ *West Side Rd. (Box 1828, 03860),* ☎ *800/533–6301,* ☎ 𝖥𝖠𝖷 *603/356–7100,* WEB *www. whitemountainhotel.com. 69 rooms, 11 suites. 2 restaurants, 9-hole golf course, tennis court, pool, health club, hot tub, sauna, hiking, cross-country skiing, bar, meeting rooms. AE, D, MC, V. BP, MAP.*

$$–$$$$ ✕🏠 **Darby Field Inn.** After a day of activity in the White Mountains, warm up by this inn's fieldstone fireplace or by the bar's woodstove. Most rooms in this unpretentious 1826 farmhouse have mountain views; three have fireplaces. The restaurant ($$$–$$$$) prepares such haute regional American fare as roast duckling in a Chambord sauce and rack of lamb with a merlot sauce. The dark-chocolate pâté with white-chocolate sauce is a knockout dessert. ☒ *185 Chase Hill (Box D, Albany 03818),* ☎ *603/447–2181 or 800/426–4147,* 𝖥𝖠𝖷 *603/447– 5726,* WEB *www.darbyfield.com. 12 rooms, 3 suites. Restaurant, some in-room hot tubs, some in-room VCRs, pool, hot tub, massage, mountain bikes, croquet, hiking, cross-country skiing, sleigh rides, bar; no-smoking rooms. AE, MC, V. Closed Apr. BP, MAP.*

$$–$$$$ 🏠 **Buttonwood Inn.** A tranquil 17-acre oasis in this busy resort area, the Buttonwood is on Mt. Surprise, 2 mi northeast of North Conway village. Rooms in the 1820s farmhouse are furnished in Shaker style. Wide pine floors, quilts, and period stenciling add warmth. Two rooms have gas fireplaces. Innkeepers Peter and Claudia Needham supply many thoughtful extras, such as backpacks and picnic baskets. ☒ *Mt. Surprise Rd. (Box 1817, 03860),* ☎ *603/356–2625 or 800/258–2625,* 𝖥𝖠𝖷 *603/356–3140,* WEB *www.buttonwoodinn.com. 8 rooms, 2 suites. Some in-room hot tubs, pool, hiking, cross-country skiing; no room TVs, no-smoking rooms. AE, D, MC, V. BP.*

$$ ⊡ **Cranmore Inn.** This gambrel-roof country inn opened in 1863, and many of its furnishings date from the mid-1800s. The stables have been remodeled to contain condo-style rooms with kitchens. A mere ⅓ mi from the base of Mt. Cranmore, the inn is within walking distance of North Conway village. Guests have privileges at a nearby health club. ⊠ *Kearsarge St. (Box 1349, 03860),* ☎ *603/356–5502,* WEB *www. cranmoreinn.com. 18 rooms. Restaurant, some kitchens, pool. AE, MC, V. BP.*

Nightlife and the Arts

Horsefeather's (⊠ Main St., ☎ 603/356–6862), a restaurant and bar, often has music on weekends. **Mt. Washington Valley Theater Company** (⊠ Eastern Slope Playhouse, Main St., ☎ 603/356–5425) stages productions from mid-June to Labor Day. The Resort Players, a local group, gives pre- and postseason performances.

Shopping

ANTIQUES

The **Antiques & Collectibles Barn** (⊠ 3425 Main St., ☎ 603/356–7118), 1½ mi north of North Conway village, is a 35-dealer colony with furniture, jewelry, coins, and other collectibles. Northern New England's largest multidealer shop, **North Conway Antiques & Collectibles** (⊠ Rte. 16/U.S. 302, ☎ 603/356–6661) has more than 80 stalls. **Richard Plusch Antiques** (⊠ Rte. 16/U.S. 302, ☎ 603/356–3333) deals in period furniture and accessories, including glass, sterling silver, Oriental porcelains, rugs, and paintings.

CRAFTS

The **Basket & Handcrafters Outlet** (⊠ Kearsarge St., ☎ 603/356–5332) sells gift baskets, dried-flower arrangements, and country furniture. **Handcrafters Barn** (⊠ Main St., ☎ 603/356–8996) stocks the work of 350 area artists and artisans. The **League of New Hampshire Craftsmen** (⊠ 2526 Main St., ☎ 603/356–2441) carries the creations of the state's best artisans. **Zeb's General Store** (⊠ Main St., ☎ 603/356–9294 or 800/676–9294) looks just like an old-fashioned country store; it sells food items, crafts, and other products—all made in New England.

FACTORY OUTLETS

More than 150 factory outlets—including L. L. Bean, Timberland, Pfaltzgraff, London Fog, Anne Klein, and Reebok—line Route 16.

SPORTSWEAR

A top pick for skiwear is **Joe Jones** (⊠ 2709 Main St., ☎ 603/356–9411).

Ski Areas

CRANMORE MOUNTAIN RESORT

This ski area on the outskirts of North Conway has been a favorite of families since it began operating in 1938. Five glades have opened more skiable terrain. ⊠ *Skimobile Rd. (Box 1640, 03860),* ☎ *603/356–5543; 603/356–8516 snow conditions; 800/786–6754 lodging,* WEB *www.cranmore.com.*

Downhill. The 39 trails are well laid out and fun to ski. Most runs are naturally formed intermediates that weave in and out of glades. Beginners have several slopes and routes from the summit; experts must be content with a few short, steep pitches. In addition to the trails, snowboarders have a terrain park and a halfpipe. One high-speed quad, one triple, and three double chairlifts carry skiers to the top. There are also two surface lifts. Night skiing is an option from Thursday to Saturday and during holidays.

Other activities. Other winter activities are outdoor skating, snowshoeing, and tubing.

Child care. The nursery takes children ages 6 months–5 years. There's instruction for children ages 3–12.

Summer and year-round activities. You can take a chairlift to the top for a panoramic view of the White Mountains or mountain bike on selected trails. The fitness center has an indoor climbing wall, tennis courts, exercise equipment, and a pool.

CROSS-COUNTRY
Sixty-four kilometers (40 miles) of groomed cross-country trails weave through North Conway and the countryside along the **Mt. Washington Valley Ski Touring Association Network** (⊠ Rte. 16, Intervale, ☎ 603/356–9920 or 800/282–5220).

KING PINE SKI AREA AT PURITY SPRING RESORT
King Pine, some 9 mi south of Conway, has been a family-run ski area for more than 100 years. Some ski-and-stay packages include free skiing for midweek resort guests. Among the facilities and activities are an indoor pool and fitness complex, ice-skating, and tubing. ⊠ *Rte. 153, East Madison 03849,* ☎ *603/367–8896 or 800/367–8897; 800/373–3754 snow conditions,* WEB *www.purityspring.com.*

Downhill. King Pine's gentle slopes are ideal for beginner and intermediate skiers; experts won't be challenged except for a brief pitch on the Pitch Pine trail. The 16 trails are serviced by two triple chairs, a double chair, and two surface lifts. There's tubing on Saturday and Sunday afternoons and night skiing and tubing on Friday and Saturday.

Cross-country. King Pine has 15 km (9 mi) of cross-country skiing.

Child care. Children from infants up to 6 years are welcome (8:30–4) at the base lodge's nursery. Children ages 4 and up can take lessons.

Kancamagus Highway

★ ③ *36 mi between Conway and Lincoln/North Woodstock.*

Interstate 93 is the fastest way to the White Mountains, but it's hardly the most appealing. The section of Route 112 known as the Kancamagus Highway passes through mountains with some of the state's most unspoiled scenery. This stretch, punctuated by overlooks and picnic areas, erupts into fiery color each fall, when photo-snapping drivers can really slow things down. Prepare yourself for a leisurely pace. There are also campgrounds off the highway. In bad weather, check with the White Mountains Visitors Bureau for road conditions.

Outdoor Activities and Sports
A couple of short hiking trails off the Kancamagus Highway (Route 112) yield great rewards for relatively little effort. The **Lincoln Woods Trail** starts from the large parking lot of the Lincoln Woods Visitor Center, 4 mi east of Lincoln. You can purchase the recreation pass ($5 per vehicle, good for seven consecutive days) needed to park in any of the White Mountain National Forest lots or overlooks here; stopping briefly to take photos or to use the rest rooms at the visitor center is permitted without a pass. The trail crosses a suspension bridge over the Pemigewasset River and follows an old railroad bed for 3 mi along the river. The parking and picnic area for **Sabbaday Falls,** about 15 mi west of Conway, is the trailhead for an easy ½-mi route a multilevel cascade that plunges through two potholes and a flume.

The White Mountains A to Z

To research prices, get advice from other travelers, and book travel arrangements, visit www.fodors.com.

AIRPORTS

Manchester Airport is about a 60- to 90-minute drive from the region. Charters and private planes land at Franconia Airport & Soaring Center and Mt. Washington Regional Airport.

➤ AIRPORT INFORMATION: **Franconia Airport & Soaring Center** (⊠ Easton Rd., Franconia, ☎ 603/823–8881). **Mt. Washington Regional Airport** (⊠ Airport Rd., Whitefield, ☎ 603/837–9532).

BUS TRAVEL

Concord Trailways connects Boston's South Station and Logan Airport with Berlin, Conway, Franconia, Gorham, Jackson, Lincoln/North Woodstock, Littleton, and Pinkham Notch.

➤ BUS INFORMATION: **Concord Trailways** (☎ 603/228–3300 or 800/639–3317).

CAR TRAVEL

I–93 and U.S. 3 bisect the White Mountain National Forest, running north from Massachusetts to Québec. The Kancamagus Highway (Route 112), the east–west thoroughfare through the White Mountain National Forest, is a scenic drive. U.S. 302, a longer, more leisurely east–west path, connects I–93 to North Conway. From the seacoast, Route 16 is the popular choice.

EMERGENCIES

➤ HOSPITAL: **Memorial Hospital** (⊠ 3073 Main St., North Conway, ☎ 603/356–5461).

LODGING

Country Inns in the White Mountains handles reservations for a wide variety of B&Bs and inns throughout the region.

APARTMENT AND VILLA RENTALS

➤ LOCAL AGENT: **Country Inns in the White Mountains** (☎ 603/356–9460, WEB www.countryinnsinthewhitemountains.com).

CAMPING

White Mountain National Forest campground reservations has 20 campgrounds with more than 900 campsites spread across the region; only some take reservations. All sites have a 14-day limit.

➤ CONTACT: **White Mountain National Forest** (⊠ U.S. Forest Service, 719 N. Main St., Laconia 03246, ☎ 603/528–8721 or 877/444–6777).

OUTDOOR ACTIVITIES AND SPORTS

CANOEING AND KAYAKING

River outfitter Saco Bound Canoe & Kayak leads gentle canoeing expeditions, guided kayak trips, and white-water rafting on seven rivers and provides lessons, equipment, and transportation.

➤ CONTACT: **Saco Bound Canoe & Kayak** (⊠ Rte. 16/U.S. 302, Conway, ☎ 603/447–2177, WEB www.sacobound.com).

FISHING

For trout and salmon fishing, try the Connecticut Lakes, though any clear White Mountain stream (there are 650 mi of them in the national forest alone) will do. Many streams are stocked. Conway Lake—the largest of the area's 45 lakes and ponds—noted for smallmouth bass and, early and late in the season, good salmon fishing. The New

Hampshire Fish and Game Department has information on fishing conditions. Hunter's North Country Angler schedules intensive guided fly-fishing weekends.

➤ CONTACTS: **Hunter's North Country Angler** (✉ 3643 White Mountain Hwy., Intervale, ☎ 603/356–6000, WEB www.flyfishamerica. com/nca). **New Hampshire Fish and Game Department** (☎ 603/271–3211).

HIKING

With 86 major mountains in the area, the hiking possibilities are endless. Innkeepers can usually point you toward the better nearby trails; some inns schedule guided day trips for guests. The White Mountain National Forest has information on hiking as well as on the parking passes ($5) that are required in the national forest.

The Appalachian Mountain Club headquarters at Pinkham Notch has lectures, workshops, slide shows, and outdoor skills instruction year-round. Accommodations include a 100-bunk main lodge, a 24-bed hostel in Crawford Notch, and two rustic cabins. The club's eight trailside huts provide meals and dorm-style lodging on several trails from June to October. The rest of the year the huts are self-serve. New England Hiking Holidays conducts hikes with lodging in country inns for two to eight nights. Hikes, each with two guides, allow for different levels of ability and cover between 5 and 10 mi per day.

➤ CONTACTS: **Appalachian Mountain Club** (✉ Rte. 16 [Box 298, Gorham 03581], ☎ 603/466–2721; 603/466–2727 reservations; WEB www.mountwashington.com/amc). **New England Hiking Holidays** (☎ 603/356–9696 or 800/869–0949, WEB www.nehikingholidays.com). **White Mountain National Forest** (✉ U.S. Forest Service, 719 Main St., Laconia 03246, ☎ 603/528–8721; 877/444–6777 campground reservations; WEB www.fs.fed.us/r9/white).

VISITOR INFORMATION
➤ TOURIST INFORMATION: **Mt. Washington Valley Chamber of Commerce** (✉ Box 2300, North Conway 03860, ☎ 603/356–5701, WEB www.4seasonresort.com). **North Country Chamber of Commerce** (✉ Box 1, Colebrook 03576, ☎ 603/237–8939 or 800/698–8939, WEB www.northcountrychamber.org). **White Mountains Trail** (WEB www.whitemountainstrail.com). **White Mountains Visitors Bureau** (✉ Kancamagus Hwy./Rte. 112 at I–93 [Box 10, North Woodstock 03262], ☎ 603/745–8720 or 800/346–3687, WEB www.whitemtn.org).

WESTERN AND CENTRAL NEW HAMPSHIRE

Western and Central New Hampshire mix village charm with city hustle across three distinct regions. The Merrimack River valley has the state's largest and fastest-growing cities of Nashua, Manchester, and Concord. To the northwest of this region are Lake Sunapee—with its year-round sporting activities and its nearby mountains and Colonial villages—and Hanover, home to the famous Dartmouth College. The least developed of the three areas, the Monadnock region occupies the state's sleepy southwestern corner. Here you'll find plenty of hiking trails as well as peaceful hilltop hamlets that appear barely changed in the past two centuries. Mt. Monadnock, southern New Hampshire's largest peak, stands guard over the area.

When you're done climbing and swimming and visiting the past, look for small studios of area artists. The region has long been an informal artists' colony where people come to write, paint, and weave in

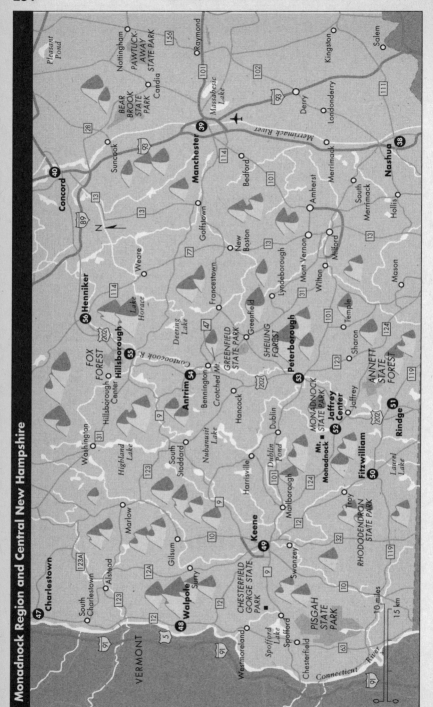

Monadnock Region and Central New Hampshire

solitude. The towns in this region, beginning with Nashua, are described in counterclockwise order.

Nashua

㊳ *98 mi south of Lincoln/North Woodstock, 48 mi northwest of Boston, 36 mi south of Concord, 50 mi southeast of Keene.*

Once a prosperous manufacturing town that drew thousands of immigrant workers in the late 1800s and early 1900s, Nashua declined following World War II, as many factories shut down or moved to where labor was cheaper. Since the 1970s, however, the metro area has jumped in population, developing into a charming, old-fashioned community. Its low-key downtown has classic redbrick buildings along the Nashua River, a tributary of the Merrimack River, which skirts the east side of town. Though not visited by tourists as much as other communities in the region, Nashua has some good restaurants and an engaging museum.

The city's impressive industrial history is retold at the **Florence Hyde Speare Memorial Building,** which houses the Nashua Historical Society. In this two-story museum you'll find artifacts, early furnishings, photos, a vintage printing press, and a research library. Adjacent to the museum, the Federal-style **Abbot-Spalding House** is furnished with 18th- and 19th-century antiques, art, and household items. You can only visit it on a guided tour, which is held at 1 on the third Saturday of every month from April through October. ⊠ *5 Abbot St.,* ☎ *603/ 883–0015.* ▨ *Free.* ☉ *Tues.–Thurs. and Sat. 10–4.*

Dining

$$–$$$ ✕ **Michael Timothy's Urban Bistro.** Part hip bistro, part jazzy wine bar
★ (with live music many nights), Michael Timothy's is so popular that even foodies from Massachusetts drive here. The regularly changing menu might offer a fricassee of seasonal mushrooms, oven-dried tomatoes, asparagus tips, and pearl onions in an herb-vegetable broth over mushroom risotto. Wood-fired pizzas are also a specialty. ⊠ *212 Main St.,* ☎ *603/595–9334. AE, D, MC, V.*

$$–$$$ ✕ **Villa Banca.** On the ground floor of a dramatic, turreted office building, this airy spot with high ceilings and tall windows specializes in both traditional and contemporary Italian cooking. Try the baked salmon topped with pistachio crumbs, shrimp scampi, tomatoes, and scallions and served over garlic-Parmesan risotto, or sample chicken-and-sausage lasagna. Note the exotic-martinis menu—a big draw at happy hour. ⊠ *194 Main St.,* ☎ *603/598–0500. AE, D, DC, MC, V.*

$–$$ ✕ **Martha's Exchange.** A casual spot with copper brewing vats, original marble floors, and booth seating, Martha's appeals both to the after-work set and office workers on lunch breaks. Burgers and sandwiches, maple-stout-barbecued chicken and ribs, Mexican fare, seafood and steak grills, and salads—all in large portions—are your options here. There's also a sweets shop attached, and you can buy half-gallon jugs of house-brewed beers to go. ⊠ *185 Main St.,* ☎ *603/883– 8781. AE, DC, MC, V.*

The Arts

American Stage Festival (⊠ 14 Court St., ☎ 603/886–7000 winter; 603/673–7515 summer), the state's largest professional theater, presents Broadway-style and newer works, music concerts, and a children's-theater series from March through October.

Manchester

③⑨ *18 mi north of Nashua, 53 mi north of the Boston.*

Manchester, with just over 100,000 residents, is New Hampshire's largest city. The town grew around the power of the Amoskeag Falls on the Merrimack River, which fueled small textile mills through the 1700s. By 1828, Boston investors had bought the rights to the Merrimack's water power and built on its eastern bank the Amoskeag Textile Mills, which became a testament to New England's manufacturing capabilities. In 1906, the mills employed 17,000 people and churned out more than 4 million yards of cloth per week. This vast enterprise formed Manchester's entire economic base; when it closed in 1936, the town was devastated.

Today Manchester is mainly a banking and business center. As part of an economic recovery plan, the old mill buildings have been converted into warehouses, classrooms, restaurants, museums, and office space. The city is also home to the state's major airport, and the Verizon Wireless Arena, which hosts minor-league hockey matches, concerts, and conventions.

☾ The **Amoskeag Mills** houses both restaurants and museums. The **SEE Science Center** is a hands-on science lab and children's museum. The **Millyard Museum** contains state-of-the-art exhibits depicting the region's history, from when Native Americans lived alongside and fished the Merrimack River to the heyday of Amoskeag Mills. The interactive Discovery Gallery is geared toward kids; there's also a lecture-concert hall and a large museum shop. ⊠ *Mill No. 3, 200 Bedford St. (entrance at 255 Commercial St.),* ☎ *603/625–2821; 603/669–0400 Science Center; 603/625–2821 Millyard Museum,* WEB *www. mv.com/org/mha.* ⊡ *Science Center $4, Millyard Museum $5.* ☉ *Science Center weekdays 10–3, weekends noon–5; Millyard Museum Tues.–Sat. 10–4, Sun. noon–4.*

At the neoclassical redbrick (1931) headquarters of the **Manchester Historic Association,** you'll find a few exhibits on this city's history and information on the Amoskeag Mills. ⊠ *129 Amherst St.,* ☎ *603/622–7531,* WEB *www.mv.com/org/mha.* ⊡ *Free.* ☉ *Tues.–Sat. 10–4.*

The **Currier Gallery of Art,** in a 1929 Italianate building, has a permanent collection of European and American paintings, sculpture, and decorative arts from the 13th to the 20th century, including works by Monet, Picasso, Hopper, and O'Keeffe. Also part of the museum is the Frank Lloyd Wright–designed Zimmerman House, built in 1950. Wright called this sparse, utterly functional living space "Usonian." It's New England's only Wright-designed residence open to the public. ⊠ *201 Myrtle Way,* ☎ *603/669–6144; 603/626–4158 Zimmerman House tours,* WEB *www.currier.org.* ⊡ *Gallery $5, free Sat. 10–1; Zimmerman House $9 (reservations essential).* ☉ *Sun.–Mon. and Wed.–Thurs. 11–5, Fri. 11–8, Sat. 10–5; call for tour times.*

☾ Salmon, shad, and river herring "climb" the **Amoskeag Fishways** fish ladder near the Amoskeag Dam from May to mid-June. The visitor center has an underwater viewing window, year-round interactive exhibits and programs about the Merrimack River, and a hydroelectric-station viewing area. ⊠ *Fletcher St.,* ☎ *603/626–3474,* WEB *www.amoskeagfishways.org.* ⊡ *$2.* ☉ *Mon.–Sat. 9–5.*

Dining and Lodging

$$$–$$$$ ✕ **Baldwin's on Elm.** Chef Nathan Baldwin has earned raves for his
★   creative renderings of regional American fare. The caramelized Nantucket Bay scallops with a celery root-and-truffle puree, squash, and

pumpkin seeds is sublime. Consider the spring roll with jasmine rice pudding, mangos, coconut, and rum anglaise for dessert. ⊠ *1105 Elm St.,* ☎ *603/622–5975. AE, D, DC, MC, V. No lunch.*

$$$–$$$$ ✕ **Richard's Bistro.** Whether you want to celebrate a special occasion or you just crave first-rate regional American cuisine, head to this romantic downtown bistro. The kitchen uses traditional New England ingredients in worldly preparations: try the char-broiled filet mignon with Gorgonzola, baked-stuffed potato, and strawberries or the broiled haddock topped with shrimp and scallops on an herb-risotto cake with a honey-peach sauce. ⊠ *36 Lowell St.,* ☎ *603/644–1180. AE, D, MC, V. No lunch Sat.*

$$–$$$ ✕ **Cotton.** Mod lighting and furnishings and an arbored patio set a
★ swanky tone at this restaurant inside one of the old Amoskeag Mill buildings. The kitchen churns out updated comfort food. Start with mussels in a red curry of coconut milk, lemongrass, and Kaffir-lime leaves. Stellar entrée picks include a casserole with yellowfin tuna, julienne vegetables, and pappardelle tossed with wild-mushroom cream and toasted lemony crumbs. ⊠ *75 Arms Park,* ☎ *603/622–5488. AE, D, DC, MC, V.*

$–$$ ✕ **Fratello's.** Despite a seemingly endless supply of seating, the wait for a table at this restaurant can be long on the weekends. The huge bi-level space inside a redbrick building at the north end of Amoskeag Mills has high timber ceilings and exposed ducts. The kitchen prepares Italian food from a lengthy menu. Try any of several mix-and-match pastas and sauces, one of the wood-fired pizzas, or one of the many grills. ⊠ *155 Dow St.,* ☎ *603/624–2022. AE, D, MC, V.*

$ ✕ **Red Arrow Diner.** A mix of hipsters and oldsters, including comedian and Manchester native Adam Sandler, favor this neon-streaked, 24-hour greasy spoon, which has been going strong since 1922. Filling fare—platters of kielbasa, French toast, and the diner's famous panfries—keep patrons happy. ⊠ *61 Lowell St.,* ☎ *603/626–1118. MC, V.*

$$$$ ✕🖪 **Bedford Village Inn.** The hayloft and milking rooms of this 1810
★ Federal farmstead, just a few miles southwest of Manchester, now contain lavish suites with king-size four-poster beds. The restaurant ($$$–$$$$)—a warren of elegant dining rooms with fireplaces and wide-pine floors—presents contemporary fare that might include a starter of Maine Jonah crab cakes with Asian slaw, a chili-soy vinaigrette, and wasabi cream, followed by apricot-and-stout-marinated venison loin with a crisp potato cake, roasted oyster mushrooms, and fennel. There's also a casual tavern ($$–$$$). ⊠ *2 Village Inn La., Bedford 03110,* ☎ *603/472–2001 or 800/852–1166,* FAX *603/472–2379,* WEB *www.bedfordvillageinn.com. 12 suites, 2 apartments. Restaurant, some in-room hot tubs, bar, meeting room; no-smoking rooms. AE, DC, MC, V.*

$$$ 🖪 **Holiday Inn Manchester.** Of Manchester's many chain properties, the 12-story Holiday Inn has the central-most location—just steps from the Amoskeag Mills and the great dining along Elm Street. Rooms are simple and clean, perfect for business travelers. ⊠ *700 Elm St., 03101,* ☎ *603/625–1000,* FAX *603/625–4595,* WEB *www.holiday-inn.com. 244 rooms, 6 suites. 2 restaurants, in-room data ports, indoor pool, hot tub, sauna, gym, bar, business services, meeting rooms, parking (fee). AE, D, DC, MC, V.*

Nightlife and the Arts

Club Merrimack (⊠ 201 Merrimack St., ☎ 603/623–9362) is New Hampshire's most popular lesbian and gay disco. Revelers come from all over to drink and mingle at the **Yard** (⊠ 1211 S. Mammoth Rd., ☎ 603/623–3545), which is also a steak house and seafood restaurant.

The **Palace Theatre** presents musicals and plays throughout the year. It also hosts the state's Philharmonic and symphony orchestras and the Opera League of New Hampshire. ⊠ *80 Hanover St.,* ☎ *603/668–5588 theater; 603/647–6476 Philharmonic; 603/669–3559 symphony; 603/647–6564 opera.*

Shopping

The enormous **Mall of New Hampshire** (⊠ 1500 S. Willow St., ☎ 603/669–0433) has every conceivable store and is anchored by Sears and Filene's.

Spectator Sport

The **Manchester Monarchs** (⊠ Elm St. and Lake Ave., ☎ 603/626–7825 or 603/868–7300), a minor-league affiliate of hockey's Los Angeles Kings, play at the Verizon Wireless Arena. The season runs from October through early April.

Concord

40 *20 mi northwest of Manchester, 67 mi northwest of Boston, 46 mi northwest of Portsmouth.*

New Hampshire's capital (population 38,000) is a quiet town that tends to the state's business but little else—the sidewalks roll up promptly at 6. The **Concord on Foot** walking trail winds through the historic district. Maps are available from the **Chamber of Commerce** (⊠ 40 Commercial St., ☎ 603/224–2508) or stores along the trail.

The **Pierce Manse** is the Greek Revival home in which Franklin Pierce lived before moving to Washington to become the 14th U.S. president. ⊠ *14 Penacook St.,* ☎ *603/225–2068 or 603/224–5954.* ⊡ *$3.* ☉ *Mid-June–Labor Day, weekdays 11–3.*

At the neoclassical, gilt-domed **State House,** the legislature still meets in its original chambers. The building, which dates from 1819, is the oldest in the United States in continuous use as a state capitol. ⊠ *107 N. Main St.,* ☎ *603/271–2154,* WEB *www.ci.concord.nh.us/tourdest/statehs.* ☉ *Weekdays 8–4:30; guided tours by reservation.*

Among the artifacts at the **Museum of New Hampshire History** is an original Concord Coach. During the 19th century, when more than 3,000 such conveyances were built in Concord, this was about as technologically perfect a vehicle as you could find—many say it's the coach that won the West. Other exhibits provide an overview of state history, from the Abenaki to the settlers of Portsmouth up to current residents. ⊠ *6 Eagle Sq.,* ☎ *603/226–3189,* WEB *www.nhhistory.org/museum.html.* ⊡ *$5.* ☉ *Jan.–June and mid-Oct.–Nov., Tues.–Wed. and Fri.–Sat. 9:30–5, Thurs. 9:30–8:30, Sun. noon–5; Dec. and July–mid-Oct., Mon.–Wed. and Fri.–Sat. 9:30–5, Thurs. 9:30–8:30, Sun. noon–5.*

The **Christa McAuliffe Planetarium** presents shows on the solar system, constellations, and space exploration that incorporate computer graphics, sound, and special effects in a 40-ft dome theater. Children love seeing the tornado tubes, magnetic marbles, and other hands-on exhibits. Outside, explore the scale-model planet walk and the human sundial. The planetarium was named for the Concord teacher—and first civilian in space—who was killed in the Space Shuttle *Challenger* explosion in 1986. ⊠ *New Hampshire Technical Institute campus, 2 Institute Dr.,* ☎ *603/271–7831,* WEB *www.starhop.com.* ⊡ *Exhibit area free, shows $8.* ☉ *Tues.–Thurs. 9–5, Fri. 9–7, weekends 10–5. Call for show times and reservations.*

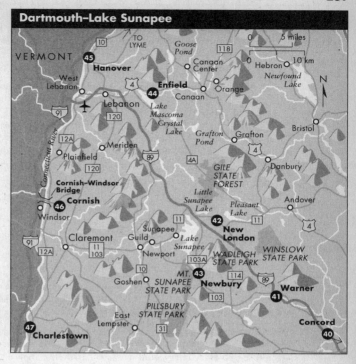

Dartmouth–Lake Sunapee

Dining and Lodging

$–$$ ✕ **Siam Orchid.** This dark, attractive Thai restaurant with a colorful rickshaw gracing its dining room serves spicy and reasonably authentic Thai food. Try the fiery broiled swordfish with shrimp curry sauce or the pine-nut chicken in an aromatic ginger sauce. ✉ *15 N. Main St.,* ☎ *603/228–3633. D, MC, V. No lunch weekends.*

$ ✕ **Foodee's Pizzas.** A local chain with additional parlors in Keene, Dover,
★ Lincoln, Milford, and Wolfeboro, Foodee's serves creative pizzas with delicious crusts (sourdough, six-grain, deep-dish). The capital branch is in the heart of downtown and serves such pies as the Polish (with kielbasa, sauerkraut, and three cheeses) and the El Greco (with sweet onions, sliced tomatoes, olive oil, and feta). You can also order pastas, salads, and calzones. ✉ *2 S. Main St.,* ☎ *603/225–3834. MC, V.*

$$–$$$ ✕⊡ **Centennial Inn.** Built in 1892 for widows of Civil War veterans, this imposing brick-and-stone building is set back from busy Pleasant Street. Much of the original woodwork has been preserved. Each room is decorated with antiques and reproduction pieces, and all have ceiling fans. The kitchen at the somewhat stodgy Franklin Pierce Dining Room ($$–$$$$) turns out surprisingly appealing Continental fare. ✉ *96 Pleasant St., 03301,* ☎ *603/225–7102 or 800/360–4839,* ⬛ *603/ 225–5031,* ⬛ *www.someplacesdifferent.com/centennialinn.htm. 27 rooms, 5 suites. Restaurant, in-room data ports, in-room VCRs, bar, meeting rooms. AE, D, DC, MC, V.*

Nightlife and the Arts

The **Capitol Center for the Arts** (✉ 44 S. Main St., ☎ 603/225–1111) has been restored to reflect its Roaring '20s origins. It hosts touring Broadway shows, dance companies, and musical acts. The lounge at **Hermanos Cocina Mexicana** (✉ 11 Hills Ave., ☎ 603/224–5669) has live jazz Sunday through Thursday nights.

Outdoor Activities and Sports

Hannah's Paddles (⊠ 15 Hannah Dustin Dr., ☎ 603/753–6695) rents canoes for use on the Merrimack River, which runs through Concord.

Shopping

CRAFTS

Capitol Craftsman and Romance Jewelers (⊠ 16 N. Main St., ☎ 603/224–6166), adjoining shops, sell fine jewelry and handicrafts. The **Den of Antiquity** (⊠ 74 N. Main St., ☎ 603/225–4505) carries hand-crafted country gifts and accessories. The **League of New Hampshire Craftsmen** (⊠ 36 N. Main St., ☎ 603/228–8171) exhibits crafts in many media. **Mark Knipe Goldsmiths** (⊠ 2 Capitol Plaza, Main St., ☎ 603/224–2920) sets antique stones in rings, earrings, and pendants.

MALL

Steeplegate Mall (⊠ 270 Loudon Rd., ☎ 603/228–0025) has more than 75 stores, including chain department stores and some smaller crafts shops.

Warner

41   *22 mi northwest of Concord.*

Three New Hampshire governors were born in this quiet agricultural town just off I–89. Buildings dating from the late 1700s and early 1800s, and a charming library welcomes you to the town's main street.

★ ☾   **Mt. Kearsarge Indian Museum, Education and Cultural Center** gives guided tours of an extensive collection of Native American artistry, including moose-hair embroidery, quilt work, and basketry. Signs on the Medicine Woods trail identify plants and explain how Native Americans use them as foods, medicines, and dyes. ⊠ *Kearsarge Mountain Rd., 03278,* ☎ *603/456–2600,* WEB *www.indianmuseum.org.* ☜ *$6.50.* ☉ *May–Oct., Mon.–Sat. 10–5, Sun. noon–5; Nov.–Dec., Sat. 10–5, Sun. noon–5.*

A 3½-mi scenic auto road at **Rollins State Park** (⊠ off Rte. 103) snakes up the southern slope of Mt. Kearsarge, where you can then hike the ½-mi trail to the summit. The road is closed November through mid-May; park admission is $3.

New London

42   *16 mi northwest of Warner, 25 mi west of Tilton.*

New London, the home of Colby-Sawyer College (1837), is a good base for exploring the Lake Sunapee region. A campus of stately Colonial-style buildings fronts the vibrant commercial district, where you'll find several cafés and boutiques. At the 10,000-year-old **Cricenti's Bog**, off Business Route 11, a short trail shows off the shaggy mosses and fragile ecosystem of this ancient pond.

Dining and Lodging

$$–$$$ ✕ **Peter Christian's Tavern.** Exposed beams, wooden tables, a smattering of antiques, and half shutters on the windows make Peter Christian's a cool summer oasis and a warm winter haven. The fare tends toward the traditional and the hearty, from beef stew to mustard-chicken cordon bleu. ⊠ *186 Main St.,* ☎ *603/526–4042. AE, D, MC, V.*

$–$$$ ✕ **Four Corners Grille and Flying Goose Brew Pub.** South of downtown, this little restaurant and pub is known for massive burgers, pit-barbecued meats, calamari in basil pesto, great ales, and exceptional views of Mt. Kearsarge. There's live folk and light rock music many nights. ⊠ *Rtes. 11 and 114,* ☎ *603/526–6899. D, MC, V.*

$$–$$$ ✕🏠 **Inn at Pleasant Lake.** This 1790s inn lies just across Pleasant Lake
★ from majestic Mt. Kearsarge. Its spacious rooms have country antiques
and modern bathrooms. The restaurant ($$$$; reservations essential) presents a nightly changing prix-fixe menu that draws raves for such entrées as roast tenderloin of Angus beef with a Calvados demiglace and
watercress pesto and such desserts as white-chocolate mousse with a trio
of sauces. ✉ *125 Pleasant St. (Box 1030, 03257),* ☎ *603/526–6271 or
800/626–4907,* FAX *603/526–4111,* WEB *www.innatpleasantlake.com. 12
rooms. Restaurant, some in-room hot tubs, gym, beach, boating, meeting rooms; no room phones, no room TVs, no smoking. MC, V.*

$$–$$$ ✕🏠 **New London Inn.** The two porches of this rambling 1792 inn over-
look Main Street. Rooms have Victorian decor; some have views of
the Colby-Sawyer campus. The restaurant's ($$–$$$) nouvelle-in-
spired menu has such starters as butternut squash with a sun-dried cranberry pesto and such entrées as grilled cilantro shrimp with a saffron
risotto. ✉ *140 Main St. (Box 8, 03257),* ☎ *603/526–2791 or 800/526–
2791,* FAX *603/526–2749. 29 rooms. Restaurant; no smoking. AE, D,
MC, V. CP.*

$$ 🏠 **Follansbee Inn.** Built in 1840, this quintessential country inn on the
shore of Kezar Lake is a perfect fit in the 19th-century village of North
Sutton, about 4 mi south of New London. The common rooms and
bedrooms are loaded with collectibles—a traveling trunk here, a
wooden school desk there. In winter, you can ice-fish on or ski across
the lake; in summer you can swim or boat from the inn's pier. A 3-mi
walking trail circles the lake. ✉ *Rte. 114, North Sutton 03260,* ☎ *603/
927–4221 or 800/626–4221,* WEB *www.follansbeeinn.com. 23 rooms,
11 with bath; 1 cottage. Some in-room hot tubs, lake, windsurfing, boat-
ing, fishing, bicycles, hiking, cross-country skiing, ice-skating; no room
phones, no room TVs, no kids under 10, no smoking. MC, V. BP.*

$ ⚠ **Otter Lake Camping Area.** The 28 sites on Otter Lake have plenty
of shade, and boating and fishing are available. Facilities include a beach,
a playground, and canoe and pedal boat rentals. ✉ *55 Otterville Rd.,
03257,* ☎ *603/763–5600. No credit cards.*

The Arts

The **New London Barn Playhouse** (✉ 209 Main St., ☎ 603/526–6710
or 800/633–2276) presents Broadway-style and children's plays every
summer in New Hampshire's oldest continuously operating theater.

Shopping

Artisan's Workshop (✉ Peter Christian's Tavern, 186 Main St., ☎ 603/
526–4227) carries jewelry, glass, and other local handicrafts.

Ski Area

NORSK CROSS COUNTRY AND SNOWSHOE CENTER
The 70 km (43 mi) of scenic cross-country ski trails here include 45
km (28 mi) that are tracked and 24 km (15 mi) that are skate-groomed.
Snowshoers have 19 km (12 mi) of groomed and backcountry trails.
✉ *Rte. 11,* ☎ *603/526–4685 or 800/426–6775,* WEB *www.skinorsk.com.*

Newbury

43 *8 mi southwest of New London.*

Newbury is on the edge of Mt. Sunapee State Park. The mountain, which
rises to an elevation of nearly 3,000 ft, and the sparkling lake are the
region's outdoor recreation centers. The popular League of New
Hampshire Craftsmen's Fair is held at the base of Mt. Sunapee each
August.

John M. Hay, who served as private secretary to Abraham Lincoln and
secretary of state for presidents McKinley and Roosevelt, built **The Fells**

on Lake Sunapee as a summer home in 1890. House tours focus on his life in Newbury and Washington. Hay's son is responsible for the extensive gardens, a mix of formal and informal styles that include a 75-ft perennial border and a hillside planted with heather. More than 800 acres of the former estate are open for hiking and picnicking. ⊠ *Rte. 103A,* ☎ *603/763–4789,* WEB *www.thefells.org.* ☜ *$4.* ☉ *House Memorial Day–mid-Oct., weekends 10–5; grounds daily dawn–dusk.*

Lodging

$ ⛺ **Crow's Nest Campground.** This campground has 100 sites, some directly on the Sugar River, as well as cabins with baths. The facilities include a recreation hall, a pool, a children's wading pool, miniature golf, and a warm-up room with a fireplace. River swimming and fishing are summer pastimes; you can skate or sled in the winter, and area snowmobile trails connect to the campground. ⊠ *529 S. Main St., Newport 03773,* ☎ *603/863–6170,* WEB *www.crowsnestcampground.com.* D, MC, V. Closed mid-Oct.–Nov. and Apr.–mid-May.

Outdoor Activities and Sports

BEACHES

Sunapee State Beach has picnic areas, a beach, and a bathhouse. You can rent canoes here, too. ⊠ *Rte. 103,* ☎ *603/763–5561.* ☜ *$3.* ☉ *Daily dawn–dusk.*

FISHING

Lake Sunapee has brook and lake trout, salmon, smallmouth bass, and pickerel.

Shopping

Overlooking Lake Sunapee's southern tip, **Outspokin' Bicycle and Sport** (⊠ Rtes. 103 and 103A, at the harbor, ☎ 603/763–9500) has a tremendous selection of biking, hiking, skateboarding, snow- and waterskiing, and snowboarding clothing and equipment.

Ski Area

MOUNT SUNAPEE

Although the resort is state-owned, it's managed by Vermont's Okemo Mountain resort, known for being family friendly. The agreement has allowed the influx of capital necessary for operating extensive lifts, snowmaking (97% coverage), and trail grooming. ⊠ *Rte. 103 (Box 2021, 03772),* ☎ *603/763–2356; 603/763–4020 snow conditions; 877/687–8627 lodging,* WEB *www.mtsunapee.com.*

Downhill. This mountain is 1,510 vertical ft and has 60 trails, mostly intermediate. Experts can take to a dozen slopes, including three nice double-black diamonds. The beginner's section is well away from other trails and has a quad chairlift. Boarders have a 420-ft-long halfpipe and a terrain park with music. Two base lodges and a summit lodge supply the essentials. One high-speed detachable quad, one fixed-grip quad, two triple and two double chairlifts, and three surface lifts transport skiers.

Child care. The Mother Goose Day Care takes children ages 1–5. Children's programs in skiing or snowboarding are available for kids 4 and up.

Summer activities. The Sunapee Express Quad zooms you to the summit. From here, it's just under a mile hike to Lake Solitude. Mountain bikers can use the lift to many trails, and an in-line skate park has beginner and advanced sections (plus equipment rentals).

Enfield

㊹ *33 mi northwest of Newbury.*

In 1782, two Shaker brothers from Mount Lebanon, New York, arrived at a community on Mascoma Lake's northeastern side. Eventually, they formed Enfield, the 9th of 18 Shaker communities in this country, and moved it to the lake's southern shore, where they erected more than 200 buildings.

★ The **Enfield Shaker Museum** preserves the legacy of the Shakers, who numbered 330 members at the village's peak. By 1923, interest in the society had dwindled, and the last 10 members joined the Canterbury community. A self-guided walking tour takes you through 13 of the remaining buildings, among them the Great Stone Dwelling (now the Shaker Inn) and an 1849 stone mill. Demonstrations of Shaker crafts techniques and numerous special events take place year-round. ⊠ *24 Caleb Dyer La.,* ☎ *603/632–4346,* WEB *www.shakermuseum.org.* ⊡ *$7.* ☉ *Memorial Day–late Oct., Mon.–Sat. 10–5, Sun. noon–5; late Oct.–Memorial Day, Sat. 10–4, Sun. noon–4.*

Dining and Lodging

$$–$$$ ✕⊡ **The Shaker Inn.** Built between 1837 and 1841, the Great Stone Dwelling on Lake Mascoma is the largest main dwelling ever built by a Shaker community. Adjacent to the Enfield Shaker Museum, it's now an inn, and the guest rooms in the original Shaker sleeping chambers have reproduction Shaker furniture and the simplicity of style for which the religious community was known. The dining room ($$) serves Shaker-inspired contemporary cuisine such as panfried buttermilk chicken breast with Vermont cheddar–whipped potatoes. ⊠ *447 Rte. 4A, 03748,* ☎ *603/632–7810 or 888/707–4257,* WEB *www.theshakerinn.com. 24 rooms. Restaurant, lake, baby-sitting; no room phones, no room TVs, no smoking. AE, D, MC, V. BP.*

Outdoor Activities and Sports

Anglers can try for rainbow trout, pickerel, and horned pout in **Lake Mascoma.**

Hanover

㊺ *12 mi northwest of Enfield, 62 mi northwest of Concord.*

Eleazer Wheelock founded Hanover's Dartmouth College in 1769 to educate the Abenaki "and other youth." When he arrived, the town consisted of about 20 families. The college and the town grew symbiotically, with Dartmouth becoming the northernmost Ivy League school. Today Hanover is still synonymous with Dartmouth, but the attractive town is also a respected medical and cultural center for the upper Connecticut River valley.

Robert Frost spent part of a brooding freshman semester at Ivy League **Dartmouth College** before giving up college altogether. The buildings that cluster around the green include the **Baker Memorial Library,** which houses such literary treasures as 17th-century editions of Shakespeare's works. The library is also well known for the 3,000-square-ft murals by Mexican artist José Clemente Orozco that depict the story of civilization on the American continents. If the towering arcade at the entrance to the **Hopkins Center** (☎ 603/646–2422) appears familiar, it's probably because it resembles the project that architect Wallace K. Harrison completed just after designing it: New York City's Metropolitan Opera House at Lincoln Center. The complex includes a 900-seat theater for film showings and concerts, a 400-seat theater for plays, and a black-box theater for new plays. The Dartmouth Symphony Orchestra performs here, as does the Big Apple Circus. In addition to African, Peruvian, Oceanic, Asian, European, and American art, the **Hood Museum of Art** owns the Picasso painting *Guitar on a Table*, silver by Paul Revere, and a set of Assyrian reliefs from the 9th century BC. Rivaling the collection is the museum's architecture: a series of austere, copper-roofed, redbrick buildings arranged around a courtyard. Free guided tours are available on request. ⊠ *Museum: Wheelock St.,* ☎ *603/646–2808,* WEB *www.dartmouth.edu/~hood.* ☎ *Free.* ☉ *Tues. and Thurs.–Sat. 10–5, Wed. 10–9, Sun. noon–5.*

NEED A BREAK?	Take a respite from museum-hopping with a cup of espresso, a ham-and-cheese scone, or a fresh-baked brownie at the **Dirt Cowboy** (⊠ 7 S. Main St., ☎ 603/643–1323), a café across from the green and beside a used bookstore.

OFF THE BEATEN PATH	**THE UPPER VALLEY** – From Hanover, you can make a 60-mi drive up Route 10 all the way to Littleton for a highly scenic tour of the upper Connecticut River valley. You'll have views of the river and Vermont's Green Mountains from many points. The road passes through groves of evergreens, over leafy ridges, and through delightful hamlets. Grab gourmet picnic provisions at **Pat Tony's General Store** (☎ 603/650–2015) on Lyme's village common, and stop at the bluff-top village green in historical Haverhill (28 mi north of Hanover) for a picnic amid the panorama of classic Georgian- and Federal-style mansions and faraway farmsteads. You can follow this scenic route all the way to the White Mountains region, or loop back south from Haverhill—along Route 25 to Route 118 to U.S. 4 west—to Enfield, a drive of about 45 mi (and 75 minutes).

Dining and Lodging

$–$$$ ✕ **Murphy's.** Students, visiting alums, and locals regularly descend upon this pub, whose walls are lined with shelves of old books. The varied menu ranges from sliced, grilled emu with caramelized onions and applewood-smoked bacon vinaigrette to Cajun salmon Caesar salads. Check out the extensive beer list. ⊠ *11 S. Main St.,* ☎ *603/643–4075. AE, D, DC, MC, V.*

$–$$ ✕ **Lui Lui.** The creatively topped thin-crust pizzas and huge pasta portions are only part of the draw at this chatter-filled eatery. It also has a dramatic setting inside a former power station on the Mascoma River. Favorite pizza picks include the BLT and the barbecue-chicken pie. Pasta fans should dive into a bowl of linguine with prosciutto, spinach, and mushrooms. The owners also run Molly's Restaurant and Jesse's Tavern, which are both nearby. ⊠ *Adjacent to Powerhouse Mall, off Rte. 12A,* ☎ *603/298–7070. AE, D, DC, MC, V.*

$–$$ ✕ **Panda House/Bamboo Garden.** In a region with few decent Asian restaurants, these two offer a welcome taste of Chinese and Japanese fare. They occupy a sedate basement space of the Hanover Park shopping arcade. Try the sashimi-sushi platters from the Bamboo Garden kitchen; Panda House favorites include the tangerine beef and the crispy fish with a spicy Hunan sauce. ⊠ *3 Lebanon St.,* ☎ *603/643–1290. AE, D, DC, MC, V.*

$ ✕ **Lou's.** A Hanover tradition for decades, this diner-cum-café-cum-bakery serves possibly the best breakfast in the valley—a plate of *migas* (eggs, cheddar, salsa, and guacamole mixed with tortilla chips) can fill you up for the better part of the day; blueberry-cranberry buttermilk pancakes also satisfy. Or grab a seat at the old-fashioned soda fountain and order an ice cream sundae. ⊠ *30 S. Main St.,* ☎ *603/ 643–3321. No credit cards. No dinner.*

$$$$ ✕🏠 **Hanover Inn.** Owned by Dartmouth College, this sprawling, Georgian-style brick structure rises four white-trimmed stories. The original building was converted to a tavern in 1780, and this expertly run inn, now greatly enlarged, has been operating ever since. Rooms have Colonial reproductions, Audubon prints, and large sitting areas. The formal Daniel Webster Room ($$–$$$$) serves regional American dishes such as grilled monkfish with tempura lobster tail and soba noodles. The swank Zins Wine Bistro ($–$$) prepares lighter but still highly innovative fare. ⊠ *The Green (Box 151, 03755)*, ☎ *603/643–4300 or 800/443–7024,* FAX *603/646–3744,* WEB *www.hanoverinn.com. 92 rooms. 2 restaurants, bar, business services, meeting rooms. AE, D, DC, MC, V.*

$$–$$$$ 🏠 **Trumbull House.** The sunny guest rooms of this white Colonial-style house—on 16 acres in Hanover's outskirts—have king- or queen-size beds, window seats, writing desks, and other comfortable touches. Breakfast, with a choice of entrées, is served in the formal dining room or in front of the living room fireplace. Rates include use of a nearby health club. ⊠ *40 Etna Rd., 03755,* ☎ *603/643–2370 or 800/651–5141,* FAX *603/643–2430,* WEB *www.trumbullhouse.com. 4 rooms, 1 suite. Dining room, some in-room data ports, some in-room hot tubs, some in-room VCRs, pond, basketball, hiking, business services, meeting room; no smoking. AE, MC, V. BP.*

$$–$$$ 🏠 **Dowds Country Inn.** This 1780 Georgian-style house on 6 pastoral acres faces the village green and the vintage country store in the frozen-in-time river village of Lyme, about 10 mi north of Hanover. Rooms have a crisp, unfussy look, with Colonial antiques, quilted bedspreads, stenciled walls, and wide-plank floors. It's a relaxed and reasonably priced alternative to the accommodations in bustling Hanover. ⊠ *On the Common (Box 58, 03768),* ☎ *603/795–4712 or 800/482–4712,* FAX *603/795–4220,* WEB *www.dowdscountryinn.com. 20 rooms, 3 suites. Pond, meeting room; no room phones, no room TVs. D, DC, MC, V. BP.*

Outdoor Activities and Sports

Ledyard Canoe Club of Dartmouth (☎ 603/643–6709) provides canoe and kayak rentals and classes on the swift-flowing Connecticut River, which isn't suitable for beginners and is safest after mid-June.

Shopping

Shops, mostly of the independent variety but with a few upscale chains sprinkled in, line Hanover's main street. The commercial district blends almost imperceptibly with Dartmouth's campus. West Lebanon, south of Hanover on the Vermont border, has many more shops. Goldsmith Paul Gross of **Designer Gold** (⊠ 3 Lebanon St., ☎ 603/643–3864) designs settings for gemstones—all one-of-a-kind or limited-edition.

The **Mouse Menagerie of Fine Crafts** (⊠ Rte. 12A, West Lebanon, ☎ 603/298–7090) sells its signature collector's series of toy mice, plus furniture, wind chimes, and other gifts. The **Powerhouse Mall** (⊠ Rte. 12A, 1 mi north of I–89 Exit 20, West Lebanon, ☎ 603/298–5236), a former power station, comprises three buildings of specialty stores, boutiques, and restaurants.

En Route From Hanover follow Route 10 south to Route 12A, and exactly 3½ mi south of I–89, bear right onto scenic **River Road.** It hugs the shore of the Connecticut River, affording outstanding views of Vermont's countryside (try to ignore the occasional glimpse of busy I–91). The bucolic road also passes several old mansions, including Plainfield's stately Home Hill Inn. The narrow lane is slow-going in places, all the better to take in the views. After about 7 mi, River Road puts you back onto the more prosaic Route 12A in Cornish.

Cornish

46 *22 mi south of Hanover.*

Today Cornish is best known for its four covered bridges and for being the home of reclusive author J. D. Salinger, but at the turn of the 20th century the village was known primarily as the home of the country's then most popular novelist, Winston Churchill (no relation to the British prime minister). His novel *Richard Carvell* sold more than a million copies. Churchill was such a celebrity that he hosted Teddy Roosevelt during the president's 1902 visit. At that time Cornish was an enclave of artistic talent. Painter Maxfield Parrish lived and worked here, and sculptor Augustus Saint-Gaudens set up his studio and created the heroic bronzes for which he is known.

★ Just south of Plainfield, where River Road rejoins Route 12A, a small lane leads to the **Saint-Gaudens National Historic Site.** Here you can tour sculptor Augustus Saint-Gaudens's (1848–1907) house, studio, gallery, and 150 acres of grounds and gardens. Scattered throughout are full-size casts of his works. The property has two hiking trails, the longer of which is the Blow-Me-Down Trail. Concerts are held every Sunday afternoon in July and August. ⊠ *Off Rte. 12A,* ☎ *603/675–2175,* WEB *www.sgnhs.org.* ☞ *$4.* ☉ *Buildings mid-May–Oct., daily 9–4:30; grounds daily dawn–dusk.*

1½ mi south of the Saint-Gaudens National Historic Site you'll reach the 460-ft **Cornish-Windsor Bridge,** which connects New Hampshire to Vermont across the Connecticut River. It dates from 1866 and is the longest covered bridge in the United States.

Dining and Lodging

$$$–$$$$ ✕⌂ **Home Hill Inn.** Set back from the Connecticut River on 25 acres
★ of meadow and woods, this tranquil 1818 mansion is best suited to adults. The owners have given the inn a French influence with 19th-century antiques and collectibles. Rooms in the main house have canopy or four-poster beds; four have fireplaces. The suite in the carriage house is romantic. The airy dining room ($$$$; closed Mon.–Tues.) serves inspired French and Mediterranean cuisine. Chef-owner Victoria du Roure runs the on-site L'École Culinaire; cooking classes are held one weekend each month in winter and spring and include two nights' accommodation and several meals. ⊠ *River Rd., Plainfield 03781,* ☎ *603/675–6165,* WEB *www.homehillinn.com. 9 rooms, 2 suites, 1 seasonal cottage. Restaurant, putting green, tennis court, pool, cross-country skiing, meeting rooms; no room phones, no room TVs, no-smoking rooms. AE, D, MC, V. CP.*

The Arts

The restored 19th-century **Claremont Opera House** (⊠ Tremont Sq., Claremont, ☎ 603/542–4433) hosts plays and musicals from September to May.

Outdoor Activities and Sports

Northstar Canoe Livery (⊠ Rte. 12A, Balloch's Crossing, ☎ 603/542–5802) rents canoes for half- or full-day trips on the Connecticut River.

Charlestown

47 *20 mi south of Cornish, 63 mi northwest of Keene.*

Charlestown has the state's largest historic district. About 60 homes, handsome examples of Federal, Greek Revival, and Gothic Revival architecture, are clustered about the town center; 10 of them were built before 1800. Several merchants on the main street distribute brochures that contain an interesting walking tour of the district.

🐌 In 1747, the **Fort at No. 4** was an outpost on the periphery of Colonial civilization. That year fewer than 50 militia men at the fort withstood an attack by 400 French soldiers, ensuring that northern New England remained under British rule. Today, costumed interpreters at this living-history museum cook dinner over an open hearth and demonstrate weaving, gardening, and candle making. Each year the museum holds reenactments of militia musters and battles of the French and Indian War. ⊠ *Rte. 111, ½ mi north of Charlestown,* ☎ *603/826–5700 or 888/367–8284,* WEB *www.fortat4.com.* 🖃 *$8.* ☉ *Mid-May–Oct., daily 10–4.*

On a bright, breezy day you might want to detour to the **Morningside Flight Park** (⊠ off Rte. 12/11, ☎ 603/542–4416, WEB www.flymorningside.com), not necessarily to take hang-gliding lessons, although you could. You can watch the bright colors of the gliders as they take off from the school's 450-ft peak.

Lodging

$$ 🛏 **MapleHedge.** The innkeepers live in the oldest section of this home, which dates from about 1755. Guest rooms, in the 1820 Federal-style part, are furnished with carefully chosen antiques. The Cobalt Room showcases an extensive collection of cobalt glass, stencil-pattern wallpaper, and mahogany furnishings. In Lt. R.A.D.'s Quarters, Marine Corps memorabilia and dark pine wainscoting lend a military academy air. A three-course breakfast is served in the formal dining room. ⊠ *355 Main St. (Box 638, 03603),* ☎ *800/962–7539,* ☎ FAX *603/826–5237,* WEB *www.maplehedge.com. 5 rooms. Internet, business services; no room TVs, no kids under 12, no-smoking rooms. MC, V. Closed Jan.–Mar. BP.*

Walpole

48 *13 mi south of Charlestown.*

Walpole possesses one of the state's perfect town greens. This one, bordered by Elm and Washington streets, is surrounded by homes built about 1790, when the townsfolk constructed a canal around the Great Falls of the Connecticut River and brought commerce and wealth to the area. The town now has 3,200 inhabitants, more than a dozen of whom are millionaires.

OFF THE BEATEN PATH

SUGARHOUSES – Maple-sugar season occurs about the first week in March when days become warmer but nights are still frigid. A drive along maple-lined back roads reveals thousands of taps and buckets catching the labored flow of unrefined sap. Plumes of smoke rise from nearby sugarhouses, where sugaring off, the process of boiling down this precious liquid, takes place. Many sugarhouses are open to the public; after a tour and demonstration, you can sample the syrup—with unsweetened doughnuts and maybe a pickle or over fresh snow. **Bacon's Sugar House** (⊠ 243 Dublin Rd., Jaffrey, ☎ 603/532–8836) ushers in the season with sugar parties that are open to the public. **Bascom Maple Farm** (⊠ Mt. Kingsbury, off Rte. 123A, Alstead, ☎ 603/835–6361) serves maple pecan pie and maple milk shakes. **Stuart & John's Sugar House & Pancake Restaurant** (⊠ Rtes. 12 and 63, Westmoreland, ☎ 603/399–4486) conducts a tour and serves a pancake breakfast.

Shopping

Boggy Meadow Farm (⊠ River Rd. S, ☎ 603/756–3300) sells the farm's Fanny Mason Farmstead Swiss cheese in its store. A window overlooks the cheese-making area. **Burdick Chocolates** (⊠ Main St., ☎ 603/756–3701) is renowned for its chocolate mice, which are shipped to trendy restaurants in New York and other cities. The staff also serves espresso and light lunches in the café; dinner is available some nights.

Keene

㊾ *17 mi southeast of Walpole; 20 mi northeast of Brattleboro, Vermont; 56 mi southwest of Manchester.*

Keene is the largest city in the state's southwest corner. Its rapidly gentrifying main street, with several engaging boutiques and cafés, is America's widest. Each year, on the Saturday before Halloween, locals use that street to hold a Pumpkin Festival, where they seek to retain their place in the record books for the most carved, lighted jack-o'-lanterns—more than 24,000 some years.

Keene State College, hub of the local arts community, is on the tree-lined main street. The **Thorne-Sagendorph Art Gallery** (☎ 603/358–2720) houses George Ridci's *Landscape* and presents traveling exhibitions. The **Putnam Lecture Hall** (☎ 603/358–2160) shows foreign and art films.

OFF THE BEATEN PATH **CHESTERFIELD'S ROUTE 63** – If you're in the mood for a country drive or bike ride, head west from Keene along Route 9 to Route 63 (about 11 mi), and turn left toward the hilltop town of Chesterfield. This is an especially rewarding journey at sunset, as from many points along the road you can see west out over the Connecticut River valley and into Vermont. The village center consists of little more than a handful of dignified granite buildings and a small general store. You can loop back to Keene via Route 119 east in Hinsdale and then Route 10 north—the entire journey is about 40 mi.

Dining and Lodging

$–$$$ ✕ **176 Main.** This grand old brick house near the campus of Keene State College in the heart of downtown has a menu that runs the gamut from pad Thai noodles to blackened catfish. The bar stocks an extensive selection of draft beers. Weekend brunch is a big event. ⊠ *176 Main St.,* ☎ *603/357–3100. AE, D, MC, V.*

$$$–$$$$ ✕🏠 **Chesterfield Inn.** Surrounded by gardens, the Chesterfield sits
★ above Route 9, the main road between Keene and Brattleboro, Vermont. Fine antiques and Colonial-style fabrics adorn the spacious guest quarters; eight have fireplaces, and eight have private decks or terraces that face the gardens and verdant Vermont hills. In the restaurant ($$$–$$$$) leg of venison with cranberry-port sauce and baked fusilli with roast squash, ham, spinach, and Asiago are among the highlights. ⊠ *Rte. 9 (Box 155, Chesterfield 03443),* ☎ *603/256–3211 or 800/365–5515,* ℻ *603/256–6131,* ⱳⒺⒷ *www.chesterfieldinn.com. 13 rooms, 2 suites. Restaurant, some in-room hot tubs, some pets allowed. AE, D, MC, V. BP.*

$$$–$$$$ 🏠 **E. F. Lane Hotel.** Lending a rare touch of urbanity to the sleepy Monadnocks, this upscale redbrick hotel is inside a retrofitted department store on Keene's gentrified Main Street. It's within earshot of local church bells and is a 10-minute walk from Colony Marketplace. Rooms are furnished with reproduction Victorian antiques. The sky-lighted Salmon Chase Bistro and Lounge serves American and Continental fare. ⊠ *30 Main St., 03431,* ☎ *603/357–7070 or 888/300–5056,* ℻ *603/357–7075,*

WEB *www.someplacesdifferent.com/eflane.htm. 33 rooms, 7 suites. Restaurant, in-room data ports, some in-room hot tubs, bar, Internet, meeting rooms. AE, D, MC, V. CP.*

$–$$ ⊡ **Carriage Barn.** Antiques and wide pine floors give this inn across from Keene State College charm. An expansive buffet is served each morning in the breakfast room, but many guests savor a second cup of coffee in the summerhouse. ⊠ *358 Main St., 03431,* ☎ *603/357–3812,* WEB *www.carriagebarn.com. 4 rooms. No room phones, no room TVs, no smoking. AE, D, MC, V. CP.*

$ ⚠ **Swanzey Lake Camping Area.** This 82-site campground for tents and RVs has a sandy beach, a dock, a ball field, a recreation area, and boat rentals. ⊠ *88 E. Shore Rd. (Box 115, W. Swanzey 03469),* ☎ *603/352–9880,* WEB *www.swanzeylake.com.*

Nightlife and the Arts

The **Colonial Theatre** (⊠ 95 Main St., ☎ 603/352–2033) opened in 1924 as a vaudeville stage. It now hosts folk and jazz concerts and has the town's largest movie screen. **Elm City Brew Co.** (⊠ 222 West St., ☎ 603/355–3335), at the Colony Mall, serves light food and draws a mix of college students and young professionals. The **Redfern Arts Center at Brickyard Pond** (⊠ 229 Main St., ☎ 603/358–2168) has year-round music, theater, and dance performances.

Outdoor Activities and Sports

The Monadnock region has more than 200 lakes and ponds. Rainbow trout, smallmouth and largemouth bass, and some northern pike swim in Chesterfield's **Spofford Lake. Goose Pond** in West Canaan, just north of Keene, holds smallmouth bass and white perch.

Shopping

ANTIQUES

The more than 200 dealers at **Antiques at Colony Mill** (⊠ 222 West St., ☎ 603/358–6343) sell everything from furniture to dolls. Just touring the six furniture- and collectibles-filled rooms is part of the fun at **Stone House Antiques** (⊠ Rte. 9, Chesterfield, ☎ 603/363–4866), a stately, restored stagecoach tavern.

BOOKS

The extraordinary collection of used books at the **Homestead Bookshop** (⊠ 221 Main St., at Rtes. 101 and 124, Marlborough, ☎ 603/876–4213) includes biographies, cookbooks, and town histories.

GIFTS

Country Artisans (⊠ 53 Main St., ☎ 603/352–6980) showcases the stoneware, textiles, prints, and glassware of regional artists. **Hannah Grimes Marketplace** (⊠ 42 Main St., ☎ 603/352–6862) overflows with mostly New Hampshire–made pottery, toys, kitchenwares, soaps, greeting cards, and specialty foods.

SHOPPING CENTERS

Colony Mill Marketplace (⊠ 222 West St., ☎ 603/357–1240), an old mill building, holds 30-plus stores and boutiques such as the Toadstool Bookshop, which carries many children's and regional travel and history books, and Ye Goodie Shoppe, whose specialty is handmade confections. There's also a food court.

Fitzwilliam

50 *14 mi southeast of Keene.*

A well-preserved historic district of Colonial and Federal-style houses has made the town of Fitzwilliam, on Route 119, the subject of thousands of postcards. Many show views of its landscape in winter, when a fine white snow settles on the oval common. Town business is still conducted in the 1817 meetinghouse.

The **Amos J. Blake House,** maintained by the Fitzwilliam Historical Society, contains a museum with period antiques and artifacts and the law office of its namesake. A town walking-tour pamphlet is available here, too. ⊠ *Village green,* ☎ *603/585–7742.* ✆ *Free.* ☉ *Late May–mid-Oct., Sat. 1–4 or by appointment.*

More than 16 acres of wild rhododendrons bloom in mid-July at **Rhododendron State Park,** which has the largest concentration of *Rhododendron maximum* north of the Allegheny Mountains. Bring a picnic lunch and sit in a nearby pine grove, or follow the marked footpaths through the flowers. ⊠ *Off Rte. 12, 2½ mi northwest of village green,* ☎ *603/239–8153.* ✆ *$3 weekends and holidays; free at other times.* ☉ *Daily 8–sunset.*

Lodging

$$$ 🖼 **Inn at East Hill Farm.** If you have kids, you'll be happy at this 1830 farmhouse resort, where children are not only allowed but seem to be expected. They can milk the cows; feed the animals; and try arts and crafts, storytelling, and hiking. The innkeepers arrange weekly sleigh (or hay) and pony rides. Twice weekly in July and August, trips are scheduled to a nearby lake for boating, waterskiing, and fishing. Rates include most activities and three meals in a camplike dining hall. ⊠ *460 Monadnock St., Troy 03465,* ☎ *603/242–6495 or 800/242–6495,* FAX *603/242–7709,* WEB *www.east-hill-farm.com. 65 rooms. Restaurant, tennis court, 3 pools (1 indoor), wading pool, sauna, hiking, horseback riding, sleigh rides, recreation room, Internet, baby-sitting, some pets allowed (fee); no room phones, no TV in some rooms, no smoking. D, MC, V. FAP.*

$–$$ 🖼 **Hannah Davis House.** This 1820 house just off the village green has
★   retained its Federal elegance. The original beehive oven still sits in the kitchen, and one suite has two Count Rumford fireplaces. Pumpkin pine floors, antique quilts, and braided rugs give the rooms cheer. Your host has the scoop on area antiquing. ⊠ *106 Rte. 119, 03447,* ☎ *603/585–3344. 3 rooms, 3 suites. No room phones, no room TVs, no smoking. MC, V. BP.*

Shopping

ANTIQUES

You'll find about 35 dealers at **Bloomin' Antiques** (⊠ Rte. 12, 3 mi south of Rte. 119, ☎ 603/585–6688). The wares of some 40 dealers are for sale at **Fitzwilliam Antiques Centre** (⊠ Rtes. 12 and 119, ☎ 603/585–9092).

Rindge

51 *8 mi southeast of Fitzwilliam.*

Tiny, hilltop Rindge overlooks the Monadnock region. Most diversions center on outdoor activities.

Cathedral of the Pines is an outdoor memorial to American soldiers and civilians who have sacrificed their lives in service to their country. There's an inspiring view of Mt. Monadnock and Mt. Kearsarge from the Altar of the Nation, which is composed of rock from every U.S. state and territory. All faiths are welcome to hold services here; organ meditations take place at midday from Tuesday to Thursday in July and August. The Memorial Bell Tower, with a carillon of bells from around the world, is built of native stone. Norman Rockwell designed the bronze tablets over the four arches. Flower gardens, an indoor chapel, and a museum of military memorabilia share the hilltop. ⊠ *75 Cathedral Entrance Rd., off Rte. 119,* ☎ *603/899–3300.* ☞ *Free; donations suggested.* ☉ *May–Oct., daily 9–5.*

Dining and Lodging

$–$$ ✕ **Lilly's on the Pond.** An appealing choice either for lunch or dinner, this rustic-timber dining room overlooks a small mill pond. The extensive menu of mostly American fare includes chicken sautéed with lime and tequila, shrimp scampi, and burgers. ⊠ *U.S. 202,* ☎ *603/899–3322. D, MC, V. Closed Mon.*

$$–$$$ ⌂ **Woodbound Inn.** A favorite with families and outdoors enthusiasts, this 1819 farmhouse became an inn in 1892. It occupies 200 acres on the shores of Contoocook Lake. Accommodations are functional but clean and cheerful; they range from quirky rooms in the main inn to modern hotel-style rooms in the Edgewood building to cabins by the water. ⊠ *62 Woodbound Rd., 03461,* ☎ FAX *603/532–8341,* ☎ *800/688–7770,* WEB *www.woodboundinn.com. 46 rooms, 42 with bath; 11 cottages. Restaurant, some refrigerators, lake, 9-hole golf course, tennis court, fishing, croquet, hiking, horseshoes, shuffleboard, volleyball, cross-country skiing, ice-skating, tobogganing, bar, recreation room. AE, MC, V. BP, MAP.*

$–$$ ⌂ **Cathedral House Bed and Breakfast.** This 1850s farmhouse on the edge of the Cathedral of the Pines was the home of the memorial's founders. Rooms have high ceilings, floral wallpaper, quilts, and well-stocked cookie jars, all of which create the sense that you've just arrived at Grandma's house. Innkeepers Don and Shirley Mahoney are well versed in area history. ⊠ *63 Cathedral Entrance Rd., 03461,* ☎ *603/899–6790 or 866/229–4519,* WEB *www.cathedralpines.com/cathedralhouse.html. 5 rooms, 1 with bath. No room phones, no room TVs, no smoking. MC, V. BP.*

Jaffrey Center

❺❷ *8 mi northwest of Rindge, 7 mi northeast of Fitzwilliam.*

Novelist Willa Cather came to Jaffrey Center in 1919 and stayed in the Shattuck Inn, which now stands empty on Old Meeting House Road. Not far from here, she pitched the tent in which she wrote several chapters of *My Ántonia.* She returned nearly every summer thereafter until her death and was buried in the Old Burying Ground. **Amos Fortune Forum,** near the Old Burying Ground, brings nationally known speakers to the 1773 meetinghouse on summer evenings.

The oft-quoted statistic about Mt. Monadnock in **Monadnock State Park** is that it's America's most-climbed mountain—second in the world to Japan's Mt. Fuji. Whether this is true or not, locals agree that it's never lonely at the top. Some days more than 400 people crowd its bald peak. Monadnock rises to 3,165 ft, and on a clear day the hazy Boston skyline is visible from its summit. The park maintains picnic grounds and a small campground (RVs welcome, but no hookups). Five trailheads branch into more than two dozen trails of varying difficulty that wend their way to the top. Allow between three and four hours for any round-trip hike. A visitor center has free trail maps as well as exhibits documenting the mountain's history. ⊠ *Off Rte. 124, 2½ mi north of Jaffrey Center, 03452,* ☎ *603/532–8862.* ☞ *$3.* ☉ *Daily dawn–dusk.*

Dining and Lodging

$$–$$$ ✕⌂ **Inn at Jaffrey Center.** Rooms here are painted in lively lavenders, yellows, or peaches. Although full of period furnishings, they have a hip sensibility as well as high-thread-count bedding, fluffy towels, and

fine toiletries. The restaurant ($$–$$$; no lunch Sat.) offers a mix of American, Asian, and Italian dishes; good bets include the veal chops with fennel and honey, the pan-seared orange-ginger scallops, or the sole piccata. Sunday brunch is impressive. ✉ *379 Main St. (Box 484, 03452),* ☎ *603/532–7800 or 877/510–7019,* FAX *603/532–7900,* WEB *www.theinnatjaffreycenter.com. 9 rooms, 2 suites. Restaurant, bar; no TV in some rooms, no-smoking rooms. MC, V. CP.*

$–$$ 🖼 **Benjamin Prescott Inn.** Thanks to the working dairy farm surrounding this 1853 Colonial house—with its stenciling and wide pine floors— you feel as though you're miles out in the country rather than just minutes from Jaffrey Center. A full breakfast of Welsh miner's cakes and baked French toast with fruit and maple syrup prepares you for a day of antiquing or hiking. ✉ *Rte. 124, 03452,* ☎ *603/532–6637 or 888/ 950–6637,* FAX *603/532–6637,* WEB *www.benjaminprescottinn.com. 10 rooms, 3 suites. No room phones, no room TVs, no kids under 10, no-smoking rooms. AE, MC, V. BP.*

Peterborough

🔵 *9 mi northeast of Jaffrey Center, 30 mi northwest of Nashua.*

The nation's first free public library opened in Peterborough in 1833. The town, which was the first in the region to be incorporated (1760), is still a commercial and cultural hub.

The **MacDowell Colony** was founded by the composer Edward Mac-Dowell in 1907 as an artists' retreat. Willa Cather wrote part of *Death Comes for the Archbishop* here. Thornton Wilder was in residence when he wrote *Our Town* (Peterborough's resemblance to the play's Grover's Corners is no coincidence). Only a small portion of the still-active colony is open to visitors. ✉ *100 High St.,* ☎ *603/924–3886.*

In **Miller State Park,** 3 mi east of town, an auto road takes you almost 2,300 ft up Pack Monadnock Mountain. The road is closed mid-November through mid-April. ✉ *Rte. 101,* ☎ *603/924–3672.* 🎟 *$3.*

Dining and Lodging

$$–$$$ ✕ **Acqua Bistro.** People like to congregate at the long bar of this smart
★   bistro. You might join them before dining on a thin-crust pizza or an entrée of wild Arctic char with roasted vegetable-dill couscous and basil-walnut pesto. Save room for the bittersweet chocolate soufflé. ✉ *9 School St.,* ☎ *603/924–9905. MC, V. No lunch.*

$$–$$$$ ✕🖼 **Hancock Inn.** This Federal-style 1789 inn is the pride of the idyllic town it anchors. Common areas possess the warmth of a tavern, with fireplaces, big wing chairs, couches, dark-wood paneling, and Rufus Porter murals. Rooms, done in Colonial style, have antique four-poster beds. Updated Yankee fare is served by candlelight in the dining room ($$$– $$$$); a specialty is roast duckling with maple-whipped sweet potatoes and a blackberry cognac sauce. ✉ *33 Main St. (Box 96, Hancock 03449),* ☎ *603/525–3318,* FAX *603/525–9301,* WEB *www.hancockinn.com. 11 rooms, 4 suites. Restaurant, bar; no smoking. AE, D, DC, MC, V. BP.*

$$–$$$ ✕🖼 **Inn at Crotched Mountain.** Three of the nine fireplaces in this 1822 inn—with stunning views of the Monadnocks—are in Colonial-style guest rooms. In the restaurant ($$–$$$) the menu lists cranberry-port pot roast as well as Indonesian charbroiled swordfish with a sauce of ginger, green pepper, onion, and lemon. Weekend rates include breakfast and dinner. ✉ *534 Mountain Rd., Francestown 03043 (12 mi northeast of Peterborough),* ☎ *603/588–6840,* FAX *603/588–6623. 13 rooms. Restaurant, 2 tennis courts, pool, cross-country skiing, bar, some pets allowed. No credit cards. Closed Apr. and Nov. BP, MAP.*

$-$$ ✕⊡ **Birchwood Inn.** Thoreau slept here, probably on his way to climb Monadnock or to visit Jaffrey or Peterborough. Country furniture and handmade quilts outfit the bedrooms, just as they did in 1775, when the house was new. Allow time to linger in the dining room ($$$; reservations essential; BYOB; closed Sun.–Mon.; no lunch). Rufus Porter murals cover the walls; she-crab soup, shrimp Parmesan, and pumpkin-applesauce tea bread are among the choices. ✉ *Rte. 45 (Box 197, Temple 03084),* ☎ *603/878–3285,* FAX *603/878–2159. 7 rooms, 5 with bath. Restaurant; no room phones, no smoking. No credit cards. BP.*

$-$$ ⊡ **Apple Gate Bed and Breakfast.** With 90 acres of orchards across the street, this B&B is appropriately named. The four rooms (and the resident yellow labrador) are named for types of apples. Some guest quarters are small, but Laura Ashley prints and stenciling make them cheery. The house dates from 1832, and the original beams and fireplace still grace the dining room. A music and reading room has a piano and a TV with a VCR tucked in the corner. From June to October, there's a two-night minimum on weekends. ✉ *199 Upland Farm Rd., 03458,* ☎ FAX *603/924–6543. 4 rooms. No room phones, no room TVs, no kids under 12, no smoking. MC, V. BP.*

$-$$ ⊡ **Jack Daniels Motor Inn.** With so many dowdy motels in south-
★ western New Hampshire, it's a pleasure to find one as bright and clean as the Jack Daniels, just ½ mi north of downtown Peterborough. The rooms are large and furnished with attractive cherrywood reproduction antiques. ✉ *U.S. 202, 03458,* ☎ *603/924–7548,* FAX *603/924–7700,* WEB *www.jackdanielsmotorinn.com. 17 rooms. AE, D, MC, V.*

The Arts

From early July to mid-September, **Monadnock Music** (☎ 603/924–7610 or 800/868–9613) produces a series of solo recitals, chamber music concerts, and orchestra and opera performances by renowned musicians. Events take place throughout the area in the evening at 8 and on Sunday at 4; many are free. In winter, the **Peterborough Folk Society** (☎ 603/827–2905) presents folk music concerts. The **Peterborough Players** (✉ Stearns Farm, off Middle Hancock Rd., ☎ 603/924–7585) have performed for more than 60 seasons. Productions are staged in a converted barn.

Outdoor Activities and Sports

You can rent bikes or get yours serviced at **Spokes and Slopes** (✉ 30 Grove St., ☎ 603/924–9961). At the Donald Ross–designed **Tory Pines Golf Course** (✉ off Rte. 47 [near Bennington town line], Francestown, ☎ 603/588–2923), you'll find a hilly, rolling 18-hole layout with nice view of the Monadnocks. Greens fee are $28–$38.

Shopping

The corporate headquarters and retail outlet of **Eastern Mountain Sports** (✉ 1 Vose Farm Rd., ☎ 603/924–7231) sells everything from tents to skis to hiking boots, gives hiking and camping classes, and conducts kayaking and canoeing demonstrations. **Harrisville Designs** (✉ Mill Alley, Harrisville, ☎ 603/827–3333) sells hand-spun and hand-dyed yarn as well as looms. The shop also conducts classes in knitting and weaving. **North Gallery at Tewksbury's** (✉ Rte. 101, ☎ 603/924–3224) stocks sconces, candlestick holders, and woodworkings. **Sharon Arts Downtown** (✉ Depot Sq., ☎ 603/924–2787) has a gallery that exhibits locally made pottery, fabric, and woodwork and other crafts.

Antrim

54 *13 mi north of Peterborough.*

Little Antrim, an attractive mill town of neatly preened brick and clapboard structures, merits a look. Shovel, tool, and cutlery factories hummed along the Contoocook River's dammed rapids for many decades, and still today—at the south end of town, just off U.S. 202—the massive redbrick Monadnock Paper Company employs hundreds of locals. Its huge, red-neon sign glows purposefully, plumes of smoke rising from its mighty stacks day and night.

Dining and Lodging

$–$$ ✕ **Rynborn Restaurant and Blues Club.** You may be surprised to find a blues club in such a quiet community, but this place serves up some vibrant sounds. The menu consists of mostly regional American fare such as blackened Cajun shrimp and pecan-crusted chicken in a honey mustard sauce. ⊠ *76 Main St.,* ☎ *603/588–6162. AE, D, MC, V. No lunch.*

$–$$ ⊞ **Maplehurst Inn.** Since 1794 this lodging in the heart of Antrim has welcomed travelers. At first glance it looks like a slightly faded boardinghouse. But wander in and you'll find a well-kept hotel with 14 comfy rooms; one has a fireplace, and several have claw-foot tubs. A fireplace glows all winter long in the homey tavern, which serves a standard lineup of American and Continental dishes. ⊠ *67 Main St. (Box 155, 03440),* ☎ FAX *603/588–8000,* WEB *www.bitwizard.com/maplehurst. 14 rooms. Restaurant; no TV in some rooms, no-smoking rooms. AE, MC, V. CP.*

Hillsborough

55 *8 mi northeast of Antrim, 23 mi southwest of Concord.*

Hillsborough comprises four villages, the most prominent of which lies along the Contoocook River and grew up around a thriving woolen and hosiery industry in the mid-1800s. This section, which is really considered Hillsborough proper, is what you'll see as you roll through town on Route 9/U.S. 202.

Turn north from downtown up School Street, however, and continue 3 mi past Fox State Forest to reach one of the state's best-preserved historic districts, Hillsborough Center, where 18th-century houses surround a green. Continue north 6 mi through the similarly quaint village of East Washington, and another 6 mi to reach the Colonial town center of Washington. One of the highest-elevation villages in New Hampshire, this picturesque arrangement of white clapboard buildings made the cover of *National Geographic* several years back. You can loop back to Hillsborough proper via Route 31 south.

The nation's 14th president, Franklin Pierce, was born in Hillsborough and lived here until he married. The **Pierce Homestead,** operated by the Hillsborough Historical Society, welcomes visitors for guided tours. The house is much as it was during Pierce's life. ⊠ *Rte. 31 just north of Rte. 9,* ☎ *603/478–3165,* WEB *www.conknet.com/~hillsboro/pierce.* ⊡ *$3.* ☉ *June and Sept., Sat. 10–4, Sun. 1–4; July–Aug., Mon.–Sat. 10–4, Sun. 1–4.*

NEED A
BREAK?
Families have been coming to **Diamond Acres Dairy Bar** (⊠ Rte. 9, ¼ mi west of Rte. 31, ☎ 603/478–3121), a short-order shanty attached to a gas station, for years to devour superfresh clam platters, lobster rolls, and frozen sweets.

Outdoor Activities and Sports

Fox State Forest (✉ Center Rd., ☎ 603/464–3453) has 20 mi of hiking trails and an observation tower.

Shopping

At **Gibson Pewter** (✉ 18 E. Washington Rd., ☎ 603/464–3410), Raymond Gibson and his son Jonathan create and sell museum-quality pewter pieces.

Henniker

56 *7 mi northeast of Hillsborough, 16 mi southwest of Concord.*

Governor Wentworth, New Hampshire's first Royal Governor, named this town in honor of his friend John Henniker, a London merchant and member of the British Parliament (residents delight in their town's status as "the only Henniker in the world"). Once a mill town producing bicycle rims and other light-industrial items, Henniker reinvented itself after the factories were damaged, first by spring floods in 1936 and then by the hurricane and flood of 1938. New England College was established in the following decade. One of the area's covered bridges is on its campus.

Dining and Lodging

$$–$$$$ ✕▥ **Colby Hill Inn.** There's no shortage of relaxing activities at this farmhouse: you can curl up with a book by the parlor fireplace, stroll through the gardens and meadows, or play badminton out back. Rooms in the main house contain antiques, Colonial reproductions, and lace curtains. In carriage-house rooms, plain country furnishings, stenciled walls, and exposed beams are the norm. The frequently changing menu ($$$–$$$$) is excellent—one fine choice is boneless breast of chicken stuffed with Maine lobster, leeks, and Boursin. ✉ *3 The Oaks (Box 779, 03242),* ☎ *603/428–3281 or 800/531–0330,* ᶠᴬˣ *603/428–9218,* ᴡᴱᴮ *www.colbyhillinn.com. 16 rooms. Restaurant, in-room data ports, pool, badminton, recreation room; no smoking. AE, D, DC, MC, V. BP.*

$–$$ ✕▥ **Meeting House Inn & Restaurant.** The owners of this 200-year-old farmhouse tout it as a lovers' getaway and start each day by serving you breakfast in bed. The old barn has become a restaurant ($$$; closed Mon.–Tues.; no dinner Sun.) that specializes in leisurely, romantic dining. Try seared medallions of pork tenderloin with spiced apples, toasted pecans, and a maple cream sauce; the chocolate-raspberry frozen mousse comes in the shape of a heart. ✉ *Rte. 114/Flanders Rd., 03242,* ☎ *603/428–3228,* ᶠᴬˣ *603/428–6334,* ᴡᴱᴮ *www.conknet.com/~meetinghouse. 6 rooms. Restaurant, hot tub, sauna; no smoking. MC, V. BP.*

Nightlife

There's often live folk music at **Daniel's Restaurant and Pub** (✉ Main St., ☎ 603/428–7621), which occupies a rambling wood-frame building with great views of the Contoocook River.

Shopping

The **Fiber Studio** (✉ 9 Foster Hill Rd., ☎ 603/428–7830) sells beads, hand-spun natural-fiber yarns, spinning equipment, and looms.

Ski Area

PATS PEAK

A quick trip up I–93 from the Mass border, Pats Peak is geared to families. Base facilities are rustic, and friendly personal attention is the rule. ✉ *Rte. 114, 03242,* ☎ *603/428–3245; 888/728–7732 snow conditions,* ᴡᴱᴮ *www.patspeak.com.*

Downhill. Despite Pats Peak's short 710 vertical ft rise, the 21 trails and slopes have something for everyone. New skiers and snowboarders can take advantage of a wide slope and several short trails; intermediates have wider trails from the top; and experts have a couple of real thrillers. Night skiing and snowboarding take place in January and February. One triple and three double chairlifts and three surface lifts serve the runs. Pats Peak also has afternoon snowtubing on weekends and holidays.

Child care. The nursery takes children ages 6 months–5 years. Ski programs operate on weekends and during vacations for kids 4–12; all-day lessons for self-sufficient skiers in this age range are scheduled daily.

Western and Central New Hampshire A to Z

To research prices, get advice from other travelers, and book travel arrangements, visit www.fodors.com.

AIRPORTS

Manchester Airport is the main airport in western and central New Hampshire. Lebanon Municipal Airport, near Dartmouth College, is served by Colgan Air (an affiliate of US Airways) from Boston and by US Airways Express from Philadelphia and New York. Private planes and charters fly to Keene Dillant-Hopkins Airport.
➤ AIRPORT INFORMATION: **Keene Dillant-Hopkins Airport** (⊠ 80 Airport Rd., off Rte. 12 south of Keene, North Swanzey, ☎ 603/357–9835). **Lebanon Municipal Airport** (⊠ 5 Airpark Rd., West Lebanon, ☎ 603/298–8878).

BUS TRAVEL

Concord Trailways runs from Concord, Londonderry, and Manchester to Boston. Dartmouth Coach connects Boston's South Station and Logan Airport with Hanover, Lebanon, and New London. Vermont Transit links Nashua, Manchester, Concord, Keene, and White River Junction, Vermont (near Hanover) with major cities in the eastern United States. Advance Transit shuttles between Hanover, West Lebanon, Enfield, Canaan, and Lebanon. Keene City Express buses serves the town from 6 AM to 7:30 PM. Manchester Transit Authority has hourly local bus service around town and to Bedford from 6 AM to 6 PM.
➤ BUS INFORMATION: **Advance Transit** (☎ 802/295–1824). **Concord Trailways** (☎ 603/228–3300 or 800/639–3317). **Dartmouth Coach** (☎ 603/448–2800 or 800/637–0123 out of state). **Keene City Express** (☎ 603/352–8494). **Manchester Transit Authority** (☎ 603/623–8801). **Vermont Transit** (☎ 800/552–8737).

CAR TRAVEL

Most people who travel up from Massachusetts do so on I–93, which passes through Manchester and Concord before cutting a path through the White Mountains. I–89 connects Concord, in the Merrimack Valley, with Vermont. Route 12 runs north–south along the Connecticut River. Farther south, Route 101 connects Keene and Manchester, then continues to the seacoast. On the western border of the state, Routes 12 and 12A are picturesque but slow-moving. U.S. 4 crosses the region, winding between Lebanon and the seacoast. Other pretty drives include Routes 101, 202, and 10.

EMERGENCIES

HospitalsCheshire Medical Center (⊠ 580 Court St., Keene, ☎ 603/354–5400). **Concord Hospital** (⊠ 250 Pleasant St., Concord, ☎ 603/225–2711). **Dartmouth Hitchcock Medical Center** (⊠ 1 Medical Center Dr., Lebanon, ☎ 603/650–5000). **Elliot Hospital** (⊠ 1 Elliot Way,

Manchester, ☎ 603/669–5300). **Monadnock Community Hospital** (✉ 452 Old Street Rd., Peterborough, ☎ 603/924–7191). **Southern New Hampshire Medical Center** (✉ 8 Prospect St., Nashua, ☎ 603/577–2200).
➤ 24-HOUR PHARMACIES: **CVS Pharmacy** (✉ 271 Mammoth Rd., Manchester, ☎ 603/623–0347; ✉ 240–242 Main St., Nashua, ☎ 603/886–1798).

LODGING
Town & Country Realty has a wide range of Lake Sunapee–area long-term rentals.

APARTMENT AND VILLA RENTALS
➤ LOCAL AGENT: **Town & Country Realty** (☎ 603/763–2334 or 800/639–9960).

OUTDOOR ACTIVITIES AND SPORTS
FISHING
For word on what's biting where, contact the New Hampshire Fish and Game Department.
➤ CONTACT: **New Hampshire Fish and Game Department** (☎ 603/271–3211).

TOURS
Narrated cruises aboard the M/V *Mt. Sunapee II* provide a closer look at Lake Sunapee's history and mountain scenery. Dinner cruises are held on the M/V *Kearsarge*. Both boats leave from the dock at Sunapee Harbor and run from late May through mid-October.
➤ CONTACTS: **M/V *Kearsarge*** (☎ 603/763–4030). **M/V *Mt. Sunapee II*** (✉ Main St., Sunapee, ☎ 603/763–4030).

VISITOR INFORMATION
➤ TOURIST INFORMATION: **Concord Chamber of Commerce** (✉ 40 Commercial St., Concord 03301, ☎ 603/224–2508, WEB www.concordnhchamber.com). **Keene Chamber of Commerce** (✉ 48 Central Sq., Keene 03431, ☎ 603/352–1303). **Lake Sunapee Region Chamber of Commerce** (✉ Box 532, Sunapee 03782, ☎ 603/526–6575 or 877/526–6575, WEB sunapeevacations.com). **Manchester Chamber of Commerce** (✉ 889 Elm St., Manchester 03101, ☎ 603/666–6600, WEB www.manchester-chamber.org). **Monadnock Travel Council** (✉ 58 Central Sq. [Box 358, Keene 03431], ☎ 800/432–7864, WEB www.monadnocktravel.com).

NEW HAMPSHIRE A TO Z

To research prices, get advice from other travelers, and book travel arrangements, visit www.fodors.com.

AIRPORTS
Manchester Airport, the state's largest airport, has rapidly become a cost-effective, hassle-free alternative to Boston's Logan International Airport. It has nonstop service to more than 20 cities thanks to scheduled flights by Air Canada, American Eagle, Continental, Delta, Northwest, Southwest, United, and US Airways. Lebanon Municipal Airport has commuter flights by US Airways.
➤ AIRPORT INFORMATION: **Lebanon Municipal Airport** (✉ 5 Airpark Rd., West Lebanon, ☎ 603/298–8878). **Manchester Airport** (✉ 1 Airport Rd., Manchester 03103, ☎ 603/624–6539).

BIKE TRAVEL

Bike the Whites, Monadnock Bicycle Touring, and New England Hiking Holidays organize bike tours.

➤ CONTACTS: **Bike the Whites** (☎ 800/448–3534, WEB www. bikethewhites.com). **Monadnock Bicycle Touring** (☎ 603/827–3925). **New England Hiking Holidays** (☎ 603/356–9696 or 800/869–0949, WEB www.nehikingholidays.com).

BUS TRAVEL

C&J Trailways serves the seacoast area of New Hampshire. Concord Trailways links Boston's South Station and Logan Airport with points all along I–93 and, around Lake Winnipesaukee and the eastern White Mountains, along Route 16. Vermont Transit links the cities of western and southern New Hampshire with major cities in the eastern United States.

➤ BUS INFORMATION: **C&J Trailways** (☎ 603/430–1100 or 800/258–7111). **Concord Trailways** (☎ 603/228–3300 or 800/639–3317). **Vermont Transit** (☎ 800/552–8737).

CAR TRAVEL

Interstate 93 is the principal north–south route through Manchester, Concord, and central New Hampshire. To the west, I–91 traces the Vermont–New Hampshire border. To the east, I–95, which is a toll road, passes through southern New Hampshire's coastal area on its way from Massachusetts to Maine. Interstate 89 travels from Concord to Montpelier and Burlington, Vermont.

Speed limits on interstate and limited-access highways are generally 65 mph, except in heavily settled areas, where 55 mph is the norm. On state and U.S. routes, speed limits vary considerably. On any given stretch, the limit may be anywhere from 25 mph to 55 mph, so watch the signs carefully. Right turns are permitted on red lights unless indicated.

Official state maps are available free from the New Hampshire Office of Travel and Tourism Development. They cite useful telephone numbers and information about bike, snowmobile, and scenic routes.

EMERGENCIES

➤ CONTACTS: **Ambulance, fire, police** (☎ 911).

LODGING

CAMPING

New Hampshire Campground Owners Association publishes a guide to private, state, and national-forest campgrounds.

➤ CONTACT: **New Hampshire Campground Owners Association** (✉ Box 320, Twin Mountain 03595, ☎ 603/846–5511 or 800/822–6764, WEB www.ucampnh.com).

OUTDOOR ACTIVITIES AND SPORTS

BIRD-WATCHING

Audubon Society of New Hampshire schedules monthly field trips throughout the state and a fall bird-watching tour to Star Isle and other parts of the Isles of Shoals.

➤ CONTACT: **Audubon Society of New Hampshire** (✉ 3 Silk Farm Rd., Concord 03301, ☎ 603/224–9909, WEB www.nhaudubon.org).

FISHING

For information about fishing and licenses, call the New Hampshire Fish and Game Department.

➤ CONTACT: **New Hampshire Fish and Game Department** (☎ 603/271–3211).

FOLIAGE AND SNOW HOT LINES

A snow and fall-foliage hot line is regularly updated with information on leaf-peeping and skiing conditions.

➤ CONTACT: **Foliage and Snow hot line** (☎ 800/258–3608).

SKIING

Ski New Hampshire has information on downhill and cross-country snow sports in the state.

➤ CONTACT: **Ski New Hampshire** (✉ Box 10, North Woodstock 03262, ☎ 603/745–9396 or 800/887–5464, WEB www.skinh.com).

VISITOR INFORMATION

➤ TOURIST INFORMATION: **New Hampshire Office of Travel and Tourism Development** (✉ 172 Pembroke Rd. [Box 1856, Concord 03302], ☎ 603/271–2343; 800/386–4664 free vacation packet; WEB www.visitnh.gov). **New Hampshire Parks Department** (☎ 603/271–3556, WEB www.nhparks.state.nh.us). **New Hampshire State Council on the Arts** (✉ 40 N. Main St., Concord 03301, ☎ 603/271–2789, WEB www.state.nh.us/nharts).

SKIING MAINE, VERMONT, AND NEW HAMPSHIRE

MAINE, VERMONT, AND NEW HAMPSHIRE resorts reflect New England values: independence, resourcefulness, thriftiness. No two are alike. Although skiing may have changed the face of some resorts, it hasn't affected the charm of a New England village: the church on the town green, the barns and homesteads brimming with antiques for sale, the country inns.

Blending Old and New. New England areas have attitude and history on their side. Some of the first lifts in North America were located here: a shovel handle tow at Black Mountain, New Hampshire; single chair-lifts at Stowe and Mad River Glen, Vermont. Many of these have given way to high-speed chairlifts, trams, and gondolas. Sugar Hill, in Franconia, New Hampshire, was the site of America's first ski school. Today most areas have instructional programs for adults and children, including clinics for women, tree skiers, bump bashers, and extreme skiers. First-timers should ask about Learn-to-Ski-or-Ride programs that package lessons with equipment and a lift ticket. Discovery Centers at Mt. Snow and Killington, Vermont; Sunday River, Maine; and Attitash Bear Peak, New Hampshire, are excellent programs for families and beginners.

Perhaps nowhere is the blend of old and new more apparent than on the hill. Old-fashioned trails ebb and flow with the mountain's contours, weaving through woods, over knolls, and providing glimpses of the surrounding countryside. Newer trails were built to accommodate snow-making and grooming equipment; they're usually wide and often follow the fall line. Often at the same mountain, you can cruise down a steep, wide, perfectly groomed slope; experience the thrills of linking tight turns on a narrow, bump-choked trail; or ramble along a trail that takes the least direct route from summit to base.

Advanced skiers have even more options: tree skiers can snake their way through glades at most resorts, with Stowe Mountain and Jay Peak, Vermont, and Sugarloaf/USA and Sunday River, Maine, providing some of the best tree skiing in the country. For the true expert, Tuckerman Ravine in New Hampshire is the Holy Grail. This hike to–only terrain on Mt. Washington, New England's tallest peak, is a rite of passage.

New England's weather can be unpredictable: rain on the coast is often snow in the mountains, and sleet at lower elevations may be feathery powder at higher ones. For the most part modern snowmaking and grooming produce reliable conditions from early December into April. Nevertheless, New England snow is not western-style snow. What New Englanders consider hard-packed powder, Westerners often consider ice. While powder days are a rare treat here, grooming means top-to-bottom cruising runs are the rule. It can get cold, but if you dress in layers and wear a neck warmer and face mask, you'll be prepared. As a general rule, the farther north the ski area, the longer the season and the more natural snow you can expect.

Riding, Gliding, Shoeing. Snowboarding has changed American resorts as riders have come to share the lifts, slopes, and trails with skiers. Most resorts have embraced snowboarding. Halfpipes and terrain parks are popular not only with riders but also with skiers. New snow toys, such as the giant Zorb ball, ski bikes, and Snow Blades, as well as tubing parks, provide alternative activities.

Off-the-hill activities abound. Cross-country centers such as Jackson, Bretton Woods, and the Balsams Wilderness, New Hampshire; Bethel, Maine; and Stowe, Vermont, have gained international recognition for their climate, terrain, and size. Bretton Woods and the Balsams are self-contained downhill and cross-country resorts anchored by historic grand resort hotels. In Jackson, you can ski from inn to inn, and Stowe has the Trapp Family Lodge. At many cross-country centers you can also snowshoe, a wonderful, easy-to-do sport.

Saving Big by Thinking Small. While day tickets at the bigger resorts approach $50, those at smaller areas can be as low as $20. Some independently owned areas are bona fide bargains for skiers who don't require the glitz of the high-profile resorts. Family pricing, multiday tickets, frequent-skier programs, junior and senior rates, Website deals, and lift-and-lodging packages can all lower the price significantly. Midweek prices are often less expensive, and many areas offer incentives then, such as two-for-one days.

Most ski areas have a variety of accommodations—lodges, condominiums, hotels, motels, inns, bed-and-breakfasts—close to the action. For stays of three days or more, a package rate may be the deal. Packages vary in composition, price, and availability; their components may include a room, meals, lift tickets, ski lessons, rental equipment, transfers to the mountain, parties, races, use of a sports center, tips, and taxes. In general, if you're willing to commute a few extra miles, off-site lodging offers good value.

Getting Practical. Rental equipment is available at all ski areas, at ski shops around resorts, and even in cities far from ski areas. Shop personnel will advise you on equipment and how to use it.

Ski areas have devised standards for rating and marking trails and slopes that offer fairly accurate guides. Trails are rated Easier (green circle), More Difficult (blue square), Most Difficult (black diamond), and Expert (double diamond). Keep in mind that trail difficulty is measured relative to that of other trails at the same ski area. A black-diamond trail at one area may rate only a blue square at a neighboring area. Unless you're able to handle any type of terrain, your best bet is to start on green-circle trails and work your way up in difficulty until you find the terrain where you're most comfortable.

If you're traveling with children, ask about programs geared to their age. Areas renowned for their family emphasis include Smugglers' Notch, Vermont, and Waterville Valley, New Hampshire. Both have plenty of activities, both on the snow and off, for all ages. Child-care centers can be found at virtually all ski areas and often accept children from ages six weeks to six years. Parents must usually supply formula and diapers for infants; reservations are advised at most, essential at some. Most programs also have instructional opportunities for children at least three years of age and older.

292

New England Ski Areas

CANADA

QUÉBEC

Colebrook

Dixville
Notch

16

Errol

Newport

Enosburg
Falls

St. Albans

Orleans

Barton

Island
Pond

North
Stratford

Groveton

91

1

2 Morrisville

3

Hardwick

4

Lyndonville

Lancaster

Berlin
Gorham

Lake
Champlain

Burlington

5

Stowe

St. Johnsbury

Littleton

Bretton
Woods

18

Montpelier

17

6

Barre

Woodsville

19

Lincoln

Bartlett

22 **20**

21

23

Conway

7

Middlebury

89

24

25

Brandon

Randolph

VERMONT

Tamworth

Ossipee

Plymouth

Meredith

Lake
Winnipesaukee

7

Rutland

Woodstock

10

Lebanon

Bristol

8

9

91

89

Laconia

26

NEW
YORK

Poultney

Ludlow

Claremont

11

12

Springfield

27 NEW HAMPSHIRE

Manchester

13

28

Concord

Arlington

14

Manchester

Bennington

15

Wilmington

Keene

Milford

Haverhill

Brattleboro

Nashua

Lawrence

Lowell

Williamstown

Athol

Fitchburg

35

34

Greenfield

Gardner

Leominster

Concord

Lexington

36

Pittsfield

Northampton

91

Amherst

Marlborough

95

37

Stockbridge

MASSACHUSETTS

Worcester

38

90

Chicopee

90

495

Otis

39

Springfield

146

Winsted

Windsor
Locks

Putnam

Providence

Taunton

40

Torrington

41

Manchester

Willimantic

Warwick

New
Britain

Hartford

95

Bristol

Bristol

CONNECTICUT

RHODE
ISLAND

42

Waterbury

43

Meriden

Middletown

395

Newport

84

Wallingford

44

Norwich

Danbury

Wakefield

95

New

Westerly

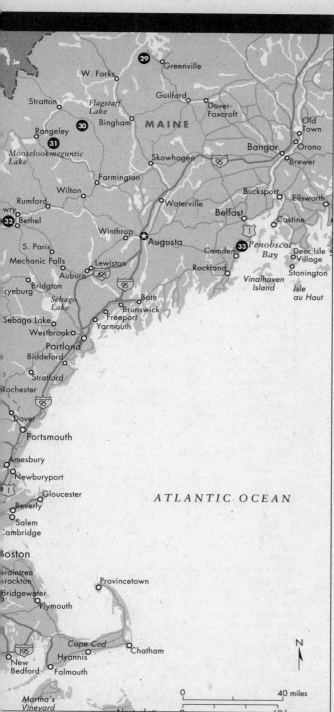

INDEX

Fodor's Key to the Guides

America's guidebook leader publishes guides for every kind of traveler. Check out our many series and find your perfect match.

Fodor's Gold Guides
America's favorite travel-guide series offers the most detailed insider reviews of hotels, restaurants, and attractions in all price ranges, plus great background information, smart tips, and useful maps.

Fodor's Road Guide USA
Big guides for a big country—the most comprehensive guides to America's roads, packed with places to stay, eat, and play across the U.S.A. Just right for road warriors, family vacationers, and cross-country trekkers.

COMPASS AMERICAN GUIDES
Stunning guides from top local writers and photographers, with gorgeous photos, literary excerpts, and colorful anecdotes. A must-have for culture mavens, history buffs, and new residents.

Fodor's CITYPACKS
Concise city coverage with a foldout map. The right choice for urban travelers who want everything under one cover.

Fodor's EXPLORING GUIDES
Hundreds of color photos bring your destination to life. Lively stories lend insight into the culture, history, and people.

Fodor's POCKET GUIDES
For travelers who need only the essentials. The best of Fodor's in pocket-size packages for just $9.95.

Fodor's To Go
Credit-card–size, magnetized color microguides that fit in the palm of your hand—perfect for "stealth" travelers or as gifts.

Fodor's FLASHMAPS
Every resident's map guide. 60 easy-to-follow maps of public transit, parks, museums, zip codes, and more.

Fodor's CITYGUIDES
Sourcebooks for living in the city: Thousands of in-the-know listings for restaurants, shops, sports, nightlife, and other city resources.

Fodor's AROUND THE CITY WITH KIDS
68 great ideas for family days, recommended by resident parents. Perfect for exploring in your own backyard or on the road.

Fodor's ESCAPES
Fill your trip with once-in-a-lifetime experiences, from ballooning in Chianti to overnighting in the Moroccan desert. These full-color dream books point the way.

Fodor's FYI
Get tips from the pros on planning the perfect trip. Learn how to pack, fly hassle-free, plan a honeymoon or cruise, stay healthy on the road, and travel with your baby.

Fodor's Languages for Travelers
Practice the local language before hitting the road. Available in phrase books, cassette sets, and CD sets.

Karen Brown's Guides
Engaging guides to the most charming inns and B&Bs in the U.S.A. and Europe, with easy-to-follow inn-to-inn itineraries.

Baedeker's Guides
Comprehensive guides, trusted since 1829, packed with A–Z reviews and star ratings.

At bookstores everywhere.   www.fodors.com/books